Communications and
Public Opinion

edited by
Robert O. Carlson

The Praeger Special Studies program—
utilizing the most modern and efficient book
production techniques and a selective
worldwide distribution network—makes
available to the academic, government, and
business communities significant, timely
research in U.S. and international economic, social, and political development.

Communications and Public Opinion

A *Public Opinion Quarterly* Reader

PRAEGER SPECIAL STUDIES IN U.S. ECONOMIC, SOCIAL, AND POLITICAL ISSUES

Praeger Publishers   New York   Washington   London

Library of Congress Cataloging in Publication Data
Main entry under title:

Communications and public opinion. Edited by Robert O. Carlson.
N.Y. Praeger Pub. 1975
   (Praeger special studies in U. S. economic, social
and political issues)
xv, 642 p. tables
   Includes index.
   1. Public opinion—Addresses, essays, lectures.
2. Communication—Social aspects—Addresses, essays,
lectures.   3. Attitude change—Addresses, essays,
lectures.   I. Carlson, Robert O.   II. Public opinion
quarterly.
HM261.C66   301.15'4   75-11687
ISBN 0-275-07510-9
ISBN 0-275-89330-8   pbk.

PRAEGER PUBLISHERS
111 Fourth Avenue, New York, N.Y. 10003, U.S.A.

Published in the United States of America in 1975
by Praeger Publishers, Inc.

Printed in the United States of America

For My Wife

Eileen Evers Carlson

Like some other relatively modern disciplines, public opinion research has had a long history but a short past. Although there had been learned speculation and publication during the eighteenth and nineteenth centuries regarding the nature of public opinion, and actual empirical studies of consumers and other groups were carried out during the early decades of the present century, it is the mid-1930s that marks the emergence of public opinion research as we know it today. It was in 1935 that George Gallup and Elmo Roper began publishing their respective data, generated from systematically selected national cross-sections of adults. In 1936, carefully designed polls of voting intentions were carried out by Gallup, Roper, and Archibald M. Crossley. You may remember that 1936 was the year when the *Literary Digest* poll provided us with an unintended demonstration of sampling bias, which minor catastrophe contributed to the credibility and the establishment of the more "scientific" pollsters. And in the midst of all of this ferment, in 1937 *The Public Opinion Quarterly* began publication at Princeton University.

Since its inception, the *Quarterly* has been central in the development and refinement of both theory and technique in public opinion studies. To some of us who were fascinated by the craft or the art of measuring public opinion, it has sometimes seemed that technique was developing much faster than theory. Quota sampling gave way to probability sampling, panel studies occasionally supplemented one-time surveys, the computer and its possibilities provided all kinds of new analytical and design opportunities. We worried a lot about theory, but did not seem to attend to its nurturance as much as we wanted to.

In this volume Robert O. Carlson demonstrates that theoretical advances have been alive and well. As the chapters in this anthology show, scholars were increasingly successful in relating quantitative results of surveys to that mysterious, invisible entity—public opinion—that had so charmed and mystified thinkers of the eighteenth and nineteenth centuries. Further work was also done on the history of the public opinion concept and in relating attitudes and opinions to behavior.

All of us who are engaged in public opinion research owe a vote of thanks to Dr. Carlson, as well as to the authors who originally contributed these articles to the *Quarterly* for this anthology. It not only highlights the development of thinking about public opinion over the past 38 years, but also helps to make current survey data more meaningful. It gives us a better understanding of how we arrived at our present "state of the art" in the assessment and understanding of public opinion.

INTRODUCTION
Robert O. Carlson

The concept of "public opinion" has fascinated scholars, politicians, and laymen for ages. Its existence is generally conceded, although there is little consensus as to its precise nature and definition. Nor is there general agreement as to the methods by which it can be identified or how its influence on behavior is best measured.

Within recent years many of our major institutions—business, organized religion, universities, and government on all levels—have been challenged from a bewildering number of quarters to justify their contributions to our society. These challenges frequently are based on the assertion that "public opinion" suggests that these institutions have not been responsive to the massive social, political, economic, and cultural changes taking place in today's world. The surfacing of the civil rights movement, consumerism, and environmentalism are cited as examples of the insensitivity of The Establishment to these changing public concerns. There is increasing evidence that many basic institutions of our society recognized that their policies in the past have been myopic and they are now seeking better ways of keeping abreast of changing public opinion on issues that may affect their operations.

For historically understandable reasons, discussions of the role of public opinion frequently have been associated with the political world and the degree to which certain segments of the public support or oppose a candidate, a public official, or a particular government policy. This continuing interest in how the public feels about current political issues is reflected in the reports of syndicated opinion polls carried out for the mass media.

The media, in turn, are interested in public opinion because they are often the object of criticism from various segments of the public as well as by some people in government for not being objective in reporting the news. Top management of the mass media, of course, recognize that the manner in which they report the news does influence the public's perception and attitudes toward events of the day.

Elusive as the concept of "public opinion" may be, and this book documents that it has many facets; it is equally certain that it is a phenomenon of major importance in our lives. In retrospect, the decision to commence publication of *The Public Opinion Quarterly* in 1937 was propitious. Throughout the ensuing years the *Quarterly* has been a forum for the reporting of significant developments in the study of public opinion. It has also served as a catalyst for the exchange of ideas by an ever-growing number of scholars and commercial researchers who are trying to understand how the force of public opinion operates in our social, political, economic, and cultural worlds.

The Foreword to the first issue of *The Public Opinion Quarterly* in January 1937 clearly states the objectives of its founding editors.

A new situation has arisen throughout the world, created by the spread of literacy among the people and the miraculous improvement of the means of communication. Always the opinions of relatively small publics have been a prime force in political life, but now, for the first time in history, we are confronted nearly everywhere by mass opinion as the final determinant of political, and economic, action. Today public opinion operates in quite new dimensions and with new intensities; its surging impact upon events becomes the characteristic of the current age—and its ruin or salvation?

For some time the phenomena of public opinion have been an object of scholarly attention. The quantity of published material dealing with the subject has increased tremendously since the early writings of Alexis de Tocqueville, James Bryce, Albert V. Dicey, Wilhelm Bauer, Ferdinand Tonnies, and A. Lawrence Lowell. A recently published bibliography of public opinion studies lists more than five thousand titles; but the attack has not much more than begun. Scholarship is developing new possibilities of scientific approach as a means of verifying hypotheses and of introducing greater precision of thought and treatment.

Under these conditions the clearest possible understanding of what public opinion is, how it generates, and how it acts becomes a vital need touching both public and private interest. The editorial staff of *The Public Opinion Quarterly* undertakes to serve that need by creating a convenient medium for regularly bringing together from all the sources indicated above—scholarship, government, business, advertising, public relations, press, radio, motion pictures—the latest available information on the phenomena and problems of public opinion and the developing thought, in connection with those phenomena and problems, of scholars, governmental officials, business men, public relations counsel, and the rest.

Of course the most active and intense interest in public opinion is usually displayed by political leaders, group leaders, advertisers, and others who wish to promote some cause—who have objectives the carrying out of which necessitates the cooperation of many minds. *The Public Opinion Quarterly* will not attempt the delicate task of evaluating these proffered causes or of discovering new ones. It will seek rather to satisfy the need of students and leaders of opinion, irrespective of their social, economic, religious, and political beliefs, for more precise information regarding the phenomena of public opinion itself. The editors will endeavor to maintain a wholly objective and scientific point of view.

To an astonishing degree the objectives and high standards that were set forth in that Foreword have remained a hallmark of the *Quarterly* in its ensuing years.

World War II broke out only two years after the founding of the *Quarterly*, and issues covering the war years report in detail on studies of propaganda, psychological warfare, and the relative effectiveness of various communications techniques in a wartime situation. World War II saw the use of propaganda and psychological warfare on a scale never approached before.

After that war ended a cadre of communications specialists returned to civilian life looking for ways of converting their skills into new careers. Some turned to journalism or to teaching. Others elected to work with the mass media or to become public relations consultants. Still others channeled their interest in public opinion by establishing commercial opinion research firms. Many of them became regular contributors to *The Public Opinion Quarterly*. Their papers documented important new developments in techniques for collecting, tabulating, analyzing, and reporting on various manifestations of public opinion. Other of their articles are case studies relating the specific application of public opinion research in clarifying problems faced by marketing and advertising firms; by business corporations and government agencies; and by political parties and candidates.

Since the founding of the *Quarterly* important changes have taken place in the role that the mass media play in our lives. For example, television has become a major force in our social, cultural, and political life. The role of magazines has changed. Radio and the press are different today than they were when the *Quarterly* began publication. The *Quarterly* provides a continuing documentation of the changing functions of these mass media for their audiences.

The early issues of *The Public Opinion Quarterly* are of special interest in revealing how the blending of academic and marketing research techniques gave birth to the methods and theories of public opinion research employed today. A lively dialogue between the "real" world of business and government and scholars has always characterized this journal. The *Quarterly* consistently attracted articles of interest and relevance to both laymen and scholars and its roster of contributors includes many of the leading students of communications research.

A complete set of all issues of the Quarterly published since 1937 stands almost seven feet high. Some of its articles were highly perishable and are of interest chiefly to historians studying a problem or issue that has largely faded into obscurity. Other of its articles represent early exploratory statements of theories about public opinion or methods of research on it and in many instances the authors of these pieces have subsequently refined and modified these theories.

Even when the foregoing material is weeded out from articles that have appeared in the *Quarterly*, there remains a rich store of data that students and practioners in the communications field can study with profit. For example, an entire book could be compiled from articles dealing with various methods for identifying attitudes and opinions and measuring changes in them. Another volume could be assembled from studies of the mass media and the influence that they exercise on the attitudes and behavior of their audiences. For students of the political process, there is a book to be put together on the role of public opinion polls in identifying key issues during a political campaign; the degree to which polls are successful in predicting election results; as well as some brilliant essays on the nature of our political system and how it operates. Other important articles deal with public opinion and the mass media in other countries and cultures.

The focus of this collection of articles from past issues of *The Public Opinion Quarterly*, however, was dictated by the title of the *Quarterly*—public opinion. For over the years the *Quarterly* has become the source for a number of outstanding articles dealing with efforts to define public opinion, to identify factors that cause it to change or to resist change, to to relate opinion change with change in behavior. Finally, there are the articles that seek to understand some of the historical roots and philosophical implications of the study of public opinion.

The articles selected for this book have stood the test of time and are as up-to-date today as when they were written. They have been sorted into four broad subject sections, each of which can be read independent of the others.

Four persons gave generously of their time and counsel in the preparation of this book and I express my gratitude to them at this time. W. Phillips Davison, a former editor of the *Quarterly*, and Bernard Roshco, the present editor, were instrumental in solving a number of problems associated with the prepublication of this reader. The late Helen S. Dinerman, Chairman of the Board of International Research Associates, Inc., and my wife Eileen provided encouragement for me to see this book through to completion. My thanks to all of them.

CONTENTS

Public opinion has been the object of formal study by social scientists and less formal study by leaders in our political and intellectual world for decades. Honest differences of opinion (or is the correct word attitude?) exist among them as to what it is and why it changes. Scholars fail to agree on the exact parameters that the term encompasses, the methods by which one can identify the phenomenon, and what represents a valid and reliable means of measuring changes in public opinion. Certainly there are sizable differences in emphasis in the academic study of public opinion depending on whether the scholar is a political scientist, historian, social psychologist, psychologist, or sociologist.

While such a situation may be confusing and frustrating to students of public opinion, this lack of consensus does not mean that the field is not responsive to meaningful study. As G. D. Wiebe has observed, the term "weather" denotes a general concept that has valid meaning for both the layman and the meteorologist, even though at any given moment they employ different criteria for describing it. The selection of articles in this book illustrates the difficulty of trying to pin a single meaning on the term public opinion.

Floyd Allport's "Toward A Science of Public Opinion" appeared in the first issue of the *Quarterly* and in it he set forth eight "Fictions and Blind Alleys" that are often associated with a discussion of public opinion.

1. The Personification of Public Opinion—the thought that it is some kind of being that dwells in or above the group.

2. The Personification of the Public—the notion of a collective, super-organic being—not the process but the public that "holds it".

3. The Group Fallacy of the Public—the practice of claiming to be talking about individuals but nevertheless employing such phrases as "the public wants so and so."

4. The Fallacy of Partial Inclusion in the Use of the Term "Public"—the failure to designate the geographic, political or psychological criteria that are employed in categorizing people.

5. The Fiction of an Ideational Entity—the Platonic "idea" that is distributed into the minds of all those who endorse it.

6. The Group Product or "Emergent" Theory—the practice of not referring to groups or agencies but only to results.

7. The Eulogistic Theory—regarding the result of group discussion and individual thought as not only different from the product of minds working individually, but as superior in character.

8. The Confusion of Public Opinion with the Public Presentation of Opinions (The Journalistic Fallacy)— the belief that if issues are the subject for reporting by the mass media that they represent matters of public opinion significance.

These eight categories serve to illustrate the confusion and lack of consensus as to the nature of public opinion. Allport seeks to resolve this murky situation by offering thirteen areas of "Common Agreements and Some Proposed Distinctions" and this effort is less productive than his identification of "Fictions and Blind Alleys." Finally, he is bold enough to offer his definition of public opinion in the final paragraph of his chapter.

> The term public opinion is given its meaning with reference to a multi-individual situation in which individuals are expressing themselves, or can be called upon to express themselves, as favoring or supporting (or else disfavoring or opposing) some definite condition, person, or proposal of widespread importance, in such a proportion of number, intensity, and constancy, as to give rise to the probability of affecting action, directly or indirectly, toward the object concerned.

Harwood Childs' "By Public Opinion I Mean—" brings together a rich sampling of definitions of this term by political scientists, psychologists, historians, and others. Childs was the first editor of the *Quarterly* and its lifelong friend and counselor. His grasp of this field of inquiry is reflected in his comments on efforts to give meaning to the concept of public opinion. He notes that the term has meaning only if it refers to a particular public and to specific opinions about definite subjects.

He feels that the word "opinion" can best be defined as a verbal expression of attitude and he stresses that "opinions differ from one another in many respects, such as content, the form in which they are expressed, their quality, their stability, their intensity, and the way in which they have been formed or elicited." He explores the question of the degree of uniformity or diversity that may characterize aspects of public opinion. He, also, offers a definition of it: "By public opinion we mean, therefore, simply any collection of individual opinions designated." But in the last sentence of this chapter he hedges on this definition: "The nature of public opinion is not something to be defined but to be studied."

David Riesman and Nathan Glazer's "The Meaning of Opinion" reflects some of the extensive discussion brought about by the failure of the public opinion polls to predict the results of the 1948 presidential election. But it deals with far broader issues as well. They suggest that efforts be made to get at the character structure of respondents in opinion surveys.

4

We have already stated our belief that group affiliation and like institutional matters are more important in predicting an election than depth psychology. . . . It is character structure, the lasting organization of personality, which lends meaning to the fleeting course of an individual's opinions; it is character structure which differentiates between opinions, verbally the same, on such scores as rootedness and susceptibility to mass media pressure; it is variations in the distribution of character types among the several social classes which give us clues to a subtly differentiated, and more accurate type of prediction.

They suggest that time pressures keep researchers from looking for the latent meaning of an answer or of no answer to a question. "Latent meaning—either of an answer or of no answer—may be understood if we grasp the socially structured interpersonal situation between poller and pollee, and search it for the residues, verbal and non-verbal, which now in our haste we throw away." Riesman and Glazer explore some of the assumptions that underlie the polling process and they are especially intrigued by what they consider its nineteenth-century-liberal concept that respondents from different social strata are "responsible citizens." What follows is a stimulating essay on the degree of saliency and importance that public issues may have for various social classes. They suggest that pollsters tend to frame questions in terms of the way reality is perceived by the broad middle classes. By structuring situations in this particular way, they get back, in effect, what they (and the mass media) have put into their studies is an interesting and disturbing observation that should bother students of public opinion.

In his chapter "Some Implications of Separating Opinions from Attitudes," G. D. Wiebe addresses himself to a topic that scholars have wrestled with for years. Early in the chapter he defines his objective: "Attitude and opinion are used as synonymous, as nearly synonymous, one is used as a sub-classification of the other, and they are used as distinctly separate concepts. The ambiguous use of words is commonplace, but if such ambiguity appears to impede progress in an area of scientific interest, clarification is of prime importance. The purpose of this paper is to propose definitions which clearly differentiate attitudes and opinion."

Wiebe reviews the writing of other students who studied this matter and notes that one body of scholars tends to think of attitudes as structural predispositions that in turn influence responses in the individual. He then offers his specific definition of an opinion.

An opinion then might be defined as a mental and neutral state perceived as a decision favoring particular behavior on a group issue—a decision which adapts attitudes related to the issue to the individual's perception of the reality in which the behavior must transpire. We have attempted to differentiate between attitudes and opinions. In so doing, a basic relationship between the two becomes apparent. Opinions adapt attitudes to the demands of social situations; but having adapted them, opinions appear to become ingredients in the constant, gradual reformulation of attitudes.

As he discusses criteria for validating his definitions Wiebe notes that the roots of attitude and opinion responses seem to reach in opposite directions, even though they have superficial similarities. "The roots of an attitude lie within the individual. The roots of an opinion lie within the life space in which the individual interacts." Wiebe proceeds to an extensive examination of how these definitions can be tested against a variety of existing research data. He offers as a hypothesis, "Opinions adapt attitudes to practical situations."

A fellow social scientist, Brewster Smith, in his article, "Comment on the 'Implications of Separating Opinions from Attitudes,' " praises Wiebe for his effort but takes exception to his conclusions.

Smith notes that Wiebe's thesis "properly cuts through at least one level of foggy thinking about the meaning of discrepancy between attitudes and actions, recognizing the interplay of personal and situational determinants of behavior." But he quarrels with some fundamental assumptions of Wiebe's, and regards as "unfortunate . . . inacceptable starting points in his chain of reasoning. These have to do with his conception of validity, his assumptions about the relation between attitudes and opinions as constructs and the behavior from which they are inferred, and his exclusive preoccupation with the analysis of single questions rather than scales."

Smith states that "Wiebe does not embrace consistently the relative conception of validity that is implied in his distinction between the appropriate criteria for validating 'opinion' and 'attitude' responses."

Continuing his comments on the Wiebe article Smith suggests, "Let us accept for the nonce Wiebe's distinction between attitude and opinion as constructs. Does a parallel distinction follow between 'attitude responses' and 'opinion responses'? Not, I think, from Wiebe's own position that emphasizes the conjoint role of personal and situational components in the determination of behavior."

"Any adequate account of opinion-attitude psychology must certainly provide for the formation of new judgments in problematic situations, and for the convergence of hitherto independent attitudes on a common complex object. If a terminology of attitudes vs. opinions makes it easier to grasp these phenomena, well and good." Brewster Smith feels that Wiebe's distinctions do not meet these criteria.

In his "Response to Smith's Comments" Wiebe observes that Smith's "basic disagreement with my point of view seems to be a matter of strategy in theory building. He appears to feel that my formulation represents the segmenting of things that should stay whole. If I understand him correctly, he feels that we should set our sights on a comprehensive understanding of human behavior that would encompass, in a single consistent theory, everything ranging from the most obscure inner motivations to the most nearly situation-bound behavior of crowds, mobs, and societies."

With a twinkle in his academic eye Wiebe suggests that Smith's orientation doesn't seem to lead to scientific rigor, but to a sort of "glorified Monday-morning quarterbacking."

Herbert Hyman's "Toward a Theory of Public Opinion" acknowledges that many scholars believe that the "imbalance between theory, on the one hand, and methodology with its concomitant collections of empirical data, on the other, must become progressively greater with the passage of time."

Speaking of the many confusing and often contradictory definitions of public opinion, Hyman offers these rational comments:

> It is bound to be harder for any mighty theory to stand the test today when relevant evidence is so much easier to come by. The stumps are found to become more numerous. And today's theorizer is sure to face, and perhaps to overstress, the "infinite thicket of psychological descriptions," for modern public opinion research in its very nature is psychologically oriented. No matter what form the analysis may ultimately take, the unit under scrutiny is always the individual and his psychic structure. If one accepts this view, the theorizer will find himself in a less and less enviable position as time goes on and our fund of knowledge increases.

Hyman is sanguine about the prospect of developing a theory of public opinion.

> Adopt an alternative view of theory and the picture brightens. If the measure of theory is not grandness or generality, but rather quality, utility, logical structure, and soundness then William Albig's description (of the tangled, matted field of opinion theory) might be less apt today. Robert K. Merton stresses the alternative view when he distinguishes systematic sociological theory, "the highly selective accumulation of those small parts of the earlier theory which have thus far survived the tests of empirical research," from the "far greater mass of conceptions which fell to bits," from "the false starts, the archaic doctrines and the fruitless errors of the past." By this standard, the field cluttered with stumps is a sign of progress, not of decay.

Hyman calls attention to Merton's "theories of the middle range, logically interconnected conceptions . . . limited and modest in scope" and thinks that this approach more correctly depicts the present state of public opinion theory. One

7

passage in his chapter points up a chronic problem: "This very movement of problem areas into and out of the sphere of public opinion research, while understandable, is perhaps the most crucial deficiency for the growth of a theory. The absence
of data which provides a sound description of even the *lack* of public opinion on a
problem, at a time when it is not under discussion, means that there is no basis for
developing adequate theory as to the formation of public opinion."

W. Phillips Davison's "The Public Opinion Process" is a down-to-earth
effort to remove some of the confusion and mystery surrounding the concept of
public opinion. A former editor of the *Quarterly*, Davison first offers a quick
review of some of the historic roots of this concept.

> Although the term "public opinion" was not used until the
> eighteenth century, the phenomenon itself has been noted and
> described by writers in ancient, medieval, and early modern times.
> Public opinion appears most often in urban societies and in those
> with relatively well-developed communication facilities, as for in-
> stance the Greek city states, but it can also be observed, even if more
> rarely, in predominantly rural societies with rudimentary communi-
> cations. The existence of phenomena bearing strong resemblances to
> public opinion has been noted by anthropologists in primitive socie-
> ties of widely varying characteristics.
>
> In ancient and medieval times writers who mention public opin-
> ion often refer to it as having mystical or divine properties. Early
> modern writers regard it as perceptible but indefinable. They usually
> agree on two of its aspects that it is a consensus among a large number
> of people, and that this consensus somehow exercises forces.

After a quick review of some of the historic roots of this term, Davison
moves to a real-life (although hypothetical) situation in Center City and gives us
a step-by-step account of the birth and growth of a specific public opinion issue
in the political world of Center City. His concept that personal opinions on
public opinion questions is built upon a process of "personal sampling" is
intriguing, even through as he notes others, such as Walter Lippmann, have also
referred to it. He also touches on, but does not fully explore, the fascinating
subject of why and how some public opinion issues dissolve and disappear.

Davison emphasizes the importance of maintaining the distinction between
the public opinion process he describes in Center City and the process that takes
place in small groups.

> We believe that there are very important differences. Perhaps most
> important is the fact that a public is formed around a single issue, or
> a number of closely related issues, while the range of issues on which
> a small group may demand conformity from its members can be very
> great indeed.

8

A second difference is that the interaction process leading to the formation of group opinions takes place among people who are in frequent association, while the public opinion process involves people who may be united in a particular interaction process only once.

Don Smith adds another dimension to understanding public opinion in his article, "Cognitive Consistency and the Perception of Others' Opinions." He begins by noting: "Few assumptions are as widely accepted as that which claims some relationship between the opinion people hold about an issue and the knowledge they possess about it. . . . Despite the universal assumption of such a relationship, the existence of any such relationship and, more so, the *nature* of such a relationship, is actually very unclear. . . . Consistency theory seems pertinent to the problem." Smith sets forth four hypotheses as providing a theoretical orientation for studying the purported relationship between knowledge and opinions:

1. Most individuals will both know and believe more facts congenial to their opinion than facts uncongenial to their opinion.
2. The proportion of individuals knowing and believing more congenial than uncongenial facts will be greater for those holding extreme opinions.
3. The proportion of individuals knowing and believing more congenial than uncongenial facts will be for those who perceive significant others agreeing with them than for those who perceive significant others disagreeing with them.
4. The greater the number of significant others perceived to disagree with one's opinion, the smaller the proportion of individuals knowing and believing more congenial than uncongenial facts.

Don't let the somewhat dense language put you off, for Smith then proceeds to report on a research study that he carried out to test these ideas. Smith's findings supported all four hypotheses indicating "that there is a clear association between the facts people know and believe about an issue and their opinions on that issue." Far from answering many questions, Smith's findings raise significant questions for public opinion research. "The results suggest that the knowledge or information component of opinions is less consistent for some individuals than for others—that similar opinions may rest on considerably different knowledge bases."

Brewster Smith's "A Psychologist's Perspective on Public Opinion Theory" makes the point that " 'Public opinion research' has mainly meant survey research. For psychologists, it has meant attitude research. Over the past generation, survey research has amply proved its utility, but neither survey research nor

9

experimental attitude research has greatly advanced our formulations of public opinion as a social force." As a psychologist he notes that his profession's longstanding bias that the very concept of public opinion is a reification is now being questioned by many psychologists who find the term meaningful and useful in their work.

Brewster Smith notes that beliefs about public opinion can influence realities and these, in turn, translate into certain actions by our political and business leaders that have discernible influences on our lives. He finds merit in the concern expressed by some scholars, such as Charles Y. Glock, in how much "free will" individuals exercise in arriving at attitudes and opinions on public as well as private issues. In a cautiously positive note, he makes a plea for students of public opinion research "to push ahead with the attempt to understand the phenomena of self-determination systematically and causally."

Smith concludes his article by calling attention to the increased academic interest in the fact that "how much self-determination a person exercises is bound up in a self-fulfilling prophecy. His feelings of efficacy, rooted in attitudes and concepts about the self, have much to do with what he will try and what he will accomplish."

Clearly there is no consensus among scholars as to the precise nature of public opinion. It is easier for them to discuss what it is not than to describe the phenomenon itself. Yet there runs through most of these articles a common thread of agreement, stated in many different forms and with countless qualifications. That thread suggests that public opinion, in part, is the expression of a predisposition by individuals to react in certain predictable ways to changing needs, interests, and pressures in their lives.

Some contributors place considerable stress on the importance of group membership, life style, and "significant others" in the shaping of public opinion. Others are more intrigued by the public opinion process itself. Often they see it as a learning experience. If there is any bias in these articles and their approach to this topic it probably is a sociological one—how group membership and the perception of reality by an individual contribute to the formation of public opinion. If these essays can be said to have generated any new theories about public opinion, they are best described by Merton's concept of "theories of the middle range."

1

TOWARD A SCIENCE
OF PUBLIC OPINION
Floyd D. Allport

Literature and popular usage with reference to public opinion contain many conceptions which impede clear thinking. These notions are drawn from analogies, personifications, and other figures of speech and are employed for journalistic terseness, for the purpose of arousing vivid imagery, or to conceal the emotional bias of the particular writer. They are so widespread in their use and are regarded with so much respect, even in textbooks of political and social science, that their reexamination is necessary as a first step in formulating a workable, scientific approach.

FICTIONS AND BLIND ALLEYS

1. *The Personification of Public Opinion*. Public opinion, according to this fiction, is thought of as some kind of being which dwells in or above the group, and there expresses its view upon various issues as they arise. The "voice of public opinion," or the "public conscience," are metaphors of this sort. The fiction arises through thinking of an expression given by a "group" at one time and another expression given by the same group at another time, and then assuming a continuity of some sort of soul principle between the two expressions. It might be said, for example, that public opinion in 1830 favored slavery, but in 1930 opposed it; and the *daemon* of the group is thus thought of as changing its mind. When viewed from the descriptive standpoint of science, this fiction, of course, disappears, and we find only groupings of specific individuals with a certain common agreement among them at one time and a different sort of agreement at another time. Though misleading from the standpoint of research, this fiction may have arisen partly from a wholly genuine situation. A certain psychological continuity

Originally published in Volume 1, Number 1, 1937 of the *Public Opinion Quarterly*.

does exist in the fact that there are established in individuals, over a period of time, a number of habitual ideas, traditions, customs, and formulations of past experience, in short, a "reservoir" of accepted beliefs and practices, upon the basis of which many current issues are decided. The error, however, consists in thinking that these habitual, neural dispositions in individuals make up collectively a soul or being called "public opinion," which contemplates and decides upon public issues as they appear.

2. *The Personification of the Public.* A related fiction is one in which the notion of a collective, super-organic being is applied not to the opinion process itself, but to the public which "holds it." A personified "Public" is spoken of as turning its gaze, now this way, now that, as deciding, and as uttering its opinion. One of the effects of this loose, journalistic manner of writing is that, since "the public" is here not an explicitly denotable reality, but a metaphor, any kind of opinion may be attributed to it without the possibility of checking the assertion.

3. *The Group Fallacy of the Public.* Somewhat less mystical, but equally uncritical, is the usage of those who renounce the idea of a collective entity or group mind, holding that when they say "the public" they mean *individuals*; but who, nevertheless, go on employing such phrases as "the public wants so and so," or "the country voted dry." Whether we personify the notion of the public or not, we are likely to commit a fallacy when we use a collective term as the subject of a verb denoting action. For the statement which the verb implies will often be true only of a part of the aggregate concerned. By this sort of terminology, which has also been called the "part-for-the-whole fallacy," one conceals facts concerning minorities which it is the business of research to uncover.

4. *The Fallacy of Partial Inclusion in the Use of the Term "Public."* Applying the foregoing criticism more specifically the question arises, "What do we mean by a *public*?" Is it a population defined by geographical, community, political jurisdiction, or other limits; or is it merely the collection of people, within such an area, who have a common interest? In the first instance the term is *totally inclusive,* that is, it is employed to include *all* of *each* individual in the area, his body, his physiological processes and needs, as well as his various opinions and reactions. This usage, however, is not common because it is too complete; it includes so much that the categories of social scientists and leaders cannot be intelligently used in dealing with it. We cannot speak of *the* opinion of this public, because it includes too many alignments of opinion, many of which may be irrelevant or even contradictory.

The second meaning of the term public is usually, therefore, the one intended. This meaning is made up, not of entire individuals, but of an abstraction of a specific interest (or set of interests) common to a certain number within the population. Those who have such a common interest are said to constitute a *"public."* We may call this usage of the term public one of *partial inclusion.* Now let us suppose that the individuals having this particular interest (that is, comprising a public from the partially inclusive standpoint) are not also members of some other partially inclusive public. That is, let us suppose their public does not overlap with any other public. If we conceive opinion to go with interest, as is likely on important issues, this public becomes coterminous with the spread of an opinion upon certain issues. The public, in other words, would be defined as the number of people holding a certain opinion, and the people holding that opinion would be identified as those belonging to that public. The definition of the term public would thus be circular. The term public, as a partially inclusive phenomenon, would thus be found superfluous for the purpose of research, and the problem would be reduced directly to the task of discovering where and in what degree these alignments of individuals having similar opinions exist among the population concerned.

Now let us suppose, on the other hand, that the publics overlap, that is, that an individual may belong simultaneously in two or more groupings because of different opinions or interests he possesses on different issues. In such a case if we try to state, or discover by a canvass, the opinion of a certain partially inclusive grouping (a "public"), we might not know where a certain individual should be placed. Since he is in two groupings, he may have attitudes which tend to contradict each other on certain questions. One of these attitudes must be suppressed in favor of the other. If we place him arbitrarily in one of the publics we may be misjudging which attitude is dominant, thus producing a false result. If we place him in *both,* we count him twice, or perhaps have him cancelling himself, both of which consequences are absurd. With terminology such as this it becomes impossible to define our problem, or to discover our empirical units of study. Opinions are reactions of individuals; they cannot be allocated to publics without becoming ambiguous and unintelligible for research.[1]

[1] Professor Dewey has recognized this confusion in the notion of a public and its result in connection with our difficulties in dealing with public problems. (See Dewey, *The Public and Its Problems.*) For further discussion of this point and of Professor Dewey's position, see F. H. Allport, *Institutional Behavior,* Essay V. For a further reference to "total and partial inclusion" in their bearing upon method in social science, see F. H. Allport, "Group and Institution as Concepts in a Natural Science of Social Phenomena," *Publications of the American Sociological Society,* Vol. XXII, pp. 83-99.

5. *The Fiction of an Ideational Entity.* Another non-scientific way of speaking about public opinion, sometimes encountered in popular usage and even in the literature, represents the opinion content as a kind of essence which, like a Platonic "idea," is distributed into the minds of all those who endorse it. The expression that a certain opinion is "public" illustrates this usage.

6. *The Group-Product, or "Emergent," Theory.* We now come to formulations which refer not to personifications or agencies, but to results. Public opinion in this sense is regarded as a new product emerging from integrated discussion in a group, a product of concerted individual thinking which is different both from an average or consensus of views and from the opinion of any particular individual.[2] A variant of this definition is that which describes public opinion as "a step on the way toward social decision, a sort of gathering point of the social will in its organization toward action."[3] This fiction will be discussed in connection with the one following.

7. *The Eulogistic Theory.* Those who are inclined to regard public opinion as the emergent result of group discussion usually carry the implications of their theory farther, viewing this result not only as different from the products of minds working individually, but as superior in character. In the process of interaction errors are thought to be weeded out so that the opinion of the more enlightened, improved by discussion, will in the end prevail. Public opinion is thus considered not as a segment of behavior common to the many, but as a single ideational product of interacting and creative personalities.[4]

The criticism of the emergent and eulogistic theories calls for some careful distinctions. It is granted at the outset that when one individual enters into a discussion with others he often reaches conclusions which are different from any conclusion he would have arrived at through solitary reflection. The assumption which we should guard against, as unworkable in scientific methodology, is that this emergent product is something floating out, as it were, in space, and belongs to a group mind rather than to individuals' reactions. Argument A must be related to argument B and argument C in a particular individual's thinking. A cannot be in one individual's mind, B in another's, and so on, and produce any emergent that can be known to human intelligence. The emergent product must be expressed by some

[2] See Krueger and Reckless, *Social Psychology*, pp. 127, 266, and Gault, R. H., *Social Psychology*, pp. 176-77.
[3] See the definition cited by J. K. Folsom, *Social Psychology*, p. 446, and Chapter IX of that work.
[4] See R. H. Gault, *op. cit.*

14

individuals or we cannot know it at all; and if it *is* expressed by some individual, it becomes difficult to show just how much the influence of integrated discussion has helped to form it. For no matter what common result individuals have reached through discussion with others, when they put that conclusion forward in overt action, in voting, for example, they are expressing not only what they *think,* but what they *want.* So-called "group thinking" may have taken place in individuals, as we have shown; but in the arena of practical affairs it is *individuals* who do things and not the integrated product of group thought. It may be that the individuals are acting *in accordance with* group thinking; but in large alignments of opinion this may be difficult to establish since it is so difficult to know what the content of this emergent opinion is.

We must realize, of course, that the questions which make up the content of public-opinion phenomena are usually not questions of ascertainable fact, but of *opinion.* There is, in such instances, no way of knowing whether the product of the interaction of individuals is of a higher or a lower order so far as truth, or even value, is concerned. Such interaction does bring out the issues more definitely, and it shows more clearly how the individuals are aligning upon different sides. In other words, it gives a clearer picture of what the individuals *want.* This result, however, does not necessarily constitute an intelligent solution of the problem. Such a solution can be known to have been reached only when time and experiment have given us some basis upon which to judge; when, in other words, the issue has become to some extent a question of fact. When this time arrives it is probable that the emergent product will be the result not of group deliberation alone, but of a considerable amount of overt experimentation as well.[5]

We are not denying the possibility that a superior product of group interaction may exist. We are merely saying that, if there is such an emergent product, we do not know where it is, how it can be discovered, identified or tested, or what the standards are by which its value may be judged. Though not discredited in the realm of possible abstract truth, theories of this sort seem to be blind alleys so far as a scientific treatment of the problem

[5] For an account of some of the effects of group discussion upon accuracy of opinion, and of the theory involved, see an account by the present writer in Achilles, P. S., *Psychology at Work,* pp. 214-18; also Jenness, Arthur, "Social Influences in the Change of Opinion," *Jn. of Abn. and Soc. Psych.,* 1932, 27, 29-34, and "The Rôle of Discussion in Changing Opinion Regarding a Matter of Fact," *Jn. of Abn. and Soc. Psych.,* 1932, 27, 279-96.

is concerned. Writers who have stressed them have perhaps been thinking of small, totally inclusive rural or pioneer communities where adjustment to nature and to one's fellow men is direct, and where the common, integrated opinion is practically synonymous with the common life; or else they may have been thinking of discussion groups in which a deliberate attempt is made to reach a result satisfactory to the wishes and judgment of all participating. In our modern vast and growing urban populations, complex in composition and organization, where face-to-face contacts of whole personalities are giving way to occupational and other groupings, it is doubtful how much real integrative effect does take place in an individual's ideas through discussion with others. Some occurs, no doubt; but it is probably mingled with the effects of emotional conditioning, with susceptibility to stereotypes, symbols, and "straddle-terms" of political leaders, as well as an undeviating regard for one's own individual interests. In any case the view that public opinion is a product of group thinking superior to the thinking of individuals and effective as a kind of super-individual group will or judgment is a scientifically sterile notion. This theory, like the others we have discussed, may be motivated by the desire of publicists for the support of a kind of "social providence" for their acts. Though comfortably optimistic, the emergent and eulogistic theories may lull us into a sense of false security in which the need for research and for facts regarding attitudes and control processes is in danger of being forgotten.

8. *The Confusion of Public Opinion with the Public Presentation of Opinion.* (*The Journalistic Fallacy.*) The preceding discussion has dealt with theories of the nature of public opinion itself. There should be added to these a common fallacy concerning the criterion by which a given opinion content should be regarded as "public" (that is, as widely accepted). This is the illusion that the item which one sees represented in print as "public opinion," or which one hears in speeches or radio broadcasts as "public information" or "public sentiment," really has this character of widespread importance and endorsement. This naïve error has been fostered by review and digest journals, and by surveys urging popular or legislative action, in which evidence presented concerning "public opinion" has consisted of news-item and editorial clippings from different sections of the country. The lack of statistical foundation, or of studies relating this material to the actual lay of attitudes in the population, is so obvious that further comment is unnecessary.

COMMON AGREEMENTS AND
SOME PROPOSED DISTINCTIONS

Notwithstanding these many futile characterizations of public opinion, there appear certain points of common agreement in the work of various scholars which may prove useful in guiding us past the blind alleys and setting us upon the proper road. These points of agreement the writer ventures to restate in his own way and to add a few other distinctions which, he believes, have value for research. The phenomena to be studied under the term public opinion are essentially *instances of behavior* of which the following conditions are true.

a. They are behaviors of human *individuals.*
b. They involve *verbalization.*
c. They are performed (or the words are expressed) by *many* individuals.
d. They are stimulated by and directed toward some *universally known object* or *situation.*
e. The object or situation they are concerned with is *important to many.*
f. They represent *action* or *readiness for action* in the nature of *approval* or *disapproval* of the common object.
g. They are frequently performed with an *awareness* that *others are reacting to the same situation* in a similar manner.
h. The attitudes or opinions they involve are *expressed* or, at least, the individuals are in readiness to express them.
i. The individuals performing these behaviors, or set to perform them, may or may not be in one another's presence. (Public-opinion situation in relation to crowd.)
j. They may involve verbal contents of both *permanent* and *transitory* character, constituting "genetic groundwork material" and *"present alignment,"* respectively.
k. They are in the nature of *present efforts to oppose or accomplish something,* rather than long-standing conformities of behavior. (Public opinion phenomena contrasted with law and custom.)
l. Being efforts toward common objectives, they frequently *have the character of conflict* between individuals aligned *upon opposing sides.*
m. They are sufficiently strong and numerous, as common behaviors, to give rise to the *probability that they may be effective* in attaining their objective.

These points of common agreement require some comment. Item (a), stating that the content of the phenomenon must be conceived as related to the actual *behavior of individuals,* is self-evident. It cannot be merely an invention, for example, of a journalist purporting to represent actual behaviors of acceptance. As for item (c), *"many individuals,"* the specific number or proportion necessary cannot be stated, since it will vary with the situation. The number required to produce an effect toward the objective (m) must be considered in this connection.

(b) *Verbalization*. The common stimulating object or situation must be something that can be expressed in words; it must be capable of being immediately and clearly named. There can be no such thing as opinion without stating the content of the opinion in language form. The *response* of individuals to this common stimulating situation may be either verbal or non-verbal. It may, for example, be a grimace, gesture, or emotional expression. This reaction, however, must be *capable* of being readily translated into words, such, for example, as expressions of agreement or approval.

(d) *Common Stimulating Object*. The object or situation toward which the individuals' responses are directed must be clearly understood, and within the experience of all. It must be sufficiently limited to be related to a definite proposal for action. It could not be, for example, the general subject of taxation; but it might be the proposal of some particular tax law. Properly speaking, public opinion does not exist about the nature of the deity, though it might well exist with regard to spoken violations of accepted theological creeds.

(e) The common stimulating situation must not only be well known; it must be a *matter of universal importance*. Mere interest is not enough; the situation must touch upon fundamental needs or desires. The hazards of a man ascending in a stratosphere balloon arouse widespread interest, but they could not ordinarily be called matters of public opinion, since they are not important to many. A government policy of building military aircraft for "national defense," however, might well become a matter of public opinion.

(f) *Readiness for Approval or Disapproval*. The responses aroused or prepared in the individuals must be in the nature of active liking or disliking, of support or opposition. For example, the common knowledge of the various methods by which the sale of alcoholic liquors may be controlled, and of the relative advantages of these methods, does not belong in the category of public opinion unless such knowledge is connected with the widespread favoring or opposing of some particular method.

(g) *Awareness of Others Reacting*. A number of writers have maintained that public-opinion phenomena involve a "consciousness of kind" in the individuals holding or expressing the accepted view. It may make a considerable difference in one's behavior, in supporting or opposing a particular measure, if he is aware, or even if he imagines, that others are reacting in the same manner.[6] Although this "impression of universality" is an impor-

[6] For a discussion of this phenomenon see F. H. Allport, *Social Psychology*, pp. 305-7.

tant part of the opinion process, it is perhaps best not to require it as an essential element in every opinion alignment to be studied. Otherwise important phases of the problem may be overlooked, such, for example, as the distribution of opinions existing at the first moment the common proposal or stimulating object appears, and before people have had a chance to become aware of, or concerned about, the reactions of others.

(h) *Opinions Expressed.* If item (g), the effect of the opinions of others, be accepted as an important phase of public-opinion phenomena, the corollary follows that the individual's opinions must be outwardly expressed, or at least capable of being readily elicited. As shown by the work of Dr. Richard Schanck, it makes a decided difference in how one feels or thinks, whether the opinion is one that the individual readily expresses or acknowledges to others, or is his own personal and private view. Dr. Schanck has called these two types of reaction "public" and "private attitudes," respectively.[7] To a publicist, the unexpressed opinion is usually unimportant since it does not represent a recognizable alignment. It is not his concern what the reasons of different personalities for holding or not holding certain common opinions may be. The fact of common acceptance or rejection is alone significant. From the scientific standpoint, however, although we recognize that a public-opinion phenomenon requires expression of opinions, we cannot neglect the field of private attitudes. In the long run, the existence of a widespread similarity of unexpressed private attitudes may be highly important, and should be discovered and measured by our techniques. Consider, for example, the potential importance of the opinion which great numbers of Germans or Italians may have about their rulers, but do not dare reveal.

(i) *Relation to Presence or Absence of Others.* A number of writers have discussed the difference between a public and a crowd.[8] They seem in general to agree, however, that the phenomena which we call public opinion can occur in either situation. The condition of partial inclusion which we have previously cited as characteristic of the usual definition of a public is recognized by implication in the general agreement that an individual can be in a number of publics at one time, but in only one crowd. Another way to state the matter is to recognize that in either case we have a situation comprising many individuals reacting to a common object or situation, but

[7] Schanck, Richard L., "A Study of a Community and Its Groups and Institutions Conceived of as Behaviors of Individuals," *Psychol. Monographs*, Vol. XLIII, No. 2 (whole No. 195), 1932.

[8] See Krueger and Reckless, *Social Psychology*, p. 266.

under different conditions of association, proximity, stimulation, and response. Where individuals are separated, for example, in their own homes, there is not the possibility of visual, touch, and olfactory sensations from the other individuals which obtains in a crowd situation. Modern radio, however, has brought *auditory* stimulation from others into this segregated domain, as when we "listen in" to the applause of an audience in a political address. This limitation of sensory modes probably has an effect in the lessening of facilitation, or reenforcement, of the responses characteristic of the crowd situation; but it probably does not abolish such reenforcement. In the main, where individuals are reacting in one another's presence, motor responses often have the possibility of being more expressive, overt, vigorous, and direct in their action. In cases where the individuals are separated, the reactions are likely to be more implicit, and can usually become effective only through some symbolic or representative mechanism, or indirect political process, such as voting. For the most part, however, the distinction between crowd-action and public-opinion phenomena seems to be one of degree rather than one of kind.

(j) *Transitory and Permanent Aspects.* In the treatment of public-opinion phenomena writers of one school have stressed the stable and rational character of the content and the aspect of its universal acceptance, while other writers have represented the opinion content as unstable, emotional, opportunistic, subject to propaganda, and divided upon controversial issues.[9] This disagreement can be resolved if we view the phenomenon as a process with a time dimension, in which the older content becomes the stabilized and universal portion, while the more recent content represents the present ever-shifting alignment. We have referred above to what we have figuratively called a "reservoir" of common beliefs, attitudes, and knowledge, which forms a part of the sociologists' "culture pattern." More specifically, these mores of thinking and feeling are merely reactions that can be predicted to occur with greater certainty, both now and in the future, than can other types of reactions. Some of these long-standing behaviors may be of a rational character; or they may be the product of trial-and-error experience on a large scale, as, for example, the doctrine of American isolation or the avoidance of inflation. Others may be equally long-standing and predictable, but more emotional in character, such, for instance, as race prejudices. Now in the process of forming the new align-

[9] One writer has taken note of this contrast by making a distinction between "public" opinion and "preponderant" opinion.

ments, publicity agents employ these universal and long-standing attitudes to secure their immediate ends, their method being that of transferring the old reaction to a new stimulus by the familiar method of the conditioned response. The old response of approaching, withdrawing, rejecting, or struggling is evoked by the old stimulus term, and while it is occurring the new stimulus to which it is desired to transfer it is introduced. The result is the association of the old response, in the future, with the new stimulus.

We now have the suggestion of a solution of the disagreement regarding public-opinion content. The old responses, stable and universally accepted as following upon their original and "rightful" stimuli, still exist in the background. They are the universal, tried, and stable aspect of the opinion. But the fact of their transfer by conditioning *to a new stimulus* is something new, unstable, opportunistic, and effective among certain portions of the population (who are more biased, more gullible, or more heavily propagandized) but not among others. Hence we have here an explanation of the shifting, irrational, and divided aspect of the public-opinion process.

To take an example of the conditioning process above described, let us consider the doctrine that "All men are created equal." This idea has long been accepted as a part of American mores. Now such an established attitude alone does not satisfy our criteria for public-opinion phenomena, since it does not, of itself, suggest definitive action toward some objective. Nevertheless, it is one of the psychological foundations upon which opinion alignments, which do satisfy our criteria, can be built. In 1776 support for the war against George III was elicited by conditioning the responses of approval aroused by this formula to the proposals for revolutionary action. Thus the older maxim of individual equality was the stable, enduring, and unanimously accepted phase of the phenomenon. Its transfer to the revolutionary cause was the new, opportunistic, and, at first, highly controversial aspect. Between 1830 and 1861 the same reaction of individual equality and liberty was increasingly connected with the argument against slavery; and after the Civil War the reaction against slavery also became a part of the basic mores. In later years the same doctrine (with aversion to slavery added) has been employed to help align individuals toward abolishing compulsory prostitution (white slavery), child labor (child slavery), and undesirable working conditions (wage slavery). In a similar manner (to take another example) a nation-wide inveterate pride in race and culture, combined with a long-standing prejudice against Jews, are being employed by Hitler as an instrument with which to unify his followers in support of the measures of the Nazi régime.

We may call this body of long-standing, common attitudes which are conditioned to newer situations the *genetic groundwork responses* of public opinion; and in contradistinction we may speak of the consensus of many individuals, induced by transferring these earlier reactions to new stimuli, as the *present alignment*. One of the important problems of research is to discover the groundwork materials of real or potential importance for opinion in a population, and to determine their relation to alignments existing at present or in the process of formation.

(k) *Action toward Present Objective.* The distinction between genetic groundwork and present alignment suggests a further contrast between public-opinion phenomena and another set of long-standing behaviors, namely, those which constitute laws, customs, and traditions. These latter phenomena are perhaps special cases of the genetic groundwork upon which opinion alignments may be built. They differ, however, from the other groundwork in the existence of a steeper mode of conformity resulting from the more vigorous coercion of punishment and public disapproval for those who fail to conform. Usually, however, the opinion phenomenon does not represent a conditioning of the legalized response to a new stimulus, but is a widespread struggle reaction against individuals or proposals which go against the customary or legally prescribed practice. Thus we do not say that a law requiring a householder to shovel the snow from his sidewalk is itself a part of a public-opinion phenomenon, so long as everyone obeys it. It is simply a common and expected practice of citizens. If, however, certain individuals in a neighborhood persistently fail to remove snow from their sidewalks, causing inconvenience and danger to their neighbors, there may arise an alignment of expressed opinion against them. In order to make such an alignment effective the existence of the common practice expected and prescribed as law is likely to be cited. Laws protecting property are not, in themselves, public-opinion situations; but should numerous unpunished burglaries occur in a community within a short time, a condition fulfilling all the criteria of public opinion might speedily arise. Public-opinion phenomena arise when non-conformists openly refuse to treat the national flag with respect, to wear clothes, or to conform with other customs. With regard to laws not established but in prospect, the situation is reversed. It is not now a case of public-opinion phenomena arising against those who violate expected or legal practice, but of the new law being championed or opposed according as it conforms or does violence to previously existing

22

groundwork (or can be made to appear to do so). An example of this relationship is afforded by the passing of legislation to prohibit Negroes from teaching in white schools in localities where they were likely to be appointed. Here the genetic groundwork of race prejudice was the response to which the newly proposed law became the conditioning stimulus.

(1) *Relation to Issue and Conflict.* Public-opinion phenomena, as we have seen, are those which involve readiness for action toward some present unattained objective. The common stimulating situation toward which the responses are directed is a plan or policy through which many individuals are trying to get what they want. This being true, situations will often arise in which the individuals are aligned in special-interest groups, members of each side trying to get what they want in opposition to individuals aligned in an opposing group. Opinions upon the two sides in this case are only aspects or symptoms of a more profound and general struggle. They may be only a rationalization of this struggle to secure favor with neutrals or stronger loyalty from adherents in the drive toward the real objective, which is often more biological or prepotent than the formulated opinions of its supporters would suggest. The Doctrine of States' Rights, for example, has been used as a rallying symbol for individuals with strong economic interests of various sorts.

We enter here the field of public opinion in relation to pressure politics, class and labor struggles, and social conflicts of every type. It becomes necessary here to transcend the view of the publicist who is usually interested only in one side of the controversy; for the alignment, or piling up in a J-curve of attitude distribution upon one side, is intelligible only in the light of a corresponding steepening upon the other side. In a two-party system of politics each party alignment has its full significance only in view of the opposing party alignment. The entire distribution becomes U-shaped. Strong communistic developments are contemporaneous with strong capitalistic and fascistic alignments; and the one grouping seems to derive its meaning in contrast with the other. The popular notion that these various "isms" arise as political philosophies gaining momentum through indoctrination as they spread is inadequate. These philosophies represent rationalizations of the more powerful factors which lie beneath. They are the verbal aspects of the total concerted struggle behaviors of individuals aligned upon the two sides. They are the verbal part of the techniques which the individuals are using to get what they want in the struggle. In international conflicts, similarly, we should take our public-opinion field as broader than the limits of one country alone. We should think of a

U-shaped distribution of the population of both countries combined; for the shifts of attitude distribution in one of the countries bears a definite, predictable relationship to the shift in the other.

(m) *Probability of Effect.* Our final criterion, that of a probable degree of effectiveness is, from the standpoint of control, the most important of all. In the entire field of the population sampled there will probably be found consensuses of individuals favoring or disfavoring all sorts of common objects, in all ranges of number, intensity of conviction, and effort put forth. A thorough program of research would include the charting of all these consensuses. From a more practical standpoint, however, we shall probably have to choose from all this array the particular alignments in which we are most interested. And in this choice the criterion of selecting those which promise to be in some degree *effective* will probably be found the most useful and natural to employ. In making such a choice the mistake is sometimes made of selecting the alignment which seems to be the largest from the standpoint of numbers of adherents. A careful consideration of the probable effect of a given alignment, in which other factors besides number are taken into account, will help us to make a better selection. There may be many cases in which a large proportion of the people favor some action, but that does not necessarily argue the highest probability of that action being taken. The variable of *intensity,* that is the *degree of feeling,* or the *strenuousness of the effort* which individuals will make toward the common objective, must also be considered. For example, a recent nationwide sample poll on birth control has revealed that a substantial majority of the people are in favor of it. Yet legislative action supporting it has not been generally forthcoming, probably because the desire for it was not sufficiently intense. That is, the need and desire for contraceptive information and help that cannot now be gained by the individual himself is not felt acutely enough by the members of this majority to press for organized action in opposition to a minority who have a very intense feeling upon the other side. Collective results are brought about by enough people holding and expressing opinions, and by their expressing them strongly enough, or acting upon them. The situation must ensure that enough people are intensely enough affected.

Other influences must, of course, be recognized in predicting or understanding the production of effects. The existence of some type of organization for bringing collective action about, and the facility of using such organization, are important. The presence of individuals of outstanding influence and ability to direct the undertaking is another factor. A third factor is the degree of reenforcement received by each individual through feeling that others have the same attitude as he; and this, in turn, depends upon the ease, quickness, and freedom of communication among the individuals. The channels through which citizens can make known their wishes to authorities must also be taken into account. We must remember also that the process through which the alignment becomes effective is complicated by a circularity of reenforcement. When, for example, an editor pretends in his columns that he is expressing "public opinion," he thereby influences authorities on the one hand and strengthens the alignment among the people on the other. The latter influence increases the popular manifestation of the attitude, with the effect of still further increasing the editor's confidence and aggressiveness in putting forth his editorials as "public opinion."

It is true that these various factors are at present difficult to isolate and measure. To separate them and study the contribution of each to the total effect is one of the problems of the new science of public opinion. For the present we must rely, in the absence of more definite knowledge, upon a practical familiarity with these complex situations. In applying the criterion of effectiveness it is, however, unnecessary to wait until the effect has already been produced. If we waited until that point, we should miss important aspects of the phenomenon as they were taking place. Nor is it necessary to be *certain* that the effect will occur, and that the opinion-alignment we are considering will play a definite part in producing it. It is sufficient that, when we survey the whole situation, there seems to be a probability above chance that this will occur. This, in fact, is the very method which political leaders use in gauging the potential importance for their programs of current opinion-movements in their communities. And although they have only this subjective weighing of the probabilities to count on, nevertheless, if they accept a certain opinion-alignment and act as if it were *going to be* effective, the responses of citizens adhering to that alignment will probably *tend to become* effective or more effective than they were before. Important as the original lay of attitude of individuals may be, we must consider also the *entire control situation,* with the numerous influencing factors we have cited, as a configuration in a multi-individual field. This phase of the problem cannot be overlooked if we are to be able to predict or even to understand effects. In the language of the new topological psychology we seem to be dealing here with vectors of force operating in a social field.[10]

[10] It might be argued that, if an alignment of individuals of given numbers and feeling intensity is thus to be regarded as a force in a social situation, the treatment of public

opinion as an entity, a formulation which we have rejected as sterile, becomes valid, and even necessary, as a working principle of research. The attempt to isolate and measure forces in a social field is, however, too new for us to make a final decision about this matter. In addition to the intangible character of the units we must handle in measuring the force of an alignment, there is the further baffling problem of the circular increase in effect. In figuring the stresses upon the pier of a bridge an engineer does not need to figure the pull of gravitation and the force of the current as augmenting one another in a circular manner. If this were true it would render his task of making calculations wellnigh impossible. The situation, however, with human organisms is different. A public official's attitude and program, let us say, are under the influence of the combined "forces" of newspaper publicity and the opinions manifested by individuals at large. But the calculation of these two forces is not an easy problem, because the newspaper appeal, as we have shown, may affect the attitudes of the citizens, and the change thus produced may in turn reaffect the newspaper editor, *this* change again *further* influencing the citizens. And so on ad infinitum. The present writer is inclined to believe that "force" calculations will fail in the multi-individual behavior field, and that we shall have to employ some other type of measuring continua, such as the telic or teleonomic, which have been described elsewhere. In such methods, however, we shall be obliged, as we have indicated, to take into account a field of reciprocally acting units, whether these units be conceived as collective entities or as single human organisms.

But granting that indices of collective alignments of "public opinion" in a social field could be developed (and all efforts in that direction should certainly be encouraged) there is still good reason for us to continue our emphasis upon measurement at the more elementary level, namely, the behaviors of individuals. We must remember that the societal patterns, or *gestalten,* are far less stable than force fields in the physical or biological sciences, by analogy with which the societal configurations are suggested. Voluntaristic action, such as we have in public affairs, is by its very nature subject to unpredictable changes which may alter the functioning of the entire pattern and the force which we assign to its various components. The position of iron particles in a magnetic field, the contributions of various bodily organs and tissues to the entire body metabolism, the rôle of sensory units in the perception of space,—all these are phenomena having a high degree of stability. The pattern of relationships is not affected by any likelihood that these component atoms, molecules, tissues, or sensations might think or feel in a certain way, or connect their old, stable ways of thinking to new issues, or communicate their reactions to the other elements of the pattern, or that it would make any difference in the patterns of magnetism, metabolism, or perception if they did. In the human field, however, the mere fact of individuals thinking or feeling in certain ways, or knowing certain facts about the "pattern" of their actions, profoundly affects that pattern itself. Let us suppose, for example, that it should suddenly become known that, in their own private feelings, the great majority of citizens had long been wishing for a law to be passed depriving the "Supreme Court" of the power of declaring enactments of "Congress" unconstitutional. What a marked readjustment this would bring about in our power field, and how it would alter the "force index" of "nine venerable gentlemen"! In contrast with this instability of the collective force field, we come back to the relative dependability of attitudes in individuals. For this instability of the collective scene is not due to shifts of personal attitudes in the citizens, at least to shifts in the groundwork-reactions of opinion, but to the control methods, political structures, sudden blockings or facilitation of communication, dispelling of "pluralistic ignorance," and the exploiting of group and institutional symbols for shifting purposes. Attitudes of course are not absolutely permanent, not even the groundwork-reactions which have been longer established. They are far more stable, however, than the force indices of the various components in a societal pattern. It is difficult to predict the *power* which, in coming decades, will be accorded to spokesmen either of the working class or of the government-controlled capitalists, or the authority which will be vested in the President, the members of Congress, or the heads of government bureaus. But we can feel fairly certain that the *opinion alignments* which will be most broadly held and most effective in this country will be those of protecting the interests of the "common man," of maintaining homes,

DEFINING THE "PUBLIC-OPINION SITUATION"

Our discussion of the fictions and blind alleys of method have shown us where the major futilities lie. When we try to find an object corresponding to the term public opinion, that is, when we regard it as an entity or a content to be discovered and then studied or analyzed, our efforts will meet with scant success. But when we distinguish by this term a multi-individual situation, or some of the relationships in such a situation, and then enter this situation and begin to study the explicit materials which it affords, some valuable results may be gained.

The question now arises as to the nature of this "public-opinion situation" and how its characteristic relationships may be recognized. And the answer to this question is to be found in the points of common agreement which we have previously discussed. We are to deal with situations involving word reactions or reactions *to* words on the part of many individuals, which are directed toward common stimulating situations important to many, these reactions showing readiness to act favorably or unfavorably toward the situation, to be influenced by the awareness of others reacting, to associate older attitudes with present issues, to be directed toward an objective different from the *status quo,* to be frequently related to concerted conflict, and to suggest the likelihood of being effective. Through the use of these criteria we thus find reality and use for the notion of public opinion, while discarding those earlier attempts at formulation which led us off upon the wrong track. We have retained and identified public-opinion phenomena, while at the same time keeping our hands upon the explicitly denotable realities before us, upon behaviors of individuals which can be measured and recorded in the form of statistical distributions. The whole argument may be summarized by the following condensed and somewhat formal statement:

The term public opinion is given its meaning with reference to a multi-individual situation in which individuals are expressing themselves, or can be called upon to express themselves, as favoring or supporting (or else disfavoring or opposing) some definite condition, person, or proposal of widespread importance, in such a proportion of number, intensity, and constancy, as to give rise to the probability of affecting action, directly or indirectly, toward the object concerned.

of liquidating public debts, of demanding security for the future, of keeping out of European politics, and of maintaining an adequate national defense.

> "Where all people talk on the same subject, they should be agreed about the vocabulary with which they discuss it: or, at any rate, they should be aware that they are *not* agreed."
>
> —*George C. Lewis*

"BY PUBLIC OPINION I MEAN"—

Reports of current developments in the fields of public relations, advertising, fund-raising, and professional services generally, are comparatively meaningless unless they are related to precisely defined concepts, problems, perspectives, standards of values, and interpretations of social purpose. It is desirable, therefore, to pause from time to time and essay this task of reorientation. Professional as well as academic students continue to use the term "public opinion" as if it were something vague and mystical, hesitantly posing the query: Is there really any such thing as public opinion? And if so, what is it? It will not be inappropriate, therefore, if we consider this question before going on to more pressing problems of analysis and assessment.

Search for a Definition

Many attempts have been made to define the meaning of the term "public opinion" in a way that will be generally acceptable. As a result there are about as many definitions as there are studies in the field. This is so perplexing that a special group of social scientists declared in 1924 that serious students of the subject should avoid use of the expression altogether.

Periodically some student will attempt to assemble a collection of definitions and classify them with a view to reconciling different points of view. Inevitably he concludes with another addition to the already long list. Virginia Sedman, after a careful analysis of the definitions of Lippmann, Lowell, Dewey, King, Holcombe, Bogardus, and others,

Originally published in Volume 3, Number 2, 1939 of the *Public Opinion Quarterly*.

concluded that "public opinion, for us, is an active or latent force derived from a composite of individual thoughts, sentiments and impressions, which composite is weighted by the varying degrees of influence and aggressiveness of the separate opinions within the aggregate."

Floyd H. Allport, in the first issue of THE PUBLIC OPINION QUARTERLY in January 1937, also tried to bring order out of the conceptual chaos by surveying the literature of the field and specifying several fallacious notions that have given rise to misconceptions. He called attention specifically to such fictions and blind alleys as (1) the personification of public opinion; (2) the personification of the public; (3) the group fallacy; (4) the fallacy of partial inclusion in the use of the term "public"; (5) what he calls the fiction of ideational entity; (6) the emergent theory; (7) the eulogistic theory; and (8) the journalistic fallacy. And he, too, contributed another definition. It reads: "The term public opinion is given its meaning with reference to a multi-individual situation in which individuals are expressing themselves, or can be called upon to express themselves, as favoring (or else disfavoring or opposing) some definite condition, person, or proposal of widespread importance, in such a proportion of number, intensity, and constancy, as to give rise to the probability of affecting action, directly or indirectly, toward the object concerned."

One of the most recent attempts at conceptualization is that of William E. Utterback who uses an imposing array of definitions as a backdrop for his own attempt. Included among the earlier definitions are those of Dicey, McDougall, Cooley, Foulke, Bernays, Sedman, Ross, King, Maxey, Hart, Gault, Bogardus, Lowell, Ellwood, Bauer, Young, Shepard, Ginsberg, Wilson, Jones, Bryce, Dewey, Lasswell, Park, Carr, Lundberg, Clark, Bentley, and Lippmann. Such a list virtually constitutes a catalogue of neo-classical writers on the subject of public opinion.

The Word "Public"

The term "public opinion" is obviously a general and rather indefinite expression like many other useful English words. By itself it has very little meaning. Only as it is related to a particular public and to specific opinions about definite subjects does it become significant. In these respects it is similar to the word "weather" which a dictionary defines merely as "a state of the atmosphere." Students of meteorology are not usually concerned about weather in general, but about the state of the atmosphere at a particular time and in a particular place. Defined in these terms the word "weather" becomes significant and can be studied. Similarly the term "public opinion" must be related to a specific public and to definite opinions about something. Then it is possible to study it, to find out what the state of public opinion is, why it is what it is, what changes have been and are taking place, and what if anything should be done.

It is obvious that there are all kinds of publics. In some cases a public will be a group of individuals with common interests and possibly a formal organization. But the public in which we are interested may be composed of a heterogeneous collection of individuals without organization and lacking identifying symbols and attributes. The number of different publics in a community is theoretically the number of distinct combinations of individuals possible in that community. Among the more significant publics, however, are such organized groups as the citizens of a state, members of political parties, of trade unions, business organizations, churches, fraternal groupings, political and professional associations, etc. Publics may also include such unorganized groups as crowds, customers, newspaper readers, and clienteles of different types. Individuals may be members of different publics simultaneously. That is to say, they may at one time be members of a football crowd, a physician's clientele, a fraternity, a church, and a

political party. Students of public opinion as well as leaders and managers of public opinion display interest in different publics and in different aspects of these publics.

Before the term "public opinion" can be profitably used, either in discussion or for purposes of special study and investigation, the word "public" must be defined in terms of a specific group of persons. The failure to be specific in this respect characterizes much of the literature in the field and leads to confusion and loose thinking.

When the historian or the politician states that public opinion in the United States favors this or that proposal we should insist that he specify what public it is that he is talking about. In other words there is no such thing as *the* public except in the sense that there may be a particular group of persons about which we are talking. As students of public affairs we are naturally interested in a great many different publics, particularly those that have and exercise an influence on public policy. Probably the most important public in this respect is the group which includes all the eligible voters in the United States. This is obviously a very important public, but one difficult to deal with because of its size. Within this larger public there are innumerable smaller publics, exercising influence on the larger, and of considerable significance with reference to it. In our thinking and study we need to identify our publics as precisely as possible and also to be on the alert to discover propositions that appear to be applicable to publics generally as well as those which apply to selected publics.

The Word "Opinion"

Perhaps the word "opinion" can best be defined as a verbal expression of attitude. There are of course many other expressions of attitude such as laughter, the shaking of the head, and the "look in one's eye." The question may be asked whether opinions expressed in words are accurate indices of attitude, and the answer must be that in many cases they are not. But what a person says is very often not only an indication of attitude but also an indication of what we may expect him to do. Whether accurate expressions of attitude or not, opinions are of such significance that hundreds of thousands of dollars are spent annually to find out what they are—and opinions as expressed in the ballot booth are determining factors in social and political life.

Some will ask for a definition of attitude, but we do not need to pursue the ultimate meaning of things indefinitely. For our purposes it is sufficient to quote the definition of attitude given by the psychologist who says that it is "the sum-total of a man's inclinations and feelings, prejudice or bias, preconceived notions, ideas, fears, threats, and convictions about any specific topic." In other words, it is a tendency to act in a particular manner, a tendency which is liberated whenever the proper stimulus is presented. Whereas attitudes are subjective, opinions are objective, taking the form of written or spoken words.

Opinions differ from one another in many respects, such as content, the form in which they are expressed, their quality, their stability, their intensity, and the way in which they have been formed or elicited. Any one or more of these aspects may assume importance depending on the interest of the observer or the investigator. A scientist may be interested primarily in the truth of the opinion, or the way in which it has been formed; a novelist in the style in which it is expressed. A national advertiser or a politician may focus his attention upon the types of persons holding a particular opinion, their wealth, social standing, influence.

It must be clear that an opinion is always the opinion of a person, not of a group as such. Public opinion always refers to a collection of individual opinions, not to some mystical entity that is floating about in the atmosphere over our heads. To find out what a given state of public opinion is, therefore, we have to collect the opinions of individuals. This point would require no emphasis were it not for the fact that some writers have thought in terms of a "group mind" quite separate and distinct from the minds of tangible persons.

Public Opinion Defined

By public opinion we mean, therefore, simply any collection of individual opinions designated. If we are studying the opinions of the individual members of a college class that is a study of public opinion quite as definitely as if we were studying the opinion of the voters in the United States. We are usually interested in those collections of opinions which exert the greater influence upon government and public policy.

Degree of Uniformity

There are many different aspects of any given collection of individual opinions that are significant. One reason for the many definitions of public opinion is that students have been interested in some particular aspect or aspects and have tried to restrict the definition of public opinion to collections of individual opinions having these aspects. It is as if they undertook to restrict the definition of the word "weather" to states of atmosphere having predefined temperatures, wind velocities, and barometric pressures. One very significant aspect of any given collection of opinions is the degree of uniformity. If 90 per cent of the voters in the United States have the same opinion on a given subject, that fact is of the greatest significance.

In a democracy the actions and policies of government officials are presumed to reflect the opinions of a majority of the citizens. This is not always the case, however, in part because of the difficulty of ascertaining precisely what public opinion is regarding a particular policy or candidate. Any state of public opinion is continually changing, and election machinery can give only periodic and rather crude information regarding these changes. Nevertheless, it is important to ascertain, if possible, the degree of uniformity existing at any given time, for election figures which reveal a majority opinion are usually acted upon.

Because of the importance of collections of individual opinions that reveal a substantial degree of agreement, many students of government and public opinion would narrow the meaning of the term to include only those collections of opinions having a specific degree of uniformity. James Bryce, for example, defines public opinion as any view, or set of views, "when held by an apparent majority of citizens." And Professor Dicey expresses much the same viewpoint when he states that public opinion comprises the "wishes and ideas as to legislation held by the people of England, or to speak with more precision, by the majority of those citizens at a given moment taking an effective part in public life."

Although mainly interested in the degree of uniformity or agreement, some writers narrow the term even further to include only those collections of opinions revealing complete or substantial unanimity. Professor Gault expresses this point of view when he states: "Gradually there emerges, as a result of a slow, but more spontaneous than deliberate analysis, a certain apprehension of common and fundamental interests by all members of the group. This is public opinion." Similarly, Professor Maxey interprets public opinion as "the coming together in common agreement on the same definite conclusion or body of conclusions." Needless to say, such common agreement is seldom if ever found, especially in a public as large as that comprising all citizens or voters in the United States.

Obviously, any given collection of individual opinions with respect to any matter under consideration may reveal degrees of unanimity varying all the way from complete unanimity to a considerable degree of diversity. The degree of unanimity is not a condition of the existence of public opinion, but an aspect to be investigated. If an investigator starts out to find a state of public opinion which represents a definite

degree of agreement such as complete unanimity or majority agreement, or such vague aspects as the "normative aspects of collective consciousness," "fairly uniform collective expressions of mental or inner behavior reactions," or "uniform mental reactions to stimuli," his focus of attention is restricted to a single aspect of public opinion, and the search will be rather fruitless.

The point I wish to underscore is simply this: Public opinion is any collection of individual opinions, regardless of the degree of agreement or uniformity. The degree of uniformity is a matter to be investigated, not something to be arbitrarily set up as a condition for the existence of public opinion.

Extent of Diversity

It is often quite as important to know the extent and character of disagreement within a given collection of individual opinions as it is to ascertain the degree of uniformity. This aspect has seemed to be of such importance to some students that they have used it as a basis for their definition of public opinion. Edward L. Bernays, for example, states that public opinion "is a term describing an ill-defined, mercurial, and changeable group of individual judgments." Professor Gettell supports the same point of view when he states that "Public opinion is usually a more or less confused mass of public opinions."

These observations undoubtedly apply to states of opinion within some publics, at certain times, with respect to specific issues. Not all collections of opinions evidence quite such a chaotic condition, however. Not infrequently there exists what may be called polarizations of opinion, or sub-groupings within which there is a considerable measure of uniformity. Aware of this, and focusing attention upon it, students of public opinion have defined public opinion as "an alignment of the individuals of the community into groups formed upon the basis of differing views as to the proper solution of questions of general concern." Professor Bogardus states that, "It is proper and more accurate, therefore, to speak of public opinion as composed of two lesser but conflicting public opinions, or sub-publics, representing two sub-publics." No better illustration of the impossibility of attempting to describe the classical elephant by focusing attention upon his tail is afforded than these attempts to describe public opinion solely in terms of a single aspect. Undoubtedly some collections of individual opinions will evidence such sub-groupings or polarizations, but their existence can be determined only by actually collecting and analyzing selected collections of opinions.

It is obvious that individual opinions will possess varying degrees of excellence. Some opinions are undoubtedly more intelligent than others; some are better informed, more mature, more practical, more liberal. Discussions of the advantages and disadvantages of democracy have frequently emphasized the shortcomings of individual opinions when collected from the rank and file and when measured in terms of some agreed standard of excellence. That some degree of excellence is necessary for the facile working of democratic government is the conclusion of most writers, even though they do not agree upon the standard to be applied. But the existence of public opinion is not dependent upon the presence of a prescribed quality of opinion as suggested by Professor Jordan who states that, "Perhaps it sounds a bit harsh, but there is no such thing as a public opinion, and it requires only a moderate understanding of human nature to show that such a thing as an intelligent public opinion is not possible."

Whose Opinions?

In the case of a particular public it is not only significant to know the quality, the extent of diversity, and the degree of uniformity of the opinions expressed, but it may also be worth while to investigate who it is that holds particular types of opinions. Again, this is no reason for restricting the meaning of the term "public opinion" to the opinions of particular types or groups of persons. But this is precisely what has happened in the case of many writers on the subject. MacKinnon, writing in the early part of the nineteenth century defined public opinion as "that sentiment on any given subject which is entertained by the best informed, most intelligent, and most moral persons in the community."

Many historians and others use the expression to refer to the opinions of newspaper editors and publishers. Others say that it is the opinion of "those who are willing to abide by the decision of the majority" or those who are "spectators but not judges of the merits of a dispute and are chiefly interested in making certain rules of the game." Professor Lasswell, by reason of his interest in political and social changes which are reflected in new "value pyramids" and new symbols, defines public opinion solely in terms of those who are "participating in debatable demands for action." Professor Wilson, a political scientist, thinking in terms of the operation of American government would limit the meaning of public opinion to the opinions of those who have "the right to participate in government."

In other words, we find that there is a considerable difference of opinion as to the precise connotation of public opinion because students cannot agree as to which group of people, which public, is important. But this is not surprising, for there are a great many different publics that are significant. The question may fairly be raised by political scientists, for example, as to which public is most important from their point of view.

The Content of Opinion

What the public thinks is probably of greater general interest than any other aspect. Polling the opinions of various publics has become a major industry. Is the existence of a state of public opinion to be determined or restricted to a collection of individual opinions regarding certain subjects only? Professor Dewey, for example, would limit the term to opinions regarding "public affairs." But what is a public affair? The importance of a subject varies with time, place, circumstance, and person. Under some circumstances the most trivial thing may become a *cause célèbre*. Walter Lippmann states that public opinion relates solely to our "opinions as to how others ought to behave," and further amplifies his meaning by stating that "those features of the world outside which have to do with the behavior of other human beings, in so far as that behavior crosses ours, is dependent upon us, or is interesting to us, we call roughly public affairs. The pictures inside the heads of these human beings, the pictures of themselves, or others, or their needs, purposes, and relationships, are their public opinions." Professor Allport would restrict the meaning of public opinion to individual opinions of "widespread importance." Unfortunately, there is no universal agreement as to what is important.

Obviously, students of public opinion will wish to study collections of individual opinions which they regard as more rather than less important. And for students of public affairs, opinions regarding great questions of public policy will usually be more significant than opinions regarding private affairs. But this is no reason for restricting the meaning of the term public opinion to expressions of individual opinion regarding a selected list of subjects.

Other Aspects

Students of public opinion will continue to call attention to old and new aspects of the subject that merit attention. Of considerable interest is the way in which particular opinions have been formed; the relative stability or constancy of different types of opinion; the intensity with which they are held; and the likelihood that they will result in action or some change in political and social institutions. All of these aspects have been considered by writers on the subject, and, as might be supposed,

have served as the basis for definitions of public opinion.

Professor King, in reaching the conclusion that "public opinion is the social judgment reached upon a question of general or civic import after conscious, rational public discussion," is not only restricting the meaning of the term to opinions formed in a prescribed manner, but assumes that it is possible to say just how a set of opinions has been formed and to earmark those which are the product of "conscious, rational public discussion." Likewise President Lowell, in his classic definition, seeks to restrict the meaning of public opinion to opinions that have been formed in a rational manner, as if it were possible to determine the part that rationality plays in the process. Professor Holcombe also seeks to limit the term to opinions which are based on a "substantial part of the facts required for a rational decision."

To confine the term "public opinion" to collections of opinions that have been formed in a specific manner is not only ignoring other aspects of public opinion of equal importance, but may be laying emphasis upon presumptions that are still incapable of scientific proof. It is very doubtful whether there are any opinions that are purely rational, whatever that may mean. It is easy to understand why students of government, particularly democratic government, have been impressed with the need for greater rationality in the formation of public opinion. To determine, if it is possible to do so, how rational a particular collection of opinions is, is a matter for study and analysis, not a condition of the existence of public opinion.

The variety of interpretations which have been given to the term public opinion are of value in that they underscore aspects of public opinion that are worthy of study. The phrase "public opinion" like the word "weather" is merely a general expression. The first step in public opinion research is to define the public to be studied, then to collect the opinions of the individuals composing this public. From that point on, the focus of attention will vary with the interests of the particular student. The nature of public opinion is not something to be defined but to be studied.

THE MEANING
OF OPINION
David Riesman and
Nathan Glazer

By the time this appears in print, various technical reasons will have been discovered for the failure of the major polls to predict the last presidential election. Very likely, answers will be looked for, and found, along the lines of sample-construction, the estimate of the number voting, the handling of the "don't know" group, etc. Yet it would be a mistake if the shock of the election did not lead to a re-examination of the assumptions behind polling, and a deeper understanding of the meaning of opinion. It may well be that election-polling and election-voting have become so similar in psychological and social meaning that the latter can, with some improvements of technique, be predicted from the former. But real understanding of American opinion will only come, we think, when polling moves away from an emphasis on set answers to set questions to an emphasis on the "latent" meaning of answers, understood in terms of an entire interview and a grasp of what went on in the interpersonal situation of the interview.

To avoid misunderstanding, we should make clear at the outset that we are not making a plea for polling conducted by "depth" interviews. We do not believe that the longer and more "freely" someone talks, the more truth he necessarily tells, nor that psychological probing is as useful as, say, study of group affiliation and activity in predicting an election. We agree with most of the penetrating remarks of Paul F. Lazarsfeld[1] on the problem of open-ended versus structured interviews: namely, that virtually all the functions for which intensive interviews

[1] "The Controversy over Detailed Interviews—an Offer for Negotiation," *Public Opinion Quarterly, 8*, No. 1 (1944), pp. 38-60.

Originally published in Volume 12, Number 4, 1948 of the *Public Opinion Quarterly*.

are used today can be met by different types of conventional poll questions, if intelligently constructed. Our point is rather that new functions, at the moment perhaps best met by intensive interviews, must be taken on by polling, if it is to serve as an effective tool in "mirroring" the public mind.

I. SOME ASSUMPTIONS WHICH UNDERLIE POLLING

To divide the total population on any given question among those who are for, those against, and those undecided, gives an inadequate report of the state of public opinion on most types of issues; and this remains so even when the report is complicated by the use of such devices as George Gallup's quintamensional plan,[2] Roper's multiple-choice, or the various types of intensity thermometers. All these reports assume, in the first place, a qualitative equality among all those who select the same alternative, an equality reflected in the expectation that people in all social classes, and of all character types, will be equally habituated to the style of thinking which "makes up its mind" in terms of such stateable alternatives. These methods generally assume, in the second place, that the most significant division of opinion on any issue is between those who are for and those who are against, and between both of these and the "don't knows." But this simply reflects the structure of opinion as our political-legal tradition supposes it to be, with each view having its partisans and its "independent voters." This tradition is in turn supported by the way the mass media handle opinion, which is again in terms of a dichotomy or trichotomy, or in terms of categories and degrees of partisanship. Public opinion research comes along and confirms the existing ideology about opinion, both in its interviewing methods and in its manner of presenting its findings.

The scientific study of public opinion is thus today in the hands of neither the poll-takers nor the respondents: both are caught in an historical process which has not only set the questions to be investigated but also the form of the answer. We should at least assume that another structure of opinion may exist, in which every question has many sides, and many perspectives in which it may be viewed, each tinged with varying degrees of meaning and affect; we should try to work with models of opinion other than the conventional two- or three-sided

[2] "The Quintamensional Plan of Question Design," *Public Opinion Quarterly*, *11*, No. 3 (1947), pp. 385-393.

one now in use. One such model, for example, might divide the population into those who had grounds for an opinion and those who did not. Among others, the National Opinion Research Center (NORC) has done much work along this line. Another model might divide those in whom the answer was deeply rooted from those to whom the answer was, so to speak, lightly attached. One might experiment with this by having the interviewer challenge or argue with the answer —contrary to the convention, which advocates of both structured and open-ended methods share, of "non-directive" interviewing.

Present-day polling, in its main assumptions, exemplifies the 19th-century liberal's approach to the individual as a social atom. By a convenient fiction, polling tends to treat its subject, in every social stratum, as a "responsible citizen"—one who considers the world in terms of "issues" and considers these issues in the terms in which they are discussed in the press and on the radio, holds a position in a political spectrum which runs in such single dimensions as left-right, or Republican-Democrat-Progressive, and feels it his duty to take sides on public issues both when polled and when called upon to vote.

To be sure, one can still find people like this—often people in the upper and upper middle classes, and many older persons of varying class position for whom opinion grows out of a feeling of responsibility, and out of a feeling of potency to affect political events which responsibility implies. Such people think that their opinion, and their vote, matter very much, and the mass media and the polling process encourage them in this belief. Maybe this is a good thing for society. But it unquestionably handicaps public opinion research to operate with assumptions which are no longer, if they ever were, a useful abstraction from the social reality of a mass society. The type of 19th-century citizen, whom we have characterized—a type we call "conscience-directed"—becomes increasingly rare under the pressures of our era.

For most people in modern society, there is no such direct relation between responsibility for having an opinion and responsibility for action. They can see no relation between their political opinions and the actual course of political life—particularly those developments, such as war, which are most crucial to them. On the contrary, the obscurity and remoteness of the more decisive national and international political happenings, the general feeling that instead of "we" (the common people), it is some alien "they" (the distant powers) who manage events (among those social groups who assume events to be manageable at all)—these developments have made politics an anxious and frustrating topic. And this leads either to an obviously apathetic reaction to politics or to attempts (functionally no less apathetic) to view politics in some more tolerable framework, such as sports (the election as a race), chit-chat (the election as gossip), or the more amiable aspects of the American past (clichés about democracy). People today seem to us to be increasingly "other-directed," rather than "conscience-directed," in their character structure: that is, they are very much concerned with the opinions of others rather than with what they themselves think, and use their own opinions not so much to orient themselves in responsible action as to please, entertain, or simply get along with others. This psychic state increases their subjective feelings of powerlessness to affect the course of political events.

Yet the great majority of people, while they are actually powerless and while they feel as alienated from politics as from the other major foci of modern life, are called upon, in our democratic tradition, to act as if they had power. They are called upon to vote, and to expose themselves to information and exhortation from the mass media and to discussion in their clique groups about political affairs. The public opinion polls play a part in this call, though perhaps a minor one, not only in the way their results are presented, but also in the specific contacts between poller and pollee. The public opinion interviewer is a pervasive symbol of the demand to be opinionated. Most polls assume that people will have—and subtly therefore, that they should have—opinions on the "issues of the day" or "news of the week," though occasionally Gallup asks people "Do you have a cold?" or "Are you happy?" or some similar question which does not come straight out of 19th-century "conscience-directed" politics.

The fact is that people do respond, in overwhelming numbers, to this social demand that they have an opinion. Perhaps 10 per cent of the population refuses to be polled at all; another 10 per cent or so gets into the no-answer or undecided box; all the rest "have an opinion." If we took this evidence of the polls at face, we might conclude that politics had in fact not changed since the last century, that the masses who had entered the historical process had not withdrawn from it. Maybe so. But we think that the polls conceal as much as they reveal on this subject, and that if we look at the polls in unorthodox ways, we can even now see that the meaning of opinion is in flux.

II. WHY DO PEOPLE HAVE OPINIONS?

To this question, we have a few tentative hypotheses to offer, which we hope can be tested by public opinion research. These hypotheses spring from our general view of American history and American social structure, and from an analysis of poll data and of a small number of intensive interviews on politics, the mass media, and other spheres of life which we have gathered during the past year. We shall attempt to describe some of the different ways people approach the problem of having—and giving—an opinion. While we group these different ways roughly according to class, the various types we describe can probably be found, in varying degrees, in all classes.

THE FUNCTIONS OF OPINION IN THE UPPER CLASS

The unrecorded experience of insightful poll interviewers seems to us one of the most important sources for discovering the meaning of opinion in the several social strata. This belief is confirmed by the opportunity given us by Herbert Hyman of NORC to read over some of his extraordinarily searching interviews with interviewers, and to interview several of these people ourselves. There is some evidence here, of course quite unsystematic, that the upper-class person—the pollers' "class A"—does not find emotional satisfaction in *voicing* an opinion to an interviewer, who is generally of lower social status, as distinguished from having and voicing an opinion at the dinner table, on the commuter train, and in clique groups generally. Perhaps the interviewer, according to the view of this social level, falls into the category of the cab-driver and the elevator man, with whom one exchanges seasonal pleasantries about the weather and the election, but with whom one is also reserved and close-mouthed.

We may interpret this reaction to the interviewer psychologically by saying that many of these upper-class respondents do not feel alienated from their opinions; they do not need to make either conversation or capital with them. Though in recent years they have often talked as if they felt politically frustrated, as if they could make no headway against "that man in the White House," or, indeed, against politicians in general, the premise of this apparent frustration is that they are not really powerless, but that they feel temporarily out of the seats of power. Actually, politics is a malleable domain for them, whether or not they are "conscience-directed" types who feel responsibility for it. Yet even they tend to overestimate their power, and therefore the social importance of their having an opinion, and it is often this feeling which allows the interviewer to get by the doormen and secretaries at all.

ILLUSIONS OF OMNIPOTENCE IN THE UPPER MIDDLE CLASS

In both the upper and upper middle class there is a high proportion of response on polls, particularly from men. People in these groups have been brought up to make choices and to consider their opinions significant: on what to do for a living, on whether to buy a Packard or a Cadillac, on what summer resort or salad dressing is "best." That is to say, they have been brought up to consider themselves as individuals—an individuality constantly reinforced by ability to make tastes, preferences, and opinions count in daily life-situations. Moreover, voicing their opinions to others increases their feeling of potency, in a way akin to the uses of word magic by children; they reassure themselves that they grasp their world—that it is *theirs*—by means of having opinions about those aspects of reality they have been brought up to attend to. In the working class, politics does not generally become a focus of interest, if ever, until after formal education is complete and the individual has entered on his work career, but in the upper middle class young people often begin to attend to political discourse earlier, in high school and college. Public opinion polling, and the election itself, meets such people on their own ground; they think about men and issues in the way that the polls, the mass media, and their clique groups all require of them.

While such "other-directed" people appear, we think, in increasing numbers in middle-class urban America today, they are not new as a social type. Indeed, one of the best descriptions of such individuals appears in *Anna Karenina*:

> "Stepan Arkadyevitch took in and read a liberal paper, not an extreme one, but one advocating the views held by the majority. And in spite of the fact that science, art and politics had no special interest for him, he firmly held those views on all these subjects which were held by the majority and by his paper, and he only changed them when the majority

changed them—or, more strictly speaking, he did not change them, but they imperceptibly changed of themselves within him.

"Stepan Arkadyevitch had not chosen his political opinions or his views, these political opinions and views had come to him of themselves, just as he did not choose the shapes of his hat and coat, but simply took those that were being worn. And for him, living in a certain society—owing to the need, ordinarily developed at years of discrètion, for some degree of mental activity—to have views was just as indispensable as to have a hat.

"... liberalism had become a habit of Stepan Arkadyevitch's and he liked his newspaper, as he did his cigar after dinner, for the slight fog it diffused in his brain."[3]

Men (and women) like Stepan Arkadyevitch are tempted by their social situation to overestimate their actual power. They are in contact with political "insiders" both in print and in person; this helps them to identify with the political world and to feel it as more malleable than it is. In our interviews we often find such people to be "inside-dopesters," possessed of a relatively high level of information about politics and a stock of opinions like a well-furnished wine-cellar, but lacking in any genuine affect about opinions which would lead them to discriminate between those opinions which have meaning in today's world from those which are mere opinionatedness.

The upper middle class tends to have a "conscience-directed" ideology about politics, so that there is much talk and action in terms of responsibility; and of course some "conscience-directed" types of personalities remain. But the trend seems to us to lie with the Stepan Arkadyevitches, whose opinions are lightly attached—hence easily secured by a poller—and yet they need opinions, for clothing, conformity, and comfort, as desperately as they need a hat.

MAKING CONVERSATION BETWEEN THE SOCIAL CLASSES

As one goes down the status ladder, one still finds an astonishingly high proportion of response on polls, both in permitting oneself to be interviewed and in having an opinion which can be fitted, without too much gerrymandering, into the dimensions of current polling work. In a sense, this is only another way of saying that America is a middle-class country and that middle-class values and styles of perception reach into all levels except perhaps the fringes at the very top and the very

[3] Modern Library edition, pp. 10-11.

bottom. The study of polling, however, suggests two perspectives on this well-accepted statement: one is that people who are actually powerless and voiceless grasp at straws of participation, and the other is that the upper and lower levels of our culture converse with each other across status lines by means of the polls and, of course, also by means of the mass media and many other forms of exchange.

In the lower middle class, there often seems to be considerable satisfaction in voicing an opinion to the interviewer, even if it has to be manufactured on the spot for the purpose. Respondents in this group are not so often consulted as they might wish—"I told that fellow from the Gallup Poll. . . "—and at the same time, they do not want to be taken for ignoramuses who do not know, and consequently are quite happy to have a chance to show that they do know. And, of course, they *do* know. For, like the upper social levels, they have been trained to exercise consumption preferences, and they are willing, if not avid, cash customers for opinions on political issues. Though national and international affairs are for them mysterious realms, though they have no way of grasping what a political figure actually does, they can listen to Walter Winchell. As the "inside dope" is spread to wider circles, it becomes one of the chief opiates of the people.

Since such people have, however, no actual experience of potency in meaningful life situations—but only the imitation of potency in the consumption of goods and opinions—they will tend to be over-impressed by "public opinion." Frightened as they are of being taken for suckers, they assume public opinion to be much more "given" and "set" than it actually is, and, if anything, underestimate what *they* might do to change opinion by taking a strong stand against a current trend. Truman, no inside-dopester, was not impressed by the massive public opinion structure which the mass media talked about. Rather, like the self-made, conscience-directed man of earlier generations, he thought it was up to him whether he got to the top, and his naïveté encouraged him where other-directed types would have despaired.

Added to the desire to participate on the part of the lower middle class is the cultural pressure, felt by both interviewer and interviewee, in favor of giving someone an answer rather than no answer. The situation is said to be different in France and some other countries, but the American attitude is summed up in the expression criticizing those who "wouldn't give anyone the right time." An opinion is considered a free gift in a culture where privacy is at a minimum, and people will feel that the interviewer is entitled to an opinion irrespective of whether they also try to guess which of several possible opinions he may want of them. Even the people who seem to enjoy slamming the door in the interviewer's face may be taking advantage of a rarely-given opportunity not to live up to expectations and to lord it over the (usually female) interviewer. It is not that they so value their privacy. And indeed, why should people not give their opinion freely when the opinions were often only created for this purpose in the first place, as part of the socialization process which has produced this "other-directed" type of character? Opinions are not felt as part of one's underlying self; on the contrary, people have been so invaded, the threshold of personality has become such a highway, that they have very little private self left anyway.

Beyond that, we think it is useful to see the interview situation, and the polling process as a whole, as one form of the continuing conversation between the upper and lower social levels of our culture. This conversation is more than mere politeness, although it is reflected in the politeness of up-to-date personnel relations and public relations, which form part of this conversation. It is an attempt to hide, on both sides, the realities of the power situation and the status disparities—an attempt which operates most openly in the movies, where, for example, a bus driver may be taken seriously by a department store executive. It would be a mistake to see this as a conscious effort to "fool the masses" by providing counselors to take the pulse of America, for the powerful in America are by no means as psychologically secure (or, indeed, as ruthless) as other ruling classes have been, and they need to be reassured by contact with the less powerful, by hearing their voices, by exchange. Since they, too, are other-directed, their character structure needs the smiles, and fears the frowns, of the weak. However, they also wish to appear, to themselves and others, as realistic and hard-boiled; hence, they must overestimate the power of the weak in order to rationalize paying so much attention to them, listening so carefully, and, on occasion, making more concessions than might be objectively required by the *Realpolitik* they profess.[4] The consequence

[4] We can illustrate this complicated mechanism by the example of the manufacturer who justifies his expenditures on a public cause by saying it is "good public relations," when in his case public relations cannot affect his sales or profit. He needs the good will of the public, though his nineteenth-century forbears—conscience-directed in at least this sense—didn't give a damn.

of their anxious attention to the polls and to other indices of opinion is that the socially weak are encouraged to overestimate *their* power, as of course they are only too ready to do.

In this perspective, the polls may be thought of as a kind of political market research. Like most commercial market research, the effort is not really to find out what people might want under quite different social conditions, but rather to offer them a monopolistically-limited range of alternatives: just as they can choose between the four big weeklies. They can be for or against Truman, for or against Taft-Hartley, even for or against the United Nations, but they cannot be, in the given spectrum, in favor of trying to start a revolution within Russia, as against fighting or appeasing her. And probably they have been so conditioned that they would not know what to do with any radically new alternatives, but would try to fit them into the style of viewing "reality" which the existing polls reflect.

RAPPORT AND OPINION IN THE LOWER CLASS

Even the lower class participates in this "conversation between the classes." Some are left out, as indicated by the fact that the proportion of "don't knows" rises sharply in the lower class, particularly among women. Many of the "don't knows" and refusals in the lower social strata are actually frightened; frightened of authorities in general, of the FBI in some places, and of the Communists in others (as we found last summer in rural Vermont). Yet even among this group it is surprising how many respond.

There are few illusions of omnipotence here, as one finds them among the upper middle class; nor is there, we suspect, as much need as in the lower middle class for verbal aggression against interviewers— telling "them" (the powers) off, through the interviewer. Why, then, do people respond? Partly, of course, it is a matter of simple courtesy and needs no complicated explanations. But we think that the emphasis on rapport which dominates so much discussion of interviewing shows that there are other elements involved. The concern for good rapport as a requirement of good interviewing seems to us partly a reflection of the need of modern middle-class people to be liked by everybody. At any rate, rapport serves to insure the success of the "conversation of the classes" when it is conducted between the middle-class interviewer and the lower-class respondent. Thus great care is taken that the lower-class individual is approached sympathetically, and the polls try to use an interviewer of his own ethnic group, though they are rarely able to use one of his own class. This is not wholly pointless if one's goal is to maximize the number of responses, since rapport, by providing some interpersonal though usually spurious warmth, helps to repress unconscious feelings of powerlessness and distrust. But this is artificial; life-situations for the interviewee in the lower class are not typically suffused with rapport, and he is rarely treated with the consideration the interviewer shows him. Thus a false picture of the actual extent of political involvement is created, though it might be argued that it is a picture which would disappear under depth-interviewing and still greater doses of rapport. This needs testing, but it seems clear that the same culture which insists on "service with a smile" can also get answers with a smile—up to a point.

DOES THE ELECTION CHANGE THINGS?

The foregoing observations were sketched out by the writers in a memorandum written a year ago; naturally, we have had to ask ourselves whether Truman's victory does not show the power of the allegedly powerless. This may be. No doubt the union locals who put Truman over in the cities have a feeling of potency and elation, though coupled with misgivings they will be "sold out." Winning an election against odds, it may be argued, is different from merely having an opinion: affect is aroused and competence learned in the very process of getting out the vote. But even in the case of the union vote, many of the rank and file were simply pressured into going to the polls by a leadership which felt threatened by the Taft-Hartley Act; and while undoubtedly for many millions of Americans—somewhat more perhaps than we believed—opinion is formed by a realistic evaluation of alternatives, for these same persons, and for many others, the social and psychological meanings of opinion we have discussed become increasingly prominent. Whether we are interested in predicting elections or in understanding what is happening in America—and while the former may be hit by dint of sheer luck, ultimately it involves the latter—we must go past the level on which opinion research is now concentrating. Individuality and idiosyncrasy of response, up to now "processed out" of the polling process, is, we feel, the key to this next stage.

III. AN APPROACH TO LATENT MEANING

The drift of our argument above may be restated as follows: the pollers—of course we speak generally, and there are exceptions— frame questions in terms of the way reality is perceived by the broad middle classes and, by structuring the situation in a particular way, get back, in effect, what they (and the mass media) have put in. We all know the same answer means different things, varying with the different satisfactions gained by each stratum and their different interpretations of the interpersonal situation. But this influences the published opinion report only very indirectly—even though a great deal of information on the meaning of answers is available which, because it is unsystematic and not easily quantifiable, is not made use of. Although opinion researchers try to formulate questions in words which have an equivalent meaning in all social groups, they can scarcely avoid distorting whatever idiosyncratic meanings they get when they assume that the same verbal answers are to be classified as identical. Moreover, the concept of rapport—the neutral, "friendly" interviewer— though it appears to be a technique for reducing interviewer bias, actually introduces another sort of bias which aids in finding out certain things but forecloses the finding out of others.

DO WORDS HAVE A MEANING?

Much current social research proceeds on the assumption that if one wants to tap idiosyncratic meaning one must dispense with interviews altogether, except perhaps the psychoanalytic interview, and substitute projective tests such as the Rorschach, or the TAT, where the stimulus is non-verbal. A number of psychoanalysts, for instance, have said that Kinsey could not possibly have discovered anything veracious by his rapid-fire poll-type questionnaire. Indeed, some of the more orthodox Freudians, occasionally joined by some extreme semanticists, tend to take the position that people *never* mean what they say, and that the manifest replies to a question are inevitably a façade to be pierced rather than anything to be taken seriously.

We think that this outlook in social science is also an over-reaction against an earlier, naïve reliance on the manifest content of answers to questions in personality inventories and other types of questionnaires. But today the best pollers no longer fall into such simplistic pitfalls;

by pretesting with intensive interviews and converting these results into interlocking sets of questions, they try to follow the lead of Professor Lazarsfeld in the article already cited. We think it most unlikely that the failure to predict the election could have been repaired by depth interviewing in its present stage of development. On the contrary, we think it most likely that a better job of prediction might have been done by a conventional interview, had it dealt with such matters as group affiliation, probed as to the decisive aspects of an opinion (e.g., what does Dewey really stand for?), challenged answers in a test for rootedness of opinion, and done a better selection job to avoid getting the more opinionated voters who scratch the ceilings of their respective socio-economic status categories.[5] Let us move away from this sterile dichotomy between over-rational belief in words per se and over-skeptical nihilism about them, and see precisely in what direction public opinion research can advance if we believe that words do, sometimes, possess their rational manifest meaning, while being also projective of underlying character structure.

When it comes to getting at deep-lying and not easily verbalized meanings of opinion, we do not believe that the check-list, the multiple-type question, and other refinements will do the trick. For this, Professor Lazarsfeld holds that one must resort to projective tests. On the other hand, Dr. Frenkel-Brunswik and her co-workers at the University of California feel that one can find "diagnostic questions," to which responses of "yes" or "no" (with different intensities) will give a characterological profile. Our own quite tentative hypothesis is that it is possible to work with answers to a relatively structured interview as if the interview itself as a whole, rather than as a set of separate questions, were a projective test.

Our interviews are not long, nor do they probe for intimate data; skill in administering them helps, but is not essential. The problem is in interpretation, not in administration. For we handle the entire interview as a unit—a *gestalt*, a record of an experience—which we try to translate into a set of latent meanings which may in any given case

[5] Rough handling of the "don't know" group—both in an effort by interviewers under central office pressure to shake them into expressing an opinion which was likely to be the opinion (namely, Dewey) which the mass media expected, and by dividing the group pro rata among the candidates, without reference to their social status—seems to us no accident; rather it shows the unconscious assumption of the pollers that one should have an opinion, and a preference for the 90 per cent who do, as against the 10 per cent who do not conform to this demand.

include some of the literal, manifest meanings, too. This is done before any single answer is coded for purposes of correlation and comparison. That is, each single answer gives clues as to the latent meaning, the plot, of the interview, and as the latter develops, so it colors the meaning of the single answer, which must frequently be reinterpreted in the light of other answers and of the whole. Eventually, in a dialectic process, we come to a point where the latent, character-based meanings of answers are consistent and are seen to spring from a total personality, no matter how seemingly contradictory the surface answers are. The method we use thus resembles that used by the more "intuitive" and less quantitative workers with Rorschach and TAT. Moreover, to get beneath ideology, chit-chat, and rationalization that are always part of the manifest responses, we must look at and rely on the way things are said, and when they are said in the sequence of answers, and on what the interviewer can tell us as to non-verbal modes of reaction to a question. (Of course, we must know something of the interviewer, too, in order to evaluate the report.)

This work is only in its preliminary stages, as we have said. It is not even in the pilot-model or handicraft stage, with the assembly-line production needed for polling far away. We are far enough along, however, to be confident that an interview, if treated as a whole, can be as revealing as most projective tests, both as to character structure (though here perhaps less valuable than a good Rorschach) and as to fundamental political orientation. By fundamental political orientation we do not refer to party affiliation and activities, though one can easily cover this in a brief, free-answer interview, but rather to the significance of politics in the individual's psychic and social economy.

CHARACTER STRUCTURE AND THE MEANING OF OPINION

What is the advantage of getting at character structure for public opinion research? We have already stated our belief that group affiliation and like institutional matters are more important in predicting an election than depth psychology. Moreover, it is undoubtedly possible to predict an election by lucky empiricism without understanding it, just as it is possible to cure a patient without knowing what ails him. It is only if we wish to understand the role of opinion in the several social strata of our society that we need to resort to expensive methods, such as ours, for processing interviews. It is character structure, the lasting organization of personality, which lends meaning to the fleeting course of an individual's opinions; it is character structure which differentiates between opinions, verbally the same, on such scores as rootedness and susceptibility to mass media pressure; it is variations in the distribution of character types among the several social classes which may give us clues to a subtly differentiated, and more accurate, type of prediction.

The point of view is not entirely new. The study by Fromm and Schachtel of German workers' attitudes is, in some respects, an exemplar of this method, as is the very careful and elaborate work being done in the Harvard study of attitudes towards Russia.

THE FEAR OF THE LATENT

Latent meaning—either of an answer or of no answer—may be understood if we grasp the socially structured interpersonal situation between poller and pollee, and search it for the residues, verbal and non-verbal, which now in our haste we throw away. But it is not only haste which often steers the academic, as well as the commercial poller, away from reliance on latent meaning. In our daily life we all know that a gesture, an inflection, a nuance of phrase, may show a latent meaning which is the opposite of the patent one. In our working life, however, we fear to rely on such human knowledge because of the difficulties of proof, of standardization, and of validation. If we are other-directed types, like the bulk of the middle-class urban professionals, we will fear to be called unscientific by our colleagues. The failure of the polls to predict the election should give us a kind of back-handed courage, by demonstrating that the alternative, highly-quantified methods may at times be equally fallible.

Depth interviewing, it is apparent, does not avoid the problem of interpretation of latent meaning. It cannot assume that the interviewee's self-revelations may be taken at face, especially if they are intimate and of the sort usually hidden. For these, too, may be as spurious as any surface rationalizations; the excellent rapport which produced them may merely have served to encourage boasting or aggression by the respondent. What we want is the whole personality, and neither what is on the surface nor what is covered up will alone suffice. There is, we conclude, no escape from the social scientist's own judgment. He must train himself to hear, and to understand, latent response, even though the whole culture, as well as the demands of his training and his colleagues, make this difficult.

At the same time the rewards of even a fragmentary approach to latent meaning are great. The election shows—as did the British Labor Party victory of 1945—how little we know, polls or no polls, about what is going on in our society. We do not know what the election meant to people in different social classes. We know almost nothing about the underlying forces in American life which are not visible—forces which cannot fit themselves into the pollers' opinion-grid. Until the election, public opinion research was largely committed to turning out products on a schedule furnished by the culture, rather than a schedule related to the curiosity and intellectual adventure of social science itself. Now, by virtue of our proven ignorance, we can justify staving off demands for quick results, and can occupy ourselves with discovering what is fundamental and how to get at it.

4

SOME IMPLICATIONS
OF SEPARATING OPINIONS
FROM ATTITUDES
G. D. Wiebe

T HE terms attitude and opinion are often used as if they were synonymous. In his book *Social Psychology,* Newcomb suggests that the term "public opinion" might be improved upon. A more accurate term for referring to what is generally designated as public opinion research might be "group attitudes."[1] Cantril uses the terms attitude and opinion as synonymous in the following statement: "We want to know if a person's attitude toward one problem has any bearing on his attitude toward another problem. Is one opinion merely something to which a person has become conditioned, or is it something related to a larger mental context?"[2] In other places, however, these authors and indeed most social scientists use the words as having different meanings.

Attitude and opinion are used as synonymous, as nearly synonymous, one is used as a sub-classification of the other, and they are used as distinctly separate concepts. The ambiguous use of words is commonplace, but if such ambiguity appears to impede progress in an area of scientific interest, clarification is of prime importance.

The purpose of this paper is to propose definitions which clearly differentiate attitudes and opinions. The difference between these two concepts will be developed by reference to differences in the criteria in terms of which attitude and opinion responses may most appropriately be validated. The definitions of attitude and opinion will be applied in dividing a sample of 100 "opinion" items into four functional categories. Certain characteristics of validity as applied to each of the four groups of items will be discussed. The fortunate degree of stability usually found

[1]Newcomb, Theodore M., *Social Psychology,* The Dryden Press, Inc., 1950, p. 176.
[2]Newcomb, Theodore M., Eugene L. Hartley, and others, *Readings in Social Psychology,* Henry Holt and Company, Inc., 1947, p. 602.

Originally published in Volume 17, Number 3, 1953 of the *Public Opinion Quarterly*.

in pre-election surveys will be contrasted with the greater degree of flux encountered in attempting to validate many other predictive opinion surveys.[3] Finally the varying degree of articulation between attitudes and opinions in a given population will serve as groundwork for an hypothesis regarding political stability.

It is maintained that if differentiation between attitudes and opinions reduces in some degree, the ambiguity surrounding the concept of validity in opinion research, and if it also suggests challenging hypotheses for further research, then the differentiation will have been worthwhile. An attempt will be made to demonstrate both of these outcomes.

ATTITUDE AS STRUCTURAL PRE-DISPOSITION

The definition of an attitude which has perhaps the widest current acceptance, and to which we subscribe, is stated by Allport as follows: An attitude is "a mental and neural state of readiness organized through experience, exerting a directive or dynamic influence upon the individual's responses to all objects and situations with which it is related."[4] Following this line of thought Newcomb says attitudes "are not themselves responses but states of readiness to respond. Hence they can be measured only indirectly."[5] Gardner Murphy defines attitude as "readiness to react in one way rather than another."[6] Doob says, "Before an attitude can be aroused, some kind of stimulus has had to be present."[7] He continues, "An attitude, in short, helps mediate a drive."[8]

There appears to be rather general agreement on the point that attitudes are not in themselves responses. Allport's definition seems to imply that attitudes may in fact be neural patterns — physical traceries within the brain. Murphy says they reside in "the tissues, specifically those involved in perceiving and valuing."[9] Although the physical existence of attitudes as nerve networks need not be maintained, the concept appears to have much merit. It is *as if* an attitude were an established route through a maze of neural connections, a route which serves to lend a characteristic

---

[3]"Opinion research" and "public opinion research" are generally accepted as synonymous and will be used interchangeably. There is no doubt, for example, regarding the .nature of the work done by the National Opinion Research Center, or by the Opinion Research Section of our Occupation Forces. Opinion research has come to mean public opinion research.

[4]Murchison, E. (Ed.): *A Handbook of Social Psychology*, "Attitudes," by G. W. Allport, (Worchester, Mass.: Clark University Press, 1935).

[5]Newcomb, Theodore M., *Social Psychology*, The Dryden Press, Inc., 1950, p. 154.

[6]Murphy, Gardner, *Personality*, Harper & Brothers, 1947, p. 980.

[7]Doob, Leonard W., *Public Opinion and Propaganda*, Henry Holt and Co., 1948, p. 27.

[8]Op cit. p. 29.

[9]Op cit. p. 489.

coloration to the stimulae that traverse it. Thus attitudes lie dormant until activated by a drive, but once activated, attitudes "mediate" the drive.

Responses to attitude items may be thought of as bearing evidence of the various attitudinal routes that a given stimulus has traversed in the minds of the respondents. The environment in which the respondent lives has an impact on a given attitude only to the extent that the environment has already been gradually internalized and incorporated in the structuring of the attitude. Thus an attitude is characteristically referred to as a relatively *stable* phenomenon. When a person expresses an attitude he is not expressing, primarily, the current impact of the world around him. He is expressing an established, subjective, private, intuitive, personal way of responding to the stimulus situation. There is a persistent, automatic toughness about an attitude, plus a satisfying history of drive reduction via its use that makes it resistant to the blandishments of intellectual arguments and altered circumstances.

In spite of the comparative toughness and stability of attitudes, however, they do change. Just as they originally took form out of the numberless individual experiences of adjusting the satisfaction of drives to the demands of the environment, so they must continue to undergo a gradual restructuring as drives and environmental factors change. But this change is slow. Perhaps it may be likened to the changing of paths across an open field in the middle of a village. A new friendship raises the need for a new diagonal. It is hardly perceptible for some time. A hedge planted partly for beauty, partly for spite, necessitates a detour, but the path remains smooth and well-marked for a long time. A low spot is muddy for days after a rain, so there is a supplementary arc of pathway that looks quite inefficient during the dry season. Its use seems automatic, however, during rainy weather. The analogy should not be pressed, but perhaps it will serve to emphasize the position being supported here, namely that attitudes are highly structured ways of responding — they are resistant to change.

An example seems appropriate. During student days the author participated in the campaign to remove the "White Clause" from the constitution of Phi Delta Kappa, an educational honorary fraternity. Following a debate on this issue, his opponent, a graduate student from a southern university told this story to illustrate his own feelings: A distinguished southern gentleman said to Booker T. Washington, following an inspired speech by Mr. Washington, "Booker, you're the greatest man in this generation." "Oh, thank you sir," replied Mr. Washington, "but you are too kind. President Teddy Roosevelt is the greatest man." "I thought so too," said the southern gentleman, "until he invited you to lunch."

We have likened an attitude to a neural pathway in the brain, that is, we have referred to an attitude in a structural sense. What then of the perception — the attitude mediated stimulus — that one hopes will be verbalized in response to an attitude item? It also is often referred to as an attitude, but this practice leads to confusion. It might more appropriately be called the product of an attitude. Instead of asking a respondent for his attitude on a given conflict situation, one is really asking him to process this conflict situation through his attitudes and to verbalize the outcome. Attitude testers know the danger that a number of respondents may answer a given item via different attitudes. For example, an item which purports to assess attitudes toward anti-Semitism may, in the case of one individual, be responded to in terms of anti-Semitism while a second individual may respond in terms of economic self-interest, and a third may respond in terms of his attitude toward foreigners.[10] So, the response illicited by an attitude item should be differentiated from the attitude that it purports to reflect. Newcomb suggests the phrase "attitude response" which will be used here.

OPINION AS DECISION IN A SOCIAL MATRIX

Discussions of opinion as a psychological entity are few in number. In many cases opinion is apparently assumed to be whatever is investigated by opinion research methods. The methodology of opinion research then receives extended and careful discussion. Among the definitions of public opinion and opinion, however, there is a helpful degree of unanimity. Reference to a few of these definitions will serve to bring this measure of apparent agreement into focus.

Albig says, "An opinion is some expression on a controversial point."[11] Doob submits "a definition that seeks to be precise and at least not sensationally different from the way in which the term is frequently employed; public opinion refers to people's attitudes on an issue when they are members of the same social group."[12] Bernays defines public opinion as "an

[10]This discussion is grossly over-simplified. For example each of these three respondents almost certainly answer, not in terms of one attitude but in terms of a complex intertwining of a number of attitudes. Another complication not discussed here is selective perception of ones own attitudinal responses. Suppose for example, that a bright senior who also works as a janitor, scores in the radical quartile of a scale on political attitudes. Two years later, as a junior executive with an adequate and increasing salary, he scores at the midpoint of the scale. Assuming that his answers were honest, did his attitudes toward politics change? Or was the crucial change in the size of the gap between his self estimate and his position in society? There seems to be at least reasonable doubt as to which explanation would be closer to the truth.

[11]Albig, William, *Public Opinion*, McGraw-Hill, New York, 1939, p. 1.
[12]Op cit. p. 35.

ill-defined and changeable group of individual judgements."[13] Smith refers to this definition by Bernays, and then continues: "James Bryce said that it was not enough to think of public opinion as the aggregate of discrepant and varying notions and beliefs on public affairs held by the people in a community. . . ."[14]

"Public opinion, then," Smith continues, "is not the sum total of the individual opinions of isolated men. It is made up of the opinions of men living an associational life and affected by their contacts with one another."

In the first issue of the Public Opinion Quarterly Floyd Allport wrote:

"The term public opinion is given its meaning with reference to a multi-individual situation in which individuals are expressing themselves, or can be called upon to express themselves, as favoring or supporting (or else disfavoring or opposing) some definite condition, person, or proposal of widespread importance, in such a proportion of number, intensity, and constancy, as to give rise to the probability of affecting action, directly or indirectly, toward the object concerned."[15]

Hart, writing with the Hartleys, differentiates opinions from attitudes as follows:

"Opinion is a fact of a different psychological order; it differs in its functional relation to behavior. It comes into being just when, and to the extent that, attitudes are not adequate to enable the individual or the group to cope with a situation. Many situations are problematic in that they involve new and strange objects or new combinations or arrangements of familiar objects, as in the old illustration of the cow in the parlor. These problem situations require that participants 'take thought', that they try to find out what the situation portends, what will happen if this or that course of action is followed. In this process of assessing the situation, participants draw upon past experience, bringing to bear attitudes that seem to be relevant; but they cannot rely, except tentatively, upon these attitudes to carry them through the situation. With a greater or lesser degree of rationality, a definition of the situation, a conception of the kind of action appropriate to it, will be worked out; it is just such a definition that seems to be referred to on both the practical and the scholarly level, as opinion. It involves, or is based in part upon, attitudes; but it is not, therefore, synonymous with attitude. It is always concerned with doubtful elements in the situation, with conflicts and uncertainties, with problems of 'issues,' and is, therefore, a more rational concept. It pertains not to a single attitude but to an attitude-complex corresponding to the object-complex comprising the extra-individual aspect of the situation. It adapts attitudes to one another and to the circumstances in which action must go on."[16]

This sampling of definitions of "opinion" and "public opinion" suggests that public opinion is the aggregate of individual opinions provided

[13]Bernays, Edward L., *Crystallizing Public Opinion*, Liveright Publishing Co., New York, p. 61.

[14]Smith, Charles W. Jr., *Public Opinion in Democracy*, Prentice-Hall Inc., New York, 1939, p. 16.

[15]Allport, Floyd H., "Toward A Science Of Public Opinion", *Public Opinion Quarterly*, Volume 1, No. 1, p. 22.

[16]Hartley, Eugene L. and Ruth E., *Fundamentals of Social Psychology*, New York, Alfred A. Knopf, 1952, p. 657.

that the individuals involved constitute a group in the sense that they have an effect on one another. The role of attitudes in these definitions varies. The distinctive characteristic of an opinion, however, on which there appears to be general agreement is the importance of current (or nearly current) social interaction in its make-up. Whereas one feels an attitude as an immediate, intuitive orientation, one thinks out, calculates an opinion as a solution to a problem, or as a reasoned choice among possible alternatives for interaction in a social matrix.

What does one infer from an opinion response? Is it not a decision favoring a particular pattern for social interaction? This is the point toward which the various definitions of opinion appear to converge; that opinion adjusts attitudes to the individual's perception of social demands to the end that his social interaction may be successful. An opinion then might be defined as *a mental and neural state perceived as a decision favoring particular behavior on a group issue — a decision which adapts attitudes related to the issue to the individual's perception of the reality in which the behavior must transpire.*

OPINIONS AS RAW MATERIALS FOR THE BUILDING OF ATTITUDES

We have attempted to differentiate between attitudes and opinions. In so doing, a basic relationship between the two becomes apparent. Opinions adapt attitudes to the demands of social situations; but having adapted them, opinions appear to become ingredients in the constant, gradual reformulation of attitudes.

Attitudes, as Allport states, are organized through experience. Many of the individual experiences which contribute to the organization of an attitude would, considered singly, involve the kind of decisions defined above as opinion. Consider an example. A young child has no attitude toward politicians. He does, however, have a well-developed attitude toward his father. His father is benevolent and powerful. On hearing about the mayor of the town as the head of the whole town, the child tends to perceive the mayor via his attitude toward his father. But due to some sleight of hand in the zoning board, instigated by the mayor, the child and his playmates are deprived of a playground which is converted into a well fenced parking lot. The child hears that "It's the mayor's fault... just like a politician." His attitudes toward father are no longer appropriate for mediating his reaction toward the mayor. His attitude toward Martian Invaders seems better. Instead of shooting Martians the next day, the child and his playmates shoot "Mayors and Politicians."

The decision to do so is an opinion. The statement, "Let's shoot mayors and politicians" is an opinion response. The mental and neural state described here lacks the history of experience and the stability that characterize an attitude. Two or three parties with refreshments furnished by the mayor could probably reverse this opinion. But given the first experience and the opinion which followed, plus many comparable ones, and the absence of counteracting ones, a negative attitude toward mayors and politicians might be expected to take form.

Suppose that an attitude of suspicion, distrust and resentment does take form, and that thirty years hence, the child has become the leading physician in his home town. He is selected to represent his town at a White House conference at which the location of a number of large hospitals will be determined. Before leaving for Washington, he addresses the Town Council as follows: "Mr. Mayor, gentlemen of the Council, I wish first to express my thanks for having been selected by this distinguished body..." The fact of the matter is that his attitude toward politicians is unchanged, but the community needs better hospital facilities, and he would like to have the best surroundings in which to practice. So he arrives at a decision favoring particular behavior on a group issue. And this decision adapts attitudes, related to the issue. He forms an opinion. He decides to pay deference to the politicians though his attitude toward them slants his intuitive responses in quite a different direction. His statement, "this distinguished body..." is an opinion response. It certainly is not an attitude response, *nor could related attitudes safely be inferred from it.*

Attitudes are mental and neural states organized and stabilized out of many experiences, each of which adds to the personal, characteristic way in which an individual is predisposed to respond to a given type of situation. Important among the experiences that go into the forming of an attitude are those decisions regarding social interaction which have been defined as opinions. Especially important, presumably, are those opinions which, when acted upon produce decisively favorable or unfavorable consequences.[17] As in all cumulative processes, the size or potency of a particular increment determines the measure of its effect on the aggregate. But other things being equal, the earlier opinions presumably have the greater

[17]Even though opinions, as defined here, involve a serious overt behavioral intention, still many opinions are not acted out because of unanticipated changes in the environment. It would seem reasonable that opinions which are acted out would have greater impact in attitude formation than would those which are not acted out. In the first place an opinion which is not acted out will, in many cases, have been reconsidered and rejected in favor of a different opinion regarding the same issue which is then acted out. The rejection of the first opinion would presumably reduce its potency as an attitude ingredient. In the second place, the acting out of an opinion, with its interpersonal consequences surely increases the significance of the opinion as a psychosocial experience.

force in determining the nature of an attitude. Without implying neat mathematical regularity in the formative process, it is perhaps appropriate to recall that the second experience in a particular area constitutes 50 per cent of one's total experience in that area. The hundredth constitutes only 1 per cent.

CRITERIA FOR VALIDATION

If the foregoing definitions have merit, then the crux of the difference between attitude responses and opinion responses may be high-lighted by reference to the criteria in terms of which they may most appropriately be validated. Validity is sometimes defined as the extent of agreement between an index and the thing the index purports to measure. But this definition is a very stringent one. A more practicable definition is: *"Validity is the extent of agreement between the index and an independent and generally accepted criterion of what the index purports to measure.*[18] Consider an example.

In Parry and Crossley's research on the validity of public opinion responses, they asked respondents whether they had library cards.[19] The respondents' answers constituted the index. The reality that this index purports to measure is actual ownership of a library card. The validity of each response could have been established by asking each respondent to produce the card if he claimed to have one, and by asking him to permit a search of his person and premises if he claimed not to have one. The difficulties in any such validation procedure are apparent. Instead of insisting on validating the index in terms of the reality the index purports to measure, Perry and Crossley chose the records of the public library as their criterion. This criterion satisfied three provisions:

a. It was independent of the index.
b. It was generally acceptable as standing in close correspondence to the reality being measured.
c. It was objective in the sense that a number of judges, assessing it independently, would reach substantial unanimity.

[18]Most discussions of validity emphasize such factors as sampling difficulties, interview bias, item bias and honest responses. These and related factors will not be discussed here. The literature is abundant, and thorough in this area. The excellence and understanding that has been achieved in handling these technical aspects of opinion research is a matter in which social scientists may well take pride. But the central requirement for assessing the degree of validity is not thereby satisfied. The concept of validity is a concept of *relationship*. It is meaningless to speak of the validity of a test, a measurement or an index without reference to the thing tested, measured or indexed. In a large number of opinion surveys the degree of validity that may be ascribed to the findings is simply unknown.

[19]Parry, Hugh J., and Helen M. Crossley, "Validity of Responses to Survey Questions," *Public Opinion Quarterly,* Volume 14, Number 1, (Spring 1950), p. 72.

Although this "ownership item" is far from typical of opinion research questions, there is no doubt that we have here a case of good validating practice in the field of *opinion* research — a validating criterion which objectifies social interaction.

Now suppose one wishes to establish the validity of an *attitude* questionnaire that purports to measure the respondent's attitudes toward his father. Such an attitude questionnaire might be validated in terms of correspondence between questionnaire findings and an independent criterion which combined findings of clinical interviews with certain findings from Rorschach and TAT tests. Certainly the use of such a multiple clinical criterion would be considered better practice than using the respondent's behavior in the presence of his or her father as the criterion. The findings of clinical psychology lead to extreme skepticism regarding any dependable correspondence between a person's attitudes toward his father and his observable behavior in the presence of his father. The characteristic that particularly seems to recommend the multiple clinical criterion is its privateness — its guarantee against the threats and pressures toward social conformity.

Although attitude and opinion responses have superficial similarities their roots seem to reach in opposite directions. The roots of an attitude lie within the individual. The roots of an opinion lie within the life space in which the individual interacts. It would appear that the closest approach to a person's attitudes is in the privileged communications of clinical interviews or in the revelations of projective techniques. Thus the best validating criteria for attitudes appear to be clinical. But opinions, as defined here, lie so close to social interaction that behavior criteria are by far the most convincing for the validation of opinions.

Ideal criteria for validating attitude responses lie on the private side of attitude indices. Ideal criteria for validating opinion responses lie on the public or social side of opinion responses. So any ambiguity as to whether an item is an attitude item or an opinion item should be reduced if the researcher or the client is pressed to state the nature of the independent criterion which would satisfy him for purposes of validation. This point of view may be paraphrased: Tell me, not what you want to ask the respondent but what you finally want to know. Do you want to know the characteristic patterns of people's spontaneous feeling, believing — quite aside from what they may subsequently do? Or do you finally want to know how people behave — how they interact with their environment and with other people? If you want to know the former, then you want attitude testing, and you want an independent validating criterion of the clinical type. If you want the latter, then you want opinion research and you want an independent validating criterion of the overt, behavioral, directly observable type.

The confusion of the two entities defined here as attitudes and opinions has led to the further confusion of attempting to validate *attitude* responses in terms of *behavior* criteria. This appears to have been the difficulty in La Piere's well-known study of proprietors' attitudes toward Chinese.[20] La Piere travelled extensively over the United States with a young Chinese couple, between the years 1930 and 1932. They entered 184 restaurants, and 67 hotels, auto camps, and tourist homes. With the exception of one auto camp, they were accommodated in all instances. La Piere reports that on many of these occasions, the courtesy extended to them exceeded ordinary expectations. Six months after each of these stops, the proprietor received a mail questionnaire from La Piere posing this item: "Will you accept members of the Chinese race as guests in your establishment?" Fifty-one per cent responded, and of these 92 per cent answered "No." This study has occasioned much discussion because a concise item and an objective criterion par excellence turned up decidedly contradictory findings. Given a clear differentiation between attitudes and opinions, these findings are understandable.

Judging by the validating criterion, the item purports to be an index of overt, observable social behavior. In terms of present definitions then, the item was meant to be an opinion item — not an attitude item. As an opinion item, it was validated in terms of a sound criterion, and found to be grossly defective. As an *attitude* item, however, the item simply has not been validated. La Piere's criterion, figuratively speaking, was located on the wrong side of the index. The criterion should have been on the private, subjective, clinical side of the index instead of on the social behavior side.

Let us speculate as to what skillful depth interviewers might have elicited from a sample of the proprietors a few days after they answered "no" to La Piere's questionnaire. Between 1930 and 1932, when the study was conducted, the depression was severe. Business was bad. People hit the road with little money and vague destinations. Minority groups were among the first to be displaced as employment decreased. In this situation the proprietors received an inquiry from an unknown individual asking, "Will you accept members of the Chinese race...?" The proprietors envisage a straggling group of indigent Orientals — dressed in strange clothing, speaking a foreign language, seeking only rice and a dry floor to sleep on before continuing their search for truck farms or laundries with "help wanted" signs. Such a fantasy might well activate attitudes regarding status, property rights and economic well being as well as attitudes regarding Chinese.

[20]La Pierre, Richard T., "Attitudes vs. Action," *Social Forces*, Volume 13, 1934, pp. 230–237.

Such speculation as this is completely without substantiation. But is it less likely than that the proprietors had this fantasy: There will be a pleasant well-dressed American man accompanied by two handsome young people who speak English with no accent, who dress and behave like upper-middle class Americans, and who arrive, equipped with good luggage. The young couple have moderately oriental features. This, according to La Piere's report, appears to have been the real situation.

If our speculation, above, can be admitted into the realm of — not probability — but possibility, then we may conclude that:

(a) La Piere's item was useless as an opinion item because it did not allow respondents to adapt related attitudes *to the reality in which social behavior would transpire,* but,

(b) The item may well have been a highly valid attitude item. Its validity as an attitude item was not measured.

Attitude items measure a reality that is internal, private, subjective. Establishing their degree of validity is primarily the task of clinicians. Opinion items measure a reality that is also internal and private in the sense that ones perceptions are invariably internal and private, but an opinion draws heavily on the immediate social surroundings. An opinion (decision) is calculated for purposes of social interaction, for use in public. So it can be said that an opinion is bona-fide symbolic behavior.

WHAT 100 ITEMS "FINALLY WANT TO KNOW"

Attitudes and opinions have been defined in a manner that clearly differentiates them, and it has been pointed out that the difference between them may be high-lighted by reference to appropriate criteria for validation. The applicability of this formulation to the general field of public opinion items was investigated as follows:

One hundred items were selected from the Cantril-Strunk volume by taking the first complete item on one of the first pages, and the first complete item on every tenth page thereafter until 100 items had been chosen.[21] The writer classified these items in terms of the following questions:

Suppose that you could observe the criterion behavior. Suppose that you were custodian of all records, seer into the future, reader of minds and emotions. What is the real thing that would have motivated you to ask this item? What is the lack of information that responses to this item would satisfy?

Items were taken at face value. It was assumed that no items were indirect, or projective in nature. For example, if an item asked whether parents should go to PTA meetings, interest was assumed to be in the "should," in the belief — not in actual frequency of attending PTA meetings. The degree of variation between the writer's classifications and the way those who phrased the items would classify them is unknown. No cross tabulation of a preceding item, and no sub-item relating to

[21]Cantril, Hadley and Mildred Strunk, *Public Opinion,* 1935–1946, Princeton: Princeton University Press, 1951.

a preceding primary item was considered. Only items reported as discrete and separate pieces of research were classified.

The following results were obtained:

I would have asked this item to find out:	*Number of Items*
(Opinion Responses)	
What respondents will do	4
What respondents would do, given specified conditions	4
What respondents think others should do	20
What respondents would like in the future	2
(Status Responses)	
What respondents do	6
What respondents did	6
What respondents have or own	3
(Attitude Responses)	
What respondents think, feel or believe	42
What respondents thought, wanted in the past	1
Why respondents did what they did	1
What respondents should do	1
What respondents think others will do	4
What respondents think others have done	1
What respondents think other people think	1
(Information Responses)	
What respondents know	4
Total	100

The first 30 items appear to seek information about people's decisions on how to adapt attitudes to a reality situation with a view to successful behavior. The criteria that seem most appropriate come *after* the survey. Gradual progress toward higher validity in this type of opinion research is a matter of doing one's best, awaiting the outcome, attempting to explain the error in retrospect, and improving the methodology accordingly on the next similar study. The pre-election study is the prototype of this group.

A question might be raised regarding the "What respondents would like in the future" items. Do they belong in the first category? To the extent that such items elicit day dreams and idle fantasies they do not. But to the extent that the researcher thinks respondents will *try to bring about* what they would like in the future, the intention of the item appears to be predictive. The two items appeared to be of this latter type.

The items grouped under *Status Responses* might be called "opinions in retrospect." Thus, "Do you have a library card?" is sensible short hand for "Did you decide to get a library card in the past and did you do it?" In terms of validity the characteristic quality of these items is the existence of concrete evidence of, or records of, criterion behavior at the time of the survey.

The items labled *Attitude Responses* appear to seek information about subjective states of mind. A question might be raised regarding the four items labled "What respondents think others will do." If an item, among these four, had been "Do you think your husband will buy a dishwasher this year?" then the wife's response would presumably denote a decision which would be implemented in social interaction. But a more appropriate wording in such a case would be, "Do *you* plan to buy..." in which case it would be under Opinion Responses. No such problems arose however. "Do you think Stalin will extend the war?" conveys the flavor of these four items.

If the items in the third group are taken at face value, they appear to seek attitude responses — states of mind unencumbered by the restrictions of deciding what one will actually do about the issue. At any rate, if this is *not* the case, and if researchers do expect respondents to behave in correspondence with their replies, the burden of proof, regarding any such correspondence between the replies and subsequent behavior is on the researcher. Assuming that these items are intended to elicit attitude responses, the appropriate criteria are clinical in nature. That is, they are criteria that may be presumed to lie closer to the respondent's subjective readiness to respond than do the words elicited by a strange doorstep interviewer.

The familiar question regarding the genuineness, or the truthfulness that can be expected from a doorstep interview is pertinent at this point. People withhold many of their attitude responses (as defined here) from the scrutiny of strangers. Social scientists realize this, and in many instances they neither want nor expect wholly candid attitude responses from "opinion" surveys. For example, sociologists, anthropologists, and clinical psychologists are rather generally agreed on the observation that few white people, reared in contemporary United States are entirely free of anti-Negro bias. But religious, social, ethical, and political rationality lead a large majority of whites to deplore this taint, and to attempt to edit it out of their thinking and behavior. Now suppose that an "opinion" researcher gathers responses to the item: "Do you feel that Negroes deserve rights and privileges equal to those of whites?" Does he really want attitude responses? Does he think he could get them if he wanted them? Does he think he could approach high validity if he checked doorstep responses on this item against a criterion combining depth interviews and projective test responses? No, he expects impulses to be tempered with rationality. He expects that first, deeply engrained, readiness to respond to be disciplined by a counterbalancing devotion to democratic ideals. Such a researcher would appear to ask for an attitude response, to expect an opinion response, and to get an ambiguous aggregate of various and irresponsible opinion responses because he would have failed to evoke, in the respondent's mind, a fantasy of the reality situation in which action would transpire.

The doorstep interviewer seems of doubtful usefulness in surveying attitudes. The situation is quite different, however, with regard to opinion responses. Opinion responses are, by definition, calculated for social interaction, for scrutiny by others. The attitudes involved in them are adapted to the perceived reality in which behavior must transpire. Here, the doorstep interviewer may be expected to function effectively. The same situation would appear to apply in the case of Status Responses. Such status elements as owning a freezer or being an officer in a club are generally divulged without reticence.

The usefulness of attitude items in public opinion surveys seems to demand reappraisal. Few of these items are validated, probably because few of the findings are considered worth the time and skill required to assess validity. Who is really concerned about what respondents think, feel, or believe — or think other people think — unless the respondents *do* something about it? Such people as one's friends, relatives, teachers, and clinicians are, of course, concerned. But these solicitous ones are concerned primarily because these thoughts and feelings do have counterparts in behavior in the intimate and subtle interaction with which they are concerned. For example, a woman reported that she felt "outraged and angry" at the corrupt officials exposed during the Kefauver Hearings.[22] Six weeks after the hearings, however, she reported that she had done "nothing about it — didn't even discuss it with my family." If these feelings caused our respondent to be irritable and resentful for a day, her husband may be presumed to have been concerned. Her feelings flowed into behavior in so far as interaction with him was concerned. But would her feelings, by any reasonable standards, have significance in a public opinion survey? They do not seem to.

A number of the items that appear to seek attitude responses also convey the impression that information regarding subsequent behavior would be most welcome. If this impression is true, then confusion about the concept of validity with regard to them is understandable. It is maintained that a number of items which appear to elicit attitude responses are inadequate items meant to seek opinion responses. This is especially true of the "What respondents think, feel or believe" category. It is further maintained that clarification of such ambiguity, restatement of the items

[22]Wiebe, G. D., "Responses to the Televised Kefauver Hearings and Some Social Psychological Implications," *Public Opinion Quarterly,* Vol. 16, No. 2, (Summer, 1952.)

as opinion items, and a forthright attack on the formidable problems of validating a greater variety of predictive surveys constitutes one of the most challenging opportunities for progress in contemporary social science.

Ambiguity as to whether an item is an attitude, or an opinion, item is probably one of the reasons for the appearance of face validity. Face validity is unacceptable as a scientific concept. It arose from a basic misunderstanding of the concept of validity. Proponents of face validity attribute scientific status to the kind of circular thinking that is lampooned in an old joke: "What is intelligence?" "Intelligence is whatever this intelligence test measures." In face validity one decides on the index, and then declares that the validating criterion is identical with the responses to that index. Confusion is frequently compounded by the assertion that face validity is based on *behavior* criteria. This is because responding to the index is behavior. The error, obviously, is in forgetting that a validating criterion must, by definition, be *independent* of the index. The achievement of validity approaching 100 per cent is a primary goal in the most highly developed sciences. To redefine this concept for use in opinion research so that one automatically gets 100 per cent validity, as proponents of face validity do, is pure sophistry.

The group labeled *Information Responses* includes items which seek the recitation of discrete units of information. Such information items are distinctly different from attitude and opinion items in so far as validity is concerned. Both attitude and opinion items are indices, that is, they are cues, short hand indications of more comprehensive states. Information items, are not indices in this sense. They do not require validation because validation is a technique for relating an index to the thing indexed. Claims of face validity for such items are not only unscientific, they are totally unnecessary. "Who is President of the United States?" The response to this item calls for "correction" not validation. The answer is right or wrong. It is not an index — it is the whole thing. If responses to the "Who is President" item were taken together with responses to other information items as an index of good citizenship, then validity should again be demonstrated by reference to an independent and generally acceptable criterion.

LIMITATIONS ON ASSESSING VALIDITY OF ATTITUDE AND OPINION RESPONSES

A basic difference between attitudes and opinions has been discussed. The relationship between the index and the reality it purports to measure in the two cases is correspondingly different. The answer that a person gives to an attitude item is a symbolic representation of a personal state of mind. To the extent that a person's state of mind is conscious, and to the extent that it can be communicated in symbols appropriate to the testing situation, an attitude response may be assumed to be true or else *deliberately* false.

A person's attitudes are private property. They are personal possessions—and they are comparatively stable. One may choose not to symbolize them for inspection by others, or one may find that he cannot accurately represent them in symbolic form; but just the same they are his, and his alone. Establishing the validity of attitude testing, then, appears to be limited only by the skill of the tester and the insight and cooperativeness of the respondent. There are, however, certain additional limitations in determining the validity of opinion surveys.

The relationships between opinion responses and the realities they purport to measure present, in some cases, fewer difficulties and in other cases more difficulties than those encountered in attitude testing. Those that present fewer difficulties were classified above as status responses. They report decisions that were made in the past and that were acted upon before the survey. In these instances criteria are, or could be, a matter of record. Objective validating criteria can generally be found in these instances. By a limited number of comparisons between index and criterion, the validity of the mass of information made available through sampling techniques can be estimated. Thus, such surveys rise above the realm of simple reporting and contribute data to the social sciences on which the degree of validity is known with a useful degree of accuracy.

The more perplexing difficulties are encountered in validating predictive items. In this area, tests of validity are not only possible, they are in many instances, unavoidable. Professional communicators (editors, politicians, businessmen, reporters) and fellow scientists exhibit remarkable spurts of critical interest in opinion research when people don't do what opinion research predicted that they would do. The limitations of validity on predictive opinion items merit special consideration. An opinion has been defined as a mental and neural state perceived as a decision favoring particular behavior on a group issue — a decision which adapts attitudes related to the issue to the individual's perception of the reality in which the behavior must transpire. Predictive opinion response is not only a symbolic representation of a personal state of mind; it is that *plus* a fantasy of a set of social circumstances *plus* a fantasy of interaction with those circumstances. The chances of deviation between the decision to behave and the corresponding behavior increase geometrically. The validity of predictive opinion items is limited not only by the skill of the researcher and the insight and cooperativeness of the respondent but also by the vagaries of social circumstances and human interactions.

Given these complexities, the outlook for reasonably high validity on predictive opinion items is not encouraging. An alternative comes to mind. Why not forego this taxing allegiance to behavior criteria, and adopt a concept of opinion which would involve validating criteria that can be controlled to a greater extent? Why not validate predictive opinion items in terms of, for example, correspondence between opinion survey responses and the impressions of family members and intimate friends as to the respondent's opinions? They, in ordinary and intimate conversation, presumably get closer to the respondent's true opinions than do strange interviewers who require answers that fit into multiple choice categories.

In spite of its methodological attractiveness, this alternative must be rejected on the basis of common sense and simple honesty. No one cares whether a pre-election poll is valid in terms of how respondents told their spouses they would vote. The proper criterion is a record of behavior at the polls. A manufacturer isn't interested in knowing that men tell both interviewers and their best friends that they would buy woolen neckties, if having manufactured 100,000 of them, men don't buy them. A decision to behave in a particular way has its validity in behaving that particular way. Opinion researchers whose findings are confirmed by social action never hesitate to claim this correspondence as proof of validity. There appears to be no satisfactory middle ground. Predictive opinion items should be validated in terms of subsequent behavior in spite of the complexities that intervene between the decision (opinion) and the behavior.

Opinion, as defined here, cannot be realistically surveyed unless the reality situation, in which criterion behavior will take place is to some degree defined by the opinion item. A particular item may solicit opinion responses on an issue that is so clearly structured in its social dimensions that bare reference to the issue will evoke a clear and consistent fantasy in the minds of respondents. But this happy situation cannot be taken for granted. The researcher must assume responsibility for evoking in the minds of his respondents a realistic fantasy of the "reality in which the (criterion) behavior must transpire." The researcher must assess the situation in which action will transpire — assess it accurately and then he must symbolize his assessment in acceptable item form.

A researcher cannot declare that he has fulfilled this requirement in phrasing a predictive item. He can only state that he has done his best. Having done his best, all of the vagaries of selective perception on the part of the respondent come into play. In spite of his best efforts, no researcher can vouch for the fantasies evoked in the minds of respondents by his carefully phrased item.

Even when the researcher has phrased the item with simplicity and insight so that it evokes a rather accurate fantasy of the social situation in which action must transpire and the respondent has perceived the item with a minimum of distortion, and responded with candor regarding his decision as to how he will behave, there remains the very real possibility that the social situation itself will change between the time the item was phrased and the time for criterion behavior. Given such intrinsic difficulties as these in predictive opinion research, the degree of validity that has been demonstrated on numerous occasions seems truly remarkable. These predictions with relatively high validity have probably occurred most often in certain types of market research[23] and in pre-election surveys. Several characteristics of research in these two areas merit mention.

STABLE FACTORS IN MARKET RESEARCH AND IN PRE-ELECTION SURVEYS

There is little ambiguity about criterion behavior in market research and pre-election surveys. Criterion behavior is specific, and it is "either — or." Intensity is ruled out as a factor. One buys, and reduces the inventory by one unit, or he doesn't. One votes for candidate A, or B, or C, or one doesn't vote. Under such circumstances, stringent tests of validity are inevitable. Why in view of the theoretical difficulties just reviewed, is rather high validity achieved?[24] An important reason appears to be that several crucial factors, beyond the present control of social scientists, are relatively stable in these types of research. Three of them follow:

1. Because criterion behavior is unambiguous, the researcher's assessing of it, and his formulation of the item, can be simple and lucid. He experiences a minimum of difficulty in communicating to the respondent the nature of the reality situation in which action (criterion behavior) must transpire.
2. Criterion behavior is similarly clear to the respondent. It is familiar, highly structured, demands a minimum of initiative, and is, in its essentials, behavior that has transpired before. It can, therefore, be fantasied by the respondent with a high degree of accuracy.
3. The reality situation in which behavior must transpire will not deviate, barring acts of God, from the researcher's and the respondent's fantasies of it.

The importance of these normally stable factors can be dramatized by imagining them in flux. If eligibility to vote, and the weight to be assigned each individual's vote were decided at the polls, at the time of voting, or if election day were not fixed by law, the researcher would have considerable difficulty fixing in his own mind, just what criterion behavior looked like. He would have corresponding difficulty in phrasing a good item. The respondent would have difficulty expressing a bona fide intention. But

[23]See, for example, Henry C. Link and A. D. Freiberg, "The Problem of Validating vs. Reliability in Public Opinion Polls," *Public Opinion Quarterly*, Vol. VI, No. 1. (Spring 1942), pp. 87–98.

[24]The author is not among those who scorn the pre-election research of 1948. Very few social phenomena are predictable, at present, with a similar degree of accuracy.

researchers can claim no credit for the stability of the real situation as contrasted with the flux of the imagined one. They don't control these variables. They achieve comparatively high validity because these variables tend to remain stable. The danger is in assuming that because variables remain stable, they are not variables.

A PREDICTIVE ITEM WITH MANY VARIABLES IN FLUX

The American Institute of Public Opinion queried nation wide samples, in 1949, and 1950 on the following question:

"Would you favor or oppose having Alaska admitted as a state in the Union?"[25]

The findings were:

Date	Favor	Oppose	No Opinion
1949	68%	7%	25%
1950	81%	8%	11%

Taken at face value, this item appears to be an attitude item. It elicits information on how the respondent feels about statehood for Alaska. The idea of depth interviews to gain a closer vantage point from which to infer a highly organized mental and neural state of readiness to respond to the political status of Alaska is surely ludicrous. This is not an attitude item.

It appears that the item is an opinion item since a suitable criterion seems to lie in the area of social interaction rather than in the precincts of privileged communication.

Since the decision to withhold or grant statehood to Alaska was being debated during 1949 and 1950, one cannot escape the conclusion that the reality indexed by these findings was meant to register some impact on congressional action. The item, then, was meant in some degree to be predictive. Not in the sense that the Senate should legislate the majority finding (this would be naive). Surely not in the sense that the Senate should legislate the minority response. But the findings, if they are presumed to mean anything at all, must be thought of as indexing something that added to the affirmative case. If this is the presumption, then the findings are valid to the extent that the expected increment on the affirmative side was in fact felt by the Senators as they came to their decision on the issue. The task of setting up an independent criterion that stands in close relationship to this increment would be a very complex undertaking. But the alternative appears to be forgetting about validity and saying, in effect, "That's what they said. We don't know what it means. Take it or leave it."

[25]"The Quarter's Polls," *Public Opinion Quarterly*, Vol. XIV, No. 4, (Winter 1950–1951), p. 817.

It is fairly obvious that the Senators leave it.[26] Furthermore, there is no evidence to show that they are foolhardy for doing so. But they certainly would not react similarly to findings of 81, 8, and 11% on a pre-election poll. Then these figures must bear an entirely different order of consequence in the two cases.

The degree of validity of the "Alaska" findings is unknown — unknown because no independent and acceptable criterion has been stated by which validity can be measured. Should the opinion findings be validated in terms of Senatorial action? At first glance this appears to be too stringent a criterion — even a little presumptuous. But there would be rather general agreement that the wishes of 81 per cent of the citizens on a public issue exert *some* influence on the Senate. And there is little reason to doubt that if 81 per cent of the people became highly excited, and fanatically determined, they could determine Senatorial action. There appears to be no sound *theoretical* reason for disqualifying Senatorial action as the criterion. The bothersome thing is a matter of common sense. One just knows that legislative action has not conformed in any regular fashion with the findings of public opinion polls, and one doesn't expect it to do so.

We are now in the position of saying:

1. That Senators are responsive in some degree to public opinion.
2. That public opinion, on occasion, may determine the behavior of Senators.
3. That one does not expect Senators to behave in any regular correspondence with public opinion.

Who is erratic — the Senators, public opinion, or both? One should examine his own house first.

One unfortunate by-product of face validity is the tendency to confuse public opinion with the findings of public opinion surveys. The latter are only an index. They are not public opinion.

Published findings of public opinion surveys should notify congressmen regarding the tangible force of public opinion that they may prepare to feel. Similarly, pre-election polls do not elect — they notify — they predict behavior by assessing the opinion out of which that behavior will flow. If predictive public opinion surveys achieved high and consistent validity, then it is conceivable that governing bodies might begin to govern in conformity with opinion research findings. Such a political leadership would be like Pavlov's dog — salivating at the sound of the bell. But if such a state of affairs should come to pass, the leaders, like the dog, would probably soon find that the meat sometimes didn't appear. So we may suppose, the leaders would return to their earlier habit of using public

[26]As of January 1954, Alaska is not a state.

73

opinion findings in preparation for the meat of tangible social action — not as a substitute for it.

What is the behavior predicted by the 81 per cent pro-Alaska vote? Whatever it is, it is rather weak stuff for the occasion; 81 per cent of a national sample is a large measure of agreement to find on any issue. Unanimity can't be expected to go much higher, but the Senate disregarded it with impugnity. Is it not appropriate to ask then, whether the "Something" that 81 per cent of the respondents affirmed was, in any consequential sense, opinion?

Consider the item. Did the researcher and the respondents perceive, or approximately perceive, the reality in which behavior would transpire? An excerpt from the Congressional Record[27] suggests that they did not. Senator Stennis of Mississippi, made the following statement:

> "Mr. President, the prize for admission of any area as a State within the United States is two seats on the floor of the United States Senate. All other arguments by relation and by primary importance vanish into the background. The real prize is two seats on the floor of the Senate....
>
> "But that is not the main power, Mr. President. The Senate of the United States and the President of the United States largely determine the foreign policy of this Nation. That is particularly important now, and it will be more important as the years come and go. It comes from one of the provisions written into the Constitution more than a century and a half ago, that treaties, when negotiated by the President and ratified by two-thirds of a quorum of the Senate, shall become the supreme law of the land. That is the present sleeping giant in our form of government.
>
> "Under the system of the two-thirds vote, if two more Senators are added, they will have the power to negate the votes of four Senators. They will have negative power equivalent to the combined power of the Senators from the Great State of New York and the Great State of Pennsylvania. The votes of the four Senators from these two States, representing roughly a population of more than 23,000,000 will be completely stymied or offset by the votes of two Senators representing a civilian population in Alaska of about 100,000."

Without attempting a detailed analysis, we may conclude that at least some Senators were coming to a decision to behave in a perceptual framework in which domestic balance of power, and relations with European nations loomed large. This frame of reference is certainly not communicated by the item. One may suppose that many respondents, left to their own devices by a simple and concise item, thought in terms of "fair play" and 49 stars in the American Flag.

Although the polls were conducted in 1949 and 1950, Senator Stennis' statement was made in 1952. If his arguments were stated and were effective during the debates of '49 and '50, then the researchers failed to convey the reality situation in which action must take place when they phrased the item, and it may be assumed that most respondents failed to perceive the reality situation with accuracy. If Senator Stennis' arguments

[27]Congressional Record, February 19, 1952, p. 1137.

appeared for the first time in '52, then the researchers suffered that completely uncontrollable situation, namely a change of the situation in which action must transpire between the time of the survey and the time for action. At any rate, one might imagine a Senator looking at the AIPO item and its findings and saying, "The survey is irrelevant because those people and we in the Senate are not thinking about the same thing."

Unlike an election situation, an individual's behavior which flows from his opinion on the Alaska issue does not have a pre-determined unit of weight in decision making. Nor do respondents or social scientists know, with a useful degree of accuracy, how much weight a given behavior by a given individual has. Election day is fixed by law, and swift totaling of votes is fixed by custom. But a citizen's behavior on the Alaska issue may be poorly or well timed, and may move swiftly to the place for decision making, or may be delayed, buried, misinterpreted, magnified, or nullified in transit. Behavior is specified and formalized in an election. It is unstructured on the Alaska issue.

These are examples of uncontrolled variables[28] — variables that the social scientist ordinarily finds conveniently stable in pre-election surveys and in certain types of market research. But stable or in flux, there are factors that characterize predictive opinion research. They challenge the social scientist. If they can not be assessed with precision, they almost certainly can be understood on a "greater or lesser" basis.

Coming to grips with such variables as these involves the assumption of a new role by the researcher. The process of predictive opinion research, as discussed in this paper, makes the *respondent* the one who does all or most of the predicting. The researcher's job is primarily that of helping the respondent to forsee his own behavior accurately. As long as his behavior, and *the implications of his behavior* can be forseen, are "visable" to the respondent, this is a profitable procedure.

But for all of its difficulties and technicalities, this method of prediction does not yet involve the prediction of effects by the understanding of causes which is the ultimate scientific method of prediction. Rather, present practice must, in most cases, be characterized as predicting effect by the appraisal of incipient effect.

As basic research accumulates,[29] prediction may be expected to move more and more toward cause and effect techniques. In practical terms, this would mean questioning respondents, not only on the issue, but questioning them on subjects which have been ascertained before hand

[28]G. D. Wiebe, "Merchandising Commodities and Citizenship on Television," *Public Opinion Quarterly*, Volume XV, No. 4, p. 679.

[29]See, for example, Helen Dinerman, "1948 Votes in the Making — A Preview," *Public Opinion Quarterly*, Vol. XII, No. 4, Winter, 1948, p. 585.

to constitute the causes on which the determination of the issue (effect) will turn.

Attention to factors which are "out of sight" of the respondent, (for example, the destiny and final impact of 1000 letters of protest addressed to a Senator or the consequences, at the executive level of a corporation, when 80 per cent of the white collar workers talk to each other about deserving a higher salary) attention to such factors do much to dispel the air of mysticism that often characterizes discussions of public opinion. Newspapers and magazines abound in statements to the effect that "public opinion will demand a change." Public opinion doesn't communicate by magic. It won't demand anything except as opinion flows into social behavior. If responses are so trivial that they do not flow into behavior, then one may question whether they have any real significance in the determination of our social and political environment.

If attention is turned to the power of public opinion rather than to the "face of the dial which purports to measure it," then a number of familiar propositions appear to invite systematic investigations.

1. A representative sample of the population is often irrelevant. A representative sample of those who will engage in effective behavior is often the more relevant sample.
2. An arbitrary value of 1 assigned to each opinion is simply poor mathematics in attempting to predict on issues where the researcher knows with practical certainty that one person's decision to behave (opinion) is at least 100 times as important as that of another person on the same issue.
3. Informed opinion may be irrelevant. Uninformed opinion may be potent.
4. Little is known about the "gates, parkways, detours, and short-cuts" that intervene between opinion and its immediate counterpart in behavior on the one hand, and effective group decision on the other.[30]
5. If a respondent is uninterested in an issue but is urged, never the less, to state an "opinion," and if social pressures are not such as to press him toward definitive corresponding behavior (e.g. to vote), then the response might better be called a whim than an opinion, for left to his own devices, the respondent will almost certainly not behave in conformity with his response.
6. Politicians and other policy makers tend to behave in terms of their own opinions, that is, they reach decisions which adapt their attitudes to their own perception of the reality in which they must take action. This reality is often a veritable storm of conflicting interest and pressures which impinge on the policy maker with all the power and persuasiveness that can be mustered. In such situations, the supposition that the politicians or policy makers will bend their ears to the whisperings of public preference which have no counterpart in the whirlwind that buffets them is — unrealistic.

When numerous and important variables are in flux, validating predictive opinion research *with precision* appears to be beyond the skills and techniques presently available. In some cases (e.g. when the reality situa-

[30]See a discussion of "social impotence" in G. D. Wiebe, "Responses to the Televised Kefauver Hearings," *Public Opinion Quarterly*, Volume XVI, No. 2, (Summer, 1952), pp. 179–200.

tion changes after the survey) it appears to be impossible. In
however, agreement on criterion behavior, and a forthright
assessing the function of known variables could result in a marke
in the significance of public opinion findings. The concept of op.
behavioral intention appears to contribute toward progress in this
It tends to reduce concern with whims and daydreams, and to focus
tion more clearly on the dynamics by which individuals function in group
living.

AN HYPOTHESIS

In concluding this attempt at a useful differentiation between attitudes
and opinions, one hypothesis regarding the relationship between these
two psychological entities is proposed. Social scientists together with many
others are concerned with morale and the social stability of large groups.
Closely related to this is concern with ideology. The definitions of attitude
and opinion stated above lead to the following hypothesis: Opinions adapt
attitudes to practical situations. The greater the required adaptation in
order to achieve a specified degree of success in social interaction, the
greater the stress that will be aroused in the process. Thus a person whose
attitudes are in harmonious accord with the requirements of the social
situation in which he must interact, will experience a sense of fulfillment
in moving from attitude to opinion to behavior. Contrariwise, a person
whose attitudes are inappropriate for successful interaction in his environment will experience stress in adjusting his attitudes to opinions which can
be acted upon without incurring failure or punishment from those with
whom he interacts. Thus the greater the differences between attitudes and
opinions, the lesser the degree of stability and morale.

The degree of stress is not only symptomatic of the degree of difference
between attitudes and opinions. It might be characterized as a dynamic
that "pushes" toward changing the reality situation so that it conforms
more closely with one's attitudes. The "push" tends to favor the attitudes
because attitudes are older, more stable, more deeply integrated. This
"push" may be thought of as a potential, driving toward, or at least recep-
tiveness to, social change.

Why do autocrats progress from the control of people's behavior and
speech to attempts at controlling their thoughts? Could it be that there
is an intuitive recognition that conformity through coercion masks a
potential for revolt that is in direct proportion to the gap between attitudes and opinions? Does the degree of success of the western strategy

[31]Floyd H. Allport states "that the content of (public opinion) must be conceived as
related to the actual *behavior of individuals,* is self evident." Op. cit. p. 13.

of sustaining hope for liberation among people under tyranny have an objective counterpart in the gap between attitudes and opinions among the tyrannized?

Opinions, especially those that are acted upon with satisfying consequences, become internalized, and so contribute to a slow modification of related attitudes. It would appear to follow from this, that the stress experienced in adapting attitudes to the requirements of society would gradually lessen (given a fairly stable reality situation). This gradual reduction of stress would occur because, as opinions are internalized, the attitudes would change in the direction of easier articulation with subsequent similar opinions.[32]

Given the existence of *attitudes* appropriate for survival in a highly coercive society, and then liberation, will a comparatively permissive environment engender more democratic attitudes, or will the "push," as hypothesized above, tend toward reshaping the reality situation toward greater conformity with attitudes? Might a comparatively permissive situation in Western Germany, for example, foster a feeling of fulfillment via a "push" toward "Neo-Nazism"?[33]

Such questions as these will, it is hoped, argue for the practical usefulness of separating attitudes and opinions. They seen too valuable, separately and in conjunction with each other, to leave undifferentiated.

[32]The important function of individual differences is recognized. The hypothesis is that over and above these, useful generalizations may exist.

[33]See *the New York Times*, Sunday, January 18, 1953. "Rise in Neo-Nazism Is Shown By Survey in West Germany," page 1.

COMMENT ON THE "IMPLICATIONS OF SEPARATING OPINIONS FROM ATTITUDES"

M. Brewster Smith

I N A RECENT article in this *Quarterly*,[1] Wiebe argues persuasively for maintaining a clear conceptual and methodological distinction between opinions and attitudes. *Attitudes,* he holds following Allport, are most profitably regarded as structural predispositions of a relatively generalized and enduring sort, while *opinions,* on the other hand, reflect particular decisions made in a social context. "Opinions adapt attitudes to the demands of social situations; but having adapted them, opinions appear to become ingredients in the constant, gradual reformulation of attitudes."[2] The different criteria that he suggests for the validation of "attitude responses" and "opinion responses" give his distinction operational meaning. "Attitude responses", he holds, have no essential relationship to overt behavior; "it would appear that the closest approach to a person's attitudes is in the privileged communications of clinical interviews or in the revelations of projective techniques. Thus the best validating criteria for attitudes appear to be clinical. But opinions, as defined here, lie so close to social interaction that behavior criteria are by far the most convincing for the validation of opinions."[3] The test he proposes for validating "opinion responses" is, essentially: Does the person's future behavior conform to the decision implied by his response?

There is much merit immediately apparent in Wiebe's formulation. It seems to fit current usage as well as any attempt at clarity can fit the ambiguities in this terminological morass. It properly cuts through at least

[1]Wiebe, G. D., "Some Implications of Separating Opinions from Attitudes", *Public Opinion Quarterly,* Vol. 17 (Fall 1953), No. 3 pp. 328–352.
[2]Ibid., p. 333.
[3]Ibid., p. 336.

Originally published in Volume 18, Number 3, 1954 of the *Public Opinion Quarterly*.

one level of foggy thinking about the meaning of discrepancy between attitudes and actions, recognizing the interplay of personal and situational determinants of behavior. It soundly questions the practical and theoretical meaningfulness of many "opinion" questions that polling organizations still put before a patient public. And it directs fresh thought toward the problem of question validity, which too often is considered a matter of pat formulae when it is not simply neglected.

There are other apparent accomplishments of Wiebe's analysis, however, which seem to me more questionable. At first glance, for example, detaching attitudes from behavior and relating them to clinical criteria would seem to provide a charter of liberation for "attitude"—as distinct from "opinion"—research. Closer inspection leads one to suspect, however, that Wiebe is actually relegating attitudes to the realm of the trivial and academic: serious and practical people should, if they follow his analysis, devote themselves to the study of opinion, where to be sure more exacting criteria of validation have to be met, but the pay-off in predictive power seems proportionately greater.

It is my contention, and the reason for this commentary, that this aspect of Wiebe's position, which I would regard as unfortunate, is a consequence of inacceptable starting points in his chain of reasoning. These have to do with his conception of validity, his assumptions about the relation between attitudes and opinions as constructs and the behavior from which they are inferred, and his exclusive preoccupation with the analysis of single questions rather than scales. The outcome of working through these sources of difficulty, unfortunately, lacks the neat symmetry of Wiebe's position, but perhaps retains some of its virtues. It indicates, however, a very different preferred strategy from his for advancing theoretical understanding and predictive power in opinion research.

VALIDITY FOR WHAT?

Let us begin with Wiebe's critical discussion of validity in opinion research. He proposes the following definition: *"Validity is the extent of agreement between the index and an independent and generally accepted criterion of what the index purports to measure."*[4] This would seem straight-forward enough, but closer inspection locates a source of ambiguity. Who does the "purporting"? Certainly not the index itself, passive and innocently inanimate as it is. Data, we have often been reminded, do not speak for themselves. The person reporting a research presents or implies the inferences he would draw from his data, and the consumer of the research may draw other inferences of his own. Since purposes are

[4]Ibid., p. 335.

many, possible directions of inference from a given body of data are also various. It is to these inferences that criteria of validity apply, not, strictly speaking, to the question that elicits the response or to the response itself. If we sometimes talk eliptically about the validity of a question, test or scale, or of responses to these, we risk confusion if there is any ambiguity about the purposes for which the responses or scores are to be used.

Wiebe does not embrace consistently the relative conception of validity that is implied in his distinction between the appropriate criteria for validating "opinion" and "attitude" responses. Consider, for instance, his discussion of La Piere's well-known study of proprietors' attitudes toward Chinese[5], in which the widest discrepancy was found between observed acceptance of a Chinese couple in La Piere's company, and asserted non-acceptance in response to a subsequent mail questionnaire. Wiebe resolves the discrepancy by concluding that La Piere's question was useless and in-valid as an "opinion item" (it did not predict behavior correctly) but that its validity as an "attitude item" (an index of how the proprietors "really" felt about Chinese) was in no way measured. Note, however, an assumption that Wiebe makes here as elsewhere. He is interested in the validity of only a single kind of inference about "opinion" items: the direct one that distributions of behavior will conform to the *marginals* of the item responses. An item is valid as an elicitor of opinion only if it asks people what they will do under specified circumstances and they do as they say they will. Inference at this level is a simple and direct business. In effect it neatly shifts the responsibility for prediction from the social scientist to his victim.

Wiebe neglects other possible lines of inference that fall within his definition of opinion since they are also concerned with behavioral out-comes in social contexts. Data may be used to support comparative pre-dictions as well as absolute ones. One might predict that respondents who give one answer to an item will be *more likely* to exhibit a particular sort of behavior than those who answer differently. While the La Piere data do not lend themselves well to this sort of use since both the response and the behavioral criterion cut the sample into groups of extremely disparate size, one might predict from such a question that the greater proportion of discriminatory behavior would occur among respondents giving prejudiced answers. Here the appropriate test of validity is com-parative, not a matter of exact correspondence. Correspondence between behavior and replies taken at their face value is a limiting case of still another sort of prediction for which indices are often employed. Item responses can be used to predict not only the relative frequency of kinds

[5]Ibid., p. 337–338; La Piere, Richard T., "Attitudes vs. Actions", *Social Forces*, Vol. 13, 1934, pp. 230–237.

of behavior associated with different response categories, as above, but their absolute frequencies as well. But this requires knowledge of the "scale value" of the item, in effect, and the relation of scale scores to behavior in the situation to which prediction is being made. An item like the La Piere question could be utterly "biased," invalid, in regard to naive use of its marginals at their face value, yet conceivably be highly valid in assigning persons to categories with known behavior characteristics.

The frame of mind induced by working with single questions is almost bound to result in excessive interest in the face value of replies, with the test of validity being applied rather to the respondent's ability to foretell his own behavior than to the scientist's ability to infer it. The use of scales, on the other hand, encourages the researcher in attaining detachment from the surface meaning of particular responses. Rational prediction then involves relating scale scores to relevant behaviors.

Predictions from either single items or scales, moreover, may be either unconditional or contingent. Prediction within the framework of scientific theory is always contingent: if this, then that. But prediction in the lay sense is often unconditional: flatly, that will happen. In sophisticated versions, unconditional predictions may be qualified with a statement of probability level, without changing their logical character. Unconditional predictions call for different tests of validity than contingent ones, and among contingent predictions, validation must be geared to the relevant contingencies. In the La Piere situation, the question asked the proprietors might perhaps have furnished the basis for valid inference of proprietors' behavior toward unaccompanied Chinese who conformed to the prevalent oriental stereotype, without having validity for other contingencies or for unconditional prediction of behavior toward Chinese regardless of circumstance.

Validity has been discussed above in relation to predictive inferences. It may perhaps be argued that inferences to the nature of a construct are of a different order, and require different criteria of validation. Wiebe would seem to hold this view in his insistence on clinical criteria for measures of attitude. One might, of course, ask why "clinical" criteria are not just as relevant to measures of opinion. If it is proper to ask what a person "really" feels (an assumption that will presently be challenged), surely it is equally appropriate to inquire whether his "real" decisions for action, his "real opinions," are adequately reflected in his responses to questioning.

The serious difficulty with this line of argument, one that Wiebe appreciates where his own concerns with opinion research are involved, is that free-floating constructs that are not anchored to consequent behavior are surplus baggage that a scientific theory can ill afford. Constructs like attitude are introduced precisely because it is hoped that they will enable us to organize our research data in ways that increase our ability to predict and to generalize our predictions appropriately to new situations. Predictive inferences are the kind that it is scientifically important to test.

What has this detour about the nature of validity to do with Wiebe's disinction between "attitudes" and "opinions" with respect to criteria for validation? Simply, that his sharp dichotomy does not stand up. There are not just two sorts of criteria, but many, corresponding to the many kinds of inferences that researcher and client may have occasion to draw from opinion and attitude data. The clinical criterion, while doubtless a useful adjunct in connection with others, is of questionable scientific value by itself, and in any case is equally applicable to measures of "opinion" and of "attitude." His predictive, behavioral criterion dissolves into a host of independent criteria, each appropriate to a different scientific or practical purpose. Contingent inferences about behavior are just as appropriately drawn from "attitude" data as from "opinion" items, while as Wiebe's article documents, "opinion" items are frequently though unwisely used for unconditional predictions. These issues will be encountered from a somewhat different perspective in a subsequent section.

CONSTRUCTS VS. RESPONSES

Underlying the foregoing argument that validity is a property of inferences, not of items or responses, is the view that attitudes and opinions in Wiebe's sense are constructs rather than directly given data of behavior. Wiebe is entirely clear and consistent about this point in regard to attitudes. Some ambiguity, however, enters into his treatment of opinions. By his definition, they are constructs: "An opinion might then be defined as *a mental and neural state perceived as a decision favoring particular behavior on a group issue.*"[6] Leaving aside the difficulty involved in *perceiving* "a mental or neural state," we can be sure from his wording, chosen to parallel Allport's definition of attitude, that he intends to regard "opinion" as a construct in the realm of individual psychology. But his discussion centers not on the construct so defined, but on what he calls "opinion response."

Let us accept for the nonce Wiebe's distinction between attitude and opinion as constructs. Does a parallel distinction follow between "attitude responses" and "opinion responses"? Not, I think, from Wiebe's own position that emphasizes the conjoint role of personal and situational components in the determination of behavior. Behavior, it is widely accepted

[6]Ibid., p. 333.

83

in principle, is a function of both the person and his situation. *Any* response to a questionnaire or interview inevitably involves both personal and situational determinants. Situational determinants are not the special feature of responses to any identifiable class of "opinion items": even a person's innermost feelings are always expressed in a situation which unavoidably influences the manner and content of their expression. In the most intensive clinical situation, psychoanalysis, it takes a high level of sophistication and training for the therapist to *infer* the patient's feelings from his responses. Conversely it is obvious that attitudinal determinants are not absent from expressions of opinion that are manifestly closely bound to particular situations.

Responses cannot, then, be neatly classified as revealing either "attitudes" or "opinions." Items cannot be sharply divided into ones that elicit one or the other kind of response. It may nevertheless be legitimate to classify items in terms of the kind of inference in connection with which a competent investigator would be likely to use them. This is essentially what Wiebe has attempted. To evaluate his success, we must turn to questions of research strategy.

TWO STRATEGIES OF OPINION-ATTITUDE RESEARCH

The problem that Wiebe poses, a legitimate and serious one, can be reformulated thus: If both the verbal raw material of opinion research and the actions—verbal and non-verbal—that the researcher wishes to predict are complex resultants of relatively stable determinants ascribable to the person, on the one hand, and situationally-bound determinants, on the other, what is the most promising direction from which to seek valid prediction?

Wiebe's strategy is the one that is characteristic of much good opinion and market research. Its philosophers' stone is the valid single question—that is, the question that elicits responses from which valid predictions can be made. Granted the situational factors that cut across and disturb the consistency of individual behavior, how are such valid questions to be achieved? Much useful lore has of course been accumulated about how to phrase good individual questions.[7] But the crucial prescription to meet the difficulty introduced by the existence of situational determinants is to make the question *situationally specific*. This, in essence, is Wiebe's advice. Rather than seeking to *disentangle* situational and attitudinal components of response, it seeks to pose questions that evoke the perfect *synthesis* of these components to permit valid contingent predictions of

[7]See, for example, Stanley L. Payne, *The Art of Asking Questions*. Princeton: Princeton University Press, 1951.

behavior. As we have already observed, the inferences involved are usually of a simple conceptual order—that the person will do as he says. This strategy, Wiebe notes, has often paid off well, as in the prediction of voting behavior.

Where does the study of "attitudes" fit into this strategy? In one sense, it doesn't fit in at all, since the respondent's inner feelings are left for those to study who need not concern themselves with predicting overt action. In another sense, however, the same strategy is carried over to the diagnosis of attitudes. Again, what is sought is the ideal valid question— or scale—that will elicit what the person *really* thinks and feels. Here the attempt is characteristically made to *eliminate* situational influences. The strategy is that of the non-directive question, the permissive interview, the "neutral" situation. Results of considerable theoretical interest have of course been obtained along these lines, though Wiebe can rightly argue that responses to such unusual stimulus situations give, by themselves, insufficient basis for predicting behavior in social situations that are differently structured.

But there is a second, quite different strategy for meeting the problem that Wiebe puts before us. Faced with the fusion of situational and attitudinal components in behavior, one may seek to disentangle these components and examine their relationships, rather than searching for items that elicit the unique synthesis that yields accurate prediction, or foregoing prediction entirely for academic research on attitudes. If behavior is a function of both person and situation, its rational prediction should stem from the attainment of diagnostic measures of each class of factors, and the determination of the functional relationship.

In the present strategy, attitudes as genotypic constructs are central to the prediction of behavior, not the epiphenomenal entities that they tend to become in Wiebe's approach. Attitudes are the variables that represent the contribution of the person to the behavior equation. It will be suggested below, however, that non-directive questioning with a clinical criterion of validity provides an insufficient basis for their measurement for this purpose.

As is usually the case with alternative strategies, there is no clear right and wrong about the present pair. Each has its advantages, and each entails sacrifices. Wiebe's strategy, in the short run, yields a technology that achieves considerable success in empirical prediction. It is undoubtedly the strategy of choice in fields of commercial application in which immediate results must pay off. But the search for "good questions" nets a yield in predictive power that is not matched by theoretical understanding. Opinion research is left to remain what it has been, a technology and a lore, not a science. One achieves an increasingly sophisticated "art of asking questions"— questions that mix together the determinants of response in proportions such that the response itself can be adopted by the opinion researcher as *his* best prediction of the respondent's behavior. Rule-of-thumb empiricism, however, has distinct limits as a research strategy, even for practical purposes. If predictions are kept specific to the situations that the questions imaginally evoke, the approach provides no rational basis for extrapolating contingent predictions to other situations.

The second strategy suggests a program for basic research rather than for immediate application. But it is my contention that only this strategy holds promise for advancing scientific understanding of opinions and attitudes in relation to behaviors-in-situations. Only a strategy such as this can carry us beyond the present achievements of untheoretical empiricism. Attitude research, particularly scaling theory, has been making progress in specifying the personal variables in the equation. Much less has been done toward formulating the situational variables in ways that can be articulated with attitudinal ones in the prediction of behavior. Until this task is carried further—with the necessary collaboration of sociologists and political scientists whose business it is to study the social contexts in which behavior occurs—attitude research will continue to be open to charges of impracticality.

WHAT IS A PERSON'S "REAL" ATTITUDE?

Let us return to the conception of attitude implied by Wiebe's strategy. It presupposes that a person's "real" attitude is describable by some unique responses that validly express the way he "really" feels. But will this work?

One source of difficulty is suggested in the circularity and limited applicability of Wiebe's following statement:

> "To the extent that a person's state of mind is conscious, and to the extent that it can be communicated in symbols appropriate to the testing situation, an attitude response may be assumed to be true or else *deliberately* false."[8]

From a purely subjective standpoint, it is no easy thing to specify how one "really" feels about anything of personal importance. Ambivalence is probably more the rule than the exception. The introspectively scrupulous, moreover, have good reason to find fault even with good attitude questionnaires for yielding a less than faithful rendition of their views. Honesty and fidelity are not to be confused.

Behaviorally, there appear to be even more serious difficulties in the conception of a simply-construed "true" attitude. If attitudes are "mental and neural states of readiness," according to Allport's definition which

[8]Ibid., p. 342-343.

Wiebe follows, they are readinesses for a wide variety of related behaviors and perceptions, not for some single state of affairs. Difficult as their organization is to conceptualize, "consistency" rather than "uniformity" seems the more appropriate term for the way in which such readinesses cohere in the behavioral and mental organization of personality.

Attitude research could draw with profit on two disparate conceptual models, from widely separated reaches of psychological theory, that each suggest possibilities for avoiding the difficulties inherent in a simple notion of a person's "true" attitude. One is Hull's concept of the habit-family hierarchy, the hierarchically organized array of response tendencies (implicit or explicit) that a given stimulus complex evokes.[9] If we are to conceptualize a person's attitude toward an object in a way compatible with predicting his behavior in particular situations involving the object, we need the kind of information about his dispositions that is conveyed by a multivalued array rather than by a single position on a scale. What is the "habit strength," we need to know, of each of his related implicit and explicit response tendencies?

McDougall's concept of sentiment, differently oriented, likewise stresses complex organization of a sort impossible to infer from a single "valid" response.[10] If a person loves an "object," says McDougall following Shand, he experiences all manner of contrasting emotions; he is motivated to the most contrasting kinds of behavior, all depending on the situation in which he discovers himself and the object. No single response, no single emotion, uniquely characterizes love; it is the organized dispositional pattern that defines the sentiment.

Yet attitude research has characteristically taken Wiebe's position, and sought to get at a person's "true" attitude by creating as neutral, permissive a situation as possible in which to question him. The persistent assumption, theoretically indefensible but undeniably convenient as a practical compromise, is that if we can only rig the situation right, we can get a person to *display* his true attitudes without the necessity for complicated inference.

A more appropriate research strategy, one more in keeping with the complexities of the attitude construct suggested by Hullian or McDougallian theory, would infer the structure of attitudes from observations of responses in multiple situations. Ideally, it would put more emphasis on

[9]Cf. Hull, Clark L., *A Behavior System*. New Haven: Yale University Press, 1952, p. 257 ff.

[10]McDougall, William, *Introduction to Social Psychology* (14th ed.) Boston: John W. Luce Co., 1921, p. 127 ff.

behavioral observation. Within the range of techniques of conventional opinion research, it would systematically vary the situational pressures rather than attempting to minimize them. Response in the permissive interview would become one among many sources of inference, no longer self-sufficient. Such response would, however, retain special significance as one of the points of reference in the "triangulation" process from which the nature of a person's attitude would be inferred. The study of attitudes would then not be isolated from research on "opinions," in Wiebe's sense. Attitudes would be inferred from their intra-personal consistency.

The technical problems of how to describe the structure of attitudes in ways that lend themselves to measurement are great. They are by-passed, not solved, in the recent concentration of effort on the development of mathematically rational scaling techniques. Attack on these problems, however, seems essential if attitude research is to achieve a sound theoretical basis.

"ATTITUDES" AND "OPINIONS"

What, then, of Wiebe's distinction between opinions and attitudes? We have seen that his distinction between "opinion responses" and "attitude responses" is hardly tenable, any concrete response having both personal and situational determinants. Is the distinction useful at the level of constructs?

As a minimum, the following seem conceptually distinguishable: attitudes as *dispositions* of varying degrees of centrality, generality, consistency, etc. (a construct); momentary *implicit behavior* (also an inferential construct); and momentary *overt behavior* (the data of observation, verbal and non-verbal). "Opinion responses" in Wiebe's sense are overt behavior. As constructs, opinions are to be allocated either to implicit behavior or to dispositions. Insofar as Wiebe talks of opinions as decisions,[11] they seem to involve momentary implicit behavior of which the "opinion response" is the overt counterpart. But to the extent that they are treated as the situationally-bound ingredients of attitudes, perhaps they become dispositional concepts.

It is, of course, possible to retain Wiebe's conceptual distinction without the particular methodological implications that he would draw from it. The passage that he quotes approvingly from Clyde Hart, writing with the Hartleys, brings out an attractive feature of the point of view that these authors share with Wiebe:

[11]Ibid., p. 334: "...those decisions regarding social interaction which have been defined as opinions".

"[Opinion] comes into being just when, and to the extent that, attitudes are not adequate to enable the individual or the group to cope with a situation.... It involves, or is based in part upon attitudes; but it is not, therefore, synonymous with attitude. It is always concerned with doubtful elements in the situation, with conflicts and uncertainties, with problems of 'issues'....It pertains not to a single attitude but to an attitude-complex corresponding to the object-complex comprising the extra-individual aspect of the situation,"[12]

Any adequate account of opinion-attitude psychology must certainly provide for the formation of new judgments in problematic situations, and for the convergence of hitherto independent attitudes on a common complex object. If a terminology of attitudes vs. opinions makes it easier to grasp these phenomena, well and good.

Adopting such a terminology, however, does not by itself solve the difficult research problems involved in teasing out these relationships in the individual and as shared in a social group; if it makes it easier to reify the distinction, giving it more absolute status than the facts warrant, it may be no help at all. For we are likely to go astray if we think of attitudes as tightly organized constructs at the same psychological level, which sometimes run off automatically into behavior when the situation is familiar and appropriate, and at other times interact to generate opinions for coping with the novel and problematic. Quite a different conception seems required by the facts.

On the dispositional side, attitudes vary in generality and specificity, in rigidity and permeability, in their hierarchical relations with other attitudes. Indeed, the research decision as to the boundaries of a particular attitude has inevitably an element of arbitrariness, governed by the purpose at hand as well as by stubborn psychological fact. In intensive studies of the individual—not just his inner life as revealed to depth psychology, but of his behavior under diverse situational stresses—one may infer the structure of his attitudes as they bear on a given range of objects and situations. We may be in a position to say, with the uncertainty still characteristic of clinical appraisal, that for John Jones, such dispositions as he has toward Russia are subsidiary to his more general orientation toward communism, and to his still more general rejection of things "un-American."

In research dealing with aggregates of people, on the other hand, the attitudinal object is usually specified in advance by the researcher. In favorable cases, tests are later applied to the data to determine whether responses to items in the universe of relevant content cohere to the minimal extent necessary for it to be useful for us to talk of the involvement of a common attitude. But the boundaries of the attitude as they

[12]Ibid., p. 332; Hartley, Eugene L. and Ruth E., *Fundamentals of Social Psychology.* New York: Alfred A. Knopf, 1952, p. 657.

emerge from research depend as much on the research procedures as on the contribution of the respondent. One may thus develop, for the same population at the same time, measures of dispositions toward as specific an object as Senator McCarthy, or as general a topic as civil liberties.

Neither are the facts simple on the situational side. Situations vary in the novelty and problem-quality with which they confront the individual: this is not a feature that is simply present or absent. And any situation is in some respects unique. Novelty seems therefore not to afford a decisive criterion for distinguishing attitude and opinion. *Issues,* for public opinion research, are in fact defined by what is *socially* problematic, not by what is problematic to the aggregate of individuals. Those who feel most strongly about an issue are typically people for whom it is *not* problematic; they have firmly made up their minds.

I hope the burden of this discussion is not entirely negative. It is intended to have positive implications for research. The urgent need that is being met neither by current good and valuable research on scale construction nor by comparable efforts on question wording, as I see it, is for fundamental research on the structure of attitudinal dispositions, on the one hand, and of social and psychological situations, on the other. At a time when it would be premature to say that we have arrived at satisfactory ways of formulating and indexing our constructs in attitude and opinion research, looseness of terminology may still have its redeeming features.

Response to Smith's Comments

By G. D. WIEBE

SMITH sets forth the basis for his comments in his third and fourth paragraphs. Having found much of merit in my paper, he feels, on second thought that it may be just a piece of special pleading: "Closer inspection leads one to suspect, however, that Wiebe is actually relegating attitudes to the realm of the trivial and academic; serious and practical people should, if they follow his analysis, devote themselves to the study of opinion, where to be sure, more exacting criteria of validation have to be met, but the pay-off in predictive power seems proportionately greater." Having stated what he *suspects,* he continues: "It is my contention, and the reason for this commentary, that this aspect of Wiebe's position, which I would regard as unfortunate, is a consequence of inacceptable starting points in his chain of reasoning."

Smith's chain of reasoning seems to merit attention: (1) He suspects that I am prejudiced against attitudes and in favor of opinions, (2) he assumes that his suspicion is true, and so re-names his suspicion as an "aspect of my position", (3) having saddled me with his suspicion, he assumes that I must have gotten into that "unfortunate" position because of inacceptable starting points. Smith and Wiebe seem to be getting all mixed up!

It is of course true that a social scientist may claim to be writing social science, but pepper his prose with inferences, innuendos, suggestions and condescensions to such an extent that the reader is led to believe that the author's subject matter is merely a vehicle for his prejudice. If the reader finds my paper falling into this category, severe criticism would be in order. I find no such double talk however, and Smith cites none. The association of "trivial" with "academic" is Smith's, not mine. So is the idea that "serious and practical people" will pass up attitudes in favor of opinions.

Perhaps then Smith's comments might be answered by saying that since the suspicion on which he says they are based is, in my opinion, groundless, I rest my case pending substantial support of the suspicion. But Smith raises some solid questions which merit serious discussion.

His basic disagreement with my point of view seems to be a matter of strategy in theory building. He appears to feel that my formulation represents the segmenting of things that should stay whole. If I understand him correctly, he feels that we should set our sights on a comprehensive understanding of human behavior that would encompass, in a single consistent theory, everything ranging from the most obscure inner motivations to the most nearly situation-bound behavior of crowds, mobs, and societies. He says, (p. 260) "If behavior is a function of both person and situation, its rational prediction should stem from the attainment of diagnostic measures of each class of factors, and the determination of the functional relationship.

"In the present strategy, (Smith's alternative to mine) attitudes as genotypic constructs are central to the prediction of behavior..." He continues, a little later, "...it is my contention that *only this strategy* (italics mine) holds promise for advancing scientific understanding of opinions and attitudes in relation to behaviors-in-situations...Attitude research, particularly scaling theory, has been making progress in specifying the personal variables in the equation. Much less has been done toward formulating the situational variables in ways that can be articulated with attitudinal ones in the prediction of behavior. Until this task is carried further—with the necessary collaboration of sociologists and political scientists...attitude research will continue to be open to charges of impracticality."

I don't know who makes this charge of impracticality. Certainly I do not. I think attitude research is both practical and important, especially in increasing understanding of the psychology of individuals, and also in understanding social behavior, provided the social situation is congenial, permissive, and familiar to the persons being studied.

But let us consider this "all or none" theory. I don't think it is a good theoretical orientation for social scientists who are primarily concerned with understanding the social behavior of people under stress; people under all gradations of pressure and coercion; people faced with unanticipated circumstances. These are the kinds of people, for the most part, who live in this second half of the twentieth century. Nor do I think it is a good theoretical orientation for those who are making constant progress in understanding the dynamics of individual psychology. Why should they deny their own very substantial and continuing progress by making its worth contingent upon the prediction of social behavior?

What would the implementation of Smith's orientation involve? First, perhaps we may assume that an excellent psychoanalyst knows more about a client who has been in analysis for a year than does a social scientist who has given the same person one or a battery of attitude scales. The analyst, at the present imperfect stage of his skill and insight, may or may not be equalled in understanding, in the future, by the social scientist armed with the yield of attitude scales. Could the analyst predict how his client would act within the next 24 hours? He would be cautions. He might predict tentatively, surrounding his prediction with contingencies. Would he predict how his client would act 6 months hence? He would have many reservations, prominent among them being the probability that 6 months more of analysis would change the way the individual would tend to behave. How about predicting for 6 months after the end of what the analyst would consider a successful analysis? The analyst would remind us that change does not cease when analysis stops. And *that* is the inconvenient thing about a human being for those who feel the need of comprehensive "alpha to omega" predicting systems. He is always a different thing today from what he was yesterday because part of yesterday's environment has become internalized as part of today's individual. A social scientist can never treat John Doe like a chemist treats H_2O. The chemist has the considerable advantage of knowing that the H_2O he used yesterday in certain interactions acted exactly like the H_2O he uses today will act. But John Doe keeps changing. Those "personal variables" in Smith's "equation" are going to kick up a lot of trouble.

Then come the "situational variables" on which we must await further "necessary collaboration of sociologists and political scientists." That is liable to take quite some time too. It would appear that Smith needs the kind of data, *on each respondent,* available from psychoanalysis, sociology and political science in order to get an admittedly crude beginning at working out his theory for predicting social behavior. As attitude scales are perfected and as sociologists and political scientists add to their understanding, progress will be made. But these kinds of data, and the interactions among them, would be required at frequent points in time because every factor in the equation would be constantly changing. I doubt whether many attitude researchers will be willing to assume that their work is open to the charge of impracticality until that day arrives. There seems to me to be something approaching escapism in holding that the only road toward scientific prediction of social behavior lies in the perfecting of a system that requires the orderly articulation of everything from attitudes as genotypic constructs, at one end, to undiscovered concepts in political science at the other.

The physicists are just beginning to cope with an "alpha to omega" orientation in their field, but suppose they had stuck with such an orientation back in the days when the basic elements were, according to the best minds, earth, fire and water.

In practice, Smith's orientation seems to lead, not to scientific rigor, but rather to a sort of glorified Monday-morning Quarterbacking. This is apparent in the confusion he encounters in his discussion of validity. Predictions, of course, always involve contingencies. But when the experimental method is stretched to the point where the responsible researcher's own criterion of validity is discarded when validity proves to be low, and when a "consumer" of the research then says, in effect, suppose it wasn't valid in terms of *that* criterion, it might be valid in terms of another one, then the concept of validity loses its usefulness. It ceases to be an attribute of *research,* and becomes, in some vague way, synonomous with the wisdom of any individual who chooses to draw inferences from research. For example, Smith seems reluctant to admit that La Piere's attitude item did not predict behavior. Even if it didn't, he says in effect, maybe it would if we just thought in terms of *different* behavior: "In the La Piere situation", he says, "the question asked the proprietors might perhaps have furnished the basis for valid inference of proprietors' behavior toward unaccompanied Chinese who conformed to the prevalent stereotype, without having validity for other contingencies or for unconditional prediction of behavior toward Chinese regardless of circumstances."

Such speculation is both permissible and important when conceived as hypothesis-building for further research. But as an attempt to salvage validity where the experimenter has failed to find a useful degree of validity, and has candidly said so, this practice would appear to subordinate experimentation to speculation. The postulate that an attitude response *ought* to predict social behavior seems to dominate the finding that in fact it did not. Where does this lead in terms of Smith's orientation? In the service of the conviction that attitudes *should* predict behavior, do we hypothesize one or twenty or a hundred "genotypic constructs" which predispose people to act in a certain way toward "unaccompanied Chinese who conform to the prevalent stereotype"..? And another set for accompanied Chinese who conform to the stereotype, and a third for unaccompanied Chinese who do *not* conform to the stereotype, and then try to incorporate them in experimental designs for predicting behavior? Or do we ask what we believe is an attitude item, get the answers, and then hunt for behavior that would make them valid?[1] The cumbersomeness of such an approach is apparent. One ends up with literally millions of "genotypic constructs," and a chaotic looseness about the behavioral counterpart of any one or combination of them.

It is my belief that the requirement that attitude researchers keep one eye on social behavior, as a species of grading system, is an undesirable impediment. How would Freud have fared if, at each step in the evolution of his theories, he had felt constrained to check his hypotheses against the observable social behavior of his subjects?

Opinion researchers have a different challenge. They may do well to remember that chemists didn't have to wait on the understanding of electrons and protons before learning a very great deal about the behavior of substances composed of electrons and protons. Navigators learned a great deal about the sea, its tides and winds and temperatures, while having only the crudest notions of the chemical content of the water.

More specifically, there appear to me to be highly important reasons why people with primarily theoretical interests as well as those with primarily applied interests might find merit in the orientation presented in my paper. I will mention only two as illustrative. First, in the context of the present discussion, neurosis and psychosis might be described as more or less disabling friction resulting from the rub between a person's inner life and his perception of outside reality. To a frightening extent this rub is left to intensify, in so far as society is concerned, until the victim must be wholly or partially disqualified for intercourse in society. These problems must be tackled before they break out into gross, observable, social-behavioral forms. There is hardly room here for hair

[1]Of course scales, as well as single items are important. See, for example, the last half of p. 349 in my paper.

splitting about the inevitable social component in repression. The fact is that, excluding a social revolution, the problems of mental health must be tackled primarily at the levels of attitudes, perceptions, repressions, dissociations, autisms and the like; levels at which disturbances, though visable and malleable to attitude researchers and clinicians, may not even register on the indices of opinion researchers, sociologists, and political scientists.

Contrary-wise, it seems to me that attitude scales, as we know them, and as we can imagine them in the forseeable future, will predict social behavior in inverse correlation with the encroachment of coercion, tyranny, authoritarianism on a society. An attitude scale may predict the behavior of an individual with considerable validity while that individual is within the walls of his home, where love and mutual respect abound. But by definition, the greater the coercion, the less freedom to behave in terms of ones predispositions. Perhaps Smith would say we must simply add the understanding of people's attitudes toward coercion to the formula, plus, of course, the understanding of the scaffolding which rises from the attitudes of the coercers, via social and political institutions and traditions, to the social gestalt which we describe as coercive. Shall opinion researchers, then, raise their eyes above the foreground and the middle ground, setting their sights resolutely on the orderly articulation of political science and psychoanalysis before attempting valid prediction of social behavior? In our day, it seems less defensible from both practical and theoretical points of view than that bridge builders and chemists should have waited for Einstein.

I have attempted to illustrate why the clear differentiation between attitudes and opinions which I proposed would tend to stimulate more meaningful research in both areas. I believe that this orientation would also tend to promote more effective articulation *between* the two. An example of this belief is discussed in the last section of my paper, headed An Hypothesis. Sills, (Winter 1953–54 POQ, p. 541) in reviewing a shorter version of my paper, read at the 1953 AAPOR Convention, finds it an "enticing hypothesis...which might give new life to much current thinking on the topic of 'attitude change'."

6

**TOWARD
A THEORY
OF PUBLIC OPINION**
Herbert H. Hyman

"There is the tangled, matted field of opinion theory. It is a field cluttered with the stumps of the once mighty theoretical particularisms, a field in which a dense underbrush has grown, in which there are confusing brambles of terminological disputation and an infinite thicket of psychological descriptions."

O N this note, William Albig begins his distinguished work, *Public Opinion*—not his recent edition, but the edition of his book published close to twenty years ago. At that time the *Public Opinion Quarterly* was still an infant. Gallup, Roper, and other major research agencies had barely begun their activities. Would the description of opinion theory he gave then still apply today?

Many would answer the question affirmatively—asserting that the major advances have been methodological and that the contribution of the last two decades has been to increase the quantity of empirical data but not the quality of theory. To endorse this answer, however, is to accept a very special view of theory, a view which equates theory with a general, even an all-embracing, set of ideas and speculations about a field. Thus it was that Albig followed his diagnosis of 1939 with a prescription which called for a "master synthesizer."[1]

Such a view would, indeed, suggest that the imbalance between theory, on the one hand, and methodology with its concomitant collections of empirical data, on the other, must become progressively greater with the

---

* This article may be identified as Publication #A-229 of the Bureau of Applied Social Research at Columbia University.

[1] William Albig, *Public Opinion*, New York: McGraw Hill, 1939, p. v.

Originally published in Volume 22, Number 2, 1958 of the *Public Opinion Quarterly*.

passage of time. The synthesis required twenty years ago had to deal only with a limited body of data. Today, the synthesizer must encompass in his theory a mass of findings based on millions of interviews with members of publics in many countries, and derived from hundreds of elaborate inquiries into many different areas of opinion. It is easier to be general when knowledge is not specific. To follow Albig's figure, when nature is plentiful, there is certain to be more underbrush, more thickets, more brambles. It is bound to be harder for any mighty theory to stand the test today when relevant evidence is so much easier to come by. The stumps are found to become more numerous. And today's theorizer is sure to face, and perhaps to overstress, the "infinite thicket of psychological descriptions," for modern public opinion research in its very nature is psychologically oriented. No matter what form the analysis may ultimately take, the unit under scrutiny is always the individual and his psychic structure. If one accepts this view, the theorizer will find himself in a less and less enviable position as time goes on and our fund of knowledge increases.

RECONCILIATION OF THEORY AND METHODOLOGY

Adopt an alternative view of theory and the picture brightens. If the measure of theory is not grandness or generality, but rather quality, utility, logical structure, and soundness, then Albig's description might be less apt today. Merton stresses the alternative view when he distinguishes systematic sociological theory, "the highly selective accumulation of those small parts of earlier theory which have thus far survived the tests of empirical research," from the "far greater mass of conceptions which fell to bits," from "the false starts, the archaic doctrines and the fruitless errors of the past."[2] By this standard, the field cluttered with stumps is a sign of progress, not of decay. Admittedly, synthesis is to be desired and a master synthesizer would be welcome, but while awaiting such a creative imagination, we may rather work with what Merton has called "theories of the middle range, logically interconnected conceptions . . . limited and modest in scope," while seeking for ultimate consolidation of one public opinion theory.[3]

With this view and strategy, theory is congenial to methodology and empirical data. Indeed, they must progress together. The empirical research permits mistaken ideas to be uncovered. It leads us to new phenomena and concepts. Instead of being irritated by the problem of fitting everything into a master-scheme, we need, for the moment, only to fit the new ideas into some smaller structure of theory. On this view, the theorizer is in a more and more enviable, but not wholly enviable, position. Our strategy demands

[2] R. K. Merton, *Social Theory and Social Structure,* (Glencoe: The Free Press, 1949), pp. 4-5.
[3] *Ibid.,* pp. 5ff.

theories of the *middle* range, not the molecular range, and our ultimate victory requires at least some direction toward still larger consolidation along the way. We have all the potential for a theory, but it must still be realized. Here there is no substitute for continuity and cumulative inquiry, and important problems cannot be neglected. Else the larger theory will never be built or will be incomplete.

In this light, a review of public opinion research in the U. S. in the last twenty years to uncover discontinuities would be especially valuable, for the discontinuities prevent the orderly growth of modest and sound theories. But not all continuities are valuable. We may concentrate on the trivial rather than the important. We may even institutionalize the neglect of some important part of our ultimate larger theory. In short, an examination of the history of public opinion research will help point the way toward a public opinion theory.

DEFICIENCIES OF DISCONTINUOUS DATA

The concept of public opinion has almost always been identified with the public's views on problems that are controversial and of general concern. Correspondingly, public opinion research has shown a persistent tendency to describe popular feelings on *issues*. As a consequence, the most striking discontinuity in our accumulated body of data is the shift from problem area to problem area with the passage of time. Thus, by way of illustration, it is inevitable that no description of American public opinion on Korea exists for the period prior to 1945. There was no issue, the public had no opinions, and no surveys were conducted. In 1950 there was an issue, there was public opinion, and there is much empirical evidence as to its nature.

This very movement of problem areas into and out of the sphere of public opinion research, while understandable, is perhaps the most crucial deficiency for the growth of a theory. The absence of data which provides a sound description of even the *lack* of public opinion on a problem, at a time when it is not under discussion, means that there is no basis for developing adequate theory as to the formation of public opinion. Similarly, the waning of an issue has generally meant the neglect of it by survey research. Thus, no theory can really be built as to either the formation or decline of public opinion. To take an example much more fundamental than Korea, compare the thorough attention of public opinion research to domestic economic and labor issues in the years before 1945 with the general neglect of it in current research. Thus, despite the speculation today as to a realignment of American ideology, as to the passing of the old cleavages of left and right, there is really very little evidence because of the lack of surveys.

The argument can be conveyed by still another type of example. The recent Supreme Court decision on desegregation stimulated considerable attention in public opinion research. A baseline of public opinion on desegregation prior to recent legislation and recent social changes would provide a most desirable body of data for use in development of theory.[4] Yet, almost without exception, the issue had not been posed in earlier years. In addition to appealing to our interest as political analysts, these examples document a crucial deficiency for the development of a general theory. Obviously, what would be desirable would be to extend public opinion research from the *ad hoc* description of whatever part of the current social world is hot to the systematic description of both the hot and the cold. With such an extension, theory could develop in a number of fruitful directions. Taking any point in time, the *structure* of public thinking, the *mental organization* of public attitudes, would be better understood by seeing the connections between different bodies of opinion. And if these same areas were dealt with over long spans of time, providing trend data, a theory of public opinion formation and opinion change would be well on its way to formulation. As a result of the rise of panels, part of that theory is now available, but only that part which deals with the flux of opinion over short ranges of time in relation to very specific stimuli or psychological factors. By contrast, long term trends in the systematic description of public opinion would enable us to relate opinion processes to much more macroscopic determinants: for example, law, social change, demographic processes, and the like.[5] And such trend data in juxtaposition with political analysis would lead not merely to theories of opinion formation, but also to theories about the *consequences* of popular opinion for political actions.

The continuous attention of opinion research to the transient issues of the day has meant a discontinuity in the study of particular content areas and a corresponding lack of a sound theory of social determinants of opinion formation and change.

SEARCH FOR THE SOCIAL SUBSTRATUM OF PUBLIC OPINION

Another persistent feature of opinion research that prevents the development of a sound theory of opinion formation has been the definition of the population to be studied. Prior to the rise of the polls, psychologists lamented the fact that our social psychology was one restricted to the "college sopho-

---

[4] For a study summarizing available information on these trends over 15 years, see Herbert Hyman and Paul B. Sheatsley, "Attitudes Toward Desegregation," *Scientific American*, December, 1956, pp. 35-39.

[5] There are fortunately some areas in which the polls have provided data on systematic long term trends, and the occasional analyses based on such data vividly demonstrate the theoretical benefits. See, for example, Gabriel Almond, *The American People and Foreign Policy*, (New York: Harcourt Brace, 1950).

more." Now, by contrast, we have an opinion inventory restricted almost exclusively to the American adult, for we have identified public opinion as the views of the electorate on the controversial issues of the day. While this was a legitimate decision and represented progress, what nostalgia one ought to feel for the good old days when we knew something about the social world of the pre-adult population! Where there is much stability in the opinions of various groups of adults, these opinions cannot be regarded as merely the product of the contemporary environment. Yet the study of the socialization of the individual with respect to the opinions he may be expected ultimately to hold can be dealt with only by infrequent and approximate retrospective questions inserted into occasional studies. Just as systematic trend studies would illuminate the macroscopic determinants of opinion formation, the parallel study of pre-adults and adults with the modern tools of opinion research would illuminate the learning process underlying opinion formation, and go far to explain the stabilizing mechanisms in public opinion.[6]

Since opinion research as it is conducted deals with the current scene, it appears always to study opinion formation *de novo*. Members of the public cannot have any prepared basis for evaluating a problem that did not exist for them at an earlier time. Yet the ease with which they form opinions on most subjects suggests that there must be some underpinnings, some precursors of an opinion. The direction theory and research have taken to deal with such problems of opinion formation has been first to search for more fundamental attitudes, and subsequently to investigate personality processes—both of these being regarded as providing a substratum for opinions. Here, in recent years, theory has been lavish and fruitful. But such a development, while especially valuable for the psychological study of an *individual's* opinions, is not adequate for the understanding of *public* opinion. The uniformities observed in opinions suggest that there are uniformities in the underlying intervening variables. We need concepts and corresponding research on what is both fundamental or deep and also *common* to a group or a society. The study of values, or the exploration of what Alpert has recently called "mentality," would enrich current theories of opinion formation and broaden what is at present an unduly narrow psychological emphasis.[7]

[6] H. H. Remmers is almost alone in the systematic exploration of public opinion among national high school populations. See the many publications of the Purdue Opinion Panel. For an illustration of the usefulness of such data, see the writer's forthcoming publication on Learning and Socialization into Politics.

[7] Harry Alpert, "Public Opinion Research as Science," *Public Opinion Quarterly,* Fall, 1956, p. 498. For an unusual and valuable study of the *values* underlying opinions, and the conditions of their engagement, see, M. B. Smith, "Personal Values as Determinants of a Political Attitude," *Journ. Psychol.,* 1949, 28, pp. 477-486.

So much for some of the deficiencies in a theory of the formation and change of opinion which could be remedied by some modification of current empirical research. There is, however, a positive side. Today we stand close to a sound theory of opinion formation, and only because of the riches and variety of empirical research. The growth of surveys in many nations provides the first real basis for comparative opinion analysis which will ground a theory of cultural and societal determinants of opinion. The elaborate attention to "areas of ignorance" in past research, perhaps waning for the moment, alas, is a basis for theory about the rational and intellectual factors governing opinions, a necessary counterweight to the stress on personality determinants. The files of opinion research bulge with data bearing on theoretical problems of structural, group membership, and reference group determinants of opinion. In these areas the deficiencies are few, and we may expect much in the way of theoretical advance.

Let me turn finally to two interrelated areas in which more empirical study and methodology are called for in the interests of better and more comprehensive theory. The first of these involves special problems of index construction. There has been great sophistication in the development of scaling methods, typological procedures, and modes of index construction, but such developments have mainly helped in the treatment of the individual and his opinions. Now, modes of index construction which characterize and capture relevant features of the social distribution of opinions are urgently needed. We need indices of *public* opinion which parallel the current indices of individual opinion. When is the social geography of opinion too polarized? When is consensus breaking down? Questions of this order call for development of imaginative indices that treat the aggregate of opinions, or what Lazarsfeld has recently called the complete attitude distribution. One area of concentration should be indices that are predicated on normative considerations about the political process. When is the distribution of opinions of such a nature that the requirements of democracy are not being met?[8]

This particular facet of index construction for public opinion leads directly to our last point. The state of our psychological theory about opinion formation is healthy; the missing social psychological and sociological elements of a theory can be remedied with some changes in emphasis in our empirical work. But what of the other fundamental aspect of a theory of public opinion; the aspect that relates public opinion to the political process, to political forms of society? Early political theory had much to say by way of speculation about the requirements opinion must meet to be compatible with a particular political process, but provided little in the way of evidence

[8] For a provocative discussion of such a problem, see, Bernard Berelson, P. F. Lazarsfeld and William McPhee, *Voting,* (Chicago: University of Chicago Press, 1954), p. 312ff.

as to the facts of the case. Attention to this relatively neglected problem, plus work on indices that treat of such normative requirements, will provide the basis for a re-invigorated body of theory.[9] Thus will we move toward a comprehensive theory of public opinion, via developments that partake of psychological, sociological and political theory and which find their support in the richness of our empirical research.

[9] A number of studies are directed to these problems. See, G. Almond, *op. cit.;* Berelson, *et al., ibid.;* H. Hyman and P. B. Sheatsley, "The Current Status of American Public Opinion," *National Council for Social Studies Yearbook,* 21, 1950, pp. 11-34; M. Janowitz and D. Marvick, *Competitive Pressure and Democratic Consent,* Michigan Governmental Studies, #32, (Ann Arbor: University of Michigan Institute of Public Administration, 1956).

THE PUBLIC
OPINION PROCESS
W. Phillips Davison

ALTHOUGH THE TERM "public opinion" was not used until the eighteenth century, the phenomenon itself has been noted and described by writers in ancient, medieval, and early modern times. Public opinion appears most often in urban societies and in those with relatively well-developed communication facilities, as for instance in the Greek city states, but it can also be observed, even if more rarely, in predominantly rural societies with rudimentary communications.[1] The existence of phenomena bearing strong resemblances to public opinion has been noted by anthropologists in primitive societies of widely varying characteristics.[2]

In ancient and medieval times writers who mention public opinion often refer to it as having mystical or divine properties. Early modern writers regard it as perceptible but indefinable. They usually agree on two of its aspects: that it is a consensus among a large number of people, and that this consensus somehow exercises force. The German poet Wieland has given us one of the first formal discussions of public opinion in his *Gespräch unter vier Augen* (1798):

> I, for my part, understand by it an opinion that gradually takes root among a whole people; especially among those who have the most influence when they work together as a group. In this way it wins the upper hand to such an extent that one meets it everywhere. It is an opinion that without being noticed takes possession of most heads, and even in situations where it does not dare to express itself out loud it can be recognized by a louder and louder muffled murmur. It then only requires some small opening that will allow it air, and it will break out with force. Then it can change whole nations in a brief time and give whole parts of the world a new configuration.

Wieland's description is similar to many others given in writings of approximately the same period.[3]

[1] Wilhelm Bauer, *Die Öffentliche Meinung in der Weltgeschichte*, Potsdam, 1930.

[2] Felix M. and Marie Keesing, *Elite Communication in Samoa: A Study of Leadership*, Stanford University Press, 1956; Margaret Mead, "Public Opinion Mechanisms Among Primitive Peoples," *Public Opinion Quarterly*, July, 1937.

[3] *Cf.* Hans Speier, "Historical Development of Public Opinion," *Social Order and the Risks of War*, New York, Stewart, 1952.

Originally published in Volume 21, Number 1, 1957 of the *Public Opinion Quarterly*.

More recently, students have been able to agree substantially on a number of distinguishing marks of public opinion. A list of characteristics, which is still one of the best, was given by Floyd Allport more than twenty years ago.[4] He noted that public opinion involved verbalization and communication among many individuals, that some widely known issue was always involved, that public opinion represented action or a readiness for action by individuals who were aware that others were reacting to the same situation, and that it was ordinarily a transitory phenomenon. Other writers have pointed out that a majority is not necessarily involved, that public opinion must be distinguished from norms and customs, and that the effectiveness of public opinion in bringing about change depends on the political and societal context in which it operates.

In spite of a considerable measure of agreement on these and other characteristics of public opinion, social scientists have been unable either to link these characteristics together into a theoretical framework or to offer a satisfactory definition of the phenomenon they are attempting to describe. Having rejected the "collective mind" explanation, which provided a theoretical basis for public opinion study even if one that was manifestly incorrect, students have been left without any concept that adequately serves to interrelate the various observed aspects of the phenomenon.

This gap has been pointed out with increasing frequency. In the twentieth anniversary issue of this journal a number of authorities noted that especially during the past two decades progress in measuring and describing various aspects of public opinion has greatly outstripped conceptualization.[5] Our ability to measure the distribution of individual opinions in a population or the thematic content of communications is now far greater than our capacity to explain how the phenomenon that we call public opinion arises in the first place or why sustained propaganda will have very little effect in one situation while in another a series of whispers will produce a riot.

While lamentable, the primitive state of public opinion theory is not surprising. The extent to which a satisfactory explanation of the phenomenon as a whole has eluded serious thinkers indicates that factors of considerable complexity are involved. And since this problem has been attacked repeatedly by psychologists, sociologists, political scientists, and representatives of other disciplines, we may suspect that insight from all these fields will be required if a solution is to be found.

Nevertheless, although the hazards are sufficiently apparent to discourage speculation in the realm of public opinion theory, and obviously have done so, the importance of the phenomenon suggested by its close relation-

[4] "Toward a Science of Public Opinion," *Public Opinion Quarterly*, January 1937.
[5] See especially William Albig, "Two Decades of Opinion Study: 1936-1956" *Public Opinion Quarterly*, Spring 1957.

ship to major problems of political, social, and economic behavior is ample justification for renewed attempts. This article represents such an attempt.

A DEFINITION OF PUBLIC OPINION

The term "public opinion" will be used here in a sense suggested by Allport and will refer to action or readiness for action with regard to a given issue on the part of members of a public who are reacting in the expectation that others in the public are similarly oriented toward the same issue.

If we accept this definition as a tool for use in further inquiry, it raises a number of questions for investigation. How is the central issue in the public opinion process defined? What is a public? How are expectations as to the behavior of others formed? What effect do these expectations have on the attitudes and behavior of individual members of the public? What is the usual sequence of steps in the process by which public opinion is formed?

That the suggested definition is not completely adequate is indicated by the fact that a number of other questions are not immediately raised. The definition says nothing about communication, about opinion leadership, or about the role of primary groups. Yet we strongly suspect that these are somehow involved in the phenomenon under study. The part they play may be illuminated, however, if we examine the process by which public opinion is formed.

GENESIS OF AN ISSUE IN THE PRIMARY GROUP

A familiar allegory uses the analogy of seeds to illustrate the growth of ideas. The seeds are numbered in thousands, and are scattered over the landscape. Some fall on the rocks and fail to germinate. Others start to take root but soon die because they lack soil in sufficient depth or because they are smothered by faster-growing weeds. Only a few fall on earth where the conditions are right for continued growth and multiplication.

Similarly, there are many more issues that might provide the basis for mass movements than ever see the light of day. All men have grievances, inspirations, and ideas for improving society, but most of these die away in mutterings or casual conversations. An issue begins to take root only when it is communicated from one person to a second, who then carries it further in his own conversation. Most potential issues disappear from attention before this human chain grows to an appreciable length, but the few that survive form the basis for public opinions.

Let us take the hypothetical case of Center City. This is a town of some 30,000 persons, situated in a predominantly agricultural region. It serves as the market place for a wide area and has a relatively large population of small business men and white collar workers. It also has a few small factories and a junior college. Center City is governed by a mayor who was returned at the last election, in which the principal issue was a proposed sales tax. The mayor successfully opposed this tax, and the issue is now less controversial.

But one day a new factor is injected into the political life of the town. Mr. Jones, who runs a dry goods store on Main Street, receives a notice that the value of his residence has been reassessed. From now on he will have to pay almost half as much again in real estate tax as he has paid in previous years. He hurries down to the assessor's office to protest, but receives no satisfaction. He complains loud and long to his wife, his brother-in-law, his neighbors, and his friends on Main Street. The valuation of his property, he says, is way out of line with that placed on similar properties in the neighborhood.

As it happens, Mr. Jones is a popular man. He has many friends and is not known as one who constantly complains or makes hasty judgments. When he discusses his grievance against the city government with others, some of them remember grievances of their own: one has been treated inconsiderately by municipal employees, another has had difficulties with trash collection, a third dislikes the mayor personally because of a family squabble several years ago. In the minds of all those who interact in these discussions a generalized picture of maladministration is built up. Soon one cannot mention the city government in the circle frequented by Mr. Jones without eliciting the opinion that it is time for a change in city hall. A political issue has arisen.

Actually, we know very little about the formative stage of issues. This part of the public opinion process is usually buried in obscurity because it is unlikely to attract the attention of historians or journalists. Students of public opinion have ordinarily given attention to issues only after they have exploded into public view. Observation of small group behavior does, however, suggest the kind of process that is at work.[6]

The history of issues is complicated further by the fact that important ideas often appear independently at various times and places.[7] To which one of these points of origin should the idea that eventually emerges into public discussion be traced? Or is it the very fact that an idea has a number of apparently independent points of origin that is in part responsible for its subsequent growth?

But, however an issue germinates, we know that in order to survive and spread it must find one or more human groupings that are hospitable to it.[8] Otherwise, the originator will usually discard it or keep it to himself, since

[6] See especially the excellent summary of small group research in Elihu Katz and Paul F. Lazarsfeld, *Personal Influence,* The Free Press, 1955, pp. 31-116.

[7] The frequency of independent, but almost simultaneous, discoveries has been noted by historians of science. *Cf.* Robert K. Merton, "Priorities in Scientific Discovery," *American Sociological Review,* December 1957.

[8] Harold D. Lasswell has pointed to the significance of the small group as "a radiating nucleus for an idea." *Cf. Psychopathology and Politics,* University of Chicago Press, 1930, p. 187.

it interferes with the harmony of his social relationships. Those few who persist in expressing ideas that find no resonance among their daily associates are usually the lonely and embittered members of society.

Let us return to Mr. Jones and his friends in Center City. Their dissatisfaction with the local government soon comes to the attention of the Opposition Party. This party knows that several similarly disaffected groups exist in the city and, since an election is scheduled for the following year, decides it is time to fan the flames of dissatisfaction. Leaders of the Opposition Party are on good terms with the publisher of the *Center City Bugle* and arrange with him for a series of articles, based largely on leads supplied by the party, on inefficiency in the local government. These deal not only with tax valuations and trash collection, but also with police protection, street lighting, and other subjects about which there have been complaints. One result of these articles is that the mayor and city councilmen prepare to defend themselves. Another is that additional complaints and more information about alleged shortcomings of the city administration flow into the offices of the *Bugle* and the Opposition Party.

While the series of articles on local mismanagement is appearing, and as indignant responses can be heard from the mayor and his friends, the leader of the Opposition Party makes a series of speeches before trade and fraternal groups. His problem is that dissatisfaction with the government comes both from those who think tax valuations are too high and from those who favor extended city services, and who therefore are inferentially in favor of added taxes. To solve this problem, the opposition leader avoids mentioning the tax problem at all and concentrates on two slogans:

PUT CENTER CITY ON A BUSINESS BASIS

and

GIVE THE CITIZEN HIS MONEY'S WORTH

He states that the aims of both these slogans can be accomplished by returning the Opposition Party to office at the next election.

Thus, at this stage of the public opinion process, leadership transcending the original primary group or groups can be distinguished. Sometimes this leadership is provided by the original exponent of the issue in question, whose influence then begins to extend beyond the circle of those he knows personally. An example of such a situation is given in a recent study of a fluoridation controversy in Northampton, Massachusetts, where one of the original opponents of fluoridation succeeded in winning election as mayor and then continued his campaign from the mayor's office.[9] A similar situation is noted in an older study of a controversy over the location of a new school in a rural community. Here the men who had personal interests in the location of the new school, and who first expressed opinions about it, became community leaders as far as this issue was concerned.[10]

More often, however, ideas that are agitating small, face-to-face groups are taken up by men who are already concerned with mass manipulation and who have at their disposal the means of organization and publicity. Such ideas may be collected and exploited by leaders in one field or another with considerable self-consciousness. Before the last presidential election a speech writer for a prominent politician asked the author whether he could suggest any lively foreign policy issue that had not recently been dealt with by some national figure. Political parties are increasingly ascertaining by public opinion polls what issues are most talked about throughout the population and then are tailoring their campaigns to fit these issues.

When leadership takes over, simplification and generalization of the original ideas can usually be observed. The leader attempts to formulate the issues in such a maner that they will be understood by and be of interest to the largest possible number of people. A classic example of this adaptation process has been provided by Walter Lippmann in his analysis of a speech made by Charles Evans Hughes following his acceptance of the Republican presidential nomination in 1916.[11]

At this point it is possible to suggest a definition of leadership that may be useful in this discussion. A leader is one who, in the course of interacting with others, influences their attitudes and behavior more than they influence his. He can be distinguished from a spokesman, who merely registers the opinions of a group, and from a prestigeful follower, who lends authority to an existing pattern of attitudes and behavior. In practice, a leader often serves as spokesman and may seek to appear as a prestigeful follower, but if he actually is limited to one or the other of these roles he cannot be regarded as a leader. This definition is illustrated by the rapidly shifting patterns of leadership that can be observed in mob action. A mob leader falls from power and a new leader emerges when the behavior of the latter exerts more influence on the actions of the mob members than does the behavior of the former, who may then become a follower.[12]

9 Bernard and Judith Mausner, "A Study of the Anti-Scientific Attitude," *Scientific American,* February 1955.

10 Richard L. Schank, "Test-Tube for Public Opinion: A Rural Community," *Public Opinion Quarterly,* January 1938.

11 *Public Opinion,* Penguin Books, 1946, pp. 150-154; also p. 156.

12 Robert C. Myers, "Anti-Communist Mob Action: A Case Study," *Public Opinion Quarterly,* Spring 1948.

The most important characteristic of communications at this stage of the public opinion process is their ability to transmit facts and opinions about the issue concerned to members of many primary groups. Mass communications have the advantage of being able to reach large numbers of people simultaneously, but even when they are not available the same effect may be achieved, although more slowly and with infinitely more difficulty, through person-to-person communication systems. It is probably because of this fact that we are able to discern public opinion phenomena in societies where mass communications are poorly developed, or are under the rigid control of the state, even though we see these phenomena more rarely than in societies where mass communication systems are easily available to all currents of opinion.

Through inter-group communications the ideas that were originally developed as a result of interaction within face-to-face groups, and were then rationalized by opinion leaders, become available to large numbers of people who are not personally acquainted with each other. Some of those exposed pay no attention. Others find the new ideas incompatible with existing ideas on which they already base their behavior or with the norms of the groups to which they belong, and either consciously or unconsciously reject the new notions. If all, or nearly all, of the audience falls into one of these two categories, then the phenomenon we call public opinion never appears. If, on the other hand, a substantial number of individuals accept the new ideas there is a chance that public opinion may develop.

Those who agree or disagree with an issue propounded in intergroup communications are not scattered at random throughout the audience but are clustered in certain population categories. Those who agree may for example, be concentrated in the ranks of low income groups, younger people, Baptists, and Midwesterners; while those who disagree may be found more frequently among higher income groups, Episcopalians, and Easterners. Studies of public opinion have repeatedly found that the distribution of individual opinions on any given issue is correlated with the group composition of the audience in question.[13]

PERSONAL OPINIONS ON PUBLIC ISSUES

When a controversial idea is received by a significant number of persons in any segment of an audience, face-to-face discussions are likely to start again.[14] This process resembles the one that takes place in the original primary group where the issue is generated, except that this time group discussion proceeds in the awareness that many other people are thinking and talk-

[13] A familiar example is provided by Paul F. Lazarsfeld, Bernard Berelson, and Hazel Gaudet in *The People's Choice,* Columbia University Press, 1948, pp. 25-27.

[14] *Cf.* Elihu Katz, "The Two-Step Process of Communication: An Up-to-Date Report on an Hypothesis," *Public Opinion Quarterly,* Spring 1957.

ing about the same thing. Out of these discussions new formulations and leaders may emerge and these may modify the formulation presented in the first wave of inter-group communication or may merely reinforce it. A circular process is thus set up: an increasing volume of public communications stimulates more and more discussions, and the involvement of new groups and individuals leads to more public communication.

It is at this point that most of us enter the public opinion process. We rarely take part in the discussions that lead to the initial emergence of an issue, nor do we attempt to formulate or manipulate it. But we are constantly bombarded with ideas originating outside the realm of our personal acquaintanceship (although these may be relayed to us by relatives or friends) and we must disregard, reject, or consider each of these ideas. If we think about the issues involved and form attitudes about them, these attitudes are likely to be shaped not only by our existing attitudes but also by the attitudes prevalent among those with whom we have day to day relationships.[15]

Our attitudes and opinions about issues under public discussion are, however, also conditioned by our knowledge of the opinions and behavior of other groups. The statement attributed to Winston Churchill to the effect that if Hitler invaded Hell, he (Churchill) would say a favorable word for the Devil in the House of Commons is an extreme example of the way in which the actions or opinions of those outside our immediate group help to shape our attitudes on broader issues. "If they are fur it, then I'm agin' it." Studies of prestige suggestion have shown that our attitudes may be shaped by the views of those with whom we have few personal contacts as well as by the attitudes of those with whom we live our daily lives. This is particularly true of people who would like to raise their social status and who therefore model their behavior on that of others with whom they may be acquainted only through press, radio, or television.

The process just described occurred in Center City. As a result of the agitation of the Opposition Party, informal discussions took place along Main Street, especially at lunch time, and in service clubs and fraternal organizations. Small businessmen tended to subscribe to the Opposition Party's slogans. Many white collar workers, who hoped some day to become store owners or managers, adjusted their opinions to those of the boss. In numerous cases their relatives and friends followed suit. Only among the mayor's immediate political following and in the ranks of labor was there strong sentiment in favor of the incumbent administration. A local union leader wrote the *Bugle* in support of the mayor, pointing out that the city government had successfully avoided a sales tax. But since the Opposition Party had said

[15] This process is illustrated by a great many studies. See especially the remarks on voting changes by social units in Bernard R. Berelson, Paul F. Lazarsfeld and William N. McPhee, *Voting,* University of Chicago Press, 1954, pp. 118-132.

nothing about imposing such a tax most skilled and unskilled workers did not feel themselves threatened. As a matter of fact, only a minority joined in the lively discussions; most citizens were not greatly concerned with local politics. They remained silent during the discussions at which they were present, and at this point did not form any personal opinions at all.

EXPECTATIONS AS TO THE BEHAVIOR OF OTHERS

In the process of forming their own attitudes on public issues, people usually learn about the opinions of others beyond their own immediate circle of acquaintances. Indeed, they often attempt self-consciously to ascertain what these opinions are. They note views reported in the mass media and may even question taxi drivers or casual acquaintances they meet on the train as to the prevailing opinion on a given issue in one part of the country or another. More often, however, people learn about the opinion of others without realizing that they are seeking them.

This process might be called "personal sampling." It leads to a picture of the way members of other groups may be expected to react. From the few opinions that are accessible to us we generalize as to the opinions of large groups or whole populations. We decide, after three or four conversations, that "all the better people in town" feel in such and such a way about a given issue; or we may read a few Paris newspapers and conclude that Frenchmen are overwhelmingly in favor of halting atom bomb tests.

A study of reactions to a radio dramatization of H. G. Wells' *War of the Worlds* provides some excellent examples of the way the personal sampling process may be carried out, although in this case the sampling was in reference to a question of fact (whether or not there had really been an invasion from Mars) rather than to a question of opinion.[16] Walter Lippmann also notes this personal sampling process.[17]

The way in which expectations are formed, and the resulting nature of these expectations, varies greatly from individual to individual and from case to case. Some people feel that they know how a given group will react even without sampling the opinions of any members of this group. ("Labor will never stand for that.") The less educated are likely to sample poorly or to project their own opinions onto the whole human race. ("Everybody knows that the earth is flat.") Or a very simple differentiation may be made between the probable difference in the views of good and bad people, or rich and poor. Those with more education are likely to make finer differentiations. But, however accurate or inacurate these expectations are, they serve to provide an individual with a picture of the way people beyond the reach of his personal observation are likely to behave on any issue in which he is interested.

[16] Hadley Cantril, *The Invasion From Mars,* Princeton University Press, 1947.
[17] *Op. cit.,* pp. 112-13.

Practical propagandists are aware of the importance of the picture people form of the attitudes of others and seek to influence this, often by "rigging" the sample. During the Berlin blockade, for instance, East German communists sought to convince West Berliners that pro-communist opinion was strong in the city. They therefore started sending groups of three or four agitators, dressed in work clothes, into West Berlin. One of these would engage a passer-by in conversation on political questions and then, if another West Berliner joined in, the second communist would come up as if by chance, and so on.[18] Similarly, during the South Sea Bubble in 18th century London, the directors of the South Sea Company sent agents into Exchange Alley, where they attempted to create the impression that the stock of the company was in great demand.[19] It has been alleged that advertising agencies have resorted to analogous tactics by stationing operatives in rush-hour subways, with instructions to make loud-voiced comments to each other about the virtues of a given product or service. Such efforts to influence an individual's picture of public attitudes are more often unsuccessful than successful, since they usually are outweighed by other observations a person can easily make in the course of his everyday life.

As a result of prior information, observation, and personal sampling, people are able to locate their own position and the position of the groups to which they belong with regard to an issue. "We" are for it, "they" are against it, and the rest don't care.

The formation of expectations about the opinions and probable behavior of others could be seen in our hypothetical case of Center City. As a result of conversations, discussions, and reading of the *Bugle,* people who were interested in local politics decided that nearly all the business and professional men, and most of the better-paid white collar employees would vote for the Opposition Party at the next election. The politically-conscious segment of labor clearly supported the mayor, but most factory workers showed little interest. White collar girls and housewives were also seen as indifferent. There were in fact very appreciable deviations from these patterns, but those who discussed politics in Center City ordinarily spoke as if the various population groups would vote as a unit.

ADJUSTMENT OF OPINIONS AND BEHAVIOR

Once expectations about the attitudes and behavior of others on a given issue have been formed, these expectations tend to influence the opinions and behavior, and even the attitudes, of the people who entertain them. They know that expressions in favor of an issue are likely to win respect or affec-

[18] Berlin *Tagesspiegel,* July 1, 1948.
[19] Charles Mackay, *Extraordinary Popular Delusions and the Madness of Crowds,* L. C. Page and Company, 1932, p. 53.

tion for them in one group and may provoke hostile reactions or indifference in other groups. Therefore, they are likely to speak or act in one way if they anticipate approbation and to remain silent or act in another way if they anticipate hostility or indifference. When emotions run high, people may even express support for a position they privately oppose.

This process can be observed most clearly in a crowd that is organized around a given issue. People who do not share the opinions as expressed by the crowd's leaders are likely to remain silent, fearing the disapproval of those around them. This very silence isolates others who may be opposed, since they conclude that, with the exception of themselves, all those present share the same attitudes. Even some who oppose the dominant opinion, or who do not care about it, may express approval by applauding, and thus adjust their behavior to the expected reactions of others present. Crowd members who gain cheers by riotous behavior will be encouraged to even greater excesses. A process is set up in which expectations produce behavioral adjustments, and these in turn reinforce expectations. When this has happened, public opinion has been formed.

It is at this last stage of the public opinion process that individuals who may be unconcerned with the issue at hand are drawn in. Although they may not have formed a personal attitude about the issue, and indeed may not be aware of its nature, they still cannot ignore the behavior of those about them who *do* feel strongly about it. They therefore adopt the opinions of these others. Most often they are involved through some primary group to which they belong, as when one politically-concerned member of a family insists that the others vote, but they may also feel the impact of the opinions of those with whom they are not acquainted.[20] Jules Verne's imperturbable hero, Phineas Fogg, who arrived in San Francisco during an election rally in the course of girdling the world in eighty days, found that having no opinion about the local election left him in a highly exposed position. Women who have little interest in the latest trends of fashion still find themselves influenced by the dominant opinion among other women as to what is suitable attire for a given occasion. The fairy tale of the emperor's new clothes is also a case in point, in that all who were sensitive to the opinions of others maintained that they saw the clothes, while only the child, belonging to a population category that is often insensitive to grown-up opinions, announced that the emperor was naked.

In Center City, the process of behavioral adjustment on the basis of expectations was clearly observable. Speakers at business men's luncheons learned that jokes at the expense of the mayor were likely to provoke laughter. Even those who did not share the views of the Opposition Party usually joined politely in the merriment, although somewhat less heartily. Office seekers

[20] *Cf.* Lazarsfeld, Berelson and Gaudet, *op. cit.,* p. 149.

whose observations convinced them that the mayor would be defeated made small contributions to the Opposition Party, or offered their services as party workers. The minority along Main Street who favored the mayor kept discreetly silent on the subject of local politics, except when talking to personal friends.

When election day came, most of those who supported the Opposition Party marched to the polls, taking with them their relatives of voting age and their friends. A good turn-out was assured by the fact that these people felt the eyes of their neighbors and associates upon them. The supporters of the mayor, who did not feel an equal degree of pressure from the less-interested members of their own group, showed a much lower incidence of voting. The headline in the *Center City Bugle* on the following morning ran:

PUBLIC OPINION SWEEPS MAYOR FROM OFFICE

Before leaving this final stage of the public opinion process, it may be useful to attempt a definition of a public in the sense that it has been referred to here. A public is a large collection of individuals (either assembled at one point or scattered throughout a wide area) who do not know each other personally but who react to an issue with the expectation that certain categories of others will display similar attitudes on the same issue. It thus includes those whose behavior is influenced by the expected approval or expected similar actions of others, even if they themselves have no strongly-held attitude about the issue in question. This definition does not, however, include those who, even if they take the expected behavior of the public into account in shaping their overt actions, feel no community of interest with it. For example, social scientists studying a riot or a political rally are not members of the rioting or rallying public when the term is used in this sense.

As this last reservation suggests, the behavior of those who are not members of a given public may still be influenced by the public opinion that has taken root there. Thus, the social scientists in question may be especially discreet in their note-taking because they do not wish to arouse hostility or suspicion on the part of the members of the public they are studying. Similarly, military or political planners often take public opinion into account as one datum, along with many others of both a social and a non-social nature. They may be concerned with public opinions in a given area along with the geographic location, raw materials, industrial plant, and political leadership of this area.

It is clear, of course, that the expression "public" is also used frequently in other ways: to refer to a population, to an audience, or to any collection of persons distinguished by a single characteristic (e.g., the stockholders of a company). In connection with discussions of public opinion, however, we believe that a definition along the lines of the one we have offered is the most useful. To use one of the other possible definitions leads to the anomaly that one can distinguish several public opinions among members of a single public.

One of the characteristics of public opinion that has been noted since early times is that it is a transitory phenomenon. It seems to arise spontaneously and to disappear imperceptibly. With the benefit of the scheme outlined above, we can offer some suggestions as to the various ways it disappears.

Since public opinion refers to attitudes and behavior polarized around an issue, it is clear that if the issue disappears the behavioral adjustment that characterizes public opinion will cease to have any purpose. A mob, for instance, will break up if the occasion for its gathering ceases to exist. Sometimes new goals are found as, for instance, when the mob turns its attention to destruction of property if the victim escapes, but this can be only a temporary stay. The mob members soon resume their normal patterns of life. A similar pattern of developments can be observed in the case of a political public after an election is over.

In other instances, public opinion on one issue is displaced by public opinion on another. At the same time that behavioral adjustment with regard to the first issue is at its height, a new wave of public opinion based on a different issue may be starting to form. This new issue attracts the attention of many members of the first public and a new public, possibly more powerful, is formed. Democratic statesmen who take actions that they know will be opposed by public opinion at the time often do so with the expectation that they will subsequently receive popular support when all the facts are known, or when the situation has been changed by new developments.

Public opinion may sometimes be broken up by superior physical force. The ringleaders may be arrested, all known adherents of a given viewpoint may be subjected to harsh penalties, or all communication among members of a public may be halted. If this repression is carried through relentlessly, individuals who initially composed the public may find their former behavioral adjustment incompatible with their personal safety or with the attainment of other values and adjust their behavior and even their attitudes to the new situation.

Public opinion may lead to the formation of customs or social norms before it is dissipated. The feminist movement managed to organize public opinion in such a manner that many of those who privately disagreed or who didn't care were led to adjust their behavior to conform to the pattern demanded by the militant minority. This pattern, subsequently buttressed by political and economic changes in many areas, then became established as a custom or norm. Feminism was no longer an issue, but people behaved in the manner demanded by the feminists because this was the way they had learned to behave. Their actions were no longer taken with reference to expected approval or hostility from others but either with no thought at all or else with reference to custom or social norms.

Finally, public opinion may also cease to exist when it has succeeded in having the issue around which it was organized embedded in formal laws or constitutions. The writers of *The Federalist* struggled hard to organize public opinion in favor of the constitution of the United States. After the constitution had been ratified, political behavior on many questions then became governed by reference to this formal instrument rather than by public opinion. It is only when a custom or law is seriously threatened that individual behavior may once again become polarized by reference to expectation of mass reactions.

Partially because of its long history and undefined character the term "public opinion" has been used to refer to a great many phenomena, in addition to phenomena of the type that have been described above. It may serve to clarify our discussion if we mention some of these usages and explain why they cannot be applied to the phenomenon we have attempted to describe.

A common usage is to refer to the findings of opinion polls as public opinion. If, for example, it is found that 80 per cent of eligible voters are in favor of increased federal grants for certain public works, it is sometimes said that public opinion supports legislation to this effect. But it may be that the issue has not been generally discussed. A majority of individual citizens may favor increased federal aid for highways, but their position is taken without reference to the expected behavior of others, because they have not been able to form an expectation about this behavior. They may not know that others share their opinions. In this case, the poll gives us the sum of individual opinions, but the process described in this article has not taken place, or has taken place among the members of only a relatively small public.

This, of course, is not to say that such survey findings are inaccurate or of no value. In some cases they enable us to predict (although not with very great accuracy) what majority and minority public opinion on an issue would be if it were to be formed. Furthermore, they may provide a useful guide for legislators, since in a democracy individual opinions may be as suitable a basis for legislative action as public opinion. The political leader who takes the sum of individual opinions as a guide, however, runs the risk that public opinion when formed later may be of a substantially different character.

An older usage treats public opinion as if it were represented by the dominant ideas expressed in public communications. This approach has been shaken by the observation that successful political candidates in hotly contested elections are often opposed by a heavy proportion of the mass media. It was dealt an even heavier blow when in 1956 the Hungarians rebelled against those who had enjoyed a near monopoly of the communication media for ten years. We are fairly certain that public communications do not necessarily reflect what people talk about in small groups, and even if the issues mentioned in headlines are discussed either approvingly or disapprovingly they may not serve as issues around which a public opinion process is centered.

A third usage refers to public opinion as an agent that enforces social norms, taboos, and so on. In a few cases this may be true, but ordinarily the process we have described does not appear to take place in such situations. A person who breaks a norm or violates a taboo is usually punished without reference to the expected attitudes or behavior of others in the group, and very little communication may take place. Those who administer the punishment play a role more like that of the traffic policeman who gives a ticket when he sees a law violated, while most group members who adhere to established norms or taboos do so not because of the expected behavior of those around them but because they feel that it is the right thing to do. That is, they will behave in the same manner even in private.

The most difficult distinction to maintain is the one between the public opinion process as we have described it here and the process that takes place in relatively small groups. In both cases we can see that similar individual predispositions and environmental influences may be involved, that communication and interaction take place, that expectations as to the attitudes and behavior of others are formed, and that the overt behavior of the self is adjusted to the expected behavior of others with respect to a given issue. At first sight it would appear that a distinction between the public opinion process and what we might call the group opinion process would be difficult to make.

Nevertheless, we believe that there are very important differences. Perhaps most important is the fact that a public is formed around a single issue, or a number of closely related issues, while the range of issues on which a small group may demand conformity from its members can be very great indeed.

A second difference is that the interaction process leading to the formation of group opinions takes place among people who are in frequent association, while the public opinion process involves people who may be united in a particular interaction process only once. Consequently, behavioral adjustment with regard to an issue on which there is concensus in a small group may actually be brought about more because of the past relations and expected future relations among members of the group than because of the dominant stand of the group members on this particular issue. Thus a faculty member may express agreement with a course of action suggested by his colleagues not because of the immediate appreciation he anticipates but because he feels he owes this support to his colleagues in view of their past indulgence to him, or perhaps because he is planning on submitting a proposal himself at a later meeting and does not want to prejudice its chances. Log-rolling in Congress is a similar case in point. A transitory public has no comparable past and future, but only a present.

A related distinction is that group members usually know each other, while members of a public may be total strangers. Adjustment in the group may therefore take place with reference to specific people ("these are my friends and I don't want to hurt their feelings"), while such a process is unlikely in a faceless public.

Indeed, the importance of the public in social processes seems to be related to the fact that, as distinct from the small group, it is a transitory, impersonal aggregate that is organized around a particular issue. These characteristics give it a great suppleness and versatility. The group opinion process is an extremely important component of the public opinion process, but the distinction between the two must be maintained if public opinion phenomena are to be explained adequately.

8

COGNITIVE
CONSISTENCY AND
THE PERCEPTION OF
OTHERS' OPINIONS

Don D. Smith

EW ASSUMPTIONS are as widely accepted as that which claims some relationship between the opinions people hold about an issue and the knowledge they possess about it.[1] Even among the readers of this report there are probably few who would disagree with the notion that the more accurately informed individuals are, the less likely they are to oppose racial desegregation or fluoridation of the city water supply. Such a relationship is certainly assumed in any attempt to create, reinforce, or convert opinions by the dissemination of factual information. Almost any research analysis that examines the variable of education in relation to respondents' opinions is making the same assumption that there is some relationship between the opinions people hold about an issue and the facts they know about it. Indeed, "common sense" literally demands that it be so.

Despite the universal assumption of such a relationship, the existence of any such relationship and, more so, the *nature* of such a relationship, is actually very unclear. Most previous research has focused on the relationship between an individual's opinion on some issue and the *amount* of information he possesses relevant to that issue. The results of such research present an utterly mixed picture. For example, studies by Schonbar; Smith; Walsh; and Reckless and

* This article is based on a doctoral dissertation submitted to the Department of Sociology at the University of North Carolina at Chapel Hill, 1964. The writer wishes to express his gratitude to Dr. Harry J. Crockett, Jr., for his invaluable advice throughout the study.

[1] In this study the term "opinion" will be used in its most conventional sense—as an overt expression of favorability or unfavorability toward some issue.

Originally published in Volume 32, Number 1, 1968 of the *Public Opinion Quarterly*.

Bringen found a clear relationship between amount of information known about a specified group and favorable opinions toward that group,[2] but research conducted by Cooper and Michiels; Deutsch and Proshansky; and Christiansen found no relationship of any kind between the information possessed by individuals and the opinions they held.[3] Newcomb found a relationship between information and opinions for those whose opinion was in the majority in the community, but none for those in the minority.[4] Hastings found some situations in which a relationship existed and some in which it did not.[5] Murphy and Likert, as well as Nettler, in finding only very modest correlations, concluded that information was a negligible element in opinions.[6]

Despite the mixed findings of this previous research, this study begins with the assertion that we do have systematic theory, supported by empirical evidence, which suggests that we certainly *should* be finding a clear association between the facts people have about some issue and their opinions on that issue. This report provides no answer about the causal direction of that relationship; it attempts only to determine clearly if there is a relationship and, if so, to explore some facets of that relationship. It is but the first step in a long-range project designed to examine the role of knowledge in the public opinion process. Such an examination is long overdue; having destroyed the myth of the "rational man" in noting the pervasive influence of psychological and sociological factors, the social sciences have never intensively re-evaluated the role of rationality in the opinion process.

[2] Rosalea A. Schonbar, "Students' Attitudes toward Communists: The Relation between Intensity of Attitude and Amount of Information," *Journal of Psychology*, Vol. 27, 1949, pp. 55-71; George H. Smith, "A Note on Attitudes and Information," *Journal of General Psychology*, Vol. 37, 1947, pp. 193-198; Warren B. Walsh, "What the American People Think of Russia," *Public Opinion Quarterly*, Vol. 8, 1944, pp. 512-522; Walter C. Reckless and H. L. Bringen, "Racial Attitudes and Information about the Negro," *Journal of Negro Education*, Vol. 2, 1933, pp. 128-138.

[3] Joseph B. Cooper and Lawrence J. Michiels, "Study of Attitudes as Functions of Objective Knowledge," *Journal of Social Psychology*, Vol. 36, 1952, pp. 59-71; Martin Deutsch and Harold Proshansky, "Information and Opinion during an International Crisis," *Journal of Social Psychology*, Vol. 54, 1961, pp. 169-175; Bjorn Christiansen, *Attitudes toward Foreign Affairs as a Function of Personality*, Oslo, Oslo University Press, 1959.

[4] Theodore Newcomb, "The Influence of Attitude Climate upon Some Determinants of Information," *Journal of Abnormal and Social Psychology*, Vol. 41, 1946, pp. 291-302.

[5] Philip K. Hastings, "Level of Information and Opinion Content," *Political Science Quarterly*, Vol. 69, 1954, pp. 234-240.

[6] Gardner Murphy and Rensis Likert, *Public Opinion and the Individual*, New York, Harper, 1938, pp. 126-132; Gwynne Nettler, "The Relationship between Attitude and Information Concerning the Japanese in America," *American Sociological Review*, Vol. 11, 1946, pp. 177-191.

Consistency theory seems pertinent to the problem. Not only does this theoretical orientation imply that we should be finding a clear relationship between the information individuals know about some issue and their opinions on that issue, but it also suggests other variables that are likely to intervene in the relationship (and that have not been controlled in previous research). This theory has the added advantages of (1) being inclusive enough to permit integrated empirical inquiry on two different levels, the internal, psychological level, and the interpersonal, sociological level, and (2) being sufficiently precise that hypotheses of predictive power are directly deducible from it.

On the internal level, the consistency orientation asserts that men are generally characterized by an effort to achieve and maintain consistency among their opinions, beliefs, and other cognitive elements.[7] There is empirical evidence that individuals do tend to expose themselves selectively to, and perceive and recall more readily, that which supports their already existing cognitive set of beliefs and opinions.[8] While the evidence is more mixed, there is also support for the idea that individuals selectively deny exposure to, misperceive, and forget more readily those stimuli contradictory to their beliefs and opinions.[9]

If people do monitor incoming stimuli in such a fashion, then why would one not expect that, at a given moment in "real life," people would know more factual information supporting their opinion than factual information contradicting it? ("Knowing information" is used

[7] For example, see Leon Festinger, *A Theory of Cognitive Dissonance*, New York, Row, Peterson, 1957; Fritz Heider, "Attitudes and Cognitive Organization," *Journal of Psychology*, Vol. 21, 1946, pp. 107-112; Charles B. Osgood and Percy H. Tannenbaum, "The Principle of Congruity and the Prediction of Attitude Change," *Psychological Review*, Vol. 62, 1955, pp. 42-55; Jack Brehm and Arthur R. Cohen, *Explorations in Cognitive Dissonance*, New York, Wiley, 1962. A review of these consistency theories is provided in Robert B. Zajonc, "The Concepts of Balance, Congruity, and Dissonance," *Public Opinion Quarterly*, Vol. 24, 1960, pp. 280-296.

[8] Cf. Wilbur Schramm and Roy Carter, "Effectiveness of a Political Telethon," *Public Opinion Quarterly*, Vol. 23, 1959, pp. 121-126; Jerome M. Levine and Gardner Murphy, "The Learning and Forgetting of Controversial Material," *Journal of Abnormal and Social Psychology*, Vol. 38, 1943, pp. 507-517; Judson Mills, Elliot Aronson, and H. Robinson, "Selectivity in Exposure to Information," *Journal of Abnormal and Social Psychology*, Vol. 59, 1959, pp. 250-253. For dissenting views, see David O. Sears and Jonathan L. Freedman, "Selective Exposure to Information: A Critical Review," *Public Opinion Quarterly*, Vol. 31, 1967, pp. 194-213, and Timothy C. Brock, "Commitment to Exposure as a Determinant of Information Receptivity," *Journal of Personality and Social Psychology*, Vol. 2, 1965, pp. 10-19.

[9] For discussion and research on this point, see Ivan D. Steiner, "Receptivity to Supportive vs. Nonsupportive Communications," *Journal of Abnormal and Social Psychology*, Vol. 65, 1962, pp. 266-267, and Judson Mills, "Avoidance of Dissonant Information," *Journal of Personality and Social Psychology*, Vol. 2, 1965, pp. 589-593.

here in the sense of having previously heard of it, or read about it, in any form, from any source whatsoever.) Thus, there should be clear evidence of an association between facts known by people and their opinions if *direction* of factual information, that is, whether it is congenial to (logically supports), or uncongenial to (logically contradicts), their own opinions, is taken into account along with *amount* of information. This assertion rests on the reasonable premise that two items may be "facts" (i.e. "true"), and yet one may be favorable to the issue and one unfavorable.[10]

One final theoretical comment is in order. An individual might know some information that conflicts with his opinion but he might, perhaps for that very reason, believe it to be "untrue." This would, in effect, prevent inconsistency between his opinions and the facts he knows. Consequently, this study examines not only the facts known to individuals but also whether they believe these facts to be "true" or not.[11] The same pressures toward consistency that apply to information known by individuals would be expected to apply to information they believe to be true.

Putting this theoretical orientation into the context of the purported relationship between knowledge and opinions, the following intrapersonal hypothesis may be deduced:

1. Most individuals will both know and believe more facts congenial to their opinion than facts uncongenial to their opinion.

One of the major variations of consistency theory asserts that the greater the magnitude of discrepancy between cognitive elements, the greater the motivation to restore consistency.[12] In the context of this study, then, we might expect that the more extreme one's opinion, the greater the motivation to maintain consistency between that opinion and other cognitive elements, such as the facts one knows relevant to the issue. It would seem likely that individuals holding more extreme opinions (whether extremely favorable or extremely unfavorable to the issue) would be more constrained to support their

---

[10] For example, the issue might be "the advisability of cigarette smoking." A "true" statement favorable to that issue is: "For many people, cigarette smoking serves as a tension release"; a "true" statement negative to that issue is: "An increasing amount of evidence suggests a relationship between cigarette smoking and lung cancer." Both of these are reasonably verified "facts"—but one is negative and one is favorable to the issue. This follows the lead of Newcomb, *op. cit.*, who was one of the first to recognize direction of information as a factor in the relationship between knowledge and opinions.

[11] For a related discussion, see Carolyn W. Sherif and Norman R. Jackman, "Judgments of Truth by Participants in Collective Controversy," *Public Opinion Quarterly*, Vol. 30, 1966, pp. 173-186.

[12] Festinger, *op. cit.*

opinions—more rigid in their exposure to congenial material and their belief in that material as "true," and more resistant to uncongenial material. Thus, the second hypothesis reads:

2. The proportion of individuals knowing and believing more congenial than uncongenial facts will be greater for those holding extreme opinions.

Up to this point, the consistency orientation treats the individual as a bounded psychological system, stating that the individual is subject to pressures to consistency within this system. However, this same consistency conception has been extended to the interpersonal level as well. On this sociological level, the theory emphasizes a strain to consistency of opinions and attitudes *between* individuals rather than *within* an individual.[13]

There is abundant sociological evidence, whether produced formally within the context of consistency theory or within the closely related reference group theory, which indisputably establishes that groups do exert pressures on their members toward consistency in opinions and beliefs.[14] For our purposes, then, it is significant to note that an individual is subject not only to internal consistency demands, but also, at the same time, to pressures toward consistency with other individuals and groups that are meaningful to him. Consequently, the ground is laid for possible consistency conflict—conflict not just within the cognitive elements of the internal system, or between individuals in the interpersonal network, but between the individual's internal and interpersonal pressures for consistency.

One way of maintaining consistency between these two demands is for the individual to perceive significant others to be in agreement with his own opinion. But for some individuals this is not possible; the cues are too clear that significant others are in disagreement with them about the issues in question. Such individuals are thus in the traditional "cross-pressure" situation—but, in this case, the cross-pressure is between the demands for consistency of their own internal psychological systems and the social demands of the interpersonal networks of which they are a part. Seemingly, such people would not have a homogeneous set with which they scan incoming stimuli; they would not be as restrictively drawn to supportive information or as resistant to uncongenial information, since such information would be, at the same time, congenial to the opinion of significant others.

---

13 Cf. Theodore Newcomb, *The Acquaintance Process*, New York, Holt, Rinehart and Winston, 1961; Fritz Heider, *The Psychology of Interpersonal Relations*, New York, Wiley, 1958.

14 For a bibliography of such studies, see A. Paul Hare, *Handbook of Small Group Research*, Glencoe, Ill., Free Press, 1962, pp. 44-45.

This mixed response to congenial and uncongenial information would presumably result in a lower association between their own opinions and the kind and amount of information they know and believe about the issue.

From such a theoretical conception, the following interpersonal hypothesis may be drawn:

3. The proportion of individuals knowing and believing more congenial than uncongenial facts will be greater for those who perceive significant others agreeing with them than for those who perceive significant others disagreeing with them.

Extending this same notion still further, past research has demonstrated that the numerical size of the significant others whose opinions oppose those of the individual is directly related to the amount of influence on the individual's opinions, and that even one source of support increases the number of times an individual will resist the opinions of these significant others.[15] In the context of this study, then, we might expect that the more significant others an individual perceives to disagree with him, the greater the cross-pressure of the situation. From this we may hypothesize that:

4. The greater the number of significant others perceived to disagree with one's opinion, the smaller the proportion of individuals knowing and believing more congenial than uncongenial facts.

METHOD

Presented as a study of college students' opinions on current political and social issues, and the factors that go into their opinions on such issues, our data were obtained by group-administered questionnaire to a volunteer sample of college students, each of whom received $1 for participation in the study. The questionnaire elicited the respondents' opinions on several social issues, their interest and concern in these issues, their perception of the opinions of significant others on these issues (and the interest of these others in the issues), dogmatism levels, and, finally, each respondent's knowledge of, and belief in, the facts concerning these issues.

In selecting the issues to be included in the study, a panel of undergraduates was used as informants on current student interests. A number of potential issues were discarded because of little discernible interest on the part of the potential respondents; other issues

---

15 Solomon Asch, "Opinions and Social Pressures," *Scientific American,* Vol. 193, 1955, pp. 31-35; K. R. Hardy, "Determinants of Conformity and Attitude Change," *Journal of Abnormal and Social Psychology,* Vol. 54, 1957, pp. 290-294.

were discarded only after the discovery that the development of information tests that could be validated as fact (i.e., "true") would be extremely difficult for such issues (e.g. United Nations, Euthanasia, Disarmament). From this examination, two issues were selected for the study; the question of Federal aid to Catholic parochial schools, and the foreign aid program of the United States. The results for only one of these issues—Federal aid to Catholic parochial schools—are presented here; the data for the foreign aid issue corroborate these results and will be presented in a later report.[16]

Because of the high educational level of the potential respondents, a lengthy introduction to the issue, which carefully prescribed the frame of reference to be utilized by the respondents in considering the issue, was presented in the questionnaire. This was followed by a single question, developed in numerous pre-tests with a student group, which elicited each respondent's opinion on the issue:

If Federal aid (in any form) is extended to public elementary and secondary schools, would you approve or disapprove of extending Federal aid (in some form) to Catholic elementary and secondary schools?

_____Approve strongly
_____Approve on the whole
_____Approve, but with qualifications
_____Disapprove, but with qualifications
_____Disapprove on the whole
_____Disapprove strongly

The use of this single question had the virtue of brevity (the information test, belief test, dogmatism test, and other variables creating a very lengthy questionnaire), and it permitted use of the same question form (and thereby encouraged use of the same frame of reference) in eliciting the respondents' perceptions of the opinions of others on this issue.[17]

Six presumably significant others were arbitrarily included for consideration. These others were chosen to provide a range from specific reference individuals (each respondent's father, mother, best friend, and opinion leader) to specific reference group (each respondent's immediate friendship group), and on to a more generalized other (the respondent's perception of the opinion of the entire student body on the issue).[18]

[16] The results for the foreign aid issue may be examined in Don D. Smith, "The Association of Factual Knowledge with Opinions about Social Issues," Chapel Hill, University of North Carolina, 1964, pp. 186-244, unpublished doctoral dissertation.

[17] Based on extensive pre-testing with student groups, the omission of a "Don't Know" response was deliberate.

[18] The entire study body was used as a reference group because the students were drawn from a small, church-related, liberal arts college. Without cars, far

The knowledge test for the issue consisted of twenty-four statements, each of which had been verified as fact (i.e. "true").[19] Twelve of these statements had been judged by a panel (in a Thurstone manner) as favorable to the issue, and twelve had been judged as unfavorable.[20] Illustrative of these statements are the following:

Favorable to the issue:

"Catholic and other parochial schools are already included in the Federal aid to school lunch and milk programs."

"Between 13 and 15 per cent of the total elementary and secondary school population of the U.S. is being educated in Catholic schools."

Unfavorable to the issue:

"The official position of the National Council of Churches of USA is that 'we do not consider it just or lawful that public funds should be assigned to support the elementary or secondary schools of any church.'"

"If Federal aid is given to parochial schools, this will be in direct violation of the constitutions of some of our states."

A knowledge score for each respondent was obtained from the difference between the total number of favorable facts the respondent "knew" (had ever heard of, or read about, in any manner, from any source whatsoever) and the total number of unfavorable facts he knew. This difference was then compared to his own opinion for

---

from the activity centers of the larger community, encumbered by a heavy academic expectation that restricted outside activity, with very few "local" students among them, it was reasonable to consider these students as forming a college "community" within which they most consistently interacted and with which they could identify.

[19] As the goal was to get factual items that were readily available to anyone who might want to obtain such information, lists of statements were developed from mass media discussions of these issues over the past two years. These lists were then examined for validation as fact. A given item was validated as fact by the following criteria: (a) consistent use of the item as fact in articles both pro and con the issue, (b) lack of contradictory items, (c) evidence cited for it as fact either in the article itself or from consulting professional sources such as official church statements, (d) citation of expert opinion of it as fact, again either in the literature or from consulting professional sources. (A group of teachers and students in Catholic parochial schools were used to confirm the validity of the items on the issue.) This process resulted in seventy-one items that were considered reasonably well-established as "fact."

[20] The seventy-one statements established as fact were given to a panel of thirty-six judges who, in a Thurstone manner, judged each statement as favorable or unfavorable to the issue. Selecting the statements which were viewed most unanimously by the judges and which offered a reasonably representative range of information on the issue resulted in the final list of twenty-four statements. The assumption is made here that these twenty-four statements offer a representative range of content on the issue. A normal curve distribution was obtained in the students' responses to these statements.

sign.[21] As a means of restricting projection of their own opinions on the knowledge items, the respondents were strongly admonished not to guess (orally during the administration of the questionnaire and also in the written instructions). Although none of our techniques of measuring reliability is particularly applicable in this situation, the corrected split-half reliability of these knowledge scores on a pre-test sample of thirty-one students was $r=.76$.

After taking the knowledge test, the respondents received the same statements again (in mixed order)—this time indicating whether they believed each item to be "true" or not (and again being strongly encouraged not to guess). *Considering only those items the respondent had previously indicated on the knowledge test that he knew,* a belief score was computed in the same manner as the knowledge score. The total number of favorable items the respondent believed to be true (of the items he knew) was compared to the total number of unfavorable items he believed to be true (of those he knew), the difference between them then being compared to the respondent's own opinion for sign.[22]

RESULTS

Eliminating Catholic respondents (because of the nature of the issue), a total of 593 usable returns were obtained from the student body of 1,200. As the college from which the respondents were obtained is a church-related institution, it is not surprising that the percentage of responses favorable to the issue was lower than that of nationally representative samples.[23] Seventy-one per cent of the respondents were against Federal aid to Catholic parochial schools and 29 per cent were in favor of such aid. Although this was a non-probability sample, analysis of the social composition of the respondents (i.e. year in school, social class) indicated no serious disproportions. As there were no significant differences in responses to the questionnaire on the basis of such variables, the results that follow are based on the entire sample.

[21] Thus, if a respondent indicated that he knew 11 of the factual statements that were negative to Federal aid and 7 of those that were favorable—and his own opinion was negative to Federal aid, this would result in a score of +4, indicating that he knew more information congenial to his own opinion. Conversely, if he indicated that he knew 6 items favorable to the issue and 9 that were unfavorable—and his own opinion was favorable to the issue, this resulted in a score of −3, indicating that he knew more information uncongenial to his own opinion.

[22] Thus, if the respondent knew 11 items favorable to the issue and believed 7 of them to be true, and knew 9 unfavorable items of which he believed 5 to be true—and his own opinion was favorable to the issue—his belief score was +2, indicating that, of the facts known by him, he believed more congenial than uncongenial facts.

[23] Cf., "The Polls," *Public Opinion Quarterly*, Vol. 29, 1965, p. 332.

Hypothesis 1. The first hypothesis of this study considers the direction of information and the amount of information known and believed to be true by the respondents. The data for the examination of this hypothesis, presented in Table 1, clearly indicate that more individuals both know and believe a greater amount of factual information congenial to their own opinion. Fifty-five per cent of the respondents knew more information congenial to their opinion, while 28 per cent knew more uncongenial information, a difference (D score) of 27.[24] The remaining 17 per cent of the respondents knew equal amounts of congenial and uncongenial information (a percentage that remains quite constant through the entire analysis). The same results may be seen for the belief scores. This same pattern of results was obtained when considering separately those favorable and those unfavorable to the issue.[25] Clearly, the first hypothesis is confirmed: when controlling for no other factors than amount and direction of factual information, there is an association between knowledge (both facts known and facts believed to be true) and opinions held about the issue.

TABLE 1

PERCENTAGE OF RESPONDENTS KNOWING AND BELIEVING
MORE CONGENIAL AND UNCONGENIAL FACTS
($N = 593$)

More Facts	Facts Known	Facts Believed
Congenial	55	55
Uncongenial	28	28
Equal	17	17
Total	100	100
	$D_k = 27$[a]	$D_b = 27$[b]

[a] In the analysis of the results, D_k refers to the difference between the percentage knowing more congenial facts and the percentage knowing more uncongenial facts.

[b] Similarly, D_b refers to the difference between the percentage believing more congenial facts and the percentage believing more uncongenial facts.

[24] For accurate evaluation, the number of individuals in a group who know more uncongenial facts, and equal facts, must be considered along with the number in that same group who know more congenial facts. Consequently, use is made here of D score—consisting of the percentage of individuals in a given group who know (or believe) more congenial facts minus the percentage of individuals in that same group who know (or believe) more uncongenial facts. Thus, the higher the D score for a group, the higher the association between knowledge and opinion within that group.

[25] See Smith, *op. cit.*, p. 102.

Hypothesis 2. On the premise that the greater the discrepancy between cognitive elements, the greater the motivation to restore consistency, this study asserted that the more extreme one's opinion, the more constrained he is to support it with congenial material and shield it from contradictory facts; consequently, at a given moment in "real life," we would expect that there would be a greater proportion of individuals knowing and believing more congenial than uncongenial facts among those with extreme opinions (whether extremely favorable or extremely unfavorable) than among those whose opinions are less extreme. Table 2 shows the results for this hypothesis.

TABLE 2

PERCENTAGE OF RESPONDENTS KNOWING AND BELIEVING MORE CONGENIAL
AND UNCONGENIAL FACTS, BY STRENGTH OF OPINION

	Strongly Favorable or Unfavorable (*197*)	*Favorable or Unfavorable* (*204*)	*Qualified Favorable or Unfavorable* (*192*)
Know:			
More congenial facts	59	55	49
More uncongenial facts	22	30	31
Equal facts	19	15	20
Total	100	100	100
	$D_k = 37$	$D_k = 25$	$D_k = 18$
Believe:			
More congenial facts	59	57	49
More uncongenial facts	26	26	32
Equal facts	15	17	19
Total	100	100	100
	$D_b = 33$	$D_b = 31$	$D_b = 17$

From these results, the hypothesis is clearly supported. More individuals whose opinion is strongly held know ($D_k=37$) and believe ($D_b=33$) more congenial information than individuals whose opinion is qualified ($D_k=18$ and $D_b=17$). Respondents who are between these points in strength of opinion provide a consistent mid-point in percentage knowing and believing more congenial than uncongenial facts.

Hypothesis 3. On the grounds that individuals are disposed to interpersonal consistency as well as to internal consistency, this hypothesis asserts that individuals who perceive significant others disagreeing with them will be in a position of cross-pressure, and that this will result in a lower proportion of them knowing and believing more congenial facts than for those who perceive significant others agreeing with them. This hypothesis was examined separately for each of six significant others: the father and mother of the respondent, his best friend, and his self-designated opinion leader on the issue (as reference individuals), the respondent's immediate friendship group (as a reference group), and the entire student body (as a more generalized reference other). For economy of space, only three of these are presented here, one from each category, the results for all six being quite similar.[26]

From Table 3 we can see that, as one would expect, most individuals do perceive significant others to be in agreement with them on the issue and that this tendency is accentuated with the more specific reference others. In confirmation of the hypothesis, it is also evident from this table that, for each significant other, the D score is notably higher for those individuals who perceive that significant other agreeing with them than it is for those who perceive the significant other disagreeing.

Having previously noted in Table 2 that respondents' strength of opinion is a variable influencing the association of knowledge and opinion, this variable was controlled simultaneously with respondents'

TABLE 3

PERCENTAGE OF RESPONDENTS KNOWING AND BELIEVING MORE CONGENIAL AND UNCONGENIAL FACTS, BY PERCEPTION OF OTHERS' OPINION

	Perception of Others					
	Father		Group		Students	
	Agrees (485)	Disagrees (107)	Agrees (473)	Disagrees (119)	Agree (444)	Disagree (149)
Know:						
More congenial facts	57	44	59	39	58	46
More uncongenial facts	26	38	26	33	25	35
Equal facts	17	18	15	28	17	19
Total	100	100	100	100	100	100
	$D_k = 31$	$D_k = 6$	$D_k = 33$	$D_k = 6$	$D_k = 33$	$D_k = 11$
Believe:						
More congenial facts	57	46	56	50	56	51
More uncongenial facts	26	38	27	32	27	33
Equal facts	17	16	17	18	17	16
Total	100	100	100	100	100	100
	$D_b = 31$	$D_b = 8$	$D_b = 29$	$D_b = 18$	$D_b = 29$	$D_b = 18$

[26] The results for the remaining significant others may be examined in *ibid.*, pp. 126-131.

perception of the opinions of significant others. This resulted in even higher D scores, indicating that both these variables are making an independent contribution to the association between knowledge and opinions.[27] It is worthy of note that this association is accentuated when controlling for still additional variables. For example, on the interpersonal level, the association between opinions and knowledge is higher for those who perceive significant others disagreeing with them and who also perceive these others to have little interest in the issue than it is for those who perceive significant others disagreeing with them and also perceive these others to be very much interested in the issue.[28] These are results that would be expected from the theoretical orientation of this study on the grounds that the pressure to consistency with others would not be as great if those others are perceived to have little interest in the issue.

Hypothesis 4. If individuals who perceive significant others disagreeing with them are in a position of cross-pressure that results in a smaller number of them knowing and believing more congenial information than those who perceive significant others agreeing with them, then we might expect this effect to be magnified by the number of significant others the respondents perceive to agree or disagree with them. Table 4 presents the data for this hypothesis (the data for all six significant others are included).

TABLE 4

PERCENTAGE OF RESPONDENTS KNOWING AND BELIEVING MORE CONGENIAL AND UNCONGENIAL FACTS, BY NUMBER OF SIGNIFICANT OTHERS PERCEIVED TO DISAGREE

	Number of Significant Others Perceived to Disagree			
	None (303)	1-2 (167)	3-4 (88)	5-6 (33)
Know:				
More congenial facts	59	56	51	21
More uncongenial facts	25	27	30	55
Equal facts	16	17	19	24
Total	100	100	100	100
	$D_k = 34$	$D_k = 29$	$D_k = 21$	$D_k = -34$
Believe:				
More congenial facts	58	50	58	33
More uncongenial facts	26	28	32	46
Equal facts	16	22	10	21
Total	100	100	100	100
	$D_b = 32$	$D_b = 22$	$D_b = 26$	$D_b = -13$

[27] *Ibid.*, pp. 133-139.
[28] *Ibid.*, pp. 148-153.

In keeping with our theory, it is evident that there is a linear decrease in the number of respondents perceiving increasing numbers of significant others to be in disagreement with them. In support of the hypothesis, it is also evident that as the number of significant others perceived to disagree with the respondent's own opinion increases, the percentage of respondents knowing more factual information congenial to their own opinion decreases. With one exception, this same linear association obtains for facts known and believed to be true.

DISCUSSION

From these results, the hypotheses in this study would appear confirmed. They indicate that there is a clear association between the facts people know and believe about an issue and their opinions on that issue. Further, they give some indication of the complexity of this association, involving both psychological and sociological variables in an intricately interrelated fashion. In evaluating these results it is useful to note that numerous other variables were examined in relation to this same issue of Federal aid to Catholic parochial schools. These additional variables were closely interrelated with those reported here and were also drawn deductively from consistency theory on both the internal and interpersonal levels. When all these theoretically interrelated variables are controlled simultaneously with those reported here (for example, adding respondents' interest in the issue, their perception of others' interest in the issue, and the respondents' dogmatism levels), D_k and D_b scores as high as 55 were obtained.[29] At this point, the variables under control are accounting for a great share of the variability in the association between knowledge and opinions.

Caution should be exercised in viewing these results as support for the consistency theory from which the hypotheses were deduced. Recent investigators have recognized alternative interpretations that could account for the same results that are often predicted from consistency theory.[30] For instance, more individuals who perceive others disagreeing with them might know more uncongenial facts than those who perceive others agreeing, not just because of lessened pressure to seek congenial facts or to resist uncongenial facts, but also because these disagreeing others may provide them with such uncongenial information. Nevertheless, the intricately consistent way the wide range of hypotheses were supported in the full study, of

[29] *Ibid.* p. 179.
[30] Cf., Natalia P. Chapanis and A. Chapanis, "Cognitive Dissonance: Five Years Later," *Psychological Bulletin*, Vol. 61, 1964, pp. 1-22.

which this report is just a part, attests to the usefulness of consistency theory as an empirical research tool.

Far from answering many questions, the results presented here raise significant questions for public opinion research. The results suggest that the knowledge or information component of opinions is less consistent for some individuals than for others—that similar opinions may rest on considerably different knowledge bases. The study indicates that the knowledge basis to support one's opinion is different for those with differing degrees of opinion, for those who perceive others agreeing with them than for those who perceive others disagreeing with them, and for those who perceive many others disagreeing with them in contrast to those who perceive only a few others disagreeing. The implications of these points for opinion stability and likelihood of opinion change are totally unexplored.

Many other questions remain unanswered, such as the role played in an individual's opinions by the erroneous facts he believes to be true. This is just one of the questions which will be examined during the course of this prolonged inquiry into the role of knowledge in the opinion process.

A PSYCHOLOGIST'S
PERSPECTIVES ON PUBLIC
OPINION THEORY
M. Brewster Smith

A TIME THAT HAS generated Panthers and Weathermen, eruptive dissent and a newly vocal "silent majority," is not a good one for the old "weatherman's prediction"—that today's alignments will persist tomorrow. Such a time compels attention to the causal dynamics of opinion processes, because existing empirical regularities may cease to hold.

"Public opinion research" has mainly meant survey research. For psychologists, it has meant attitude research. Over the past generation, survey research has amply proved its utility, but neither survey research nor experimental attitude research has greatly advanced our formulations of public opinion as a social force. Here I will first briefly take stock of psychological contributions to the understanding of public opinion. This will lead me to emphasize the need for joining forces with sociologists and political scientists in the attempt to understand how the opinions of individuals articulate to become a politically effective force—a problem that psychologists may have a trained incapacity to face. I will conclude with some suggestions from the psychologists' own territory that bear on politically effective opinion in our present day.

AN APPRAISAL OF THE PSYCHOLOGICAL CONTRIBUTION

An honest stocktaking of psychological research on opinion processes should be the occasion for considerable modesty. We can now look back on a double wave of theoretically interesting research on

* Revised from a paper presented in the symposium, "Toward a Theory of Public Opinion," American Association for Public Opinion Research, May 22, 1970. On this date, the aftermath of President Nixon's speech announcing the extension of the Vietnam War to Cambodia was salient to all. I would revise minor aspects of some of the judgments expressed were I rewriting the paper in the quite different atmosphere of January, 1971.

Originally published in Volume 34, Number 3, 1970 of the *Public Opinion Quarterly*.

persuasive communication and opinion change, associated with the names of Carl Hovland and of Leon Festinger. As we scan what this double wave has left behind on the beach as it recedes, we cannot be self-satisfied. True, many factors that affect the formation and change of individual opinion have been identified and mapped, and accounts of these processes have been brought into contact with theories about general psychological processes of learning, judgment, cognitive organization, and personality dynamics. That is all to the good, and not to be minimized. It has shaped the discipline of experimental social psychology as we have known it in the past two decades. But Nathan Maccoby's metaphor of the "new scientific rhetoric"[1] overstates what psychologists are in a position to export to students of public opinion.

A quarter century of experimental research actually leaves us quite vulnerable. The initial strategy of experimental work appropriately focused on trivial, superficial beliefs and opinions, where measureable change could be produced efficiently by brief and easily conducted "manipulations." This made good sense in an initial mapping of the terrain. But there has been little follow-through with more consequential attitudes and with parametric studies of several variables in interaction (there have been some notable exceptions in the work of Sherif[2] and of Janis[3]). The result is that a quite comprehensive map is filled in with entries that are suggestive rather than definitive. And meanwhile, Orne, Rosenthal, and Rosenberg[4] have come on the scene with their skeptical "social psychology of the psychological experiment" to imply that subjects in many of our experiments may unwittingly have been conning the experimenter rather than vice versa.

Apart from these uncertainties, three general features of this line of psychological research limit its relevance for the understanding of consequential public opinion. First, the prevailing emphasis on experimental manipulation has deflected attention from the longer-term

[1] Nathan Maccoby, "The New Scientific Rhetoric," in Wilbur Schramm, ed., *The Science of Communication: New Directions and New Findings in Communication Research*, New York, Basic Books, 1963, pp. 41-53.

[2] E.g. Muzafer Sherif, *Social Interaction: Process and Products*, Chicago, Aldine, 1967; Caroline W. Sherif, Muzafer Sherif, and Roger E. Nebergal, *Attitude and Attitude Change: The Social Judgment-Involvement Approach*, Philadelphia and London, W. B. Saunders, 1965.

[3] E.g Irving L. Janis, "Effects of Fear Arousal on Attitude Change: Recent Developments in Theory and Experimental Research," in Leonard Berkowitz, ed., *Advances in Experimental Social Psychology*, New York and London, Academic Press, Vol. 3, 1967, pp. 166-224; Irving L. Janis and Leon Mann, "A Conflict-Theory Approach to Attitude Change and Decision Making," in Anthony G. Greenwald, Timothy Brock, and Thomas M. Ostrom, eds., *Psychological Foundations of Attitudes*, New York and London, Academic Press, 1968, pp. 327-360.

[4] *Cf.* Robert Rosenthal and Ralph L. Rosnow, eds., *Artifact in Behavioral Research*, New York and London, Academic Press, 1969.

processes by which a person's deeper commitments and orientations become established and may subsequently be dislodged. Second—this point has been stressed by Leon Festinger[5]—the relevance of opinion change to behavior change is still shockingly in doubt. While we have learned to talk about the relation of attitudes to behavior in more sophisticated terms than we did at the time of LaPiere's study,[6] the realm of psychological research on opinions and attitudes largely remains an encapsulated verbal world. And, third, psychologists have not concerned themselves with how individual opinions aggregate or articulate to produce social and political consequences. They have not dealt with public opinion as a social force. This can hardly be charged as a fault of laboratory research, but psychologists are likely to be biased by training and preoccupation against taking the problem of articulation seriously.

THE PROBLEM OF ARTICULATION

According to the old individualistic view that used to be the psychologist's predictable bias—the view that Floyd Allport[7] once proclaimed—the very concept of public opinion is a reification. All we can deal with scientifically is distributions of individual opinions, and that is that. While our methodological premises have become less dogmatic, our habits of research still take for granted the doctrine of one man—one vote, which is fine for voting but not for the processes of influence and decision-making that constitute the stuff of politics outside the voting booth.

A skeptical, reductionist view of public opinion in this individualist tradition has its constructive side. We do well to doubt the substantiality of public opinion as a supraindividual entity. That is, there is no reason to suppose that the opinions of individuals articulate in the same way in different political contexts. In maintaining or questioning the legitimacy of the political and legal order; in influencing the

[5] Leon Festinger, "Behavioral Support for Opinion Change," *Public Opinion Quarterly*, Vol. 28, 1964, pp. 404-417.

[6] Richard T. LaPiere, "Attitudes versus Actions," *Social Forces*, Vol. 13, 1934, pp. 230-237; Donald T. Campbell, "Social Attitudes and Other Acquired Behavioral Dispositions," in Sigmund Koch, ed., *Psychology: A Study of a Science*, New York, McGraw-Hill, Vol. 6, 1963, pp. 94-176; Martin Fishbein, "Attitude and the Prediction of Behavior," in Martin Fishbein, ed., *Readings in Attitude Theory and Measurement*, New York, Wiley, 1967, pp. 477-492; Allan W. Wicker, "Attitudes versus Actions: The Relationship of Verbal and Overt Behavioral Responses to Attitude Objects," *Journal of Social Issues*, Vol. 25, No. 4, 1969, pp. 41-78.

[7] Floyd H. Allport, *Institutional Behavior: Essays toward a Reinterpretation of Contemporary Social Organization*, Chapel Hill, University of North Carolina Press, 1933.

Congress, the presidency, the military, or local government; in the different content spheres of domestic and foreign policy issues, effective *public* opinion is surely composed from individual opinions along different lines. The relevant attentive publics are different, as is the role of the inattentive citizenry; the paths from opinion to influence very likely differ. This has to be worked out empirically, and I take it that the job falls in the customary sphere of political science and political sociology.

One component of the problem of articulation is more social psychological. According to Kurt Lewin's methodological premise, anything that has effects is "real," and this surely applies to reifications of public opinion as they enter the belief systems of legislators and policymakers, as they are purveyed by the mass media, and as they are entertained by different segments of the general citizenry. What people in these various roles believe public opinion to be obviously affects what they do.

Recent events provide some interesting illustrations of how beliefs about public opinion can influence realities. One involves President Nixon's invention of the "silent majority," which has my grudging admiration as an inspired piece of political tactics. By giving an explicit label to a segment of the population whose general agreement with many of his less liberal policies would otherwise be neutralized politically by its normal tendency to be politically inert, Mr. Nixon would seem to have reaped an immediate dividend in self-fulfilling political perception. Verbal magic is obviously only part of the story, but I think it improves the prospects of his intended new coalition. I admire the strategy but fear for the consequences. I hope that public opinion research in progress may capture enough of what is happening to advance our understanding of how the manipulation of political perception can alter the political facts.

The recent events on our campuses as I interpret them provide another example of feedback processes whereby perceptions of public opinion change political realities. Since the assassinations of King and the Kennedys, the playing out of the McCarthy crusade, the 1968 convention, and the fragmentation of SDS, the campuses that had previously been swept by activist protest seemed to be settling into a kind of sullen peace. Although Astin's[8] data show some trends toward increasing polarization among students, the mood of those sympathetic to the left was tending toward hopelessness—grounds for copping out in quietism and drugs or for nihilistic expressive violence.

8 Alan E. Bayer, Alexander W. Astin, and Robert F. Boruch, "Social Issues and Protest Activity: Recent Student Trends," Washington, D. C., American Council on Education, *ACE Research Reports,* Vol. 5, No. 2, February 1970.

Mr. Nixon's speech on Cambodia and the Kent State killings that followed in close sequence, at the height of spring, evoked an immediate response of outrage. The common and compelling stimuli triggered a simultaneous response that organized and made manifest what had previously been latent and disorganized—and also brought into the picture the less elite campuses that had thus far been quite inactive. In good part, the initial response had the destructiveness of a reflex reaction by the hopeless; it was more expressive than instrumental. But campus *perception* of this massive response, by students, faculties, and administrators, paradoxically created grounds for new hope, expectations of political effectiveness, that substantially changed the setting and nature of student protest, and involved faculties and administrators as well to an unprecedented extent. The initial expressive reaction laid the basis for a burst of instrumental activity. As we know, the floundering student protest movement has found new life, and student energies on many campuses are now directed once more toward normal political channels, which for the sake of the country I hope they find effective.

In this interpretation of what has happened, the visibility of widespread immediate reaction to a common stimulus created a sense of efficacy that started a new chain of political events the end of which is not in sight. The perception of public opinion is a fact, describable at the individual level, that mediates and complicates how individual opinions aggregate or articulate to produce political effects.

SELF-DETERMINATION AND OPINION THEORY

My final point bears on perceived and real efficacy as involved in the just preceding example. Recent research and theory in psychology, I think, is in a position to contribute, at long last, to formulating the conditions and consequences of self-determination, an issue at the heart of normative political theory that is also basic to recent protest politics on and off the campus. Claims for self-determination are involved not only in the rebellious protests of students, blacks, and former colonials, but also in the reactive backlash of people whose own freedom and privilege seem threatened by the new claims pressed by the insurgent groups. *Can* self-determination be given an intelligible psychological meaning? Can the gap between the normative theory of democracy and the deterministic theories of the behavioral sciences be bridged?

That the problem has long been before AAPOR is readily documented. As early as 1952, Bernard Berelson devoted his presidential address to "Democratic Theory and Public Opinion".[9] After tallying point by point the imperfect match between facts gleaned in public opinion research and the ideal requirements for a democratic polity, he noted as a problem for negotiation that "the theorists tend to use descriptive categories (e.g. rationality) and the researchers prefer predictive categories (e.g. group memberships) in 'explaining' political preferences" (p. 330). Is there a place for rational choice in a causal theory of opinion and political behavior?

More recently, that master of political research, V. O. Key,[10] argued posthumously from presidential voting data:

In the large, the electorate behaves about as rationally and responsibly as we should expect, given the clarity of the alternatives presented to it and the character of the information available to it. In American presidential campaigns of recent decades the portrait that emerges is not one of an electorate strait-jacketed by social determinants or moved by subconscious urges. . . . It is rather one of an electorate moved by concern about central and relevant questions of public policy, of governmental performance, and of executive personality. (p. 7–8)

Key proclaimed the importance of rational choice, but saw it as antithetical to the role of social and psychological determinants.

As I have noted elsewhere,[11] Key's characteristically vivid rhetoric creates a needless theoretical dilemma:

. . . Social determinants do not have their influence by any mysterious process of "strait-jacketing" the electorate. . . . Their influence . . . lies primarily in the fact that common experience and common social position yield similar perceptions of interest, and over time lead to the emergence of norms that reflect these perceptions. Social determination is by no means incompatible with political rationality. (pp. 99-100)

Nor is psychological determination.

Charles Glock, in his 1964 AAPOR presidential address,[12] raised the problem that I want to highlight still more pointedly—"How much free will is man thought to have?" For Glock as for Key, freedom or rationality and causal determination are at opposite, mutually exclusive poles. This way of thinking is so much a part of our intellectual heritage that we can hardly escape from it.

[9] Bernard Berelson, "Democratic Theory and Public Opinion," *Public Opinion Quarterly*, Vol. 16, 1952, pp. 313-330.

[10] V. O. Key, Jr., with the assistance of Milton C. Cummings, Jr., *The Responsible Electorate: Responsibility in Presidential Voting*, Cambridge, Mass., Harvard University Press, 1966.

[11] M. Brewster Smith, "Personality in Politics: A Conceptual Map with Application to the Problem of Political Rationality," in Oliver Garceau, ed., *Political Research and Political Theory*, Cambridge, Mass., Harvard University Press, 1968, pp. 77-101.

[12] Charles Y. Glock, "Images of Man and Public Opinion," *Public Opinion Quarterly*, Vol. 28, 1964, pp. 539-546.

My suggestion is that the time has come for us to break free of what I think is a false polarity, and that we now have the conceptual resources to do so. As social scientists, true enough, we must be committed to determinism as a methodological premise. But freedom, in the sense of self-determination, is not a matter of chance and randomness; it is itself subject to causal analysis. Recent psychological research is beginning to treat free will not as a paradox or as an illusion, but as an empirical variable that has causes and consequences. Some people have more free will than others. Some people that for pretty obvious reasons had little of it before are now developing more of it; they are getting "pushy."

I draw upon the ideas and research of Robert White[13] and Richard de Charms[14] and evidence from Julian Rotter[15] to propose that to a considerable extent, how much self-determination a person exercises is bound up in a self-fulfilling prophecy. His feelings of efficacy, rooted in attitudes and concepts about the self, have much to do with what he will try and what he will accomplish.[16] And these feelings of efficacy have their own social and personal determinants. The other side of the coin, psychological "reactance" as a motivational state produced when a person's perceived options or degrees of freedom are reduced, has been explored by Brehm.[17]

What has this way of viewing matters to do with the theory of public opinion? The close relationship between general feelings of personal effectiveness and the sense of political efficacy has been established by Douvan and Walker.[18] In *The Civic Culture*, Almond and Verba[19] made clear that the sense of political efficacy is a key ingredient that differentiates political cultures. Melvin Seeman,[20] another contributor to this line of development, draws on Rotter's work

---

[13] Robert W. White, "Motivation Reconsidered: The Concept of Competence," *Psychological Review*, Vol. 66, 1959, pp. 297-333; "Ego and Reality in Psychoanalytic Theory: A Proposal for Independent Energies," *Psychological Issues*, Vol. 3, 1963, No. 3.

[14] Richard de Charms, *Personal Causation*, New York and London, Academic Press, 1968.

[15] Julian Rotter, "Generalized Expectancies for Internal versus External Control of Reinforcement," *Psychological Monographs*, Vol. 80, 1966, No. 1 (Whole Number 609).

[16] M. Brewster Smith, "Competence and Socialization," in John A. Clausen, ed., *Socialization and Society*, Boston, Little, Brown, 1968, pp. 271-320.

[17] Jack W. Brehm, *A Theory of Psychological Reactance*, New York and London, Academic Press, 1966.

[18] Elizabeth Douvan and Alan M. Walker, "The Sense of Effectiveness in Public Affairs," *Psychological Monographs*, Vol. 70, No. 22, 1956, pp. 1-19.

[19] Gabriel A. Almond and Sidney Verba, *The Civic Culture: Political Attitudes and Democracy in Five Nations*, Princeton, N. J., Princeton University Press, 1963.

[20] E.g. Melvin Seeman, "Alienation, Membership, and Political Knowledge," *Public Opinion Quarterly*, Vol. 30, 1966, pp. 354-367.

to relate psychological propositions about a person's sense of control over the outcomes of his endeavors to sociological propositions about alienation in mass society. I am therefore not adding new ideas or facts: I am rather trying to put what we are beginning to know in a new focus. I am suggesting that a psychological ingredient unknown to the deterministic psychologies of the past, be they behavioristic or psychoanalytic, and not explicitly encompassed in my early work with Bruner and White,[21] is turning out to be important in psychological research and relevant to political analysis. Sense of person control or efficacy, as a self-fulfilling source of initiative and political action, is a psychological variable of which I predict we will be hearing much more.

It would be good for the ethical and political posture of the theory of public opinion if I am right. Accounts of psychological and social determinants *seem* to have a "straightjacketing" effect on individual political freedom even though, as I maintain, this is a metatheoretical mistake. Behavioral science has projected a mechanistic view of man, which again in a self-fulfilling prophecy has lent weight to dehumanizing trends in modern life and to disrespectful, manipulative trends in the marketplace and political arena. My colleagues in experimental social psychology have focused on the techniques of manipulating opinions and behavior, and in the very style of their research they have unintentionally advanced the dehumanizing trend.[22] Now that the young and the Movement types are calling stridently for more self-determination, it behooves our behavioral science to push ahead with the attempt to understand the phenomena of self-determination systematically and causally. Additions to our knowledge of the conditions and consequences of personal control and autonomy in politics should better prepare us for some difficult times to come.

[21] M. Brewster Smith, Jerome S. Bruner, and Robert W. White, *Opinions and Personality*, New York, Wiley, 1956.
[22] Herbert C. Kelman, *A Time to Speak: On Human Values and Social Research*, San Francisco, Jossey Bass, 1968.

II

UNDERSTANDING
CHANGES IN
PUBLIC OPINION

The phenomenon of change has fascinated philosophers, historians, novelists, social scientists, and politicians for ages. Attitudes and interests change as the individual grows older. Is this because he has incorporated certain trial and error experiences into his thinking or is it merely a response to the pressures of his peer groups? Some attitudes or "prejudices" persist in spite of clear evidence that they do not reflect reality. What social and psychological rewards are met by retaining them?

Peter Odegard in his chapter, "Social Dynamics and Public Opinion," reviews some of the paradoxes of trying to understand the process of opinion change. He reminds us, for example, of the debate over the F. A. Lange-William James theory that prefers to believe that we are afraid because we run, rather than that we run because we are afraid. Odegard points out "there is a tendency to forget that words are instruments not only of reason but of will . . . but they are equally and more commonly serviceable, without,regard for logic and indeed in flagrant violation of the so-called laws of thought, as symbols to rationalize, i.e. give meaning to, impulsive demands." Finally he quotes Karl Mannheim who observes, "We tend 'to be content to attribute importance to what is measurable merely because it happens to be measurable.' "

Although Arnold Rose's fame as a sociologist rests on his work in areas other than public opinion theory, he has some keen observations to offer regarding this matter. In his "Public Opinion Research Techniques Suggested by Sociological Theory" he notes that academic psychologists and sociologists did not participate significantly in public opinion polling until the mid-1930s, and research procedures were developed before social science theory could influence them very much. He then proceeds to suggest a number of general sociological principles that have relevance for public opinion research.

The first such general principle stems from a distinction made by Robert E. Park between a public and a mass. The public is a social grouping in which all the members are actively in communication with each other, either directly or indirectly. A mass, on the other hand, is an agglomeration of people who are recipients of communication from a central source and who are not in communication with each other. An archetype of a public would be the informal group that meets at the village store when the mail comes in. . . . An archetype of a mass would be a movie audience. . . .

A second sociological principle which has implication for public opinion research is that in contemporary urbanized society an individual is likely to belong to a variety of unintegrated groups which make different demands on him. The very heterogeneity of our society which creates the diverse viewpoints that we wish to measure by polling people also creates a lack of uniformity in attitudes within a single individual. Probably few people anywhere have a completely uniform and consistent attitude toward any significant social object, and probably least of all in our own society.

Rose's third point is "that different groups or social roles have different significances for those who participate in them. It is a continuing interest of sociologists to determine what social groups do most to satisfy needs or confer status, and what social roles are perceived as most desirable or most important." Hyman and others have subsequently developed the "reference group theory" as a way of studying this phenomenon.

The fourth point is "that broad population divisions—such as those of class and caste—may have excellent communication within them but that informal communication will much less readily cross into another class or caste. . . . Such broad social groupings as class and caste also embody culture differences which manifest themselves in public opinion research as differences in the connotation of words."

Rose reminds us of William G. Sumner's concept of "mores" and speculates on the degree to which mores and pseudo-mores may inhibit the researcher from asking certain kinds of questions or may encourage respondents,to give the socially acceptable answer to a question. Finally, he refers to Georg Simmel's theory of the "Stranger" and how the public opinion interviewer's anonymity allows him to secure some of his most confidential and honest answers from his respondents.

Daniel Katz's "The Functional Approach to the Study of Attitudes" is a classic statement on this topic. In a very real sense it cannot and should not be subjected to a summary for the elegance of its construction and the precision of its logic is lost. The best apparent resolution of this dilemma is to quote directly from the opening two paragraphs of his chapter and from his summary last paragraph.

The study of opinion formation and attitude change is basic to an understanding of the public opinion process even though it should not be equated with this process. The public opinion process is one phase of the influencing of collective decisions, and its investigation involves knowledge of channels of communication, of the power structures of a society, of the character of mass media, of the relation between elites, factions and masses, of the role of formal and informal leaders, of the institutionalized access to officials. But the raw material out of which public opinion develops is to be found in the attitudes of individuals, whether they be followers or leaders and whether these attitudes be at the general level of tendencies to conform to legitimate authority or majority opinion or at the specific level of favoring or opposing the particular aspects of the issue under consideration. The nature of the organization of attitudes within the personality and the processes which account for attitude change are thus critical areas for the understanding of the collective product known as public opinion.

At the psychological level the reasons for holding or for changing attitudes are found in the functions they perform for the individual, specifically the function of adjustment, ego defense, value expression, and knowledge. The conditions necessary to arouse or modify an attitude vary according to the motivational basis of the attitude. Ego-defensive attitudes, for example, can be aroused by threats, appeals to hatred and repressed impulses, and authoritarian suggestion, and can be changed by removal of threat, catharsis, and self-insight. Expressive attitudes are aroused by cues associated with the individual's values and by the need to reassert his self-image and can be changed by showing the appropriateness of the new or modified beliefs to the self-concept. Brain washing is primarily directed at the value-expressive function and operates by controlling all environmental supports of old values. Changing attitudes may involve generalization of change to related areas of belief and feeling. Minimal generalization seems to be the rule among adults; for example, in politics voting for an opposition candidate does not have much effect upon party identification.

The purpose of this paper was to provide a psychological framework for the systematic consideration of the dynamics of public and private attitudes. Four functions which attitudes perform for the personality were identified: the adjustive function of satisfying utilitarian needs, the ego-defensive function of handling internal conflicts, the value-expressive function of maintaining self-identity and of enhancing the self-image, and the knowledge function of giving understanding and meaning to the ambiguities of the world about us. The role of these functions in attitude formation was described. Their relevance for the conditions determining attitude arousal and attitude change were analyzed. Finally, constellations of variables such as group contact and legislate control of behavior were considered in terms of their motivational impact.

Percy Tannenbaum provides a significant and new analytical concept to our understanding of the formation of public opinion in his theory, "The Indexing Process in Communication." He notes that traditionally research has tended to focus on the nature and the predispositions of the intended audience for a message on the one hand, and on an examination of the totality of the message and its content on the other hand.

There has been little attention to the distinctive components of this stimulus pattern. . . . The notion of an indexing process in communications effects is an outgrowth of regarding the communication message as a set of distinctive stimulus elements—of individual signs or cues usually (e.g., language), but not necessarily (e.g., pictorial communication), arranged in a sequential order of some kind. The nature of the basic message unit—is it the morpheme, the word, the phrase, the sentence, etc?—remains undecided at present and is the undefined term of the system. This issue, however, is a vital one in communication theory and will ultimately have to be resolved.

Tannenbaum offers a theory to answer this question:

For our purposes here it is sufficient to make the assumption of the message being a *set* (in mathematical set theory terminology) of such undefined elements. An *index* is considered to be a single such stimulus element or a stimulus complex that may serve to predispose a particular interpretation or meaning of the total stimulus pattern or of some segment of this stimulus pattern other than itself. . . . One way in which an index may influence the effects of a communication is, of course, in terms of *attracting attention* to that message.

He offers examples of this phenomenon by citing studies of the impact of different newspaper headlines, newscast "leads," picture captions, and qualifying words such as "but" on how audiences reaction to similar messages. In the area of nonverbal indices he cites research on the impact of political symbols, color, and even music on the perception of messages.

In his article, "Processes of Opinion Change," Herbert Kelman suggests two foci of social-psychological theorizing and research that offer promise for understanding opinion formation and change. One is the study of processes of social interaction as such. He is interested in the expectations that the respondent brings to the interview situation and the goals he seeks to achieve by his interaction with the interviewer. His second concern is the study of processes of social influence and the induction of behavior change—"the social conditions under which they were adopted, the motivations that underlie them, and the social and personal systems in which they are embedded."

Kelman moves on to offer a theoretical framework for the study of three processes of social influence in the study of opinion change—compliance, identification, and internalization. More important, he reports on research data that test these concepts. He concludes his piece by stating that his model for the analysis of public opinion appears promising because "by tying together certain antecedents of influence with certain of its consequents, it enables us to infer the motivations underlying a particular opinion from a knowledge of its manifestations, and to predict the future course of an opinion from a knowledge of the conditions under which it was formed."

Nathan and Eleanor Maccoby's "Homeostatic Theory in Attitude Change" has a passage early in the article that summarizes current theories regarding attitude change: "Most of these theoretical approaches to attitude change have at least one major characteristic in common. They involve a kind of balance-of-forces approach in which the overloading of one type of factor gives rise to changes designed to restore balance. In short, all employ homeostasis in some form or other." They review highlights of the writings of Leon Festinger, F. Heider, Morris Rosenberg, Charles E. Osgood and Percy H. Tannenbaum, and Theodore M. Newcomb as examples of this approach to explaining attitude change. They then turn attention to the relationship between learning theory and homeostatic theory and the degree that each point of view has in fact produced "considerably different emphases—a different choice of research problems. The learning theorist would think of cognitive dissonance or imbalance in terms of conflict. . . . Learning theory also differs from the homeostatic theories in the amount of attention it gives to *practice* of the content of a persuasive communication." They conclude on an affirmative note: "The test of a theory, of course, lies not only in its ability to organize existing knowledge but also its ability to generate new knowledge. There is no doubt that the homeostatic theories have proved themselves in this respect."

The special merit of Philip Converse's "Information Flow and the Stability of Partisan Attitudes" is that it offers a rich interweaving of historic theories of attitude change in the political arena with specific research findings that clarify, question, and occasionally keep unanswered major facets of these theories. Converse's particular attention in this article is on one of the long-standing puzzles facing students of our political life. "Not only is the electorate as a whole quite uninformed, but it is the least informed members within the electorate who seem to hold the critical 'balance of power,' in the sense that alterations in governing party depend disproportionately on shifts in their sentiment." He tests this hypothesis against a conceptual background that he formulates as follows: "Any theory of mass voting behavior must come to grips at the outset not only with the fact of low public information about politics, but also with the fact that information about politics is as inequitably distributed as wealth in the mass public." Much of the substantive portion of his article devotes itself to the "shifting" or "floating" voters—those whose information about politics is relatively impoverished.

Although the focus of Converse's material is the American political system, his conclusions deserve to be studied by those who seek to understand attitude change in any context and his final paragraph merits careful thought by all students of communications research. "Since changes in the information-propagating capacities of a society occur at a fairly slow rate, it is in such historical perspective that a link between the volume of information flow and the partisan stability of an electoral system has its most interesting implication." We need only substitute the phrase "value and attitude system" for his "electoral system" to make the reading of this article significant for understanding attitude change.

"Apocalyptic and Serial Time Orientation and the Structure of Opinion" by Kurt Back and Kenneth Gergen finds that much existing research on attitude change is focused on characteristics of respondents and their group memberships. Their approach looks to still another factor that influences opinion and attitude change.

> We shall avoid either of these approaches and define personal traits that relate to the basic situation of a human being before he identifies himself as part of either a social or a personal system. We shall deal with the relation between personality structure and public opinion on the basis of certain assumptions about a person's orientation in time and space. Thus, we shall deal with opinions as if a person were making decisions to act and direct our attention to the meaning of the future for a person.

In brief, they set out to relate "time perspective" as a force in the shaping of attitudes. The authors offer four propositions to support their thesis:

1. Decision making is partially a function of repeatable events, hence is usually more effective if a long-range time perspective is maintained. . . .

2. The more crucial the decision, the shorter the time perspective and the greater the tendency toward the apocalyptic pole. . . .

3. Besides its relations to the kind of decision, time perspective is an individual characteristic and a function of over-all range of life space. . . .

4. The size of life space is partially a function of such characteristics as age, education, occupation, and social class, and may indeed be the essential factor in the relation of these traits to social attitudes.

Unfortunately, these seminal theses have not been tested in much of the attitude and opinion research carried out since the publication of this article.

Leo Bogart's chapter, "No Opinion, Don't Know, and Maybe No Answer," is a philosophical treatise on the changing moral, cultural, political, and personal impact of the enormous growth in the use of public opinion polls in recent decades. Early in his essay he states:

> No doubt the character and quality of public opinion have changed over years, with the growth of literacy and mass communications. Such change has been subtle, gradual, and continuous, whereas in the academic discussion of public opinion there is a sharp discontinuity between the periods before and after the development of the systematic opinion survey. . . . The paradox of scientific method is that we change phenomena by measuring them. An interview acts as a catalyst. The confrontation of interviewer and respondent forces the crystallization and expression of opinions where there were no more than chaotic swirls of thought.

With concern widespread today about the threats to our freedom of information, Bogart raises several salient points. "Opinions always start from certain factual premises. But the information we have at hand is usually limited. Our opinion invariably transcends our knowledge. Today's mass media can produce the illusion of knowing the inside story of what in fact we know only selectively and incompletely. . . . How sensitive should a leader be to opinion formed without knowledge of important information?" It would be unfair to select all "the raisins" from his article, but one more example will suggest the scope of the points he makes.

> What an individual defines as important cannot be separated from what he feels he has within his control. Compared to the questions of consumer choice with which we most commonly confront our survey respondents, political questions may have more objective importance. Yet the average individual has no control over political questions, or over the problems that they represent, except within the framework of collective social action. The questions asked in opinion surveys often seem irrelevant to a world of barricades, guerrilla warriors, and lumbering armies.

The final chapter in this section is Phillips Davison's "Public Opinion Research as Communication." He asks: "What role do we as public opinion researchers play within the social organism of which we are a part? . . . to recognize that survey research provides information that has a wide-range of utilities does not tell us what kind of social role we are playing. How would society as a whole differ if we were not a part of it?"

He answers his rhetorical question in part by noting: "We can think of public opinion research as part of the communication system of our society and of a world community." Davison suggests that in a highly simplified view,

> one could also see our society, at least, as an amalgam of several different pyramids. . . . Within the three main segments of the pyramids, one can also visualize lateral communications, linking together different groups within the elite, the sub-elite, and the mass. Public opinion research contributes in no small measure to each of these communication flows. As part of the upward flow of communication it helps to explain public opinion on any given issue, putting it into context, defining who is involved and why, explaining whether this aggregation of opinions represents a small minority or a large wave of popular sentiment. Second, our research provides a feedback mechanism to decision-makers. . . . A third implication of our work for the upward flow of communication is less well understood and poorly documented. This is that we may, on occasion, provide a *substitute* for public opinion . . . we have the capability to identify grievances, inequities, and resentments in all sectors of our society— before they become acute enough to be manifested in widespread suffering or in violent and disruptive behavior.

Davison regrets that lateral and diagonal flows of communication have been so infrequently studied, but he notes that this type of communication does perform some valuable social functions—for example, enabling a particular group to shape its activities and opinions in light of what other groups are doing and thinking.

Several themes recur in these articles dealing with how public opinion changes. One is the notion that public opinion is characterized by a sizeable degree of instability and that it is sustained by the operation of a little understood process of psychic, social, and economic trade-offs resulting in a dynamic equilibrium. Still another point that surfaces in many of these essays is the need to understand the function that is served when an individual changes his opinion, and how this may be supportive or dysfunctional for his ties to the groups to which he claims membership. Several scholars suggest that the extent to which people believe they have power may explain their level of involvement in the public opinion process. While these articles offer no unified theory as to why changes take place in public opinion, they do offer some very constructive ideas as to how this process may be studied more effectively.

10

Peter H. Odegard

Students of public opinion are in final analysis students of human thought and behavior. Whether as political scientists, economists, psychologists, sociologists or philosophers our universe of discourse is the same. We are in short, whether we realize it or not, students of the sociology of knowledge, belief and conduct. There are few, if any, areas of human experience toward which we can safely assume an attitude of unconcern. The "flower in the crannied wall" leads no less surely to every frontier of thought and feeling than does the form and function of social action and belief. I know of no field of inquiry where vision, imagination, and insight are so vitally necessary. The description of a philosopher as one who sees life steadily and sees it whole is equally applicable to the student of public opinion at his best. He must constantly ask not only *how* but *why* we behave like human beings. He must be concerned with human *drives* or *motives* no less than with the *structure* and *mechanism* of social conduct, with *social dynamics* as well as social *statics*. Above all he must remember that the particular inquiry upon which he may be for the moment engaged is but a segment of a larger whole to which it must somehow be related. Otherwise he comes to resemble the blind man who undertook to describe an elephant by feeling its tail.

What has been said assumes, of course, that students of public opinion are interested in the functional etiology of attitudes as well as in the description and measurement of opinion. (An opinion is at best merely a crude representation of an attitude.) Our position

Originally published in Volume 3, Number 2, 1939 of the *Public Opinion Quarterly*.

today is not unlike that of the psychologists nearly fifty years ago. The so-called brass instrument school under the leadership of Weber, Fechner, and Wundt in Europe and the Titchenerian structuralists in America, in seeking to emancipate psychology from philosophy and metaphysics indentured it in its infancy to physiology and mechanics. The vague generalizations of arm-chair inquiries concerning human understanding seemed naïve and unscientific when contrasted with the precision of Weber's law, reaction time studies and the careful measurement of neuro-muscular twitches. It required the vigorous protestations and research of instinctivists like James and McDougall, functionalists like Dewey and Angell, dynamists and psychoanalysts like Woodworth and Freud, and gestaltists like Koffka and Koehler to restore psychology as the science of human nature rather than as a branch of Newtonian physics. Even today a rereading of William James's *Principles of Psychology* is a healthy antidote to the nickel-in-the-slot mechanistic psychology of the extreme behaviorists.

The analogy is by no means exact—but a not altogether dissimilar situation prevails today among students of public opinion. Many of us in our revolt against the methods of Bagehot, Bryce, Bauer and Lowell have turned to the precise measurement of minutiae in a feverish search for instruments of understanding and control. The sphygmograph and the calculus have become standard equipment for the 1939 model of public opinion research. Nor is this altogether to be lamented. August Comte described the emergence of scientific method as the transition from imagination and fantasy to observation and experiment. Whatever makes for more precise and objective observation must be put down therefore as scientific advance. It is certainly true, too, that more accurate methods of measurement help to increase the possibility of control. The studies of Thurstone, Pressey, Terman, and Murphy among psychologists and of Beyle, Gosnell, Gallup, Ogburn, Rice and others among political scientists and sociologists represent notable contributions to the study of public opinion. Psycho-metrics and sociometrics are well on the way to becoming as rigorously scientific as physics and chemistry.

The sad paradox of this development for students of public opinion is that refinements of method too often lead to a progressive narrowing of the field of vision and yield increasingly precise descriptions of what is superficial or fragmentary, or both. There is, moreover, real danger that, in carrying over to the social sciences the methods of the natural sciences, we will avoid qualitative analysis in our preoccupation with quantitative analysis. We are likely to ask only How? How many? or How much? and to fight shy of asking Why? and To what purpose? As Karl Mannheim observes, we tend "to be content to attribute importance to what is measurable merely because it happens to be measurable." It may be true that quality is spread on quantity like butter on bread, but this is not always discernible in most of the quantitative studies that have thus far appeared.

There is an unfortunate tendency also to assume that verbal opinions bear a 1-to-1 relation to attitudes and that what a man says at any given time is an accurate representation of what he feels or what he will do at some future time. It is of course important and valuable to know that a given percentage of a scientifically selected sample of voters in October 1938 expressed a continuing loyalty to the New Deal or to the Wagner Act or to Martin Dies. It is at least equally important and valuable to know *why,* and yet on this question most current surveys throw precious little light. Unless we know why certain preferences or antipathies are expressed, we are almost as much in the dark as to what should be done to accelerate or retard a tendency, after the survey as before. It may be that by progressive particularization we can achieve results that will give us the answers we seek. But to follow this course will inevitably involve not only an elaboration of apparatus indescribably complex and costly, but may land us in such a wilderness of detail, in such an impenetrable forest of particulars, as to defy classification or generalization.

Nor is our position much improved if we turn from the statisticians who count and classify verbalisms to the physiological psychologists who measure neuro-muscular or cardiac reactions. It is no doubt true that alternations in blood pressure, psychogalvanic reflexes, and pulse rates, accompany, if they do not cause, emotional disturbances and psychophysical tensions which we describe as attitudes. The Lange-James theory which prefers to believe that we are afraid because we run, rather than that we run because we are afraid, has never been scientifically established. Indeed the studies of C. G. Sherrington, *The Integrative Action of the Nervous System,* and W. B. Cannon, *Bodily Changes in Pain, Hunger, Fear and Rage,* cast considerable doubt upon its validity. Professor Lasswell and others have demonstrated that significant physiological changes do occur in the psychoanalytical interview, without indicating whether this is cause or effect, and the Marston Lie Detector Test has made its way from the laboratory into the law courts. But the bearing of all this on the opinion and behavior of publics is by no means clear. The question remains whether, except by a process of dubious extrapolation, such refined analyses have any very significant relation to the dynamic factors involved in the current contest between labor and management or the innumerable other conflicts that arrest the attention of scientist and layman alike.

It may be true that psychophysical tensions in the individual personality are ultimately reflected in an accumulation of social tensions out of which mutual antagonisms grow, and that these may or may not be accurately represented by the verbal symbols of social intercourse. But in final analysis these social tensions arise out of impulses and drives which not even the most delicate instruments can detect, but which may nevertheless be common knowledge to every normal adult. The mechanisms and structures through which these drives operate are provided by the biological and social heritage which may be well or poorly adapted to their satisfaction.

When the customs and institutions of mankind stand inescapably in the way of primordial strivings for prestige, security, new experience, and the recreational satisfactions of procreation, the result will be either immorality or psychosis on the one hand, or social readjustment or revolution on the other. The resistance may be great or small, the threshold of social inhibition high or low, social customs and institutions flexible or rigidly inflexible. The degree of inflexibility and the extent of the resistance marks the difference between orderly progress and revolution. What I am saying is that the dynamics of social change are to be found in the continuous conflict between visceral hungers and the mores or between the libido and the law, using both terms in their widest sense. It is essentially what Freud means when he speaks of the ambivalent character of human behavior manifested in the struggle between the *id* and the *superego*. The resulting tensions form the basis for any real analysis of the etiology of attitudes. Where tension is great we speak of what Doob calls *dominant* attitudes or of what Wilhelm Bauer calls *dynamic* opinion; where tension approaches a minimum we speak of *latent* attitudes or *static* opinion. Compared to the task of understanding what is involved in the transition from latent or static to dominant or dynamic attitudes, the counting and classification of verbalisms or the recording of neuromuscular reactions is child's play.

If the student of opinion management is to assist in the release or resolution of those tensions which make for antagonism and conflict he will have to develop a broader view and a deeper insight than is displayed in a preoccupation with precise description of cultural superficialities. Once he realizes this he will see why such studies as Sumner's *Folkways,* Tawney's *Religion and the Rise of Capitalism,* Troeltsch's *Die Soziallehren der Christlichen Kirchen und Gruppen,* Veblen's *Theory of the Leisure Class,* Laski's *Rise of Liberalism,* Mannheim's *Ideology and Utopia,* Freud's *Totem and Taboo,* and *Civilization and Its Discontents,* Lasswell's *World Politics and Personal Insecurity,* the Lynds' *Middletown,* and even Arnold's *Folklore of Capitalism* are among the very best textbooks on public opinion.

AMBIVALENT BEHAVIOR PATTERNS

Whether we take the intellectualistic, naturalistic, or what Robert Binkley called the phenomenological view of opinion, we are compelled to consider the relation between verbal responses and overt behavior. The hiatus between the world of will and idea which troubled Arthur Schopenhauer is of no less concern to contemporary students of social control. It is a matter of common observation that what men say they believe is not always an accurate representation of what they really believe when measured in terms of behavior. Not infrequently an avowal of belief in the Christian beatitudes, or in Jeffersonian democracy, or state rights, or any one of a hundred other social myths bears little or no relation to actual behavior patterns. So great is this gap in the case of the Christian public that one wag was led to observe that Christians are people who believe in the Way of the Cross on Sunday and the Way of the Double-Cross on the other six days of the week. Who has not known the business or professional man who, having loudly declared his belief in free enterprise and rugged individualism proceeds to demand, almost in the same breath, legal restrictions, discriminating taxation, strict regulation, or outright suppression of his competitors? How many unfortunate Negroes have been lynched by lawless mobs in the name of law and order?

Such ambivalent behavior cannot be understood or predicted by elaborate compilations of verbal responses. Nor can it be smugly condemned or dismissed as the conduct of hypocrites and ignorant *untermensch*. Nor do we throw much light on the processes involved by asserting that the symbols used are meaningless or the conduct logically indefensible. What we are confronted with here is the ancient conflict between the worlds of will and idea. Or, to put the matter more bluntly, we are faced with a conflict between standards of conduct rationalized in social myths and the visceral hungers or drives which are the dynamic and impelling forces in human conduct.

There is a tendency to forget that words are instruments not only of reason but of will. When used logically according to the laws of identity, contradiction, excluded middle, and sufficient reason they are, as Thomas Hobbes said, wise men's counters. But they are equally and more commonly serviceable, without regard for logic and indeed in flagrant violation of the so-called laws of thought, as symbols to rationalize, i.e. give meaning to, impulsive demands. Used logically, words are among the major tools of science. Used non-logically they are the propagandists' stock in trade. They become fool's gold only when they cease to be of use to both science and sentiment, or when they are taken at face value without regard for the life situation of those who use them. It is then that we can realistically speak of the tyranny of words—i.e. when symbols become the masters rather than the servants of intelligence and will.

"I don't know what you mean by 'glory,'" said Alice.

Humpty Dumpty smiled contemptuously. "Of course you don't—till I tell you. I meant 'there's a nice knock-down argument for you.'"

"But," Alice objected, "'glory' doesn't mean a 'nice knock-down argument.'"

"When *I* use a word," Humpty Dumpty said, "it means just what I choose it to mean—neither more or less."

"The question is," said Alice, "whether you can make words mean so many different things."

"The question is," said Humpty Dumpty, "which is to be master—that's all."

Most words in common non-scientific usage are veritable boxes of Pandora—or, as Humpty Dumpty insisted, they are like capacious portmanteaux, out of which any number of meanings can be extracted to serve the person and his wishes. Symbols of identification, demand, and expectation, which comprise a large part of the language of social intercourse, are necessarily abstract. But, unlike the abstractions of science, they are universals under which many different, conflicting, and even contradictory particulars may be subsumed. The larger and more varied the public which they serve, the greater will be the variety of meanings to which they must give sanctuary and the more abstract and universal must they be. Their usefulness as propaganda is destroyed by particularization, since the more precise they become the smaller will be the public to which they afford suitable rationalizations of psychic tensions arising from the stress of social adjustment. For the function of social beliefs is to enable the individual or group to utilize the familiar psychopathological mechanisms of projection, introjection, transfer, etc., under the aegis of culturally commendable myths.

It follows, therefore, that any inquiry into the etiology of attitudes must take account of the function they fulfill for various publics and the individuals of which they are composed. Such an inquiry, as Franz Alexander says, "must always be a historical one, cultural, political and economic history, corresponding to the individual life history in psychoanalysis." We cannot exercise the demons of race prejudice, class hatred, religious bigotry, and political paranoia, unless we first know how such attitudes and beliefs function to make tolerable and meaningful the lives of those who hold them. We need to know more about the dynamic factors involved in the will to believe. This is particularly important for those of us who are interested in the rôle of propaganda in society.

Those symbol specialists whom we call propagandists merely offer symbolic representations, rationalizations if you will, of personal wishes and insecurities. Their programs win support in so far as they offer opportunity for the resolution of psychic tensions and an outlet for private aggressions. This is merely another way of saying with Harold Laski (*The State in Theory and Practice*) that the propagandist "does not influence the multitude unless the grievances for which he demands redress are grievances they profoundly feel." Essentially the same view was expressed by Aldous Huxley when he wrote, "Men accept the propagandists' theology or political theory because it apparently justifies and explains the sentiments and desires evoked in them by circumstances."

THE FUNCTION OF SYMBOLS

The validity of any ideology, symbol, slogan, or program depends not upon its logical form but upon its psychological function in any given culture. It is well to remember that although technology rests on logic and science, civilization, as a complex of routines, habits, institutions and loyalties, rests on sentiment. In a very real sense propagandists may be regarded as the architects of civilization since it is they who provide the symbols in terms of which men can unite with common loyalties in pursuit of common programs of action. The battle among rival political propagandas is at bottom a conflict between those who seek to perpetuate existing institutions and customs and those who seek to change them. Those who enjoy security, prestige, power and wealth (income, defense, and safety) under the prevailing system stand opposed to those who feel themselves thwarted and victimized by it. The outcome, barring perhaps the forcible suppression of opposition, will depend upon the extent and intensity of satisfaction or dissatisfaction with things as they are and the skill of myth makers, propagandists, in rationalizing existing loyalties or current discontents. Extensive and intensive preoccupation with competing ideologies is a crude measure of social instability just as the gap between science and technology on the one hand and social custom and usage on the other is a measure of social lag. The first indicates the predominance of dynamic attitudes generated by widespread discontent and the impoverishment of traditional myths. The second, social lag, indicates the predominance of static opinion or attitudes, characteristic of a culture which is unenlightened, perhaps, but contented and satisfied with its traditional mythology.

What I wish to make clear is that social beliefs or myths, abstract and meaningless as they may appear to the logician, have a vital function in the lives of human beings. That function is to give communicable meaning to actual experience and behavior or to serve as a compensatory device for the satisfaction of elementary human hungers. Our visceral itches and the habits growing out of them become meaningful when symbolized as love, or liberty, or justice, or democracy. Our individual wishes are glorified when translated into symbols claiming universal validity. Flight into the fantasy of racial or national grandeur is a soul-satisfying experience for anyone oppressed by a sense of personal fear or ineptitude.

There is more truth than poetry in George Schuyler's assertion that the Negro's greatest gift to America is flattery. "Look," he says, "for example, at Isadore Shankersoff. . . . In Russia he was a nobody—hoofed by everybody—the Mudsill of society. Quite naturally his inferiority complex was Brobdingnagian. Arriving under the shadow of the Statue of Liberty, he is still Isadore Shankersoff, the prey of sharpers and cheap grafters, but now he has moved considerably higher in the social scale. Though remaining mentally adolescent, he is no longer at the bottom; he is a white man! Over night he has become a member of the superior race. . . . For the first time in his life he is better than somebody." The same applies to Cyrus Dumbell, Anglo-Saxon textile slave from the Blue Ridge Mountains. Ignorant, propertyless, poor, exploited, "Cy has never had cause to think himself of any particular importance in the scheme of things, but his fellow workers tell him differently. He is a white man, they say, and therefore divinely appointed to 'keep the nigger down.' . . . Like the ancient Greeks and Romans, he now believes himself superior. . . . Whatever his troubles may be, he has learned . . . to blame it all on the dark folks, who are, he is now positive, without exception his inferiors." The lavish praise which we bestow upon the group with which we are identified affords satisfaction for narcissistic tendencies not otherwise realizable. Worship of the group becomes an oblique form of personal adoration.

It is comforting to believe that our successful offspring are merely chips off the old block or, contrariwise, that our problem children are products of an unfortunate environment and bad associates, outside their own home. There is abundant evidence to show that belief in heredity, as distinguished from knowledge of genetics, is correlated with social prestige, security, and income. Nor is it wholly unrelated to the desire for survival.

How joyful for the poor and disadvantaged to believe that heaven is their destination and that on the day of final judgment they will be first while their oppressors, real or fancied, roast in hell within full view of the elect as they sit in paradise! Or that $200 a month or $30 Every Thursday awaits them once their dear leader has routed the forces of darkness. To understand the full significance of these beliefs it is necessary to look beyond the symbols themselves to the dynamic factors, material or otherwise, affecting the lives of those who proclaim their devotion to them. The elaboration of symbols without regard for the social milieu in which they are to function is like building castles in the air. This, I take it, is what Marx meant when he said that "Man makes his own history but he does so only out of the materials at hand."

To discover what these materials are requires more careful research than the description and analysis of isolated S-R (stimulus-response) relationships. Our task is the study of the entire form and content of society—an inquiry into the nature and significance of social *gestalten*. For such is the character of social life that to shatter a myth is to shake to their roots the individuals concerned in it. It is to assail not only the pillars of society but the structure of the soul.

The Constitution of the United States, for example, is more than a brooding omnipresence in the sky. The parchment upon which the sacred words are inscribed is no more the Constitution than the New Testament is Christianity. The words, it is true, are there for everyone to read, but their significance—literal, analogical, or anagogical—does not depend upon the exigetical pronouncements of students skilled in the law. It depends upon acts of will and considerations of interest by those whose conduct it is sought to circumscribe within the ambit of the script as set forth. Demand for constitutional change is likely to represent not merely discontent with a particular clause or construction but revolt against an entire social order of which the Constitution as construed is the symbol. Similarly the cry "Preserve the Constitution" may be more than a liturgical mask for resistance to a particular amendment, although of course it may be that too. It may arise from a profound fear that the society in which those who raise the cry have prospered is in danger and the Constitution stands as the ark and covenant of what they know as civilization. It is not without significance, to cite one other example, that Professor Ferrero called his book on the fall of Rome *The Ruin of Ancient Civilization and the Triumph of Christianity.*

And so I return to my original proposition, namely, that students of public opinion must concern themselves with weightier matters than the precise description of trivialities, if they are to

163

understand the etiology of attitudes and the function of belief in society. They must inquire into the foundations, both material and psychological, of civilization and the dynamic forces which give it life. Such an inquiry will need not only the specialized competence of the scientist but something of the philosopher's vision to see life steadily and see it whole. Only if we do that can we hope to throw much light into the darkness that lies ahead.

11

PUBLIC OPINION
RESEARCH TECHNIQUES
SUGGESTED BY SOCIOLOGICAL
THEORY
Arnold M. Rose

PUBLIC OPINION research got its start in the practical hands of market researchers, industrial engineers, and newspaper or magazine editors. Academic psychologists and sociologists had an early interest in attitude studies in small groups, but did not participate significantly in public opinion polling until the mid-1930's. As a consequence, the research procedures were developed before social science theory could influence them very much. That lag has existed to the present time, although periodically psychologists and sociologists issue critiques of one or another aspect of public opinion research in terms of the knowledge built up in their specialized disciplines.[1] The lag is likely to continue far into the future, since public opinion polling faces its own dynamic problems, since the academic critics make their points didactically without illustrating them with concrete research, and since inertia or expense provide motives for the pollsters not to change their policies. Nevertheless, theoretical suggestions from the academic people will continue to flow into the public opinion literature, and will probably gradually influence public opinion research as they have in the past.

[1] See, for example: (1) Katz, Daniel, "Three Criteria: Knowledge, Conviction, and Significance," *Public Opinion Quarterly*, Vol. 4, No. 2 (1940), 277-284; (2) McNemar, Quinn, "Opinion-Attitude Methodology," *Psychological Bulletin*, 43 (1946), 289-374; (3) Lee, Alfred McClung, "Sociological Theory in Public Opinion and Attitude Studies," *American Sociological Review*, XII (1947), 312-323; (4) Lee, Alfred McClung, "Social Determinants of Public Opinion," *International Journal of Opinion and Attitude Research*, I (1947), 12-29; (5) Dollard, John, "Under What Conditions Do Opinions Predict Behavior?", *Public Opinion Quarterly*, Vol. 12, No. 4 (1948), 623-632.

Originally published in Volume 14, Number 2, 1950 of the *Public Opinion Quarterly*.

This article will take up some general sociological principles which have relevance for public opinion research but which do not seem to have been adequately presented in the public opinion literature.

"MASS" VERSUS "PUBLIC"

The first such general principle stems from a distinction made by Robert E. Park[2] between a public and a mass. The public is a social grouping in which all the members are actively in communication with each other, either directly or indirectly. A mass, on the other hand, is an agglomeration of people who are recipients of communication from a central source and who are not in communication with each other. An archetype of a public would be the informal group that meets at the village store when the mail comes in, and it might extend to a whole nation if there is some object of common interest about which people form chains of communication. An archetype of a mass would be a movie audience in which the participants—unaware of each other's identity—sit passively for several hours absorbing the communication from the screen, and it might extend to a whole nation if a widely scattered poster attracts their attention but is not considered interesting enough to talk about. In a public all points of view are brought to bear on an issue, each member is made aware of the varying viewpoints and of other relevant facts, and he is encouraged to present his own point of view to members of his community who engage him in conversation. In a mass, however, the only communication is from a single source (a "propagandist" in the broadest sense of the term), and the only opposition to the passive acceptance of this communication by an individual as his own point of view depends on incidental experience he may have had with the subject of the communication.

The result for the opinion itself is that public opinion is rational or rationalized, whereas mass opinion is superficial. That is, public opinion—as a resultant of many communications, of conflicts of diverse viewpoints, of modifications arising from the need to integrate the

[2] First presented in a doctor's dissertation, *Masse und Publikum* (Bonn, 1904), and later re-stated in Park, R. E., and Burgess, E. W., *Introduction to the Science of Sociology*, Chicago: University of Chicago Press, 1921, Chapters XII and XIII. For a recent statement, see: Blumer, Herbert, in Lee, A. M. (ed.), *An Outline of the Principles of Sociology*, New York, Barnes and Noble, 1947, pp. 241-250.

opinion with heterogeneous experiences and cultural backgrounds—is a product of much thought and may therefore be said to be rational. It is not necessarily logical in the sense that all fact and value premises are made explicit, and all relevant facts may not be available. But public opinion is rational in the sense that it has been thought over and integrated into the framework of existing ideas and attitudes. Mass opinion, on the other hand, is simply the resultant of an experience that is added to, not integrated into, the mind. It has no supports except that given to it by repetition.

The consequences for public opinion research are fairly obvious. If the opinion investigated meets the criteria of public opinion, it will come out without much probing (assuming there are no moral blocks to its expression), the individual respondent will have his mind fairly well made up and will not have to "hunt around" for an answer, and different wordings of the question should elicit the same answer. Sometimes the respondent will not find a check-list answer to the question sufficient to express his opinion fully and he will tend to inform the interviewer of conditions under which he would answer differently. If the opinion investigated is part of mass opinion, on the other hand, the respondent will have to hunt around for an answer. He will always be satisfied with a brief answer to the question, and different wordings of the question may elicit different answers from him.

We might also distinguish public opinion from mass opinion in terms of the greater stability of the former, since it is less subject to modification by propaganda. But this may be a misleading distinction, since public opinion is flexible and will change when social conditions change. Public opinion can also be changed if new facts and new points of view are brought to public attention. The distinction might better be stated in terms of the greater reliability of public opinion, in the technical sense of the term reliability. If an issue is talked over, thought over, and subjected to divergent points of view and varying considerations, then varying forms of a question, asked under varying circumstances, are much more likely to elicit the same results than if the issue is newly or superficially presented to the respondents. Public opinion is more stable than mass opinion also because propaganda which makes only an emotional appeal, and does not present new facts or new insights, is less able to influence it.

A second sociological principle which has implications for public opinion research is that in contemporary urbanized society an individual is likely to belong to a variety of unintegrated groups which make differing demands on him.[3] The very heterogeneity of our society which creates the diverse viewpoints that we wish to measure by polling people also creates a lack of uniformity in attitudes within a single individual. Probably few people anywhere have a completely uniform and consistent attitude toward any significant social object, and probably least of all in our own society. Each social role we take requires that we have a somewhat different attitude toward a social object. Just as we are somewhat different persons in our offices, in our homes, in our churches, in our various clubs, on our vacations, on our business trips, in our contacts with close friends and with superficial acquaintances, so we frequently have and express different attitudes toward the same social object in these varying social roles. It would be a valuable study in public opinion if the same questions on such subjects as international policy, race relations, women's role, or social security, were to be asked of the same group of subjects in two diverse social situations.

Public opinion researchers are accustomed to controlling their sample on "background factors" such as economic status, rural-urban residence, etc., in order to make sure that each segment of the population receives its proper weight in the expression of public opinion. They may also have to learn to control their sample for the type of social situation in which the opinion is expressed. The man who voices one opinion toward the role of women at the front door of his home may express a quite different attitude as he leaves his lodge. The person who holds forth on his political attitudes while relaxing in a park may manifest different political attitudes when confronted with a ballot in the privacy of a polling booth. These diversities may not exist for all kinds of attitudes or for all kinds of persons, but we do not yet know the conditions under which we may expect a single individual to hold different attitudes toward the same social object. Social psychologists have long observed that an individual's *behavior* is frequently not consistent; we must assume that his *attitudes* are also not consistent under varying circumstances. Since the public opinion researcher is con-

[3] See, for example: Cooley, C. H., *Social Process*, New York: C. Scribner's Sons, 1918; L. Wirth, "Urbanism as a Way of Life," *American Journal of Sociology*, XLIV (1938), 1-24.

cerned not with the attitudes of a single individual but with the net consequences of the attitudes of a whole population, he need not bother with all the possible variations. He must, however, if he is to present an accurate picture, weight his sample for the types of situations under which the opinion is expressed.

THE VARYING INTENSITY OF ORGANIZATIONAL INFLUENCES

A third sociological principle is that different groups or social roles have different significances for those who participate in them.[4] It is a continuing interest of sociologists to determine what social groups do most to satisfy needs or confer status, and what social roles are perceived as most desirable or most important. We are as yet far from having satisfactory knowledge; degree or intensity of group loyalty is still analyzed in terms of the factors influencing it rather than measured for comparisons among groups. There are studies which trace the declining influence of the family and nationality groups on adult attitudes, and others which suggest the growing influence of the occupational group. But these are hardly in a form to be used systematically by public opinion researchers in assigning weights to opinions from different groups or elicited in different situations. They can be used, however, for considerations such as the following: if a group known to have strong and growing value for its members begins to swing its weight to influence their attitudes in a certain direction, their attitudes are likely to move in that direction. This is probably one of the things that happened in the 1948 national elections, when the labor and farm organizations put more and more effort into their campaigns to get members to vote for certain candidates. The implication for the public opinion researcher, if he wishes to estimate trends, is to keep his eye on the activities of powerful social organizations as they increase or decrease their efforts to influence the opinions of their members.

COMMUNICATION BLOCKS IN SOCIETY

A fourth sociological principle is that broad population divisions —such as those of class and caste—may have excellent communication within them but that informal communications will much less readily

---

[4] The early sociologist who contributed most to the understanding of social roles was C. H. Cooley. See his *Human Nature and the Social Order*, New York: C. Scribner's Sons, 1902, and his *Social Organization*, New York: C. Scribner's Sons, 1909.

cross into another class or caste.[5] Since communication is the basis of public opinion formation, we should expect sharp divisions between classes and castes in both the content and trends of public opinion. In the past election or two, public opinion researchers were aware that factors considered important in making up the minds of whites had little influence among Negroes. We must be prepared for even more discoveries of that sort. It may be, for example, that as whites are more and more swayed by a fear of Communism and Russia, Negroes will have little of that experience. If this should be, the two groups will react quite differently to propaganda put out by the two dominant political parties. The same might be true of class divisions. For example, increasing exposure to the Republican campaign against the "welfare state" may gain that party increasing support from the middle class but decreasing support from the lower class. The public opinion researcher cannot assume that no change in the proportion of the total population favoring a certain policy means that there is stability in public opinion on this issue. He must, as he frequently does, break down his total population into those groups within which different communications or varying interpretations of the same communication may be circulating.

Such broad social groupings as class and caste also embody culture differences which manifest themselves in public opinion research as differences in the connotations of words. Public opinion researchers have become aware of the need for changing both the form and wording of a question when they wish to secure comparable findings in two different countries. They need to adapt the same principle—although in lesser degree—when they move from one class to another. The procedure now widely used is to try and find words and question forms which transcend culture differences within our society. But this is not always possible, as for example Kinsey found in the study of the most common forms of sex behavior. Variations in wording can be used to increase the comparability and generalizability of findings, if we recognize significant culture differences within the American population.

MORES AND PSEUDO-MORES AS A PROBLEM FOR POLLSTERS

A familiar sociological concept is that of the mores. Its very popu-

5 See, for example: Davis, Allison, Burleigh B. Gardner and Mary R. Gardner, *Deep South*, Chicago: University of Chicago Press, 1941.

larity has lessened its scientific usefulness, since its extended use has changed the meaning which Sumner[6] originally gave it. Sumner used the concept "mores" to refer to those traditional ways of doing things from which no deviation could be tolerated, as any deviation was regarded as a threat to the existence of the group and all its moral standards. To most people who use the term "mores" today, it simply means "customs" without any connotation of necessity or social welfare. Although few practices in our society correspond to Sumner's use of the term, occasionally in the course of public opinion research we come across people who regard it as grossly indecent or socially dangerous to express certain attitudes. The question may then be raised as to whether we have encountered a true example of the mores and had better not ask questions on that subject of certain groups in the population. Subjects on which such experiences have been had include religion, sexual practices, certain kinds of race relations, and violent crimes. Since mores are never matters of public opinion, there can be no discussion of them or questions about them.

Before we reach the conclusion that we are up against the mores when we ask questions that elicit strong or violent resistances, and that the subject under study cannot be explored by opinion research, we might examine the possibility that they are rather pseudo-mores. Pseudo-mores may be defined as those customs which people believe to be mores —for other people—but from which they personally deviate secretly. Occasionally good friends will exchange information about these deviations, but they would be afraid to speak about them publicly. The Kinsey study has, of course, revealed that several behavior patterns and attitudes which were previously thought to be in the mores actually are pseudo-mores. On the surface, the pseudo-mores are as difficult to investigate through public opinion research techniques as are the mores themselves, although for different reasons. However, by stating questions indirectly rather than directly, and by creating an assumption that the interviewer is aware and tolerant of deviant practices, the pseudo-mores can frequently be successfully studied in public opinion surveys. During World War II, such an approach revealed a surprisingly large proportion of persons (in a non-representative sample) who admitted a hope that the war would continue for some time.

[6] Sumner, William Graham, *Folkways*, Boston: Ginn and Company, 1906.

171

The whole matter of public versus private attitudes used to intrigue social psychologists,[7] but has recently been ignored in the quest for practical and measurable results. In earlier decades, perhaps too much was made of the difference. It was then maintained that most people held both public and private attitudes about most subjects, and that it was impossible to learn about private attitudes simply by asking questions. Since it was later found that public opinion research techniques elicited much of what researchers and practical people wanted, the distinction gradually came to be ignored. The distinction might prove valuable, however, in studying opinions about certain subjects (even outside the pseudo-mores). A number of recent sociological studies have indicated that subjects which involve the highest types of group ideals are probably the focus of at least two kinds of attitudes. Questions regarding the role of fairness and impartiality in behavior toward minority groups, for example, will usually elicit a large proportion of expressions of desire to be fair and yet of willingness to practice discrimination.[8] Both of these are public attitudes in response to two different kinds of questions—some of the general kind, others referring specifically to minority groups. The inconsistency suggests that there are private attitudes behind both of these public attitudes which can only be inferred, and that behavior is predicated on private as well as public attitudes. People who express attitudes of prejudice toward a minority group do not manifest only discriminatory behavior patterns toward them; nor do people who express general principles of fairness and equalitarianism manifest only non-discriminatory behavior patterns. This suggests to the public opinion researcher that he should try to elicit the entire gamut of public attitudes which might be relevant to a given behavior pattern, so that private attitudes might more readily be inferred. Or, better still, the public opinion researcher may try to experiment with the behavior of his respondents and then ask them questions as they respond in varying ways. The rationalized answers obtained under those circumstances are very revealing of private attitudes.

[7] See, for example, Faris, Ellsworth, *The Nature of Human Nature*, New York: McGraw-Hill Book Company, 1937, pp. 144-154.

[8] Myrdal, Gunnar, with the assistance of Richard Sterner and Arnold Rose, *An American Dilemma*, New York: Harper and Brothers, 1944.

To illustrate, we shall cite two findings from a fascinating study by Gerhart Saenger,[9] throughout which the author recognizes the need to plumb for private attitudes as the basis for understanding actual behavior. Saenger interviewed persons who had just been waited on by Negro sales clerks in a large department store but who did not know they had been observed by the interviewers, and an equal number who had been waited on by white sales clerks at the same counters. The proportions opposing Negro sales clerks in department stores were about the same in both groups! He also found that some of those who had just been waited on by Negro sales clerks in food departments said they would not be opposed to being waited on by Negroes in food departments but would be in clothing departments, while some of those who had just been waited on by Negro sales clerks in clothing departments said they would not be opposed to Negroes in clothing departments but would be opposed in food departments. On the basis of these and similar findings he was able to predict that the department store would not lose customers by hiring Negro sales personnel—a prediction later verified as accurate by the manager. To have accepted the simple proportion of those opposed to Negro sales clerks as an indication that the new policy would hurt sales, without having observed the respondents' behavior, would have led to an error.

THE VALUE OF ANONYMITY

One other sociological theory may be called on for guidance to the public opinion researcher. This is Simmel's theory of the "Stranger."[10] The public opinion interviewer—even though he identifies his purpose and indicates the organization for which he works—is a stranger to practically all his respondents. It is by virtue of his stranger's role, especially the anonymity which he can allow the respondent to maintain toward him, that the interviewer can secure some of his most confidential and honest answers. Having a mistaken idea of rapport, some interviewers strive to establish their personal identity and a possible relation to the respondent. If the interviewer's effort is successful, the respondent can no longer answer the questions freely and with the sense of security that comes from the belief that his answers can

[9] "Customer Reactions to the Integration of Negro Sales Personnel," paper read to the American Psychological Association, Boston, September 1948.

[10] Simmel, Georg, *Soziologie*, Leipzig: Duncker and Humblot, 1908, 685-691.

never reflect back on him or be used against him. If he loses his anonymity, the respondent will answer in a social role—as an acquaintance whose statements might be repeated to those who know him as a certain type of person. This may well serve to inhibit the fullness or accuracy of his answers. It is necessary, of course, for the interviewer to establish his authenticity by indicating his innocent purpose and the legitimacy of his organization. He may also seek to establish confidence in himself as a person. But beyond that he should remain a stranger, for the purposes of most kinds of public opinion research. The suggestion is of greatest value in small towns, where the chances are large that the interviewer has an acquaintanceship with the respondent. In such a setting it is most often wise to import an interviewer from outside the town.

The sociological theories from which our suggestions for public opinion research are drawn have a long and respected tradition of thought and empirical research to support them. They are not completely verified, of course, and when transferred from one scientific setting to the new one of public opinion research they are in special need of further testing. They are therefore presented in the form of suggestions. They are especially valuable, however, as they help to throw additional light on some problems which have long disturbed the more thoughtful public opinion researchers and on other matters which have never been questioned in public opinion research. The older and more theoretical disciplines need to be probed constantly for such suggestions if the new field of research is to have maximum validity.

12

THE FUNCTIONAL
APPROACH TO THE
STUDY OF ATTITUDES
Daniel Katz

THE STUDY of opinion formation and attitude change is basic to an understanding of the public opinion process even though it should not be equated with this process. The public opinion process is one phase of the influencing of collective decisions, and its investigation involves knowledge of channels of communication, of the power structures of a society, of the character of mass media, of the relation between elites, factions and masses, of the role of formal and informal leaders, of the institutionalized access to officials. But the raw material out of which public opinion develops is to be found in the attitudes of individuals, whether they be followers or leaders and whether these attitudes be at the general level of tendencies to conform to legitimate authority or majority opinion or at the specific level of favoring or opposing the particular aspects of the issue under consideration. The nature of the organization of attitudes within the personality and the processes which account for attitude change are thus critical areas for the understanding of the collective product known as public opinion.

EARLY APPROACHES TO THE STUDY OF ATTITUDE AND OPINION

There have been two main streams of thinking with respect to the determination of man's attitudes. The one tradition assumes an irra-

Originally published in Volume 24, Number 2, 1960 of the *Public Opinion Quarterly*.

tional model of man: specifically it holds that men have very limited powers of reason and reflection, weak capacity to discriminate, only the most primitive self-insight, and very short memories. Whatever mental capacities people do possess are easily overwhelmed by emotional forces and appeals to self-interest and vanity. The early books on the psychology of advertising, with their emphasis on the doctrine of suggestion, exemplify this approach. One expression of this philosophy is in the propagandist's concern with tricks and traps to manipulate the public. A modern form of it appears in *The Hidden Persuaders*, or the use of subliminal and marginal suggestion, or the devices supposedly employed by "the Madison Avenue boys." Experiments to support this line of thinking started with laboratory demonstrations of the power of hypnotic suggestion and were soon extended to show that people would change their attitudes in an uncritical manner under the influence of the prestige of authority and numbers. For example, individuals would accept or reject the same idea depending upon whether it came from a positive or a negative prestige source.[1]

The second approach is that of the ideologist who invokes a rational model of man. It assumes that the human being has a cerebral cortex, that he seeks understanding, that he consistently attempts to make sense of the world about him, that he possesses discriminating and reasoning powers which will assert themselves over time, and that he is capable of self-criticism and self-insight. It relies heavily upon getting adequate information to people. Our educational system is based upon this rational model. The present emphasis upon the improvement of communication, upon developing more adequate channels of two-way communication, of conferences and institutes, upon bringing people together to interchange ideas, are all indications of the belief in the importance of intelligence and comprehension in the formation and change of men's opinions.

Now either school of thought can point to evidence which supports its assumptions, and can make fairly damaging criticisms of its opponent. Solomon Asch and his colleagues, in attacking the irrational model, have called attention to the biased character of the old experiments on prestige suggestion which gave the subject little opportunity to demonstrate critical thinking.[2] And further exploration of subjects in these stupid situations does indicate that they try to make sense of a nonsensical matter as far as possible. Though the same statement is presented by the experimenter to two groups, the first time as coming from a positive source and the second time as coming from a negative

[1] Muzafer Sherif, *The Psychology of Social Norms*, New York, Harper, 1936.
[2] Solomon E. Asch, *Social Psychology*, New York, Prentice-Hall, 1952.

source, it is given a different meaning dependent upon the context in which it appears.[3] Thus the experimental subject does his best to give some rational meaning to the problem. On the other hand, a large body of experimental work indicates that there are many limitations in the rational approach in that people see their world in terms of their own needs, remember what they want to remember, and interpret information on the basis of wishful thinking. H. H. Hyman and P. Sheatsley have demonstrated that these experimental results have direct relevance to information campaigns directed at influencing public opinion.[4] These authors assembled facts about such campaigns and showed conclusively that increasing the flow of information to people does not necessarily increase the knowledge absorbed or produce the attitude changes desired.

The major difficulty with these conflicting approaches is their lack of specification of the conditions under which men do act as the theory would predict. For the facts are that people do act at times as if they had been decorticated and at times with intelligence and comprehension. And people themselves do recognize that on occasion they have behaved blindly, impulsively, and thoughtlessly. A second major difficulty is that the rationality-irrationality dimension is not clearly defined. At the extremes it is easy to point to examples, as in the case of the acceptance of stupid suggestions under emotional stress on the one hand, or brilliant problem solving on the other; but this does not provide adequate guidance for the many cases in the middle of the scale where one attempts to discriminate between rationalization and reason.

RECONCILIATION OF THE CONFLICT IN A FUNCTIONAL APPROACH

The conflict between the rationality and irrationality models was saved from becoming a worthless debate because of the experimentation and research suggested by these models. The findings of this research pointed toward the elements of truth in each approach and gave some indication of the conditions under which each model could make fairly accurate predictions. In general the irrational approach was at its best where the situation imposed heavy restrictions upon search behavior and response alternatives. Where individuals must

[3] *Ibid.*, pp. 426-427. The following statement was attributed to its rightful author, John Adams, for some subjects and to Karl Marx for others: "those who hold and those who are without property have ever formed distinct interests in society." When the statement was attributed to Marx, this type of comment appeared: "Marx is stressing the need for a redistribution of wealth." When it was attributed to Adams, this comment appeared: "This social division is innate in mankind."

[4] Herbert H. Hyman and Paul B. Sheatsley, "Some Reasons Why Information Campaigns Fail," *Public Opinion Quarterly*, Vol. 11, 1947, pp. 413-423.

give quick responses without adequate opportunities to explore the nature of the problem, where there are very few response alternatives available to them, where their own deep emotional needs are aroused, they will in general react much as does the unthinking subject under hypnosis. On the other hand, where the individual can have more adequate commerce with the relevant environmental setting, where he has time to obtain more feedback from his reality testing, and where he has a number of realistic choices, his behavior will reflect the use of his rational faculties.[5] The child will often respond to the directive of the parent not by implicit obedience but by testing out whether or not the parent really meant what he said.

Many of the papers in this issue, which describe research and theory concerning consistency and consonance, represent one outcome of the rationality model. The theory of psychological consonance, or cognitive balance, assumes that man attempts to reduce discrepancies in his beliefs, attitudes, and behavior by appropriate changes in these processes. While the emphasis here is upon consistency or logicality, the theory deals with all dissonances, no matter how produced. Thus they could result from irrational factors of distorted perception and wishful thinking as well as from rational factors of realistic appraisal of a problem and an accurate estimate of its consequences. Moreover, the theory would predict only that the individual will move to reduce dissonance, whether such movement is a good adjustment to the world or leads to the delusional systems of the paranoiac. In a sense, then, this theory would avoid the conflict between the old approaches of the rational and the irrational man by not dealing with the specific antecedent causes of behavior or with the particular ways in which the individual solves his problems.

In addition to the present preoccupation with the development of formal models concerned with cognitive balance and consonance, there is a growing interest in a more comprehensive framework for dealing with the complex variables and for bringing order within the field. The thoughtful system of Ulf Himmelstrand, presented in the following pages, is one such attempt. Another point of departure is represented by two groups of workers who have organized their theories around the functions which attitudes perform for the personality. Sarnoff, Katz, and McClintock, in taking this functional approach, have given primary attention to the motivational bases of attitudes and the

[5] William A. Scott points out that in the area of international relations the incompleteness and remoteness of the information and the lack of pressures on the individual to defend his views results in inconsistencies. Inconsistent elements with respect to a system of international beliefs may, however, be consistent with the larger system of the personality. "Rationality and Non-rationality of International Attitudes," *Journal of Conflict Resolution*, Vol. 2, 1958, pp. 9-16.

processes of attitude change.[6] The basic assumption of this group is that both attitude formation and attitude change must be understood in terms of the needs they serve and that, as these motivational processes differ, so too will the conditions and techniques for attitude change. Smith, Bruner, and White have also analyzed the different functions which attitudes perform for the personality.[7] Both groups present essentially the same functions, but Smith, Bruner, and White give more attention to perceptual and cognitive processes and Sarnoff, Katz, and McClintock to the specific conditions of attitude change.

The importance of the functional approach is threefold. (1) Many previous studies of attitude change have dealt with factors which are not genuine psychological variables, for example, the effect on group prejudice of contact between two groups, or the exposure of a group of subjects to a communication in the mass media. Now contact serves different psychological functions for the individual and merely knowing that people have seen a movie or watched a television program tells us nothing about the personal values engaged or not engaged by such a presentation. If, however, we can gear our research to the functions attitudes perform, we can develop some generalizations about human behavior. Dealing with nonfunctional variables makes such generalization difficult, if not impossible.

(2) By concerning ourselves with the different functions attitudes can perform we can avoid the great error of oversimplification—the error of attributing a single cause to given types of attitude. It was once popular to ascribe radicalism in economic and political matters to the psychopathology of the insecure and to attribute conservatism to the rigidity of the mentally aged. At the present time it is common practice to see in attitudes of group prejudice the repressed hostilities stemming from childhood frustrations, though Hyman and Sheatsley have pointed out that prejudiced attitudes can serve a normative function of gaining acceptance in one's own group as readily as releasing unconscious hatred.[8] In short, not only are there a number of motivational forces to take into account in considering attitudes and behavior, but the same attitude can have a different motivational basis in different people.

(3) Finally, recognition of the complex motivational sources of behavior can help to remedy the neglect in general theories which lack

[6] Irving Sarnoff and Daniel Katz, "The Motivational Bases of Attitude Change," *Journal of Abnormal and Social Psychology*, Vol. 49, 1954, pp. 115-124.

[7] M. Brewster Smith, Jerome S. Bruner, and Robert W. White, *Opinions and Personality*, New York, Wiley, 1956.

[8] Herbert H. Hyman and Paul B. Sheatsley, "The Authoritarian Personality: A Methodological Critique," in Richard Christie and Marie Jahoda, editors, *Studies in the Scope and Method of the Authoritarian Personality*, Glencoe, Ill., Free Press, 1954, pp. 50-122.

specification of conditions under which given types of attitude will change. Gestalt theory tells us, for example, that attitudes will change to give better cognitive organization to the psychological field. This theoretical generalization is suggestive, but to carry out significant research we need some middle-level concepts to bridge the gap between a high level of abstraction and particularistic or phenotypical events. We need concepts that will point toward the types of motive and methods of motive satisfaction which are operative in bringing about cognitive reorganization.

Before we attempt a detailed analysis of the four major functions which attitudes can serve, it is appropriate to consider the nature of attitudes, their dimensions, and their relations to other psychological structures and processes.

NATURE OF ATTITUDES: THEIR DIMENSIONS

Attitude is the predisposition of the individual to evaluate some symbol or object or aspect of his world in a favorable or unfavorable manner. Opinion is the verbal expression of an attitude, but attitudes can also be expressed in nonverbal behavior. Attitudes include both the affective, or feeling core of liking or disliking, and the cognitive, or belief, elements which describe the object of the attitude, its characteristics, and its relations to other objects. All attitudes thus include beliefs, but not all beliefs are attitudes. When specific attitudes are organized into a hierarchical structure, they comprise *value systems*. Thus a person may not only hold specific attitudes against deficit spending and unbalanced budgets but may also have a systematic organization of such beliefs and attitudes in the form of a value system of economic conservatism.

The dimensions of attitudes can be stated more precisely if the above distinctions between beliefs and feelings and attitudes and value systems are kept in mind. The *intensity* of an attitude refers to the strength of the *affective* component. In fact, rating scales and even Thurstone scales deal primarily with the intensity of feeling of the individual for or against some social object. The cognitive, or belief, component suggests two additional dimensions, the *specificity* or *generality* of the attitude and the *degree of differentiation* of the beliefs. Differentiation refers to the number of beliefs or cognitive items contained in the attitude, and the general assumption is that the simpler the attitude in cognitive structure the easier it is to change.[9] For simple structures there is no defense in depth, and once a single item of belief has been changed the attitude will change. A rather different dimension of attitude is the *number and strength of its linkages to a related*

[9] David Krech and Richard S. Crutchfield, *Theory and Problems of Social Psychology*, New York, McGraw-Hill, 1948, pp. 160-163.

value system. If an attitude favoring budget balancing by the Federal government is tied in strongly with a value system of economic conservatism, it will be more difficult to change than if it were a fairly isolated attitude of the person. Finally, the relation of the value system to the personality is a consideration of first importance. If an attitude is tied to a value system which is closely related to, or which consists of, the individual's conception of himself, then the appropriate change procedures become more complex. The *centrality* of an attitude refers to its role as part of a value system which is closely related to the individual's self-concept.

An additional aspect of attitudes is not clearly described in most theories, namely, their relation to action or overt behavior. Though behavior related to the attitude has other determinants than the attitude itself, it is also true that some attitudes in themselves have more of what Cartwright calls an action structure than do others.[10] Brewster Smith refers to this dimension as policy orientation[11] and Katz and Stotland speak of it as the action component.[12] For example, while many people have attitudes of approval toward one or the other of the two political parties, these attitudes will differ in their structure with respect to relevant action. One man may be prepared to vote on election day and will know where and when he should vote and will go to the polls no matter what the weather or how great the inconvenience. Another man will only vote if a party worker calls for him in a car. Himmelstrand's work is concerned with all aspects of the relationship between attitude and behavior, but he deals with the action structure of the attitude itself by distinguishing between attitudes where the affect is tied to verbal expression and attitudes where the affect is tied to behavior concerned with more objective referents of the attitude.[13] In the first case an individual derives satisfaction from talking about a problem; in the second case he derives satisfaction from taking some form of concrete action.

Attempts to change attitudes can be directed primarily at the belief component or at the feeling, or affective, component. Rosenberg theorizes that an effective change in one component will result in changes in the other component and presents experimental evidence to confirm this hypothesis.[14] For example, a political candidate will

[10] Dorwin Cartwright, "Some Principles of Mass Persuasion," *Human Relations*, Vol. 2, 1949, pp. 253-267.

[11] M. Brewster Smith, "The Personal Setting of Public Opinions: A Study of Attitudes toward Russia," *Public Opinion Quarterly*, Vol. 11, 1947, pp. 507-523.

[12] Daniel Katz and Ezra Stotland, "A Preliminary Statement to a Theory of Attitude Structure and Change," in Sigmund Koch, editor, *Psychology: A Study of a Science*, Vol. 3, New York, McGraw-Hill, 1959, pp. 423-475.

[13] See pages 224-250 of this issue of the *Quarterly*.

[14] See pages 319-340 of this issue of the *Quarterly*.

often attempt to win people by making them like him and dislike his opponent, and thus communicate affect rather than ideas. If he is successful, people will not only like him but entertain favorable beliefs about him. Another candidate may deal primarily with ideas and hope that, if he can change people's beliefs about an issue, their feelings will also change.

The major functions which attitudes perform for the personality can be grouped according to their motivational basis as follows:

1. *The instrumental, adjustive, or utilitarian function* upon which Jeremy Bentham and the utilitarians constructed their model of man. A modern expression of this approach can be found in behavioristic learning theory.
2. *The ego-defensive function* in which the person protects himself from acknowledging the basic truths about himself or the harsh realities in his external world. Freudian psychology and neo-Freudian thinking have been preoccupied with this type of motivation and its outcomes.
3. *The value-expressive function* in which the individual derives satisfactions from expressing attitudes appropriate to his personal values and to his concept of himself. This function is central to doctrines of ego psychology which stress the importance of self-expression, self-development, and self-realization.
4. *The knowledge function* based upon the individual's need to give adequate structure to his universe. The search for meaning, the need to understand, the trend toward better organization of perceptions and beliefs to provide clarity and consistency for the individual, are other descriptions of this function. The development of principles about perceptual and cognitive structure have been the contribution of Gestalt psychology.

Stated simply, the functional approach is the attempt to understand the reasons people hold the attitudes they do. The reasons, however, are at the level of psychological motivations and not of the accidents of external events and circumstances. Unless we know the psychological need which is met by the holding of an attitude we are in a poor position to predict when and how it will change. Moreover, the same attitude expressed toward a political candidate may not perform the same function for all the people who express it. And while many attitudes are predominantly in the service of a single type of motivational process, as described above, other attitudes may serve more than one purpose for the individual. A fuller discussion of how attitudes serve the above four functions is in order.

1. The adjustment function. Essentially this function is a recognition of the fact that people strive to maximize the rewards in their external environment and to minimize the penalties. The child develops favorable attitudes toward the objects in his world which are associated with the satisfactions of his needs and unfavorable attitudes toward objects which thwart him or punish him. Attitudes acquired in the service of the adjustment function are either the means for reaching the desired goal or avoiding the undesirable one, or are affective associations based upon experiences in attaining motive satisfactions.[15] The attitudes of the worker favoring a political party which will advance his economic lot are an example of the first type of utilitarian attitude. The pleasant image one has of one's favorite food is an example of the second type of utilitarian attitude.

In general, then, the dynamics of attitude formation with respect to the adjustment function are dependent upon present or past perceptions of the utility of the attitudinal object for the individual. The clarity, consistency, and nearness of rewards and punishments, as they relate to the individual's activities and goals, are important factors in the acquisition of such attitudes. Both attitudes and habits are formed toward specific objects, people, and symbols as they satisfy specific needs. The closer these objects are to actual need satisfaction and the more they are clearly perceived as relevant to need satisfaction, the greater are the probabilities of positive attitude formation. These principles of attitude formation are often observed in the breach rather than the compliance. In industry, management frequently expects to create favorable attitudes toward job performance through programs for making the company more attractive to the worker, such as providing recreational facilities and fringe benefits. Such programs, however, are much more likely to produce favorable attitudes toward the company as a desirable place to work than toward performance on the job. The company benefits and advantages are applied across the board to all employees and are not specifically relevant to increased effort in task performance by the individual worker.

Consistency of reward and punishment also contributes to the clarity of the instrumental object for goal attainment. If a political party bestows recognition and favors on party workers in an unpredictable and inconsistent fashion, it will destroy the favorable evaluation of the importance of working hard for the party among those whose motivation is of the utilitarian sort. But, curiously, while consistency of reward needs to be observed, 100 per cent consistency is not as effective as a pattern which is usually consistent but in which there are some lapses. When animal or human subjects are invariably rewarded for a correct performance, they do not retain their learned responses as well as when the reward is sometimes skipped.[16]

15 Katz and Stotland, *op.cit.*, pp. 434-443.
16 William O. Jenkins and Julian C. Stanley, "Partial Reinforcement: A Review and Critique," *Psychological Bulletin*, Vol. 47, 1950, pp. 193-234.

2. *The ego-defensive function*. People not only seek to make the most of their external world and what it offers, but they also expend a great deal of their energy on living with themselves. The mechanisms by which the individual protects his ego from his own unacceptable impulses and from the knowledge of threatening forces from without, and the methods by which he reduces his anxieties created by such problems, are known as mechanisms of ego defense. A more complete account of their origin and nature will be found in Sarnoff's article in this issue.[17] They include the devices by which the individual avoids facing either the inner reality of the kind of person he is, or the outer reality of the dangers the world holds for him. They stem basically from internal conflict with its resulting insecurities. In one sense the mechanisms of defense are adaptive in temporarily removing the sharp edges of conflict and in saving the individual from complete disaster. In another sense they are not adaptive in that they handicap the individual in his social adjustments and in obtaining the maximum satisfactions available to him from the world in which he lives. The worker who persistently quarrels with his boss and with his fellow workers, because he is acting out some of his own internal conflicts, may in this manner relieve himself of some of the emotional tensions which beset him. He is not, however, solving his problem of adjusting to his work situation and thus may deprive himself of advancement or even of steady employment.

Defense mechanisms, Miller and Swanson point out, may be classified into two families on the basis of the more or less primitive nature of the devices employed.[18] The first family, more primitive in nature, are more socially handicapping and consist of denial and complete avoidance. The individual in such cases obliterates through withdrawal and denial the realities which confront him. The exaggerated case of such primitive mechanisms is the fantasy world of the paranoiac. The second type of defense is less handicapping and makes for distortion rather than denial. It includes rationalization, projection, and displacement.

Many of our attitudes have the function of defending our self-image. When we cannot admit to ourselves that we have deep feelings of inferiority we may project those feelings onto some convenient minority group and bolster our egos by attitudes of superiority toward this underprivileged group. The formation of such defensive attitudes differs in essential ways from the formation of attitudes which serve the adjustment function. They proceed from within the person, and the objects and situation to which they are attached are merely con-

17 See pp. 251-279.
18 Daniel R. Miller and Guy E. Swanson, *Inner Conflict and Defense*, New York, Holt, 1960, pp. 194-288.

venient outlets for their expression. Not all targets are equally satisfactory for a given defense mechanism, but the point is that the attitude is not created by the target but by the individual's emotional conflicts. And when no convenient target exists the individual will create one. Utilitarian attitudes, on the other hand, are formed with specific reference to the nature of the attitudinal object. They are thus appropriate to the nature of the social world to which they are geared. The high school student who values high grades because he wants to be admitted to a good college has a utilitarian attitude appropriate to the situation to which it is related.

All people employ defense mechanisms, but they differ with respect to the extent that they use them and some of their attitudes may be more defensive in function than others. It follows that the techniques and conditions for attitude change will not be the same for ego-defensive as for utilitarian attitudes.

Moreover, though people are ordinarily unaware of their defense mechanisms, especially at the time of employing them, they differ with respect to the amount of insight they may show at some later time about their use of defenses. In some cases they recognize that they have been protecting their egos without knowing the reason why. In other cases they may not even be aware of the devices they have been using to delude themselves.

3. The value-expressive function. While many attitudes have the function of preventing the individual from revealing to himself and others his true nature, other attitudes have the function of giving positive expression to his central values and to the type of person he conceives himself to be. A man may consider himself to be an enlightened conservative or an internationalist or a liberal, and will hold attitudes which are the appropriate indication of his central values. Thus we need to take account of the fact that not all behavior has the negative function of reducing the tensions of biological drives or of internal conflicts. Satisfactions also accrue to the person from the expression of attitudes which reflect his cherished beliefs and his self-image. The reward to the person in these instances is not so much a matter of gaining social recognition or monetary rewards as of establishing his self-identity and confirming his notion of the sort of person he sees himself to be. The gratifications obtained from value expression may go beyond the confirmation of self-identity. Just as we find satisfaction in the exercise of our talents and abilities, so we find reward in the expression of any attributes associated with our egos.

Value-expressive attitudes not only give clarity to the self-image but also mold that self-image closer to the heart's desire. The teenager who by dress and speech establishes his identity as similar to his own peer group may appear to the outsider a weakling and a craven conformer.

To himself he is asserting his independence of the adult world to which he has rendered childlike subservience and conformity all his life. Very early in the development of the personality the need for clarity of self-image is important—the need to know "who I am." Later it may be even more important to know that in some measure I am the type of person I want to be. Even as adults, however, the clarity and stability of the self-image is of primary significance. Just as the kind, considerate person will cover over his acts of selfishness, so too will the ruthless individualist become confused and embarrassed by his acts of sympathetic compassion. One reason it is difficult to change the character of the adult is that he is not comfortable with the new "me." Group support for such personality change is almost a necessity, as in Alcoholics Anonymous, so that the individual is aware of approval of his new self by people who are like him.

The socialization process during the formative years sets the basic outlines for the individual's self-concept. Parents constantly hold up before the child the model of the good character they want him to be. A good boy eats his spinach, does not hit girls, etc. The candy and the stick are less in evidence in training the child than the constant appeal to his notion of his own character. It is small wonder, then, that children reflect the acceptance of this model by inquiring about the characters of the actors in every drama, whether it be a television play, a political contest, or a war, wanting to know who are the "good guys" and who are the "bad guys." Even as adults we persist in labeling others in the terms of such character images. Joe McCarthy and his cause collapsed in fantastic fashion when the telecast of the Army hearings showed him in the role of the villain attacking the gentle, good man represented by Joseph Welch.

A related but somewhat different process from childhood socialization takes place when individuals enter a new group or organization. The individual will often take over and internalize the values of the group. What accounts, however, for the fact that sometimes this occurs and sometimes it does not? Four factors are probably operative, and some combination of them may be necessary for internalization. (1) The values of the new group may be highly consistent with existing values central to the personality. The girl who enters the nursing profession finds it congenial to consider herself a good nurse because of previous values of the importance of contributing to the welfare of others. (2) The new group may in its ideology have a clear model of what the good group member should be like and may persistently indoctrinate group members in these terms. One of the reasons for the code of conduct for members of the armed forces, devised after the revelations about the conduct of American prisoners in the Korean War, was to attempt to establish a model for what a good soldier does and does not do. (3) The activities of the group in moving toward its goal permit the individual genuine opportunity for participation. To become ego-involved so that he can internalize group values, the new member must find one of two conditions. The group activity open to him must tap his talents and abilities so that his chance to show what he is worth can be tied into the group effort. Or else the activities of the group must give him an active voice in group decisions. His particular talents and abilities may not be tapped but he does have the opportunity to enter into group decisions, and thus his need for self-determination is satisfied. He then identifies with the group in which such opportunities for ego-involvement are available. It is not necessary that opportunities for self-expression and self-determination be of great magnitude in an objective sense, so long as they are important for the psychological economy of the individuals themselves. (4) Finally, the individual may come to see himself as a group member if he can share in the rewards of group activity which includes his own efforts. The worker may not play much of a part in building a ship or make any decisions in the process of building it. Nevertheless, if he and his fellow workers are given a share in every boat they build and a return on the proceeds from the earnings of the ship, they may soon come to identify with the ship-building company and see themselves as builders of ships.

4. The knowledge function. Individuals not only acquire beliefs in the interest of satisfying various specific needs, they also seek knowledge to give meaning to what would otherwise be an unorganized chaotic universe. People need standards or frames of reference for understanding their world, and attitudes help to supply such standards. The problem of understanding, as John Dewey made clear years ago, is one "of introducing (1) *definiteness* and *distinction* and (2) *consistency* and *stability* of meaning into what is otherwise vague and wavering."[19] The definiteness and stability are provided in good measure by the norms of our culture, which give the otherwise perplexed individual ready-made attitudes for comprehending his universe. Walter Lippmann's classical contribution to the study of opinions and attitudes was his description of stereotypes and the way they provided order and clarity for a bewildering set of complexities.[20] The most interesting finding in Herzog's familiar study of the gratifications obtained by housewives in listening to daytime serials was the unsuspected role of information and advice.[21] The stories were liked "because they explained things to the inarticulate listener."

19 John Dewey, *How We Think*, New York, Macmillan, 1910.
20 Walter Lippmann, *Public Opinion*, New York, Macmillan, 1922.
21 Herta Herzog, "What Do We Really Know about Daytime Serial Listeners?" in Paul F. Lazarsfeld and Frank N. Stanton, editors, *Radio Research 1942-1943,* New York, Duell, Sloan & Pearce, 1944, pp. 3-33.

The need to know does not of course imply that people are driven by a thirst for universal knowledge. The American public's appalling lack of political information has been documented many times. In 1956, for example, only 13 per cent of the people in Detroit could correctly name the two United States Senators from the state of Michigan and only 18 per cent knew the name of their own Congressman.[22] People are not avid seekers after knowledge as judged by what the educator or social reformer would desire. But they do want to understand the events which impinge directly on their own life. Moreover, many of the attitudes they have already acquired give them sufficient basis for interpreting much of what they perceive to be important for them. Our already existing stereotypes, in Lippmann's language, "are an ordered, more or less consistent picture of the world, to which our habits, our tastes, our capacities, our comforts and our hopes have adjusted themselves. They may not be a complete picture of the world, but they are a picture of a possible world to which we are adapted."[23] It follows that new information will not modify old attitudes unless there is some inadequacy or incompleteness or inconsistency in the existing attitudinal structure as it relates to the perceptions of new situations.

The articles in this issue by Cohen, Rosenberg, Osgood, and Zajonc discuss the process of attitude change with respect to inconsistencies and discrepancies in cognitive structure.

DETERMINANTS OF ATTITUDE AROUSAL AND ATTITUDE CHANGE

The problems of attitude arousal and of attitude change are separate problems. The first has to do with the fact that the individual has many predispositions to act and many influences playing upon him. Hence we need a more precise description of the appropriate conditions which will evoke a given attitude. The second problem is that of specifying the factors which will help to predict the modification of different types of attitude.

The most general statement that can be made concerning attitude arousal is that it is dependent upon the excitation of some need in the individual, or some relevant cue in the environment. When a man grows hungry, he talks of food. Even when not hungry he may express favorable attitudes toward a preferred food if an external stimulus cues him. The ego-defensive person who hates foreigners will express such attitudes under conditions of increased anxiety or threat or when a foreigner is perceived to be getting out of place.

[22] From a study of the impact of party organization on political behavior in the Detroit area, by Daniel Katz and Samuel Eldersveld, in manuscript.
[23] Lippmann, op.cit., p. 95.

The most general statement that can be made about the conditions conducive to attitude change is that the expression of the old attitude or its anticipated expression no longer gives satisfaction to its related need state. In other words, it no longer serves its function and the individual feels blocked or frustrated. Modifying an old attitude or replacing it with a new one is a process of learning, and learning always starts with a problem, or being thwarted in coping with a situation. Being blocked is a necessary, but not a sufficient, condition for attitude change. Other factors must be operative and will vary in effectiveness depending upon the function involved.

AROUSING AND CHANGING UTILITARIAN ATTITUDES

Political parties have both the problem of converting people with antagonistic attitudes (attitude change) and the problem of mobilizing the support of their own followers (attitude arousal). To accomplish the latter they attempt to revive the needs basic to old attitudes. For example, the Democrats still utilize the appeals of the New Deal and the Republicans still talk of the balanced budget. The assumption is that many people still hold attitudes acquired in earlier circumstances and that appropriate communication can reinstate the old needs. For most people, however, utilitarian needs are reinforced by experience and not by verbal appeals. Hence invoking the symbols of the New Deal will be relatively ineffective with respect to adjustive attitudes unless there are corresponding experiences with unemployment, decreased income, etc. Though the need state may not be under the control of the propagandist, he can exaggerate or minimize its importance. In addition to playing upon states of need, the propagandist can make perceptible the old cues associated with the attitude he is trying to elicit. These cues may have associated with them favorable affect, or feeling, though the related needs are inactive. For example, the fighters for old causes can be paraded across the political platform in an attempt to arouse the attitudes of the past.

The two basic conditions, then, for the arousal of existing attitudes are the activation of their relevant need states and the perception of the appropriate cues associated with the content of the attitude.

To change attitudes which serve a utilitarian function, one of two conditions must prevail: (1) the attitude and the activities related to it no longer provide the satisfactions they once did, or (2) the individual's level of aspiration has been raised. The Chevrolet owner who had positive attitudes toward his old car may now want a more expensive car commensurate with his new status.

Attitudes toward political parties and voting behavior are often difficult to change if there is no widespread dissatisfaction with economic conditions and international relations. Currently, however, the polls show that even Republicans in the age group over sixty are worried about increased costs of medical care and the general inadequacy of retirement incomes. Thus many old people may change their political allegiance, if it becomes clear that the Democratic Party can furnish a program to take care of their needs.

Again the mass media play a role secondary to direct experience in changing attitudes directly related to economic matters. Once dissatisfaction exists, they can exert a potent influence in suggesting new ways of solving the problem. In the field of international affairs, mass media have a more primary role because in times of peace most people have no direct experience with other countries or their peoples. The threat of war comes from what they read, hear, or see in the mass media.

The area of freedom for changing utilitarian attitudes is of course much greater in dealing with methods of satisfying needs than with needs themselves. Needs change more slowly than the means for gratifying them, even though one role of the advertiser is to create new needs. Change in attitudes occurs more readily when people perceive that they can accomplish their objectives through revising existing attitudes. Integration of white and Negro personnel in the armed forces came to pass partly because political leaders and military leaders perceived that such a move would strengthen our fighting forces. And one of the powerful arguments for changing our attitudes toward Negroes is that in the struggle for world democracy we need to put our own house in order to present a more convincing picture of our own society to other countries. Carlson has experimentally demonstrated that discriminatory attitudes toward minority groups can be altered by showing the relevance of more positive beliefs to such individual goals and values as American international prestige and democratic equalitarianism.[24]

Just as attitudes formed in the interests of adjustment can be negative evaluations of objects associated with avoidance of the harmful effects of the environment, so too can attitudes change because of unpleasant experiences or anticipation of harmful consequences. The more remote the cause of one's suffering the more likely he is to seize upon a readily identifiable target for his negative evaluation. Public officials, as highly visible objects, can easily be associated with states of dissatisfaction. Thus there is truth in the old observation that people vote more against the candidates they dislike than for the candidates they like. In the 1958 elections, in a period of mild recession, unemployment, and general uneasiness about atomic weapons, the incumbent governors (the more visible targets), whether Republican or Democratic, fared less well than the incumbent legislators.

[24] Earl R. Carlson, "Attitude Change through Modification of Attitude Structure," *Journal of Abnormal and Social Psychology*, Vol. 52, 1956, pp. 256-261.

The use of negative sanctions and of punishment to change utilitarian attitudes is more complex than the use of rewards. To be successful in changing attitudes and behavior, punishment should be used only when there is clearly available a course of action that will save the individual from the undesirable consequences. To arouse fear among the enemy in time of war does not necessarily result in desertion, surrender, or a disruption of the enemy war effort. Such channels of action may not be available to the people whose fears are aroused. The experiment of Janis and Feshback in using fear appeals to coerce children into good habits of dental hygiene had the interesting outcome of a negative relationship between the amount of fear and the degree of change. Lurid pictures of the gangrene jaws of old people who had not observed good dental habits were not effective.[25] Moreover, the group exposed to the strongest fear appeal was the most susceptible to counterpropaganda. One factor which helps to account for the results of this investigation was the lack of a clear-cut relation in the minds of the children between failure to brush their teeth in the prescribed manner and the pictures of the gangrene jaws of the aged.

The necessity of coupling fear appeals with clear channels of action is illustrated by a study of Nunnally and Bobren.[26] These investigators manipulated three variables in communications about mental health, namely, the relative amount of message anxiety, the degree to which messages gave apparent solutions, and the relative personal or impersonal phrasing of the message. The high-anxiety message described electric shock treatment of the psychotic in distressing detail. People showed the least willingness to receive communications that were high in anxiety, personalized, and offered no solutions. When solutions were offered in the communication, there was more willingness to accept the high-anxiety message.

The use of punishment and arousal of fear depend for their effectiveness upon the presence of well-defined paths for avoiding the punishment, i.e. negative sanctions are successful in redirecting rather than suppressing behavior. When there is no clearly perceptible relation between the punishment and the desired behavior, people may continue to behave as they did before, only now they have negative attitudes toward the persons and objects associated with the negative sanctions. There is, however, another possibility, if the punishment is severe or if the individual is unusually sensitive. He may develop a defensive avoidance of the whole situation. His behavior, then, is not directed at solving the problem but at escaping from the situation,

[25] Irving L. Janis and Seymour Feshback, "Effects of Fear-arousing Communications," *Journal of Abnormal and Social Psychology*, Vol. 48, 1953, pp. 78-92.

[26] Jum C. Nunnally and Howard M. Bobren, "Variables Governing the Willingness to Receive Communications in Mental Health," *Journal of Personality*, Vol. 27, 1959, pp. 38-46.

even if such escape has to be negotiated by absorbing extra punishment. The attitudes under discussion are those based upon the adjustive or utilitarian function, but if the individual is traumatized by a fearful experience he will shift from instrumental learning to defensive reactions.

AROUSAL AND CHANGE OF EGO-DEFENSIVE ATTITUDES

Attitudes which help to protect the individual from internally induced anxieties or from facing up to external dangers are readily elicited by any form of threat to the ego. The threat may be external, as in the case of a highly competitive situation, or a failure experience, or a derogatory remark. It is the stock in trade of demagogues to exaggerate the dangers confronting the people, for instance, Joe McCarthy's tactics with respect to Communists in the State Department. Many people have existing attitudes of withdrawal or of aggression toward deviants or out-groups based upon their ego-defensive needs. When threatened, these attitudes come into play, and defensive people either avoid the unpleasant situation entirely, as is common in the desegregation controversy, or exhibit hostility.

Another condition for eliciting the ego-defensive attitude is the encouragement given to its expression by some form of social support. The agitator may appeal to repressed hatred by providing moral justification for its expression. A mob leader before an audience with emotionally held attitudes toward Negroes may call out these attitudes in the most violent form by invoking the good of the community or the honor of white womanhood.

A third condition for the arousal of ego-defensive attitudes is the appeal to authority. The insecurity of the defensive person makes him particularly susceptible to authoritarian suggestion. When this type of authoritarian command is in the direction already indicated by his attitudes of antipathy toward other people, he responds quickly and joyously. It is no accident that movements of hate and aggression such as the Ku Klux Klan or the Nazi Party are authoritarian in their organized structure. Wagman, in an experimental investigation of the uses of authoritarian suggestion, found that students high in ego-defensiveness as measured by the F-scale were much more responsive to directives from military leaders than were less defensive students.[27] In fact, the subjects low in defensiveness were not affected at all by authoritarian suggestion when this influence ran counter to their own attitudes. The subjects high in F-scores could be moved in either

[27] Morton Wagman, "Attitude Change and the Authoritarian Personality," *Journal of Psychology,* Vol. 40, 1955, pp. 3-24. The F-scale is a measure of authoritarianism comprising items indicative of both defensiveness and ideology.

direction, although they moved more readily in the direction of their own beliefs.

A fourth condition for defensive arousal is the building up over time of inhibited drives in the individual, for example, repressed sex impulses. As the drive strength of forbidden impulses increases, anxiety mounts and release from tension is found in the expression of defensive attitudes. The deprivations of prison life, for example, build up tensions which can find expression in riots against the hated prison officials.

In other words, the drive strength for defensive reactions can be increased by situation frustration. Though the basic source is the long-standing internal conflict of the person, he can encounter additional frustration in immediate circumstances. Berkowitz has shown that anti-Semitic girls were more likely than less prejudiced girls to display aggression toward an innocent bystander when angered by a third person.[28] In a subsequent experiment, Berkowitz and Holmes created dislike by one group of subjects for their partners by giving them electric shocks which they thought were administered by their partners.[29] In a second session, subjects worked alone and were threatened by the experimenter. In a third session they were brought together with their partners for a cooperative task of problem solving. Aggression and hostility were displayed by subjects toward one another in the third session as a result of the frustration produced by the experimenter, and were directed more against the disliked partner than toward an innocuous partner.

Studies outside the laboratory have confirmed the principle that, where negative attitudes exist, frustration in areas unrelated to the attitude will increase the strength of the prejudice. Bettelheim and Janowitz found that war veterans who had suffered downward mobility were more anti-Semitic than other war veterans.[30] In a secondary analysis of the data from the Elmira study, Greenblum and Pearlin report that the socially mobile people, whether upward or downward mobile, were more prejudiced against Jews and Negroes than were stationary people, provided that the socially mobile were insecure about their new status.[31] Though it is clear in these studies that the situation

[28] Leonard Berkowitz, "Anti-Semitism and the Displacement of Aggression," *Journal of Abnormal and Social Psychology*, Vol. 59, 1959, pp. 182-188.

[29] Leonard Berkowitz and Douglas S. Holmes, "The Generalization of Hostility to Disliked Objects," *Journal of Personality*, Vol. 27, 1959, pp. 565-577.

[30] Bruno Bettelheim and Morris Janowitz, *Dynamics of Prejudice*, New York, Harper, 1950.

[31] Joseph Greenblum and Leonard I. Pearlin, "Vertical Mobility and Prejudice," in Reinhard Bendix and Seymour M. Lipset, editors, *Class, Status and Power*, Glencoe, Ill., Free Press, 1953.

frustration strengthens a negative attitude, it is not clear as to the origin of the negative attitude.

Most research on ego-defensive attitudes has been directed at beliefs concerning the undesirable character of minority groups or of deviants, with accompanying feelings of distrust, contempt, and hatred. Many ego-defensive attitudes, however, are not the projection of repressed aggression but are expressions of apathy or withdrawal. The individual protects himself from a difficult or demanding world and salvages his self-respect by retreating within his own shell. His attitudes toward political matters are anomic: "It does not make any difference to people like me which party is in power" or "There is no point in voting because I can't influence the outcome." Threat to people of this type takes the form of a complexity with which they cannot cope. Thus, they daydream when the lecturer talks about economic theories of inflation or the public official talks about disarmament proposals.

The usual procedures for changing attitudes and behavior have little positive effect upon attitudes geared into our ego defenses. In fact they may have a boomerang effect of making the individual cling more tenaciously to his emotionally held beliefs. In the category of usual procedures should be included increasing the flow of information, promising and bestowing rewards, and invoking penalties. As has already been indicated, punishment is threatening to the ego-defensive person and the increase of threat is the very condition which will feed ego-defensive behavior. The eneuretic youngster with emotional problems is rarely cured by punishment. Teachers and coaches know that there are some children who respond to censure and punishment by persevering in the forbidden behavior. But what is not as well recognized is that reward is also not effective in modifying the actions of the ego-defensive person. His attitudes are an expression of his inner conflicts and are not susceptible to external rewards. The shopkeeper who will not serve Negroes because they are a well-fixated target for his aggressions will risk the loss of income incurred by his discriminatory reactions.

Three basic factors, however, can help change ego-defensive attitudes. In the first place, the removal of threat is a necessary though not a sufficient condition. The permissive and even supportive atmosphere which the therapist attempts to create for his patients is a special instance of the removal of threat. Where the ego-defensive behavior of the delinquent is supported by his group, the social worker must gain a measure of group acceptance so as not to be perceived as a threat by the individual gang members. An objective, matter-of-fact approach can serve to remove threat, especially in situations where people are accustomed to emotional appeals. Humor can also be used to establish a nonthreatening atmosphere, but it should not be directed against the audience or even against the problem. Cooper and Jahoda attempted to change prejudiced attitudes by ridicule, in the form of cartoons which made Mr. Biggott seem silly, especially when he rejected a blood transfusion which did not come from 100 per cent Americans.[32] Instead of changing their attitudes, the subjects in this experiment found ways of evading the meaning of the cartoons.

In the second place, catharsis or the ventilation of feelings can help to set the stage for attitude change. Mention has already been made of the building up of tension owing to the lack of discharge of inhibited impulses. When emotional tension is at a high level the individual will respond defensively and resist attempts to change him. Hence, providing him with opportunities to blow off steam may often be necessary before attempting a serious discussion of new possibilities of behavior. Again, humor can serve this purpose.

There are many practical problems in the use of catharsis, however, because of its complex relationship to other variables. In his review of the experimental work on the expression of hostility Berkowitz reports more findings supporting than contradicting the catharsis hypothesis, but there is no clear agreement about the mechanisms involved.[33] Under certain circumstances permitting emotional outbursts can act as a reward. In a gripe session to allow individuals to express their complaints, group members can reinforce one another's negative attitudes. Unless there are positive forces in the situation which lead to a serious consideration of the problem, the gripe session may have boomerang effects. The technique often employed is to keep the group in session long enough for the malcontents to get talked out so that more sober voices can be heard. Catharsis may function at two levels. It can operate to release or drain off energy of the moment, as in the above description. It can also serve to bring to the surface something of the nature of the conflict affecting the individual. So long as his impulses are repressed and carefully disguised, the individual has little chance of gaining even rudimentary insight into himself.

In the third place, ego-defensive behavior can be altered as the individual acquires insight into his own mechanisms of defense. Information about the nature of the problem in the external world will not affect him. Information about his own functioning may have an influence, if presented without threat, and if the defenses do not go too deep into the personality. In other words, only prolonged therapy can help the psychologically sick person. Many normal people, how-

32 Eunice Cooper and Marie Jahoda, "The Evasion of Propaganda: How Prejudiced People Respond to Anti-prejudice Propaganda," *Journal of Psychology,* Vol. 23, 1947, pp. 15-25.
33 Leonard Berkowitz, "The Expression and Reduction of Hostility," *Psychological Bulletin,* Vol. 55, 1958, pp. 257-283.

ever, employ ego defenses about which they have some degree of awareness, though generally not at the time of the expression of such defenses. The frustrations of a tough day at work may result in an authoritarian father displacing his aggression that night on his family in yelling at his wife, or striking his youngsters. Afterward he may recognize the cause of his behavior. Not all defensive behavior, then, is so deep rooted in the personality as to be inaccessible to awareness and insight. Therefore, procedures for arousing self-insight can be utilized to change behavior, even in mass communications.

One technique is to show people the psychodynamics of attitudes, especially as they appear in the behavior of others. Allport's widely used pamphlet on the A B C's of Scapegoating is based upon the technique.[34] Katz, Sarnoff, and McClintock have conducted experimental investigations of the effects of insightful materials upon the reduction of prejudice.[35] In their procedure the psychodynamics of prejudice was presented in the case history of a subject sufficiently similar to the subjects as to appear as a sympathetic character. Two findings appeared in these investigations: (1) Subjects who were very high in defensiveness were not affected by the insight materials, but subjects of low or moderate defensiveness were significantly affected. (2) The changes in attitude produced by the arousal of self-insight persisted for a longer period of time than changes induced by information or conformity pressures. In a further experiment Stotland, Katz, and Patchen found that involving subjects in the task of understanding the dynamics of prejudice helped arouse self-insight and reduce prejudice.[36] McClintock compared an ethnocentric appeal, an information message, and self-insight materials, with similar results.[37] There was differential acceptance of these influences according to the personality pattern of the subject. McClintock also found a difference in F-scale items in predicting attitude change, with the projectivity items showing a different pattern from the conformity items.

Of practical concern are four general areas in which insufficient attention has been paid to the ego-defensive basis of attitudes with respect to the role of communication in inducing social change:

[34] Gordon W. Allport, *The Nature of Prejudice*, Cambridge, Mass., Addison-Wesley, 1954.

[35] Daniel Katz, Irving Sarnoff, and Charles McClintock, "Ego Defense and Attitude Change," *Human Relations*, Vol. 9, 1956, pp. 27-46. Also their "The Measurement of Ego Defense as Related to Attitude Change," *Journal of Personality*, Vol. 25, 1957, pp. 465-474.

[36] Ezra Stotland, Daniel Katz, and Martin Patchen, "The Reduction of Prejudice through the Arousal of Self-insight," *Journal of Personality*, Vol. 27, 1959, pp. 507-531.

[37] Charles McClintock, "Personality Syndromes and Attitude Change," *Journal of Personality*, Vol. 26, 1958, pp. 479-593.

1. Prejudices toward foreigners, toward racial and religious out-groups, and toward international affairs often fall into this category. The thesis of the authors of *The Authoritarian Personality* that the defenses of repression and projectivity are correlated with racial prejudice has seen more confirmation than disproof in spite of the fact that not all racial prejudice is ego-defensive in nature. In a review of studies involving the California F-scale, Titus and Hollander report investigations where positive correlations were obtained between high scores on authoritarianism and prejudice and xenophobia.[38]

Of course not all the variance in social prejudice can be accounted for by ego-defensiveness. Pettigrew has shown that a sample of Southern respondents was almost identical with a sample of Northern respondents on the F-scale measure of authoritarianism, but the Southern sample was much more negative toward Negroes with respect to employment, housing, and voting.[39]

Relations have also been found between authoritarianism and attitudes toward nationalism and internationalism. Levinson constructed a scale to give an index of internationalism which included such items as opinions about immigration policy, armaments, the get-tough with Russia policy, cooperation with Red China, our role in the UN, etc. This measure of internationalism correlated .60 with the F-scale.[40] A study by Lane in 1952 showed that a larger proportion of authoritarians than of equalitarians were against working toward a peaceful settlement of the Korean issue. The authoritarians either favored the bombing of China and Manchuria or else were for complete withdrawal.[41] And Smith and Rosen found such consistent negative relations between world-mindedness and the dimension of authoritarianism that they suggested in the interest of parsimony the two be considered as slightly different aspects of the same basic personality structure.[42]

2. A related area of attitudes consists of opinions toward deviant types of personalities, e.g. delinquents, the mentally ill, Beatniks, and other nonconformers. The problem of the rehabilitation of the ex-convict or the discharged mental patient is sometimes impeded by the

[38] H. Edwin Titus and E. P. Hollander, "The California F-Scale in Psychological Research: 1950-1955," *Psychological Bulletin*, Vol. 54, 1957, pp. 47-64.

[39] Thomas F. Pettigrew, "Personality and Socio-cultural Factors in Intergroup Attitudes: A Cross-national Comparison," *Journal of Conflict Resolution*, Vol. 2, 1958, pp. 29-42.

[40] Daniel J. Levinson, "Authoritarian Personality and Foreign Personality," *Journal of Conflict Resolution*, Vol. 1, 1957, pp. 37-47.

[41] Robert E. Lane, "Political Personality and Electoral Choice," *American Political Science Review*, Vol. 49, 1955, pp. 173-190.

[42] Howard P. Smith and Ellen W. Rosen, "Some Psychological Correlates of Worldmindedness and Authoritarianism," *Journal of Personality*, Vol. 26, 1958, pp. 170-183.

emotional attitudes of the public toward individuals with a record of institutionalization.

3. Attitudes toward public health measures, whether the fluoridation of the water supply of a community, the utilization of X-ray examinations for the prevention of disease, or the availability of information about birth control, often have their roots in unacknowledged anxieties and fears. Davis, for example, believes that opposition to fluoridation is not so much a matter of ignorance of the specific problem as it is a function of a deeper attitudinal syndrome of naturalism.[43] Governmental interference with natural processes is regarded as the source of many evils, and this general ideology is tinged with suspicion and distrust suggestive of defensive motivation.

4. Apathy toward political issues and especially toward atomic weapons may reflect a defensive withdrawal on the part of some people. The information officer of a government agency or the public relations officer in charge of a health campaign faces the difficult problem of changing public attitudes which may satisfy different needs for different people. To present information designed to show the dangerous situation we are in may be effective for some people but may prove too threatening for others. What is needed in such cases is research which will get at the reasons why people hold the attitudes they do. There are times when dramatically confronting the public with the dangers of a situation may be more effective strategy than a more reassuring approach. But there are also occasions when the first strategy will merely add to defensive avoidance. Gladstone and Taylor presented communications to their students, two of which were news stories from the *New York Times*.[44] One reported speeches made by Malenkov and Khrushchev about the peaceful intentions of the Soviet Union but its readiness to crush aggressors. The second news story reported British reactions to the American opinion about the situation in Indo-China. A third communication concerned the H-bomb and its dangers. Students were previously tested on their susceptibility to being threatened. Those who were threat-prone tended to deny the truth of the points in the communications or to overlook them entirely. For these subjects the communications had no effect on existing attitudes.

The use of mass communication has been better adapted to supplying information and to emphasizing the advantages of a course of action than to changing defensive attitudes. A new field in communica-

[43] Morris Davis, "Community Attitudes toward Fluoridation," *Public Opinion Quarterly*, Vol. 23, 1959, pp. 474-482.
[44] Arthur I. Gladstone and Martha A. Taylor, "Threat-related Attitudes and Reactions to Communication about International Events," *Journal of Conflict Resolution*, Vol. 2, 1958, pp. 17-28.

tion to large publics is the creation of self-understanding, which so far has been pre-empted by personal advice columns. The specifics for this new development remain to be worked out, but they may well start with techniques based upon attitude research of the basic reasons for resistance to an objectively desirable program.

CONDITIONS FOR AROUSING AND CHANGING VALUE-EXPRESSIVE ATTITUDES

Two conditions for the arousal of value-expressive attitudes can be specified. The first is the occurrence of the cue in the stimulus situation which has been associated with the attitude. The liberal Democrat, as a liberal Democrat, has always believed in principle that an income tax is more just than a sales tax. Now the issue has arisen in his state, and the group in which he happens to be at the moment are discussing an increase in sales tax. This will be sufficient to cue off his opposition to the proposal without consideration of the specific local aspects of the tax problem. The second condition for the arousal of this type of attitude is some degree of thwarting of the individual's expressive behavior in the immediate past. The housewife occupied with the routine care of the home and the children during the day may seek opportunities to express her views to other women at the first social gathering she attends.

We have referred to voters backing their party for bread and butter reasons. Perhaps the bulk of voting behavior, however, is the elicitation of value-expressive attitudes. Voting is a symbolic expression of being a Republican or a Democrat. Party identification accounts for more variance in voting behavior than any other single factor.[45] Though there is a minority who consider themselves independent and though there are minor shifts in political allegiance, the great majority of the people identify themselves as the supporters of a political party. Their voting behavior is an expression of this self-concept, and it takes a major event such as a depression to affect their voting habits seriously.

Identification with party is in good measure a function of the political socialization of the child, as Hyman has shown.[46] An analysis of a national sample of the electorate in 1952 by Campbell, Gurin, and Miller revealed that of voters both of whose parents were Democrats, 76 per cent identified themselves as Democrats, another 10 per cent as independent Democrats, and 12 per cent as Republicans.[47] Similarly,

[45] Angus A. Campbell, Philip Converse, Warren Miller, and Donald Stokes, *The American Voter*, New York, Wiley, 1960.

[46] Herbert H. Hyman, *Political Socialization*, Glencoe, Ill., Free Press, 1959.

[47] Angus A. Campbell, Gerald Gurin, and Warren Miller, *The Voter Decides*, Evanston, Ill., Row, Peterson, 1954.

of those with Republican parents 63 per cent considered themselves Republican and another 10 per cent as independent Republicans. Attachment to party, Hyman suggests, furnishes an organizing principle for the individual and gives stability to his political orientation in the confusion of changing issues.

Even in European countries, where we assume greater knowledge of issues, political behavior is the symbolic expression of people's values. Members of the Labor Party in Norway, for example, are little more conversant with the stand of their party on issues than are voters in the United States. In fact, the policy of their party in international affairs and armament in recent years has been closer to the views of Conservative voters than to their own. Nevertheless, they consider themselves supporters of the party which reflects their general values.

The problem of the political leader is to make salient the cues related to political allegiance in order to arouse the voters who consider themselves party supporters to the point of expressing their attitudes by voting on election day. One technique is to increase the volume and intensity of relevant stimulation as the election approaches. If the relevant cues could be presented to each voter on election day— for example, a ballot box in his home—then the appropriate behavior would follow. But the citizen must remember on the given Tuesday that this is election day and that he must find time to go to the polls. The task of party organization is to try to remind him of this fact the weekend before, to call him that very day by phone, or even to call for him in person.

Again, two conditions are relevant in changing value-expressive attitudes:

1. Some degree of dissatisfaction with one's self-concept or its associated values is the opening wedge for fundamental change. The complacent person, smugly satisfied with all aspects of himself, is immune to attempts to change his values. Dissatisfaction with the self can result from failures or from the inadequacy of one's values in preserving a favorable image of oneself in a changing world. The man with pacifist values may have become dissatisfied with himself during a period of fascist expansion and terror. Once there is a crack in the individual's central belief systems, it can be exploited by appropriately directed influences. The techniques of brain washing employed by the Chinese Communists both on prisoners of war in Korea and in the thought reform of Chinese intellectuals were essentially procedures for changing value systems.

In the brain washing of Chinese intellectuals in the revolutionary college, the Communists took advantage of the confused identity of the student.[48] He had been both a faithful son and a rebellious reformer and perhaps even an uninvolved cynic. To make him an enthusiastic Communist the officials attempted to destroy his allegiance to his parents and to transfer his loyalty to Communist doctrines which could meet his values as a rebel. Group influences were mobilized to help bring about the change by intensifying guilt feelings and providing for atonement and redemption through the emotional catharsis of personal confession.

To convert American prisoners of war, the Communists made a careful study of the vulnerability of their victims. They found additional weaknesses through a system of informers and created new insecurities by giving the men no social support for their old values.[49] They manipulated group influences to support Communist values and exploited their ability to control behavior and all punishments and rewards in the situation. The direction of all their efforts, however, was to undermine old values and to supply new ones. The degree of their success has probably been exaggerated in the public prints, but from their point of view they did achieve some genuine gains. One estimate is that some 15 per cent of the returning prisoners of war were active collaborators, another 5 per cent resisters, and some 80 per cent "neutrals." Segal, in a study of a sample of 579 of these men, found that 12 per cent had to some degree accepted Communist ideology.[50]

2. Dissatisfaction with old attitudes as inappropriate to one's values can also lead to change. In fact, people are much less likely to find their values uncongenial than they are to find some of their attitudes inappropriate to their values. The discomfort with one's old attitudes may stem from new experiences or from the suggestions of other people. Senator Vandenburg, as an enlightened conservative, changed his attitudes on foreign relations from an isolationist to an internationalist position when critical events in our history suggested change. The influences exerted upon people are often in the direction of showing the inappropriateness of their present ways of expressing their values. Union leaders attempt to show that good union men should not vote on the old personal basis of rewarding friends and punishing enemies but should instead demand party responsibility for a program. In an experiment by Stotland, Katz, and Patchen there was suggestive evidence of the readiness of subjects to change attitudes which they

[48] Robert J. Lifton, "Thought Reform of Chinese Intellectuals: A Psychiatric Evaluation," *Journal of Social Issues*, Vol. 13, No. 3, 1957, pp. 5-20.

[49] Edgar H. Schein, "Reaction Patterns to Severe, Chronic Stress in American Army Prisoners of War of the Chinese," *Journal of Social Issues*, Vol. 13, No. 3, 1957, pp. 21-30.

[50] Julius Segal, "Correlates of Collaboration and Resistance Behavior among U.S. Army POW's in Korea," *Journal of Social Issues*, Vol. 13, No. 3, 1957, pp. 31-40.

found inappropriate to their values.[51] Though an attempt was made to change the prejudices of the ego-defensive subjects, individuals who were not basically ego-defensive also changed. These subjects, who already approved of tolerance, apparently became aware of the inappropriateness of some of their negative evaluations of minority groups. This second factor in attitude change thus refers to the comparatively greater appropriateness of one set of means than another for confirming the individual's self-concept and realizing his central values.

We have already called attention to the role of values in the formation of attitudes in the early years of life. It is also true that attitude formation is a constant process and that influences are continually being brought to bear throughout life which suggest new attitudes as important in implementing existing values. An often-used method is to make salient some central value such as the thinking man, the man of distinction, or the virile man, and then depict a relatively new form of behavior consistent with this image. The role of motivational research in advertising is to discover the rudimentary image associated with a given product, to use this as a basis for building up the image in more glorified terms, and then to cement the association of this image with the product.

AROUSING AND CHANGING ATTITUDES WHICH SERVE THE KNOWLEDGE FUNCTION

Attitudes acquired in the interests of the need to know are elicited by a stimulus associated with the attitude. The child who learns from his reading and from his parents that Orientals are treacherous will not have the attitude aroused unless some appropriate cue concerning the cognitive object is presented. He may even meet and interact with Orientals without identifying them as such and with no corresponding arousal of his attitude. Considerable prejudice in this sense is race-name prejudice and is only aroused when a premium is placed upon social identification. Since members of a minority group have many other memberships in common with a majority group, the latent prejudiced attitude may not necessarily be activated. Prejudice based upon ego-defensiveness, however, will result in ready identification of the disliked group.

The factors which are productive of change of attitudes of this character are inadequacies of the existing attitudes to deal with new and changing situations. The person who has been taught that Orientals are treacherous may read extended accounts of the honesty of the Chinese or may have favorable interactions with Japanese. He finds his old attitudes in conflict with new information and new ex-

[51] Stotland, Katz, and Patchen, *op.cit.*

perience, and proceeds to modify his beliefs. In this instance we are dealing with fictitious stereotypes which never corresponded to reality. In other cases the beliefs may have been adequate to the situation but the world has changed. Thus, some British military men formerly in favor of armaments have changed their attitude toward disarmament because of the character of nuclear weapons. The theory of cognitive consistency later elaborated in this issue can draw its best examples from attitudes related to the knowledge function.

Any situation, then, which is ambiguous for the individual is likely to produce attitude change. His need for cognitive structure is such that he will either modify his beliefs to impose structure or accept some new formula presented by others. He seeks a meaningful picture of his universe, and when there is ambiguity he will reach for a ready solution. Rumors abound when information is unavailable.

GLOBAL INFLUENCES AND ATTITUDE CHANGE

In the foregoing analysis we have attempted to clarify the functions which attitudes perform and to give some psychological specifications of the conditions under which they are formed, elicited, and changed. This material is summarized in the table on page 192. We must recognize, however, that the influences in the real world are not as a rule directed toward a single type of motivation. Contact with other peoples, experience in foreign cultures, group pressures, group discussion and decision, the impact of legislation, and the techniques of brain washing are all global variables. They represent combinations of forces. To predict their effectiveness in any given situation it is necessary to analyze their components in relation to the conditions of administration and the type of population toward which they are directed.

The effect of contact and intercultural exchange. Contact between peoples of different races, nations, and religions has been suggested as an excellent method of creating understanding and reducing prejudice. Research studies have demonstrated that such an outcome is possible but not that it is inevitable. People in integrated housing projects have developed more favorable attitudes toward members of the other race;[52] the same findings are reported from children's camps,[53] industry,[54] and army units.[55] But some studies report increased prejudice with in-

[52] Morton Deutsch and Mary E. Collins, *Interracial Housing: A Psychological Evaluation of a Social Experiment*, Minneapolis, University of Minnesota Press, 1951.
[53] Marian R. Yarrow, editor, "Interpersonal Dynamics in a Desegregation Process," *Journal of Social Issues*, Vol. 14, No. 1, 1958, pp. 1-63.
[54] Allport, *op.cit.*, pp. 274-276.
[55] Samuel A. Stouffer *et al.*, *The American Soldier*, Vol. 1, Princeton, N.J., Princeton University Press, 1949, pp. 566-599.

Function	Origin and Dynamics	Arousal Conditions	Change Conditions
Adjustment	Utility of attitudinal object in need satisfaction. Maximizing external rewards and minimizing punishments	1. Activation of needs 2. Salience of cues associated with need satisfaction	1. Need deprivation 2. Creation of new needs and new levels of aspiration 3. Shifting rewards and punishments 4. Emphasis on new and better paths for need satisfaction
Ego defense	Protecting against internal conflicts and external dangers	1. Posing of threats 2. Appeals to hatred and repressed impulses 3. Rise in frustrations 4. Use of authoritarian suggestion	1. Removal of threats 2. Catharsis 3. Development of self-insight
Value expression	Maintaining self identity; enhancing favorable self-image; self-expression and self-determination	1. Salience of cues associated with values 2. Appeals to individual to reassert self-image 3. Ambiguities which threaten self-concept	1. Some degree of dissatisfaction with self 2. Greater appropriateness of new attitude for the self 3. Control of all environmental supports to undermine old values
Knowledge	Need for understanding, for meaningful cognitive organization, for consistency and clarity	1. Reinstatement of cues associated with old problem or of old problem itself	1. Ambiguity created by new information or change in environment 2. More meaningful information about problems

creased contact.[56] Obviously, contact as such is not a statement of the critical variables involved.

Contact carries with it no necessary conditions for alleviating the internal conflicts of the ego-defensive. If anything, the immediate presence of hated people may intensify prejudice. For less defensive people, contact with other groups depends upon the cooperative or competitive nature of the interaction. Prejudice against a minority can increase in a community as the minority grows in numbers and competes successfully with the majority group. Contact has increased but

[56] Muzafer Sherif and Carolyn W. Sherif, *An Outline of Social Psychology*, rev. ed., New York, Harper, 1956, pp. 548-551.

so too has prejudice. On the other hand, the successful effects of integrating white and Negro soldiers during World War II occurred under conditions of joint effort against a common enemy. Sherif has experimentally demonstrated the importance of cooperation toward common goals in a camp situation.[57] First he created two antagonistic groups of boys, established the identity of each group, and placed them in a series of competitive and conflicting situations. As a result the two groups felt mutual dislike and held negative stereotypes of each other. The groups then were brought together for a picnic, but the antagonistic attitudes persisted; food was hurled back and forth between the two gangs. Finally, superordinate goals were created by sending all the boys on an expedition during which the water supply broke down. Group differences were forgotten as the boys worked together to solve the common problem. Favorable interactions continued after the incident.

Contact, then, can change adjustive attitudes in the direction of either more positive or more negative evaluations depending upon whether the conditions of contact help or hinder the satisfaction of utilitarian needs. Contact can also change attitudes which serve the knowledge function, provided that little ego defensiveness and little competitiveness are present. The usual negative stereotypes toward other groups are gross simplifications and exaggerations of the characteristics of large numbers of human beings. Contact will provide richer and more accurate information about other people and will show them to be very much like members of one's own group.

A special case of contact is experience in a foreign culture. Our cultural-exchange program is predicated upon the assumption that sending representatives of our nation abroad to teach, study, entertain, or work with the citizens of other countries and bringing their students, scientists, and representatives here will aid in international understanding and in mutually improved attitudes. The bulk of the research evidence supports this assumption. Reigrotski and Anderson have conducted one of the most extensive investigations in this area, involving interviews with sizable samples in Belgium, France, Holland, and Germany.[58] Foreign contact, as measured by visiting abroad and having friends and relatives abroad, was found to increase favorable images of other peoples and to make individuals more critical of their compatriots. But again we need to make more specific the conditions of such experiences as they relate to the motivations of the principals in the drama. The importance of such specification is documented by the findings of Selltiz, Hopson, and Cook, who interviewed some 348 foreign

---

[57] Sherif and Sherif, *op.cit.*, pp. 287-331.

[58] Erich Reigrotski and Nels Anderson, "National Stereotypes and Foreign Contacts," *Public Opinion Quarterly*, Vol. 23, pp. 515-528.

students in thirty-five colleges and universities in the United States shortly after their arrival and again five months later.[59] They found no relationship between amount of personal interaction with Americans and attitude change, and they suggest as one possible explanation that "other factors may be of overriding importance."

The importance of the utilitarian and value-expressive functions in attitude change through cross-cultural experience is indicated in the study of Watson and Lippitt of twenty-nine Germans brought here by the State Department for advanced study.[60] These visitors were interviewed while in the United States, shortly after their return to Germany, and six months after their return. They were eager to learn techniques which would help them with their own problems in areas where they regarded us as more expert. They were also willing to adopt new attitudes which were implementations of their own value systems. At first they had negative evaluations of American patterns of child rearing. However, they placed a high value on individualism and were ready to learn how to be successfully individualistic. When they saw the relation of the American child-rearing practices to individualism they developed favorable attitudes toward these practices.

Perhaps the reason most of the evidence suggests positive outcomes from cross-cultural experiences stems from the selective nature of the people engaged in visiting and traveling. Students and visitors who come from abroad come for specific purposes related to their needs and values. They do not come for the ego-defensive purposes of venting their aggression on a scapegoat or expressing their superiority, though some may come to escape problems at home. Once the visitor is in a foreign country, however, many circumstances can arouse ego-defensiveness. He is in a strange world where his usual coping mechanisms are no longer successful. He lacks the customary social support of his group. He may be forced to accept a lower status than he enjoys at home. The wife of the American Fulbrighter, who bears the brunt of the adjustment problem, may become defensive and negative toward the host country. The status problem is often in evidence when Indian scholars who enjoy privilege and position in their own country are reduced to the lowly status of a first-year graduate student. Another interesting issue arises with respect to the status of the country of the visitor as perceived by the people he meets in the host country. Morris studied

[59] Claire Selltiz, Anna L. Hopson, and Stuart W. Cook, "The Effects of Situational Factors on Personal Interaction between Foreign Students and Americans," *Journal of Social Issues*, Vol. 12, No. 1, 1956, pp. 33-44.

[60] Jeanne Watson and Ronald Lippitt, "Cross-cultural Experience as a Source of Attitude Change," *Journal of Conflict Resolution*, Vol. 2, 1958, pp. 61-66. Also, Jeanne Watson and Ronald Lippitt, *Learning across Cultures*, Ann Arbor, Mich., Institute for Social Research, Research Center for Group Dynamics, 1955.

318 foreign students at U.C.L.A. and noted that finding one's country occupying a low status in America did not matter so much unless there was a discrepancy between the status expected and the status accorded.[61] Thus, if the visitor expected a moderately low evaluation he was not upset when he encountered it. But if with the same expectation he met an even lower evaluation, he was affected. Of the visiting students who found that their national status was higher than anticipated, some 66 per cent held favorable attitudes toward the United States. Of those who experienced a relative loss in national status, only 38 per cent were favorable.

Group influences. In any practical attempt to change attitudes, social support and group influence assume first importance. The power of the group over the individual, however, needs to be assessed carefully with respect to the dynamics of the influence exerted. The concept of *group identification* points to an emotional tie between the individual and the group symbols. This can be a matter of individual incorporation of group values as expressing his own inner convictions, as in the case of the dedicated union member. Or it can result from the insecure person's attachment to the strength of the group to compensate for his own weakness. The concept of *reference group* implies less emotional attachment and suggests that many people turn to particular groups for their standards of judgment. In this narrow sense the reference group has the function of helping to supply cognitive structure for the individual's uncertainties. Sherif's early experiments demonstrated that in ambiguous situations people would turn to the group norms for support.[62]

Whatever definition is used for terms to describe the relation between the individual and the group, groups do serve all three of the functions described above. They also serve the fourth function of aiding the individual in his utilitarian attempt to maximize satisfactions. He gains recognition and other rewards through becoming a good group member. Since all four basic motivations can be present in group settings, we need to know the function involved if we are to predict the effectiveness of various types of appeal from the group. The defensive person can be used by the group more readily than the person motivated by utilitarian needs, who is more likely to want to use the group for his own purposes. The man who has internalized the group's values can be moved markedly by group leaders in the direction of their attainment but may prove to be very resistant to leaders who attempt to move him in the opposite direction.

[61] Richard T. Morris, "National Status and Attitudes of Foreign Students," *Journal of Social Issues,* Vol. 12, No. 1, 1956, pp. 20-25.
[62] M. Sherif, *Psychology of Social Norms, op.cit.*

Control over behavior: change through legislation. Attitudes can be expressed in overt action, but actions can also determine attitudes. Often behavior change precedes attitude change. People enter new groups, they take on new jobs, and in their new roles behave in a fashion appropriate to the expectations of those roles. In time they will develop attitudes supportive of the new behavior. Lieberman tested workers before and after their assumption of new roles as foremen and union stewards.[63] As workers they were very much alike in attitudes and beliefs. As foremen and stewards they quickly acquired the distinctive standards and values appropriate to the new roles.

Attitudes may change when people take on new roles for a number of reasons, but the two most likely causes are: (1) Both appropriate attitudes and appropriate behavior are necessary to receive the full rewards and anticipated benefits of the system the newcomers have entered. (2) It is confusing to have conflicting beliefs and behavior. Some people will maintain private attitudes at variance with their public behavior, but this becomes difficult if the public behavior has to be maintained fairly constantly.

The implications of the strategy of changing attitudes by requiring new behavior have long been recognized. Efforts are made, for example, to control juvenile delinquency by providing new recreational, educational, and social activities for teenagers; the critics in the group are given some responsibility for running these activities.

The use of legislation has been of special interest in the desegregation controversy. Its opponents contend that if change is to come about it should come about through education. Its advocates assert their belief in the efficacy of legislation. At least three conditions are important to the outcome of this debate: (1) Law in our culture is effective when directed against behavior and not against attitudes. We can legislate against specific discriminatory practices but not against prejudice as such. (2) Laws are accepted when the behavior is regarded as being in the public domain and not the private domain. People will not support measures directed at personal matters such as the length of women's skirts. (3) When the behavior is in the public domain, regulatory acts still may not work if they are not applied quickly and consistently. The basis of legal authority is in acceptance of what is properly legal. Hence if there is doubt, delay, and confusion in the administration of the law, with Federal authorities saying one thing and state authorities another, the legitimacy of the act is in question. Lack of powerful Federal legislation and a strong administrative enforcement program to implement the Supreme Court de-

[63] Seymour Lieberman, "The Relationship between Attitudes and Roles: A Natural Field Experiment," University of Michigan, 1954, unpublished doctoral dissertation.

cision on desegregation gave local resistance a chance to form and to confuse the issue.

The problem of whether behavior is in the private or public domain is in good part a matter of public opinion and can be ascertained on borderline matters. Public schools, public housing, and government employment are, almost by definition, not in question. With respect to private housing there may be more of a question in the public mind, though it is recognized that the community has the right to pass zoning laws. Since people will resist legislation in what they regard as purely private matters, a survey of a representative sample of the public including both whites and Negroes can provide useful information.

Though legislation about desegregation can change behavior and the attitudes corresponding to it, the generalization to other attitudes and other forms of behavior is more difficult to predict.[64] The basic problem of the generalization of change will be considered in a later section.

Brain washing. Though brain-washing methods are directed at changing the self-concept and its related values, they differ from other procedures by virtue of the complete control acquired over the individual. In a prisoner-of-war camp or in some institutions, the leaders have control over all information reaching their charges, all punishments and rewards, the composition of groups, and the formation of group life. Repressive methods and manipulation of people through reward and punishment are old devices. What is new in brain washing is the more thorough use of old procedures, on the one hand, and the development of techniques for controlling group life with respect to both its formal and informal structure, on the other—a perverted group dynamics, in fact.

Eight procedures can be identified from the experience of the Korean camps.[65] (1) Leaders or potential leaders were segregated from the other prisoners, making group resistance to the Communists more difficult. (2) All ties and informational support from home were removed through systematic censorship of letters and materials from the outside world. (3) Distrust of their fellows was created among the prisoners through the use of informers and suspicion of informers. Generally, when formal group controls are in operation, informal communication and informal standards develop to protect the lowly against the decision makers. With potential ringleaders already screened out of the group and with the inculcation of fear of communication with comrades, no effective informal group structure developed. (4) Group life was made available to the prisoners if they participated

64 Stuart Cook, "Desegregation, A Psychological Analysis," *American Psychologist,* Vol. 12, 1957, pp. 11-13.
65 Schein, *op.cit.*

in activities prescribed by the Communists. If a unit of men all participated in a study group they could then take part in a ball game or other group sport. Pressure to conform and participate in the discussion session was thus generated among the men themselves. At a later stage, self-criticism in group sessions was encouraged under threat of withholding the reward of group games. (5) The first instances of real or distorted collaboration by prisoners were used with telling effect upon their fellows. A testimonial from a prisoner or a lecture by a collaborator destroyed any illusion of group resistance and, moreover, made it seem pointless for others to resist further. (6) The Communists paced their demands so that they required little from the prisoner in the early stages. Once he made some concessions it was difficult for him to resist making further ones. (7) The Communists always required some behavioral compliance from the prisoners, no matter how trivial the level of participation. (8) Rewards and punishments were carefully manipulated. Extra food, medicine, and special privileges were awarded for acts of cooperation and collaboration. Punishments were threatened for acts of resistance, but only imprisonment was consistently used as a penalty.

These techniques were, of course, carried out with varying degrees of thoroughness and effectiveness in the different camps and at different stages of the war. Unfamiliarity with American culture on the part of many Chinese leaders made for difficulties in breaking down informal group processes of the prisoners, some of whom would indulge in ridiculous caricature during the self-criticism session. The over-all effect of brain washing was not so much the production of active collaboration and of ideological conversion to the Communist cause as it was the creation of apathy and withdrawal. The environment was so threatening that the prisoners resorted to primitive defense mechanisms of psychological escape and avoidance. There is some evidence to indicate that this apathetic reaction resulted in a higher death rate, since many men refused to marshal their strength to combat the rigors of the situation.

Perhaps the two most important lessons of the Korean experience are (1) the importance of central values in sustaining the ego under conditions of deprivation and threat and (2) the necessity of maintaining some form of group support in resisting the powerful manipulations of an opponent.

GENERALIZATION OF ATTITUDE CHANGE

Perhaps the most fascinating problem in attitude change has to do with consequences to a person's belief systems and general behavior of changing a single attitude. Is the change confined to the single target of the attitude? Does it affect related beliefs and feelings? Is so, what types of related belief and feeling are affected, i.e. on what does the change rub off? Teachers and parents, for example, are concerned when a child acquires an immoral attitude or indulges in a single dishonest act, for fear of the pernicious spread of undesirable behavior tendencies. Responsible citizens are concerned about the lawless actions of extremists in the South in combatting integration, not only because of the immediate and specific implications of the behavior but because of the general threat to legal institutions.

Research evidence on the generalization of attitude change is meager. In experimental work, the manipulations to produce change are weak and last for brief periods, sometimes minutes and at the most several hours. It is not surprising, therefore, that these studies report few cases of change which has generalized to attitudes other than the one under attack. Even in the studies on self-insight by Katz *et al.*, where the change in prejudice toward Negroes was still in evidence some two months after the experiment, there were no consistent changes in prejudice toward other minority groups.[66] In real-life situations outside the laboratory, more powerful forces are often brought to bear to modify behavior, but again the resulting changes seem more limited than one would expect on an a priori logical basis. Integration of whites and Negroes in the factory may produce acceptance of Negroes as fellow workers but not as residents in one's neighborhood, or as friends in one's social group. Significant numbers of Democrats were influenced by the candidacy of Dwight Eisenhower to help elect him President in 1952 and 1956, but, as Campbell *et al.* have established, this change in voting behavior did not rub off on the rest of the Republican ticket.[67] Most of the Democratic defectors at the presidential level voted for a Democratic Congress. Nor did they change their attitudes on political issues. And the chances are that this change will not generalize to other Republican presidential candidates who lack Eisenhower's status as a national figure.

It is puzzling that attitude change seems to have slight generalization effects, when the evidence indicates considerable generalization in the organization of a person's beliefs and values. Studies of authoritarian and equalitarian trends in personality do find consistent constellations of attitudes. It is true that the correlations are not always high, and Prothro reports that, among his Southern subjects, there was only a slight relationship between anti-Semitism and Negro prejudice.[68] But studies of the generalization hypothesis in attitude structure give positive findings. Grace confirmed his prediction that the attitudes people

66 Stotland and Katz, *op.cit.*

67 Campbell, Converse, Miller, and Stokes, *op.cit.*

68 E. Terry Prothro, "Ethnocentrism and Anti-Negro Attitudes in the Deep South," *Journal of Abnormal and Social Psychology*, Vol. 47, 1952, pp. 105-108.

displayed in interpersonal relations toward their friends and colleagues carried over to their attitudes toward international matters.[69] He studied four types of reaction: verbal hostility, direct hostility, intropunitiveness, and apathy. People characteristically giving one type of response in everyday situations would tend to respond similarly in professional and international situations. Stagner concluded on the basis of his empirical investigation of attitudes toward colleagues and outgroups that the evidence supported a generalization theory rather than a displacement or sublimation theory.[70] Confirmation of the generalization hypothesis comes from a Norwegian study by Christiansen in which reactions were classified on two dimensions: (1) threat-oriented versus problem-oriented and (2) outward-directed versus inward-directed. Thus, blaming oneself would be a threat-oriented, inwardly directed reaction. Christiansen found that (a) people tend to react consistently toward everyday conflict situations, (b) they react consistently to international conflicts, (c) there is a correlation between reactions to everyday conflicts and to international conflicts, and (d) this correlation is lower than the correlations among reactions to everyday conflicts and among reactions to international conflicts, respectively.[71]

Three reasons can be suggested for the failure to find greater generalization effects in attitude change:

1. The over-all organization of attitudes and values in the personality is highly differentiated. The many dimensions allow the individual to absorb change without major modification of his attitudes. A Democrat of long standing could vote for Eisenhower and still remain Democratic in his identification because to him politics was not involved in this decision. Eisenhower stood above the political arena in the minds of many people. He was not blamed for what his party did, as the Gallup polls indicate, nor did his popularity rub off on his party. In 1958, in spite of Eisenhower's urgings, the people returned a sizable Democratic majority to Congress. There are many standards of judgment, then, which pertain to content areas of belief and attitude. An individual uses one set of standards or dimensions for a political decision but will shift to another set when it is more appropriate.

2. The generalization of attitudes proceeds along lines of the individual's own psychological groupings more than along lines of conventional sociological categories. We may miss significant generalized change because we do not look at the individual's own pattern of beliefs and values. One man may dislike foreigners, but to him foreign-

69 H. A. Grace, *A Study of the Expression of Hostility in Everyday Professional and International Verbal Situations*, New York, Columbia University Press, 1949.

70 Ross Stagner, "Studies of Aggressive Social Attitudes," *Journal of Social Psychology*, Vol. 20, 1944, pp. 109-120.

71 Bjorn Christiansen, *Attitudes towards Foreign Affairs as a Function of Personality*, Oslo, Norway, Oslo University Press, 1959.

ers are those people whose English he cannot understand; to another person foreigners are people of certain physical characteristics; to a third they are people with different customs, etc.

People will utilize many principles in organizing their own groupings of attitudes: (a) the objective similarities of the referents of the attitudes, (b) their own limited experiences with these referents, (c) their own needs, and (d) their own ideas of causation and of the nature of proper relationships. Peak has used the concept of psychological distance and difference between events in psychological space to describe attitude structure and generalization.[72]

The liberal-conservative dimension, for example, may be useful for characterizing large groups of people, but individuals may differ considerably in their own scaling of attitudes comprising liberalism-conservatism. Some conservatives can stand to the left of center on issues of the legal rights of the individual or on internationalism. Social classes show differences in liberal and conservative ideology, the lower socio-economic groups being more liberal on economic and political issues and the upper income groups more liberal on tolerance for deviants and on democratic values in interpersonal relationships. Stouffer found that during the McCarthy period the low-status groups were more intolerant, and other studies have shown more authoritarian values among these groups.[73]

3. Generalization of attitude change is limited by the lack of systematic forces in the social environment to implement that change. Even when people are prepared to modify their behavior to a considerable extent they find themselves in situations which exert pressures to maintain old attitudes and habits. The discharged convict who is ready to change his ways may find it difficult to find a decent job and his only friends may be his former criminal associates. It does not necessarily help an industrial firm to train its foremen in human relations if the foremen must perform in an authoritarian structure.

ASSESSMENT OF MOTIVATIONAL BASES OF ATTITUDES

If an understanding of the nature of attitudes and the conditions for their change depends upon a knowledge of their functional bases, then it becomes of first importance to identify the underlying motivational patterns. The traditional advertising approach is to give less attention to the research assessment of needs and motives and more attention to multiple appeals, to gaining public attention, and to

[72] Helen Peak, "Psychological Structure and Person Perception," in Renato Tagiuri and Luigi Petrullo, editors, Person Perception and Interpersonal Behavior, Stanford, Calif., Stanford University Press, 1958, pp. 337-352.

[73] Samuel A. Stouffer, Communism, Conformity and Civil Liberties, New York, Doubleday, 1955.

plugging what seems to work. Multiple appeals will, it is hoped, reach some members of the public with an effective message. In political campaigns, there is more concern with gearing the approach to the appropriate audience. If the political party makes serious mistakes in its assessment of the needs of particular groups, it is not a matter of losing a few potential customers but of losing votes to the opposing party, and so losing the election. Political leaders are, therefore, making more and more use of public opinion polls and a number of the major candidates for high office enlist their own research specialists. So true is this that we may no longer have political conventions naming a dark-horse candidate for the presidency. If the leaders are not convinced by poll results that a candidate has a good chance to win, they are not likely to support him.

There are no reliable short-cuts to the assessment of the needs which various attitudes satisfy. Systematic sampling of the population in question by means of interviews or of behavioral observation is a necessity. A growing number of devices are becoming available to supplement the depth interview. Objective scales for determining personality trends, such as the F-scale or the Minnesota Multiphasic Inventory, have been widely used. Projective methods which call for the completion of sentences and stories or furnishing stories about ambiguous pictures are just beginning to be exploited. In a nationwide survey of attitudes toward public health, Veroff *et al.* successfully used a picture test to obtain scores for people with respect to their needs for achievement, for affiliation, and for power.[74] Methods for measuring motivation are difficult, but the basic logic in their application is essentially that of any research tool. If early abuses of these instruments do not prejudice the research field, they will in the future have almost as wide a use as the polls themselves. Moreover, polling methods can be adapted to measuring people's needs with indirect questions which have been validated against more projective tests.

In many situations inferences can be made about people's needs without elaborate measures. If farm income has fallen drastically in a given section of the country, or if unemployment has risen sharply in a certain city, obvious inferences can be drawn. The extent and depth of the dissatisfaction will be better known through adequate measurement.

Measures of the four types of motivational pattern discussed indicate wide individual differences in the extent to which the patterns characterize the person. Though all people employ defense mechanisms, there are wide differences in the depth and extent of defensiveness. And

[74] Joseph Veroff, John W. Atkinson, Sheila C. Feld, and Gerald Gurin, "The Use of Thematic Apperception to Assess Motivation in a Nationwide Interview Study," *Psychological Monographs*, in press.

Cohen has shown that the need for knowledge varies even in a college population.[75] Subjects were assigned scores on their need to know by a questionnaire with forced-choice alternatives to a wide variety of hypothetical situations. One of three alternatives indicated a desire for more information. In the experimental situation which followed, one group was given fear-arousing communications about the grading of examinations and then given information about grading on the basis of the normal curve. Their need for information was thus aroused before the presentation of the information. A second group was given the information about grading on the basis of the curve and then given the fear-arousing communication. Measures were taken of the acceptance of the information at a subsequent period. The subjects who had scored low on need for knowledge were definitely affected by the order of presentation. When they received information before their anxieties had been aroused about grades, they were much less receptive than were the low-need scorers who had their anxieties aroused before they received the information. On the other hand, the subjects scoring high on the need to know were not affected by the order of the presentation. Their needs for knowledge were sufficiently strong that they were receptive to information without the specific need arousal of the experimental situation. In other words, the need to know, like other needs, varies in intensity among people as a characteristic of personality.

In spite of characteristic differences in the strength of needs and motives, we cannot predict attitude change with precision solely on the basis of measures of need. We must also have measures of the related attitudes. Knowledge of the need state indicates the type of goal toward which the individual is striving. But the means for reaching this goal may vary considerably, and for this reason we need to know the attitudes which reflect the evaluation of the various means. Farmers with depressed incomes may still vote for the Republican Party if they have confidence in Nixon's farm program. Some need patterns furnish more direct predictions than others. The defensive person who is extrapunitive will be high in prejudice toward outgroups. Even in this case, however, his prejudices toward specific outgroups may vary considerably.

THE FACTOR OF GENERAL PERSUASIBILITY

We have emphasized the fact that appeals to change attitudes must be geared to the relevant motivational basis of the attitude. An opposed point of view would be that there is a general personality characteristic of persuasibility according to which some people are easier to convince

[75] Arthur R. Cohen, "Need for Cognition and Order of Communication as Determinants of Opinion Change," in Carl Hovland *et al.*, editors, *The Order of Presentation in Persuasion*, New Haven, Conn., Yale University Press, 1957, pp. 79-97.

than others no matter what the appeal. Hovland and Janis have tested this hypothesis in a series of experiments.[76] In one investigation ten different communications were presented to 185 high school students. The communications ranged from logical arguments to fear-arousing threats on five topics, on both the pro and con sides of the issue. In general there was some tendency for the acceptance of the influence of one communication to be associated with the acceptance of other influences. Of the 45 correlation coefficients for the ten communications, 39 were positive but only 11 were significant at the .01 confidence level and only 6 were over .40. Though there may be some general susceptibility to influence, it is apparently not a potent factor and accounts for a small amount of variance in attitude change. For certain purposes, however, it deserves consideration, especially in situations where attitudes are not supported by strong motivational patterns.

SUMMARY

The purpose of this paper was to provide a psychological framework for the systematic consideration of the dynamics of public and private attitudes. Four functions which attitudes perform for the personality were identified: the *adjustive function* of satisfying utilitarian needs, the *ego-defensive function* of handling internal conflicts, the *value-expressive function* of maintaining self-identity and of enhancing the self-image, and the *knowledge function* of giving understanding and meaning to the ambiguities of the world about us. The role of these functions in attitude formation was described. Their relevance for the conditions determining attitude arousal and attitude change were analyzed. Finally, constellations of variables such as group contact and legislative control of behavior were considered in terms of their motivational impact.

[76] Carl I. Hovland and Irving L. Janis, editors, *Personality and Persuasibility*, New Haven, Conn., Yale University Press, 1959.

THE INDEXING PROCESS
IN COMMUNICATION
Percy H. Tannenbaum

F ROM a broad viewpoint, we may conceive of two major classifications of variables that are operative in a given communication message having some effect, intended or otherwise. There are, on the one hand, factors in the recipients of the message which may enhance or limit its effectiveness. A variety of such audience variables has been studied,[1] but we still lack adequate measures to explore many of the presumably critical factors.

The other major classification consists of factors in the message itself. Obviously the content of a message will determine, to an extent, its effects. But what is the effective content? One obvious answer is to regard the *total* message as the single gross stimulus input into a communication situation, and to attribute any measurable effect of the communication to that single entity, as such. This has been the approach that has characterized most of the hundreds of studies that have demonstrated communication effects of one kind or another. There has been little attention to the distinctive components of this stimulus pattern.

Some investigations of content analysis[2] represent a certain degree of refinement from this gross approach. Here the focus is usually on the determination of the relative frequencies of arbitrarily-established content categories, or in the isolation of basic themes or appeals. But in most studies of this kind, the causal relationship between content categories and effects is more often assumed than demonstrated.

*Grateful acknowledgement is due Drs. Wilbur Schramm and Charles E. Osgood for their many helpful suggestions and guidance throughout the conduct of the experiments reported here, and in the writing of this paper. Financial support for most of these studies came from the Institute of Communications Research at the University of Illinois.
[1]Hovland, C. I., I. L. Janis and H. H. Kelley, *Communication and Persuasion*, New Haven: Yale University Press, 1953.
[2]Berelson, B., *Content Analysis in Communication Research*, Glencoe, Illinois: Free Press, 1952.

Originally published in Volume 19, Number 3, 1955 of the *Public Opinion Quarterly*.

The notion of an indexing process in communication effects is an outgrowth of regarding the communication message as a set of distinctive stimulus elements—of individual signs or cues usually (e.g., language), but not necessarily (e.g., pictorial communication), arranged in a sequential order of some kind. The nature of the basic message unit—is it the morpheme, the word, the phrase, the sentence, etc?—remains undecided at present and is the undefined term of the system. This issue, however, is a vital one in communication theory and will ultimately have to be resolved. For our purposes here it is sufficient to make the assumption of the message being a *set* (in mathematical set theory terminology) of such undefined elements.

An *index* is considered to be a single such stimulus element or a stimulus complex that may serve to predispose a particular interpretation or meaning of the total stimulus pattern or of some segment of this stimulus pattern other than itself.[3] Or, continuing the set theory analogy further, an index is a subset of the total message set; more precisely, it is a *proper subset,* in that it may be composed of one or more of the elements, but is never all of them. In a given communication message, then, there may be one or more such subsets which may or may not overlap (or intersect) one another, depending on the conditions of membership imposed.

One way in which an index may influence the effects of a communication is, of course, in terms of *attracting attention* to that message. If a particular cue or cue combination within the total message structure somehow raises the threshold of attention for that message and guides its selection over other messages, then it has served to influence its potentiality for effect. This is particularly true of the *mass* communication situation. Schramm has referred to this aspect of the indexing process as follows: "Communications is a buyer's market. Far more stimuli come to us than we are able to attend to. . . . There is good reason to think that we scan our communication environment like an index, selecting among cues and concentrating our attention on the signs associated with the cues that specially attract us. . . . For example, we habitually listen to a newscast at a relatively low level of attention until a cue word or phrase awakens our attention and invites us to respond to a group of signs associated with the cue."[4]

This illustration stems directly from one of Schramm's own studies.[5] He found that the presence of the name of a well-known person—in this

[3]A more precise definition of an index is given in the "Discussion" section of this paper.
[4]Schramm, W., *Personal Communication.*
[5]Related to the writer by Dr. Wilbur Schramm, and reported herein with his permission.

case, a popular campus athlete—in association with a particular radio newscast item significantly enhanced the recall of that item. Moreover, some sort of generalization effect seemed to exist: items closely adjacent to the name-linked one were recalled significantly more frequent than when the name cue was absent.

Another way in which an index may function is in influencing the *decoding* the message. An incoming stimulus pattern impinges on and interacts with the predisposing, subjective factors within the recipient of the communication. The result of such integration of the message complex within the subjective frame of reference of the individual is the precipitation of the meaning of that message for that person.[6] This internal activity also serves to mediate any responses the individual may make to the message in that it provides the distinctive self-stimulation for such responses. If a particular message segment influences this central perceptual process in some way, it has then served as an index.

In the nomenclature of perception, the focus of inquiry here is whether the part can influence the perception of the whole, or, in some cases, whether it can influence the perception of another of the parts. As a problem in perception this is not novel. The literature of traditional perception abounds with examples of this,[7] as does that of the more contemporary "new look" perception.[8]

VERBAL INDICES

There is considerable evidence for the influence of verbal indices on perception. Asch found that the simple substitution of the word "cold" for "warm" in a list of eight descriptive adjectives significantly altered the impression of the personality these adjectives were supposed to describe.[9] And there is further evidence for the operation of the warm-cold variable as an index.[10] Several experiments have shown that the verbal applied to

[6]For a more thorough treatment of this identification of "meaning" with perception, see Osgood, C. E., *Method and Theory in Experimental Psychology*, New York: Oxford University Press, 1953, pp. 194–195.

[7]See, e.g., E. G. Boring, *Sensation and Perception in the History of Experimental Psychology*, New York: Appleton-Century, 1942, and M. D. Vernon, *A Further Study of Visual Perception*, Cambridge, England: Cambridge University Press, 1952.

[8]See Bruner, J. S., "Personality Dynamics and the Process and Perceiving," in Blake, R. R. and G. V. Ramsey (Eds.), *Perception: An Approach to Personality*, New York: Ronald Press, 1951.

[9]Asch, S. E., "Forming Impressions of Personality." *Journal of Abnormal and Social Psychology*, Vol. 41 (1946), pp. 258–290.

[10]Kelley, H. H., "The Warm-Cold Variable in First Impressions of Persons." *Journal of Personality*, Vol. 18 (1950), pp. 431–439; Mensh, I. M. and J. Wishner, "Asch on 'Forming Impressions of Personality': Further Evidence." Journal of Personality, Vol. 16 (1947), pp. 188–191, and Cofer, C. N. and J. T. Dunn, "Personality Ratings as Influenced by Verbal Stimuli." *Journal of Personality*, Vol. 21 (1952), pp. 223–227.

an ambiguous design in many cases determined the nature of the reproduction of that design.[11] Following another line of study, Farnsworth and Beaumont demonstrated that aesthetic evaluation of paintings was significantly affected by a statement of their commercial value.[12] Not least, the study in rumor transmission by Allport and Postman contains abundant evidence of the role of both verbal and non-verbal parts on the perception of the whole.[13]

The Newspaper Headline. In an experiment by Tannenbaum, two stories were planted in a regular front page of a college daily.[14] Three different headlines, each emphasizing a separate segment of the story, were presented to different groups of subjects with the main body of the story held constant. One story, for example, dealt with a report of a day's proceedings in a murder trial, with one headline indicating innocence of the defendant, one guilt, and the third non-commital.

Differential effects of the headline, in reply to a question regarding the innocence or guilt of the defendant, were significant beyond the 5 per cent level. On the other story, the headline effect was significant at the .15 level. It was also shown that the effect of the headline was inversely related to the extent to which the story was read—i.e., the more thorough the reading, the less the effect of the headline *per se*, and vice-versa.

The Newscast "Lead." Tannenbaum and Kerrick repeated the headline experiment in the form of a radio newscast.[15] A regular newscast was written from the front-page stories, including the two experimental items. Three variations of the newscast were recorded, the variable being the introductory statement or "lead" to the experimental stories. Here again, differences in the effect of the "lead" index were significant beyond the 5 per cent level. No significant effect was noted on the second story, but this can be attributed to the fact that we were dealing with well-structured attitudes that were not susceptible to change.

Picture Captions. Can slightly different captions alter the meaning of

[11]Carmichael, L., H. P. Hogan and A. A. Walter, "An Experimental Study of the Effect of Language on the Reproduction of Visually Perceived Forms." *Journal of Experimental Psychology*, Vol. 15 (1932), pp. 73–86; Gibson, J. J., "The Reproduction of Visually Perceived Forms." *Journal of Experimental Psychology*, Vol. 12 (1929), pp. 1–39, and Luchins, A. S., "Social Influence on Perception of Complex Drawings." *Journal of Social Psychology*, Vol. 21 (1945), pp. 257–275.

[12]Farnsworth, P. R. and H. Beaumont, "Suggestion in Pictures." *Journal of General Psychology*, Vol. 2 (1929), pp. 362–366.

[13]Allport, G. W. and L. Postman, *The Psychology of Rumor*, New York: Holt, 1947.

[14]Tannenbaum, P. H., "The Effect of Headlines on the Interpretation of News Stories." *Journalism Quarterly*, Vol. 30 (1953), pp. 189–197.

[15]Tannenbaum, P. H. and Jean S. Kerrick, "The Effect of the Lead on Radio Newscast Interpretation," *Journalism Quarterly*, Vol. 31 (1954), pp. 33–37.

the same accompanying pictorial material?[16] Using Osgood's semantic differential technique[17] as the measuring device, this problem was investigated with five selected pictures of the Thematic Aperception Test. Each picture was presented in three variations: without a caption, with a caption loading the meaning in one direction, and with a caption loading the meaning in the opposite direction.

The results showed a significant index effect of the two opposing captions.[18] On the direction of loading on the intended scales (e.g., toward *happy* in the case of a picture captioned AT THE STATION: RE-UNION, and toward *sad* when the caption was AT THE STATION: PARTING). Moreover, the effect of the caption generalized to other scales so that the total interpretation was congruent with the aspect made explicit in the caption. In some instances where the caption was quite opposite to the basic content of the picture, the effect was sufficient to cause a shift in judgment in the direction of the caption.

The Word "But." In another study in verbal indexing, the effect of a single word—the common conjunction "but"—immersed in a stream of conversation was studied.[19] A tape recording was made of two individuals discussing the use of radio for adult educational purposes. The script was written in this manner: One discussant would make a point, then the second discussant would say something of the order of: "I agree with you BUT . . .", and would then proceed to make essentially the same point but in somewhat different words. In this manner the discussion went back and forth—first one person making a point, and then the other indicating agreement, adding the word "but," and proceeding to make the same point with a different vocabulary.

Two recordings of this conversation were made. One was left intact and the other was edited so that all the "but's" were deleted. The two recordings, then, were identical except for the absence or presence of the index word. Two groups of subjects were exposed to the respective tapes, and, following exposure, were asked a series of questions relating to the content. The main question for purposes of analysis was: "Is it your opinion that the discussants agreed with each other or that they disagreed?" A Chi-square analysis of the replies indicated a significant difference between the two groups beyond the 5 per cent level, with the index word "but" apparently creating a predisposition of disagreement.

[16]This study was conducted by Jean S. Kerrick.

[17]Osgood, C. E., "The Nature and Measurement of Meaning." *Psychological Bulletin*, Vol. 49 (1952), pp. 197–237.

[18]For reasons of economy, the actual results of this and the following experiments are not reported. In most cases, these results can be presented only in the form of lengthy and numerous tables. Interested readers may obtain the actual results by contacting the writer.

[19]This study was conducted by the writer.

Most people exposed to an undergraduate psychology course are well acquainted with the common optical illusions to be found in most texts— e.g., the Muller-Lyre, Poggendorf and Zollner illusions.[20] These are prime examples of the effect of non-verbal indices in visual perception. Similarly, the more recent experiments in social perception contain evidence of non-verbal indexing. Bruner and Postman found that the presence of differently-valued symbols (a swastika, a dollar sign, and an abstract geometric design) drawn on identically-sized discs influenced the perceived size of those discs.[21] In the same way, the studies of Ansbacher[22] and of Bruner and Goodman[23] on the perceived size of postage stamps and coins, respectively, can be considered as cases of indexing.

Political Symbols. As part of a study in pictorial symbolism, the effect of commonly-used political symbols on judgments of various animal drawings was investigated.[24] The animals dealt with were the bear, eagle, lion, donkey, and elephant. To various groups of subjects the following modes of presentation were offered for each animal for judgment on the semantic differential: (a) drawing of the animal itself (e.g., plain drawing of the bear); (b) drawing of the animal in a typical non-political situation (e.g., a dancing bear); and (c) political cartoon of the animal (e.g., the Russian bear, with the hammer-and-sickle symbol clearly indicated on his chest). In addition, subjects rated the orthographic forms of the symbol and the thing symbolized—e.g., the word "bear" and the word "Russia."

The results clearly indicate significant differences between the profiles of judgment for the three forms of pictorial representation. And, whereas judgments of the non-political symbols showed some evidence of compromise (e.g., judgments of the dancing bear shifted from those of the plain drawing of the bear only on those scales of the semantic differential appropriate to the stereotyped situation), judgments of the political drawings showed no such compromise, differing on almost all of the ten scales from those of the other two stimulus situations. Indeed, the profile of the political cartoon of the bear was almost identical with that for the word "Russia." It is to be noted that subjects were asked to judge the *total* drawing.

Color. Can different colors significantly alter the judgments of articles

[20]See Boring, E. G., *Op. cit.*

[21]Bruner, J. S. and L. Postman, "Symbolic Value as an Organizing Factor in Perception." *Journal of Social Psychology*, Vol. 27 (1948), pp. 203–208.

[22]Ansbacher, H., "Number Judgment of Postage Stamps: A Contribution to the Psychology of Social Norms." *Journal of Psychology*, Vol. 5 (1938), pp. 347–350.

[23]Bruner, J. S. and C. C. Goodman, "Value and Need as Organizing Factors in Perception." *Journal of Abnormal and Social Psychology*, Vol. 42 (1947), pp. 33–44.

[24]This study was conducted by the writer and Jean S. Kerrick.

with which they are associated?[25] A latin-square analysis of variance design was set up in which five nationally-advertised products (a shirt, ice cream, rug, automobile, and cake) and a control (color spot)—making six objects of judgment—were judged by six groups of subjects against 20 bi-polar scales of the semantic differential. Subjects were instructed to rate the *products* only. The same design was applied to four different conditions of color-usage—intense (80 per cent saturation) color in product, pale (20 per cent saturation) color in product, intense color in background, and pale color in background. Separate analyses were conducted for each scale under each condition.

The findings of this study can be summarized as follows: (a) Using the product-color interaction as the error term, *F*-values between colors were significant for several of the non-evaluative[26] descriptive scales such as warm-cool, heavy-light, rough-smooth, flimsy-sturdy and exciting-dull, and only for the condition of intense color on product; using the less stringent error term of within-cells variance, several additional scales, still non-evaluative ones, showed significant color effects. (b) Particularly on the evaluative scales (e.g., good-bad, tasty-distasteful, etc.) the color-product interaction was the significant factor, indicating the importance of selecting appropriate, culturally-accepted colors to go with particular advertised products. (c) Pastel colors, both in the product and background, elicited small but consistently more favorable judgments.

Music. A recently-completed experiment indicates that background music can have a significant effect on the impact of dramatic material presented over television.[27] Three conditions of presentation of a one-act play were used: the stage presentation, a one-camera kinescope recording made at the same time as the stage presentation with the single camera situated on the center aisle of the theatre, and a two-camera studio presentation utilizing all the techniques of TV production, including close-ups, super-imposed images, etc. Six groups of subjects were employed—three groups for the conditions indicated, and another three groups where an appropriate musical background score was *added* to the presentation. Subjects were asked to rate the play, as such, on ten selected scales of the semantic differential.

The results indicate that the musical index was not effective on the evaluative judgments, but that it exercised a significant effect over all

[25]This study was conducted by Charles E. Osgood and the writer.

[26]The terms "non-evaluative" and "evaluative," as used here in application to the scales of the semantic differential, are based on the relative loadings of these scales on a set of empirically-derived factors. See Osgood, C. E., *Report on Development and Application of the Semantic Differential*, Urbana, Illinois: Institute of Communication Research, University of Illinois, 1953 (mimeo).

[27]This study was conducted by the writer.

three conditions of presentation in terms of judgments of the strength or potency of the drama and along an active-passive continuum. For the particular play and the particular music used, the music background effect was one of making the play appear stronger and more active. No significant interaction between the music and the presentation was indicated.

DISCUSSION

It is apparent from the foregoing results that what we have referred to as the indexing process is a general phenomenon that may be operative in many kinds of communication situations. In each of the seven experimental studies reported, the manipulation of a single index under conditions of single communication exposures produced significant effects on the judgments of the total message. These findings are somewhat spectacular in themselves. They are even more so when we consider the implications they hold for the more common communication situations where we have repeated exposures to similar, related messages, each accompanied by a number of cues pointing in the same direction. Under such conditions, the cumulative index effects may completely dominate the interpretation of the communication.

What is the mechanism by which an index exercises its influence on the perception of message, and thus on their effects? As part of the general body of perception theory, this is still an unresolved issue. Similarly, lacking a precise knowledge of the dynamics of the communication process, it is impossible to give a complete account of the functioning of the indexing process in communication.

However, within the domain of the communication studies reported here, there are certain aspects of its operation that become evident. To begin with, an index does not achieve its status as an index merely by virtue of being a part—even a highly-structured part—of the total stimulus content and structure. It is effective as an index to the extent, first, that it has meaning for the recipient of the message. In other words, it is the significance or meaning that the communicatee attributes to the particular message segment—and not its mere existence as a message segment—that is of importance. And, second, it is the way in which the communicatee then integrates his meaning of this one segment into his interpretation of the total message that promotes its influence. It is not the communicator's or the experimenter's decision that determines what is and what is not an index. It is the communicatee's or subject's meaning and consequent utilization thereof that is the critical factor.[28] It follows, then, that if two

[28]For similar and more thorough expressions of this view, see D. Krech and R. S. Crutchfield, *Theory and Problems of Social Psychology*, New York: McGraw-Hill, 1948, pp. 81 ff. on their treatment of structural and functional factors in perception, and Bruner, *op. cit.*, pp. 131–133, on his discussion of relevant and non-relevant cues.

individuals have different meanings of the particular message part under consideration, the functioning of this part as an index will differ in kind if not in extent. Similarly, if one individual utilizes this part in his final interpretation of the message more than the other, then the difference will be in extent.

In a sense, most message parts may be considered as indices, since it is reasonable to assume that the final interpretation of a communication is a result of the integration of the meanings and significances of its individual units. But the notion of an indexing process, as advanced here, is that some parts may *exercise an inordinate effect* in this integrative process, and that their "contribution" to the final meaning may be out of all proportion to that of the other parts. It is when a message part exercises such excessive influence that we refer to it as an index.

For analytic purposes, the indexing process may be conveniently considered within the general framework of Osgood's mediation theory.[29] Figure 1 represents a symbolic model. The cues of the message $(S_1, S_2 \ldots S_n)$ each elicit mediational processes $(r_m - - - \rightarrow S_m)$ within the individual exposed to them, according to previous experience. Each of these mediation processes represents, at this level, the meaning or significance of that cue for that individual. Within the context of a communication message, the mediating reactions (r_m) of the cues may be further thought of as becoming integrated into a higher-order mediating reaction to the communication per se. This mediating reaction (r_{mc}) produces a distinctive pattern of self-stimulation (S_{mc}) which is at once the awareness or significance of the message and a necessary condition for evoking appropriate responses (R_c), such as, e.g., ratings on an attitude scale in a typical experimental situation.

Thus, this central mediation process represents a distinct psychological state of the individual at a given time. As outlined above, this state is the representation of the meaning of the message—i.e., how it is decoded by its recipient. On the encoding side, it represents the intentions of the communicator.

The particular mediating reaction thus elicited is obviously only one of a number of such available reactions. In other words, just as there may be a number of different meanings of a single sign or cue, there are also a number of different significances within a mature individual's repetoire for the particular message. That is, the particular r_{mc} elicited is only one of a number of such possible mediating reactions, each of which has associated with it its own distinctive pattern of self-stimulation, and thus may lead to differential

[29]See Osgood, *Method and Theory in Experimental Psychology*, for the general learning theory model, and his article, "The Nature and Measurement of Meaning" for an application to the communication process. A more elaborate treatment is to be found in *A General Model of the Human Communication Process*, Urbana, Illinois: Institute of Communication Research, University of Illinois, 1953 (mimeo.).

meanings and responses. This set of possible reactions may be thought of as belonging to a *hierarchy*. The specific reaction that, for some reason or other, goes to the top of the hierarchy in a given communication situation, is the one that is responsible for the specific meaning attributed to that message, or for the way in which it is perceived.

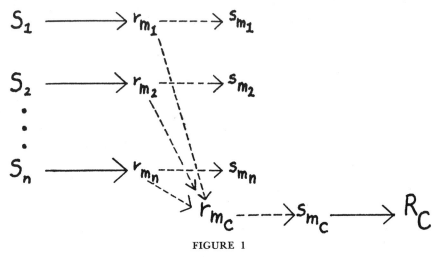

FIGURE 1

SYMBOLIC ACCOUNT OF THE DEVELOPMENT OF
THE SIGNIFICANCE OF A COMMUNICATION

Within this general paradigm, presented here all too briefly, the indexing process may be operationally stated: A message part serving as an index is one which selectively sensitizes a particular perception of the message by channeling a particular mediating reaction to the top of the hierarchy. To put it another way, the hierarchy may be considered as a set of possible reactions each with a certain probability of occurrence at a given time. An index serves to raise the probability of one of these reactions occurring over all others. In Figure 1, each of the cues shown tend to produce a single mediating reaction to the communication. Let us suppose, however, that another in this set of message cues, say S_k, exercises a more profound effect than the other cues combined, and leads to the evoking of a different mediating reaction to the communication ($r_{m_{ck}}$) which has a higher probability of occurrence. This mediating reaction will produce its own stimulation ($S_{m_{ck}}$) and will thus lead to a different response. We then speak of S_k as an index.

This analysis still fails to define the mechanism by which an index influences the probabilities or how it channels a particular reaction to the top of the hierarchy. It is the writer's contention that the mechanics of this process rest in the neurophysiological system of the individual, and will ultimately have to be accounted for on that microscopic level of analysis. For example, it may well be that in the case of sequentially-organized messages where the index appears at the beginning of the message—e.g., the "lead" in the radio newscast study—the operation of the index may be accounted for on the basis of a *stimulus trace* persisting through time in the central nervous system. Such a notion is entirely plausible, but for the present is only speculative.

14

PROCESSES OF
OPINION CHANGE
Herbert C. Kelman

A PERSISTENT concern in the analysis of public opinion data is the "meaning" that one can ascribe to the observed distributions and trends—and to the positions taken by particular individuals and segments of the population. Clearly, to understand what opinion data mean we have to know considerably more than the direction of an individual's responses or the distribution of responses in the population. We need information that will allow us to make some inferences about the characteristics of the observed opinions—their intensity, their salience, the level of commitment that they imply. We need information about the motivational bases of these opinions—about the functions that they fulfill for the individual and the motivational systems in which they are embedded.[1] We need information about the cognitive links of the opinions—the amount and the nature of information that supports them, the specific expectations and evaluations that surround them.

The need for more detailed information becomes even more apparent when we attempt to use opinion data for the prediction of subsequent behavior. What is the likelihood that the opinions observed in a particular survey will be translated into some form of concrete action?

* This paper is based on a research program on social influence and behavior change, supported by grant M-2516 from the National Institute of Mental Health.

[1] For discussions of the different motivational bases of opinion see I. Sarnoff and D. Katz, "The Motivational Bases of Attitude Change," *Journal of Abnormal and Social Psychology*, Vol. 49, 1954, pp. 115-124; and M. B. Smith, J. S. Bruner, and R. W. White, *Opinions and Personality*, New York, Wiley, 1956.

Originally published in Volume 3, Number 2, 1939 of the *Public Opinion Quarterly*.

What is the nature of the actions that people who hold a particular opinion are likely to take, and how are they likely to react to various events? How likely are these opinions to persist over time and to generalize to related issues? What are the conditions under which one might expect these opinions to be abandoned and changed? Such predictions can be made only to the extent to which we are informed about the crucial dimensions of the opinions in question, about the motivations that underlie them, and about the cognitive contexts in which they are held.

INFERRING THE MEANING OF OPINIONS

In a certain sense, the need for more detailed information about opinions can (and must) be met by improvements and refinements in the methodology of opinion assessment. A great deal of progress in this direction has already been made in recent years. Thus, many widely accepted features of interviewing technique are specifically designed to elicit information on which valid inferences about the meaning of opinions can be based: the creation of a relaxed, nonjudgmental atmosphere; the emphasis on open-ended questions; the progressive funneling from general to specific questions; the use of probes, of indirect questions, and of interlocking questions; and so on. These procedures facilitate inferences (1) by maximizing the likelihood that the respondent will give rich and full information and thus reveal the motivational and cognitive structure underlying the expressed opinions, and (2) by minimizing the likelihood that the respondent will consciously or unconsciously distort his "private" opinions when expressing them to the interviewer.

Similarly, when attitudes are assessed by means of questionnaires, it is possible to approximate these methodological goals. In part, this is accomplished by the instructions, which can motivate the subject to respond fully and honestly and assure him of confidentialness or anonymity. In part it is accomplished by the use of indirect and projective questions, and by the inclusion of a series of interrelated items in the questionnaire. And, in part, it is possible to make inferences about the meaning of opinions by the use of various scaling devices in the analysis of the data.

There is no question about the importance of these methodological advances, but in and of themselves they do not solve the problem of inference. They increase the investigator's ability to obtain rich and relatively undistorted information on which he can then base valid inferences. But, no matter how refined the techniques, they do not provide direct information about the meaning of the opinions and do not permit automatic predictions to subsequent behavior: the investigator still has to make inferences from the data.

To make such inferences, the student of public opinion needs a theoretical framework which accounts for the adoption and expression of particular opinions on the part of individuals and groups. Such a framework can serve as a guide in the collection of data: it can provide a systematic basis for deciding what information is relevant and what questions should be asked in order to permit the drawing of inferences. Similarly, it can serve as a guide for interpreting the data and deriving implications from them.

The need for such a framework is particularly apparent when one attempts to make predictions about subsequent behavior on the basis of opinion data. For example, in a relaxed interview situation a particular respondent may express himself favorably toward socialized medicine. What are the chances that he will take the same position in a variety of other situations? To answer this, we would need a theoretical scheme for the analysis of interaction situations, in terms of which we could make some inferences about the structure and meaning of this particular interview situation as compared to various other situations in which the issue of socialized medicine might arise. How would we expect this same respondent to react to a concerted campaign by the Medical Association which links Federal insurance programs with creeping socialism? To answer this, we would need a theory of opinion formation and change, in terms of which we could make some inferences about the characteristics of opinions formed under different conditions.

Progress in the analysis of public opinion, then, requires theoretical development along with methodological improvements. For this development, it should be possible to draw on some of the current theoretical thinking and associated research in social psychology. There are two foci of social-psychological theorizing and research that would appear to be particularly germane to the analysis of public opinion. One is the study of processes of social interaction as such. Such diverse approaches to the analysis of social interaction as those of Getzels,[2] Goffman,[3] and Jones and Thibaut,[4] for example, can be useful for con-

[2] J. W. Getzels, "The Question-Answer Process: A Conceptualization and Some Derived Hypotheses for Empirical Examination," *Public Opinion Quarterly*, Vol. 18, 1954, pp. 80-91.

[3] See, for example, E. Goffman, "On Face-work: An Analysis of Ritual Elements in Social Interaction," *Psychiatry*, Vol. 18, 1955, pp. 213-231; and "Alienation from Interaction," *Human Relations*, Vol. 10, 1957, pp. 47-60.

[4] E. E. Jones and J. W. Thibaut, "Interaction Goals as Bases of Inference in Interpersonal Perception," in R. Tagiuri and L. Petrullo, editors, *Person Perception and Interpersonal Behavior*, Stanford, Calif., Stanford University Press, 1958, pp. 151-178.

ceptualizing the determinants of *opinion expression*. Thus, by using one or another of these schemes, the investigator can make some formulations about the expectations that the respondent brought to the interview situation and the goals that he was trying to achieve in this interaction. On the basis of such a formulation, he can make inferences about the meaning of the opinions expressed in this situation and about their implications for subsequent behavior—for example, about the likelihood that similar opinions will be expressed in a variety of other situations.

The second relevant focus of social-psychological theorizing and research is the study of processes of social influence and the induction of behavior change. Theoretical analyses in this area can be useful for conceptualizing the determinants of *opinion formation* and *opinion change*. They can help the investigator in making formulations about the sources of the opinions expressed by the respondent—the social conditions under which they were adopted, the motivations that underlie them, and the social and personal systems in which they are embedded. On the basis of such a formulation, again, he can make inferences about the meaning and implications of the opinions ascertained.

The model that I shall present here emerged out of the second research focus—the study of social influence and behavior change. It is, essentially, an attempt to conceptualize the processes of opinion formation and opinion change. It starts with the assumption that opinions adopted under different conditions of social influence, and based on different motivations, will differ in terms of their qualitative characteristics and their subsequent histories. Thus, if we know something about the determinants and motivational bases of particular opinions, we should be able to make predictions about the conditions under which they are likely to be expressed, the conditions under which they are likely to change, and other behavioral consequences to which they are likely to lead. Ideally, such a model can be useful in the analysis of public opinion by suggesting relevant variables in terms of which opinion data can be examined and predictions can be formulated.

THE STUDY OF SOCIAL INFLUENCE

Social influence has been a central area of concern for experimental social psychology almost since its beginnings. Three general research traditions in this area can be distinguished: (1) the study of social influences on judgments, stemming from the earlier work on prestige suggestion;[5] (2) the study of social influences arising from small-group

[5] See, for example, S. E. Asch, *Social Psychology*, New York, Prentice-Hall, 1952.

interaction;[6] and (3) the study of social influences arising from persuasive communications.[7] In recent years, there has been a considerable convergence between these three traditions, going hand in hand with an increased interest in developing general principles of social influence and socially induced behavior change.

One result of these developments has been that many investigators found it necessary to make qualitative distinctions between different types of influence. In some cases, these distinctions arose primarily out of the observation that social influence may have qualitatively different effects, that it may produce different kinds of change. For example, under some conditions it may result in mere public conformity—in superficial changes on a verbal or overt level without accompanying changes in belief; in other situations it may result in private acceptance—in a change that is more general, more durable, more integrated with the person's own values.[8] Other investigators found it necessary to make distinctions because they observed that influence may occur for different reasons, that it may arise out of different motivations and orientations. For example, under some conditions influence may be primarily informational—the subject may conform to the influencing person or group because he views him as a source of valid information; in other situations influence may be primarily normative—the subject may conform in order to meet the positive expectations of the influencing person or group.[9]

My own work can be viewed in the general context that I have outlined here. I started out with the distinction between public conformity and private acceptance, and tried to establish some of the distinct determinants of each. I became dissatisfied with this dichotomy as I began to look at important examples of social influence that could

[6] See, for example, D. Cartwright and A. Zander, editors, *Group Dynamics*, Evanston, Ill., Row, Peterson, 1953.

[7] See, for example, C. I. Hovland, I. L. Janis, and H. H. Kelley, *Communication and Persuasion*, New Haven, Yale University Press, 1953.

[8] See, for example, L. Festinger, "An Analysis of Compliant Behavior," in M. Sherif and M. O. Wilson, editors, *Group Relations at the Crossroads*, New York, Harper, 1953, pp. 232-256; H. C. Kelman, "Attitude Change as a Function of Response Restriction," *Human Relations*, Vol. 6, 1953, pp. 185-214; J. R. P. French, Jr., and B. Raven, "The Bases of Social Power," in D. Cartwright, editor, *Studies in Social Power*, Ann Arbor, Mich., Institute for Social Research, 1959, pp. 150-167; and Marie Jahoda, "Conformity and Independence," *Human Relations*, Vol. 12, 1959, pp. 99-120.

[9] See, for example, M. Deutsch and H. B. Gerard, "A Study of Normative and Informational Social Influence upon Individual Judgment," *Journal of Abnormal and Social Psychology*, Vol. 51, 1955, pp. 629-636; J. W. Thibaut and L. Strickland, "Psychological Set and Social Conformity," *Journal of Personality*, Vol. 25, 1956, pp. 115-129; and J. M. Jackson and H. D. Saltzstein, "The Effect of Person-Group Relationships on Conformity Processes," *Journal of Abnormal and Social Psychology*, Vol. 57, 1958, pp. 17-24.

not be encompassed by it. I was especially impressed with the accounts of ideological conversion of the "true believer" variety, and with the recent accounts of "brainwashing," particularly the Chinese Communist methods of "thought reform."[10] It is apparent that these experiences do not simply involve public conformity, but that indeed they produce a change in underlying beliefs. But it is equally apparent that they do not produce what we would usually consider private acceptance— changes that are in some sense integrated with the person's own value system and that have become independent of the external source. Rather, they seem to produce new beliefs that are isolated from the rest of the person's values and that are highly dependent on external support.

These considerations eventually led me to distinguish three processes of social influence, each characterized by a distinct set of antecedent and a distinct set of consequent conditions. I have called these processes *compliance, identification*, and *internalization*.[11]

THREE PROCESSES OF SOCIAL INFLUENCE

Compliance can be said to occur when an individual accepts influence from another person or from a group because he hopes to achieve a favorable reaction from the other. He may be interested in attaining certain specific rewards or in avoiding certain specific punishments that the influencing agent controls. For example, an individual may make a special effort to express only "correct" opinions in order to gain admission into a particular group or social set, or in order to avoid being fired from his government job. Or, the individual may be concerned with gaining approval or avoiding disapproval from the influencing agent in a more general way. For example, some individuals may compulsively try to say the expected thing in all situations and please everyone with whom they come in contact, out of a disproportionate need for favorable responses from others of a direct and immediate kind. In any event, when the individual complies, he does what the agent wants him to do—or what he thinks the agent wants him to do—because he sees this as a way of achieving a desired response from him. He does not adopt the induced behavior—for example, a particular opinion response—because he believes in its content, but because it is instrumental in the production of a satisfying social effect. What the individual learns, essentially, is to say or do the expected thing in special situations, regardless of what his private beliefs may

10 For instance, R. J. Lifton, " 'Thought Reform' of Western Civilians in Chinese Communist Prisons," *Psychiatry*, Vol. 19, 1956, pp. 173-195.

11 A detailed description of these processes and the experimental work based on them will be contained in a forthcoming book, *Social Influence and Personal Belief: A Theoretical and Experimental Approach to the Study of Behavior Change*, to be published by John Wiley & Sons.

be. Opinions adopted through compliance should be expressed only when the person's behavior is observable by the influencing agent.

Identification can be said to occur when an individual adopts behavior derived from another person or a group because this behavior is associated with a satisfying self-defining relationship to this person or group. By a self-defining relationship I mean a role relationship that forms a part of the person's self-image. Accepting influence through identification, then, is a way of establishing or maintaining the desired relationship to the other, and the self-definition that is anchored in this relationship.

The relationship that an individual tries to establish or maintain through identification may take different forms. It may take the form of classical identification, that is, of a relationship in which the individual takes over all or part of the role of the influencing agent. To the extent to which such a relationship exists, the individual defines his own role in terms of the role of the other. He attempts to be like or actually to *be* the other person. By saying what the other says, doing what he does, believing what he believes, the individual maintains this relationship and the satisfying self-definition that it provides him. An influencing agent who is likely to be an attractive object for such a relationship is one who occupies a role desired by the individual—who possesses those characteristics that the individual himself lacks—such as control in a situation in which the individual is helpless, direction in a situation in which he is disoriented, or belongingness in a situation in which he is isolated.

The behavior of the brainwashed prisoner in Communist China provides one example of this type of identification. By adopting the attitudes and beliefs of the prison authorities—including *their* evaluation of *him*—he attempts to regain his identity, which has been subjected to severe threats. But this kind of identification does not occur only in such severe crisis situations. It can also be observed, for example, in the context of socialization of children, where the taking over of parental attitudes and actions is a normal, and probably essential, part of personality development. The more or less conscious efforts involved when an individual learns to play a desired occupational role and imitates an appropriate role model would also exemplify this process. Here, of course, the individual is much more selective in the attitudes and actions he takes over from the other person. What is at stake is not his basic sense of identity or the stability of his self-concept, but rather his more limited "professional identity."

The self-defining relationship that an individual tries to establish or maintain through identification may also take the form of a reciprocal role relationship—that is, of a relationship in which the roles of the two parties are defined with reference to one another. An individual may be involved in a reciprocal relationship with another specific individual, as in a friendship relationship between two people. Or he may enact a social role which is defined with reference to another (reciprocal) role, as in the relationship between patient and doctor. A reciprocal-role relationship can be maintained only if the participants have mutually shared expectations of one another's behavior. Thus, if an individual finds a particular relationship satisfying, he will tend to behave in such a way as to meet the expectations of the other. In other words, he will tend to behave in line with the requirements of this particular relationship. This should be true regardless of whether the other is watching or not: quite apart from the reactions of the other, it is important to the individual's own self-concept to meet the expectations of his friendship role, for example, or those of his occupational role.

Thus, the acceptance of influence through identification should take place when the person sees the induced behavior as relevant to and required by a reciprocal-role relationship in which he is a participant. Acceptance of influence based on a reciprocal-role relationship is similar to that involved in classical identification in that it is a way of establishing or maintaining a satisfying self-defining relationship to another. The nature of the relationship differs, of course. In one case it is a relationship of identity; in the other, one of reciprocity. In the case of reciprocal-role relationships, the individual is not identifying with the other in the sense of taking over *his* identity, but in the sense of empathically reacting in terms of the other person's expectations, feelings, or needs.

Identification may also serve to maintain an individual's relationship to a group in which his self-definition is anchored. Such a relationship may have elements of classical identification as well as of reciprocal roles: to maintain his self-definition as a group member an individual, typically, has to model his behavior along particular lines and has to meet the expectations of his fellow members. An example of identification with a group would be the member of the Communist Party who derives strength and a sense of identity from his self-definition as part of the vanguard of the proletarian revolution and as an agent of historical destiny. A similar process, but at a low degree of intensity, is probably involved in many of the conventions that people acquire as part of their socialization into a particular group.

Identification is similar to compliance in that the individual does not adopt the induced behavior because its content per se is intrinsically satisfying. Identification differs from compliance, however, in that the individual actually believes in the opinions and actions that he adopts. The behavior is accepted both publicly and privately, and its manifestation does not depend on observability by the influencing agent. It does depend, however, on the role that an individual takes at any given moment in time. Only when the appropriate role is activated—only when the individual is acting within the relationship upon which the identification is based—will the induced opinions be expressed. The individual is not primarily concerned with pleasing the other, with giving him what he wants (as in compliance), but he is concerned with meeting the other's expectations for his own role performance. Thus, opinions adopted through identification do remain tied to the external source and dependent on social support. They are not integrated with the individual's value system, but rather tend to be isolated from the rest of his values—to remain encapsulated.

Finally, *internalization* can be said to occur when an individual accepts influence because the induced behavior is congruent with his value system. It is the content of the induced behavior that is intrinsically rewarding here. The individual adopts it because he finds it useful for the solution of a problem, or because it is congenial to his own orientation, or because it is demanded by his own values—in short, because he perceives it as inherently conducive to the maximization of his values. The characteristics of the influencing agent do play an important role in internalization, but the crucial dimension here—as we shall see below—is the agent's credibility, that is, his relation to the content.

The most obvious examples of internalization are those that involve the evaluation and acceptance of induced behavior on rational grounds. A person may adopt the recommendations of an expert, for example, because he finds them relevant to his own problems and congruent with his own values. Typically, when internalization is involved, he will not accept these recommendations *in toto* but modify them to some degree so that they will fit his own unique situation. Or a visitor to a foreign country may be challenged by the different patterns of behavior to which he is exposed, and he may decide to adopt them (again, selectively and in modified form) because he finds them more in keeping with his own values than the patterns in his home country. I am not implying, of course, that internalization is always involved in the situations mentioned. One would speak of internalization only if acceptance of influence took the particular form that I described.

Internalization, however, does not necessarily involve the adoption of induced behavior on rational grounds. I would not want to equate internalization with rationality, even though the description of the process has decidedly rationalist overtones. For example, I would characterize as internalization the adoption of beliefs because of their congruence with a value system that is basically *irrational*. Thus, an authoritarian individual may adopt certain racist attitudes because they fit into his paranoid, irrational view of the world. Presumably, what is involved here is internalization, since it is the content of the induced behavior and its relation to the person's value system that is satisfying. Similarly, it should be noted that congruence with a person's value system does not necessarily imply logical consistency. Behavior would be congruent if, in some way or other, it fit into the person's value system, if it seemed to belong there and be demanded by it.

It follows from this conception that behavior adopted through internalization is in some way—rational or otherwise—integrated with the individual's existing values. It becomes part of a personal system, as distinguished from a system of social-role expectations. Such behavior gradually becomes independent of the external source. Its manifestation depends neither on observability by the influencing agent nor on the activation of the relevant role, but on the extent to which the underlying values have been made relevant by the issues under consideration. This does not mean that the individual will invariably express internalized opinions, regardless of the social situation. In any specific situation, he has to choose among competing values in the face of a variety of situational requirements. It does mean, however, that these opinions will at least enter into competition with other alternatives whenever they are relevant in content.

It should be stressed that the three processes are not mutually exclusive. While they have been defined in terms of pure cases, they do not generally occur in pure form in real-life situations. The examples that have been given are, at best, situations in which a particular process predominates and determines the central features of the interaction.

ANTECEDENTS AND CONSEQUENTS OF
THE THREE PROCESSES

For each of the three processes, a distinct set of antecedents and a distinct set of consequents have been proposed. These are summarized in the table below. First, with respect to the antecedents of the three processes, it should be noted that no systematic quantitative differences between them are hypothesized. The probability of each process is presented as a function of the same three determinants: the importance of the induction for the individual's goal achievement, the power of the influencing agent, and the prepotency of the induced response. For each process, the magnitude of these determinants may vary over the entire range: each may be based on an induction with varying degrees of importance, on an influencing agent with varying degrees of power, and so on. The processes differ only in terms of the *qualitative* form that these determinants take. They differ, as can be seen in the table,

	Compliance	Identification	Internalization
Antecedents:			
1. Basis for the *importance of the induction*	Concern with social effect of behavior	Concern with social anchorage of behavior	Concern with value congruence of behavior
2. Source of *power of the influencing agent*	Means control	Attractiveness	Credibility
3. Manner of achieving *prepotency of the induced response*	Limitation of choice behavior	Delineation of role requirements	Reorganization of means-ends framework
Consequents:			
1. Conditions of performance of induced response	Surveillance by influencing agent	Salience of relationship to agent	Relevance of values to issue
2. Conditions of change and extinction of induced response	Changed perception of conditions for social rewards	Changed perception of conditions for satisfying self-defining relationships	Changed perception of conditions for value maximization
3. Type of behavior system in which induced response is embedded	External demands of a specific setting	Expectations defining a specific role	Person's value system

in terms of the *basis* for the importance of the induction, the *source* of the influencing agent's power, and the *manner* of achieving prepotency of the induced response.

1. The processes can be distinguished in terms of the basis for the importance of the induction, that is, in terms of the nature of the motivational system that is activated in the influence situation. What is it about the influence situation that makes it important, that makes it relevant to the individual's goals? What are the primary concerns that the individual brings to the situation or that are aroused by it? The differences between the three processes in this respect are implicit in the descriptions of the processes given above: (a) To the extent that the individual is concerned—for whatever reason—with the *social effect* of his behavior, influence will tend to take the form of compliance. (b) To the extent that he is concerned with the *social anchorage* of his behavior, influence will tend to take the form of identification. (c) To the extent that he is concerned with the *value congruence* of his be-

havior (rational or otherwise), influence will tend to take the form of internalization.

2. A difference between the three processes in terms of the source of the influencing agent's power is hypothesized. (a) To the extent that the agent's power is based on his *means control*, influence will tend to take the form of compliance. An agent possesses means control if he is in a position to supply or withhold means needed by the individual for the achievement of his goals. The perception of means control may depend on the agent's *actual* control over specific rewards and punishments, or on his *potential* control, which would be related to his position in the social structure (his status, authority, or general prestige). (b) To the extent that the agent's power is based on his *attractiveness*, influence will tend to take the form of identification. An agent is attractive if he occupies a role which the individual himself desires[12] or if he occupies a role reciprocal to one the individual wants to establish or maintain. The term "attractiveness," as used here, does not refer to the possession of qualities that make a person likable, but rather to the possession of qualities on the part of the agent that make a continued relationship to him particularly desirable. In other words, an agent is attractive when the individual is able to derive satisfaction from a self-definition with reference to him. (c) To the extent that the agent's power is based on his *credibility*, influence will tend to take the form of internalization. An agent possesses credibility if his statements are considered truthful and valid, and hence worthy of serious consideration. Hovland, Janis, and Kelley[13] distinguish two bases for credibility: expertness and trustworthiness. In other words, an agent may be perceived as possessing credibility because he is likely to *know* the truth, or because he is likely to *tell* the truth. Trustworthiness, in turn, may be related to over-all respect, likemindedness, and lack of vested interest.

3. It is proposed that the three processes differ in terms of the way in which prepotency is achieved. (a) To the extent that the induced response becomes prepotent—that is, becomes a "distinguished path" relative to alternative response possibilities—because the individual's choice behavior is limited, influence will tend to take the form of compliance. This may happen if the individual is pressured into the induced response, or if alternative responses are blocked. The induced response thus becomes prepotent because it is, essentially, the only response permitted: the individual sees himself as having no

---

[12] This is similar to John Whiting's conception of "Status Envy" as a basis for identification. See J. W. M. Whiting, "Sorcery, Sin, and the Superego," in M. R. Jones, editor, *Nebraska Symposium on Motivation*, Lincoln, University of Nebraska Press, 1959, pp. 174-195.

[13] *Op.cit.*, p. 21.

choice and as being restricted to this particular alternative. (b) To the extent that the induced response becomes prepotent because the requirements of a particular role are delineated, influence will tend to take the form of identification. This may happen if the situation is defined in terms of a particular role relationship and the demands of that role are more or less clearly specified; for instance, if this role is made especially salient and the expectations deriving from it dominate the field. Or it may happen if alternative roles are made ineffective because the situation is ambiguous and consensual validation is lacking. The induced response thus becomes prepotent because it is one of the few alternatives available to the individual: his choice behavior may be unrestricted, but his opportunity for selecting alternative responses is limited by the fact that he is operating exclusively from the point of view of a particular role system. (c) Finally, to the extent that the induced response becomes prepotent because there has been a reorganization in the individual's conception of means-ends relationships, influence will tend to take the form of internalization. This may happen if the implications of the induced response for certain important values— implications of which the individual had been unaware heretofore— are brought out, or if the advantages of the induced response as a path to the individual's goals, compared to the various alternatives that are available, are made apparent. The induced response thus becomes prepotent because it has taken on a new meaning: as the relationships between various means and ends become restructured, it emerges as the preferred course of action in terms of the person's own values.

Depending, then, on the nature of these three antecedents, the influence process will take the form of compliance, identification, or internalization. Each of these corresponds to a characteristic pattern of internal responses—thoughts and feelings—in which the individual engages as he accepts influence. The resulting changes will, in turn, be different for the three processes, as indicated in the second half of the table. Here, again, it is assumed that there are no systematic quantitative differences between the processes, but rather qualitative variations in the subsequent histories of behavior adopted through each process.

1. It is proposed that the processes differ in terms of the subsequent conditions under which the induced response will be performed or expressed. (a) When an individual adopts an induced response through compliance, he tends to perform it only under conditions of *surveillance* by the influencing agent. These conditions are met if the agent is physically present, or if he is likely to find out about the individual's actions. (b) When an individual adopts an induced response through identification, he tends to perform it only under conditions of *salience* of his relationship to the agent. That is, the occurrence of the behavior

will depend on the extent to which the person's relationship to the agent has been engaged in the situation. Somehow this relationship has to be brought into focus and the individual has to be acting within the particular role that is involved in the identification. This does not necessarily mean, however, that he is consciously aware of the relationship; the role can be activated without such awareness. (c) When an individual adopts an induced response through internalization, he tends to perform it under conditions of *relevance of the values* that were initially involved in the influence situation. The behavior will tend to occur whenever these values are activated by the issues under consideration in a given situation, quite regardless of surveillance or salience of the influencing agent. This does not mean, of course, that the behavior will occur every time it becomes relevant. It may be outcompeted by other responses in certain situations. The probability of occurrence with a given degree of issue relevance will depend on the strength of the internalized behavior.

2. It is hypothesized that responses adopted through the three processes will differ in terms of the conditions under which they will subsequently be abandoned or changed. (a) A response adopted through compliance will be abandoned if it is no longer perceived as the best path toward the attainment of social rewards. (b) A response adopted through identification will be abandoned if it is no longer perceived as the best path toward the maintenance or establishment of satisfying self-defining relationships. (c) A response adopted through internalization will be abandoned if it is no longer perceived as the best path toward the maximization of the individual's values.

3. Finally, it is hypothesized that responses adopted through the three processes will differ from each other along certain qualitative dimensions. These can best be summarized, perhaps, by referring to the type of behavior system in which the induced response is embedded. (a) Behavior adopted through compliance is part of a system of external demands that characterize a specific setting. In other words, it is part of the rules of conduct that an individual learns in order to get along in a particular situation or series of situations. The behavior tends to be related to the person's values only in an instrumental rather than an intrinsic way. As long as opinions, for example, remain at that level, the individual will tend to regard them as not really representative of his true beliefs. (b) Behavior adopted through identification is part of a system of expectations defining a particular role—whether this is the role of the other which he is taking over, or a role reciprocal to the other's. This behavior will be regarded by the person as representing himself, and may in fact form an important aspect of himself. It will tend to be isolated, however, from the rest of the person's values—

to have little interplay with them. In extreme cases, the system in which the induced response is embedded may be encapsulated and function almost like a foreign body within the person. The induced responses here will be relatively inflexible and stereotyped. (c) Behavior adopted through internalization is part of an internal system. It is fitted into the person's basic framework of values and is congruent with it. This does not imply complete consistency: the degree of consistency can vary for different individuals and different areas of behavior. It does mean, however, that there is some interplay between the new beliefs and the rest of the person's values. The new behavior can serve to modify existing beliefs and can in turn be modified by them. As a result of this interaction, behavior adopted through internalization will tend to be relatively idiosyncratic, flexible, complex, and differentiated.

RESEARCH BASED ON THE MODEL

The model itself and its possible implications may be seen more clearly if I present a brief summary of the research in which it was used. This research has moved in three general directions: experimental tests of the relationships proposed by the model, application of the model to the study of personality factors in social influence, and application of the model to the analysis of a natural influence situation.

Experimental tests of the proposed distinctions between the three processes. The relationships proposed by the model can be tested by experiments in which the antecedents postulated for a given process are related to the consequents postulated for that process. The first experiment on this problem[14] varied one of the antecedents—the source of the influencing agent's power—and observed the effects of this variation on one of the consequents—the conditions of performance of the induced response. Subjects (Negro college freshmen) were exposed to a tape-recorded interview dealing with an aspect of the Supreme Court decision on school segregation. Four versions of this communication were developed and played to different groups of subjects. The four communications contained the same message, but they differed in the way in which the communicator was introduced and presented himself at the beginning of the interview. These differences were designed to vary the source and degree of the communicator's power: in one communication the speaker was presented as possessing high means control, in the second as possessing high attractiveness, in the third as possessing high credibility, and in the fourth (for purposes of comparison) as being low in all three of these sources of power.

[14] H. C. Kelman, "Compliance, Identification and Internalization: Three Processes of Attitude Change," *Journal of Conflict Resolution,* Vol. 2, 1958, pp. 51-60.

The subjects filled out attitude questionnaires designed to measure the extent of their agreement with the communication. To vary the conditions of performance, we asked each subject to complete three separate questionnaires, one under conditions of salience and surveillance, one under conditions of salience of the communicator—but without surveillance, and a third under conditions of nonsurveillance and nonsalience. It was predicted that attitudes induced by the communicator high in means control would tend to be expressed only under conditions of surveillance by the communicator (the mediating process here being compliance), attitudes induced by the communicator high in attractiveness would tend to be expressed only when the subject's relationship to the communicator was salient (the mediating process here being identification), and attitudes induced by the communicator high in credibility would tend to be expressed when they were relevant in content, regardless of surveillance or salience (the mediating process here being internalization). These predictions were confirmed to a most encouraging degree.

One implication of this study for the analysis of public opinion is that we can make certain predictions about the future course of a given opinion if we know something about the interpersonal circumstances under which it was formed. An interview might reveal the predominant dimensions in terms of which the respondent perceives those individuals and groups to whom he traces the opinion in question. For example, does he see them primarily as potential sources of approval and disapproval? Or as potential reference points for his self-definition? Or as potential sources of information relevant to his own concern with reality testing and value maximization? From the answers to these questions we should be able to predict the future conditions under which this opinion is likely to come into play.

The study also suggests possible "diagnostic" devices that would make it possible to infer the process by which a particular opinion was adopted and hence the level at which it is held. If, for example, an opinion is expressed only in the presence of certain crucial individuals, one can assume that it is probably based on compliance and one can make certain further inferences on that basis. In other words, by observing the "conditions of performance of the induced response" (one of the consequents in our model), we can deduce the process on which this response is based.

It would, of course, be considerably easier and safer to make such inferences if several diagnostic criteria were available. It would be useful, therefore, to derive—from the list of consequents postulated by the model—further indicators in terms of which compliance-based, identification-based, and internalized opinions can be distinguished from one another, and to test the validity of these indicators. This is particularly true for identification and internalization. Since both of these processes, presumably, produce changes in "private belief," it is difficult to pin down the distinction between opinions based on them. There is a need, therefore, to develop a number of indicators that can capture the qualitative differences in the nature of opinions produced by these two processes, subtle though these differences may be. A second experiment addressed itself to this problem.[15]

The experimental situation, again, involved the use of tape-recorded communications. Three versions of the communication were used, each presented to a different group of college students. In each of the communications a novel program of science education was described and the rationale behind it was outlined. The basic message was identical in all cases, but the communications differed in terms of certain additional information that was included in order to produce different orientations. In one communication (*role-orientation* condition) the additional information was designed to spell out the implications of the induced opinions for the subject's relationship to certain important reference groups. Positive reference groups were associated with acceptance of the message, and—in a rather dramatic way—negative reference groups were associated with opposition to it. The intention here was to create two of the postulated antecedents for *identification*: a concern with the social anchorage of one's opinions, and a delineation of the requirements for maintaining the desired relationship to one's reference groups (see the table). In the second communication (*value-orientation* condition) the additional information was designed to spell out the implications of the induced opinions for an important value—personal responsibility for the consequences of one's actions. The communication argued that acceptance of the message would tend to maximize this value. The intention here was to create two of the postulated antecedents of *internalization*: a concern with the value congruence of one's opinions, and a reorganization of one's conception of means-ends relationships. The third communication was introduced for purposes of comparison and contained only the basic message.

On the basis of the theoretical model it was predicted that the nature of the attitude changes produced by the two experimental communications would differ. Role orientation would presumably produce the consequences hypothesized for identification, while value orientation would produce the consequences hypothesized for internalization. A number of measurement situations were devised to test these predic-

[15] H. C. Kelman, "Effects of Role-orientation and Value-orientation on the Nature of Attitude Change," paper read at the meetings of the Eastern Psychological Association, New York City, 1960.

tions: (1) In each group, half the subjects completed attitude questionnaires immediately after the communication, under conditions of salience, and half completed them a few weeks later, under conditions of nonsalience. As predicted, there was a significant difference between these two conditions of measurement for the role-orientation group but not for the value-orientation group. (2) The generalization of the induced attitudes to other issues involving the same values, and to other situations involving similar action alternatives, was measured. The prediction that the value-orientation group would show more generalization than the role-orientation group on the value dimension tended to be confirmed. The prediction that the reverse would be true for generalization along the action dimension was not upheld. (3) Flexibility of the induced attitudes was assessed by asking subjects to describe their doubts and qualifications. As predicted, the value-orientation group scored significantly higher on this index. (4) Complexity of the induced attitudes was assessed some weeks after the communication by asking subjects to list the things they would want to take into account in developing a new science education program. The total number of items listed was greater for the role-orientation group, but the number of items showing an awareness of relevant issues (as rated by a naïve judge) was clearly greater in the value-orientation group. (5) Half the subjects in each group were exposed to a countercommunication presenting a new consensus, the other half to a countercommunication presenting new arguments. It was predicted that the role-orientation group would be relatively more affected by the first type of countercommunication, and the value-orientation group by the second. The predicted pattern emerged, though it fell short of statistical significance.

The results of this study are not entirely unambiguous. They are sufficiently strong, however, to suggest that it should be possible to develop a number of criteria by which identification-based and internalized attitudes can be distinguished from one another. On the basis of such distinctions, one can then make certain inferences about the meaning of these attitudes and further predictions about their future course.

The relation between personality factors and social influence. This research starts with the assumption that the specific personality variables that are related to the acceptance of influence will depend on the particular process of influence involved. There is a further assumption that relationships depend on the type of influence situation to which the person is exposed. In other words, the concern is with exploring the specific personality variables that predispose individuals to engage in each of the three processes, given certain situational forces.

In the first study of this problem[16] we were interested in the relationship between one type of personality variable—cognitive needs and styles—and the process of internalization. We wanted to study this relationship in a situation in which people are exposed to new information that challenges their existing beliefs and assumptions. This is a situation in which at least some people are likely to re-examine their beliefs and—if they find them to be incongruent with their values in the light of the new information—they are likely to change them. A change under these particular motivational conditions would presumably take the form of internalization.

It was proposed that people who are high in what might be called the *need for cognitive clarity* would react more strongly to a situation of this type. They would be made uncomfortable by the incongruity produced by such a situation and the challenge it presented to their cognitive structures. The *nature* of their reaction, however, may differ. Some people may react to the challenge by changing their beliefs, while others may react by resisting change. Which of these directions an individual would be likely to follow would depend on his characteristic *cognitive style*. A person who typically reacts to ambiguity by seeking clarification and trying to gain understanding (a "clarifier") would be likely to open himself to the challenging information and perhaps to reorganize his beliefs as a consequence. A person who typically reacts to ambiguity defensively, by simplifying his environment and keeping out disturbing elements (a "simplifier"), would be likely to avoid the challenging information.

Measures of cognitive need and cognitive style were obtained on a group of college students who were then exposed to a persuasive communication that presented some challenging information about American education. Change in attitudes with respect to the message of the communication was measured on two occasions for each subject: immediately after the communication, under conditions of salience, and six weeks later under conditions of nonsalience.

We predicted that, among people high in need for cognitive clarity, those whose characteristic style is clarification would be the most likely to manifest attitude change in the induced direction, while those whose characteristic style is simplification would be the most likely to manifest resistance to change and possibly even negative change. This difference should be especially marked under conditions of nonsalience, which are the conditions necessary for a reasonable test of internalization. Among the people who are low in need for cognitive clarity, it was

[16] H. C. Kelman and J. Cohler, "Reactions to Persuasive Communication as a Function of Cognitive Needs and Styles," paper read at the meetings of the Eastern Psychological Association, Atlantic City, 1959.

predicted that cognitive style would be unlikely to produce consistent differences since they are less motivated to deal with the ambiguity that the challenging information has created.

The results clearly supported these predictions. High-need clarifiers showed more change than high-need simplifiers (who, in fact, changed in the negative direction). This difference was small under conditions of salience, but became significant under conditions of nonsalience— suggesting that the difference between clarifiers and simplifiers is due to a difference in their tendency to internalize. Among low-need subjects, no consistent differences between the two style groups emerged.

This study suggests that one can gain a greater understanding of the structure of an individual's opinions on a particular issue by exploring relevant personality dimensions. In the present case we have seen that, for some of the subjects (those concerned with cognitive clarity), the opinions that emerge represent at least in part their particular solution to the dilemma created by incongruous information. In studies that are now under way we are exploring other personality dimensions that are theoretically related to tendencies to comply and identify. If our hypotheses are confirmed in these studies, they will point to other ways in which emerging opinions may fit into an individual's personality system. Opinions may, for example, represent partial solutions to the dilemmas created by unfavorable evaluations from others or by finding oneself deviating from the group. Since these relationships between opinions and personality variables are tied to the three processes of influence in the present model, certain predictions about the future course of the opinions for different individuals can be readily derived.

The application of the model to the analysis of a natural influence situation. We are currently engaged in an extensive study of Scandinavian students who have spent a year of study or work in the United States.[17] We are interested in the effects of their stay here on their self-images in three areas: nationality, profession, and interpersonal relations. Our emphasis is on learning about the processes by which changes in the self-image come about or, conversely, the processes by which the person's existing image maintains itself in the face of new experiences. Our subjects were questioned at the beginning of their stay in the United States and at the end of their stay, and once again a year after their return home.

This study was not designed as a direct test of certain specific hypotheses about the three processes of influence. In this kind of rich field situation it seemed more sensible to allow the data to point the

[17] Lotte Bailyn and H. C. Kelman, "The Effects of a Year's Experience in America on the Self-image of Scandinavians: Report of Research in Progress," paper read at the meetings of the American Psychological Association, Cincinnati, 1959.

way and to be open to different kinds of conceptualizations demanded by the nature of the material. The model of influence did, however, enter into the formulation of the problem and the development of the schedules and is now entering into the analysis of the data.

In a preliminary analysis of some of our intensive case material, for example, we found it useful to differentiate four patterns of reaction to the American experience which may affect various aspects of the self-image: (1) An individual may change his self-image by a reorganization of its internal structure; here we would speak of a change by means of the process of *internalization*. (2) His self-image may be changed by a reshaping of the social relationships in which this image is anchored; here we would speak of a change by means of *identification*. (3) The individual may focus on the internal structure of the self-image but maintain it essentially in its original form; here we would speak of the process of *confirmation*. Finally, (4) he may maintain his self-image through a focus on its original social anchorage; here maintenance by the process of *resistance* would be involved. We have related these four patterns to a number of variables in a very tentative way, but the analysis will have to progress considerably farther before we can assess the usefulness of this scheme. It is my hope that this kind of analysis will give us a better understanding of the attitudes and images that a visitor takes away from his visit to a foreign country and will allow us to make some predictions about the subsequent history of these attitudes and images. Some of these predictions we will be able to check out on the basis of our post-return data.

CONCLUSION

There is enough evidence to suggest that the distinction between compliance, identification, and internalization is valid, even though it has certainly not been established in all its details. The specification of distinct antecedents and consequents for each of the processes has generated a number of hypotheses which have met the experimental test. It seems reasonable to conclude, therefore, that this model may be useful in the analysis of various influence situations and the resulting opinion changes. It should be particularly germane whenever one is concerned with the quality and durability of changes and with the motivational conditions that produced them.

I have also attempted to show the implications of this model for the analysis of public opinion. By tying together certain antecedents of influence with certain of its consequents, it enables us to infer the motivations underlying a particular opinion from a knowledge of its manifestations, and to predict the future course of an opinion from a knowledge of the conditions under which it was formed. Needless to say, the usefulness of the model in this respect is limited, not only because it is still in an early stage of development but also because of the inherent complexity of the inferences involved. Yet it does suggest an approach to the problem of meaning in the analysis of public opinion data.

HOMEOSTATIC THEORY
IN ATTITUDE CHANGE
Nathan Maccoby and
Eleanor E. Maccoby

I N recent years a number of theoretical formulations have been made to account for attitude change. Some of these have been applications of more general theory, while others were devised especially to deal with attitude change. All are concerned with attitude change as an effect of communications. The more general theories that have been applied specifically to attitude change problems include Festinger's theory of cognitive dissonance, Heider's balance theory, and learning theory.[1] Some of the especially devised approaches are Rosenberg's affective-cognitive consistency approach, McGuire's rational-syllogistic formulation, Osgood and Tannenbaum's congruity theory, and Newcomb's strain toward symmetry.[2] Brehm, Cohen, Adams, Romney, and the Maccobys have recently applied dissonance theory to attitude change problems.[3] Cartwright and Harary have developed theo-

[1] L. Festinger, *A Theory of Cognitive Dissonance*, Evanston, Ill., Row, Peterson, 1957. F. Heider, "Attitudes and Cognitive Organization," *Journal of Psychology*, Vol. 21, 1946, pp. 107-112.

[2] M. J. Rosenberg, "An Analysis of Affective-Cognitive Consistency," in C. I. Hovland and M. J. Rosenberg, editors, *Attitude Organization and Change*, New Haven, Conn., Yale University Press, 1960. M. J. Rosenberg, "A Structural Theory of Attitude Dynamics," *Public Opinion Quarterly*, Vol. 24, 1960, pp. 319-340. W. J. McGuire, "A Syllogistic Analysis of Cognitive Relationships," in Hovland and Rosenberg, *op.cit.*, C. E. Osgood and P. H. Tannenbaum, "The Principle of Congruity in the Prediction of Attitude Change," *Psychological Review*, Vol. 62, 1955, pp. 42-55. C. E. Osgood, "Cognitive Dynamics in the Conduct of Human Affairs," *Public Opinion Quarterly*, Vol. 24, 1960, pp. 341-365. T. M. Newcomb, "An Approach to the Study of Communicative Acts," *Psychological Review*, Vol. 60, 1953, pp. 393-404.

[3] J. W. Brehm, "Attitudinal Consequences of Commitment to Unpleasant Behavior," *Journal of Abnormal and Social Psychology*, Vol. 60, 1960, pp. 379-383. J. W. Brehm and A. R. Cohen, "Choice and Chance Relative Deprivation as Determinants of Cognitive Dissonance," *Journal of Abnormal and Social Psychology*, Vol. 58, 1959, pp. 383-387. A. R. Cohen, "Attitudinal Consequences of Induced Discrepancies between Cognitions and Behavior," *Public Opinion Quarterly*, Vol. 24,

Originally published in Volume 25, Number 4, 1961 of the *Public Opinion Quarterly*.

retical applications to attitude change from Heider's balance theory.[4] And there are others.

Most of these theoretical approaches to attitude change have at least one major characteristic in common. They involve a kind of balance-of-forces approach in which the overloading of one type of factor gives rise to changes designed to restore balance. In short, all employ homeostasis in some form or other.[5]

GENERAL THEORIES

Festinger's theory of cognitive dissonance states that two cognitive elements are in a dissonant relation if, considering these two alone, the obverse of one element would follow from the other. X and Y are dissonant if not X follows from Y. Dissonance can result not only from the perception of such logical inconsistencies, but also from conflicting motivations or desired consequences. Dissonance could take place from cultural mores—Festinger gives the example of picking up a chicken bone at a formal dinner to get at the meat. When an opinion is a derivation or special case of a more general attitude, such as not favoring a particular Democratic candidate when one is a Democrat, or when past experience makes clear that what is being perceived is all wrong, for example staying dry while standing in the rain, dissonance is also said to occur.

The occurrence of such dissonance, says Festinger, gives rise to motivation to reduce it, that is, to change the cognitive dissonance to cognitive consonance. One way of doing this (and there are others) is by changing one of the dissonant cognitions or changing an attitude. Thus let us assume that one's initial position is that President Kennedy should not have permitted the recent abortive Cuban revolt to take place, and that a communication is presented asserting that it was necessary for Castro to be overthrown by such and such a date or he would obtain such effective Russian weapons that the Cuban people would never be able to overthrow him (assuming they wanted to!). Dissonance is thus created by conflicting cognitions. This dissonance gives rise to a drive to reduce it. One of the ways—clearly not the only way—to reduce the dissonance is to change one's attitude toward Presi-

---

1960, pp. 297-318. J. S. Adams, "The Reduction of Cognitive Dissonance by Seeking Consonant Information," *Journal of Abnormal and Social Psychology*, Vol. 62, 1961, pp. 74-78. Eleanor E. Maccoby, N. Maccoby, A. K. Romney, and J. S. Adams, "Social Reinforcement and Attitude Change," *Journal of Abnormal and Social Psychology*, Vol. 63, 1961, pp. 108-114.

[4] D. Cartwright and F. Harary, "Structural Balance: A Generalization of Heider's Theory," *Psychological Review*, Vol. 63, 1956, pp. 277-293.

[5] Zajonc has pointed out the similarity in Heider's, Festinger's, and Osgood's approaches, R. B. Zajonc, "The Concepts of Balance, Congruity, and Dissonance," *Public Opinion Quarterly*, Vol. 24, 1960, pp. 280-296.

dent Kennedy's role in the revolt. Since, however, there are other means of reducing dissonance, if this particular attitude is to be surely changed these other ways must be closed off or at least sharply limited in attractiveness.

Heider applied balance theory to attitude theory in 1946 in his article "Attitudes and Cognitive Organization."[6] This general theory was presented more fully in his 1958 book, *The Psychology of Interpersonal Relations*.[7] If P and O are persons and X is an impersonal object, idea, or event, the problem is how P's cognitions of the relations of P, O, and X are organized. These cognitions are in balance if all three are positive in all respects or if two are negative and one is positive. If P likes O and X, and O is perceived to like X, P's cognitions are balanced. Similarly if P likes O and perceives that both he and O dislike X, P's cognitions with respect to O are balanced. Variations from this state of affairs result in unbalanced states. Unbalanced states generate forces designed to restore balance. As in the case of dissonance, a homeostatic model is again proposed. Cartwright and Harary have applied linear graph theory to the Heider concept. In their model there can be degrees of balance and imbalance.[8]

ESPECIALLY DEVISED APPROACHES

One of the most interesting formulations of recent vintage is that of Rosenberg.[9] This psychologist argues that when the cognitive and affective, or emotional, components of an attitude are in conflict, something has to give. He argues that people seek congruence between their beliefs and their feelings toward an object, and from this develops what he calls a "structural theory" of attitude dynamics. Rosenberg points out that while a number of studies have already demonstrated cases in which the affective component changed following cognitive change, few have been done in which the *cognitive* component was the one changed to achieve congruence following a change in feelings. In a series of dramatic experiments, Rosenberg hypnotized subjects and suggested a radical change in belief without giving reasons, plus an instruction to forget afterward that such a suggestion had been made. The results were quite startling. Not only did the changes in belief occur, but all sorts of arguments were invented to support these new beliefs. For instance, in one study hypnotized subjects who believed strongly in United States aid to foreign countries were told that upon awakening the very idea of such United States aid would displease and disgust them. Upon awakening they strongly opposed the principle of United

[6] *Op.cit.*
[7] F. Heider, *The Psychology of Interpersonal Relations*, New York, Wiley, 1958.
[8] Cartwright and Harary, *op.cit.*
[9] Rosenberg, "An Analysis of Affective-Cognitive Consistency," as cited.

States aid and were completely convinced that they took their new positions as a result of hard reasoning. Rosenberg thus also stresses a homeostatic model with the factors in balance, the factors in his case being cognition and affect, with affect stressed as the modifier of cognition.

While Rosenberg is concerned with the role of drive produced by inconsistency in the cognitive and affective elements in promoting attitude change, McGuire has taken a somewhat different tack.[10] His approach is in terms of logical thinking and wishful thinking. A person's belief system is seen as being comprised of a series of interrelated propositions. In McGuire's model, when a series of propositions implies an *illogical* relationship or a logical *inconsistency*, wishful thinking is involved. Motivation to change one or more of the propositions so as to restore logic takes place when the wishful thinking is exposed. The Socratic method is employed as one of the ways of exposing such logical inconsistencies.

Osgood and Tannenbaum's congruity approach provides another consistency or balance model.[11] They state that cognitive modification (attitude change) results from the psychological stress produced by cognitive inconsistencies that are in some relation to one another. If these inconsistencies are present in sufficient strength, the stress to change occurs. As in the case in several of the other approaches cited above, Osgood and Tannenbaum's theory has led to formal model building and has permitted some degree of quantification. In some respects congruence theory is closest to Heider's and Cartwright and Harary's balance theory. The latter have been mostly concerned with problems of interpersonal perception, while Osgood and his associates have been much more concerned with the effects of mass communications. For example, in both Heider and Cartwright and Harary the illustrations most often used involve persons liking or disliking other persons and the effect of this on attitudes toward something else. Osgood and his colleagues typically refer to public affairs problems as cited in the press. Both stress the drive to restore the equilibrium when it is disturbed or placed in an unbalanced position.

Finally, there is Newcomb's strain toward symmetry approach.[12] When two people are oriented toward a common object, the strain toward symmetry influences communication between them so as to bring about a congruence in their attitudes toward the common objects. In his study of a special experimental dormitory at Michigan, Newcomb found that those who liked one another tended to agree on a great many things, including their attitudes toward some external matter, and the degree of agreement increased with time.

[10] *Op.cit.*   [11] *Op.cit.*   [12] *Op.cit.*

A large body of work on attitude change stems from traditional learning theory, notably the work of Hovland and his colleagues Lumsdaine, Sheffield, Janis, Kelley, and others.[13] How is this work related to that of the homeostatic theorists described above? While one can make derivations from learning theory to dissonance or balance theory, it is our position that the two points of view have in fact produced considerably different emphases—a different choice of research problems.

1. The learning theorist would think of cognitive dissonance or imbalance in terms of conflict. We are aware that Festinger distinguishes between conflict and dissonance, reserving the term dissonance for a post-decisional rather than pre-decisional state. Yet, when we study attitude change, the tension produced in the individual through hearing a message contrary to his existing beliefs is post-decisional in nature in that the pre-existing attitude was previously "decided on." Festinger's term, then, applies to the impact of communication upon attitudes. We believe that conflict theory also applies. One cannot comfortably hold inconsistent attitudes or beliefs, because they produce conflicting action tendencies, and in the presence of such tendencies the state of conflict itself becomes a drive which spurs the individual into some activity designed to resolve the conflict. So, to the learning theorist, the conflict produced by holding incompatible attitudes would be theoretically comparable to the conflict of incompatible motor habits arising when one changes, for example, from a stick-shift car to one with an automatic transmission. To the learning theorist, cognitive conflict does produce a drive state, but there are other motivational states which are relevant to the problem of attitude change too, and the learning theorists have tended to range farther afield in their choice of motive systems to manipulate in order to produce attitude change. For example, Janis used a fear appeal, Cohen aroused need achievement as part of a study of various orders of presentation of a persuasive communication, and Weiss and Fine aroused anger as a pre-condition for the acceptance of a punitive message.[14] The homeostatic theorists have

[13] C. I. Hovland, A. A. Lumsdaine, and F. D. Sheffield, *Experiments in Mass Communication*, Princeton, N.J., Princeton University Press, 1949. C. I. Hovland, I. L. Janis, and H. H. Kelley, *Communication and Persuasion: Psychological Studies of Opinion Change*, New Haven, Conn., Yale University Press, 1953. C. I. Hovland, editor, *The Order of Presentation in Persuasion*, New Haven, Conn., Yale University Press, 1957. C. I. Hovland and I. L. Janis, editors, *Personality and Persuasability*, New Haven, Conn., Yale University Press, 1959. C. I. Hovland and M. J. Rosenberg, editors, *Attitude Organization and Change*, New Haven, Conn., Yale University Press, 1960.

[14] W. Weiss and B. J. Fine, "The Effect of Induced Aggression on Opinion Change," *Journal of Abnormal and Social Psychology*, Vol. 52, 1956, pp. 109-114.

largely confined their attention to attitude change as it occurs under the pressure of a single motive: that arising from incompatibility between different elements in attitudes or beliefs.

2. Learning theory also differs from the homeostatic theories in the amount of attention it gives to *practice* of the content of a persuasive communication. It may be true that if one is dealing with a small enough "bit" or stimulus-response unit, learning occurs in a single trial. An attitude, however, is not this smallest irreducible element. Therefore, when we are talking about attitude change we are talking about a process that presumably does not occur in a single instant of time. This is true even though the overt manifestation of a change in attitude may occur as a single event when sufficient covert "bits" have been learned to result in a kind of "flopover" in response to a question. The underlying process may still be thought of as a cumulative one to which the concept of the learning curve applies. The learning theorists have pointed to the importance of covert practice, or rehearsal, of a message during the post-communication period and have been concerned with the conditions which facilitate or interfere with such practice. The dissonance and balance theorists have tended to ignore this process, and their interest in the post-communication has centered on the motivational consequences which follow from having accepted or not accepted the message at the time of initial impact. These motivational consequences may produce attitude change or information seeking in support of either the initial or the changed attitude, but the amount of practice of the content of the original message is not a variable that is given much attention except by those whose thinking stems fairly directly from traditional learning theory. We would urge that it is an important variable.

CHANNELING OF MOTIVATION INTO ATTITUDE CHANGE

Whether one is thinking in terms of conflict drive, dissonance, imbalance, or strain toward symmetry, a central issue concerns the way in which the aroused motivation is channeled into attitude change. To say that people are made uncomfortable when they catch themselves in an inconsistency and are motivated to get rid of the discomfort would be to say nothing new, and if this were *all* the homeostatic theorists were saying, few of us would be much interested. The interest lies in the nature of the behavior to which the motive state leads. The theorists we have discussed differ in the amount of attention they give to alternative stratagems for dealing with the unsteady state, but all are agreed that attitude change does not necessarily result from the arousal of this state. Indeed, it is here that the homeostatic theorists have made some of their greatest contributions, and much research and theorizing has been centered around the identification of the conditions which determine whether dissonance or imbalance or inconsistency will result in attitude change or in some alternative course of action. The possible alternatives have been frequently noted: they include (1) strengthening the original attitude by discounting the source of the disturbing communication, or by seeking additional information which will support the initial attitude; (2) refusal to attend to the message, or repressing or de-verbalizing it once it is received; and (3) compartmentalizing or fractionating the attitude so that the inconsistencies are not so readily apparent. In addition to these stratagems for restoring balance, we must consider the conditions which might lead individuals simply to endure the tension of dissonance or inconsistency. We are familiar with the concept of tolerance for ambiguity and recognize that in scientific work problems may be in the process of solution over a very long period of time, during which dissonant elements must continue to be cognized as exactly what they are—dissonant elements. In one of the last paragraphs of the last book in the Yale studies in attitude and communications, Hovland and Rosenberg point out that there are people who not only can endure dissonance but who appear to seek it. This brings us to the important matter of individual differences in the ability to tolerate inconsistency, and the implications of such differences for attitude change. Festinger has commented that individual differences in the tolerance for dissonance should be measurable, and that they should relate to variance in attitude change. When such measures are developed, it will be interesting to compare the resulting work, at the level of both concepts and findings, with Janis's work on persuasibility.[15]

USES OF HOMEOSTATIC THEORIES

The test of a theory, of course, lies not only in its ability to organize existing knowledge but also in its ability to generate new knowledge. There is no doubt that the homeostatic theories have proved themselves in this respect. The book *Attitude Organization and Change*, edited by Hovland and Rosenberg, is proof enough.[16] A group of us working on attitude change at Stanford have found dissonance theory useful, in that it has led us to select problems that we otherwise might not have studied, and to put different questions to our data than we would otherwise have asked.

A recent study by Adams will illustrate how we have made use of the theory.[17] The initial positions of a group of mothers were obtained on the roles of hereditary vs. environmental factors in personality development. Some of these mothers were then subjected to a lecture which was consonant, and some to a lecture which was dissonant, with their position. Adams found that those mothers in whom dissonance

[15] Hovland and Janis, *op.cit.*   [16] *Op.cit.*   [17] *Op.cit.*

256

had been produced were more likely to seek further information on the topic than were those who had received consonant information. In a study of post-communication behavior, Eleanor E. Maccoby, N. Maccoby, A. K. Romney, and J. S. Adams found that people who had been influenced by a message sought out post-communication conversations which would reinforce their newly acquired beliefs; furthermore, these conversations served the function of preventing the respondents from backsliding to their original positions: their attitude change was maintained over a period of six months.[18]

Dissonance theory is also being employed in this series of studies to predict the effect of persuasive communication in relation to the initial position of the subject. We expect the greatest attitude change where there is greatest discrepancy between the subject's initial position and that of the communication, *provided* other avenues for reducing dissonance are closed off.

It is interesting to note that these studies grew out of the application of dissonance theory to problems of attitude and behavior change. It is not so much the case that other theoretical approaches of the type discussed in this paper cannot encompass the findings in these and other studies as that these other formulations would not have been so likely as dissonance theory to have led to these particular studies. Similarly, the other theoretical efforts have already led, and will no doubt continue to lead, to the formulation of other interesting and important hypotheses.

When Hovland and his associates, in their pioneer volume *Experiments on Mass Communication*, called for the establishment of a science of communication, they obtained a vigorous and productive response.[19] Carl Hovland died knowing that the field of theoretical and experimental communication to which he contributed so brilliantly and prolifically was indeed well launched.

18 *Op.cit.*
19 Hovland, Lumsdaine, and Sheffield, *op.cit.*

16

INFORMATION FLOW
AND THE STABILITY
OF PARTISAN ATTITUDES
Philip E. Converse

THE low level of public information about politics has been documented with monotony ever since sample survey techniques developed several decades ago. While the critic of public opinion studies is fond of citing Pareto, De Maistre, LeBon, and other anti-democrats of the nineteenth century to show that "we knew this all along," it is worth remembering that these elite theorists represented but one side of a debate, and it was, furthermore, a debate that they lost. It is ironic that what might be used as documentation for their premises about "the common man" has come along in depth only after the conclusion argued from these premises—that mass democracy was not viable—has lost a good deal of its impact.

This irony has been compounded by a second prime finding of public opinion studies. Not only is the electorate as a whole quite uninformed, but it is the least informed members within the electorate who seem to hold the critical "balance of power," in the sense that alternations in governing party depend disproportionately on shifts in their sentiment. In one form of accounting, of course, the stable vote has equal weight with the shifting vote in any given election. Nonetheless, it is easy to take the stable vote for granted: what commands attention as the governor of party success at the polls, and hence administrations and policies, is the changing vote. And "shifting" or "floating" voters

---

* Elaboration of a paper read at meetings of the American Psychological Association, New York, September 1961. The author gratefully acknowledges the skilled assistance of Aage Clausen.

Originally published in Volume 26, Number 4, 1962 of the *Public Opinion Quarterly*

tend to be those whose information about politics is relatively impoverished.

While most major investigations of voting behavior have converged on this finding in one vocabulary or another, the evidence mustered in support has not been striking. Of course any data would be disillusioning if one imagines that an electorate is definitively split into two portions, one made up of fairly informed voters who never shift parties, and the other of uninformed voters who account for any electoral change. This is of course not the intended picture. There are very highly informed voters—should Walter Lippmann be cited?—who shift parties at occasional junctures. And there are as well myriads of extremely uninformed voters who have never crossed party lines. Instead, we think at most in terms of potentials and probabilities: susceptibility to party shifting seems higher for some types of voters than for others, and in any given shift between two elections, the hypothesis argues that the less involved and less informed voters are disproportionately represented.

Even with such an amendment, however, proof of the hypothesis has generally been rather weak. Indeed, a recent intensive review of the major voting studies asserts that none of the published data has adequately supported the notion of a "floating voter," much less hypotheses as to his character.[1] Part of the problem has been that the dependent variable (vote shifts from election to election) is a dynamic one, while most studies have either been single-interview studies or panels nestled in a single campaign period. On common-sense grounds, individuals who vacillate in forming their voting decisions during the campaign period are likely to contribute disproportionately to such *inter*-election voting shifts as do occur, and the Lazarsfeld Erie County study in 1940 showed that these waverers tended to be the less involved and less informed.[2] However, the authors hesitated to generalize the finding to inter-election vote changes. More recent studies have asserted the more inclusive version of the hypothesis quite baldly, basing the judgment in the clearest cases upon recall of a previous vote.[3] The

[1] H. Daudt, *Floating Voters and the Floating Vote: A Critical Analysis of American and English Election Studies*, Leiden, Holland, H. E. Stenfert Kroese N.V., 1961.

[2] P. Lazarsfeld, B. Berelson, and H. Gaudet, *The People's Choice*, New York, Columbia University Press, 1944, pp. 69ff.

[3] Almost all the major studies might be cited. A partial list that indicates variety of national setting and emphasizes inter-election partisan change, as well as campaign vacillation, includes M. Janowitz and D. Marvick, *Competitive Pressures and Democratic Consent: An Interpretation of the 1952 Presidential Election*, Ann Arbor, Mich., University of Michigan Institute of Public Administration, 1956; R. Milne and H. Mackenzie, *Marginal Seat, 1955*, London, The Hansard Society for Parliamentary Government, 1958; A. Girard and J. Stoetzel, "Le Comportement

data shown, however, usually consist of weak correlations at best.

In our own sequence of Survey Research Center studies we have also been impressed with the amount of presumptive evidence for the general hypothesis, once again without definitive long-term panel tables.[4] It has been a standard static finding, for example, that more involved voters are more strongly identified with one of the major parties, and hence could be supposed to have a higher probability of remaining faithful to it over time. A similar mild correlation exists between indices of political involvement and recall of party fidelity in voting. Voters who split their tickets have been found to be less politically involved than straight party voters.[5] A relatively strong negative correlation emerged between a scale measuring sophistication of political conceptions and the crossing of normal party lines in the 1956 presidential vote, although here once again the evidence of inter-election shifts in party is presumptive.[6]

Belief in the broad hypothesis has been stronger than actual evidence might warrant in part because of obvious measurement problems, all of which act in the direction of weakening positive results. For example, if we try to establish the fact of a vote shift from the individual's recall of his next prior vote, we are at the mercy of the accuracy of his report. The same theory which predicts that the less involved are more susceptible to party change suggests that the less involved will also give less accurate accounts of past political behavior. For simple psychological reasons, we would expect them to distort past behavior in the direction of current preference. Such distortions build in a false impression of stability; and if they are more frequent among the less involved, then they act to weaken empirical results in the most direct way.

Similarly, the frailties of involvement measures can affect the clarity of findings.[7] People usually shift parties in a state of what is, for them,

Electoral et le Mécanisme de la Décision," in *Le Referendum de Septembre et les Elections de Novembre 1958*, Paris, Librairie Armand Colin, 1960.

[4] This article draws freely from election studies conducted by the Survey Research Center of the University of Michigan in 1952, 1954, 1956, 1958, and 1960. These projects have been supported variously by grants from the Carnegie Corporation, the Rockefeller Foundation, and the Social Science Research Council.

[5] A. Campbell and W. Miller, "The Motivational Basis of Straight and Split Ticket Voting," *American Political Science Review*, Vol. 51, No. 2, 1957.

[6] A. Campbell, P. E. Converse, W. Miller, and D. E. Stokes, *The American Voter*, New York, Wiley, 1960, p. 264.

[7] It must be noted, of course, that the hypothesis has its greatest interest when the independent variable is political comprehension or political information, rather than political involvement per se. We tend to use involvement as a surrogate for comprehension because it is more readily measured and because it is a fair assumption that there is a high correlation between involvement (motivation to attend to information about matters political) and breadth of comprehension about what is

relative political excitement. Such a transient surge of excitement, if it occurs among people who normally pay little attention to elections and still less to politics outside the campaign, has little to do with political involvement as a durable, year-to-year concern about things political. Yet it is likely that such excitement registers in our measures as involvement and further blurs findings concerning the floating voter.

Two- and four-year longitudinal studies of the national electorate have served to confirm such methodological suspicions and to throw more light on the character of inter-election vote shifts. The table below, employing panel information for the 1956 and 1960 presidential elections, lends rather clear support to the standard "floating voter" hypothesis. The final column, involving persistent nonvoters, has no bearing on vote change in this period, and is inserted merely as an informative anchor to the table. The voters in the two central columns fashioned the shift in the national vote division, 1956-1960, and they compare quite poorly in political information with the stable partisans of the first column. A similar table employing a summary measure of durable political involvement expressed over the entire four-year period gives very comparable results.

THE ASSOCIATION BETWEEN STABILITY OR CHANGE IN PRESIDENTIAL VOTING OVER TIME AND POLITICAL INFORMATION LEVEL, 1956-1960

(*in per cent*)

Information Level*	Voted Twice and for Same Party (N = 712)	Voted Twice but Shifted Parties (N = 207)	Failed to Vote in One of Two Elections† (N = 220)	Twice a Nonvoter† (N = 201)
High	49	33	19	11
Medium	32	32	35	17
Low	19	35	46	72
Total	100	100	100	100

* By and large, knowledge of the more obvious items of political information turns out to show cumulative scale properties for a cross-section of the national population. This is a preliminary measure based on a scaling of items concerning such knowledge about the 1960 presidential candidates as the region from which they came and knowledge about which party controlled the 1960 Congress.

† The table is restricted to individuals who were eligible to vote in both the 1956 and 1960 elections, where the "eligible" include all noninstitutionalized adult citizens over twenty-one.

going on in politics. One of the better estimates of this relationship is presented in Campbell, Converse, Miller, and Stokes, *op.cit.*, p. 252. The uninvolved voter is, by and large, the uninformed voter, and we shall presume this loose equation frequently in the course of this paper.

The broad normative implications of the floating voter hypothesis have been frequently discussed. It is less our purpose here to repeat these discussions than to suggest a refinement in the hypothesis itself. While this modification does not render earlier treatments obsolete, it does have some interesting implications of its own. Since the modification can be seen as a simple logical deduction from the general view of mass voting phenomena that we have been developing in our studies, let us briefly recapitulate the position.

CONCEPTUAL BACKGROUND

Any theory of mass voting behavior must come to grips at the outset not only with the fact of low public information about politics, but also with the fact that information about politics is as inequitably distributed as wealth in the mass public. There are obvious problems involved in the construction of models to embrace at one and the same time the voting decisions of the avid college-educated follower of politics in one of our large urban centers, and those of the Kentucky farmer who has not yet heard at the time of his October interview that a national election is impending, and who goes to the polls to make his ultimate "choice" without any knowledge whatever of the identity of the two presidential candidates.

Given such a "range of talent," it is congenial to work initially with attitudes toward the major political parties. This is so in part because the two parties are virtually the only interesting political objects that are surely perceived by the quasi-totality of the population. Nearly all Americans are capable of locating themselves on a seven-point scale that runs from strongly identified Democrats through independents at the neutral midground to strongly identified Republicans at the opposite end. The same long-term panel studies cited above have shown not only that these self-locations are very meaningful in terms of the prediction of other political evaluations and behavior, but also that they are remarkably stable for individuals over time.

These data lead naturally to a picture of mass voting in the United States in which there is a fundamental two-party division of loyalties remaining constant over long periods of time. If no other factors intervened in a systematic way, the two-party division of the popular vote at a national level would remain constant from election to election, reflecting nothing more than this underlying division of loyalties. There must, therefore, be a crucial phenomenon of short-term deviation from one's preferred party in actual voting choice, for the two-party division of the national vote has shifted rather violently (e.g. from a 42 per cent Democratic vote for President in 1956 to a 56 per cent Democratic vote for Congress two years later) even in the years for which our data show a profound stability of loyalties. And, indeed, we do find in our samples enough avowed partisans crossing party lines in any given election to account for swings in the actual vote.

Usually, certain perturbations or oscillations around the constant baseline are fashioned by forces associated with the immediate election—such transient factors as Eisenhower's great personal attractiveness to the public, or Kennedy's Catholicism, which served to draw Catholics and repel Protestants in 1960.[8] In other words, party identification may be seen as an inertia or momentum component which determines the partisan direction of any individual decision *unless there are short-term forces in the immediate situation acting with sufficient strength in an opposite partisan direction to deflect the momentum and shift the behavior.*

If we wish to locate the floating voter in the general scheme, it is worth pursuing the Newtonian metaphor one step further. Quite obviously, the oscillations of the actual vote around the constant baseline are, by the hypothesis, attributable disproportionately (although not completely, of course) to shifts in short-term evaluations on the part of less informed voters. Now "mass" is not entirely wild as an analogue for information level, in the sense that the highly informed voter operates with a large storage of political lore, and the uninformed voter is characterized by an impoverished storage of political information retained from the past. Our prior comments about the staggering differences in information level in the electorate are, then, comments about great differences in this "mass" from voter to voter.[9] And *the probability that any given voter will be sufficiently deflected in his partisan momentum to cross party lines in a specified election varies directly as a function of the strength of short-term forces toward the opposing party and varies inversely as a function of the mass of stored information about politics.* The latter part of this proposition is, of course, no more than a restatement of the floating voter hypothesis.

A PUZZLE AND A PREDICTION

As we have already implied, our data permit us to determine, for any of the elections that we have observed, which citizens were defecting and hence were responsible for the departure of the national vote

[8] It is not hard to see this model as a special case of what Lewin discussed as "quasi-stationary social equilibria." See Kurt Lewin, in Dorwin Cartwright, editor, *Field Theory in Social Science*, New York, Harper, 1951, pp. 202 ff. A more general discussion of the behavior of this type of equilibrium over longer periods of time is included in Campbell, Converse, Miller, and Stokes, *op.cit.*, Chap. 19.

[9] From a psychological point of view, any cognitive modeling of these propositions could rapidly capitalize upon the many hypotheses concerning the development of structure and interconnectedness as the mass of information increases. For our purposes here, however, the spare notion of mass itself suffices.

263

division from its underlying constant baseline. Furthermore, our general argument would predict that the magnitude of the correlation between party identification and the actual vote for any election, being an index of the gross amount of defection from party, should vary within the population as a direct function of political comprehension or involvement. In the 1952 and 1956 presidential election data we were able to observe some faint variation of this sort, although the relationship was more ragged than anticipated. Subsequent methodological demonstrations have provided one answer as to why this pattern of variation is not stronger.[10]

Accepting the fact that there is a partially obscured relationship is, however, where our puzzle begins. For if the relationship was ragged for presidential materials in 1952 and 1956, the picture was even murkier for the 1958 congressional elections. Here, if we subdivided the lower end of the involvement continuum somewhat more finely, it appeared that the expected relationship was actually reversed: the least involved were less likely to have departed from their party in the 1958 voting than were the somewhat more involved!

Now we know several interesting distinctions between presidential and off-year congressional elections. For example, the oscillations of the actual vote over time around the constant term reflecting the underlying division of party loyalties seem weaker in amplitude in congressional voting than in presidential voting. This phenomenon has led to one of the most reliable rules of thumb in the game of mass voting statistics: the party which has won the Presidency in any given quadrennial election is almost certain to lose ground in Congress in the ensuing off-year election. This rule has been broken only once since 1860, although it has remained an "empirical rule" without solid theoretical explanation.

Campbell has provided such explanation, employing the general theoretical framework used in this paper. In essence, a presidential election tends to be a "high-stimulus election" that attracts a relatively large turnout, dipping rather deeply into the less involved elements of the electorate. An off-year congressional election must be considered a "low-stimulus election" with a much lower turnout. The less in-

[10] Not only is it true that less involved people recall their prior votes with greater distortion, but they also are relatively labile in their responses to items concerning current partisan identification. If we look at turnover tables on measures of party identification drawn from the same respondents after a two-year interval, subdivided into thirds on political involvement, we find that despite no significant changes in the marginals, the correlation (Pearson product-moment) for the most involved third is over .9, is over .8 for those only moderately involved, and is in the .7 range for the weakly involved. Hence the reports of the least involved hide instability in voting, for even the underlying loyalties "float" quite considerably.

volved people who rejoin the active electorate in a presidential year are those who are most responsive to short-term tides of opinion, and their re-entry creates a wider oscillation of the vote away from the constant baseline than would be observed if they had failed to vote. When in the next off-year election stimuli are much weaker, this floating contingent either floats back to normal partisanship or drops out of the voting altogether. Hence it is natural that the division of the two-party vote for Congress should regress toward the division of underlying loyalties.[11]

This explanation has resolved quite well one of the older riddles facing the political scientist. However, it would not in itself lead us to expect any reversal of the gradient of magnitude of the party-vote correlation in the off-year election. Nor does it explain (although intuitively the reason may be apparent enough) why it is that even in presidential years, when floating voters go to the polls, the congressional vote is more nearly a party vote, with less crossing of party lines by individual voters, than is the accompanying presidential vote.[12]

We would have no difficulty guessing that the congressional vote in a presidential year is more nearly a party vote in large measure because the flow of information about the congressional candidates is a good deal weaker than that for the two presidential candidates. Voters go to the polls primarily to vote for President in a presidential year, and have been supplied by the media with a great deal more information about the presidential candidates. Democrats who were seduced to an Eisenhower vote in 1956 had a choice at lower levels of the ballot: continue with a straight Republican ticket, or switch back to their normal Democratic choices. Some Democrats chose one way, and some the other, and the inevitable result was a national congressional vote less extremely Republican than the Eisenhower vote, yet more Republican than a straight party vote would have been.

The same conditions of low information mark the off-year congressional voting as well. Indeed, this is the source of turnout reduction in what Campbell called the "low-stimulus election." In a presidential

11 Angus Campbell, "Surge and Decline: A Study of Electoral Change," *Public Opinion Quarterly*, Vol. 24, 1960, pp. 397-418.
12 The clearer "party vote" at the individual level contributes to the phenomenon of a two-party congressional vote showing oscillations of a smaller amplitude even in years of presidential elections. In the presidential year, the congressional vote summed nationally tends to fall between the baseline set by the constant loyalty term and the direction in which the actual presidential vote has swung. Another major source of this muffled variation is the simple aggregation of voting units at the congressional level. In some races, an attractive Democrat induces Republican defections, while in others a more attractive Republican wins an unusual vote. Cumulation over three-hundred-odd congressional races will find many local swings of the vote balancing one another out.

election, the public is so massively bombarded by information about the two presidential aspirants than only a remote and indifferent citizen could fail to absorb some few meaningful items of information about each. The actual flow of information about local candidates for the national Congress, on the other hand, is extremely weak.[13]

The short-term forces mentioned above that either reinforce partisanship or deflect the voter from his normal partisan course obviously depend for their life on the flow of current information. Something of a ceiling is set upon the strength of these forces by the volume of information flow. Other things equal, both the individual rates of defection from party and the amplitude of the vote oscillations will be limited if the flow of information is weak. If the flow of information is strong, no particular prediction is safe, in the sense that the partisan valences of the incoming information may be so varied that net pressures toward change are weak, or in the sense that other canceling processes may arise between individuals whose current reactions polarize. If the flow of information is weak, however, very potent limits on defections and vote oscillation are established. And, most important, if there is no new information input at all, there will be no defection and no oscillation: the vote will be a pure party vote. The latter deduction is more interesting than might appear.

The ultimate information intake of the voter is limited in two directions, (1) by the volume of output of the formal and informal systems of political communication in the society, and (2) by the voter's motivation to attend to political communications, once some flow exists. As we have seen, there is systematic variation in output volume between presidential and off-year elections, as well as between various levels of office. There is obviously systematic variation across individuals in the motivational term as well. Quite specifically, there is a strong correlation between the mass of stored political information and the motivation to monitor communication systems for additional current information. The highly involved voter draws a much larger sample of the current information flow than does the uninvolved voter.

We can see at once, then, that the very uninvolved voters, who we have come to expect will tend to "float" politically, present us with some-

[13] In 1958, when there was no presidential ballyhoo to occupy newspaper space, we initiated an analysis of newspaper content relating to local congressional candidates campaigning for re-election. The project was rapidly dropped because examination of newspapers even after the campaign was well under way showed that information about such candidates was printed only sporadically, and then was usually buried in such a remote section of the paper that the item would go unheeded by all but the more avid readers of political news. It is no wonder that data that we have collected over the years show a large portion of citizens who fail to be aware of their congressional candidates as individuals at all.

thing of a paradox in this regard. On the one hand, such voters show a high susceptibility to short-term change in partisan attitudes *provided that any new information reaches them at all*. On the other hand, when the flow of information through the society is weak, these are the individuals who are *most* likely to experience no new information intake, and hence are individuals *least likely to show changes in patterns of behavior*, if indeed they are constrained to behave at all.[14]

It should be stressed that our propositions do little to disturb the basic floating voter hypothesis associating "mass" with partisan stability. If we order voters on a continuum of increasing stored "mass," we have only to imagine that the gradient of current information intake, while positively sloped as well, increases less steeply than the stored mass itself, in order to preserve the flavor of the basic prediction.[15] The modification occurs at the lower end of the involvement continuum. That is, let us suppose that along the abscissa of a coordinate system respondents are arrayed in terms of enduring political involvement, and that this array is a very good surrogate for arrays in terms of (1) current information intake and (2) mass of stored information from the past. If stability of partisan attitudes were to be plotted along the ordinate, then our propositions would predict a very sudden "step change" at the lowest levels of involvement, from perfect stability where information input is zero, dropping precipitously to a minimum just above the zero point. Beyond this minimum, of course, stability would increase as a function of involvement.

Since we obviously have not monitored all the intake of political information for our respondents during any political campaign, empirical tests to which we might put these predictions are certain to be crude. However, we have traditionally asked our respondents after each campaign whether or not they had listened to any political broadcasts on radio or television, or had read any political articles in newspapers or magazines. While such questions fail to cover the sector of informal

[14] One might wonder why individuals with no new relevant information should ever stir themselves to vote, but it is clear that they do, although quite naturally at lower rates of turnout. Party loyalties, along with generalized values concerning citizen duty, appear to be sufficient stimuli. A concrete example is the Nebraska woman who considered herself a strong Republican and voted with some regularity. Probed in 1960 as to her political perceptions, she displayed no awareness of any current political issues or figures. The lone shred of political content came when she was asked what she disliked about the Democratic Party: "I've never liked them ever since they got rid of Prohibition way back. I don't just know what the parties have been up to lately."

[15] This is a crude simplification for the sake of brevity. In the more elaborated model that underlies the discussion, the partisanship of different communications and communication channels is taken more explicitly into account. These, along with some commonplace psychological propositions, threaten if anything to "overaccount" for increasing stability, rather than to "underaccount" for it.

social communication about politics, they do cover the major mass media and should provide a rough index of intake during the campaign, an index superior for our purposes to traditional measures of political involvement.

We wished to avoid the body of data which had first stimulated our thinking, so we returned to data collected from an entirely independent sample of the nation in connection with the 1952 election. For measures of stability of partisan attitudes we employed two rather different indices. The first had to do with the rate of turnover between the statement of vote intentions prior to the election and the actual voting behavior. A high correlation would indicate high stability of intentions, a lower correlation, relative instability. Since the ultimate voting act consisted in a Republican vote, a Democratic vote, or a failure to vote, it was inconvenient to consider any respondents who were unclear as to their vote intention before the election. Thus a three-by-three table could be constructed, and a rank-order (tau-beta) correlation computed for it within subsets of the population, according to whether no media were used or some higher number. Since there might be some question as to the effect of differences in proportions of nonvoters upon the correlation, a comparable coefficient was also calculated for the two-by-two table reflecting constancy or change in choice of candidates. These are obviously not independent tests.

The second portion of the test had to do with the correlation between party identification and final vote. For the theoretical reasons given above, a low rate of defection from party (a high party-vote correlation) should reflect high attitude stability, while a low correlation should reflect relative instability under the short-term forces of this particular election. The second test once again is not independent of the first, having been performed on the same units of analysis. However, their distribution is somewhat different for the two tests, and in this sense some weight is added by the second set of computations.

Despite the crudity of the measures, the accompanying chart indicates that the predicted curve did indeed emerge very clearly.[16] Furthermore, the same phenomenon has been visible at other points in our data. For example, it can be shown that the relatively small portion of the population that failed to see any of the television debates between Kennedy and Nixon in 1960 was made up of voters less likely to have revised their voting intentions before the final decision than were

[16] While the minimum in the test involving party identification is farther to the right than predicted, it must be remembered that the measurement difficulties described above—the tendency of the most weakly involved to bring their statements of party loyalty into line with current vote—would affect this particular test in this fashion. The other tests are true "panel" tests.

MEASURES OF ATTITUDE STABILITY, BY NUMBER OF MASS MEDIA THAT
RESPONDENT MONITORED FOR POLITICAL INFORMATION
DURING THE 1952 CAMPAIGN

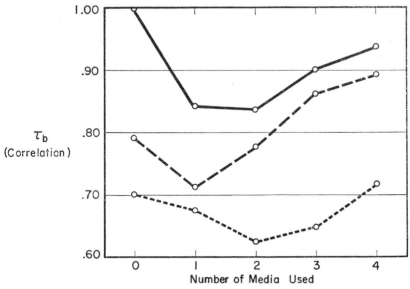

KEY: The solid line represents the 2 × 2 table, party intention by party choice. The dashed line represents the 3 × 3 table, vote intention by vote. The dotted line indicates party identification by vote.

people who watched the debates. The rank-order correlation between vote intention and vote in the two-by-two case for nonwatchers whom we had interviewed before the debates was .96, but for the watchers it was .89. In the three-by-three case, taking into account intentions as to whether or not one would vote, the correlation was .88 among nonwatchers, but only .64 among watchers. While the first of these two comparisons is relatively weak, further investigation shows that the only nonwatchers who changed their choice of candidate between the pre-debate period and the election fell in a subset of nonwatchers who distinguished themselves by indicating to our interviewers that they had not watched the debates because of some mechanical barrier (they worked a night shift, their television set was broken, and the like). Some of these people may have heard the debates on the radio; in any event, they stand as the most involved subset that can be isolated among nonwatchers. Among the remaining majority of nonwatchers (who either said that they were too uninterested in politics to watch the debates or else failed to give a reason for their inattention), there was no change at all in vote intention, the correlation thereby being

269

1.00 in the two-by-two case (N of 52 voters). As indicated, this second subset of nonwatchers was the less politically involved of the two, and by the simple floating voter hypothesis should have been the more unstable. Thus throughout these debate materials in 1960 we find evidence of the newly predicted reversal: the more remote the respondent was from the flow of information represented by the debates, the more stable his vote intention, despite the general correlation within the large set of watchers (80 per cent of the population) between partisan stability and political involvement.

In sum, then, our predictions are confirmed in several bodies of data. And their parent propositions serve to explain our initial puzzles. That is, we can now understand why in the off-year congressional vote the gradient of correlations between party identification and vote should show some reversal, with the least involved being more likely to follow normal behavior patterns than the more involved who do manage to pick up some new information from the weaker flow. Of course, the original reversal was not strong: it did not suggest that the more involved were *more* likely to defect in the off-year than in the presidential year. Over-all, the amount of defection was notably reduced relative to the presidential year voting. This fact, as well as the reversal of gradients, is embraced by simple recognition of the weaker information flow.

Second, we have thrown new light on the indifferent empirical confirmation that the floating voter hypothesis has tended to receive. In this regard, we may point out that the number of people involved in our "no-media" data points was few (for the 1952 test, an N of 22 in the two-by-two case, 92 in the three-by-three case). Normally, in crude divisions of a sample by involvement, the investigator would lose such no-media cases from sight in the larger number of uninvolved who are represented on the media scale as having received some little information. This adulteration of the highly unstable slight-information people with a set of perfectly stable no-information people would inevitably cloud the relationship, although not sufficiently either to obscure it completely or to betray the underlying curvilinearity.

DISCUSSION

A question frequently posed is: How large is the floating vote? From our point of view, the question is unanswerable in this form, presuming as it does an unrealistic division of the electorate into two camps, floaters and nonfloaters. As we have observed, the matter is one of differential susceptibility to partisan change, and hence we must think in terms of gradients rather than sharp dichotomization. Even in these terms, however, an analogous question may be posed concerning the susceptibility of a mass public to swings in partisan voting patterns of greater or lesser magnitude, in response to varying short-term forces.

In the course of this paper we have taken for granted one factor that is, in the larger view, itself a variable—the aggregate development of partisan loyalties in an electorate. We have explored elsewhere the implications of the fact that partisan loyalties are less strongly developed in some segments of a society than in others, with young voters and rural populations as cases in point.[17] There are, furthermore, interesting cross-national variations in the development of such loyalties, and it seems clear if fairly obvious that the mere passage of time is an important factor in the "jelling" of deep partisan identifications in large portions of a mass population. When democratic systems are newly launched, or when their traditional party structures have been shattered by war, some time must elapse before stabilizing loyalties are developed or redeveloped.

In a system where partisan loyalties are fully developed, however, the volume of information flow can be seen as an important governor upon the magnitude of oscillations in party fortunes. In the United States of the 1960's, our modification of the floating voter hypothesis may appear to be of limited significance, simply because of the meager proportion of voters who fall in the "no media" cell where presidential campaigns are concerned. In 1952, less than 2 per cent of the voters, or 6 per cent of the potential electorate, were so classified. On the other hand, it can be argued that in times past (as well as for off-year elections currently) this proportion must have been very much larger, given what we know of changes in conditions of information flow in the past century. In a historical perspective, then, not to mention one which looks toward less developed nations, the refinement is by no means trivial.

The dramatic changes in information propagation are too familiar to require much elaboration. In brief, two broad trends have converged: (1) rising levels of education have given increased proportions of the adult population access to the printed media; and (2) the development of the spoken media has provided channels of information accessible even to those not motivated to read. The cumulative change has been of awesome proportions. Historical trends hinging on shifts of 5 or 10 per cent in relevant societal rates often draw comment; here, conditions of information propagation have shifted in ways that affect a vast majority of the population.

Of these two changes, it can be argued that the advent of the spoken media has been even more crucial than the upgrading of education,

[17] Campbell, Converse, Miller, and Stokes, *op.cit.*, pp. 402-440, 497-498.

where mass political behavior is concerned. In the first place, of course, a number of states even outside the South have had literacy requirements for the franchise, thereby "neutralizing" any effects on the electorate of variations in literacy rates. The spoken media loom even more important, however, as we come to realize that the critical phenomenon is less illiteracy in the strict sense than what is sometimes called "functional illiteracy." Even currently, after more than a century of expansion in education, the proportion of adults who eschew any serious reading that is not imperative (and most printed information on politics is of this sort) is often estimated to be as high as 60 per cent.

In modern data we typically find that 70 to 80 per cent of the electorate reports having read "something" about the presidential campaign in one of the printed media. This figure is quite high, and eighty years ago it must have been substantially lower. Nonetheless, it leaves a fair residual population that received its *only* current information from the spoken media. If we can imagine that prior to 1920 such a residuum simply went without information, then the ranks of our "no media" people would be increased by a factor of three, and the proportion of "no media" voters by a factor of six. We would then be talking of a significant fraction of the voting public, enough to create noticeable differences in the cast of election returns.

Furthermore, we must bear in mind that this 70 to 80 per cent that learns "something" from a printed medium passes only the weakest of tests: merely discovering from a headline the names of the candidates would qualify. Indeed, the slight amount of information gleaned from the printed media by many of these "readers" is betrayed by another datum: less than one-third of the current population, when asked the medium from which it draws most political information, mentions a printed medium. In other words, a majority of those who do notice some political news in the printed media nonetheless feel that they learned more about what is going on politically from the spoken media. Given the sketchy coverage of politics in the spoken media by contrast with the written, this is quite a commentary on the relative "reach" and impact of the newer spoken media.

All this being so, we find that we have traversed a rather strange circle. We began by remarking upon the extremely low levels of political information in the current period. Now we adduce evidence in some depth that the effective reach of the communication system has advanced enormously, and that the citizen himself recognizes a greater information intake than he would have had short of the newer media. Naturally, this juxtaposition of findings underscores among other things a fundamental motivation problem. At one time it might have been argued that electorates were uninformed for lack of realistic access to information. Now a fair flow of information is *accessible* to almost everybody in the society; the fact that little attention is paid to it even though it is almost hard to avoid is a fair measure of lack of public interest. But all these facts do no more than stir our curiosity: if levels of public information are extremely low now, when access to rudimentary information is not a primary problem, what must this level have been a century ago?

There is, of course, a considerable literature that makes of nineteenth-century America a Golden Age of democratic politics. In effect, it is argued that the conditions of life entailed by modern industrialized society have destroyed the free give and take of political discussion that once characterized the small towns and rural hamlets of the relatively agrarian nation. The public is less capable now than it once was of approximating the assumptions of normative democratic theory. Among recent versions of this panorama, perhaps that by C. Wright Mills in *The Power Elite* is as imaginative as any.[18] Since this view is diametrically opposed to any reconstruction we can suggest, it is worth a moment to consider points of divergence.

Mills's account is somewhat difficult to address because of the range of disparate phenomena that flow into and out of the argument. If, for example, the point is to compare a restricted elite of functionally literate voters with modern universal suffrage, then one would grant out of hand that a major change has occurred. In context, however, this is hardly the point Mills wished to press. Or if the point is to compare the informed character of a debate between villagers as to the laying of a local drainpipe and the information the same villagers can bring to the debates of national politics (often equally crucial to their lives), then once again there can be little argument, and the difference is of profound importance. Or, finally, if the point is that the modern mass media leave a good deal to be desired in terms of breadth of alternatives presented or general level of discussion, the contention is as readily granted.[19]

Despite fleeting attention to all of these points, the true burden of Mills's argument seems to be that the modern mass media stifle what once was free discussion. Most concretely, it is argued that the modern media have decreased the number of "opinion givers" relative to the number of "opinion receivers." "More than anything else," Mills ob-

18 C. Wright Mills, *The Power Elite*, New York, Oxford, 1956, Chap. 13.
19 Although we should not lose sight of the apparent fact that one reason people who both read and listen feel they get more information from the spoken media is precisely this lower level of presentation. The printed media are less palatable in part because their somewhat more elevated discussions presuppose more information.

serves, "it is the shift in this ratio which is central to the problems of the public and public opinion in latter-day phases of democracy." Here our arguments collide most directly, for it seems patent that opinion giving presupposes opinion formation, and opinion formation presupposes information that there is something to form a political opinion about.[20] We have suggested that opinion-stimulating information about national politics must have been a much rarer commodity in the mass public a century ago.

Despite the evidence we have already presented, there remain ways in which we might try retrospectively to bootleg increased amounts of information to the nineteenth-century voter. It might be argued, for example, that nowadays people read *less* political material than in the past simply because they now can fill their needs with less effort through the spoken media. In other words, there are some fixed needs for political information, and in an era when such information was less accessible, more energy would have been expended in compensation to secure it. Direct evaluation of such a hypothesis would require data that do not and will not exist, since turning back the clock empirically is impossible. However, none of the indirect ways in which we may turn back the clock lend any credence to this possibility.

There are, for example, pockets of modern American society—remote rural areas—that tend toward a rough representation of the older conditions of communication, in that they have newspaper distribution but up until recently have had inadequate service by electronic media. In such areas, of course, it may be demonstrated to any reasonable degree of satisfaction that the intake of political information is less in an absolute sense, political interest is lower, and the incidence of opinion giving is lower as well, relative to more urban areas. Or again, we may turn back the clock by considering data from societies somewhat behind us in industrial evolution. France, with less popular access to the spoken media and an educational distribution that roughly resembles that of the United States several decades ago, shows no heavier public con-

[20] One might distinguish two classes of events here, both of which require information before political opinions are stimulated. The first includes events that have no discernible effect on the life of the individual, at least as he comprehends his existence. Here the outside information is required even to know there is a debatable problem. There is a second class of events that *do* bear directly upon him (e.g. the loss of a job as part of a general economic contraction in his community), which he cannot fail to cognize as events. Even here, however, further information is important: that politics is relevant to such an event is hardly a "given," an innate idea. Perception of a potential link requires other information. Even now, this "other" information cannot be presupposed for all American voters. Since a century ago a potential link between such an event and national politics was not invariably perceived by well-educated people who left written traces, one would certainly hesitate to presuppose it for most mass voters.

sumption of political news through the printed media. Instead, rates of information intake via newspapers and magazines seem very much like those in the United States for comparable levels of education; since the education level is lower in France, so is the intake of information from printed media.[21]

The fact of the matter is that in the current period the tendencies to monitor different media for political information follow Guttman scalar patterns very closely, with magazines the "hardest" item, and the spoken media the easiest.[22] Such a scale is, of course, highly correlated with education: 74 per cent of college graduates fall in the top category, as opposed to 17 per cent of the grade-school educated; 6 per cent of college graduates monitor only a spoken medium or none at all, as opposed to 40 per cent of the grade-school people. In other words, the stratum most vitally affected by the new currents of information is that which would have had least option in times past of compensating for an absence of these media with newspapers or magazines.

A rather different means of bootlegging information to the nineteenth-century voter is to shift weight to informal social communication for the transmission of political information. Before the mass media corrupted the majority of voters with "direct information," it can be claimed that the nets of informal communication buzzed with all the political information inaccessible through other channels. This is a particularly interesting argument, since it hews very closely to the spirit of the Mills contentions about free and fervent informal political discussion.

We are less interested here in the "power to persuade" of informal communications as opposed to the mass media than we are in (1) the characteristics of informal communication as a source of information supply, and (2) the motivation to sustain transmission of political information along the chain. With regard to the nature of the information transmitted, our interviews frequently represent the respondent's

21 P. E. Converse and G. Dupeux, "Politicization of the Electorate in France and the United States," *Public Opinion Quarterly*, Vol. 26, 1962, pp. 1-23. The French example is of added interest because another claim is frequently made that the state of public information about politics in America reflects a political indifference that has grown up recently as a result of the absence of "real" policy alternatives offered by the two major parties. Few voters are provided with the wealth of clear-cut policy alternatives available to French voters, yet, if anything, mass political interest in France over recent years has been slightly less than that in the United States.

22 That is, people who report having drawn political information from magazines are very likely to report having monitored newspapers and a spoken medium as well. People who report the monitoring of newspapers do not in large measure read magazines, but are very likely to have monitored radio or television. Among people who have monitored one of the spoken media, there are a disproportionate number who have monitored nothing else.

transmission of things he has recently seen, heard, or read in the media. This is information at only a first remove, yet the "sea change" in content emphasis and accuracy is quite striking. It is not at all unusual that a voter who exposes himself to an information presentation that is 95 per cent current issues and 5 per cent personal background of a political personality comes away with the personal oddments burning in the memory and the rest lost. While political content in the spoken media may strike an academic observer as somewhat light, its devaluation at one remove is hardly calculated to raise regard for informal transmission involving multiple steps. Our point is not that people are more capable today of absorbing critical information than they were a century ago, but rather that if information depends on informal communication, any potential receiver who might have stronger policy interests is at the mercy of the weakest link in the informal communication chain prior to him. Since currently the flow of information is directly accessible to him, he at least may select the information that strikes him as important, for better or for worse. A person at third or fourth remove in a chain during the Golden Age would have had a much greater probability of hearing something about Cleveland's love life than he would of hearing that labor problems, tariffs, or free silver were subjects for debate.

And even this devaluation process supposes that there is some motivation to communicate about politics, or the chain is broken. Indeed, Mills assumes quite directly that prior to the incursions of the mass media, people were *more* motivated to communicate informally about politics. Current data make this position hard to accept. Studies of the 1960 television debates, for example, suggest that these performances were responsible in the most direct way for live spates of informal political discussion which undoubtedly would not otherwise have taken place.[23]

We have more direct data on "opinion giving" that tells exactly the same story. For several elections we have asked respondents, "Did you talk to any people and try to show them why they should vote for one of the parties or candidates?" The probability of opinion giving thus defined is tied in the most extreme fashion to information intake. In 1960, for example, 52 per cent of the people who drew information from four media were opinion givers; for three media, the figure was

23 E. Katz and J. Feldman, "The Debates in the Light of Research and Vice Versa," in Sidney Kraus, editor, *The Great Debates,* Bloomington, Indiana University Press, 1962. No judgment is implied here that the quality of such discussions was high—it is almost axiomatic that over the electorate as a whole they must have been something below the quality of the debates themselves. The critical matter is that the alternatives were not good discussion or poor discussion, but rather some discussion or no discussion at all.

44 per cent; for two, 23 per cent; for one, 15 per cent. Among the no-media people, who are currently few in number but who we contend bulked larger a century ago, 0 per cent reported opinion giving (N of 82).[24]

None of these data establishes any causal link between the stimulation of information reception and the motivation to communicate informally about politics. That is, prior political involvement clearly predisposes both to a more vigorous information search *and* to an increased tendency to form and give opinions. But the data do make it extremely difficult to argue that somehow a weaker information flow from the mass media generates a vacuum that people attempt to fill by increasing informal communication about politics. With regard to the Mills argument, then, it seems much simpler to conclude that the historical alternative to the strong information flow of the mass media was not more and better opinions, but rather no opinion formation at all.

Attempts to reconstruct historical conditions that affected large populations are often unsatisfying because direct proof is impossible. Historians have become painfully aware of the optical illusions created by history where trends in ideas are concerned, since the populations that have left ideational traces of their days and ways become increasingly narrow (and elite) as we probe more deeply into the past. Whether we are studying trends in wit, conformity, or political acumen, to lay an implicit eighteenth-century population of Voltaires, Diderots, and Ben Franklins against the current Everyman, as revealed by all

[24] These are familiar data of the opinion-leader type. It is unfortunate that we lack comparable materials on "opinion receiving" from informal sources. Within any given milieu, the "two-step flow of communication" helps to spread opinions, along with the information they presuppose, beyond the immediate receivers. However, the effects of such communications upon our argument fall far short of what one would expect were the who-to-whom matrices of communication random. Thus, for example, the most prevalent special case of the two-step flow where politics is concerned runs between the husband who is somewhat attentive to political information and the wife who is content to receive it second-hand. This pattern occurs within all milieux. However, the lower-class wife, who is less likely than anyone else in the society to receive information from the media, at the same time has a husband who is less likely than any other male in the society to receive such information, or to bother transmitting it in the instances when he does receive something. In point of fact, our no-media people who reported no opinion giving departed from the question sequence in marked numbers to note as well that they had simply not conversed about politics with *anyone*. In sum, then, were these informal political communications to be aggregated over the society as a whole, there is every reason to believe that opinion receiving would show a high positive correlation with opinion giving, and not the negative correlation required for an efficient diffusion of information through the system. These facts have been recognized quite explicitly by theorists developing the two-step flow hypothesis. See E. Katz, "The Two-Step Flow of Communication: An Up-to-Date Report on an Hypothesis," *Public Opinion Quarterly*, Vol. 21, 1957, especially pp. 76-77.

the mass feedback techniques of modern research, is to assure terrifying conclusions about man's evolution. It is ironic that in the voting case, however, we do have one of the few bodies of systematic records—mass voting statistics—struck off by the hand of Everyman himself.

While we are only on the brink of extracting more sophisticated information from these records, one comment is worth venturing. If our model has merit, and if it is true that for any given election the cell comprised of no-current-information voters must once have bulked much larger than it does today, then it would follow that the amplitude of the oscillations in voting for political objects at a national level must have been materially less in an earlier period, for precisely the same reason of weakened information flow that limits swings of the congressional vote in the current period. And, conversely, there should be an increasing amplitude of these swings as the information flow has increased during the current century.

In a cursory inspection of the vote trends, at least, this is precisely what we *do* find. The general cast of the American historical statistics suggests three rough periods. In the first, terminated abruptly by the Civil War, the parties were undergoing frequent splits and shifts in manifest identity. In this period, relatively large voting oscillations were quite common, and it is likely that party loyalties in the broad public had not as yet had a chance to develop in any wide degree. The abrupt "settling down" after the Civil War creates the impression that conditions surrounding the war filled the mass of voters with deep-seated party feeling.[25] For several decades after the Civil War, vote oscillations were extremely muffled, producing the sort of record we would associate today with prevalence of partisan attachment accompanied by extremely weak information flow. Just as the Nebraska woman cited above has continued to vote Prohibition for thirty years, so there must have been a much larger pool of poorly informed and *potentially* mobile voters in the late nineteenth century who for decades voted the Civil War not only because of the impress of that tragic episode, but in part as well because of an absence of information as to what political elites were currently competing about or, for that matter,

[25] Outside of the ravaged South, this galvanizing process did not penetrate the more remote rural areas, which continued to show great voting lability on into the early twentieth century, and which even now manifest weaker levels of partisan identification. Such urban-rural discrepancies in partisan stability are very frequent evolutionary phenomena, with one of the most noteworthy cases being that of the Weimar Republic. Nazi party workers stumbled to their surprise upon the fact that, while the movement was essentially urban and recruited its activists from the the cities, the harvest of mass votes that could not be dislodged in the distressed cities because of prior development of party loyalties could be had for the asking in distressed rural areas. See Campbell, Converse, Miller, and Stokes, *op.cit.*, Chap. 15.

who the current political elites were. As such information has become more accessible, this cell of perfectly stable voters has dwindled and the oscillations of the vote have regained amplitude.

Such historical reconstruction is of necessity loose and crude. Probably our extrapolations from current data are in the final analysis more solidly anchored. But the fact remains that there is historical evidence that seems of a piece with our theoretical understanding of more thorough modern data, and this is encouraging. Since changes in the information-propagating capacities of a society occur at a fairly slow rate, it is in such historical perspective that a link between the volume of information flow and the partisan stability of an electoral system has its most interesting implications.

17

APOCALYPTIC AND SERIAL TIME ORIENTATION AND THE STRUCTURE OF OPINIONS

Kurt W. Back and
Kenneth J. Gergen

THE STRUCTURE of opinions about public events can be based on a number of different criteria. It can be based on the events themselves, assuming a logical connection between the events and attitudes concerning them. Thus a person approving of a war in the near future should also approve of an increase in armaments. It can be based on the assumption that a person will accept the program of a party or group to which he belongs, regardless of whether the items in the program have any other relationship to him. It can be based on informal membership in social groups, such as economic or ethnic groups. And, it can also be based on a person's own world view and be related to the ways in which he acts in several aspects of his life.

Investigations of public opinion have freely used the first three systems of organization. The intrinsic logic of the events themselves has been used for grouping questions and for the construction of indices and scales. Group memberships, both formal and inferred, have been used as independent or control factors, and their influence on public opinion has been amply demonstrated. However, the personal factors have generally been left unexplained. Some of the so-called "background characteristics," especially age, education, and sex, have no manifest meaning that would explain their influence on the many atti-

* Revision of a paper read at the annual meeting of the American Association for Public Opinion Research, May 1962. This study was supported by a grant from the Ford Foundation on socio-economic studies in aging, and by a faculty grant from the Duke University Research Council. The data were made available through the cooperation of the Roper Public Opinion Center, Williamstown, Massachusetts.

Originally published in Volume 27, Number 3, 1963 of the *Public Opinion Quarterly*.

tudes they so powerfully predict. A basic orientation is often assumed to account for differences between population groups, but frequently we cannot say just what it is.

This paper will attempt to define such an orientation. This approach has proved somewhat recalcitrant to analysis. If taken simply as a problem of personality organization and public opinion, it is forced to deal with a great many variables, none of which has an intrinsic relationship to public events. While the logic of the events themselves, the influence of organized political movements, and the influence of social self-interest groups are at least partially defined by their relation to public issues, description of the individual has proceeded on different grounds. Personality orientation is a self-contained system, as is public opinion in relation to social structure. Thus, in attempting to predict public opinion from a purely individual trait, there is no obvious reason for selecting one trait over another.

The great variety of personal characteristics that could be influential makes any systematic progress in theory and research in this field difficult. Common observation would indicate that there is a strong relation between expressions of the personality and stands on public issues. Accordingly, even roughly defined variables, such as impressions of conviviality and body build, have been shown to be possible determinants of opinion.[1] The real problem in relating personality traits and opinions is precisely the plethora of possible relationships, which can obscure any comprehensible model.

The problem arises primarily from the fact that we are dealing here with two different systems.[2] Man can act as an integrating force on the total of his own traits (as an individual system), or as a unit within society (as part of a social system). The traditional approaches, mentioned above, have tended to relate the individual and social systems in two ways. Either they have defined personal traits as reflections of society or society as a reflection of the individual. Methodologically, one approach has led to the construction of personality scales based on certain kinds of social attitudes; prominent examples have been the construction of scales on such traits as authoritarianism, anomie, tough-mindedness, dogmatism, or Machiavellianism. The other approach has led to a series of case studies demonstrating the continuity in an individual's life, from his personal affairs to his position in society.[3] We

[1] Jan Stapel, "The Convivial Respondent," *Public Opinion Quarterly*, Vol. 11, 1947, pp. 524-529.

[2] Kurt W. Back, "The Proper Scope of Social Psychology," *Social Forces*, Vol. 41, May 1963, pp. 368-377.

[3] For the social-trait approach, see such works as: Theodore W. Adorno, Else Frenkel-Brunswick, Daniel J. Levinson, and R. Nevitt Sanford, *The Authoritarian*

shall avoid either of these approaches and define personal traits that relate to the basic situation of a human being before he identifies himself as part of either a social or a personal system. We shall deal with the relation between personality structure and public opinion on the basis of certain assumptions about a person's orientation in time and space. Thus, we shall deal with opinions as if a person were making decisions to act and direct our attention to the meaning of the future for a person. Historically, much of the theory of decision making has been prescriptive, first ethical and later rational, rather than descriptive. A descriptive analysis of a decision problem must admit other kinds of decisions.[4]

THE APOCALYPTIC-SERIAL DIMENSION

Let us discuss first some of the general considerations regarding time perspective that can lead to subsequent hypotheses about public opinion. To begin with, reactions to a specific situation will depend on the perspective in which one sees the situation. Individual development, as Frank has shown in introducing the term "time perspective," leads to characteristic changes.[5] Babies at first react immediately to physiological stimuli. Experiments have shown that young children prefer minimal immediate gain to greater rewards that are accompanied by delay, while older children learn to see events in larger perspective, and when faced with choice situations they take into account additional circumstances with greater time perspective.[6] There is some evidence of a reversal of this process at the other end of the age range, especially with regard to future time perspective. Other social characteristics have shown similar relations with time perspective, on the one hand, and reactions to critical situations on the other. Education, for instance, is intended to lead to an enlarged perspective and to an increased ability to handle critical situations. Similarly, membership in the

Personality, New York, Harper, 1959; Leo Srole, "Social Integration and Certain Corollaries: An Exploratory Study," *American Sociological Review*, Vol. 21, 1956, pp. 709-716; Hans J. Eysenck, *The Psychology of Politics*, London, Routledge, 1954; Milton Rokeach, *The Open and the Closed Mind*, New York, Basic Books, 1960; Richard Christie and Robert K. Merton, "Procedures for the Sociological Study of the Values Climate of Medical Schools," *Journal of Medical Education*, Vol. 33, December 1958, pp. 125-153. A good example of the personal setting approach is M. Brewster Smith, Jerome S. Burner, and Robert K. White, *Opinions and Personality*, New York, Wiley, 1956.

[4] Kurt W. Back, "Decisions under Uncertainty: Rational, Irrational, and Nonrational," *American Behavioral Scientist*, Vol. 4, February 1961, pp. 14-19.

[5] Lawrence E. Frank, "Time Perspectives," in his *Society as the Patient*, New Brunswick, N.J., Rutgers University Press, 1948, pp. 339-358.

[6] Walter Mischel, "Preference for Delayed Reinforcement and Social Responsibility," *Journal of Abnormal and Social Psychology*, Vol. 62, 1961, pp. 1-7.

middle class is characterized by the delayed gratification pattern as opposed to the more immediate rewards emphasized in the lower classes.[7] We also find evidence that the middle class does not tend to as extreme solutions as working-class members.[8] Professionals in particular tend, through their education as well as their occupation, to take the long-range view both in regard to success and to a number of other issues.[9]

We can conclude from the above that the value of an act depends, to a great extent, on the span of time that is to be taken into consideration. The rational model has, since the time of Bentham and the utilitarians, been based on the decision that will be best in the long run if followed in all similar cases. Although it is possible to attach a personal probability value to a single event, the evaluation of the utility of the choice will depend on how much and what aspects of the future are taken into consideration.[10] Thus, the rational model is normative under conditions in which the repeatability of events is assumed. Clearly, if these conditions are not met, acting as if they were is not very rational, and therefore this term can be a misnomer.

Objectively, some events may be repeatable and some may not. It would be possible in certain instances to state the range of future events that would be more reasonable to consider as repeatable. On the other hand, some people may be more likely than others to believe that events are repeatable and would be inclined to a longer-range view. The dimension that interests us especially in relation to decision making is thus the extent of time perspective and, within this, the be-

[7] Urie Bronfenbrenner, "Socialization and Social Class through Time and Space," in Eleanor E. Maccoby, Theodore M. Newcomb, and Eugene L. Hartley, editors, *Readings in Social Psychology*, New York, Holt, 1958; Allison Davis, "The Motivation of the Underprivileged Worker," *ETC, A Review of General Semantics*, Vol. 3, Summer 1946, pp. 243-253; M. Spinley, *The Deprived and the Privileged: Personality Development in English Society*, London, Routledge, 1953; Richard Hoggart, *The Uses of Literacy*, New York, Oxford University Press, 1957; Arthur J. Vidich and Joseph Bensman, *Small Town in Mass Society*, Princeton, N.J., Princeton University Press, 1958.

[8] Seymour M. Lipset, "Democracy and Working-class Authoritarianism," *American Sociological Review*, Vol. 24, 1959, pp. 482-501.

[9] Everett C. Hughes, "Mistakes at Work," *Canadian Journal of Economics and Political Science*, Vol. 17, 1951, pp. 320-327.

[10] Probability can be defined as a psychological concept without recourse to actual repetition, as shown by the "neo-Bayesian school," cf. Frank P. Ramsey, *The Foundations of Mathematics*, London, Routledge, 1931; Leonard J. Savage, *The Foundations of Statistics*, New York, Wiley, 1954; Howard Raiffa and Robert Schlaifer, *Applied Statistical Decision Theory*, Boston, Harvard University, Graduate School of Business Administration, 1961. Whether the indicated psychological experiments would give a clear-cut answer, however, is doubtful. Thornton B. Roby ("Utility and Futurity," *Behavioral Science*, Vol. 7, April 1962, pp. 194-210) has shown that time perspective is still necessary if probability and utility are considered jointly.

lief in a second chance. One pole of this attitude can be called "apocalyptic"—each event is the last one. The other pole can be called "serial."

As an example of the importance of apocalyptic-serial contrast to rational behavior, let us consider the discussion of civil defense preparations. If the assumption is made that a future nuclear war is one in a series, then it is possible to plan behavior during a war in such a way that repetition of this behavior in a series of wars will have a high probability of success. If, however, one assumes that only one nuclear war is possible, then one cannot talk about rational behavior. Here the only meaningful discussion can be whether one wants to avoid this war or not, whatever the subjective hope of doing so. The complementary relationship occurs regarding the attitude toward the fight against communism. If one thinks a Communist victory would be a unique event leaving no hope for any future struggle, then the only question is what kind of immediate action to take, and a rational, long-range plan would seem futile. On the other hand, those who believe that social changes will go on as long as there are people could take the outcome of any incident, even the most drastic one, as one point in a series, and plan accordingly. A variety of political predispositions and of reality situations will make people look at one event as apocalyptic and another one as not. What we are interested in here is whether there is a predisposition to see any kind of event as repeatable or not.

To summarize our speculations thus far, we can advance four propositions:

1. Decision making is partially a function of repeatable events, hence is usually more effective if a long-range time perspective is maintained.

Rational decisions are generally those that work over the long run, and they imply short-range losses for a long-range gain. If the decision is nonrepeatable, the tendency will be to go for an all-or-none solution.

2. The more crucial the decision, the shorter the time perspective and the greater the tendency toward the apocalyptic pole.

Crises are by definition situations in which the individual will not get a second chance. Further, stressful situations lead to the perception of dichotomies, while less important repeatable situations lead to perception of gradations and acceptance of medium risks.

3. Besides its relation to the kind of decision, time perspective is an individual characteristic and a function of over-all range of life space.

The relation of the self to the world includes the extent of the relevant environment, both in time and in space. Consideration of immediate versus distant future can manifest itself in various aspects of planning, risk taking, and reactions to personal and public problems.

4. The size of the life space is partially a function of such characteristics as age, education, occupation, and social class, and may indeed be the essential factor in the relation of these traits to social attitudes.

Adolescence can be viewed as coping with a rapidly expanding life space, while disengagement in aging is partially equivalent to a decrease in life space to the present and immediate environment.[11] Similarly, education leads to an increase in life space, especially through its emphasis on symbol manipulation. In so far as social classes and occupations are characterized by emphasis on symbol manipulation, these factors will accentuate the expansion of the life space, and especially of time perspective.

As a first approach, it would be difficult to test all the ramifications of these hypotheses in one case study. It seems better to collect many instances to see the implications of what we are calling "time perspective" in a wide variety of situations, and to see whether a personal point of view has been important in all kinds of cases. To do this we have used a number of national surveys and analyzed the relationship between indicators of belief in repeatability and handling of personal and public crises. By necessity, in this secondary analysis, we have used some oblique measures of the concepts with which we are dealing. However, from the wealth of material available only those questions were originally selected that could be presumed to be indirect measures of time perspective. As an additional safeguard against capitalizing on chance relationships in such a large universe of relationships, divisions in independent variables were kept consistent, as will be seen in the tables below, although stronger confirmation could have been presented in certain instances had different divisions been used. Judiciously used, this technique gives the opportunity to deal with a wide variety of public affairs and personal problems and to utilize a variety of objective conditions over the years.

We shall start by adapting some questions from national surveys to the measurement of time perspective. We shall then relate these measures to attitudes on public issues before showing the distribution of this perspective in different population groups. According to the hypotheses listed above, time perspective can be considered as an explanatory variable underlying the relationships between background characteristics and attitudes. There is, after all, no magic reason for the effect of, say, education and age; they affect attitudes because of some

[11] Elaine Cumming and William E. Henry, *Growing Old*, New York, Basic Books, 1961.

change brought about by education and aging that in turn modifies these attitudes. For this reason, we shall first demonstrate the importance of time perspective and then show its relation to the so-called "background characteristics" of the respondents.

MEASURES OF APOCALYPTIC AND SERIAL ORIENTATIONS

An apocalyptic orientation may be based on either a very short or very long time perspective. Lawrence Frank has clearly described these two approaches and their common implications:

> If we focus ahead for only a brief span, life becomes insignificant, meaningless and dreary, since the present leads to nothing of enduring value. Such a short time perspective means only eat, drink, be merry for tomorrow we die, but man cannot live for long on a purely organic level. On the other hand, if we focus toward the most remote future the present is rendered equally valueless and dreary because nothing humanly desirable or satisfying is permissible.[12]

On the other hand, the serial orientation and its associated rational model imply that the person gives consideration to an intermediate length of time.

These two different orientations, apocalyptic and serial, may be based either on a general world view or on the person's individual estimation of available time span. The first world view may be represented by the feeling that "there is nothing new under the sun," and the individual estimate by the feeling that "my peak is behind me." Both statements imply a lessened emphasis on a time span sufficiently long for rational decision making. They were measured to a certain degree in two different studies. In one study, a measure of general lack of future perspective was obtained from the following set of statements:

1. In spite of all our efforts for peace, nations just can't live together peacefully so we might as well expect a war every few years.
2. Since life is so short, we might as well eat, drink and be merry and not worry too much about what happens to the world.
3. Human lives are too important to be sacrificed for the preservation of any form of government.
4. The world is in such a muddle that no one really knows what people should do, so why try?

These items were sufficiently intercorrelated to form an index, which represented the attitude that "there is nothing new under the sun," and the time of one human is too short to be interested in a series of events. This was labeled a Futility Scale. The second measure was derived from the question, "When does a person reach his peak of mental

[12] Frank, *op.cit.*, pp. 355-356. Cf. Kurt Lewin, "Time Perspective and Morale," in Goodwin Watson, editor, *Civilian Morale*, New York, Houghton Mifflin, 1942, pp. 48-70.

ability?" By comparing the answer with the respondent's actual age, it was possible to determine the respondent's view of his extent of personal time. This measure, although obviously related to chronological age (cf. Table 7), can be considered to be a subjective component of age. As stated before, the influence of age on opinions and attitudes may be mediated as much through changes in time perspective as through effects of the aging process.

Tables 1 and 2 show the relation of time perspective to several ques-

TABLE 1

FUTILITY SCALE AND REACTIONS TO PUBLIC ISSUES
(in per cent)

Public Issue	Sample 1 (18-25 Years)			Sample 2 (40-55 Years)		
	1 (Serial)	*2*	*3-5* (Apocalyptic)	*1* (Serial)	*2*	*3-5* (Apocalyptic)
More power for labor right away	10.6 (905)	15.8 (728)	27.5 (346)	5.9 (690)	9.5 (453)	14.2 (267)
Outlaw the Communist Party right away	53.0 (907)	60.2 (730)	65.1 (347)	55.0 (695)	63.0 (454)	62.1 (269)
Fight Russia before they get any stronger	11.4 (906)	14.2 (731)	19.4 (346)	9.0 (691)	12.7 (455)	12.6 (269)
Something seriously bad will happen to U.S.	39.8 (903)	44.5 (730)	52.4 (347)	17.5 (691)	23.3 (455)	23.5 (268)

NOTE: Figures given in parentheses in Tables 1 to 7 indicate the number of persons forming the base of the percentage immediately above.
SOURCE: Roper Survey 71, October 1948.

TABLE 2

ESTIMATE OF MENTAL PEAK AND FUTURE ORIENTATION
(in per cent)

Orientation	Peak Behind	Peak Ahead
For foreign aid	49.8 (554)	59.3 (703)
Not at all worried about bombs	38.1 (554)	43.0 (702)
Estimate less unemployment in 6 months	36.8 (552)	41.8 (705)
Predict U.S. strongest in 10 years	73.2 (541)	75.6 (709)

SOURCE: Gallup Survey 596, March 1958.

tions on public issues asked in the same surveys. People who feel that they have little time before them can be expected to prefer immediate solutions to those problems whose outcomes cannot be ascertained for a long time. Thus apocalyptically oriented persons want extreme changes to occur, such as more power for labor, outlawing the Communist party, or fighting Russia right away, while they oppose a long-range program, such as foreign aid. Confirming Frank's inference of pessimism from apocalyptic orientation, they predict both economic decline and decrease in power of the United States.

THE FUNCTION OF GAMES OF CHANCE

The situations to which the serial model are most applicable are the games of chance. In fact, rational behavior in the face of uncertainty is theoretically based on a probability model, and the model is taken from the use of chance devices. A person who likes to engage in these games can be expected to take a serial attitude toward many events. We can compare this view of gambling with Roger Caillois' discussion of the development of rational society in terms of competitive and chance games, as contrasted to Dionysian societies, which depend on the one-time experiences of vertigo and the mask.[13] Engaging in a game or contest entails a belief in continuity and concern with a finite time span. Socially, this view is reflected in rational societies (in Weber's sense) and, individually, in serial time perspective.

The questions available in surveys asked whether the respondent had used a variety of chance devices at all during the last year. The large play of individual differences in this respect is shown by the surprisingly low incidence of any game of chance. They ranged from church raffles to horse races and poker games, and this wide range probably eliminated any differences in moral attitude toward gambling. In spite of this broad interpretation, about 40 per cent of the population in most surveys say that they have not engaged in any such behavior during the preceding year. This high proportion seems to indicate that we are dealing here with an individual predisposition covering all aspects of chance and competition and which can provide a measure of serial time perspective.

This interpretation seems to be justified if we look at the relation of the games-of-chance reports to optimism about the future, as depicted in Table 3. Favoring games of chance leads to optimism about the future similar to serial time perspective measured in the two earlier

[13] Roger Caillois, *Man, Play and Games*, Glencoe, Ill., Free Press, 1961, especially Chap. 8, "Competition and Chance."

ways. That is, people having played these games are likely to be more optimistic about the future, including their own economic conditions, general economic conditions, and events in international conflict.

TABLE 3

GAMBLING AND OPTIMISM AND CONSISTENCY
(in per cent)

	Nongamblers	Gamblers
Optimism:		
Better off today than a year ago	21.7	28.6
	(1,256)	(1,647)
Will spend more next month than last	20.0	28.4
	(1,256)	(1,647)
Own stocks or bonds	16.6	27.0
	(1,256)	(1,647)
Estimate war with Germany will last		
less than 6 months	9.9	12.8
	(1,443)	(1,497)
Consistency:		
Vote for every Roosevelt bill		
(1936 Roosevelt voters only)	42.8	35.8
	(507)	(745)
Per cent of those who would vote		
Democratic today	82.5	82.4
	(217)	(267)

SOURCE: Optimism: Gallup Surveys 128 and 338, July 1938 and December 1944. Consistency: Gallup Survey 128, July 1938.

Another indication of the probability view of the game-of-chance man is his acceptance of inconsistency. It is easier for him to disagree partially with a point of view. Roosevelt voters were asked in 1938 whether they agreed with all of the administration-sponsored legislation. As Table 3 demonstrates, the nongamblers were more likely to have agreed with all Roosevelt legislation, while the gamblers did not try to stay consistent with their earlier commitment. As there was little difference in the party loyalty of the two groups, chance players were more able to disagree with party legislation and to stay with the Democratic party in spite of this. A similar direct relationship between time perspective and consistency is found among the sample who gave their distance from their peak of mental efficiency. In this study it was possible to see whether a person's party affiliation corresponded to what he perceived to be his economic self-interest. Respondents were asked which party represented the interests of economic groups such as businessmen, skilled workers, or farmers, and then to which group they felt they belonged. Later they were asked their own party preference. Of the respondents who felt that their peak was still ahead, only 33.6 per cent identified with the party that was consistent with their perceived economic self-interest, while 40.3 per cent of the respondents who felt their peak was behind identified.

Time orientation, as far as it can be measured in these national studies, underlies a variety of reactions to public events. Let us see now how an interpretation of time orientation can account for consistency in reactions to both public events and personal problems. If we want to compare a person's reactions to several kinds of problems, we can do so from two points of view. A person can judge each situation according to its own merits, or he can treat them all the same, according to his disposition. In one of the studies, we have available a comparison of action toward two situations, one of which was intrinsically favorable, the other potentially dangerous. The survey, taken at the end of 1944, asked the question: "Do you think we have any chance of losing the war in Europe?" At that time, of course, the great majority said "No." Another, unrelated question referred to personal danger: "Is there any harm in nonpasteurized milk?" Here, objectively speaking, the danger is considerable. In both cases there exists a rational action in face of danger: one can try to conclude a negotiated peace and one can drink pasteurized milk. As can be seen in the first column of Table 4, people who believe in the danger are more likely to prefer this kind of action. The relation is definite but far from perfect. Does personal orientation influence this correspondence between belief in danger and corresponding rational decisions?

We can approach this question by distinguishing between people who view each situation separately and those who bring the same set of expectations into many decisions. This is the distinction between rational decision making according to the situation and irrational decision making according to constant personal dispositions;[14] further, according to our discussion above, the rational decision maker has a serial time orientation. Persons swayed by personal dispositions will tend to view both situations in the same way: they will either deny the danger both times or accept it both times. Persons judging each situation by itself should consider one dangerous and the other not. Table 4 shows the effect of this division. The opinion about the outcome of the war is controlled by opinion on the danger of nonpasteurized milk. Among people who feel the same way about both dangers—both dangerous or both not dangerous—there is little relationship between

14 Kurt W. Back, "Decisions under Uncertainty: Rational, Irrational, and Nonrational," as cited.

TABLE 4

Types of Orientation and Reactions to Public and Private Danger
(in per cent)

	All	Personal Orientation*	Situational Orientation†
Per cent wanting to negotiate peace of:			
Those who believe in chance to lose war	35.1 (296)	29.9 (194)	45.1 (102)
Those who believe in no chance to lose war	21.7 (2,016)	25.5 (608)	20.0 (1,408)
Difference	13.4	4.4	25.1
Per cent drinking pasteurized milk of:			
Those who believe in danger from nonpasteurized milk	73.3 (1,602)	72.7 (194)	73.4 (1,408)
Those who believe in no danger from nonpasteurized milk	61.8 (710)	63.3 (608)	58.8 (102)
Difference	11.5	9.4	14.6

* Either both dangerous or neither dangerous.
† Danger only in one situation.
Source: Gallup Survey 338, December 1944.

belief in the possibility of losing the war and desire for a negotiated peace. Among those who judge both situations differently, there is a strong congruence between belief and proposed action. A similar condition holds if we control belief in danger of milk by belief in danger about the outcome of the war. However, the differences are smaller (9 per cent among the personal predisposition people and 14 per cent among the situationally oriented). We can thus tentatively infer a correspondence between personal and situational orientation on one side and apocalytic and serial time perspective on the other.

The distinction we are making here is analogous to the one made frequently between response tendencies (acquiescence, yea-saying, social desirability) and answers to the content of the questions. People who are swayed primarily by personal dispositions—and these are not response errors—show little relation among their belief, action, and time perspective. People who react to the situation will tend to the more rational solution as we have previously defined it.

An amplification of this aspect appears when we consider directly the concept of personal safety. Can persons who refuse controls for their own safety be said to "gamble"? In the sense in which we have used games of chance before, it would seem so. That is, they do not feel that any act has to be certain, but that they will always have another chance. A person feeling this way should be inclined to take risks with his personal safety and should not accept safety devices that tend to stress the finality of each venture. An example of this attitude toward safety is given in a survey that included, among other issues, a question on the willingness to keep a speed governor on one's car. Like games of chance, unwillingness to use the governor related to optimism, in this case disbelief in a war in the near future. The effect of the short-range answers to both items—that is, the use of the governor and belief in proximity of war—is the same on a variety of questions, and joint effect of both questions is also quite strong. Thus, as can be seen in Table 5, people who would use governors and think war imminent

TABLE 5

TIME PERSPECTIVE AND PUBLIC AND PRIVATE ATTITUDES
(in per cent)

	Speed Governor		No Speed Governor	
	War Predicted (Apocalyptic)	No War	War Predicted	No War (Serial)
Public attitudes:				
No fear of local plant powered by atomic energy	60.8 (194)	79.6 (201)	75.9 (54)	89.1 (119)
Approve 4 billion dollar foreign aid appropriation to fight Communism	56.7 (191)	64.5 (200)	50.0 (52)	65.0 (117)
Attitude toward self:				
Do not abstain from consumption of alcoholic beverages	50.0 (196)	66.2 (201)	63.0 (54)	91.6 (119)
Took some form of bodily exercise yesterday	56.6 (196)	60.2 (201)	66.7 (54)	70.6 (119)

SOURCE: Gallup Survey 558, January 1956.

are most afraid of an uncontrollable force in their midst, either generally (an atomic plant) or personally (use of alcohol). On the other hand, they object to actions that might produce improvements, if they are repeated over and over, e.g. taking personal exercise or giving foreign aid (cf. Table 2). Gambling with personal safety combined with optimism about the existence of a future is characteristic of serial time perspective.

SOCIAL CHARACTERISTICS AND TIME PERSPECTIVE

Belief in the repeatability of events is not a purely individual matter, but is partly determined by social conditions. Some social conditions are more likely to lead to apocalyptic or to serial attitudes and, in fact, their effects on public attitudes may be mediated by time orientation. As we have indicated previously, advanced education is intended to lead to a wider view of the world, and this means a more confident view of the future, including the belief that no single event is necessarily the only one in a series to consider. Especially, professional training stresses this probabilistic view of the universe; to a lesser degree, any position of responsibility implies this attitude. We would therefore expect education, and, similarly, occupational status, to be related to the indications of time perspective, and this is indeed the case, as evidenced in Table 6.

TABLE 6

Time Perspective Indicators and Social Factors
(in per cent)

Social Factors	Non-gamblers	Gamblers	Peak Behind	Peak Ahead	Speed Governor, Predict War*	No Governor, No War*
Education:						
Grade school	59.1	40.9	66.7	33.3	58.3	6.6
High school	44.1	55.9	36.1	63.9	29.4	22.0
College	41.4	58.6	34.3	65.7	18.5	33.9
Age:						
Under 40	35.7	64.3	1.3	98.7	24.7	24.7
40-59	49.8	50.2	64.4	35.6	38.4	20.7
60 and over	75.3	24.7	95.0	5.0	62.5	5.6
Occupation:						
Professional	28.4	71.6	42.7	57.3	22.5	29.1
White-collar	27.9	72.1	61.1	38.7	28.6	15.6
Skilled	35.2	64.8	40.1	59.9	40.7	17.3
Unskilled	41.6	58.4	42.4	57.6	46.9	21.0

* See Table 5.
Source: Gallup Surveys 128, 558, and 596, July 1938, January 1956, and March 1958.

Another important determinant of time perspective is age. It is reasonable to assume that with advancing age the likelihood of a given event to repeat tends to decrease. This is again confirmed by the relation of age to the time perspective questions.

Regarding the questions on the direction of the peak of mental ability, it is almost tautological that older people would be more likely to feel that they were past their peak, and, indeed, Table 6 indicates that this is so. Education is also correlated with the feeling that one's peak of mental ability lies in the future. The occupational breakdown shows more interesting irregularities. The professionals, skilled, and unskilled workers are all more likely to place their peak ahead than behind. The white-collar workers, though in general more highly educated, showed as a lone exception. The white-collar worker also estimates the peak of mental maturity to be earlier. Whereas the mean estimate of the peak for professionals is 44 years, the skilled worker 41 years, and the unskilled laborer 39 years, the white-collar mean estimate is only 35 years. This seems to correspond to the ambiguous status of the nonprofessional white-collar worker in our society and is reflected in more pessimistic and apocalyptic attitudes, as seen above. In many respects, the white-collar worker is closer to the lower-status groups than to the professional.

Additional data show how the apocalyptic-serial attitudes (as measured by the Futility Scale), gambling orientation, and economic achievement, are related.[15] The young (18-25-year-old) sample for whom the futility index was available were asked about their preference for different types of jobs and their expected peak income. As seen in Table 7, respondents with an apocalyptic orientation preferred a secure, though low-paying, job and also expected less income. The greater willingness to take risks of the serial-oriented youth corresponds to his expectation of having greater economic success.

The above examples show how time perspective is an explanatory concept for the common effect of education, occupation, and age on many attitudes. The effects of these variables alone have often been established, but they do present a puzzle. After all, people do not necessarily learn in school to feel certain ways about public events, nor is there any reason that through biological changes or accumulation of experience these different attitudes should become prevalent in advancing age. Taking the stance toward repeatability of events as basic, we can see how it would be affected by age and education and how, on the other hand, it would lead to a pattern of attitudes that would be consistent with this stance.

[15] This survey was done on a national basis, but with two restricted age samples, a "young" sample between 18 and 25, and an "old" sample between 40 and 55. Consequently, the old sample could not be used for income aspirations and the young sample could not be used for occupational achievement (see also Table 1).

TABLE 7

FUTILITY SCALE AND OCCUPATIONS
(in per cent)

Occupations	Sample 1 (18-25 Years)			Sample 2 (40-55 Years)		
	1 (Serial)	2	3-5 (Apocalyptic)	1 (Serial)	2	3-5 (Apocalyptic)
Would choose least	34.8	44.8	55.6	42.2	50.0	65.4
risky job	(904)	(728)	(345)	(689)	(452)	(268)
Mean estimate of peak earnings (in thousands per annum)	4.26 (614)	4.15 (497)	3.45 (220)	(Not Asked)		
Actual occupation:						
Professional				34.8	28.0	20.3
White collar	(Not Applicable)			23.6	29.8	26.6
Skilled worker				24.5	18.8	28.1
Unskilled worker				17.1	23.4	25.0

SOURCE: Roper Survey 71, October 1948.

SUMMARY

If we discuss personal reactions to public events, we have to consider several facts: the structure of events, the social differentiations, and personality traits. Clearly, the possible multiplicity of variables makes even the most sophisticated multivariate analysis hard put to disentangle the possible relationships. A basic orientation, however, may underlie much of a person's behavior, both in his individual life and in his attitude toward the social order. Assessment of either apocalyptic or serial time orientations can lead to the discovery of a common thread through many attitudes: the apocalyptic person is pessimistic, uncompromising, cautious, and consistent; all these traits seem to be compatible with his time orientation, that is, his consideration of only one event at a time, because events are not repeatable. In addition, we find a consistent selection of background factors that predict the person's orientation in time. Higher education and professional training lead to the serial orientation. In the individual life cycle, the apocalyptic orientation is manifested in the immediacy of the child, which yields to a more mature serial attitude, followed by a return to a more apocalyptic orientation as the aging individual realizes his diminishing life span.

IN JULY 1945 General Leslie Groves, head of the Manhattan Project, asked Arthur Compton to do "an opinion poll among those who know what is going on."[1] The resulting survey was conducted among 150 staff members of the Chicago laboratory. They may have had private thoughts about what to do with the bomb, but they had not been involved in the discussions at higher levels. To many of them the poll was their first encounter with the problem. According to the atomic physicist Eugene Rabinowich, "We were not given more than a few minutes to answer. . . . The man distributing [the questionnaires] said, 'Put your mark in one of the places reflecting your opinion'."

Compton's analysis of the poll's results was that "there were a few who preferred not to use the bomb at all, but 87 per cent voted for its military use, at least if after other means were tried this was found necessary to bring surrender." But within that 87 per cent there were 46 per cent who said, "Give a military demonstration in Japan to be followed by a renewed opportunity for surrender before full use of the weapons is employed," and an additional 26 per cent who said, "Give an experimental demonstration in this country with representatives of Japan present, followed by a new opportunity for surrender before full use of the weapon is employed."

The poll results were turned over to Secretary Stimson five days

[1] Len Giovanitti and Fred Freed, *The Decision to Drop the Bomb*, New York, Coward-McCann, 1965, pp. 166-167.

Originally published in Volume 31, Number 3, 1967 of the *Public Opinion Quarterly*.

before the bomb burst over Hiroshima. It seems unlikely that this survey could have had much influence on Harry Truman. What is of more than passing interest is both the use of the opinion polling method in arriving at so momentous a decision, and also the vulnerability of that method to debatable and perhaps distorted interpretations of the results.

Today, opinion surveys, professional and amateur, are an integral part of the administrative structure of power, in both political and business life. The strong interest taken in polls by both Presidents Kennedy and Johnson is a matter of common knowledge,[2] and such interest extends down the line in government. More and more Congressmen have used polls of their own to try to overcome their ignorance of what their constituents think.[3]

A public official who does something that is disapproved of by a plurality of respondents in a survey risks the accusation that he has "defied" public opinion, even though the very exercise of his leadership is likely to shift opinion toward the course of action he supports. What bearing *should* the answers given on opinion surveys, amateur *or* professional, have on legislative or administrative action? In the domain of consumer research, it is easy enough to say that a manufacturer should give his toothpaste the flavor preferred by a majority of his customers. But the tendency to regard policy as a commodity that should obey the laws of supply and demand becomes scandalous when it is extended from the realm of marketing (where it is dubious enough) to the realm of politics. In the words of Edmund Burke, "Your representative owes you not his industry only, but his judg-

[2] The *New York Times* of Feb. 18, 1966, states that "the White House is keeping a sharp eye on the state of American public opinion with respect to the war, as reflected in widely published polls and private surveys taken at its instigation. . . . The White House will not disclose the identity of polltakers who do work for it."

[3] This ignorance can be substantial. Warren E. Miller and Donald E. Stokes report that there is only a .19 correlation between the attitudes on foreign policy of people in a congressional constituency and the perception of these attitudes by the Congressman. Cf. "Representation in Congress," quoted by Bernard C. Cohen, *The Press and Foreign Policy*, Princeton, Princeton University Press, 1963, p. 240.

Congressional polls, run in an amateur and often incompetent fashion, raise questions in the minds of both legislators and the public about the essential validity of opinion research. For example, the *New York Times* of Apr. 2, 1967, reports that 66 per cent of respondents in a mail survey conducted by Representative Seymour Halpern, a Queens Republican, answered "Yes" to the question: "Do you approve of the recent decision to extend bombing raids in North Vietnam aimed at oil reserves and other strategic supply depots around Hanoi and Haiphong?" At about the same time a Manhattan Democrat, Representative William Ryan, found only 14 per cent in *his* poll answering "Yes" to the direct question: "Do you believe the United States should bomb Hanoi and Haiphong?" Not only to the uninformed layman but to the congressional user of such polls, the enormous disparity in the replies (far beyond the differences one would expect between Queens and the upper west side of Manhattan) must seem to reflect discredit upon survey research.

ment; and he betrays instead of serving you if he sacrifices it to your opinion."

It has now become quite common for candidates cynically to adapt their campaign utterances to what their private polls show to be publicly acceptable. In Los Angeles, Hal Every, who runs two affiliated organizations, the Public Relations Center and the Western Opinion Research Center, advertises: "You can be elected state senator; leading public relations firm with top flight experience in statewide campaigns wants a senator candidate." Every envisions that "in the world of 1984 voters . . . will first be polled as to what type of candidate they want, even on physical and personal characteristics. The information will be fed into a computer and the candidate most closely reflecting the voters' choice will be selected to run for office. "In the presidential race," he says, "the government will sample the nation to find 1,000 typical voters and they will make the final selection."[4]

This advanced line of thought is not limited to southern California public relations men. Vladimir K. Zworykin, the renowned electronics expert, suggests that "modern technology makes it possible to give the people the ability to communicate their wishes and opinions to the government with a directness and immediacy comparable with that realized at present only in the opposite direction."[5] He foresees a system in which every telephone would be provided with simple auxiliary equipment that would convert it into a voting station. Registered voters would express their preferences on specific questions submitted over broadcast channels in much the same manner as citizens today use voting machines to express their opinions in a referendum. According to Zworykin, "Government leaders would be able to align their policies more closely with the popular will, which would be known rather than a subject for speculation."

Zworykin echoes a widely held view that in a democracy those in authority should respond directly to public opinion. This assumes that the right questions can be asked and that everybody's responses are equally valid. It also assumes that opinions can be regarded atomistically, one by one, without regard to the context in which they come into play with each other, and without regard to the intensity with which they are held. None of these assumptions is correct.

[4] Every's formula for success is to look for a catchy campaign slogan and to keep the candidate from making personal appearances, since the candidate who talks is a bad risk. "He makes a speech and then exposes himself to foolish questions from some nut who makes him look bad." Every points out that 80 per cent of the people do not even know the name of their Congressman; "99 per cent don't know whether an incumbent running for reelection has kept his earlier campaign promises." *New York Times*, Jan. 9, 1966.

[5] "Communications in Government," in Nigel Calder, ed., *The World in 1984*, New York, Penguin Books, 1965, Vol. 2, pp. 51-57.

No doubt the character and quality of public opinion have changed over the years, with the growth of literacy and mass communications. Such change has been subtle, gradual, and continuous, whereas in the academic discussion of public opinion there is a sharp discontinuity between the periods before and after the development of the systematic opinion survey. The world of public opinion in today's sense really began with the Gallup Polls of the mid-1930's, and it is impossible for us to retreat to the meaning of public opinion as it was understood by Tocqueville and Jefferson—or even by Walter Lippmann in 1922.[6]

For many years, philosophers and political scientists dealt with public opinion as though it represented a natural force, constrained perhaps by certain regularities and laws, but capricious and unpredictable like human nature itself. It was one force among many in the complex flux of politics. These forces were like currents of the air or ocean, constantly changing in their contours and directions. The public opinion survey method requires that these elusive currents be treated as though they were static, that we define and measure what was formerly undefinable and unmeasurable. Once this is done, and done over and over again, it is easy to succumb to the illusion that our measurements represent reality rather than a distorted, dim, approximate reflection of a reality that alters its shape when seen from different angles.

Opinion surveys are often dubious indicators of actual behavior because they do not, and perhaps cannot, measure the seething, changing character of the public temper. They generally fail to embody the rich context of motivation and cross-communication out of which opinions arise and activate people in the mass. When a working committee arrives at a consensus after a prolonged, many-sided discussion, it may do so as a matter of voting and majority rule. More commonly, when there is intense feeling on the part of some individual members of a committee, and comparative indifference on the part of others, this finds expression in the decision that is

[6] There is no place for public opinion in the political theory of Marxism-Leninism, because the concept of "the public" implies a single body politic, whether or not it is considered to be composed of uniform and homogeneous individual components—as implied in the philosophy of one man—one vote. As long as one puts emphasis on the separate publics represented by social classes, to each of which an appropriate political ideology corresponds, the significant clash of opinion must be that of the publics themselves, of their powers and essential interests, which opinions serve only to rationalize. Opinions that deviate from those appropriate to one's class are irrational; those unrelated to class interest are irrelevant. Thus, half a century after the October Revolution, there is still in the Soviet Union only the most primitive and reluctant acceptance of the notion that survey techniques may be usefully applied to the study of serious matters.

eventually reached. The process by which a group comes to take a position is not amenable to study by a technique that approaches people one by one.

The paradox of scientific method is that we change phenomena by measuring them. An interview acts as a catalyst. The confrontation of interviewer and respondent forces the crystallization and expression of opinions where there were no more than chaotic swirls of thought. The respondent's statements themselves represent a form of behavior; they are commitments. A question asked by an interviewer changes an abstract and perhaps irrelevant matter into a genuine subject of action; the respondent confronts a voting decision, exactly as he might on a choice of candidates or on a proposition in a plebiscite. The conventional poll forces expression into predetermined channels, by presenting clear-cut and mutually exclusive choices. To accomodate one's thoughts to these channels represents for the respondent an arousal of interest, an affirmative act.

An opinion stated spontaneously in speech or writing is different in quality from one offered in answer to a structured questionnaire. The process of setting words down on paper forces a writer to eliminate the inconsistencies in his position. The public relations man who writes speeches for a corporate president learns that his boss rapidly comes to imagine that the ideas were his own. He begins to believe the words he reads simply because he has uttered them. This kind of commitment is the basis for Leon Festinger's theory of cognitive dissonance, which applies to situations in which an individual "takes a stand" and shifts his views to reduce incongruities. But a large proportion of the ideas that float through our minds do *not* represent "commitments" in which the ego is involved. They are ideas which are part of the common currency of the mass media, and with which people have a *passive* familiarity.

We think of public opinion as polarized on great issues; we think of it as intense, because polarized opinion must be intense almost by definition. Because of the identification of public opinion with the measurements of surveys, the illusion is easily conveyed of a public which is "opinionated"—which is committed to strongly held views. The publication of opinion poll results undoubtedly acts as a reinforcing agent in support of the public's consciousness of its own collective opinions as a definable, describable force. These published poll data may become reference points by which the individual formulates and expresses his opinions.

A 1964 NORC survey reported by Charles Y. Glock and Rodney Stark[7] found that 7 per cent of U.S. adults agreed that Hitler was

[7] *Christian Beliefs and Anti-Semitism,* New York, Harper and Row, 1966, p. 199.

right to try to kill all the Jews. We attribute no particular importance to this 7 per cent, which projects to some 8 million individuals, each one a potential mass murderer, because the sentiments they express to an interviewer are made individually without awareness of their collective strength. By contrast, we may feel enormous concern about the similarly small percentage of people who now vote for the neo-Nazi party in Germany, precisely because their opinions are crystallized and their political force is known.

The surveys on the subject of the Vietnam war illustrate the perils of interpreting answers to single questions as though they really summarized the state of public opinion.[8] The questions commonly asked gauge public sentiment in terms of support or opposition for the administration's conduct of the war and (in the case of opposition) define it as being of the hawk or dove variety. In early 1966, when a group of researchers at Stanford explored attitudes toward Vietnam war in much greater depth than had been done in any previously published survey, their data revealed a number of apparent contradictions. For example, a majority of the public supported the President's handling of the Vietnam situation but at the same time a majority also approved a policy of de-escalating the war effort. Press coverage of the Stanford poll, Nelson Polsby has pointed out, tended to dismiss the contradictions among people's opinions as signs of "confusion."[9] The survey illustrates how people withdraw from the difficult issues with which they are confronted and defer to their leaders the task of making decisions. But polls are themselves news, and the "confusion" of the public is thus itself converted into a public issue.

Today, an individual's opinions on any public matter are likely to follow a *system* of opinion already expressed in the mass media.[10] Such systems of opinion, in which all the ambiguities are straightened and all the loose ends are tied up, surround the great public issues of

[8] As a typical example, under the headline "Poll Finds More Back Escalation," the *New York Times* of May 17, 1967, refers to "rising public support for escalation of the American war effort in Vietnam." Forty-five per cent of those polled said they favored "total military victory." The corresponding figure in February was 43 per cent.

[9] "Hawks, Doves, and the Press," *Trans/action*, April 1967, pp. 35-40.

[10] The individual media function differently in this respect. Opinions expressed in print are apt to follow an orderly and systematic exposition of thoughts, presented sequentially and without opposition. Opinions expressed on television are apt to be expressed within a framework of discussion and debate, with all the heat generated by a direct clash of ideas. It is far more difficult to get one's ideology in a straight and consistent line from a television discussion program than from a newspaper editorial.

our time. They need not extend to the comprehensive scope of a doctrinaire ideology, but they carry with them a full panoply of arguments and rationalizations.

Opinions always start from certain factual premises. But the information we have at hand is usually limited. Our opinions invariably transcend our knowledge.[11] Today's mass media can produce the illusion of knowing the inside story of what in fact we know only selectively and incompletely. When governments engage in secret diplomacy, propaganda, and military actions at the same time, opinions must be based on what the public knows. If, as is often the case, a substantial percentage of the public is uninformed about and uninterested in a subject, then actions contrary to the apparent will of the polled majority may nonetheless fall within the latitude that a compliant body politic permits its leaders.[12] How sensitive should a leader be to opinion formed without knowledge of important information?

Perhaps the most important and accurate thing that surveys can tell us is the extent of public ignorance on matters of fact. Substantial sectors of the population are unable to answer correctly such questions as whether mainland China is Communist or not, who the Vietcong are, or what NATO or the Alliance for Progress is. One American in four in 1966 thought that Chiang Kai-shek was the head of the Chinese Communist Party. Such ignorance certainly does not reflect a lack of attention to the subject by the mass media. Rather, it reflects the selective inattention of large masses of the population to matters they interpret as having no direct meaning, relevance, or importance to them. The question of *what* people think about public issues is really secondary to the question of whether they think about them at all.

We measure public opinion for and against various causes, with the "undecided" as the residue. Often what we should be doing instead is measuring the degrees of apathy, indecision, or conflict on the part of the great majority, with the opinionated as the residual left over. The first question to ask is: "Have you thought about this at all? Do you *have* an opinion?"

---

[11] A *New Yorker* cartoon shows a respondent telling an interviewer, "I'm afraid I have no opinion at the moment. All my journals of opinion have been late this week."

[12] Public opinion provides a wide tolerance for obedience to leadership. The sense of deference to authority is deeply instilled in all human beings by the basic biological conditions of our infantile dependence. This is what often makes the source of information so much more important than its coherence; it can cause wide swings of agreement or disagreement with controversial statements, depending on whether they are attributed to one source or to another.

Most of what passes for public opinion research is devoted to the study of trivia; it is the study of minor preferences in the market place and in the media. To a very large extent it is not a study of opinion at all but of purchasing or consumption behavior as the respondent reports it. Of the remainder, which is really devoted to the study of public issues, much deals with subjects of transitory interest that are unfamiliar to most people or incapable of arousing strong feelings pro or con.

What an individual defines as important cannot be separated from what he feels he has within his control.[13] Compared to the questions of consumer choice with which we most commonly confront our survey respondents, political questions may have more objective importance. Yet the average individual has no control over political questions, or over the problems that they represent, except within the framework of collective social action. The questions asked in opinion surveys often seem irrelevant to a world of barricades, guerrilla warriors, and lumbering armies.

When an interviewer confronts me with questions about my brand choice in beer or automobiles, he is dealing with preferences that relate to past and possible future actions over which I exercise the primary control regardless of what influences may be brought to bear upon me. When the same interviewer asks my opinions about China, Rhodesia, or the Latin-American Common Market, he is asking about matters on which my opinions can be translated into action only through the legitimized institutions of society or through noninstitutional social behavior, from a be-in to a riot.

Seen in this light, pre-election polls are closer to consumer studies than are most other kinds of opinion surveys. In market research we may ask about brand preference, but we usually also go on to find out from the record of past purchases whether or not the respondent is a likely prospect for the product. By the same token, since 1948 we have accepted the idea that it is not enough in political polls to

[13] Paul Goodman says pessimistically, "People believe that the great background conditions of modern life are beyond our power to influence. . . . History is out of control, it is no longer something that we make but something that happens to us." *New York Review of Books,* Nov. 3, 1966.

A similar view is voiced by Tom Wicker, who refers to the "growing sense of dismay and despair at the inability of the individual to make an impact on public policy through the accepted channels of dissent." Wicker refers to "the malaise beyond dissent—the fear that dissent does not matter any more; that only action counts; but that no one really knows what action to take. More and more 20th-century man crouches like an old woman on her stoop, pointing her rusty shotgun at the oncoming expressway, knowing all the time that in the end the bulldozers will go through." *New York Times,* Mar. 12, 1967.

determine what candidate people favor; we also need their past voting record to assess the likelihood that they will act on their preferences on Election Day. Voting intentions, like brand preferences, may change, but votes, like purchases, are irrevocable. Both voting intentions and brand preferences reflect a different order of phenomenon from the kinds of opinion which are not expected to eventuate in action, which are understood to be in the hands of more powerful outside forces.

When does a statement of opinion on a public matter reflect the kind of personal engagement that characterizes our statements about acts that are within our power to control? In our impersonal, industrial, urban society no one wants to get involved in the problems of strangers. On an inside page of the newspaper, a 2-inch UPI dispatch of May 3, 1967, from Miami reports that "a wounded driver of a bakery truck bled to death tonight while 20 witnesses to the shooting stood by without notifying the authorities." Such an incident seems commonplace, barely meriting attention; from it a direct line can be traced to the world's complacent acceptance of starvation and mass murder.

Bruno Bettelheim observes that concentration camp inmates living just a few hundred yards away from the gas chambers and crematoria denied knowledge of them.

The separation of behavior patterns and values inside and outside of camp was so radical, and the feelings about it so strong that most prisoners avoided talking about it; it was one of many subjects that were "taboo." . . . This attitude of denying "reality" to events so extreme as to threaten the prisoner's integration was a first step toward developing new mechanisms for surviving in the camp. By denying reality to overwhelming situations, they were somehow made bearable; but at the same time it constituted a major change in experiencing the world.[14]

Chaim Aron Kaplan's remarkable journal of the Warsaw ghetto has the following entry for June 7, 1942: "When the news doesn't tell us what we want to hear, we twist and turn it until it seems full of hints, clues and secrets that support our views . . . and the news from Reuters always contains a certain intonation or expression to satisfy and comfort a spirit thirsting for a speedy and quick redemption."[15]

If, under such conditions, people can deny the imminence of their own doom, how much easier it is to deny reality to the unpleasant events which we know about only at second or third hand, which happen to faceless statistics rather than to individual human beings with whom we can empathize! Why should we have opinions about such

14 *The Informed Heart*, Glencoe, Ill., Free Press, 1963.
15 *Commentary*, November 1965, pp. 52-53.

matters? If we "think about the unthinkable," must this not become an obsession that makes all normal activity impossible?

Opinions become real when those who hold them feel a responsibility for action. John Darley and Bibb Latané[16] found that experimental subjects responded more slowly to an "emergency" affecting another individual when a third person was present as a bystander. When there were four other bystanders present, nearly half the experimental subjects did not report the emergency at all; the reaction time of those who did respond was exactly half as fast as when there was no other bystander and the subject had to take on all the responsibility. In the latter case, the subject had to perceive the situation as one in which he alone could summon help.

PUBLIC AND PRIVATE OPINIONS AND THE FUNCTION OF ROLES

In our bureaucratized world it is easier than ever before in history for individuals to abjure responsibility not only for their acts but also for the consequences of the opinions they hold. Eichmann, as we know, "only followed orders." It now seems to be quite well established that one can ascribe to one's superiors the motivation and blame for one's own socially unacceptable acts. It is no less common for those superiors to pass the blame to their subordinates or (again) to "The System."

In *War and Peace*, Tolstoy describes Napoleon on the battlefield at Borodino as a hostage to history, powerless to control the destinies of the armies he had set in motion:

Even before he gave that order the thing he did not desire, and for which he gave the order only because he thought it was expected of him, was being done. And he fell back into that artificial realm of imaginary greatness, and again—as a horse walking a treadmill thinks it is doing something for itself—he submissively fulfilled the cruel, sad, gloomy and inhuman role predestined for him. . . .[17]

Even Heinrich Himmler, at war's end, when he harbored the fantasy that he would be accepted by the West as the leader of postwar Germany, made no effort to argue in favor of the policy of exterminating Jews; he simply denied that it was taking place. Receiving a representative of the World Jewish Congress, Himmler complained of "distorted" reports about the concentration camps: "The bad connotation of these camps is due to their inappropriate name. They

16 "Bystander Intervention in Emergency Situations I: Diffusion of Responsibility" (as yet unpublished). Paper delivered to the American Psychological Association, Sept. 6, 1966.

17 Leo Tolstoy, *War and Peace*, translated from the Russian by Constance Garnett, New York, McGraw-Hill, 1963, p. 909.

should have been called 'reformatories'. . . . The treatment in the camps was hard but just." Himmler conceded that crimes occasionally happened in the camps but added, "I also punish the persons responsible."[18] Was this "acting"? Or was Himmler, *while* he lied, expressing genuine opinions that he had held all along *at the same time* he was engineering the "final solution"?

This is an outrageously extreme case, of course, but the psychological mechanism is a commonplace among politicians. Who is the real Kurt Kiesinger—the highly placed Nazi propagandist of the forties or America's staunch ally of the sixties? Who is the real Lester Maddox —the racist wielding axe handles to bar Negroes from his restaurant, or the great statesman who as Governor of Georgia has his picture taken shaking hands with (the militant Negro leader) Julian Bond?

In the biographies and memoirs of important political figures it is not unusual to read that in private they expressed opinions in contradiction to the views they expressed publicly. We may be shocked when Arthur M. Schlesinger, Jr., tells us that John Kennedy was disdainful of Dean Rusk.[19] If such an attitude truly represented Kennedy's opinion, expressed to Schlesinger within the framework of friendship and close collaboration, does it acquire greater meaning or validity than the esteem the President professed in public and confirmed by maintaining Mr. Rusk in his very high position? Can we assume that the public statements of public men reflect less of their personal convictions than their private statements do? The man who is in the public eye necessarily speaks in accordance with a role, but it is a role that he has chosen, and one that carries with it the responsibility of withholding his doubts and indecisions from view.[20]

The rest of us are no more immune to ambivalence and self-contradiction merely because our thoughts go unrecorded. Our increasingly segmented lives demand that we play a diversity of roles, each with its appropriate set of attitudes. Honesty may have little relevance to the task of weeding rationalizations and role-play from "true" opinions. Men believe their own lies when they repeat them often

---

18 John Toland, *The Last 100 Days,* New York, Random House, 1966, p. 415.

19 *A Thousand Days,* Boston, Houghton Mifflin, 1965.

20 Self-consciousness of role has always linked politics and the stage. The entry of movie stars into public life is not unique to the United States. In India, N. G. Ramachandran, the "Tamil Errol Flynn," was shot in the neck and critically wounded by another film star, M. R. Radha, who has generally played villain roles. Both men were prominent in political life and Ramachandran was at last reports sure of election in spite of the fact that he had to campaign from a hospital bed and was unable to talk. At the same time, according to the *New York Times* of Feb. 7, 1967, his latest movie is "a stupendous success. What makes it irresistible is the casting of the real-life assailant in the villain's role." Cf. also Orrin E. Klapp, *Symbolic Leaders,* Chicago, Aldine, 1964.

enough. Yesterday's rationalization becomes today's conviction. What opinion analyst can tell when a lie becomes a truth?

An American who at home is highly critical of U.S. foreign policy may defend that policy when he travels abroad. We all express judgments, prejudices, and emotions in the bosom of our family that would be outrageous if we heard them on the lips of strangers. Are these any less our opinions than the more reflective statements we make when we are on our best behavior?

After the military take-over of the Greek government, in the spring of 1967, a reporter interviewed an old man in a small Greek village. He asked (a typical unbiased reporter's question): "Are people unhappy with the new regime?" " 'They like it,' he said firmly. Then with a smile, 'They have to like it.' And finally with a shrug, 'Most don't like it.' "[21]

I am not proposing that on any given subject an individual has one public opinion and one private opinion which may or may not be the same. I am rather suggesting that one may at the same time hold a *variety* of opinions, articulated or vague, public shading into private. These multiple opinions, which correspond to different roles or reference groups, may be contradictory or incongruent. They may be actively at war with each other and arouse in us an uncomfortable sense of conflict, or they may be no more than low-charge reflections of the opposing viewpoints to which we are subjected through mass media and in conversation. Just as the same object may arouse alternating emotions of love and hate, depending on circumstances, so we are capable of simultaneously incorporating a belief and its opposite or seeing the best and worst in two alternative courses of action.

To "change one's mind" may mean painfully reworking an entire system of belief. More often, it means starting with an emotional judgment from which a ready-made structure of rationalizations follows automatically. In a recent experiment, John Wallace found that rewarding a subject by complimenting him on his success in playing a role produced substantial attitude change in the direction of the debating position he had taken (contrary to his private opinion).[22]

[21] *New York Times*, May 14, 1967.

[22] John Wallace, "Role Reward and Dissonance Reduction," *Journal of Personality and Social Psychology*, Vol. 3, No. 3, 1966, pp. 305-312. Wallace followed the lead of Irving L. Janis and B. T. King, who found some years ago that experimental subjects who were placed in a "forced compliance" situation in which they had to argue a point of view opposite to their own tended to change their attitudes in the direction that they expressed. The subject was "impressed by his own cogent arguments, clarifying illustrations, and convincing appeals which he is stimulated to think of in order to do a good job of 'selling' the idea to others." Cf. Irving L. Janis and B. T. King, "The Influence of Role Playing on Opinion Change," *Journal of Abnormal and Social Psychology*, Vol. 49, 1954, p. 218.

As one subject put it, "I tend to think of myself as an honest and sincere person. When you told me that the others considered me 'a very good actor,' I was somewhat baffled . . . actually, a little offended. The more I thought about it, the more I became convinced that what I had said in the debate was what I truly believed." By contrast, when experimental subjects were praised for the *content* of what they said, they did not move nearly as strongly in the expected direction. The reason for this, Wallace suggests, was that the subjects knew they were just repeating "hack" arguments that were in the "public domain." "Hence, the subject could verbalize such ideas, receive reward for the reasonableness, logical nature of, and persuasiveness of such arguments but experience little dissonance over and above that expected from simple voluntary compliance." Wallace hypothesizes that "success in role playing increases the subject's involvement in the role. And the greater the involvement of the subject, the more one would expect him to strive for self-consistency."

On the day in 1939 when Franco's Fascist armies marched into Madrid, the streets were alive with cheering crowds. When these same streets had been full of crowds applauding the troops of the Republic, were these different people altogether or were some of them the same? And did either ovation echo the mass sentiments of the moment? Throughout this century we have lived with this phenomenon over and over again.

At the end of World War II, I participated in the project of recruiting high officers of the Luftwaffe to assist the American Air Force in the continuing war against Japan. When these gentlemen were asked if they would turn against their former allies, there was not the slightest glimmer of hesitation, doubt, or ambiguity in their response. Nor, indeed, was there any that I know of in the case of the Italians, Rumanians, and other military forces whose rulers switched sides in the course of the war.

Does this kind of sharp reversal of sides reflect a change of opinion? Does not the phenomenon of sudden political change rather reflect the coexistence of antagonistic systems of thought, alignment, loyalty, and opinion in the minds of the same people? These coexisting systems can reverse their dominance when this seems to be called for by the objective realities of the situation or by immediate short-run personal self-interest.

For the highly political man who recognizes the inconsistencies, weaknesses, gaps, and fallacies in his own intellectual value system, there already exists in embryo the contradictory argument, the antithesis to his thesis. It was not necessary for Bukharin, Radek, and the other defendants in the great Moscow trials to be coached on the details of their imaginary crimes any more than it was necessary for Galileo to receive indoctrination in Ptolemaic astronomy in order to present a "disproof" of what he had demonstrated.

An act of political or religious conversion represents a reorganization of one's perceptions, ideas, past experiences, and beliefs. Such an act may perhaps be akin to the achievement of insight in psychotherapy, when forgotten, suppressed, or previously ignored relationships suddenly assume coherence and emotional significance. The secret of such insight is very often the recognition of ambivalence of feeling. The patient recognizes the strain of hatred for his objects of love and his love for the objects of his hatred. We know better than to call such events "changes of opinion," for they are indeed much more than that; they are deep changes of the heart, and they are beyond the cunning of statistics.

CONCLUDING NOTE

Today presidents—of the United States and of TV networks—gauge the success of their policies by their ratings. Surveys are taken as literal descriptions of public opinion. This easily leads to the proposition that a democracy should be ruled by the public will as described by the polls. But, too often, the polling method gets people to answer questions on matters they have not thought about and for which they feel no sense of responsibility. We are apt to answer questions differently when we know the decision is really up to us, but it is harder and harder to have this feeling when we are told who is going to win an election before we have decided whom to vote for, or who has won before we have voted. "Don't know" in response to a survey question often means "Don't want to know," which is another way of saying, "I don't want to get involved."

The prevailing model underlying our discipline is that of the single opinion. A person holds an opinion, which he communicates to an interviewer. When he is influenced to change his mind, he replaces his former opinion with another one. This model has the virtue of great simplicity but it makes no sense, because conflicting and contradictory opinions may be held simultaneously and because they constantly jostle each other for dominance.

It has taken the opinion research profession a third of a century to gain acceptance for the principle of systematic sampling. It may take the next third to dispel the illusion that descriptive measurements of public opinion represent the "real thing," and to establish that our primary task is to understand how opinions come to be held at all, and how they evolve and change.

E. M. Forster has drawn the distinction between "flat" and "round" fictional characterizations.[23] Most opinion studies, like most works of fiction, employ flat, abbreviated treatments of their subjects. We reject the reality of comic-book characters who are predictably heroes or villains, yet we too often settle for comic-book statistics on infinitely complex matters of opinion. It is the rare poll that allows us to see opinion as multi-faceted, multi-layered, and intricate.

[23] E. M. Forster, *Aspects of the Novel*, New York, Harcourt, Brace & World, 1947.

19

**PUBLIC OPINION
RESEARCH AS
COMMUNICATION**
W. Phillips Davison

O N ANY SINGLE DAY, the chances are one in several thousand that you will receive a visit or a telephone call from a special kind of stranger.[1] If you ask him what he wants, he may reply: "I'm collecting standardized information from a sample chosen to represent the component units of a predefined universe."[2] Or he may say: "I'm taking a poll." In either case the content of his message is the same.

But what do this interviewer's activities signify for society as a whole? Or, to bring the question closer to home, what role do we as public opinion researchers play within the social organism of which we are a part? It is obvious that we provide a mechanism for describing, and sometimes explaining, certain opinions, attitudes, and behaviors. Our services are used, at one time or another, by practically all organized groups and interests. Still, to recognize that survey research provides information that has a wide range of utilities does not tell us

---

[1] Data on the total number of persons polled in the United States are surprisingly sparse. POQ Polls Editor Hazel Erskine reports that her files show very few questions asked of nationwide samples that might indicate the probability of any particular person being polled on a particular day. In October 1964, the Opinion Research Corporation found that 29 percent of 2,053 adults remembered having been interviewed "at some time" by a legitimate research firm. A 1966 survey by the Sperry and Hutchinson Company obtained similar results: 35 percent of a national cross-section reported having been interviewed at some prior time. This figure included mail questionnaires (mentioned by 12 percent) as well as face-to-face and telephone interviews. (*Cf.* Elizabeth L. Hartmann, H. Lawrence Isaacson, and Cynthia M. Jurgell, "Public Reaction to Public Opinion Surveying," *Public Opinion Quarterly,* Vol. 32, 1968, pp. 295-96.)

[2] Apologies to Charles Y. Glock, ed., *Survey Research in the Social Sciences,* New York, Russell Sage Foundation, 1967, p. 5.

Originally published in Volume 36, Number 3, 1972 of the *Public Opinion Quarterly*.

what kind of social role we are playing. How would society as a whole differ if we were not a part of it?

A thorough exploration of this question would require a more extensive inquiry than I am able to undertake, but I can suggest one perspective that may provide partial answers. We can think of public opinion research as part of the communication system of our society and of the world community. A communication system is one of the mechanisms, and perhaps the most important one, that holds groups, subcultures, and nations together. How well communication systems function has a lot to do with how smoothly social systems function. The question then becomes: What do we, as public opinion researchers, contribute to these communication systems?

Before attempting to deal with this question, let us look quickly at the structure of society and the way communication systems operate within it. Here a simple model may be useful. If you think of a society or a nation as a pyramid you will recognize that it is segmented horizontally into several sections. At the top are the decision-makers, or the elite. Below them come one or more layers of the sub-elite, those who exercise direct influence on the decision-makers and who help them carry out their decisions. At the broad base of the social pyramid are the masses, those who are affected by decisions made elsewhere.[3]

Of course, this is a highly simplified view. One could also see our society, at least, as an amalgam of several different pyramids. A member of the political elite may be a voiceless member of the mass when it comes to cultural questions; or a member of the business elite may rank, when it comes to politics, as part of the sub-elite. But, by and large, the pyramidal picture of society is a useful one for analytic purposes.

Within this structure, one can visualize communications moving in different directions. *From* the elite *to* the sub-elite and the mass go laws, instructions, exhortations, and so on. One might also include here certain products, dress styles, and scientific information. *From* the mass and the sub-elite *to* the elite come expressions of needs, desires, preferences, and grievances. These upward-moving communications have been defined by some scholars as public opinion. As Hans Speier puts it: "Public opinion . . . is primarily a communication from the citizens to their government."[4] Within the three main segments of the pyramid, one can also visualize lateral communications,

[3] I am indebted for this concept to Hans Speier. *Cf.* "The Historical Development of Public Opinion," in *Social Order and the Risks of War*, New York, George W. Stewart, 1952.

[4] *Ibid.*, p. 324.

linking together different groups within the elite, the sub-elite, and the mass.

Public opinion research contributes in no small measure to each of these communication flows. Most obviously, it helps to inform decision-makers about currents of thought and behavior in all sectors of society. Almost every day, we provide information that goes from the mass to the elite—on acceptance of products, policies, or political personalities; on hopes, fears, and aspirations; on crime, drug abuse, and poverty; and on many other subjects.

This part of the upward flow of communication, for which we are responsible, performs at least three functions. The first is that it helps to explain public opinion on any given issue, putting it into context, defining who is involved and why, explaining whether this aggregation of opinions represents a small minority or a large wave of popular sentiment. This function of survey research has often been discussed.[5]

Second, our research provides a feedback mechanism to decision-makers. How many people are informed about a given issue, and to what degree? Are the pronouncements made by governmental or other leaders understood? What are the reactions to policy decisions? The feedback function of public opinion research has also received frequent attention.[6]

A third implication of our work for the upward flow of communication is less well understood and poorly documented. This is that we may, on occasion, provide a *substitute* for public opinion. Such a proposition, baldly stated, may appear to involve a contradiction in terms; it becomes more plausible if viewed in historical perspective. When scholars first began to concern themselves with the study of public opinion during the eighteenth and nineteenth centuries, they noted that it was a process that could be likened to a gathering storm. First there were soft whispers, many of them blowing in the same direction. These merged with each other, to form a stronger current, which, feeding on itself, gained in intensity. Other air masses were drawn in from outside the center. The force and volume of the disturbance increased, with the result that the government, the church hierarchy, and members of the aristocracy suddenly saw the roof blown off.

To express the same idea in a different way, the decision-makers of

[5] *Cf.*, for example, George Gallup, "Polls and the Political Process," *Public Opinion Quarterly*, Vol. 29, 1965, p. 548.

[6] One of the first systematic studies in this area was that of Herbert H. Hyman and Paul B. Sheatsley, "Some Reasons Why Information Campaigns Fail," *Public Opinion Quarterly*, Vol. 11, 1947, pp. 412-23; see also Martin Kriesberg, "Dark Areas of Ignorance," in Lester Markel, *et al., Public Opinion and Foreign Policy*, New York, Harper, 1948.

that era usually learned about public opinion *after* many individuals had become confident in their own positions through knowing that others shared them. This public opinion was then expressed through mass demonstrations, riots, boycotts, or other forms of popular expression that could be more or less violent. It is no wonder that most eighteenth-century rulers looked upon public opinion with something akin to terror.

Of course, we still have mass demonstrations, riots, and rent strikes, but I submit that, without public opinion research, we would have had many more such disturbances, and more violent ones. Indeed, when violent expressions of public opinion occur, we should look carefully at our own performance and ask whether, in some respect, we have failed to do our job. We may be partially responsible for disturbances that interfere with the productive division of labor on which our civilization is based.

Our responsibility derives from the fact that we have the capability to identify grievances, inequities, and resentments in all sectors of our society—before they become acute enough to be manifested in widespread suffering or in violent and disruptive behavior. Of course, we may do our job and the decision-makers may not pay attention to what we say. But it is certainly a blot on the escutcheon of survey research that it was left primarily for journalists to describe the extent and cruelty of the grinding poverty that was widespread in this country during the prosperous postwar era.[7]

Our role in regard to the plight of the black population may have been somewhat better, but not much. The first national poll question dealing in some way with race relations seems to have been asked by the American Institute of Public Opinion in March, 1939. At that time, 67 percent of a cross-section said they supported Mrs. Eleanor Roosevelt in her decision to resign from the DAR because of this organizations's discriminatory practices.[8] In May and June of 1942, the National Opinion Research Center used two batteries of questions about race relations, but none of these questions appear to have been cross-tabulated by race: we are given only the marginals reflecting, essentially, the opinions of the white majority.[9] Only in 1946 do some cross-breaks by race appear. At this point, NORC asked: "Do you

---

[7] One thinks of Michael Harrington's *The Other America,* and such television documentaries as "Hunger in America" and "Harvest of Shame."

[8] Hadley Cantril and Mildred Strunk, *Public Opinion: 1935-46,* Princeton, N.J., Princeton University Press, 1951, p. 988.

[9] It is possible that cross-breaks were made, but were not picked up in the Cantril/Strunk volume or by the "Polls" section of the *Public Opinion Quarterly.* In that case, the question becomes: Why were they not considered important enough to pick up?

think most Negroes in the United States are being treated fairly or unfairly?" Two-thirds of the white cross-section replied "fairly;" somewhat surprisingly, one third of the blacks in the sample agreed. In a review of polling on race relations, Hazel Erskine has pointed out that questions about this subject were rarely asked until after the Supreme Court decision on public school segregation in 1954.[10] This is not a very good record. We could have done more to give a comprehensive picture of the situation of minority groups.

These observations about our past shortcomings in identifying the needs of specific groups within our population, and communicating these needs to decision-makers, suggest that we may be failing to identify other needs and other groups at present. In a society that is now changing as rapidly as ours, strains and dislocations inevitably develop. If we can determine the nature and extent of these at the level of the individual, before they aggregate into a body of unhappy or angry public opinion, we may be able to contribute materially to new solutions or corrective policies. To the extent that we do this, we are serving as a communication channel from the mass to the decision-makers, and are substituting for public opinion in the classical sense.[11]

By looking at public opinion research as a mechanism that sometimes can substitute for public opinion, we may be able to clear up at least partially a rather old controversy. In a paper given at the 1947 meetings of the American Sociological Society, Herbert Blumer sharply criticized polls. He maintained that public opinion was an organism, and that one could not sample an object matter that was a complicated system of interacting parts.[12] His paper drew rejoinders from Julian Woodward, an associate of Elmo Roper, and also from Theodore Newcomb of the University of Michigan, both of whom vigorously defended the utility of sampling individual opinions.

I think that both Blumer and those who criticized his reasoning were essentially correct: polls cannot by themselves describe the complicated process by which individual opinions become aggregated, but, insofar as they convey the attitudes of the masses to the decision-

---

[10] Hazel G. Erskine, "The Polls: Race Relations," *Public Opinion Quarterly,* Vol. 26, 1962, p. 137. To be fair to those researchers engaged in national sampling, it should be noted that academic students of public opinion did no better. In the 17 volumes of the *Public Opinion Quarterly* that appeared before the Supreme Court decision, there were eight articles having something to do with race relations; in the next 17 volumes there were 26 such articles.

[11] One could also argue that survey research may be dysfunctional for society if it leads not to the alleviation of grievances but merely to the imposition of new controls. (*Cf.* Arthur L. Smith, Jr., "Life in Wartime Germany: Colonel Ohlendorf's Opinion Service," *Public Opinion Quarterly,* Vol. 36, 1972, pp. 1-7.) Even when research is misused, however, it still serves as a communication channel.

[12] "Public Opinion and Public Opinion Polling," *American Sociological Review,* Vol. 13, 1948, pp. 542-554.

makers, they themselves may properly be regarded as a manifestation of public opinion.

Thus far, we have been examining the role of surveys in the upward flow of communication within the social pyramid. Opinion research plays an important part in the downward flow as well. Much of the work we do is devoted to helping decision-makers formulate policies or create products. In addition, we advise decision-makers on how to reach certain publics: which media to use, and how to express an idea so that it will receive attention and be understood. We are heavily involved in providing inputs to advertising, public relations, political propaganda, and mass persuasion in general. This role of public opinion research has drawn substantial criticism in recent years, on the grounds that it can provide a basis for manipulative communications.[13] It is also the role that is perhaps most familiar to us, so I shall not discuss it further at this point.

Our contributions to lateral and diagonal flows of communication in society have received less attention. They deserve more, since opinion research is one of the most important mechanisms through which people can become acquainted with their extended social environment.

Within our immediate circle, we can make direct observations about our friends, neighbors, and co-workers. But we are coming to rely more and more on surveys to inform us about groups outside this circle. The further removed these groups are, the more we have to look to polls to find information that goes beyond superficial characteristics, stereotypes, and political slogans. The news media tell us what the leaders of other countries say and report major events involving other peoples. Through opinion research we can also learn that inhabitants of far-off lands share certain common values with us, differ with regard to other values, and give their attention to some issues and not others. We can become acquainted, at least to some extent, with the shape of the daily life of the "average" person. The late Hadley Cantril's study, *The Pattern of Human Concerns,* was based on sampling national populations totaling more than one third of all the people in the world. It not only revealed significant differences among nations, but also highlighted certain aspirations that seem to be shared almost universally.[14]

Within our own national borders, we are increasingly dependent on survey research to become better acquainted with our fellow na-

[13] Some of these criticisms have been embodied in popular literature: for example, Vance Packard's *Hidden Persuaders,* and Joe McGuinness' *The Selling of the President.*

[14] New Brunswick, N.J., Rutgers University Press, 1965.

tionals who live in other geographical regions, belong to other ethnic groups, have a different socioeconomic status, or are separated from us by a generation gap. The recent book by Daniel Yankelovich on changing values among college students is an excellent example of the way opinion research can interpret one segment of society to other segments.[15]

We contribute to the lateral flow of social communication when we provide data on other populations for books and journal articles, but even more when we serve as part of the infrastructure of the general press. Students of the mass media point out that journalists gather relatively little of their information by personal observation, or by interviewing those who participate directly in newsworthy events. Most of the information carried by the media is prepackaged or aggregated in some way, and furnished to the journalist in semi-finished form.[16] This infrastructure, on which the journalist depends heavily, is composed of: news releases, which may be issued by almost any individual or organized body; local newspapers, especially when it comes to international reporting; experts, who are able to package information on a given subject when interviewed; and various other sources. Among these other sources, the survey organization occupies an important place. Without the information provided and pre-packaged by opinion researchers, the mass media would have a far more difficult job of reporting social trends and interpreting one sector of society to another.

Lateral communication in our society, and particularly the role of survey research in such communication, has been studied surprisingly little. There are few hard data to which reference can be made. Nevertheless, it seems probable that this mode of communication performs a number of vital social functions. For one thing, it enables one group to shape its opinions and activities in the light of what other groups are doing, thinking, and feeling. As Leo Bogart points out in *Silent Politics:* "Opinion research forces this kind of awareness by illuminating the differences in values and goals among different sections of society."[17] Intergroup communication by itself rarely solves problems that are rooted in social differences, but without it such problems are even less likely to be resolved.

Another function of lateral communication is to enable organized public opinion to form—to make it possible for like-minded individuals to offer each other mutual encouragement and support. It seems

15 *The Changing Values on Campus,* New York, Pocket Books, 1972.
16 Bernard Roshco, "The Phoney Issue of News Management," *Interplay,* April 1970.
17 *Silent Politics: Polls and the Awareness of Public Opinion,* New York, Wiley, 1972, p. 208.

probable that polls and surveys play an important part in this process, by which individual opinions are aggregated into larger units. In theory, at least, opinion research can help public opinion to form by letting individuals know that they are not alone; that appreciable numbers of others share their attitudes on given issues. These individuals are therefore more likely to let their voices be heard; they will be encouraged to search out and join others who share their attitudes. I believe, although I cannot prove, that public opinion on such issues as population control and the environment has formed so rapidly in part because surveys showed that many individuals shared common attitudes on these issues.

A NON-SERIOUS LOOK AT THE FUTURE

To identify our work as serving important functions for communication flows in our society is merely a first step toward inquiring how these functions might be served better. Here one enters a dangerous area—that of prescription and recommendation. For self-protection, I am going to adopt a device skillfully used by a distinguished predecessor. Twenty-one years ago Julian Woodward delivered an AAPOR presidential address entitled, "Public Opinion Research, 1951-1970." He was speaking, of course, in 1951, and prefaced his remarks with the following caveat: "What I propose to do is to engage in a few serious and a few not-so-serious predictions confined to the field of public opinion surveying, with the serious and non-serious so carefully mixed that I later can say that the predictions that did *not* come true were not seriously made and that the ones that did were clearly the result of superior scientific foresight and imagination."[18]

Following President Woodward's excellent precedent, I shall also take an irreverent look into the future in order to discover what kind of role public opinion research might play in the years ahead. At this point, one might recall the parody of a familiar remark by Lincoln Steffens: "I have looked into the future—and it does not work." But, disregarding such discouraging thoughts, let us press on. I shall take 1984 as the year from which to look back, since Paul Lazarsfeld, also in an AAPOR presidential address, concurred with George Orwell that 1984 was an appropriate historical cutting point.[19]

By 1984, opinion researchers were fully conscious of their role in the social communication system. Consequently, their procedures differed markedly from those that had been used as little as twelve years earlier. For one thing, it was no longer fashionable to issue brief

[18] *Public Opinion Quarterly*, Vol. 15, 1951, p. 406.
[19] "The Obligations of the 1950 Pollster to the 1984 Historian," *Public Opinion Quarterly*, Vol. 14, Winter 1950-51.

news stories, larded with percentage distributions, or to present a client with a report consisting largely of charts and tables. Instead, leading opinion research firms included departments that produced tapes and films. Here, professional actors were used to replicate survey findings in dramatic form. Quantitative values were reflected by such factors as intensity of voice and length of time on screen; qualitative values, of course, came through clearly. These tapes and films were able to give the client or the public—a *feeling* for public opinion, not merely a distribution of replies to individual questions.

Cassettes depicting the conditions and opinions of all major subgroups in American society were standard equipment in the schools, and no child was allowed to graduate from the eighth grade until he or she had achieved a satisfactory score on an empathy test, thus demonstrating an ability to understand the problems and points of view of people in very different ethnic and socioeconomic strata.

At times of international tension, it was common for worldwide television to carry dramatized public opinion surveys from the various nations involved. These were broadcast directly from satellites to home receivers, and almost invariably led to a situation in which publics in all countries agreed that there was something to be said on both sides.

Print was still used to communicate survey findings, but the statistical scaffolding had retreated into the background. Instead, emphasis was placed on the people behind the numbers. By this time, both clients and the public had learned that it was not terribly important whether 10 percent or 25 percent of a given population was suffering from some condition or had an unfulfilled need. The significant point was to know that the condition or need was widespread, and to understand its nature.

On the other hand, statistical inference achieved importance in new fields, and survey researchers were instrumental in bringing about certain long-overdue constitutional changes. You all remember the headline from the 1980 election: "Senator Blowhard Fails to Achieve .05 Confidence Level! Election Thrown into House of Representatives."

Recognizing their responsibility to facilitate communication among the various segments of society, opinion researchers changed their approach to sampling and interviewing. Samples of from 800 to 2,000 cases, formerly popular because they produced marginals with a satisfactory degree of statistical reliability, were less frequently used. The interview of from 30 to 60 minutes also became a thing of the past. It was more common, and no more expensive, to conduct 16,000 five-minute interviews via phonovision. These quickie interviews enabled researchers to identify members of social subgroups, certain personality types, or people with particular problems or needs. Persons so identified, sometimes as few as 50 or 100 in number, would then be interviewed intensively for periods of four hours or more, and would be paid a fair price for their time.

It was two-stage research of this nature that enabled the Acme Music Corporation to develop the product that since has proved so popular among left-handed clarinet players. Similar research designs made it possible to establish the relationship between specific forms of psychopathology and resulting patterns of political behavior. This discovery led to the requirement, which we all now take for granted, that candidates for political office devote at least 15 per cent of their campaign communications to therapeutic messages.

Perhaps the greatest change in opinion research during the past decade has been the shift from a primary focus on measuring popular reactions to a new focus on discovering needs and preferences. In 1972, it was common for an interviewer to confront a respondent with an existing situation, a product, or a personality who was already well known, and to ask for an opinion with regard to this situation, product, or personality. By 1984, researchers had learned how to enter societal processes at an earlier stage. They were providing decision-makers with more information about the kinds of social institutions that were needed and the types of candidates who should be persuaded to run for political office. They also furnished explicit guidance to the mass media with regard to the kinds of information that were required by various segments of the population to protect and promote their legitimate interests and to live a fuller life. In other words, the emphasis had shifted from assisting decision-makers in framing their downward communications, to promoting upward and lateral communication.

A particularly interesting development was in the relationship of survey research to advertising and marketing. Prior to 1974, advertisers and marketers had used research primarily to sell more products and services. But in the following years, emphasis began to be placed on producing as few items as possible. This was because of the rise of consumerism, growing concern about exhaustion of the earth's basic resources, and increasing realization that the United States would have to reduce its disproportionate consumption of the world's raw materials.

At first, the advertising and marketing fraternities were dismayed, but then they began to see the silver lining. With fewer products being produced, it became more and more important to match the product to the individual. Marketers found that they required more information about the needs and preferences of the diverse elements of our population. For this, they turned to the researcher. Advertisers found that each individual, before he would pay the staggering prices characteristic of the late seventies and early eighties, insisted on far more information about a product than he had previously wanted. For instance, before buying his lifetime ballpoint pen, a person in 1982 demanded to know 17 facts about it, in contrast to the average of one and one quarter facts that he had wanted ten years earlier. Naturally, advertising revenues soared, and equally naturally, survey researchers were kept busy finding out what kinds of product information were most needed by consumers.

One result of this intensified marketing and advertising activity was that shoddy goods disappeared from the market. TV sets were ordinarily sold with a lifetime guarantee, while automobile sales contracts commonly included a grandfather clause, providing that worn-out parts would be replaced free of charge as long as the owner was not more than two generations removed from the original purchaser. A concomitant development was that survey researchers were employed to identify products and services that were no longer necessary and could be dispensed with.

At the same time, all exaggerated and deceptive advertising was squeezed out of the communication channels by the public's insatiable demand for factual information. The creative departments of advertising agencies gave up attempts to develop attention-getting devices and emotional appeals; instead, they became adept at increasing the information content per square inch of advertising space by the use of double exposures, runic inscriptions, and concise algebraic formulae.

A BRIEF RETURN TO THE PRESENT

Beneath this overlay of fantasy are a few notions that might be stated somewhat more baldly. If public opinion research is a significant component of our national information network, then it follows that we should constantly seek ways of communicating our findings more clearly and making them accessible to wider circles of nonspecialists. We should take care that our statistical tools remain our servants rather than becoming our masters, and should not allow them to obscure the human values implicit in our work. Experimentation with new techniques for the presentation of survey findings is desirable.

We should try to ensure that our communication system is an open one; that as many groups as possible have access to it. This implies not only diversification of sponsorship but also working with larger samples that will enable us to discover and describe population categories that have not previously been heard from.

Communication is a two-way process. We should be on guard

against pressures that would make survey research primarily a tool that helps the elite manipulate the mass, and should make full use of our capabilities to serve as a communication channel from the mass to the elite. This involves constant attention to identifying wants and needs, problems and expectations, within all population groups. We should also keep in mind our responsibility to inform various segments of society about each other.

Finally, as part of a national and international communication network, we should be jealous of our independence. Controls over survey research, whether imposed by political, economic, or other interests, carry with them many of the same dangers as controls of the press. We must be largely self-regulating. This means not only establishing high professional standards, but also maintaining competition. The most effective cure for low-quality or one-sided research is better research, just as the cure for poor news reporting is better news reporting. We will be of greater service to society in the years ahead if we think of public opinion research as one of the institutions responsible for ensuring the free flow of ideas.

Much of the study and research in the field of attitude formation and change is predicated on the assumption that some kind of link exists between an individual's attidude and his probable behavior with respect to some public issue or private decision.

For example, the business community each year spends considerable money in trying to find out whether advertisements for products, institutional messages, or point-of-sale displays are effective in promoting the sale of products. The political world has witnessed a mushrooming growth in the use of polls to guide candidates in the choice of issues that they address themselves to and in molding "images" for candidates designed to win audience attention and voter support. Government agencies and nonprofit organizations depending upon community understanding and financial support are interested in learning whether their messages are effective in winning support for their programs.

Chapters in this section present a range of theories and opinions as to the degree to which attitudes and opinions are related to behavior. The first, John Dollard's "Under What Conditions Do Opinions Predict Behavior?" makes some down-to-earth observations on why such studies are needed.

In the common sense of life we are forever testing mental responses for validity, attempting to sort out the thoughts and opinions which have proved correct from those which have been false. . . . Valid prediction of behavior is not a mere luxury of morality, but a vital social necessity. . . . As we grow up we tend to acquire a stock of sentences with which we deal with the future. Some of these sentences are pronounced, and we call these 'opinions.' Others are silently and swiftly rehearsed, and we call these 'thoughts.' From the standpoint of learning theory, both are *anticipatory*, that is, fore-casting responses. . . . If there is a strain toward consistency between *verbal expression* and overt behavior, there is likewise a strong compulsion to match *thoughts* and *overt behavior.*

Dollard identifies and illustrates three social situations affecting opinion surveys —labeling them origin, test, and criterion stiuations. His final contribution is to offer seven "common-sense" conditions that affect survey validity.

1.   Neurotics will find it difficult to predict their behavior when their own serious conflicts are involved.

2. Persons with poor verbal skills may find it difficult to forecast their own behavior.
3. People who habitually go into effective action after thinking things over can best predict their own actions.
4. The test situation should not be corrupted by extraneous threats or rewards.
5. A man can best predict what he will do in a future situation if he has been in about the same situation before and thus knows what it's all about.
6. A man can predict what he will do in a future situation, provided he doesn't have an experience which changes his mind before this situation occurs.
7. A man can better predict what he will do in a future dilemma if he is told exactly what this dilemma will be.

Dollard's common-sense propositions are as relevant today as when he first presented them and they serve as a useful checklist for a discussion of the relationship of opinion change to behavior change.

Elihu Katz's chapter restates and updates the theoretical basis and the research design leading to the formulation of the concepts of "opinion leader" and "the two-step flow of communication" first identified by Paul F. Lazarsfeld, Bernard Berelson and Hazel Gaudet in *The People's Choice.* Three distinct sets of findings came out of that book.

I. *The impact of personal influence*—personal contacts appear to have been both more frequent and more effective than the mass media in influencing voting decisions.
2. *The flow of personal influence*—opinion leaders are to be found on every level of society and presumably, therefore, are very much like the people whom they influence.
3. *Opinion leaders and the mass media*—compared with the rest of the population, opinion leaders were found to be considerably more exposed to the radio, to the newspapers and to magazines, that is to the formal media of communication.

Katz reviews four subsequent research studies that support these major findings from *The People's Choice* and presents some new observations on the nature of personal influence,in the communication of ideas. "Broadly, it appears that influence is related (1) to the *personification of certain values* (who one is); (2) to *competence* (what one knows); and (3) to *strategic social location* (whom one knows). Social location, in turn, divides into whom one knows within a group and 'outside.' "

He notes in closing two additional aspects of the two-step flow hypothesis.

The main emphasis on the two-step flow hypothesis appears to be on only one aspect of interpersonal relations—interpersonal relations as channels of communication. But from the several studies reviewed, it is clear that these very same interpersonal relations influence the making of decisions in at least two additional ways. In addition to serving as networks of communication, interpersonal relations are also sources of pressure to conform to the group's way of thinking and acting, as well as sources of social support.

Joseph T. Klapper's "What We Know About the Effects of Mass Communication: The Brink of Hope" notes that many scholars are pessimistic about finding answers to this inquiry. He is not. He states: "We already know a good deal more about communications than we thought we did, and we are on the verge of being able to proceed toward even more abundant and more fruitful knowledge." His optimism is based on two phenomena. The first he labels the phenomenistic approach.

It can perhaps be described, in a confessedly oversimplifed way, as a shift away from the concept of 'hypodermic effect' towards an approach which might be called 'situational, phenomenistic, or functional.' It is a shift away from the tendency to regard mass communication as a necessary and sufficient cause of audience effect, toward a view of the media as influences, working amid other influences, in a total situation.

A second basis for Klapper's optimism is "the emergence, from the new approach, of a few generalizations. It is proposed that these generalizations can be tied together, and tentatively developed a little further, and that when this is done the resulting set of generalizations can be extremely helpful." He cites the following generalizations:

1. Mass communication ordinarily does not serve as a necessary and sufficient cause of audience effects, but rather functions among and through a nexus of mediating factors and influences.
2. These mediating factors are such that they typically render mass communication a contributory agent, but not the sole cause, in a process of reinforcing the existing conditions. . . .
3. On such occasions as mass communications does function in the service of change, one of two conditions is likely to obtain. Either: a. the mediating factors will be found to be inoperative, and the effect of the media direct; or b. the mediating factors, which normally favor reinforcement we found to be themselves impelling toward change.

4.　There are certain residual situations in which mass communication seems to wreak direct effects, or to directly and of itself serve certain psycho-physical functions.

5.　The efficacy of mass communications, either as contributory agents or as agents of direct effect, is affected by various aspects of the media themselves or of the communications situation. . . . (including, for example, aspects of contextual organization, the availability of channels for overt action, etc.)

W. Phillips Davison's earlier chapter in this book dealt with the public opinion process and he used a hypothetical example to illustrate how this process operates. In his chapter "On the Effects of Communications" he proposes a theory of communication that goes beyond the body of existing research data dealing with social and psychological factors that facilitate or impede successful communications. "The purpose of this article is to suggest another method of interpreting the existing body of knowledge about the effects of communications. According to this mode of interpretation, communications serve as a link between man and his environment, and their effects may be explained in terms of the role they play in enabling people to bring about more satisfying relationships between themselves and the world around them." Davison draws data in support of his thesis from psychological warfare studies, research into voting behavior, communications studies in other cultures and studies of elite groups. He sees communications as leading to adjustive behavior in those exposed to them in at least three ways.

> First, they can report an actual or expected change in the environment, or a previously unknown fact about the environment, that is important to the person at the receiving end of the communication. . . . A second way that communications can lead to behavioral adjustments is by pointing out an existing feature of the environment (not a change or a completely new fact) and reminding the individual that his needs would be served if he adjusted his behavior in a given manner. . . . The third way in which communications may cause a behavioral adjustment is by bringing to a person's attention a new way of patterning his relationship to the environment.

In his concluding observations he states: "This way of looking at the effect of communication suggests that the communicator can influence attitudes or behavior only when he is able to convey information that may be utilized by members of his audience to satisfy their wants and needs."

Charles Wright's "Functional Analysis and Mass Communication" makes a case for subjecting the communications process to functional analysis. His article incorporates a modification of Lasswell's concept of the three major activities carried out by communication specialists: the surveillance of the environment, the correlation of the parts of society in responding to the environment, and the transmission of the social heritage from one generation to the next. To these he adds a fourth category: entertainment. For Wright

> the development of a functional theory of mass communications treats the question of what are the consequences of handling the *basic communication activities* by means of mass communication.... It goes without saying that each of these four activities pre-dates mass communication, and in some form each is still conducted on a "nonmass" basis in every society.... In its simplest form, then, the question posed here is: What are the consequences of performing such activities through mass communications, rather than through some other form of communication?

Wright is mindful that the mass media can prove dysfunctional as well as functional for society and the individual and offers examples of each. Not every social scientist or student of communications subscribes to the value of "functional analysis" in studying social phenomena, but even those who harbor doubts about the merits of this analytical method should find Wright's article of interest.

"High Noon in the Research Marketplace" by Robert Carlson is concerned with the manner by which decisions are made to study or not to study a particular issue or question. Most public opinion research is carried out because a client has some specific questions he wants answered. Thus the corporate and institutional interests of the sponsoring client can play a major role in public opinion research. Yet little attention has been given to the role the client plays in deciding which topics are deserving of study and what methods of research are best suited for the research in question. Even less has been written about how well or poorly the researcher and the client communicate during and after the research project has been carried out.

Some public opinion studies win high praise from the clients who commission them. Their findings lead to important administrative and policy decisions. Other public opinion studies are seen as next to worthless. These seemingly inadequate opinion research studies contribute to the feeling in some circles that such public opinion research is, at best, of marginal value and often downright misleading.

This chapter sets forth six propositions about the client-researcher relationship and suggests ways in which each contributes to the quality of the final research study and, more importantly, to the layman's degree of trust and interest in efforts to study and understand the elusive thing we label "public opinion." The six propositions are:

1. There often is a lack clarity on the part of both client and researcher as to their mutual roles, obligations, and responsibilities.
2. The client and the research agency may bring different time horizons to the study of a problem.
3. Breakdowns in communication within the client's organization, as well as faulty communication between the client and his research agency, contribute to disappointing research studies.
4. The client-researcher relationship represents an ever-changing distribution of power, and this shifting of power affects the way research problems are structured and the extent to which research findings are accepted and utilized by the client.
5. There is considerable evidence that clients and researchers employ different criteria in evaluating a completed study, and seldom do they communicate these judgments to one another.
6. Finally, both researchers and clients are disturbed by charges that the field of public opinion research is not a true profession, that it lacks standards for membership and performance, and that its work must therefore be viewed with a decent amount of reservation and question.

Early in his article, "Behavioral Support for Opinion Change," Leon Festinger states:

> I am not raising the question of whether or not attitudes are found to relate to relevant behavior. Let us accept the conclusion that they are related, at least to some extent, although even here relatively few studies in the literature address themselves to this question. . . . The fact that existing attitudes relate to overt behavior does not tell us whether or not an attitude *change* brought about by exposure to a persuasive communication will be reflected in a *change* in subsequent behavior.

Festinger provides a detailed critique of the three studies he was able to locate that sought to deal with this question. In the closing paragraphs of his article he reports: "It is my present contention that, in order to produce a stable behavior change following opinion change, an environmental change must also be produced which, representing reality, will support the new opinion and the new behavior. Otherwise, the same factors that produced the initial opinion and the behavior will continue to operate to nullify the effect of the opinion change."

David Sears and Jonathan Freedman's "Selective Exposure to Information: A Critical Review" provides exactly the information, that its title promises. It is a full and thought provoking review of the sometimes paradoxical findings in studies of the existence of selectivity in voluntary exposure to information.

330

The authors do not seriously quarrel with the formulation of Bernard Berelson and Gary A. Steiner that "people tend to see and hear communications that are favorable or congenial to their predispositions; they are more likely to see and hear congenial communications than neutral or hostile ones." But as they point out, "expressed in this form, the selective exposure hypothesis offers no explanation for *why* audiences are biased."

This chapter offers a far-reaching review of relevant literature on this topic and its underlying assumption that people have a preference for supportive, rather than nonsupportive, information. Sears and Freedman identify two aspects of selective exposure, referred to as "de facto selectivity" and "selective exposure."

De facto selectivity is most often encountered in mass meetings and in the exposure to extended propaganda programs. The authors feel there are problems associated with measuring the magnitude of this type of selectivity. "Many reports of de facto selectivity may well overestimate the magnitude of the effect because of the kinds of measures used. Perhaps the most obvious problem is that only one interview has been used in most studies. If, in this interview, attitudes and exposure favor the same side of an issue, the interpretation is ambiguous: The congruence may reflect either the attitude change or de facto selectivity."

The authors report on a series of studies designed to test the thesis that people have a preference for supportive information and they conclude that "a considerable amount of experimental research has uncovered no general psychological preference for supportive information." They then raise the intriguing question based on available research data, "How can it be that people are in fact selective, yet display no trace of a general preference for supportive information?" A number of plausible explanations are offered but perhaps the most original comes in the final paragraph of this chapter: "It has generally been assumed that selective exposure and other processes that bar information reception are prime mechanisms by which people resist influence. Perhaps such processes are not very important at all. . . . Perhaps resistance to influence is accomplished most often and most successfully at the level of information evaluation, rather than at the level of selective seeking and avoiding of information."

It is almost impossible to summarize the many stimulating ideas and propositoins in Milton Rokeach's "Attitude Change and Behavioral Change". Several, however, deserve special mention.

An *attitude* is a relatively enduring organization of beliefs about an object or situation predisposing one to respond in some preferential manner. *Attitude change* would then be a change in predisposition. . . . Especially important for the major thesis of this study is that an attitude may be focused either on an object or on a situation. . . . Social scientists have generally been far more inter-

331

ested in the theory and measurement of attitudes toward situations, across objects. Thus, we have scales that measure attitudes toward the Negro, the Jew, liberalism-conservatism, and religion. But we do not have scales that measure attitudes toward such situations as managing or being a guest in a Southern hotel, being a passenger or a driver of a bus, buying or selling real estate. As a result, the study of attitudes-toward-situations has become more or less divorced from the study of attitude-toward-objects.

Rokeach reviews some studies that seem to have found some inconsistency between attitudes and real life behavior. One was R.T. La Piere's study in which restaurant owners and innkeepers showed marked discrepancies between their verbal expression of discrimination toward Chinese and Negroes by letter or phone and their nondiscriminatory, face-to-face behavior. He offers one possible explanation for such apparent inconsistency. "The investigators did not obtain all the relevant attitudinal information needed to make accurate predictions. The subjects not only had attitudes toward Chinese and Negroes, but, as managers of businesses, also had attitudes about the proper conduct of such businesses. The investigator's methods, however, are typically focused on attitude-toward-object and are generally insensitive to attitude-toward-situation."

Two other points related to his main thesis are presented. "First a given attitude-toward-objective, whenever activated, need not always be behaviorally manifested or expressed in the same way or to the same degree. Second, in principle there is no difference between the verbal and the nonverbal expression of a given attitude. . . . Thus, any verbal expression of opinion, like any non-verbal behavior, is also a function of at least two attitudes—attitudes-toward-object and attitude-toward-situation."

Alan Weinstein's "Predicting Behavior form Attitudes" reports on his research based on the hypothesis that improved prediction of behavior will result if attitudes toward action, as well as attitudes toward an issue, are incorporated into the research design. "Although an individual may evaluate an issue positively, he may act as if he did not. This is well illustrated in the political arena, where liberals may have similar attitudes toward an issue but disagree on which action to support."

To test this hypothesis Weinstein utilized "a unidimensional concept of attitude as an evaluative or affective response (paralleling M. Fishbein's position) and focusing attention on whether or not a specific overt behavior will occur, the following hypotheses were developed.

Hypothesis I (H_1): The attitudinal assessment of both issue and potential action yields a superior prediction of behavior than an assessment of the issue or potential action alone.

Hypothesis 2 (H_2): Predictions are *less* accurate when the referent attitude favors action than when it does not. Given an action choice *re* a particular issue, affect consistent with that choice, i.e. in favor of the action, will generate poorer prediction of behavior than will affect less favorable to the action choice."

Research on two different groups of students led Weinstein to conclude that both hypotheses were given support by his research data. He also found his research offered greater accuracy of prediction based on negative affect. "This finding suggests that for behavior to occur as a tension-reducing mechanism, more conditions must be fulfilled than in the case where the action (choice) is rejected. First, the available action must be appraised as being desirable. Second, it must be appraised as more desirable than alternative courses of action. Rejection *can occur if either or both* of these conditions is not met."

Conventional wisdom tells us that if we are successful in communicating to our publics we shall probably have some success in modifying their behavior. Common sense experience supports this idea. So do many academic research studies. In discussing the relationship between opinion changes and behavior changes, many of these articles note that the concept of change itself needs to be specified, and a differentiation made between lasting change and that which is more transitory.

Some provocative suggestions are offered as to how the study of the relationship between opinions and behavior can be made more productive. One approach is to distinguish between attitudes toward situations and attitudes toward objects. Another is to study attitudes toward action as well as attitudes toward issues. Several of these articles address themselves primarily to the role of the mass media in bringing about opinion and behavioral change. Others deal with the fascinating question of why people indulge in selective information seeking or avoidance. But whatever their intellectual foci, the articles give general support to the proposition that there is a relationship between attitude change and behavior change, even though our understanding of it is limited.

UNDER WHAT
CONDITIONS DO OPINIONS
PREDICT BEHAVIOR?

John Dollard

T HIS PAPER IS AN ATTEMPT to apply our knowledge of behavior theory[1] to the problem of the validity of prediction from the public opinion survey.[2]

The popular confidence in polls is in part a result of transfer from other scientific operations. Numbers have come to have an awesome quality for the layman. Faith in polls may also be transferred from the many situations in ordinary life in which people keep their promises, the straw vote being taken as a kind of promise to perform.

But can we assume that surveys which are properly conducted and statistically reliable are also behaviorally valid? The Saturday-to-Tuesday political poll carries its own warrant as to validity but can such validity be imputed by analogy to any other survey? My feeling is that

[1] See Hull, Clark L., *Principles of Behavior*, New York: D. Appleton-Century, 1943; and Miller, Neal E., and Dollard, John, *Social Learning and Imitation*, New Haven: Yale University Press, 1941.

[2] This paper was prepared for a joint meeting of the Washington Statistical Society and the Washington chapter of the Institute of Mathematical Statistics, and was given in Washington March 9, 1944. Plans had been made to publish this and other papers given at the meeting but these plans miscarried. Hence the delay. The problem of validity had been under intensive discussion at the Research Branch of the Army's Division of Information and Education. Professor Samuel A. Stouffer initiated that discussion and stimulated this paper. Profitable discussions were held with Professor Carl I. Hovland and Mr. Lionel Florent, since unfortunately deceased.

Originally published in Volume 12, Number 4, 1948 of the *Public Opinion Quarterly*.

it cannot. Validation must be independently established in each opinion-action situation.[3]

PREDICTING OUR OWN BEHAVIOR

The problem of prediction from opinion to act is not a new problem in psychology. Indeed, mental life is apparently a mechanism for prediction. It is a forecasting device in which the experience units of the past are assembled to test the as yet unknown future. In the common sense of life we are forever testing mental responses for validity, attempting to sort out the thoughts and opinions which have proved correct from those which have been false. Even when people "lie" they try never to do so unwittingly.

Keller[4] has pointed out that "honesty," which is a special case of the validity of expression, has high social utility. It enables men to participate in organized social life with good confidence that others will do what they say they will do, will be where they say they will be. Valid prediction of behavior is not a mere luxury of morality, but a vital social necessity. Every man is under compulsion to keep his promises, to make his acts correspond with his verbal expressions. He constantly watches others to see that they do likewise.

As we grow up we tend to acquire a stock of sentences with which we deal with the future. Some of these sentences are pronounced, and we call these "opinions." Others are silently and swiftly rehearsed, and we call these "thoughts." From the standpoint of learning theory, both are *anticipatory*, that is, forecasting responses. The anticipatory response is a portion of a later, fuller, stronger response which the subject can make. Anticipatory responses are not all of a verbal character. Salivation, for instance, may become anticipatory; the eye wink may become anticipatory; flinching to a blow may become anticipatory. But like other anticipatory responses, sentences are learned and follow the laws of learning. They are responses which produce cues. They are patterned

---

[3] I might discuss at this point another fiction, not of pollers, but of propagandists who use poll results. This is the idea that public opinion as expressed in polls is a result of cross-roads discussion, a by-product of inquiring minds, chewing tobacco and pot-bellied stoves. The operators who "send up trial balloons" and have a plan "to sell the people" are supposed not to have anything to do with it. Undoubtedly the trial balloons have to have some support from local breezes, but all good technicians in the propaganda field know the tricks of manipulating, creating or even blocking naive public reaction. The real question here is often not *what* does Charlie McCarthy tell George Gallup, but *who* is whispering in his ear while he is saying it.

[4] Keller, A. G., *Net Impressions*, New Haven: Yale University Press, 1942, pp. 62-63.

with one another. When learned they must be rewarded, or else some other sentence will be tried out. They can be extinguished by non-reward. They can be discriminated so that they are called forth by exactly one and no other stimulus pattern. They can be generalized from one similar stimulus context to another.

Sometimes sentence responses are so organized that they produce other sentences, as one thought follows another. Again, they are integrated with behavior which requires the expenditure of more energy from a physical standpoint, as when a "good idea" sets in motion an arduous series of acts. In conversation a sentence of one person may stimulate a sentence response in another. The stimulus question on a questionnaire may produce a written response from the informant. I emphasize that all such behavior is learned, is strengthened by reward and weakened by non-reward.

The matching of opinions with more effortful behavior is not left to chance. Our children are given careful training in "truthful" behavior. They are impressed with the social importance of keeping promises. They are trained in rehearsing directions received from parents and policed to see that they follow these directions correctly. It is probably this unacknowledged training which gives us all the spontaneous confidence that verbal behavior on surveys very frequently predicts action in real life. No one can lie with impunity, that is, without anxiety, even to a surveyor.

If there is a strain toward consistency between *verbal expression* and overt behavior, there is likewise a strong compulsion to match *thoughts* and *overt behavior*. The social scene is so arranged that persons often get rewarded for "thinking straight" and get punished for thinking inaccurately. When a child is asked to solve an arithmetic problem or to spell a word, he goes through a process of inner rehearsal which is a kind of prediction of what the explicit answer will be. If his predictions prove frequently to be invalid, the psychologist may lay on him the curse of Binet and state that he has a low IQ. Correct problem solutions in later life tend to increase the esteem of one's friends or the size of one's salary. Through constant experience incorrect forecasting tends to be punished and eliminated. In the *implicit* or mental phase when an individual is juggling the sentences he has, following each one to its respective end of reward or punishment, while abstaining from action, he is said to be in mental conflict.

Sentences, whether of the thought or opinion type, are changed in dilemma situations. If the end sentences do not work, new ones are hit upon. If the new sentence, or series of sentences, brings reward, it is strengthened and is likely to remain as a firm opinion or attitude.

Sentences are usually interwebbed, in a way not well understood, with stronger responses of an emotional type. Sentences can, on the one hand, produce strong emotional responses and, on the other, comforting and tension-reducing reactions. Ideally, the sentence texture which an individual commands should cover all the voluntary responses which he is capable of making.

SOCIAL SITUATIONS AFFECTING OPINION SURVEYS

There are three social situations which bear on the validity of a verbal response made in a survey. We shall call them the *origin, test,* and *criterion* situations.

The *origin* situation is the one in which the opinion sentence is first hit upon and rehearsed. It may be a dramatic dilemma of the "I-will-never-do-so-and-so-again" type. Likewise, sentences may be slowly reorganized in a period of reflection after action. In this case, the origin is not a point of time but a period of time. For example, several years of contact with a new social group may gradually create an opinion or set of opinions. Some sentence elements in an opinion may have a long history, as is the case with our adult moral attitudes.

In yet a third case, an opinion may be borrowed from the experiences of a prestigeful person. Such opinions may be swiftly acquired. In all cases it would seem that one condition of such borrowing is the rehearsal of the borrowed sentence. One must repeat the message of the newspaper editor or radio commentator under conditions of drive and reward in order to fix the new response. This rehearsal may be so light and swift as merely to seem "understanding what he says," or it may be slow and heavy as when one tries to memorize a joke. Rehearsal of other's speech is one of the strongest human habits.

Finally, an opinion may be an immediate, "on-the-spot" reorganization of sentences at the moment of test. In any case, it is argued that every opinion or complex of opinions has an origin and stems from a definable origin situation.

In the *test* situation, the social surveyor intervenes with his question or questionnaire. He taps a stream of thought sentences or opinion sentences which are presumably orienting the behavior of the person surveyed. He provides the stimuli which will evoke the relevant responses.[5]

The *criterion* situation is the dilemma situation around which prediction is centered. In it the respondent must act and take whatever rewards and punishments ensue upon his action. Often these rewards and punishments are of a fairly immediate character. The subject is provoked to bring his best predictive powers to bear inasmuch as failure to act correctly may seriously and immediately affect his welfare. The criterion response may be a symbolic act like casting a vote. It may involve great economic deprivation. It may involve the exhausting labor of combat or the risk of sudden annihilation. It may involve the choice of war or peace in another twenty-five years.

To illustrate the relationship of origin, test, and criterion situations, let us take the case of a survey which was under discussion at the Research Branch of the Army's Division of Information and Education.[6] This survey concerned the validity of the opinions of given respondents when asked if they would contribute to a Red Cross Blood Bank. Some such question as, "Do you intend to make a contribution to the Blood Bank during the next three months?", might put the issue concretely.

1. *Origin situation*: There are several elements in the origin situation of the eventual opinion. Most people have learned to behave very conservatively on the score of losing blood. Opinions concerning loss of blood have been formed in dilemmas of being hurt, in situations of instructions and threat, and out of a fund of childhood notions of physiology. These experiences leave a fund of negative sentences indicating aversion to the loss of blood.

On the other hand, people have well learned to copy and rehearse various patriotic sentences, such as, "Do your part," "You can save a life," etc. Those people who have experienced transfusions or who are familiar with scientific medical practice may have somewhat modified their original negative reactions.

The resultant, then, is a conflict between "approach" opinions and

[5] A "relevant response" is one which is designed to be predictive of the criterion behavior. It is an honest and complete expression of what the individual "thinks he will do" in the criterion situation.

[6] This survey was never carried out, as I thought when the above was written it might be. Despite strong support from Stouffer and Hovland, it was crowded out by the demand for applied research.

the "avoidance" opinions. From this conflict there will occur a resultant opinion. It might be stressed in this connection that while some few opinions may be strongly learned and therefore strongly dominant so that very little conflict occurs, many opinions will be "resultants," that is, will be the end product of a conflict.

Although both blood-avoidance and patriotic attitudes are old in the life of the individual, these attitudes came into conflict only recently, when the war broke out. The origin of the conflict is therefore recent.

2. *Test situation*: The test is, of course, the actual survey as designed, carefully pretested and administered to an adequate sample.

3. *Criterion situation*: The criterion behavior is that of offering one's self at the Blood Bank—not necessarily, be it noted, actually becoming a blood donor. Some people who offer themselves may not be accepted by the medical authorities.

The reality of the conflict centering around blood transfusions is clear when one considers that many people keep "putting it off"; some set a date for the transfusion but keep finding other responsibilities which make it impossible to carry through; and still others "refuse" by fainting after having presented themselves.

CONDITIONS AFFECTING SURVEY VALIDITY

The validity of a survey obviously entails a close match between the verbal response in the test and the terminal response in the criterion dilemma. Here follow some conditions which if kept in mind may assist in predicting the criterion action on the basis of the test opinion. I hope that these conditions may seem to others, as they seem to me, simple common sense. Everyone knows some of these conditions. Many workers have at one time or another hit upon all of them. The attempt here is to give a systematic statement or check-list, handy perhaps for examining a particular survey problem.

In the case of each condition two statements will be made: first, a common-sense statement and then a more technical statement. Thereafter, in each case, an example will be given.

CONDITION I:

COMMON-SENSE STATEMENT: *Neurotics will find it difficult to predict their behavior when their own serious conflicts are involved.*

TECHNICAL STATEMENT: *Prediction is favored if in the test situation no relevant response element is disconnected from thought and speech. If some relevant elements are thus disconnected (i.e., unconscious) these elements will remain at play in the criterion situation though not registered in the test situation.* Obviously they will tend to distort prediction.

A case in point might be that of a man who is not aware of his jealous tendencies toward his wife because they have never been excited. He might well think, upon questioning, that he would not be jealous should a rival appear, but might find himself painfully so in the event.

CONDITION II:

COMMON-SENSE STATEMENT: *Persons with poor verbal skills may find it difficult to forecast their own behavior.*

TECHNICAL STATEMENT: *Prediction is favored if the sentences of the respondent cover all response elements relevant to the criterion situation. Even where an automatic repression process does not exist, some respondents may have poor skills at verbalizing their feelings and wishes. If the sentence apparatus of the respondent does not stretch over all relevant responses, he will hardly be able to make accurate verbal predictions about his actions in the criterion situation. Inarticulate persons or persons of low intelligence may have this difficulty.*

For example, if one asks on a survey, "Do you feel well most of the time?", some persons may give much more accurate answers than others. Some people may have had much practice in noticing and talking about how they feel. Others may not. Many may say they feel "fine" when a closer observation of their behavior would show them to be depressed or anxious. In the latter case, the individual may actually be making the responses inquired about but may never have attached sentences to them.

CONDITION III:

COMMON-SENSE STATEMENT: *People who habitually go into effective action after thinking things over can best predict their own actions.*

TECHNICAL STATEMENT: *Prediction from test to criterion is likely to be favored if the connection between sentence responses and overt action responses has been strongly rewarded in previous learning. Thoughts and opinions are characteristically used to guide and orient*

behavior. But in some persons a split occurs between thought and action.
Such people have not been rewarded for thinking first and then acting.
They are the dreamers who do not make their dreams come true, the
"phantasy" types. The end sentences of the thought process should be
strongly connected with the initial responses in the action series if
prediction from opinion is to be serviceable.

In counselling we frequently see the apathetic individual who is
more or less indifferent to the environment and does not act strongly
to gain his ends. We are, however, always surprised at what a lively
mental life he leads. But, if action is imminent he says, "What's the
use?" It has been found that such people have often been non-rewarded
or punished for action. They have lost hope that effective action against
the environment will reduce drive. They can think of possible good
courses of action but do not try to carry them out. Therapy consists of
getting the person to "try" again, thus, in favorable cases, restoring the
strength of connection between verbal cues and more overt responses.

CONDITION IV:

COMMON-SENSE STATEMENT: *The test situation should not be cor-*
rupted by extraneous threats or rewards.

TECHNICAL STATEMENT: *Prediction is favored if the test situation*
provides stimuli only to the verbal response relevant to the criterion
dilemma. If the test situation stimulates fear in the respondent he may
respond to the fear and not to the criterion problem. If the test situation
seems to reward some other than the relevant opinion, that other opinion
may be forthcoming. The test situation must be clean of stimuli which
produce irrelevant responses.

Any form of fear illustrates this condition. Thus, a factory worker
may deny that he intends joining a union out of fear that the interro-
gator represents his employer. The anonymity of the informant is a
common safeguard against the intervention of the fear variable. Evi-
dently the respondent argues that you cannot punish a man if you
don't know who he is.

CONDITION V:

COMMON-SENSE STATEMENT: *A man can best predict what he will*
do in a future situation if he has been in about the same situation before
and thus knows what it's all about.

TECHNICAL STATEMENT: *Prediction from test to criterion is favored if the origin situation corresponds closely to the criterion situation.* Otherwise the respondent is predicting what he would do in a situation different from the criterion dilemma. When there is a poor match between origin and criterion, the criterion dilemma is bound to seem obscure to the respondent. Once in it he is likely to say, "I didn't know it was going to be like this."

If origin and criterion situations are very similar, as in the polling-voting situation, prediction is highly favored. The voting situation is very familiar and has been well rehearsed in the past. The question asked is the same. The verbal elements of the response may be the same in the two situations.

But if you are asking a soldier, "Do you expect to go back to school after the War?", the situation is more obscure. In actual Army surveys very considerable numbers of men expressed such an expectation. Our analysts saw fit, however, to make certain corrections in the over-all percentages. They subtracted the responses of men over twenty-five. They subtracted the responses of married men, and they excluded men who had been out of school for more than a year. These subtractions had a single effect, that is, to make the after-war criterion situation more like the known origin situation. Most people who intend to go to school are under twenty-five, single, and already in school. Their test responses had, therefore, a much greater presumption of validity.

CONDITION VI:

COMMON-SENSE STATEMENT: *A man can predict what he will do in a future situation, provided he doesn't have an experience which changes his mind before this situation occurs.*

TECHNICAL STATEMENT: *Prediction is favored providing that no new origin dilemma intervenes between the test and criterion situation. If such a new origin occurs it may generate an opinion competing with the test opinion.* In this case, the test opinion will, of course, less accurately forecast the criterion action. It may be that such new origin situations are more likely to occur as time passes and that therefore length of time between test and criterion situations roughly measures the likelihood of invalidity. This seems to be a matter-of-fact presumption in current surveying.

For example, a Southerner coming North for the first time might have the opinion that he would never sit behind a Negro on a bus, or never eat at the same table with a Negro. Once in the North, however, a new learning dilemma occurs. The Southerner does not want to appear strange or bigoted to his Northern associates. He does not like to make himself conspicuous. The Southern punishments for breaking caste etiquette have been withdrawn. Old rewards for his old habits are gone. On the contrary, he may be punished by unpleasant notice or even social isolation for not adapting himself to the new situation. He might not want to miss a particular dinner where a Negro is present. Under the pressure of new drives and rewards he changes his habits. A new origin situation has come into being and the old test of opinion is no longer predictive.

CONDITION VII:

COMMON-SENSE STATEMENT: *A man can better predict what he will do in a future dilemma if he is told exactly what this dilemma will be.*

TECHNICAL STATEMENT: *Prediction is favored if the test question explicitly presents the conflict, i.e., anticipations of rewards and punishments, of the criterion dilemma.* Otherwise responses will show up in the criterion situation which were not evoked in the test situation. If the criterion situation is vague in the mind of the tester, it is difficult for him to form useful questions. This condition cautions particular care in evoking the criterion situation vividly and specifying exactly the behavior which is to be predicted.

In short, if we could pick out the neurotics, the apathetic people, and the poor verbalizers in our samples we could probably make better estimates of validity. If the test situation is not corrupted by extraneous stimuli, prediction is likewise favored. If origin and criterion dilemmas are similar, and no new origin occurs between the time of test and criterion, the likelihood of validity is increased. If the test stimuli adequately present the criterion dilemma, prediction is favored.

The usefulness of the foregoing formulation must be determined in the construction of surveys where validity is actually checked. Perhaps it can thus be refined into something more useful and more complete. In any case, this paper may be seen as an attempt to relate the data of the social survey to the framework of a more general science of human behavior.

THE TWO-STEP
FLOW OF COMMUNICATION:
AN UP-TO-DATE REPORT
ON A HYPOTHESIS
Elihu Katz

A NALYSIS OF THE PROCESS of decision-making during the course of an election campaign led the authors of *The People's Choice* to suggest that the flow of mass communications may be less direct than was commonly supposed. It may be, they proposed, that influences stemming from the mass media first reach "opinion leaders" who, in turn, pass on what they read and hear to those of their every-day associates for whom they are influential. This hypothesis was called "the two-step flow of communication."[1]

The hypothesis aroused considerable interest. The authors themselves were intrigued by its implications for democratic society. It was a healthy sign, they felt, that people were still most successfully persuaded by give-and-take with other people and that the influence of the mass media was less automatic and less potent than had been assumed. For social theory, and for the design of communications research, the hypothesis suggested that the image of modern urban society needed revision. The image of the audience as a mass of disconnected individuals hooked up to the media but not to each other could not be reconciled with the idea of a two-step flow of communication implying, as it did, networks of interconnected individuals through which mass communications are channeled.

* This may be identified as Publication No. A-225 of the Bureau of Applied Social Research, Columbia University. It is an abridged version of a chapter in the author's "Interpersonal Relations and Mass Communications: Studies in the Flow of Influence," unpublished Ph.D. thesis, Columbia University, 1956. The advice and encouragement of Dr. Paul F. Lazarsfeld in the writing of this thesis are gratefully acknowledged.
[1] Paul F. Lazarsfeld, Bernard Berelson and Hazel Gaudet, *The People's Choice*, New York: Columbia University Press, 1948 (2nd edition), p. 151.

Originally published in Volume 21, Number 1, 1957 of the *Public Opinion Quarterly*.

Of all the ideas in *The People's Choice,* however, the two-step flow hypothesis is probably the one that was least well documented by empirical data. And the reason for this is clear: the design of the study did not anticipate the importance which interpersonal relations would assume in the analysis of the data. Given the image of the atomized audience which characterized so much of mass media research, the surprising thing is that interpersonal influence attracted the attention of the researchers at all.[2]

In the almost seventeen years since the voting study was undertaken, several studies at the Bureau of Applied Social Research of Columbia University have attempted to examine the hypothesis and to build upon it. Four such studies will be singled out for review. These are Merton's study of interpersonal influence and communications behavior in Rovere;[3] the Decatur study of decision-making in marketing, fashions, movie-going and public affairs, reported by Katz and Lazarsfeld;[4] the Elmira study of the 1948 election campaign reported by Berelson, Lazarsfeld and McPhee;[5] and, finally, a very recent study by Coleman, Katz and Menzel on the diffusion of a new drug among doctors.[6]

These studies will serve as a framework within which an attempt will be made to report on the present state of the two-step flow hypothesis, to examine the extent to which it has found confirmation and the ways in which it has been extended, contracted and reformulated. More than that, the studies will be drawn upon to highlight the successive strategies which have been developed in attempting to take systematic account of interpersonal relations in the design of communications research, aiming ultimately at a sort of "survey sociometry." Finally, these studies, plus others which will be referred to in passing, will provide an unusual opportunity to reflect upon problems in the continuity of social research.[7]

[2] For the discussion of the image of the atomized audience and the contravening empirical evidence, see Elihu Katz and Paul F. Lazarsfeld, *Personal Influence: The Part Played by People in the Flow of Mass Communications,* Glencoe, Illinois: The Free Press, pp. 15-42; Eliot Friedson, "Communications Research and the Concept of the Mass," *American Sociological Review,* Vol. 18, (1953), pp. 313-317; and Morris Janowitz, *The Urban Press in a Community Setting,* Glencoe, Illinois: The Free Press, 1952.

[3] Robert K. Merton, "Patterns of Influence: A Study of Interpersonal Influence and Communications Behavior in a Local Community," in Paul F. Lazarsfeld and Frank N. Stanton, eds., *Communications Research, 1948-9,* New York: Harper and Brothers, 1949, pp. 180-219.

[4] Elihu Katz and Paul F. Lazarsfeld, *op. cit.,* Part Two.

[5] Bernard R. Berelson, Paul F. Lazarsfeld and William N. McPhee, *Voting: A Study of Opinion Formation in a Presidential Campaign,* Chicago: University of Chicago Press, 1954.

[6] A report on the pilot phase of this study is to be found in Herbert Menzel and Elihu Katz, "Social Relations and Innovation in the Medical Profession," *Public Opinion Quarterly,* Vol. 19, (1955), pp. 337-52; a volume and various articles on the full study are now in preparation.

[7] Other authors who have drawn upon the concepts of opinion leadership and the two-step flow of communication, and developed them further, are Matilda and John Riley, "A Sociological Approach to Communications Research," *Public Opinion Quarterly,* Vol. 15 (1951), pp. 445-460; S. N. Eisenstadt, "Communications Processes Among Immigrants in Israel," *Public Opinion Quarterly,* Vol. 16 (1952), pp. 42-58 and "Communication Systems and Social Structure: An Exploratory Study," *Public Opinion Quarterly,* Vol. 19 (1955), pp. 153-167; David Riesman,

The starting point for this review must be an examination of the evidence in the 1940 voting study which led to the original formulation of the hypothesis. Essentially, three distinct sets of findings seem to have been involved. The first had to do with *the impact of personal influence.* It is reported that people who made up their minds late in the campaign, and those who changed their minds during the course of the campaign, were more likely than other people to mention personal influence as having figured in their decisions. The political pressure brought to bear by everyday groups such as family and friends is illustrated by reference to the political homogeneity which characterizes such groups. What's more, on an average day, a greater number of people reported participating in discussion of the election than hearing a campaign speech or reading a newspaper editorial. From all of this, the authors conclude that personal contacts appear to have been both more frequent and more effective than the mass media in influencing voting decisions.[8]

The second ingredient that went into the formulation of the hypothesis concerned *the flow of personal influence.* Given the apparent importance of interpersonal influence, the obvious next step was to ask whether some people were more important than others in the transmission of influence. The study sought to single out the "opinion leaders" by two questions: "Have you recently tried to convince anyone of your political ideas?", and "Has anyone recently asked you for your advice on a political question?" Comparing the opinion leaders with others, they found the opinion leaders more interested in the election. And from the almost even distribution of opinion leaders throughout every class and occupation, as well as the frequent mention by decision-makers of the influence of friends, co-workers and relatives, it was concluded that opinion leaders are to be found on every level of society and presumably, therefore, are very much like the people whom they influence.[9]

A further comparison of leaders and others with respect to mass media habits provides the third ingredient: *the opinion leaders and the mass media.* Compared with the rest of the population, opinion leaders were found to be

---

The Lonely Crowd, New Haven: Yale University Press, 1950; Leo A. Handel, *Hollywood Looks at its Audience,* Urbana: University of Illinois Press, 1950. The program of research in international communications at the Bureau of Applied Social Research has given considerable attention to opinion leadership; see Charles Y. Glock, "The Comparative Study of Communications and Opinion Formation," *Public Opinion Quarterly,* Vol. 16 (1952-53), pp. 512-523; J. M. Stycos, "Patterns of Communication in a Rural Greek Village," *Public Opinion Quarterly,* Vol. 16 (1952), pp. 59-70; and the forthcoming book by Daniel Lerner, Paul Berkman and Lucille Pevsner, *Modernizing the Middle East.* Forthcoming studies by Peter H. Rossi and by Robert D. Leigh and Martin A. Trow are also concerned with the interplay of personal and mass media influences in local communities.

[8] Lazarsfeld, Berelson and Gaudet, *op. cit.,* pp. 135-152.

[9] *Ibid.,* pp. 50-51.

considerably more exposed to the radio, to the newspapers and to magazines, that is, to the formal media of communication.[10]

Now the argument is clear: If word-of-mouth is so important, and if word-of-mouth specialists are widely dispersed, and if these specialists are more exposed to the media than the people whom they influence, then perhaps "ideas often flow from radio and print to opinion leaders and from these to the less active sections of the population."[11]

DESIGN OF THE VOTING STUDY

For studying the flow of influence as it impinges on the making of decisions, the study design of *The People's Choice* had several advantages. Most important was the panel method which made it possible to locate changes almost as soon as they occurred and then to correlate change with the influences reaching the decision-maker. Secondly, the unit of effect, the decision, was a tangible indicator of change which could readily be recorded. But for studying that part of the flow of influence which had to do with contacts among people, the study design fell short, since it called for a random sample of individuals abstracted from their social environments. It is this traditional element in the design of survey research which explains the leap that had to be made from the available data to the hypothesis of the two-step flow of communication.

Because every man in a random sample can speak only for himself, opinion leaders in the 1940 voting study had to be located by self-designation, that is, on the basis of their own answers to the two advice-giving questions cited above.[12] In effect, respondents were simply asked to report whether or not they were opinion leaders. Much more important than the obvious problem of validity posed by this technique is the fact that it does not permit a comparison of leaders with their respective followers, but only of leaders and non-leaders in general. The data, in other words, consist only of two statistical groupings: people who said they were advice-givers and those who did not. Therefore, the fact that leaders were more interested in the election than non-leaders cannot be taken to mean that influence flows from more interested persons to less interested ones. To state the problem drastically, it may even be that the leaders influence only each other, while the uninterested non-leaders stand outside the influence market altogether. Nevertheless, the tempta-

---

[10] *Ibid.,* p. 51.

[11] *Ibid.,* p. 151.

[12] Strictly speaking, of course, if a respondent reports whether or not he is a leader he is not speaking for himself but for his followers, real or imagined. Furthermore, it ought to be pointed out for the record that it is sometimes possible for a respondent to speak for others besides himself. The voting studies, for example, ask respondents to report the vote-intentions of other family members, of friends, of co-workers, though this procedure is of undetermined validity.

tion to assume that the non-leaders are the followers of the leaders is very great, and while *The People's Choice* is quite careful about this, it cannot help but succumb.[13] Thus, from the fact that the opinion leaders were more exposed to the mass media than the non-leaders came the suggestion of the two-step flow of communication; yet, manifestly, it can be true only if the non-leaders are, in fact, followers of the leaders.

The authors themselves point out that a far better method would have been based on "asking people to whom they turn for advice on the issue at hand and then investigating the interaction between advisers and advisees. But that procedure would be extremely difficult, if not impossible, since few of the related 'leaders' and 'followers' would happen to be included in the sample."[14] As will be shown immediately, this is perhaps the most important problem which succeeding studies have attempted to solve.

DESIGNS OF THREE SUBSEQUENT STUDIES

To this point, two aspects of the original statement of the two-step flow hypothesis have been reviewed. First of all, the hypothesis has been shown to have three distinct components, concerning respectively the impact of personal influence; the flow of personal influence; and the relationship of opinion leaders to the mass media. The evidence underlying each has been examined. Secondly, the design of the study has been recalled in order to point up the difficulty that arises from attempting to cope with the fundamentally new problem of incorporating *both* partners to an influence transaction into a cross-sectional study.

From this point forward, the major focus will turn to those studies that have succeeded *The People's Choice*. We will first report the different ways in which three of the four studies selected for review approached the problem of designing research on interpersonal influence.[15] Thereafter, the substantive findings of the several studies will be reviewed and evaluated so as to constitute an up-to-date report on the accumulating evidence for and against the hypothesis of the two-step flow of communication.

1. *The Rovere Study*. Undertaken just as the 1940 voting study was being completed, the earliest of the three studies was conducted in a small town in New Jersey. It began by asking a sample of 86 respondents to name the

[13] There is an alternative procedure which is something of an improvement. Respondents can be asked not only whether they have given advice but whether they have taken advice. This was done in the Decatur and Elmira studies which are cited below. Thus the non-leaders can be classified in terms of whether or not they are in the influence market at all, that is, whether or not they are "followers."

[14] Lazarsfeld, Berelson and Gaudet, *op. cit.*, pp. 49-50.

[15] The Elmira study will be omitted at this point because its design is essentially the same as that of the 1940 voting study except for the important fact that it obtained from each respondent considerably more information about the vote-intentions of others in his environment, the kinds of people he talks with, etc., than was done in *The People's Choice*.

people to whom they turned for information and advice regarding a variety of matters. Hundreds of names were mentioned in response, and those who were designated four times or more were considered opinion leaders. These influentials were then sought out and interviewed.[16]

Here, then, is the initial attempt, on a pilot scale, to solve the problem of research design posed by *The People's Choice*. To locate influentials, this study suggests, begin by asking somebody, "Who influences you?" and proceed from the persons influenced to those who are designated as influential.

Two important differences between this study and the 1940 voting study must be pointed out. First, there is a difference in the conception of opinion leadership. Whereas the voting study regards any advice-giver as an opinion leader if he influences even one other person (such as a husband telling his wife for whom to vote), the leaders singled out by the criterion employed in Rovere were almost certainly wielders of wider influence.

Secondly, the voting study, at least by implication, was interested in such questions as the extent of the role of interpersonal influence in decision-making and its relative effectiveness compared to the mass media. The Rovere study took for granted the importance of this kind of influence, and proceeded to try to find the people who play key roles in its transmission.

A final point to make in connection with the design of this study is that it makes use of the initial interviews almost exclusively to *locate* opinion leaders and hardly at all to explore the *relationships* between leaders and followers. Once the leaders were designated, almost exclusive attention was given to classifying them into different types, studying the communications behavior of the different types and the interaction among the leaders themselves, but very little attention was given to the interaction between the leaders and the original informants who designated them.

2. *The Decatur Study,* carried out in 1945-46, tried to go a step further.[17] Like the voting study, but unlike Rovere, it tried to account for decisions— specific instances in which the effect of various influences could be discerned and assessed. Like Rovere, but unlike the voting study, it provided for interviews with the persons whom individuals in the initial sample had credited as influential in the making of recent decisions (in the realms of marketing, movie-going, and public affairs). The focus of the study this time was not on the opinion leaders alone, but (1) on the relative importance of personal influence and (2) on the person who named the leader as well as the leader— the advisor-advisee dyad.

Ideally, then, this study could ask whether opinion leaders tended to be from the same social class as their followers or whether the tendency was for

16 Merton, *op. cit.,* pp. 184-185.
17 Katz and Lazarsfeld, *op. cit.,* Part Two.

influence to flow from the upper classes downwards. Were members of the dyads likely to be of the same age, the same sex, etc.? Was the leader more interested in the particular sphere of influence than his advisee? Was he more likely to be exposed to the mass media?

Just as the dyad could be constructed by proceeding from an advisee to his adviser, it was also possible to begin the other way around by talking first to a person who claimed to have acted as an adviser, and then locating the person he said he had influenced. The Decatur study tried this too. Using the same kind of self-designating questions employed in the voting study, persons who designated themselves as influential were asked to indicate the names of those whom they had influenced. By "snowballing" to the people thus designated, there arose the opportunity not only to study the interaction between adviser and advisee but also to explore the extent to which people who designated themselves as influential were confirmed in their self-evaluations by those whom they allegedly had influenced. Proceeding in this way, the researchers hoped to be able to say something about the validity of the self-designating technique.[18]

The authors of *The People's Choice* had said that "asking people to whom they turn and then investigating the interaction between advisers and advisees . . . would be extremely difficult if not impossible." And, in fact, it proved to be extremely difficult. Many problems were encountered in the field work, the result of which was that not all the "snowball" interviews could be completed.[19] In many parts of the analysis of the data, therefore, it was necessary to revert to comparisons of leaders and non-leaders, imputing greater influence to groups with higher concentrations of self-designated leadership. Yet, in principle, it was demonstrated that a study design taking account of interpersonal relations was both possible and profitable to execute.

But about the time it became evident that this goal was within reach, the goal itself began to change. It began to seem desirable to take account of chains of influence longer than those involved in the dyad; and hence to view the adviser-advisee dyad as one component of a more elaborately structured social group.

These changes came about gradually and for a variety of reasons. First of all, findings from the Decatur study and from the later Elmira study re-

[18] About two-thirds of the alleged influencees confirmed the fact that a conversation had taken place between themselves and the self-designated influential on the subject-matter in question. Of these, about 80 per cent further confirmed that they had received advice. The extent of confirmation is considerably less in the realm of public affairs than it is in marketing or fashion. *Ibid.*, pp. 149-161 and 353-362.

[19] Partly this was due to inability to locate the designated people, but partly, too, to the fact that original respondents did not always know the person who had influenced them as is obvious, for example, in the case of a woman copying another woman's hat style, etc. See *Ibid.*, pp. 362-363.

vealed that the opinion leaders themselves often reported that their own decisions were influenced by still other people.[20] It began to seem desirable, therefore, to think in terms of the opinion leaders of opinion leaders.[21] Secondly, it became clear that opinion leadership could not be viewed as a "trait" which some people possess and others do not, although the voting study sometimes implied this view. Instead, it seemed quite apparent that the opinion leader is influential at certain times and with respect to certain substantive areas by virtue of the fact that he is "empowered" to be so by other members of his group. Why certain people are chosen must be accounted for not only in demographic terms (social status, sex, age, etc.) but also in terms of the structure and values of the groups of which both adviser and advisee are members. Thus, the unexpected rise of young men to opinion leadership in traditional groups, when these groups faced the new situations of urbanization and industrialization, can be understood only against the background of old and new patterns of social relations within the group and of old and new patterns of orientation to the world outside the group.[22] Reviewing the literature of small group research hastened the formulation of this conception.[23]

One other factor shaped the direction of the new program as well. Reflecting upon the Decatur study, it became clear that while one could talk about the role of various influences in the making of fashion *decisions by individuals,* the study design was not adequate for the study of fashion in the aggregate—*fashion as a process of diffusion*—as long as it did not take account of either the content of the decision or the time factor involved. The decisions of the "fashion changers" studied in Decatur might have cancelled each other out: while Mrs. X reported a change from Fashion A to Fashion B, Mrs. Y might have been reporting a change from B to A. What is true for fashion is true for any other diffusion phenomenon: to study it, one must trace the flow of some specific item over time. Combining this interest in diffusion with that of studying the role of more elaborate social networks of communication gave birth to a new study which focused on (1) a specific item, (2) diffusion over time, (3) through the social structure of an entire community.

3. *The Drug Study.* This study was conducted to determine the way in which doctors make decisions to adopt new drugs. This time, when it came to de-

---

[20] *Ibid.*, p. 318; Berelson, Lazarsfeld and McPhee, *op. cit.,* p. 110.

[21] This was actually tried at one point in the Decatur study. See Katz and Lazarsfeld, *op. cit.,* pp. 283-287.

[22] See, for example, the articles by Eisenstadt, *op. cit.,* and Glock, *op. cit.;* the Rovere study, too, takes careful account of the structure of social relations and values in which influentials are embedded, and discusses the various avenues to influentiality open to different kinds of people.

[23] Reported in Part I of Katz and Lazarsfeld, *op. cit.*

signing a study which would take account of the possible role of interpersonal influence among physicians, it became clear that there were so few physicians (less than one and one-half per 1000 population) that it was feasible to interview all members of the medical profession in several cities. If all doctors (or all doctors in specialties concerned with the issue at hand) could be interviewed, then there would be no doubt that all adviser-advisee pairs would fall within the sample. All such pairs could then be located within the context of larger social groupings of doctors, which could be measured by sociometric methods.

Doctors in the relevant specialties in four midwestern cities were interviewed. In addition to questions on background, attitudes, drug-use, exposure to various sources of information and influence, and the like, each doctor was also asked to name the three colleagues he saw most often socially, the three colleagues with whom he talked most frequently about cases, and the three colleagues to whom he looked for information and advice.[24]

In addition to the opportunity of mapping the networks of interpersonal relations, the drug study also provided for the two other factors necessary for a true diffusion study: attention to a specific item in the course of gaining acceptance, and a record of this diffusion over time. This was accomplished by means of an audit of prescriptions on file in the local pharmacies of the cities studied, which made it possible to date each doctor's earliest use of a particular new drug—a drug which had gained widespread acceptance a few months before the study had begun. Each doctor could thus be classified in terms of the promptness of his decision to respond to the innovation, and in terms of other information provided by the prescription audit.

Altogether, compared with the earlier studies, the drug study imposes a more objective framework—both psychological and sociological—on the decision. First of all, the decision-maker himself is not the only source of information concerning his decision. Objective data from the prescription record are used as well. Secondly, the role of different influences is assessed not only on the basis of the decision-maker's own reconstruction of the event, but also on the basis of objective correlations from which inferences concerning the flow of influence can be drawn. For example, doctors who adopted the new drug early were more likely to be participants in out-of-town medical specialty meetings than those who adopted it later.

Similarly, it is possible to infer the role of social relations in doctor's decision-making not only from the doctor's own testimony concerning the role of social influences but also from the doctor's "location" in the interpersonal networks mapped by the sociometric questions. Thus, on the basis of sociometric data, it is possible to classify doctors according to their integration into the medical community, or the degree of their influence, as measured by *the*

---

[24] See footnote 6.

352

number of times they are named by their colleagues as friends, discussion-partners, and consultants. They can also be classified according to their membership in one or another network or clique, as indicated by *who* names them. Using the first measure makes it possible to investigate whether or not the more influential doctors adopt a drug earlier than those who are less influential. From the second kind of analysis one can learn, for example, whether or not those doctors who belong to the same sub-groups have similar drug-use patterns. In this way, it becomes possible to weave back and forth between the doctor's own testimony about his decisions and the influences involved, on the one hand, and the more objective record of his decisions and of the influences to which he has been exposed, on the other hand.

Note that the networks of social relations in this study are mapped "prior" to the introduction of the new drug being studied, in the sense that friendship, consultation, and so on, are recorded independently of any particular decision the doctor has made. The study is concerned with the potential relevance of various parts of these sociometric structures to the transmission of influence. For example, it is possible to point to the parts of the structure which are "activated" upon the introduction of a new drug, and to describe the sequence of diffusion of the drug as it gains acceptance by individuals and groups in the community. While the Decatur study could hope to examine only the particular face-to-face relationship which had been influential in a given decision, the drug study can locate this relationship against the background of the entire web of *potentially* relevant relationships within which the doctor is embedded.

THE FINDINGS OF STUDIES SUBSEQUENT TO *The People's Choice*

Having examined the *designs* of these studies, the next step is to explore their *findings* insofar as these are relevant to the hypothesis about the two-step flow of communication. It will be useful to return to the three categories already singled out in discussing *The People's Choice:* (1) the impact of personal influence; (2) the flow of personal influence; and (3) opinion leaders and the mass media. Evidence from the three studies just reported, as well as from the 1948 Elmira study[25] and from others, will be brought together here; but in every case the characteristics of each study's design must be borne in mind in evaluating the evidence presented.

A. THE IMPACT OF PERSONAL INFLUENCE

1. *Personal and the Mass Media Influence.* The 1940 study indicated that personal influence affected voting decisions more than the mass media did,

[25] Berelson, Lazarsfeld, and McPhee, *op. cit.*

particularly in the case of those who changed their minds during the course of the campaign. The Decatur study went on to explore the relative impact of personal influences and the mass media in three other realms: marketing, fashions and movie-going. Basing its conclusions on the testimony of the decision-makers themselves, and using an instrument for evaluating the relative effectiveness of the various media which entered into the decisions, the Decatur study again found that personal influence figured both more frequently and more effectively than any of the mass media.[26]

In the analysis to date, the drug study has not approached the problem of the relative effectiveness of the various media from the point of view of the doctor's own reconstruction of what went into the making of his decision. Comparing mere frequency of mention of different media, it is clear that colleagues are by no means the most frequently mentioned source. Nevertheless, exploration of the factors related to whether the doctor's decision to adopt the drug came early or late indicates that the factor most strongly associated with the time of adoption of the new drug is the extent of the doctor's integration in the medical community. That is, the more frequently a doctor is named by his colleagues as a friend or a discussion partner, the more likely he is to be an innovator with respect to the new drug. Extent of integration proves to be a more important factor than any background factor (such as age, medical school, or income of patients), or any other source of influence (such as readersip of medical journals) that was examined.

Investigation of why integration is related to innovation suggests two central factors: (1) interpersonal communication—doctors who are integrated are more in touch and more up-to-date; and (2) social support—doctors who are integrated feel more secure when facing the risks of innovation in medicine.[27] Thus the drug study, too, provides evidence of the strong impact of personal relations—even in the making of scientific decisions.

2. *Homogeneity of Opinion in Primary Groups.* The effectiveness of interpersonal influence, as it is revealed in the studies under review, is reflected in the homogeneity of opinions and actions in primary groups. The medium of primary group communication is, by definition, person-to-person. Both of the voting studies indicate the high degree of homogeneity of political opinion among members of the same families, and among co-workers and friends. The effectiveness of such primary groups in pulling potential deviates back into line is demonstrated by the fact that those who changed their vote inten-

[26] Katz and Lazarsfeld, *op. cit.,* pp. 169-186.

[27] On the relationship between social integration and self-confidence in a work situation, see Peter M. Blau, *The Dynamics of Bureaucracy,* Chicago: University of Chicago Press, 1955, pp. 126-129.

tions were largely people who, early in the campaign, had reported that they intended to vote differently from their family or friends.[28]

The drug study, too, was able to examine the extent of homogeneity in the behavior of sociometrically related doctors, and was able to demonstrate that there were situations where similar behavior could be deserved. For example, it was found that, when called upon to treat the more puzzling diseases, doctors were likely to prescribe the same drug as their sociometric colleagues. The study also showed that, very early in the history of a new drug, innovating doctors who were sociometrically connected tended to adopt the new drug at virtually the same time. This phenomenon of homogeneity of opinion or behavior among interacting individuals confronting an unclear or uncertain situation which calls for action has often been studied by sociologists and social psychologists.[29]

3. *The Various Roles of the Media.* The 1940 voting study explored some of the reasons why personal influence might be expected to be more influential in changing opinions than the mass media: It is often non-purposive; it is flexible; it is trustworthy. It was suggested that the mass media more often play a reinforcing role in the strengthening of predispositions and of decisions already taken. Nevertheless, it was assumed that the various media and personal influence are essentially competitive, in the sense that a given decision is influenced by one *or* the other. The Decatur study tended toward this assumption too, but at one point the study does attempt to show that different media play different parts in the decision-making process and take patterned positions in a sequence of several influences. The drug study elaborates on the roles of the media even further, distinguishing between media that "inform" and media the "legitimate" decisions. Thus in doctors' decisions, professional media (including colleagues) seem to play a legitimating role, while commercial media play an informing role.

B. THE FLOW OF PERSONAL INFLUENCE

The 1940 voting study found that opinion leaders were not concentrated in the upper brackets of the population but were located in almost equal proportions in every social group and stratum. This finding led to efforts in subsequent studies to establish the extent to which this was true in areas other than election campaigns and also to ascertain what it is that *does* distinguish opinion leaders from those whom they influence.

[28] Lazarsfeld, Berelson and Gaudet, *op. cit.*, pp. 137-145; Berelson, Lazarsfeld and McPhee, *op. cit.*, pp. 94-101, 120-122.

[29] That men, faced with an unstructured situation, look to each other to establish a "social reality" in terms of which they act, is a central theme in the work of Durkheim, Kurt Lewin and his disciples, H. S. Sullivan ("consensual validation"), and in the studies of Sherif, Asch and others.

The first thing that is clear from the series of studies under review is that the subject matter concerning which influence is transmitted has a lot to do with determining who will lead and who follow. Thus, the Rovere study suggests that within the broad sphere of public affairs one set of influentials is occupied with "local" affairs and another with "cosmopolitan" affairs.[30] The Decatur study suggests that in marketing, for example, there is a concentration of opinion leadership among older women with larger families, while in fashions and movie-going it is the young, unmarried girl who has a disproportionate chance of being turned to for advice. There is very little overlap of leadership: a leader in one sphere is not likely to be influential in another unrelated sphere as well.[31]

Yet, even when leadership in one or another sphere is heavily concentrated among the members of a particular group—as was the case with marketing leadership in Decatur—the evidence suggests that people still talk, most of all, to others like themselves. Thus, while the marketing leaders among the older "large-family wives" also influenced other kinds of women, most of their influence was directed to women of their own age with equally large families. In marketing, fashions, and movie-going, furthermore, there was no appreciable concentration of influentials in any of the three socio-economic levels. Only in public affairs was there a concentration of leadership in the highest status, and there was some slight evidence that influence flows from this group to individuals of lower status. The Elmira study also found opinion-leaders in similar proportions on every socio-economic and occupational level and found that conversations concerning the campaign went on, typically, between people of similar age, occupation, and political opinion.

What makes for the concentration of certain kinds of opinion leadership within certain groups? And when influential and influencee are outwardly alike—as they so often seem to be—what, if anything, distinguishes one from the other? Broadly, it appears that influence is related (1) to the *personification of certain values* (who one is); (2) to *competence* (what one knows); and (3) to *strategic social location* (whom one knows). Social location, in turn, divides into whom one knows within a group; and "outside."

Influence is often successfully transmitted because the influencee wants to be as much like the influential as possible.[32] That the young, unmarried girls

[30] Merton, *op. cit.*, pp. 187-188.

[31] For a summary of the Decatur findings on the flow of interpersonal influence, see Katz and Lazarsfeld, *op. cit.*, pp. 327-334.

[32] That leaders are, in a certain sense, the most conformist members of their groups—upholding whatever norms and values are central to the group—is a proposition which further illustrates this point. For an empirical illustration from a highly relevant study, see C. Paul Marsh and A. Lee Coleman, "Farmers' Practice Adoption Rates in Relation to Adoption Rates of Leaders," *Rural Sociology*, Vol. 19 (1954), pp. 180-183.

are fashion leaders can be understood easily in a culture where youth and youthfulness are supreme values. This is an example where "who one is" counts very heavily.

But "what one knows" is no less important.[33] The fact is that older women, by virtue of their greater experience, are looked to as marketing advisers and that specialists in internal medicine—the most "scientific" of the practicing physicians—are the most frequently mentioned opinion leaders among the doctors. The influence of young people in the realm of movie-going can also be understood best in terms of their familiarity with the motion picture world. The Elmira study found slightly greater concentrations of opinion leadership among the more educated people on each socio-economic level, again implying the importance of competence. Finally, the influence of the "cosmopolitans" in Rovere rested on the presumption that they had large amounts of information.

It is, however, not enough to be a person whom others want to emulate, or to be competent. One must also be accessible. Thus, the Decatur study finds gregariousness—"whom one knows"—related to every kind of leadership. The Rovere study reports that the leadership of the "local" influentials is based on their central location in the web of interpersonal contacts. Similarly, studies of rumor transmission have singled out those who are "socially active" as agents of rumor.[34]

Of course, the importance of whom one knows is not simply a matter of the number of people with whom an opinion leader is in contact. It is also a question of whether the people with whom he is in touch happen to be interested in the area in which his leadership is likely to be sought. For this reason, it is quite clear that the greater interest of opinion leaders in the subjects over which they exert influence is not a sufficient explanation of their influence. While the voting studies as well as the Decatur study show leaders to be more interested, the Decatur study goes on to show that interest alone is not the determining factor.[35] In fashion, for example, a young unmarried girl is considerably more likely to be influential than a matron with an equally great interest in clothes. The reason, it is suggested, is that a girl who is interested in fashion is much more likely than a matron with an equally high interest to know other people who share her preoccupation, and thus is more likely than the matron to have followers who are interested enough to ask for her advice. In other words, it takes two to be a leader—a leader and a follower.

Finally, there is the second aspect of "whom one knows." An individual

[33] The distinction between "what" and "whom" one knows is used by Merton, *op. cit.*, p. 197.

[34] Gordon W. Allport and Leo J. Postman, *The Psychology of Rumor*, New York: Henry Holt, 1943, p. 183.

[35] Katz and Lazarsfeld, *op. cit.*, pp. 249-252.

may be influential not only because people within his group look to him for advice but also because of whom he knows outside his group.[36] Both the Elmira and Decatur studies found that men are more likely than women to be opinion leaders in the realm of public affairs and this, it is suggested, is because they have more of a chance to get outside the home to meet people and talk politics. Similarly, the Elmira study indicated that opinion leaders belonged to more organizations, more often knew workers for the political parties, and so on, than did others. The drug study found that influential doctors could be characterized in terms of such things as their more frequent attendance at out-of-town meetings and the diversity of places with which they maintained contact, particularly far-away places. It is interesting that a study of the farmer-innovators responsible for the diffusion of hybrid seed-corn in Iowa concluded that these leaders also could be characterized in terms of the relative frequency of their trips out of town.[37]

C. THE OPINION LEADERS AND THE MASS MEDIA

The third aspect of the hypothesis of the two-step flow of communication states that opinion leaders are more exposed to the mass media than are those whom they influence. In *The People's Choice* this is supported by reference to the media behavior of leaders and non-leaders.

The Decatur study corroborated this finding, and went on to explore two additional aspects of the same idea.[38] First of all, it was shown that leaders in a given sphere (fashions, public affairs, etc.) were particularly likely to be exposed to the media appropriate to that sphere. This is essentially a corroboration of the Rovere finding that those who proved influential with regard to "cosmopolitan" matters were more likely to be readers of national news magazines, but that this was not at all the case for those influential with regard to "local" matters. Secondly, the Decatur study shows that at least in the realm of fashions, the leaders are not only more exposed to the mass media, but are also more affected by them in their own decisions. This did not appear to be the case in other realms, where opinion leaders, though more exposed to the media than non-leaders, nevertheless

[36] It is interesting that a number of studies have found that the most integrated persons within a group are also likely to have more contacts outside the group than others. One might have expected the more marginal members to have more contacts outside. For example, see Blau, *op. cit.*, p. 128.

[37] Bryce Ryan and Neal Gross, *Acceptance and Diffusion of Hybrid Seed Corn in Two Iowa Communities,* Ames, Iowa: Iowa State College of Agriculture and Mechanic Arts, Research Bulletin 372, pp. 706-707. For a general summary, see Ryan and Gross, "The Diffusion of Hybrid Seed Corn in Two Iowa Communities," *Rural Sociology*, Vol. 8 (1942), pp. 15-24. An article, now in preparation, will point out some of the parallels in research design and in findings between this study and the drug study.

[38] Katz and Lazarsfeld, *op. cit.*, pp. 309-320.

reported personal influence as the major factor in their decisions. This suggests that in some spheres considerably longer chains of person-to-person influence than the dyad may have to be traced back before one encounters any decisive influence by the mass media, even though their contributory influence may be perceived at many points. This was suggested by the Elmira study too. It found that the leaders, though more exposed to the media, also more often reported that they sought information and advice from other persons.[39]

Similarly, the drug study showed that the influential doctors were more likely to be readers of a large number of professional journals and valued them more highly than did doctors of lesser influence. But at the same time, they were as likely as other doctors to say that local colleagues were an important source of information and advice in their reaching particular decisions.

Finally, the drug study demonstrated that the more influential doctors could be characterized by their greater attention not only to medical journals, but to out-of-town meetings and contacts as well. This finding has already been discussed in the previous section treating the *strategic location* of the opinion leader with respect to "the world outside" his group. Considering it again under the present heading suggests that the greater exposure of the opinion leader to the mass media may only be a special case of the more general proposition that opinion leaders serve to relate their groups to relevant parts of the environment through whatever media happen to be appropriate. This more general statement makes clear the similar functions of big city newspapers for the Decatur fashion leader; of national news magazines for the "cosmopolitan" influentials of Rovere; of out-of-town medical meetings for the influential doctor; and of contact with the city for the farmer-innovator in Iowa[40] as well as for the newly-risen, young opinion leaders in underdeveloped areas throughout the world.[41]

CONCLUSIONS

Despite the diversity of subject matter with which they are concerned, the studies reviewed here constitute an example of continuity and cumulation both in research design and theoretical commitment. Piecing together the findings of the latter-day studies in the light of the original statement of the two-step flow hypothesis suggests the following picture.

[39] Berelson, Lazarsfeld and McPhee, *op. cit.*, p. 110.

[40] Ryan and Gross, *op. cit.*, choose to explain "trips to the city" as another index of the non-traditional orientation of which innovation itself is also an index. In the case of the drug of-town meetings, trips to out-of-town centers of learning, etc., but the latter were also mentioned as key sources of advice by doctors who were innovators and influentials.
sources of advice by doctors who were innovators and influentials.

[41] See the forthcoming book by Lerner, *et. al* cited above.

Opinion leaders and the people whom they influence are very much alike and typically belong to the same primary groups of family, friends and co-workers. While the opinion leader may be more interested in the particular sphere in which he is influential, it is highly unlikely that the persons influenced will be very far behind the leader in their level of interest. Influentials and influencees may exchange roles in different spheres of influence. Most spheres focus the group's attention on some related part of the world outside the group, and it is the opinion leader's function to bring the group into touch with this relevant part of its environment through whatever media are appropriate. In every case, influentials have been found to be more exposed to these points of contact with the outside world. Nevertheless, it is also true that, despite their greater exposure to the media, most opinion leaders are primarily affected not by the communication media but by still other people.

The main emphasis of the two-step flow hypothesis appears to be on only one aspect of interpersonal relations—interpersonal relations as channels of communication. But from the several studies reviewed, it is clear that these very same interpersonal relations influence the making of decisions in at least two additional ways. In addition to serving as networks of communication, interpersonal relations are also sources of pressure to conform to the group's way of thinking and acting, as well as sources of social support. The workings of group pressure are clearly evident in the homogeneity of opinion and action observed among voters and among doctors in situations of unclarity or uncertainty. The social support that comes from being integrated in the medical community may give a doctor the confidence required to carry out a resolution to adopt a new drug. Thus, interpersonal relations are (1) channels of information, (2) sources of social pressure, and (3) sources of social support, and each relates interpersonal relations to decision-making in a somewhat different way.[42]

The central methodological problem in each of the studies reviewed has been how to take account of interpersonal relations and still preserve the economy and representativeness which the random, cross-sectional sample affords. Answers to this problem range from asking individuals in the sample to describe the others with whom they interacted (Elmira), to conducting "snowball" interviews with influential-influencee dyads (Decatur), to interviewing an entire community (drug study). Future studies will probably

---

[42] These different dimensions of interpersonal relations can be further illustrated by reference to studies which represent the "pure type" of each dimension. Studies of rumor flow illustrate the "channels" dimension; see, for example, Jacob L. Moreno, *Who Shall Survive*, Beacon, N. Y.: Beacon House, 1953, pp. 440-450. The study by Leon Festinger, Stanley Schachter and Kurt Back, *Social Pressures in Informal Groups*, New York: Harper and Bros., 1950, illustrates the second dimension. Blau, *op. cit.*, pp. 126-129, illustrates the "social support" dimension.

find themselves somewhere in between. For most studies, however, the guiding principle would seem to be to build larger or smaller social molecules around each individual atom in the sample.[43]

[43] Various ways of accomplishing this have been discussed for the past two years in a staff seminar on "relational analysis" at the Bureau of Applied Social Research. The recent study by Seymour M. Lipset, Martin A. Trow and James S. Coleman, *Union Democracy,* Glencoe, Ill.: The Free Press, 1956, illustrates one approach in its study of printers within the varying social contexts of the shops in which they are employed. The study by Riley and Riley, *op. cit.,* is another good example.

WHAT WE KNOW
ABOUT THE EFFECTS
OF MASS COMMUNICATION:
THE BRINK OF HOPE
Joseph T. Klapper

T WENTY YEARS ago writers who undertook to discuss mass communication typically felt obliged to define that unfamiliar term. In the intervening years conjecture and research upon the topic, particularly in reference to the effects of mass communication, have burgeoned. The literature has reached that stage of profusion and disarray, characteristic of all burgeoning disciplines, at which researchers and research administrators speak wistfully of establishing centers where the cascading data might be sifted and stored. The field has grown to the point at which its practitioners are periodically asked by other researchers to attempt to assess the cascade, to determine whither we are tumbling, to atempt to assess, in short, "what we know about the effects of mass communication." The present paper is one attempt to partially answer that question.

The author is well aware that the possibility of bringing any order to this field is regarded in some quarters with increasing pessimism. The paper will acknowledge and document this pessimism, but it will neither condone nor share it. It will rather propose that we have come at last to the brink of hope.

THE BASES OF PESSIMISM

The pessimism is, of course, widespread and it exists both among the interested lay public and within the research fraternity.

* This paper may be identified as publication A-242 of the Bureau of Applied Social Research, Columbia University. It was originally presented as an address at the National Education Association's Centennial Seminar on Communications, at Dedham, Mass., May 21-22, 1957.

Originally published in Volume 21, Number 4, 1957 of the *Public Opinion Quarterly*.

Some degree of pessimism, or even cynicism, is surely to be expected from the lay public, whose questions we have failed to answer. Teachers, preachers, parents, and legislators have asked us a thousand times over these past fifteen years whether violence in the media produces delinquency, whether the media raise or lower public taste, and just what the media can do to the political persuasions of their audiences. To these questions we have not only failed to provide definitive answers, but we have done something worse: we have provided evidence in partial support of every hue of every view. We have on the one hand demonstrated that people's existing tastes govern the way they use media,[1] and on the other hand reported instances in which changed media usage was associated with apparently altered tastes.[2] We have hedged on the crime and violence question, typically saying, "Well, probably there is no causative relationship, but there just might be a triggering effect."[3] In reference to persuasion, we have maintained that the media are after all not so terribly powerful,[4] and yet we have reported their impressive successes in such varied causes as promoting religious intolerance,[5] the sale of war bonds,[6] belief in the American Way,[7] and disenchantment with boy scout activities.[8] It is surely no wonder that a bewildered public should regard with cynicism a research tradition which supplies, instead of definitive answers, a plethora of relevant but inconclusive, and at times seemingly contradictory, findings.

Considerable pessimism, of a different hue, is also to be expected within the research fraternity itself. Such anomalous findings as have been cited above seemed to us at first to betoken merely the need of more penetrating and rigid research. We shaped insights into hypotheses and eagerly set up research designs in quest of the additional variables which we were sure would bring order out of chaos, and enable us to describe the process of effect with sufficient precision to diagnose and predict. But the variables emerged in such a cataract that we almost drowned. The relatively placid waters of

[1] E.g., Lazarsfeld (1940), pp. 21-47; Wiebe (1952), pp. 185 ff. (*For complete bibliographical details, refer to Bibliography.*)

[2] E.g., Lazarsfeld (1940), pp. 126 ff.; Suchman (1941). Both Lazarsfeld and Suchman point out that although media may seem to be causative agents, further research reveals that their influence was energized by other factors. The point is discussed at length below.

[3] This is the typical, if perhaps inevitable conclusion, of surveys of pertinent literature and comment. See, for example, Bogart (1956), pp. 258-274.

[4] E.g., Lazarsfeld and Merton (1949); Klapper (1948). The point is elaborately demonstrated in regard to political conversion in Lazarsfeld, Berelson, and Gaudet (1948), and in Berelson, Lazarsfeld, and McPhee (1954).

[5] Klapper (1949), pp. II-25, IV-47, IV-52.

[6] Merton (1946).

[7] The efficacy, as well as the limitations, of media in this regard, are perhaps most exhaustively documented in the various unclassified evaluation reports of the United States Information Agency.

[8] Kelley and Volkhart (1952).

"who says *what* to *whom"* were early seen to be muddied by audience pre-dispositions, "self-selection," and selective perception. More recent studies, both in the laboratory and the social world, have documented the influence of a host of other variables, including various aspects of contextual organization;[9] the audiences' image of the source;[10] the simple passage of time;[11] the group orientation of the audience member and the degree to which he values group membership;[12] the activity of opinion leaders;[13] the social aspects of the situation during and after exposure to the media,[14] and the degree to which the audience member is forced to play a role;[15] the personality pattern of the audience member,[16] his social class, and the level of his frustration;[17] the nature of the media in a free enterprise system,[18] and the availability of "social mechanism[s] for implementing action drives."[19] The list, if not endless, is at least overwhelming, and it continues to grow. Almost every aspect of the life of the audience member and the culture in which the communication occurs seems susceptible of relation to the process of communicational effect. As early as 1948, Berelson, cogitating on what was then known, came to the accurate if perhaps moody conclusion that "some kinds of *communication* on some kinds of *issues,* brought to the attention of some kinds of *people* under some kinds of *conditions* have some kinds of *effects."*[20] It is surely no wonder that today, after eight more years at the inexhaustible fount of variables, some researchers should feel that the formulation of any systematic description of what effects are how effected, and the predictive application of such principles, is a goal which becomes the more distant as it is the more vigorously pursued.

[9] The effect of such variables as the number of topics mentioned, the order of topics, camera angles, detail of explanation, explicitness vs. implicitness, one side vs. both sides, and a host of other contextual variables has been exhaustively studied in virtually thousands of experiments conducted under the auspices of the U. S. Navy, the U. S. Army, and Pennsylvania State University, as well as by individual investigators. Summaries of several such studies will be found, *passim,* in Hovland, Lumsdaine, and Sheffield (1949) and Hovland, Janis, and Kelley (1953).

[10] E.g., Merton (1946), pp. 61 ff.; Freeman, Weeks and Wertheimer (1955); Hovland, Janis, and Kelley (1953), ch. 2, which summarizes a series of studies by Hovland, Weiss, and Kelman.

[11] Hovland, Lumsdaine, and Sheffield (1949), in re "sleeper effects" and "temporal effects."

[12] E.g., Kelley and Volkhart (1952); Riley and Riley (1951); Ford (1954); Katz and Lazarsfeld (1955) review a vast literature on the subject (pp. 15-133).

[13] Katz (1957) provides an exhaustive review of the topic.

[14] E.g., Friedson (1953). For an early insight, see Cooper and Jahoda (1947).

[15] Janis and King (1954), King and Janis (1953), and Kelman (1953), all of which are summarized and evaluated in Hovland, Janis, and Kelley (1953); also Michael and Maccoby (1953).

[16] E.g., Janis (1954); also Hovland, Janis, and Kelley (1953), ch. 6.

[17] E.g., Maccoby (1954).

[18] E.g., Klapper (1948); Klapper (1949), pp. IV-20-27; Wiebe (1952).

[19] Wiebe (1951-2).

[20] Berelson (1948), p. 172.

This paper, however, takes no such pessimistic view. It rather proposes that we already know a good deal more about communications than we thought we did, and that we are on the verge of being able to proceed toward even more abundant and more fruitful knowledge.

This optimism is based on two phenomena. The first of these is a new orientation toward the study of communication effects which has recently become conspicuous in the literature. And the second phenomenon is the emergence, from this new approach, of a few generalizations. It is proposed that these generalizations can be tied together, and tentatively developed a little further, and that when this is done the resulting set of generalizations can be extremely helpful. More specifically, they seem capable of organizing and relating a good deal of existing knowledge about the processes of communication effect, the factors involved in the process, and the direction which effects typically take. They thus provide some hope that the vast and ill-ordered array of communications research findings may be eventually molded, by these or other generalizations, into a body of organized knowledge.

This paper undertakes to cite the new orientation, to state what seem to be the emerging generalizations, and to at least suggest the extent of findings which they seem capable of ordering. In all of this, the author submits rather than asserts. He hopes to be extremely suggestive, but he cannot yet be conclusive. And if the paper bespeaks optimism, it also bespeaks the tentativeness of exploratory rather than exhaustive thought. Explicit note will in fact be taken of wide areas to which the generalizations do not seem to apply, and warnings will be sounded against the pitfalls of regarding them as all-inclusive or axiomatic.

The Phenomenistic Approach. The new orientation, which has of course been hitherto and variously formulated, can perhaps be described, in a confessedly oversimplified way, as a shift away from the concept of "hypodermic effect"[21] toward an approach which might be called "situational," "phenomenistic," or "functional." It is a shift away from the tendency to regard mass communication as a necessary and sufficient cause of audience effects, toward a view of the media as influences, working amid other influences, in a total situation. The old quest of specific effects stemming directly from the communication has given way to the observation of existing conditions or changes—followed by an inquiry into the factors, including mass communication, which produced those conditions and changes, and the roles which these factors played relative to each other. In short, attempts to assess a stimu-

[21] Berelson, Lazarsfeld, and McPhee (1954), p. 234.

lus which was presumed to work alone have given way to an assessment of the role of that stimulus in a total observed phenomen.

Examples of the new approach are fairly numerous, although they still represent only a small proportion of current research. The so-called Elmira[22] and Decatur[23] studies, for example, set out to determine the critical factors in various types of observed decisions, rather than focussing exclusively on whether media did or did not have effects. McPhee, in theoretical vein, proposes that we stop seeking direct media effects on taste and inquire instead into what produces taste and how media affect that.[24] The Rileys and Maccoby focus on the varying functions which media serve for different sorts of children, rather than inquiring whether media do or do not affect them.[25] Some of the more laboratory-oriented researchers, in particular the Hovland school, have been conducting ingeniously designed controlled experiments in which the communicational stimulus is a constant, and various extra-communicational factors are the variables.[26]

This new approach, which views mass media as one among a series of factors, working in patterned ways their wonders to perform, seems to the author to have made possible a series of generalizations which will now be advanced. They are submitted very gingerly. They seem to the author at once extremely generic and quite immature; they seem on the one hand to involve little that has not been said, and on the other hand to be frightfully daring. They do seem, however, to be capable of relating a good deal of data about the processes, factors, and directions of communication effects, and of doing this in such a way that findings hitherto thought anomalous or contradictory begin to look like orderly variations on a few basic themes.

Emerging Generalizations. The entire set of generalizations will first be presented in their bare bones, and without intervening comment. The remainder of this paper will be devoted to justifying their existence and indicating the range of data which they seem able to organize. Without further ado, then, it is proposed that we are as of now justified in making the following tentative generalizations:

1. Mass communication ordinarily does not serve as a necessary and sufficient cause of audience effects, but rather functions among and through a nexus of mediating factors and influences.

2. These mediating factors are such that they typically render mass communication a contributory agent, but not the sole cause, in a process of reinforcing the existing conditions. (Regardless of the condition in question—

---

[22] *Ibid.*

[23] Katz and Lazarsfeld (1955).

[24] McPhee (1953).

[25] Riley and Riley (1951), and Maccoby (1954).

[26] E.g., the experimental program described in Hovland, Janis, and Kelley (1953).

be it the level of public taste, the tendency of audience members toward or away from delinquent behavior, or their vote intention—and regardless of whether the effect in question be social or individual, the media are more likely to reinforce than to change.)

3. On such occasions as mass communication does function in the service of change, one of two conditions is likely to obtain. Either:

a. the mediating factors will be found to be inoperative, and the effect of the media direct; or

b. the mediating factors, which normally favor reinforcement, will be found to be themselves impelling toward change.

4. There are certain residual situations in which mass communication seems to wreak direct effects, or to directly and of itself serve certain psychophysical functions.

5. The efficacy of mass communication, either as contributory agents or as agents of direct effect, is affected by various aspects of the media themselves or of the communication situation (including, for example, aspects of contextual organization, the availability of channels for overt action, etc.).

Therewith the generalizations, and herewith the application. The schemata will be applied first to the field of persuasive communication, and then, much more briefly, to the data dealing with the effects of mass communication on the levels of audience taste. The hope, in each case, is to show that the data support the generalizations, and that the generalizations in turn organize the data and suggest new avenues of logically relevant research.

THE GENERALIZATIONS APPLIED: PERSUASION

Persuasive communication here refers to those communications which are intended to evoke what Katz and Lazarsfeld have called "campaign" effects,[27] i.e., to produce such short term opinion and attitude effects as are typically the goals of campaigns—political, civic, or institutional. Long-range phenomena, such as the building of religious values, are not here a focus of attention, nor are the marketing goals of most advertising.

Reinforcement. It is by now axiomatic that persuasive communication of the sort we are discussing is far more often associated with attitude reinforcement than with conversion. The now classic *People's Choice* found reinforcement, or constancy of opinion, approximately ten times as common as conversion among Erie County respondents exposed to the presidential campaign of 1940,[28] and a nine to one ratio was found in the more elaborate study of Elmira voters in 1948.[29] Various other studies have attested that, in

[27] Katz and Lazarsfeld (1955), pp. 17 ff.
[28] Lazarsfeld, Berelson, and Gaudet (1948).
[29] Berelson, Lazarsfeld, and McPhee (1954).

367

general, when the media offer fare in support of both sides of given issues, the dominant affect is stasis, or reinforcement, and the least common effect is conversion.

But we are not here proposing merely that the media are more likely to reinforce than to convert. We are also proposing, as some others have proposed before us,[30] and as we have stated in generalization number 1, that the media typically do not wreak direct effects upon their audiences, but rather function among and through other factors or forces. And we are going slightly farther by proposing, in generalization number 2, that it is these very intervening variables themselves which tend to make mass communication a contributing agent of reinforcement as opposed to change. We shall here note only a few such variables, deliberately selecting both from among the long familiar and the newly identified, in order to suggest the extent of findings for which this generalization seems able to account, and which, seen in this light, become logically related manifestations of the same general phenomenon.

Audience predispositions, for example, have been recognized since the very beginnings of communications research as a controlling influence upon the effect of persuasive mass communication. A plethora of studies, some conducted in the laboratory and some in the social world, have demonstrated that such predispositions and their progeny—selective exposure,[31] selective retention, and selective perception—intervene between the supply of available mass communication stimuli and the minds of the audience members.[32] They wrap the audience member in a kind of protective net, which so sifts or deflects or remolds the stimuli as to make reinforcement a far more likely effect than conversion.

Let us turn from these very old friends to newer acquaintances. Communications research has recently "rediscovered" *the group.* Katz and Lazarsfeld, drawing on the literature of small group research, have proposed, with considerable supporting evidence, that primary-type groups to which the audience member belongs may themselves function as reinforcing agents and

[30] For explicit statements, see McPhee (1953) and Meyersohn (1957). Similar orientations are implicit in Katz (1957), in all studies cited in footnotes 22-26 above, and in various other works.

[31] "Selective exposure" seems to the author a somewhat more realistic term than the classic "self-selection." It is in a sense true that a given program "selects its audience before it affects it" (Lazarsfeld, 1940, p. 134), i.e., that it acts like a sieve in screening its particular audience from among the vast potential audience of all media offerings. But the sieve works, after all, only because the people, rather than the program are, consciously or unconsciously, selective.

[32] No attempt can be made to cite here the hundreds of studies which demonstrate one or more of these processes. Summaries of a considerable number which appeared during or before the late 1940's will be found in Klapper (1949), pp. Intro 11-12, I-15-26, and IV-27-33. For a particularly intriguing demonstration of selective exposure, see Geiger (1950), and for an extraordinarily elaborate demonstration of selective perception, see Wilner (1951).

may influence mass communication to do likewise.[33] People tend, for example, to belong to groups whose characteristic opinions are congenial with their own; the opinions themselves seem to be intensified, or at least made more manifest, by intra-group interaction; and the benefits, both psychological and social, of continued membership in good standing act as a deterrent against opinion change. Group-anchored norms thus serve, on a conscious or unconscious level, to mediate the effects of communications. The proposition has been empirically demonstrated by Kelley and Volkart,[34] who found that, in general, persuasive communications were more likely to be rejected if they were not in accord with the norms of groups to which the audience member belonged; there were indications, furthermore, that the tendency was intensified in regard to issues more salient to the group, and among persons who particularly valued their membership. Groups are further likely to supplement the reinforcing effect by providing areas for oral dissemination. Various studies have shown that communications spread most widely among persons of homogeneous opinion, and espically among those who agree with the communication to begin with.[35] The "rediscovered group," in short, intervenes between the media stimuli and the people who are affected, and it does so, other conditions being equal, in favor of reinforcement.

Consider another phenomenon which is now in the limelight of communication research: *opinion leadership,* or, as it is sometimes called, "the two-step flow of communication."[36] The operation of such leadership is by definition interventive. And opinion leaders, it turns out, are usually supernormative members of the same groups to which their followers belong— i.e., persons especially familiar with and loyal to group standards and values.[37] Their influence therefore appears more likely to be exercised in the service of continuity than of change, and it seems therefore a reasonable conjecture—although it has not, to the author's knowledge, been specifically documented—that their role in the process of communication effect is more likely to encourage reinforcement than conversion.

All the intervening phenomena which have thus far been cited pertain, in one way or another, to the audience members—to the element of *whom* in the old Lasswell formula. But the range of mediating influences is not so restricted. *The nature of mass communication* in a free enterprise society, for example, falls under this same rubric. It is surely not necessary to here rehearse in detail the old adage of how the need for holding a massive audi-

[33] Katz and Lazarsfeld (1955), pp. 15-133.
[34] Kelley and Volkhart (1952), and Kelley (1955), both of which are summarized in Hovland, Janis, and Kelley (1953), Ch. 5.
[35] E.g., Katz and Lazarsfeld (1955), pp. 82-115; also Katz (1957).
[36] Katz and Lazarsfeld (1955), pp. 309-320, and Katz (1957).
[37] Katz and Lazarsfeld (1955), pp. 82-115, and 219-334 *passim,* especially pp. 321 ff.; also Katz (1957).

ence leads the media, particularly in their entertainment fare, to hew to the accepted, and thus to tend to resanctify the sanctified.[38] But it should here be noted that this is to say that the demands of the socio-economic system mediate the possible effects of mass communication in the direction of social reinforcement.

Such phenomena as these lend some credence to the proposition that the media typically work among and through other forces, and that these intervening forces tend to make the media contributing agents of reinforcement. And the generalization, to which these factors lend credence, in turn serves to organize and relate the factors. Diverse though they may be, they are seen to play essentially similar roles. One is tempted to wonder if they do not constitute a definable class of forces—whether, if the process of communicational effect were reduced to symbolic formulation, they might not be severally represented as, say, Q_1, Q_2, and so forth to Q_n. The author does not propose anything so drastic. He merely notes that the generalization suggests it. It suggests, simultaneously, relevant topics for further research. *Do* opinion leaders actually function, as the generalization suggests, to render mass communication a more likely agent of reinforcement than of change? And what of all those Q's between Q_3 or Q_8 and Q_n? What other phenomena function in a similar manner and toward the same end?

We may note also that this generalization, simple though it is, not only accounts for such factors as provide its life blood. It provides as well a sort of covering shed for various bits and pieces of knowledge which have hitherto stood in discrete isolation.

Consider, for example, the phenomenon of *"monopoly propaganda"*—i.e., propaganda which is vigorously and widely pursued and nowhere opposed. Monopoly propaganda has been long recognized as widely effective, and monopoly position has been cited as a condition which virtually guarantees persuasive success.[39] But monopoly propaganda can exist only in favor of views which already enjoy such wide sanction that no opposition of any significance exists. Viewed in the light of the generalization, monopoly position is seen not as an isolated condition of propaganda success, but as a specific combination of known factors. It is a name for the situation in which both the media and virtually all the factors which intervene between the media and the audience, or which operate co-existently with the media, approach a homogeneity of directional influence. Monopoly position is, as it were, a particular setting of the machine, and its outcome is logically predictable.

Change, with mediators inoperative. Generalization number 3 recognizes that although the media typically function as contributory agents of reinforce-

[38] E.g., Klapper (1948); Klapper (1949), pp. IV-20-27; Wiebe (1952).
[39] E.g., Lazarsfeld and Merton (1949); Klapper (1948) and Klapper (1949), pp. IV-20-27.

ment, they also function as agents of attitude change. In reference to this simple point, there is surely no need for lengthy documentation: the same studies that find reinforcement the predominant effect of campaigns typically reveal as well some small incidence of conversion, and a plethora of controlled experiments attest that media, or laboratory approximations of media, can and often do shift attitudes in the direction intended by the communicator. But the generalization further proposes—and in this it is more daring than its predecessors—that such attitude changes occur when either of two conditions obtain: when the forces which normally make for stasis or reinforcement are inoperative, or when these very same forces themselves make for change.

Let us consider first the proposition that change is likely to occur if the forces for stasis are inoperative. A set of experiments which has already been mentioned above is extremely indicative in reference to this proposition. Kelley and Volkhart, it will be recalled, found that, in general, communications opposed to group norms were likely to be rejected if the issue was particularly salient to the group, and that they were more likely to be rejected by persons who particularly valued their group membership. But there is another side to the Kelley-Volkhart coin, viz., the findings that the communication opposed to group norms was more likely to be *accepted when the issue was not particularly salient* to the group, and that it was more likely to be accepted *by persons who did not particularly value their membership* in the group.[40] Put another way, *changes were more likely to occur in those situations in which the mediating effect of the group was reduced.*

·A whole slew of other findings and bits of knowledge, both old and new, and previously existing as more or less discrete axioms, seem susceptible of being viewed as essentially similar manifestations of this same set of conditions. It has long been known, for example, that although the media are relatively ineffectual in conversion, they are quite effective in forming opinions and attitudes in regard to *new issues,* particularly as these issues are the more unrelated to "existing attitude clusters."[41] But it is precisely in reference to such issues that predispositions, selective exposure, and selective perception are least likely to exist, that group norms are least likely to pertain, that opinion leaders are least ready to lead—that the mediating forces of stasis, in short, are least likely to mediate. The intervening forces, in short, are likely to be inoperative, and the media are more likely to directly influence their audience.

Much the same explanation can be offered for the observed ability of the

[40] Kelley and Volkhart (1952), and Kelley (1955), both of which are summarized in Hovland, Janis, and Kelley (1953), Ch. 5. As noted above, the findings are highly indicative, but not absolutely clear cut.

[41] Berelson (1948), p. 176.

media to influence their audience on peripheral issues[42] while simultaneously failing in the major mission of the moment, and the same situation probably obtains in regard to media's ability to *communicate facts or even change opinions on objective matters without producing the attitude changes* that such facts and opinions are intended to engender.[43] It may well be that the facts and opinions are not related to the desired attitude change sufficiently strongly to call the protective mediating forces into play: the communication content is probably not recognized as necessarily relevant to the attitude, as not salient, and mediation does not occur. This interpretation, by the way, could very easily be tested.[44]

The inverse correlation between the capability of the media to wreak attitude change and the degree to which the attitude in question is ego-involved may well be another case in point.[45] But this paper cannot analyze and rehearse, nor has the author wholly explored, the entire range of phenomena which might be explained on the basis of the forces for stasis being inoperative. If the generalization is at all valid, it will gather such phenomena unto itself. Let it be the role of this paper to present it, to germinate as it will.

Changes through Mediators. Let us turn now to the second part of the proposition about the conditions under which media may serve as agents of opinion change. It has been suggested that such an effect is likely when either of two conditions obtain: when the forces for stasis are inoperative—as in the cases which have just been discussed—and, secondly, when the intervening forces themselves favor change.

Let us look again, for example, at the influence of group membership and of group norms. These typically mediate the influences of mass communication in favor of reinforcement, but under certain conditions they may abet communicational influences for change.

[42] E.g., McPhee (1953), pp. 12-13; also Hovland (1954).

[43] Hovland, Lumsdaine, and Sheffield (1949), pp. 42 ff. and elsewhere, *passim;* summarized in Klapper (1949), pp. IV-9-17.

[44] A rather simple controlled experiment might be set up, for example, in which two groups were exposed to communications, one of which merely presented the objective facts, and the other of which explicitly pointed out the implications for attitude change of accepting the objective facts. In line with the interpretation presented above, we would hypothesize that in the latter communication the *objective facts themselves* would be more likely to be rejected. Such an experiment would differ from the numerous studies of the relative efficacy of "implicit" vs. "explicit" conclusions, which have to date been primarily concerned with whether the *conclusions,* rather than the facts themselves, were more or less likely to be accepted.

[45] For what, after all, is an "ego-involved attitude," other than an attitude which is particularly salient to the person who holds it, and thus particularly well protected by predispositions, selective perception and the like? For an amusing statement of a similar view, see "John Crosby's Law," as quoted in Bogart (1956), p. 215. Suggestively relevant studies are numerous and include, e.g., Cooper and Jahoda (1947); Cooper and Dinerman (1951); Wilner (1951); Cannel and MacDonald (1956); and various others.

In an ingeniously designed experiment by McKeachie,[46] for example, communications regarding attitudes toward Negroes, and the discussion which these communications engendered, made some group members aware that they had misperceived the pertinent group norms. The great majority of such individuals showed opinion changes in the direction of the norm, which was also the direction intended by the communication. The *newly perceived norms* impelled the audience toward the communicationally recommended change.

A *switch in group loyalties or in reference groups* may likewise predispose an individual toward consonant opinion changes suggested by mass communication.[47] Studies of satellite defectors, for example, suggest that persons who have lived for years as respected members of Communist society, and then fall from grace, develop a new susceptibility to Western propaganda. As their lot deteriorates, they turn their eyes and minds to the west, and their radio dials to VOA and RFE. By the time they defect they have developed a set of extremely anti-Communist and pro-Western attitudes, quite out of keeping with their previous lives, but in accord with what they regard as normative to their new refugee primary group.[48]

Group norms, or predispositions otherwise engendered, may furthermore become dysfunctional; in learning theory terminology, the response they dictate may cease to be rewarding, or may even lead to punishment. In such situations the individual is impelled to find a new response which does provide reward, and communications recommending such a changed response are more likely to be accepted. Some such phenomenon seems to have occurred, for example, in the case of Nazi and North Korean soldiers who remained immune to American propaganda appeals while their military primary group survived, but became susceptible when the group disintegrated and adherence to its normative attitudes and conduct ceased to have survival value.[49] The accustomed group norms in such instances had not merely become inoperative; they had become positively dysfunctional and had sensitized and predisposed their adherents to changes suggested by the media.

Personality pattern appears to be another variable which may mediate the influence of communications, and particular syndromes seem to abet change. Janis, for example, found in a laboratory study that those of his subjects "who manifested social inadequacy, inhibition of aggression, and depressive tendencies, showed the greatest opinion change" in response to persuasive

[46] McKeachie (1954).

[47] E.g., Katz and Lazarsfeld (1955), pp. 66-81.

[48] The phenomenon has not been explicitly detailed, but is implicit in various studies performed for the United States Information Agency, and in Kracauer and Berkman (1956).

[49] E.g., Shils and Janowitz (1948); also Schramm (1954), pp. 17-18.

communication. They appeared, as Hovland puts it, to be "predisposed to be highly influenced."[50]

In sum, it appears that the generalization is supported by empirical data —that intervening variables which mediate the influence of mass communication, and which typically promote reinforcement, may also work for change. And again, the generalization, in turn, accounts for and orders the data on which it is based. Group membership, dysfunctional norms, and particular personality patterns can be viewed as filling similar roles in the process of communicationally stimulated opinion change. Other similarly operative variables will doubtless be identified by a continued phenomenistic approach, i.e., by the analysis of accomplished opinion changes.

The generalization furthermore serves, as did the others, to relate and explain various discrete findings and isolated bits of knowledge. It would appear to cover, for example, such hitherto unrelated phenomena as the susceptibility to persuasive appeals of persons whose primary group memberships place them under cross-pressures, and the effects of what Hovland has called "role playing."[51]

The first case—*the susceptibility to persuasive communications of persons whose primary group membership places them under cross-pressure*[52]—is fairly obvious. In terms of the generalization, such people can be said to be at the mercy of mediating factors which admit and assist communicational stimuli favoring both sides of the same issue. We may also observe that any attitude shift which such a person may make toward one side of the issue does not necessarily entail any reduction of the forceful mediation toward the other direction. On the basis of the generalization, we would therefore predict not only change, but inconstancy, which has in fact been found to be the case.[52a]

The effects of role playing seem another, if less obvious, example of opinion change occurring as a result of a mediating, or, in this case, a superimposed factor which in turn rendered a communication effective. Hovland reported that if persons opposed to a communication are forced to defend it, i.e., to act in a public situation as though they had accepted the recommended opinion, they become more likely actually to adopt it.[53] The crucial element of role playing is, of course, artificially superimposed. But in any case, the entire phenomenon might be viewed as something very akin to what occurs when an old norm, or an old predisposition, ceases to lead to reward. Successful role playing in fact invests the opposing response with reward. The

[50] Janis (1954), which is summarized in Hovland, Janis, and Kelley (1953), pp. 276 ff. (Quotes are from p. 277.)

[51] Hovland, Janis, and Kelley (1953), Ch. 7.

[52] E.g., Berelson, Lazarsfeld, and McPhee (1954); also Kriesberg (1954).

[52a] Lazarsfeld, Berelson, and Gaudet (1948), p. 70.

[53] Hovland, Janis, and Kelley (1953), Ch. 7.

communication is thus given an assist by the imposition of new factors which favor change. The potentialities of this technique, incidentally, are of course appalling. The Communists have already developed and refined it and we have christened the process "brain-washing."

Various other bits of knowledge about communication effect can be viewed as related manifestations of this same general phenomenon, i.e., the phenomenon of communications inducing attitude change through the assistance of mediating factors which themselves favor change. But it is the goal of this paper to be only suggestive, rather than exhaustive or exhausting, and thus generalization number three may be here left, to suggest whatever it will.

So much, then, for the first three generalizations, which attempt to relate the processes, the factors, and the directions of effect. It is hardly germane, at this juncture, to belabor generalizations four and five. They serve only to recognize residual categories. Thus number four merely points out that some persuasive or quasi-persuasive effects do appear, at least to our present state of knowledge, to be direct. The apparently unmotivated learning of sufficiently repeated facts or slogans is a case in point. And generalization number five merely points out that the persuasive efficacy of the media is known to be affected by numerous variables pertaining to the content, the medium itself, or the communication situation—by such matters, for example, as the number and order of topics, the degree of repetition, the likelihood of distraction, the objective possibilities of action, and the like. The proposed schemata suggests that these variables are of a different and residual order as compared with the kind of *mediating* variables which we have just been discussing.

We have thus far been laboring to make and document three points, viz., (1) the set of generalizations is supported by our knowledge of the effects of persuasive communications; (2) the generalizations organize, or bring into logical relation, or, if you will, "predict" in an *a posteriori* sense, a large portion of that knowledge; and (3) in so ordering the data they simultaneously suggest new and logically related avenues for further research.

It is proposed that the same set of generalizations is similarly applicable to other types of communication effect. To spell this out in detail is beyond the scope of a single paper.[54] It may be well for the sake of the argument, however, to at least suggest the applicability of the generalizations to one other area, the effects of mass communication upon levels of public taste.

[54] A forthcoming book by the present author, tentatively scheduled for publication in 1958, will attempt to indicate the degree to which the schemata is applicable to a much wider array of effects.

Reinforcement. It has been long known that the media do not seem to determine tastes, but rather to be used in accordance with tastes otherwise determined. The typical audience member selects from the media's varied fare those commodities which are in accord with his existing likes, and typically eschews exposure to other kinds of material. His existing likes, in turn, seem largely to derive from his primary, secondary, and reference groups, although they are not uncommonly affected by his special personality needs.[55] Whatever their origin, they intervene between the audience member and the vast array of media fare, and between the specific content and his interpretation of it.[56] The media stimuli are thoroughly sifted and molded, and they serve, typically, as grist for the existing mill. Put in a now familiar way, the effects of mass communication are mediated, and the media serve as contributing agents of reinforcement.

Changes. But the media are also associated with changes in taste. Oddly enough, little attention has been paid to the one change which occurs continually—the changing tastes of growing children. Wolf and Fiske seem to be the only researchers who explicitly noted that the pattern of development in children's comic book preferences precisely parallels the changing needs of their developing personalities,[57] as expressed, for example, in games. And no one, to the author's knowledge, has ever pointed out that the pattern of development in comic book and TV preferences also parallels the previously characteristic patterns of development in regular reading preferences. In short, the development and its integral changes in taste are culturally wholly catholic. In terms of our present set of generalizations, this is to say that such mediating variables as personality, cultural norms, and peer group interests impel the media to function as contributory agents of taste change.

The media have also been observed, although rarely, to play a role in elevating the tastes of adults. Suchman, for example, investigated the previous habits of some 700 persons who regularly listened to classical music broadcasts, and found that in the case of 53 per cent the radio had either "initiated" their interest in music or had "nursed" a mild but previously little exercised interest. But—and here is the essential point—the radio had functioned in almost all of these cases not as a necessary and sufficient cause, but as an "energizing agent" or implementer of tendencies otherwise engendered. The so-called initiates had been urged to listen by friends, or in some cases fiancés, whose tastes they respected and whose good opinion they sought, or by their

[55] E.g., Lazarsfeld (1940), pp. 21-47; Wiebe (1952), pp. 185 ff.; Macoby (1954); Johnstone and Katz (1957).

[56] For a curious demonstration of primary-type groups affecting *interpretation* of content, see Bogart (1955).

[57] Wolf and Fiske (1949).

own belief that a taste for classical music would increase their social prestige.[58] The mediating factors, in short, were at it again.

The literature on taste effects is relatively sparse, and seems to offer no illustration of changes which could be ascribed to the forces of stasis being inoperative. It might be conjectured that such effects occur among extreme isolates, but the possibility seems never to have been investigated.

In any case, our two generalizations which regard both reinforcement and change as essentially products of mediating factors account for virtually all of the hard data on the effect of mass communication on public taste. The generalizations furthermore suggest that the data are neither contradictory nor anomalous, but logically related. Stasis, reinforcement, developmental patterns, and individual change appear as different but understandable and predictable products of the same machines.

Residual Matters. There remains a certain residuum of related data and respectable conjecture for which the generalizations do not account. They do not explain why tastes in the development of which media has played a large role tend to have a sort of pseudo-character—why music lovers whose passions have been largely radio-nurtured, for example, appear to be peculiarly interested in the lives of composers and performers, and to lack real depth of musical understanding.[59] Nor do the generalizations cover the phenomenon of media *created* pseudo-interests, about which much speculation exists. McPhee has noted, for example, that the tremendous availability of newscasts seems to have created in some people an addiction, an ardent hunger which is sated by the five-minute newscast, despite its lack of detail and regardless of its irrelevance to the addict's life and interests. McPhee notes a similar passion for big-league baseball results, even among people who have never been in a ball park nor even seen a game on TV.[60] Meyersohn regards this sort of thing as an indication that media create their own common denominators of national taste.[61]

We know little about this phenomenon. Perhaps it is a direct effect, or perhaps it involves mediators as yet unspotted. In any case, deeper understanding seems likely to come from what we have called the phenomenistic approach—from an inquiry into the functions which such addiction serves

[58] Suchman (1941).

[59] E.g., Suchman (1941), pp. 178 f.; Lazarsfeld (1940), p. 255; Bogart (1949). The generalizations are *relevant* to this phenomenon, in that such extramedia forces as the urging of friends are necessary causes of the changed tastes. But there is nothing in the generalization to *account* for the stoppage. There is no reason to assume that extra-media forces which impel the media toward wreaking particular effects also limit the extent of the effect, and in reference to the Suchman data there is not even any reason to presume that people who urge others to listen to good music are themselves possessed of "pseudo-tastes."

[60] McPhee (1953). The comment in footnote 59 is equally applicable here.

[61] Meyersohn (1957), pp. 352-4.

for the addict, and into the role of the media in creating or serving the addiction.

APPLICATION TO OTHER FIELDS

We have now considered the extent to which the proposed generalizations are applicable to existing data regarding the effects of mass communication on opinions and attitudes, and upon levels of taste. It is proposed that they are equally applicable to questions about the effect of specific types of media fare, such as fantasy or depictions of crime and violence, on the psychological orientations and behavior of the audience. In the interests of brevity, these other areas of effect will not be discussed, except to note that the classic studies, both old and new, seem particularly suggestive. The old studies of soap opera listeners by Warner and Henry[62] and Herzog,[63] for example, and the more recent and differently focused work of the Rileys and of Maccoby,[64] all relate such variables as group orientation and personality needs to media use and media effects. They speak, implicitly and explicitly, of the *functions* served by media, and of the role of the media in effects of which they are not the sole cause.

SUMMATION AND CONCLUSIONS

It is time now to look quickly back over the ground we have covered, and to evaluate the set of generalizations which have been proposed—to inquire into what they have enabled us to do, and to note their weaknesses.

On the positive side, they appear to serve three major functions:

First, as this paper has been at some pains to demonstrate, the generalizations have permitted us in some measure to organize, or to account for, a considerable number of communications research findings which have previously seemed discrete, at times anomalous, and occasionally contradictory. The author submits, tentatively and with due humility, that the schemata has in fact made possible organization of several different orders:

. . . it has enabled us to relate the *processes* of effect and the *direction* of effect, and to account for the relative incidence of reinforcement and of change.

. . . it has provided a concept of the process of effect in which both reinforcement and change are seen as related and understandable outcomes of the same general dynamic.

. . . it has enabled us to view such diverse phenomena as audience predispositions, group membership and group norms, opinion leadership, personality patterns, and the nature of the media in this society, as serving similar functions in the process of effect—as being, if you will, all of a certain order, and distinct from such other factors as the characteristics of media content.

[62] Herzog (1944).
[63] Warner and Henry (1948).
[64] Riley and Riley (1951) and Maccoby (1954).

... it has enabled us to view such other unrelated phenomena as monopoly propaganda, new issues, and role-playing as manifestations of the same general process—as specific combinations of known variables, the outcomes of which were predictable.

So much for the organizational capabilities of the media. But note that this organization of existing data, even within so sketchy a framework as these generalizations provide, permitted us to see gaps—to discover, for example, that certain presumed outcomes have to date been neither documented nor shown not to occur. And thus the second contribution: the generalizations seem capable of indicating avenues of needed research, which are logically related to existing knowledge. Put another way, even this simple schemata seems capable of contributing to the cumulatibility of future research findings. This is in no way to gainsay that future thought and research must inevitably change the generalizations themselves. As presently formulated, they constitute only a single tentative step forward, and their refinement or emendation seems more likely to enlarge than to reduce the area of their applicability.

Finally, it is in the extent of this applicability, coupled with the foetal nature of the generalizations, that the author finds particular bases for hope. Sketchy and imperfect as they are, these propositions regarding the process and direction of effect seem applicable to the effects of persuasive communications, to the effects of mass communication on public taste, and, though it has not here been demonstrated, to the effects of specific media fare upon the psychological orientations and overt behavior patterns of the audience. Furthermore, the mediating variables to which they point—variables such as predisposition, group membership, personality patterns and the like—seem to play essentially similar roles in all these various kinds of effect. Even if these generalizations turn out to be wholly in error—and certainly they are imperfect—they seem nevertheless sufficiently useful and sufficiently applicable to justify the faith that *some* generalizations can in due time be made.

These particular generalizations, however, do not usher in the millenium. They are imperfect, and underdeveloped; they are inadequate in scope, and in some senses they are dangerous.

They do not, for example, cover the residuum of direct effects except to note that such effects exist. They are less easy to apply, and perhaps inapplicable, to certain other broad areas of effect, such as the effect of the existence of the media on patterns of daily life, on each other, and on cultural values as a whole. We have here spoken of cultural values as a mediating factor, which in part determines media content, but certainly some sort of circular relationship must exist, and media content must in turn affect cultural values.

Such concepts suggest what is perhaps the greatest danger inherent both in these generalizations and in the approach to communications research from which they derive. And that is the tendency to go overboard in blindly minimizing the effects and potentialities of mass communication. In reaping the fruits of the discovery that mass media function amid a nexus of other influences, we must not forget that the influences nevertheless differ. Mass media of communication possess various characteristics and capabilities distinct from those of peer groups or opinion leaders. They are, after all, media of *mass* communication, which daily address tremendous cross-sections of the population with a single voice. It is neither sociologically unimportant nor insignificant that the media have rendered it possible, as Wiebe has put it, for Americans from all social strata to laugh at the same joke,[65] nor is it insignificant that total strangers, upon first meeting, may share valid social expectations that small talk about Betty Furness or Elvis Presley will be mutually comprehensible. We must not lose sight of the peculiar characteristics of the media, nor of the likelihood that of this peculiar character there may be engendered peculiar effects.

In any case, the most fruitful path for the future seems clear enough. It is not the path of abstract theorizing, nor is it the path, which so many of us have deserted, of seeking simple and direct effects of which media are the sole and sufficient cause. It appears rather to be the path of the phenomenistic approach, which seeks to account for the known occurrence and to assess the roles of the several influences which produced it, and which attempts to see the respondents not as randomly selected individuals each exchangeable for the other, but rather as persons functioning within particular social contexts. It is likewise the path of the cumulating controlled experiments in which the multifarious extra-media factors being investigated are built into the research design. These are the paths which have brought us to what seems the verge of generalization and empirically documented theory. They are the paths which have brought us to the brink of hope.

[65] Wiebe (1952).

BIBLIOGRAPHY

Note: Groups of works by the same author(s) are arranged *in order of their publication dates, not alphabetically by title.*

1. Bernard Berelson (1948), "Communications and Public Opinion," in Schramm (1948).
2. Bernard R. Berelson, Paul F. Lazarsfeld, and William N. McPhee (1954), *Voting: A Study of Opinion Formation During A Presidential Campaign*, Chicago, University of Chicago Press, 1954.
3. Leo Bogart (1949), "Fan Mail for the Philharmonic," *Public Opinion Quarterly*, 13, 3 (Fall, 1949), pp. 423-434.
4. Leo Bogart (1955), "Adult Talk About Newspaper Comics," *American Journal of Sociology*, 61, 1 (July, 1955), pp. 26-30.

5. Leo Bogart (1956), *The Age of Television,* New York: Frederick Ungar Publishing Co., 1956.

6. Charles F. Cannel and James MacDonald (1956), "The Impact of Health News on Attitudes and Behavior," *Journalism Quarterly,* 1956 (Summer), pp. 315-23.

7. Eunice Cooper and Marie Jahoda (1947), "The Evasion of Propaganda," *Journal of Psychology,* 23 (1947), pp. 15-25.

8. Eunice Cooper and Helen Dinerman (1951), "Analysis of the Film 'Don't Be A Sucker': A Study in Communication," *Public Opinion Quarterly,* 15, 2 (Summer, 1951).

9. Joseph B. Ford (1954), "The Primary Group in Mass Communication," *Sociology and Social Research,* 38, 3 (Jan.-Feb., 1954), pp. 152-8.

10. Howard E. Freeman, H. Ashley Weeks, and Walter I. Wertheimer (1955), "News Commentator Effect: A Study in Knowledge and Opinion Change," *Public Opinion Quarterly,* 19, 2 (Summer, 1955), pp. 209-215.

11. Eliot Friedson (1953), "The Relation of the Social Situation of Contact to the Media of Mass Communication," *Public Opinion Quarterly,* 17, 2 (Summer, 1953), pp. 230-238.

12. Theodore Geiger (1950), "A Radio Test of Musical Taste," *Public Opinion Quarterly,* 14, 3 (Fall, 1950), pp. 453-60.

13. Herta Herzog (1944), "What Do We Really Know About Daytime Serial Listeners," in Lazarsfeld and Stanton (1944).

14. Carl I. Hovland (1954), "Effects of the Mass Media of Communication," in Lindzey, Gardiner, *Handbook of Social Psychology,* Cambridge, Mass.: Addison-Wesley Publishing Co., 1954, Vol. II.

15. Carl I. Hovland, Irving L. Janis, and Harold H. Kelley (1953), *Communication and Persuasion,* New Haven: Yale University Press, 1953.

16. Carl I. Hovland, Arthur A. Lumsdaine, and Fred D. Sheffield (1949), *Experiments in Mass Communications* (Studies in Social Psychology in World War II, Vol. III), Princeton, N. J.: Princeton University Press, 1949.

17. I. L. Janis (1954), "Personality Correlates of Susceptibility to Persuasion," *Journal of Personality,* 22 (1954), pp. 504-518.

18. I. L. Janis and B. T. King (195-), "The Influence of Role Playing on Opinion Change," *Journal of Abnormal and Social Psychology,* 49 (1954), pp. 211-218.

19. John Johnstone and Elihu Katz (1957), "Youth and Popular Music," *American Journal of Sociology,* 62, 6 (May, 1957).

20. Elihu Katz and Paul F. Lazarsfeld (1955), *Personal Influence: The Part Played by People in the Flow of Mass Communications,* Glencoe, Ill.: The Free Press, 1955.

21. Elihu Katz (1957), "The Two-Step Flow of Communication: An Up-to-Date Report on an Hypothesis," *Public Opinion Quarterly,* 21, 1 (Spring, 1957), pp. 61-78.

22. Herbert C. Kelman, (1953), "Attitude Change as a Function of Response Restriction," *Human Relations,* 6, 3 (1953), pp. 185-214.

23. H. H. Kelley (195-), "Salience of Membership and Resistance to Change of Group Anchored Attitudes," *Human Relations,* 8 (1958), pp. 275-289.

24. H. H. Kelley and E. H. Volkhart (1952), "The Resistance to Change of Group-Anchored Attitudes," *American Sociological Review,* 17, (1952), pp. 453-465.

25. B. T. King and I. L. Janis (1953), as reported in Hovland, Janis and Kelley (1953), pp. 222-228.

26. Joseph T. Klapper (1948), "Mass Media and the Engineering of Consent," *The American Scholar*, 17, 4 (Autumn, 1948), pp. 419-429.

27. Joseph T. Klapper (1949), *The Effects of Mass Media*, New York: Bureau of Applied Social Research, Columbia University, 1949.

28. Siegfried Kracauer and Paul L. Berkman (1956), *Satellite Mentality*, New York: Frederick A. Praeger, Inc., 1956.

29. Martin Kriesberg (1949), "Cross-Pressures and Attitudes: A Study of the Influence of Conflicting Propaganda on Opinions Regarding American Soviet Relations," *Public Opinion Quarterly*, 13, 1 (Spring, 1949) pp. 5-16.

30. Paul F. Lazarsfeld (1940), *Radio and the Printed Page*, New York: Duell, Sloan and Pearce, 1940.

31. Paul F. Lazarsfeld, Bernard Berelson, and Hazel Gaudet (1948), *The People's Choice*, New York: Columbia University Press, 1948.

32. Paul F. Lazarsfeld and Robert K. Merton (1949), "Mass Communication, Popular Taste and Organized Social Action," in Schramm (1949), Q.V.

33. Paul F. Lazarsfeld and Frank N. Stanton (1941), *Radio Research, 1941*, New York: Duell, Sloan and Pearce, 1941.

34. Paul F. Lazarsfeld and Frank N. Stanton (1944), *Radio Research, 1942-3*, New York: Duell, Sloan and Pearce, 1944.

35. Paul F. Lazarsfeld and Frank N. Stanton (1949), *Communications Research, 1948-1949*, New York: Harper & Brothers, 1949.

36. Eleanor E. Maccoby (1954), "Why Do Children Watch Television?" *Public Opinion Quarterly*, 18, 3 (Fall, 1954), pp. 239-244.

37. Wilbert J. McKeachie (1954), "Individual Conformity to Attitudes of Classroom Groups," *Journal of Abnormal and Social Psychology*, 49, (1954), pp. 282-9.

38. William N. McPhee (1953), *New Strategies for Research in the Mass Media*. New York: Bureau of Applied Social Research, Columbia University, 1953.

39. Robert K. Merton (1946), *Mass Persuasion*, New York: Harper and Brothers, 1946.

40. Rolf B. Meyersohn (1957), "Social Research in Television," in Rosenberg and White (1957).

41. Donald M. Michael and Nathan Maccoby (1953), "Factors Influencing Verbal Learning under Varying Conditions of Audience Participation," *Journal of Experimental Psychology*, 46 (1953), pp. 411-418.

42. Matilda W. Riley and John W. Riley, Jr. (1951), "A Sociological Approach to Communications Research," *Public Opinion Quarterly*, 15, 3 (Fall, 1951), pp. 444-460.

43. Bernard Rosenberg and David Manning White (1957), *Mass Culture: The Popular Arts in America*, Glencoe, Ill.: The Free Press, 1957.

44. Wilbur Schramm (1948), *Communications in Modern Society*, Urbana, Ill.: U. of Illinois Press, 1948.

45. Wilbur Schramm (1949), *Mass Communications*, Urbana, Ill.: U. of Illinois Press, 1949.

46. Wilbur Schramm (1954), "How Communication Works," in his *The Process and Effects of Mass Communication*, Urbana, Ill.: U. of Illinois Press, 1954.

47. Edward Suchman (1941), "Invitation to Music," in Lazarsfeld and Stanton (1941).

48. Edward A. Shils and Morris Janowitz (1948), "Cohesion and Disintegration in the Wehrmacht in World War II," *Public Opinion Quarterly*, 12, 2 (Summer, 1948), pp. 280-315.

49. W. Lloyd Warner and William E. Henry (1948), *The Radio Day Time Serial: A Symbolic Analysis*, Genetic Psychology Monographs, 37 (1948).

50. Gerhart D. Wiebe (1951-2), "Merchandizing Commodities and Citizenship on Television," *Public Opinion Quarterly,* 15, 4 (Winter, 1951-2), pp. 679-691.
51. Gerhart D. Wiebe (1952), "Mass Communications" in Hartley, Eugene L. and Ruth E. Hartley, *Fundamentals of Social Psychology,* New York: Alfred E. Knopf, 1952.
52. Daniel M. Wilner (1951), *Attitude as a Determinant of Perception in the Mass Media of Communication: Reactions to the Motion Picture "Home of the Brave,"* Unpublished doctoral dissertation, U. of California, Los Angeles, 1951.
53. Katherine Wolf and Marjorie Fiske (1949), "The Children Talk About Comics," in Lazarsfeld and Stanton (1949).

QUANTITATIVE STUDIES conducted in recent years, many of them laboratory experiments, have made it possible to formulate an impressive number of propositions about the effects of communication. Progress has also been made in collecting and systematizing these propositions, and in putting them to work in education, public relations, advertising, and other fields.[1] The qualitative literature on the effects of communication has been less well explored. Much of it still lies unrecognized in historical treatises, biographies, and the writings of reporters in all eras. Attempts to systematize or derive propositions from the relatively small segment of qualitative experience that has been sifted have been made largely in the literature of rhetoric, political communication, and psychological warfare.[2]

[1] One of the most comprehensive summaries is the chapter by Carl I. Hovland, "Effects of the Mass Media of Communication," in Gardner Lindzey, editor, *Handbook of Social Psychology*, Cambridge, Mass., Addison-Wesley, 1954. Literature summarizing a greater or lesser portion of what is known about the effects of communication and applying this knowledge to a variety of problem areas is now so voluminous that only a few examples can be given: Erik Barnoiw, *Mass Communications*, New York, Rinehart, 1956; W. L. Brembeck and W. S. Howell, *Persuasion—A Means of Social Control*, Englewood Cliffs, N.J., Prentice-Hall, 1952; Rex F. Harlow, *Social Science in Public Relations*, New York, Harper, 1957; *Mass Communication and Education*, National Education Association, Educational Policies Commission, 1958.

[2] Aristotle's *Rhetoric* is still a widely used text in courses on public opinion and communication. A brief summary of experience in psychological warfare is presented by John W. Riley, Jr., and Leonard S. Cottrell, Jr., in "Research for Psychological Warfare," *Public Opinion Quarterly*, Vol. 21, 1957, pp. 147-158. The principal anthologies on political communication and psychological warfare also include collections of qualitative as well as quantitative data on effect: William E. Daugherty and Morris Janowitz, *A Psychological Warfare Casebook*, Baltimore, Johns Hopkins Press, 1958; Daniel

Originally published in Volume 23, Number 3, 1959 of the *Public Opinion Quarterly*.

While knowledge about communication effects has increased steadily, although unevenly, many of the insights gained have tended to remain discrete. It has proved difficult to relate propositions to each other, and to the larger body of knowledge about human behavior. Some of the effects produced by communication have been identified and found to be associated with certain characteristics of the audiences being studied, but it has less often been possible to specify why these relationships rather than other ones have existed. Nevertheless, several major steps in the direction of linking the accumulated knowledge about communication effects more closely to social and psychological theory have been taken recently by Festinger; Hovland, Janis, and Kelley; Katz and Lazarsfeld; and others.[3] The most comprehensive proposal for a theoretical structure—at least in the case of mass communication—has been made by Klapper, who accounts for many of the observed variations in response to identical communication stimuli by the role played by certain mediating factors, such as audience predispositions, group affiliation, and opinion leadership.[4]

The purpose of this article is to suggest another method of interpreting the existing body of knowledge about the effects of communication. According to this mode of interpretation, communications serve as a link between man and his environment, and their effects may be explained in terms of the role they play in enabling people to bring about more satisfying relationships between themselves and the world around them.

In order to introduce this approach to the study of communication effects it will be necessary to restate briefly some familiar, even though not uncontroversial, assumptions about the needs of man and the ways these needs are satisfied.

BEHAVIORAL "EFFECTS" AND THEIR CAUSES

Our first assumption is that all human actions and reactions, including changes in attitude and knowledge, are in some way directed toward the satisfaction of wants or needs. That is, whatever we do is in response to some conscious or subconscious requirement or purpose. This is not to say that the action in question is always the most appropriate one, or that actions taken to satisfy one need may not work against the satisfaction of another. Nevertheless, it can be maintained that all actions can be traced to needs,

Lerner, *Propaganda in War and Crisis*, New York, Stewart, 1951; Wilbur Schramm, *The Process and Effects of Mass Communication*, Urbana, Ill., University of Illinois Press, 1954.

[3] Leon Festinger, *A Theory of Cognitive Dissonance*, Evanston, Ill., Row, Peterson, 1957; Carl I. Hovland, Irving L. Janis, and Harold H. Kelley, *Communications and Persuasion: Psychological Studies of Opinion Change*, New Haven, Yale University Press, 1953; Elihu Katz and Paul F. Lazarsfeld, *Personal Influence: The Part Played by People in the Flow of Mass Communication*, Glencoe, Ill., Free Press, 1955.

[4] Joseph T. Klapper, "What We Know about the Effects of Mass Communication: The Brink of Hope," *Public Opinion Quarterly*, Vol. 21, 1957, pp. 453-474.

that these in turn can be related to more generalized needs, and so on.[5]

There have been many attempts to draw up lists of basic human needs and wants. The physical requirements for human existence—food, clothing, and shelter—are fairly well agreed upon. Lists of other desiderata that people pursue vary widely in their degree of generality and in their terminology, but there is a heavy degree of overlapping when it comes to values such as power, security, love, and respect. Cooley, for instance, captured in a few words several of the most widespread forces motivating human action when he wrote: "Always and everywhere men seek honor and dread ridicule, defer to public opinion, cherish their goods and their children, and admire courage, generosity, and success."[6] Lasswell lists eight goals which he finds pursued in nearly all cultures, although some are emphasized more in one culture than in another: power, respect, affection, rectitude, well-being, wealth, enlightenment, and skill.[7] Festinger suggests that the existence of inharmonious attitudes or conflicting elements of knowledge within an individual (a state that he labels "dissonance") produces a striving for consistency on the part of that individual, and that dissonance is thus a motivating factor in its own right.[8] A large number of lists and observations concerning human wants and needs could be cited. Indeed, consideration of the forces motivating human action and (to view the other side of the coin) the qualities that people pursue has always been one of the most persistent interests of those who have studied man's behavior. These forces and qualities vary from individual to individual and from culture to culture, but nearly all students agree that they can be identified—at least on a descriptive level—and that they are useful in explaining human actions.

Our second basic assumption is that man's wants and needs are dependent for their satisfaction on his environment. Some requirements can be satisfied from within the individual in the first instance—for example, some tensions can be relieved by yawning or stretching—but our self-sufficiency is exhausted when we must satisfy the more fundamental desires of which these tensions are an expression. Most of our needs or wants can be satisfied only if we are able to manipulate parts of the world outside ourselves, or to adjust in some

[5] The definition of needs or motives can, of course, easily be reduced to absurdity if one attempts to achieve extremes either of generality or of specificity. At one extreme, all actions can be explained as efforts to relieve some type of tension, or as ultimately traceable to one single "drive"; at the other extreme, the explanation refers only to the immediate object of the action: e.g. the reason I buy a magazine is because I want a magazine. Intermediate levels of description, at which categories of specific actions can be related to more generalized needs, seem to be the most fruitful for purposes of social inquiry. (Cf., Gardner Murphy, "Social Motivation," in Lindzey, op.cit., p. 608.)

[6] Charles Horton Cooley, Social Organization, Glencoe, Ill., Free Press, reprinted 1956, p. 28.

[7] Harold D. Lasswell, Power and Personality, New York, Norton, 1948; also Lasswell and Abraham Kaplan, Power and Society, New Haven, Yale University Press, 1950, especially pp. 55-58.

[8] Op.cit.

way to this environment. In the case of requirements for food or clothing the sources of satisfaction are in our physical environment; needs for affection, esteem, or even self-respect, can ordinarily be satisfied only by other people. Our desires for some other goals, such as security and power, can be met in part from our material and in part from our social surroundings. Actions thus occur when we attempt to satisfy needs by manipulating or adjusting to certain aspects of the environment.[9]

Just as it is possible to subdivide needs or motives almost infinitely, if one should wish to engage in this exercise, the content of the environment could be arranged and rearranged in an impressive number of categories. For our purposes, however, it may be most useful to mention four aspects of the environment, as it is experienced by human beings: the physical, the social, the expected, and the imagined. Some may object that the latter two categories are of a different order from the first two (and overlap the first two because expectations and imagery include content from the real environment). This objection can be conceded or it can be disputed; a decision either way makes no difference to the argument that follows.

Different kinds of people depend on each of these different aspects of the environment for the satisfaction of their needs to varying degrees. The farmer's requirements are filled to a larger degree from the physical realm than, say, those of the entertainer, who is as dependent for success on the approval of other people as the farmer is on the weather. The young student may live largely in the world of the future, the mystic in the realm of the supernatural. To some degree, all of us orient our activities toward environmental circumstances in all four categories.

The trend of recent research has been to stress increasingly the importance of the social environment for most people. Satisfaction of physical needs often turns out to be largely a means to the end of achieving a relationship with the social environment that will satisfy other needs. From Veblen to the motivation researchers, students have emphasized that in the process of obtaining food, clothing, and air-conditioned shelter we usually are attempting to bolster our status in the community or elicit approval from the neighbors, or are in some other way orienting our actions toward the social environment. The willingness of human beings to bind their feet, wear corsets, or observe stringent diets, where norms or customs provide that such behavior will be socially rewarded, seems once again to underline the importance of adjustment to the social environment at the expense of the physical.

[9] Kornhauser and Lazarsfeld observe, in another context, that any action is determined on the one hand by the total make-up of the individual and on the other by the total situation in which he finds himself. Explanations must refer both to the objective and the subjective. (Arthur Kornhauser and Paul F. Lazarsfeld, "The Analysis of Consumer Actions," in Paul F. Lazarsfeld and Morris Rosenberg, *The Language of Social Research*, Glencoe, Ill., Free Press, 1955, p. 393.)

Our third assumption is that human attention is highly selective.[10] From birth, people learn that satisfaction of their needs is dependent more on certain aspects of their environment than on other aspects. They therefore focus their attention on these aspects. As wants and needs become more complicated the important aspects of the environment become more numerous, but in view of the almost infinite complexity of the world the selective principle remains and becomes even more rigid. We don't often examine the pattern on the wallpaper, listen to the ticking of the clock, or notice what color socks one of our colleagues is wearing, because we don't need this information.[11]

In view of the importance of the social environment for the satisfaction of most people's needs, we would expect that this would occupy a heavy share of their attention and be involved in a large proportion of their actions. This seems to be the case, although reliable information about the quantitative division of attention is difficult to obtain. Nevertheless, indirect evidence is afforded by such indices as the prominence of the social environment in informal conversations and in the content of people's worries and problems.[12]

ATTITUDES AS GUIDES TO ACTION

A fourth assumption is that people gradually accumulate and carry around with them a substantial quantity of information about those aspects of the environment that are important to them. This information, in the form of habits, stereotypes, attitudes, maxims, generalizations, and facts, has been accumulated in the course of their experience. In the past it has helped them to satisfy some of their needs, or they may think that it will be useful in the future. With the aid of these stored impressions people are able to decide easily and quickly what actions are appropriate in most of the situations in which they find themselves.[13]

The existence of the various aspects of this internal picture of the world has often been noted. Habits take us up and down stairs in our own houses,

[10] William James refers to this "narrowness of consciousness" as one of the most extraordinary facts of our life. "Although we are besieged at every moment by impressions from our whole sensory surface, we notice so very small a part of them." *Psychology—Briefer Course*, New York, Holt, 1892.

[11] A familiar classroom illustration of the selectivity of perception is for the instructor, half-way through the period, to cover his necktie with a large handkerchief and then ask the students what color the tie is. Ordinarily, fewer than half the students will be able to name the color correctly. This is, of course, as it should be, since there is usually no reason why they should pay attention to the color.

[12] *Cf.* Samuel A. Stouffer, *Communism, Conformity, and Civil Liberties*, New York, Doubleday, 1955, especially pp. 58-71; also Jeanne Watson, Warren Breed, and Harry Posman, "A Study in Urban Conversation: Sample of 1001 Remarks Overheard in Manhattan," *Journal of Social Psychology*, Vol. 28, 1948, pp. 121-133.

[13] *Cf.* Hadley Cantril, *The "Why" of Man's Experience*, New York, Macmillan, 1950, pp. 66 and 77.

guide us to our offices in the morning, and do much of the work of driving our cars, leaving our consciousness free for other things. Stereotypes, as Walter Lippmann has pointed out, are also useful in reducing the burden on our capacities of perception: "For the attempt to see all things freshly and in detail, rather than as types and generalities, is exhausting. . . ."[14] Lippmann refers to these images as "pictures in our heads." Cantril mentions the "assumptive form world" that we build up on the basis of past experience. Festinger sees the body of our attitudes and beliefs as constituting a fairly accurate mirror or map of reality.[15]

An attitude is particularly important as a labor-saving device, since it usually provides some key to the behavior that is appropriate when we encounter the subject of the attitude or when it comes up in conversation.[16] If we regard another person as "a good man" or "a bad man" this gives us some crude but useful guidance as to how we should act toward him. Likes and dislikes regarding food provide an even more obvious guide to behavior. Very frequently, attitudes have little relevance to action toward the object of the attitude itself, but instead provide a key to the proper behavior in a given social group. Thus people may be for or against a given foreign country (or baseball team) because this is the attitude one should display in the group in which they move, although they have little idea of what the country (or team) in question is actually like.

When attitudes, stereotypes, and the other forms of information that we have internalized are based on little experience and serve a minor need they tend to be lightly held and easily changed. When they are based on extensive experience and/or serve a deeply felt need, it is difficult to affect them. But if a person's needs change, or if his environment is altered, then he usually has to abandon at least some of his stored-up information, since this leads him to follow lines of action that are inefficient in gaining for him a satisfactory adjustment to his environment.[17]

[14] Walter Lippmann, *Public Opinion*, Baltimore, Penguin, 1946, p. 66.

[15] Cantril, *op.cit.*, pp. 103-104; Festinger, *op.cit.*, p. 10. An application of Cantril's approach in a study of policy makers in seven countries has been made recently by Lloyd A. Free, *Six Allies and a Neutral*, Glencoe, Ill., Free Press, 1959.

[16] M. Brewster Smith, in connection with an intensive study of opinions toward Soviet Russia, found one function of attitude to be that of providing a person with an evaluation of the salient aspects of his world. "The greater the extent to which this evaluation takes account of the important harms and benefits that he may expect from his surroundings, the more adequately will it serve his adjustment in the longest run." (*Functional and Descriptive Analysis of Public Opinion*, Harvard University, 1947, pp. 34ff.) Unpublished doctoral dissertation.

[17] In his autobiography, Benjamin Franklin reports that at one time he was a vegetarian and considered the taking of fish a kind of unprovoked murder. On a voyage from Boston to Philadelphia, however, his ship became becalmed off Block Island and the crew diverted themselves by catching cod. When the fish came out of the frying pan, they smelled "admirably well." "I balanced some time between principle and inclination till I recollected that when the fish were opened, I saw smaller fish

Changing one's attitudes, stereotypes, and so on, is additionally complicated by the necessity of maintaining as much consistency as possible within this body of internalized information. If two stored-up cognitions indicate two inconsistent courses of action the resulting conflict may be painful. A not excessively painful conflict can be observed in the case of the man in the coffee advertisement, who snaps: "I love coffee, but it keeps me awake." He "snaps" because of the discomfort caused by the inconsistency between his attitude and his experience. Fortunately, his problem can be solved by drinking caffeine-free coffee. The position of the man who is persuaded of the virtues of Presidential Candidate A, while his family and friends continue to admire Candidate B, is likely to be more difficult. One set of attitudes leads him to support his candidate in conversations; another set impels him either to recognize that Candidate B has some virtues or to remain silent. Recent voting studies have found that persons subject to these "cross-pressures" are most likely to shift their opinions during a campaign.[18] Changing one important attitude, stereotype, or piece of information may necessitate an exhausting process of adjustment in other cognitions and even patterns of action. Most people would like to avoid this and therefore make important changes only when forced to do so.[19]

COMMUNICATION AS A LINK TO THE ENVIRONMENT

Habits, attitudes, and an accumulated stock of knowledge about those aspects of the environment that concern us most go a long way toward shaping our actions, but this stored-up information must be supplemented by a flow of current data about the world around us. The more complicated our needs and the more shifting the environment, the greater our requirements for current information become.

We need this current information for several different reasons. Some of it tells us about changes in the physical or social environment that may require an immediate adjustment in our behavior (a colleague is annoyed; our house is on fire). Other incoming information is stored in one form or another as of possible utility in the expected environment (Main Street is going to be turned into a four-lane highway; a vacation always costs more than you expect). It is probable, however, that a large proportion of our current informational intake primarily serves the purpose of reassuring us that our existing action patterns, attitudes, stereotypes, and so on, are indeed correct—i.e. that they are likely to satisfy our wants and needs.

---

taken out of their stomachs. 'Then,' thought I, 'if you eat one another, I don't see why we mayn't eat you.' So I dined upon cod very heartily. . . ."

[18] Bernard Berelson, Paul F. Lazarsfeld, and William M. McPhee, *Voting*, Chicago, University of Chicago Press, 1954.

[19] *Cf.* Smith, *op.cit.*: "Since his attitudes are inextricably involved in his psychological economy, . . . [a person] cannot alter them without at the same time carrying out more or less complicated readjustments" (pp. 37-38).

Most of this information can be acquired by direct observation or personal conversation. The immediate physical surroundings are subject to our scrutiny. In the family, in the neighborhood, and on the job we learn about the most important things by observing, by talking to people, or by overhearing others talk among themselves. But there is still some important information that cannot be acquired at first hand. If a person enters employment in any skilled capacity, if he takes his citizenship seriously, or if he seeks to broaden his knowledge in almost any sphere, he tends to pay at least some attention to the media of mass communication. This attention to the mass media does not necessarily diminish his participation in personal conversation; on the contrary, it may give him more to talk about.[20]

Our attention to the mass media, as to other aspects of the world around us, is highly selective. We scan the newspaper headlines and select a few stories to sample further or even to read in full. We can expose ourselves to only a very small proportion of the available radio fare, and when it comes to magazines and books our attention must be selective in the extreme.

All the information that we are exposed to through personal experience or the mass media can be divided into three categories according to our behavior toward it: some we seek out eagerly; some we attend to on the chance that it may prove useful; some we attempt to exclude because we have reason to believe that it would make satisfaction of our wants and needs more difficult.[21]

In this formidable task of sorting incoming information we are assisted by habits and attitudes, many of them culturally defined, just as habits and attitudes assist us in other aspects of our behavior. On the basis of past experience (either our own or that of others that has been handed on to us) we believe that useful facts are most likely to come from a particular person or group, or are to be found in a given newspaper, in certain radio programs, or in other specified information sources. Conversely, we know, or sense, that there are some sources of information that are likely to make

---

[20] At least, this is the case with opinion leaders in many fields, who typically belong to more organizations, have more social contacts, and in general are more gregarious than others. They also are likely to follow the mass media appropriate to their sphere of interest. Cf. Elihu Katz, "The Two-step Flow of Communication," *Public Opinion Quarterly*, Vol. 21, 1957, pp. 61-78.

[21] Principal mechanisms of exclusion appear to be nonperception (the small boy simply doesn't hear his mother tell him to keep his hands out of the cookie jar); distortion (we note that crime in our town is due mainly to visitors from outside); and, most commonly, forgetting (many people have trouble remembering how little money is left in their checking accounts). All these exclusion mechanisms have been described in connection with systematic studies: e.g. Frederic C. Bartlett, *Remembering*, New York, Cambridge University Press, 1932; Gordon W. Allport and Leo J. Postman, *The Psychology of Rumor*, New York, Holt, 1947; Eunice Cooper and Marie Jahoda, "The Evasion of Propaganda," *Journal of Psychology*, Vol. 23, 1947, pp. 15-25. Distortion is, however, not only a mechanism for excluding information. It can also be used to make some information more useful or more comprehensible.

it more difficult for us to satisfy our requirements, and we make strenuous efforts to avoid exposure to these. Students have often noted the tendency of the listener to turn off his radio when a speaker of a political party he opposes comes on the air.

A related category of devices that help us select for attention those communications that are likely to contain useful information might be called "indicators." We learn that (at least in some newspapers) the more important news is likely to be given larger headlines than the less important news. Certain tones of voice indicate urgency; others indicate sincerity. Some colors and symbols signify danger. These and many other indicators help us to give our attention to communications that are likely to be important to us, although we not infrequently find that a widely accepted indicator has been used by someone who wants to direct our attention to a message of very little importance to us.

By these and other sorting processes, we try to obtain useful information from the stream of communications. For most of us, information about our personal social environment, or information that we can use in this social environment, is important, and we give particular attention to learning about anything that may affect our relationship to those with whom we live and work. Most of us are particularly interested in knowing what other people think about us and what they think about each other. We also like to have information about those aspects of the physical environment that affect our needs, or are likely to affect them, and information that may be professionally useful, but for most of us these categories, although important, are in the second rank.

In connection with the relative attention given "personally useful" as opposed to "professionally useful" information, a small experiment conducted by the author may prove suggestive. Forty-nine government officials concerned with foreign affairs, most of them with about fifteen years' experience in this area of activity, were exposed for twenty seconds to a poster showing ten greatly enlarged newspaper headlines, and were asked to read these headlines over to themselves. No reason for the request was given. Immediately afterward, they were asked to write down as many of the headlines, or approximations of the headlines, as they could remember.[22]

The original hypothesis behind this experiment was that the officials would be most likely to remember those headlines that referred to matters with which they had been professionally concerned. This was not the case. The headline that was remembered most often was a dramatic one of a type that would be likely to provide conversational material. The next two apparently had to do with personal interests of many of the respondents.

[22] The forty-nine responses were obtained from several smaller groups. This made it possible to vary the order in which the headlines were presented. With minor exceptions, the rank order of the headlines in each subgroup remained the same.

Next came matters of professional interest, and at the bottom came matters that apparently were of little personal or professional interest to most of the men. These results are shown in Table 1.

TABLE 1

FREQUENCY WITH WHICH HEADLINES WERE RECALLED BY
FORTY-NINE OFFICIALS CONCERNED WITH FOREIGN AFFAIRS

	Number of Mentions
Fallen Jet Is Hit by Train on Coast	29
LSU Rated No. 1 in Football Polls	28
Stock Offerings Rose Last Month	25
UN to Withdraw Group in Lebanon	23
Tunisia Will Buy Arms from Reds	16
Easing of Tension over Berlin Seen	13
Soviet Asks Curb on Atomic Planes	7
Railroads Yield on Tax in Jersey	7
Transport Unity Urged as U.S. Need	7
West Tries to End Nuclear Impasse	5
	160

To summarize our thesis thus far, it may be said that communications provide a link between the individual and the world outside himself. But they do not link him with all aspects of his environment; this would be impossible in view of the limited capacity of the single human being for attention and action. Instead, each person must somehow select for attention those communications that deal with aspects of the environment that are most likely to affect his needs.[23] In this selection process he is aided by habits and attitudes, as well as by his ability to choose consciously. If it were possible to judge objectively whether a person's selection of environmental aspects about which to inform himself was "good" or "bad" from the point of view of satisfying his basic needs, it would probably be concluded that most people choose fairly well but that there is always room for improvement.

The fact that we tend to perceive and remember things that are important

[23] The same communications may be used in various ways to satisfy different needs. On the basis of a study of children's attention to comics and TV programs, the Rileys observed that "the same media materials appeared to be interpreted and used differently by children in different social positions." The principle of selectivity was also illustrated by this study. Peer group members, for example, appeared to select materials from the media which would in some way be immediately useful for group living. (Matilda White Riley and John W. Riley, Jr., "A Sociological Approach to Communications Research," *Public Opinion Quarterly*, Vol. 15, 1951, p. 456.) Similar observations were made by Merton in his study of Kate Smith's marathon drive to sell war bonds by radio. Listeners who perceived the same aspects of the broadcast sometimes "used" this information in different ways. In other cases people's attention to different aspects of the performance could be related to their psychological requirements. (Robert K. Merton, *Mass Persuasion*, New York, Harper, 1946.)

to us is neither startling nor novel. It underlies many psychological tests and its implications have been taken into account by social workers, students of public opinion interviewing, and psychotherapists. It is also taken into account, although not always consciously formulated, by practical politicians, teachers, and many others.[24] The reason for going over this familiar ground here is that, in the opinion of the author, it provides a useful link in the chain of relationships between communication and action.

COMMUNICATIONS AND BEHAVIOR

It has been maintained above that the explanation of most human actions, at least those of interest to the social scientist, should be sought in people's efforts to establish a relationship with their environment that is likely to satisfy their needs. According to this way of thinking, a communication cannot properly be said to produce behavioral effects itself, since it merely serves to link the individual to some aspect of his environment, thus enabling him to react to it or manipulate it.

One might express the environment-communication-action relationship in its simplest terms as follows: a given situation exists in the environment; this situation is reported by a communication that comes to the attention of the individual; the individual then adjusts his behavior in a manner calculated to help satisfy some want or need. Or, to translate this formula into experiential terms, we come into our house alone on a dark night; we hear a voice growl "stick 'em up—I gotya covered"; we probably then do as advised or else try to escape. In taking this action we are reacting not directly to the communication but to the situation we think exists in the environment—i.e. a burglar with a gun. If we know that our eight-year-old son is home or that someone has left the television on, we will respond to an identical communication in a different manner.

Communications can lead to adjustive behavior in those exposed to them in at least three ways. First, they can report an actual or expected change in the environment, or a previously unknown fact about the environment, that is important to the person at the receiving end of the communication: a death in the family, the poor financial condition of a local bank, or the fact that a favorite clothing store will start its annual sale next Wednesday.

Tactical psychological warfare communications during World War II were often of this type. They attempted to influence the behavior of enemy personnel by telling them about developments (or developments to be anticipated) in the military situation: "You have been cut off"; "The units defending your flank have already surrendered"; "Stay away from rail junc-

<hr>

[24] The politician who mingles with the crowd, looking friendly and receptive but saying little, "just to see what people have on their minds," is practicing somewhat the same technique as the nondirective interviewer or the psychologist who administers a projective test.

394

tions—they will all be bombed." Application of this principle in advertising is even more familiar: "Now for the first time you can buy Product A with a leather carrying case"; "Hurry and order your copy of Book B before the limited edition is exhausted."

A second way that communications can lead to behavioral adjustments is by pointing out an existing feature of the environment (not a change or a completely new fact) and reminding the individual that his needs would be served if he adjusted his behavior in a given manner. Much of the strategic propaganda in World War II was of this type: Axis personnel were told again and again about the overwhelming economic superiority of the Allied powers, and were advised to surrender to avoid senseless destruction. Allied audiences, for their part, were reminded of the great victories that the Axis forces had already achieved, and were urged to give up —also to avoid further destruction. In some cases, these communications may have contained information that was new to recipients of the propaganda, but in most instances leaflets or broadcasts served merely to remind people of facts they knew already and of needs they had already experienced. Similarly, many consumer items have been used for a long time in substantially the same form, but this does not deter advertisers from calling attention to the virtues of these products and trying to persuade people that it is to their advantage to buy them.

Communications that serve as reminders—either about conditions in the environment or about needs—have been observed to lead to substantial behavioral responses. Election studies have shown that those who lean toward a particular political party are more likely to get out and vote if they are exposed to this party's propaganda. Reminders may also strengthen existing attitudes by providing information that is in accord with them. These phenomena of activation and reinforcement were observed, for instance, in the election study of Lazarsfeld, Berelson, and Gaudet in Erie County, Ohio.[25] They are also likely to come into play on any hot day when we see a sign showing a picture of an ice-cold beverage and telling us where it may be obtained.

The third way in which communications may cause a behavioral adjustment is by bringing to a person's attention a new way of patterning his relationships to the environment. Those who have experienced a religious conversion or adopted a new philosophy may see the same environment about them, but they interpret it differently. Their basic needs may not have changed, but they find that a new pattern of behavior will serve these needs better than the pattern they had followed previously, or the relative emphasis they place on different values may have changed. A similar reorganization of behavior is sometimes brought about by education. Such

[25] Paul F. Lazarsfeld, Bernard Berelson, and Hazel Gaudet, *The People's Choice*, New York, Columbia University Press, 1948.

organizing principles do not, of course, have to be presented *in toto* by specific communications; they sometimes are worked out by the individual on the basis of exposure to many diverse communications.

In all three cases, assuming that the information in question is perceived as "useful," immediate behavioral adjustments may take place, or (when immediate action is not appropriate) the information contained in the communications may be stored in the form of attitudes or remembered facts to guide future behavior.

In some respects, a communication is thus analogous to a conductor of electricity, whose characteristics influence the work done by the electricity only insofar as the conductor is a good or a poor one. The "conductivity" of a communication seems to be influenced primarily by two factors: whether or not it is clearly organized, uses the language best understood by the audience, etc.; and whether or not it is set off by the proper "indicators" and takes advantage of the communication habits of the audience.

Most research results on the effects of communication can be translated into these terms, although it is usually necessary to supplement the reported data with unsupported assumptions and untested inferences in order to trace the steps of the hypothesized process. For instance, a recent study sponsored by the United States Information Agency in Greece found that those Greeks who were favorably predisposed toward the United States were more likely than those who were not so predisposed to notice and remember a series of United States–sponsored newspaper advertisements.[26] Furthermore, the advertisements, which dealt with basic human rights supported by both Americans and Greeks, appeared to have the effect of strengthening the pro-American attitudes of those who held such attitudes already.

To interpret these observations in accordance with the scheme suggested here, we would have to assume that those affected by the advertisements were people who had found that information about the principles of democracy or about Greek-American ties had tended to satisfy certain of their needs in the past. It may have reassured them of the correctness of their decision in voting for a party supporting Greece's NATO ties. Some of them may have had relatives in the United States. Similar information may previously have helped them to maintain good relations with those among their associates who had similar attitudes or to defend themselves against the arguments of those opposed. The number of possibilities is very large. In any event, their experience had taught them to be on the lookout for— or at least not to resist—information of the type offered in the advertisements.

We also have to assume that the communications habits of those who noticed the advertisements were such that they looked upon the newspaper

[26] Leo Bogart, "Measuring the Effectiveness of an Overseas Information Campaign: A Case History," *Public Opinion Quarterly*, Vol. 21, 1957, pp. 475-498.

as a valuable source of information, and that the advertisements were written in a manner that easily conveyed meaning to the readers.

Very similar observations were made as a result of a postwar information campaign to make Cincinnati United Nations conscious. After an intensive six months' effort to inform people in the area about the United Nations, it was found that the people reached by the campaign tended to be those who were already interested in and favorably disposed toward the world organization.[27] In this case, to follow the interpretation suggested here, we would have to assume that the population of Cincinnati could be divided into those who had some use for information about the United Nations and those who did not. Most of those for whom such information was useful had already assembled at least some information from sources available to them prior to the campaign, but the campaign enabled them to obtain a little more. Those who had no use for information about the United Nations, however, continued to have no use for it and therefore disregarded the campaign along with other content of the communication flow for which they had no use.

Studies reported in the large body of literature on experimental modification of attitudes through communications can also be interpreted in these terms. To take a very simple example, subjects are sometimes given attitude tests, then exposed to communications for or against an issue or a political figure, and finally retested. If the issue or the political figure is one that is relatively unknown to them, their attitude changes in the direction of the communication are likely to be great.[28] If, on the other hand, the subject of the communication is one with which they already are well acquainted their attitudes are likely to change little or not at all. In the former case, the communication may be the only link or the most important link with a sector of the environment that hitherto has been largely unknown to them. Therefore, when they are faced with the necessity of expressing an opinion about this subject, they are forced to rely on information from the experimental communication. Conversely, in the latter case, the communication is only one of several links with this aspect of the environment, and when it comes to expressing an opinion, information that has already been stored from other sources may be quite adequate.

That utility influences the retention and also forgetting of facts is indi-

[27] Shirley A. Star and Helen MacGill Hughes, "Report on an Educational Campaign: The Cincinnati Plan for the United Nations," *American Journal of Sociology*, Vol. 55, 1950, pp. 389-400.

[28] *Cf.* A. D. Annis and Norman C. Meier, "The Induction of Opinion through Suggestion by Means of 'Planted Content,'" *Journal of Social Psychology*, Vol. 5, 1934, pp. 65-81. In this experiment a pronounced change in attitude toward a little-known Australian prime minister was achieved through exposure to material about him "planted" in a campus newspaper. One must assume that a much smaller change would have been achieved if the individual concerned had been better known to the respondents.

cated by two observations of widely varying nature. McKown at Stanford (in an as yet unpublished study) found that the ability of a reader to conjure up a personal image of the supposed writer of a research report correlated highly with his ability to recall the content of the report. In this instance, the possibility that the report's contents might be useful in social relations as well as in professional activities appeared to result in its making a stronger impression.

The other observation comes from the experience of an interviewer of Soviet military personnel who had been captured by the Nazis. Many of the Soviet soldiers reported that they had been in Poland when Russian forces occupied the Eastern half of that country in 1940 and had been amazed at the high standard of living they found. Then, when they returned to Poland during the Soviet advance in 1944-45, they again had been amazed at the high standard of living. When the interviewer expressed surprise at the fact that they reported being amazed twice, his respondents explained that it had been wise to forget what they had seen in 1940.

A small experiment was conducted by the author to contrast the effectiveness of a communication in influencing an attitude that had little basis in knowledge or experience with the almost total inability of a communication to influence an attitude that was rooted in a substantial body of knowledge or personal experience. Sixty-nine government officials with an average of fifteen years' experience in foreign affairs were given tests to establish their attitudes on a four-point scale toward the United States foreign service and toward two German politicians.[29] They were then exposed to a speech (purportedly by a retired foreign service officer) sharply criticizing the foreign service and also to a speech (by a political scientist) highly praising *one* of the German politicians but not mentioning the other.

The results of the experiment were as expected. On the "after" test designed to elicit attitudes toward the foreign service, only one respondent appears to have shifted his rating by one point on the scale. (The possibility of compensating changes exists, but is very slight.) Most of these officials had had personal experience with the foreign service over a period of years, and had built up attitudes of considerable stability. Even though the criticisms made in the speech were shared by many of them, these criticisms had already been taken into account in their thinking and consequently gave them insufficient reason to revise the image of the foreign service they had already formed.

Although not unexpected, the results regarding the two German politicians—von Brentano and Erhard—were more interesting. Responses on these questions were divided into two groups: those from men who had had experience with reference to Western Europe and those from men who re-

[29] The attitude tests were given in three groups and the responses totaled later.

ported no such experience. With regard to Erhard, about whom no communication was presented, the scale ratings on the "before" and "after" tests were identical (or there were compensating changes, which is unlikely). The results in the case of von Brentano showed a pronounced influence of the persuasive communication among those with no Western European experience, while it had almost no influence in the case of those who were European experts. These results are shown in Table 2.[30]

TABLE 2

Evaluation by 69 Foreign Affairs Experts of the Choice of von Brentano as Foreign Minister of the German Federal Republic before and after Reading a Speech Praising Him*

	Before	After
Those with Western European experience:		
Excellent	12	14
Good	16	16
Satisfactory	4	4
Poor	2	1
No opinion	4	3
Those with no Western European experience:		
Excellent	5	18
Good	11	10
Satisfactory	5	1
Poor	0	0
No opinion	10	2

* The question was: "In 1955, Dr. Heinrich von Brentano was appointed Foreign Minister of the German Federal Republic. On the basis of what you know about Dr. von Brentano, would you say that this choice was excellent, good, satisfactory, or poor?"

Experiments such as this offer certain difficulties of interpretation, since they make use of communication habits that do not play a role in other situations. When confronted with a communication in the classroom or laboratory, the subject usually makes the conscious or subconscious assumption that the instructor or experimenter wants him to pay attention to it. Furthermore, by the time he has reached high school or college he presumably has the habit of paying attention in the classroom. Therefore, he may assimilate information that in another context he would regard as not having sufficient utility to justify his attention. For instance, in the case reported in Table 2 it is unlikely that most of those who were not experts on Western

[30] The question used to divide respondents into experts and nonexperts on Western Europe did not discriminate perfectly, as the four "no opinion" responses of the experts in the "before" test indicate. If a more accurate division could have been obtained, the changes probably would have been even fewer among the experts and more pronounced among the nonexperts.

Europe would have read the speech about von Brentano if they had not been specifically asked to do so. Another aspect of the classroom or experimental situation is that it does not ordinarily reward an individual for maintaining a consistent opinion (as is usually the case in other situations) or penalize him for changing his opinion. Indeed, the opposite may be the case. Emphasis on keeping an open mind may even predispose him toward exposure to information that he would otherwise ignore, and may encourage him to revise his opinions in the light of new data. In experimental situations where subjects have been rewarded in some way for maintaining a consistent opinion, observed changes have been considerably less. Finally, in experimental situations, the social setting of the respondent is often ignored. We usually pay little attention to his relations with the other respondents or with the experimenter; yet these relationships may exercise an important influence on his responses. To translate these remarks into the terms that have been used above, we might say that in the experimental situation a subject's needs are often different from those in other situations and therefore somewhat different habits, including communication habits, are appropriate to this situation.

SOME IMPLICATIONS FOR PERSUASION

This way of looking at the effects of communication suggests that the communicator can influence attitudes or behavior only when he is able to convey information that may be utilized by members of his audience to satisfy their wants or needs. If he has control of some significant aspect of his audience's environment, his task may be an easy one. All he must do is tell people about some environmental change or expected change that is important to them. For example, he may offer a large sum of money to anyone who does a certain thing. If he is a merchant, he may sell a product at a very low cost. We all have control over an aspect of the environment that is significant for members of the primary groups to which we belong—our own behavior.

Most communicators are in a more difficult position when they are trying to effect persuasion outside their own group, since they do not control aspects of the environment that are significant to their audiences. Furthermore, they usually do not have a monopoly of the channels of information, and must ordinarily assume that people have already located sources of information about aspects of the environment that are important to them. To influence behavior under these conditions the communicator's information must be more accurate or otherwise more useful than information from competing sources. He can, it is true, sometimes build on tendencies toward action that are already present by reminding people of existing needs and of how they may be satisfied. But to bring about any basic behavioral changes is very difficult. Attitudes and behavior patterns that are based on extensive information or on personal experience are likely to have already proved their utility and to be tough and highly resistant to change. Furthermore, the capacity of people to disregard information that is not useful (either because it is irrelevant or because it conflicts with already established patterns of thought and action) appears to be almost unlimited.[31]

This approach to the study of communication effects also suggests that soundly based knowledge about the principles of persuasion will be attainable only as a result of basic advances within psychology and sociology. A better understanding of the way people perceive their social environment and how they adjust to it appears to be particularly important. The advances that can be made independently in the field usually labeled "communication" are likely to be limited and tentative.

Nevertheless, communication studies, while they cannot stand alone, contribute to our understanding of human needs and the way these are satisfied. A substantial quantity of information on the various ways communications are utilized by different people is already available but has not been systematically organized. For most Americans, for example, news carried in the press of a totalitarian country is not very useful because of its incompleteness and inaccuracy. But for the citizen of such a country this news may be vital to preferment or even survival, since it lets him know what the power holders *want* him to believe.[32] Similarly, it has frequently been observed (e.g. in studies of prejudice) that communications from within the group have more effect on attitudes than identical communications from outside the group. This seems to be true in cases where the utility of the information to the recipient is not in its objective content but in the fact that a member of his group believes it.

Finally, this approach emphasizes that the communicator's audience is not a passive recipient—it cannot be regarded as a lump of clay to be molded by the master propagandist. Rather, the audience is made up of individuals who demand something from the communications to which they are exposed, and who select those that are likely to be useful to them. In other words, they must get something from the manipulator if he is to get something from them. A bargain is involved. Sometimes, it is true, the manipulator is able to lead his audience into a bad bargain by emphasizing one need at the expense of another or by representing a change in the significant environment as greater than it actually has been. But audiences, too, can drive a hard bargain. Many communicators who have been widely disregarded or misunderstood know that to their cost.

[31] The communicator may be able, however, to *make* his information useful—the very fact that certain people are talking about a subject makes this subject relevant for others.

[32] *Cf.* Paul Kecskemeti, "Totalitarian Communications as a Means of Control," *Public Opinion Quarterly*, Vol. 14, 1950, pp. 224-234. Some case material that illustrates Kecskemeti's observations very well is presented by Alex Inkeles and Raymond A. Bauer in *The Soviet Citizen*, Cambridge, Mass., Harvard University Press, 1959, p. 175.

THIS PAPER discusses certain theoretical and methodological points relevant to the growth of a functional theory of mass communications. In recent years various studies have explicitly or implicitly used a functional framework for examining different aspects of mass communications. The current discussion occasionally draws from such studies to illustrate the problems at hand, with no attempt, however, at a comprehensive survey of the field. Three specific topics are explored here:

1. Items suitable for functional analysis. There is a need for specification and codification of the kinds of phenomena in mass communication which have been, or can be, clarified by means of the functional approach, together with formal statements of the basic queries which are raised in each instance. A few examples of such basic functional queries—there are others, of course—are presented in the first section.

2. Organization of hypotheses into a systematic functional framework. Future research and theory would be helped by the introduction of a larger organizing framework into which can be fitted a variety of hypotheses and findings about the functions and dysfunctions of mass communication. One such organizing procedure—*a functional inventory*—is proposed in the second section.

3. Rephrasing hypotheses in functional terms. Additional hypotheses need to be formulated in terms which are specifically related to such important components of functionalism as, for example, functional requirements and the equilibrium model. A few hypotheses of this sort are suggested in the third section.

What is meant here by "mass communication"? In its popular usage the term refers to such particular mass media as television, motion pic-

* This is a revised version of a paper contributed to the Fourth World Congress of Sociology, Milan and Stresa, Italy, September 1959. It is my pleasure to acknowledge an indebtedness to Herbert H. Hyman, Leonard Broom, Mary E. W. Goss, and Raymond J. Murphy for their thoughtful and critical readings of earlier drafts of the paper.

Originally published in Volume 24, Number 4, 1960 of the *Public Opinion Quarterly*.

tures, radio, newspapers, and magazines. But the use of these technical instruments does not always signify mass communication. To illustrate, a nationwide telecast of a political speech is mass communication; closed-circuit television over which a small group of medical students observe an operation is not. Modern technology, then, appears to be a necessary but not sufficient component in defining mass communication, which is distinguishable also by the nature of its audience, the communication itself, and the communicator. Mass communication is directed toward relatively large and heterogeneous audiences that are anonymous to the communicator. Messages are transmitted publicly; are timed to reach most of the audience quickly, often simultaneously; and usually are meant to be transient rather than permanent records. Finally, the communicator tends to be, or to operate within, a complex formal organization that may involve great expense.[1]

SUBJECTS FOR FUNCTIONAL ANALYSIS

Functional analysis, to a great extent, is concerned with examining those consequences of social phenomena which affect the normal operation, adaptation, or adjustment of a given system: individuals, subgroups, social and cultural systems.[2] To what kinds of social phenomena can functional analysis be applied? The basic general requirement, according to Merton, is "that the object of analysis represent a *standardized (i.e.* patterned and repetitive) item, such as social roles, institutional patterns, social processes, cultural pattern, culturally patterned emotions, social norms, group organization, social structure, devices for social control, *etc.*"[3] This basic requirement, however, is very broad. Hence a necessary first step in the application of functional analysis to mass communications consists of *specifying* the kinds of "standardized item" with which the analyst is concerned. As a step in this direction several of the more obvious types of item are distinguished here.

First, at the broadest level of abstraction, mass communication itself, as a *social process*, is a patterned and repetitive phenomenon in many modern societies; hence it is suitable for functional analysis. The basic question at this level is: What are the consequences—for the individual, subgroups, social and cultural systems—of a form of communication that addresses itself to large, heterogeneous, anonymous audiences publicly and rapidly, utilizing a complex and expensive formal organi-

[1] A fuller discussion of the characteristics of mass communication appears in C. Wright, *Mass Communication: A Sociological Perspective*, New York, Random House, 1959.

[2] Types of systems to which functional analysis can be applied are developed in R. K. Merton, *Social Theory and Social Structure*, Glencoe, Ill., Free Press, 1957, Chap. I.

[3] *Ibid.*, p. 50.

zation for this purpose? Thus formulated, however, the query is so gross as to be unmanageable empirically, and essential evidence cannot be obtained.[4] Obviously it is useful to have comparative data from several societies in which mass communications are absent or developed to varying degrees, e.g. underdeveloped *versus* industrialized societies; pre-modern *versus* modern periods of the same society. But it is hardly possible to analyze the consequences of the dissimilar communications systems under such circumstances; their effects cannot be readily separated from those resulting from the host of other complex organizational differences between the societies under study. There remains, of course, the possibility of a speculative "mental experiment" in which the analyst imagines what would happen if mass communication did not exist, but such hypotheses are not empirically verifiable.[5]

Nor are the difficulties reduced if the analyst delimits the problem by considering concrete communication structures rather than the abstract total mass communication process. Lazarsfeld and Merton have underscored such difficulties with reference to the analysis of the social role of the mass media:

What role can be assigned to the mass media by virtue of the fact that they exist? What are the implications of a Hollywood, a Radio City, and a Time-Life-Fortune enterprise for our society? These questions can of course be discussed only in grossly speculative terms, since no experimentation or rigorous comparative study is possible. Comparisons with other societies lacking these mass media would be too crude to yield decisive results and comparisons with an earlier day in American society would still involve gross assertions rather than precise demonstrations. . . .[6]

Functional analysis at this level, then, appears currently to be dependent primarily on speculation, and holds little immediate promise for the development of an empirically verifiable theory of mass communication.

A second major type of functional analysis, slightly less sweeping than the first, considers each particular *method* of mass communication (e.g. newspapers, television) as the item for analysis. An early example is an essay by Malcolm Willey, in which he asks, "What, then, are the functions performed by the newspaper? What are the social and individual needs that it has met and still meets?" As an answer, he isolates six distinguishable functions: news, editorial, backgrounding, entertain-

---

[4] For one discussion of methods of testing functional theory see N. S. Timasheff, *Sociological Theory*, New York, Random House, 1958, pp. 229-230.

[5] For a discussion of the dangers in such an approach see M. Weber, *The Theory of Social and Economic Organization*, translated by A. Henderson and T. Parsons, Glencoe, Ill., Free Press, 1947, pp. 97-98.

[6] P. Lazarsfeld and R. Merton, "Mass Communication, Popular Taste and Organized Social Action," in L. Bryson, editor, *The Communication of Ideas*, New York, Harper, 1948, p. 98.

ment, advertising, and encyclopedic.[7] Sometimes the analyst focuses on the interrelations among several media as they affect total communication as a system. Janowitz's study of the role of the local community press within a metropolitan setting provides a case in point. Janowitz found, among other things, that the community weekly newspaper does not simply duplicate the services of the larger metropolitan daily but plays a quite distinct role, such as providing information about local residents, local issues, and neighborhood organizations.[8] Touching on several media, one might ask: What are the functions and dysfunctions of multiple coverage of the news by television, radio, and newspapers? Opportunities to test hypothesized functions at this level are available when circumstances provide societies in which a particular medium is absent (e.g. countries without television) or when the normal operation of a medium is disturbed (e.g. by a strike), providing one can account for the influence of factors in the situation other than the absence or malfunctioning of the mass medium.

As a third major instance, the functional approach can be used in the *institutional* analysis of any mass medium or organization in mass communication, examining the function of some repeated and patterned operation within that organization. Here, clearly, there is a good possibility of obtaining essential data for empirical verification of hypotheses, through case studies, comparative analysis of differently organized media, or direct experimentation. Warren Breed's study of the middle-sized daily newspaper illustrates such institutional analysis.[9] Breed examines, among other things, the ways in which the paper's presentation of the news is affected by such institutionalized statuses in the newsroom as publisher, editor, and staff member, and by the professional norms and regularized activities surrounding the newspaperman's work.

Finally, a fourth type of analysis—and one which we believe offers great promise for the development of a functional theory of mass communications—treats the question of what are the consequences of handling the *basic communication activities* by means of mass communication. What is meant by basic communication activities? Lasswell notes three major activities of communication specialists: "(1) the surveillance of the environment; (2) the correlation of the parts of society in responding to the environment; (3) the transmission of the

[7] M. Willey, "The Functions of the Newspaper," *Annals of the American Academy of Political and Social Science*, Vol. 219, 1942, p. 19.

[8] M. Janowitz, *The Community Press in an Urban Setting*, Glencoe, Ill., Free Press, 1952.

[9] W. Breed, "The Newspaperman, News, and Society," Columbia University, 1952, unpublished doctoral dissertation.

social heritage from one generation to the next."[10] Modifying these categories slightly and adding a fourth—entertainment—provides a classification of the major communication activities which concern us here. Surveillance refers to the collection and distribution of information concerning events in the environment, both outside and within any particular society, thus corresponding approximately to what is popularly conceived as the handling of news. Acts of correlation, here, include interpretation of information about the environment and prescriptions for conduct in reaction to these events. In part this activity is popularly identified as editorial or propagandistic. Transmission of culture includes activities designed to communicate a group's store of social norms, information, values, and the like, from one generation to another or from members of a group to newcomers. Commonly it is identified as educational activity. Finally, entertainment refers to communication primarily intended to amuse people irrespective of any instrumental effects it might have.

It goes without saying that each of these four activities pre-dates mass communication, and in some form each is still conducted on a "nonmass" basis in every society. But where mass media exist, each activity is also conducted as mass communication. In its simplest form, then, the question posed here is: What are the consequences of performing such activities through mass communication, rather than through some other form of communication? For example, what are the effects of surveillance through mass communication rather than through face-to-face reporting? What are the results of treating information about events in the environment as items of news to be distributed indiscriminately, simultaneously, and publicly to a large, heterogeneous, and anonymous audience? Similarly, what are the consequences of handling prescription, interpretation, cultural transmission, and entertainment as mass-communicated activities? Thus formulated, the basic query of functional analysis at this level calls for—at the least—an *inventory* of functions of mass-communicated activities, a subject to which we turn now.

TOWARD A FUNCTIONAL INVENTORY FOR MASS COMMUNICATIONS

Functional analysis does not restrict itself to the study of useful consequences. On the contrary, several types of consequences are now recognized in functional theory, each of which must be taken into account if an inventory is to be complete. For example, Merton distinguishes between consequences and the motives for an activity.[11]

---

[10] H. Lasswell, "The Structure and Function of Communication in Society," in Bryson, *op.cit.*

[11] The cited distinction and others to be discussed are from Merton, *op.cit.*

Clearly, these two need not be, and often are not, identical. To illustrate, a local public health campaign may be undertaken to encourage the people in the area to go to a clinic for a check-up. In the process of pursuing this goal, the campaign may have an unanticipated consequence of improving the morale of the local public health employees, whose everyday work has suddenly been given public attention.[12] Results that are intended are called *manifest* functions; those that are unintended, *latent* functions. Not every consequence has positive value for the social system in which it occurs, or for the groups or individuals involved. Effects which are undesirable from the point of view of the welfare of the society or its members are called *dysfunctions.* Any single act may have both functional and dysfunctional effects. For example, the public health campaign might also have frightened some people so much that they failed to report for a check-up.

Combining Merton's specification of consequences with the four basic communication activities provides a fuller query that serves to guide the inventory. Stylized into a "formula," the basic question now becomes:

	(1) manifest	(3) functions	
What are the	and	and	of mass communi-
	(2) latent	(4) dysfunctions	

cated	(5) surveillance (news)	for the	(9) society
	(6) correlation (editorial activity)		(10) subgroups
	(7) cultural transmission		(11) individual
	(8) entertainment		(12) cultural systems?

The twelve elements in the formula can be transformed into categories in a master inventory chart which organizes many of the hypothesized and empirically discovered effects of mass communication. Its essential form is illustrated in the accompanying chart, in which some hypothetical examples of effects have been inserted. A full discussion of the content of the chart cannot be undertaken here, but the method of organization will be illustrated through a limited discussion of certain functions and dysfunctions of mass-communicated surveillance.[13]

Consider what it means to society and to its members to have available a constant flow of data on events occurring within the society or in the larger world. At least two positive consequences or functions occur for the total society. First, such a flow of information often provides speedy *warnings* about imminent threats and dangers from outside the society, e.g. impending danger from hurricanes or from military attack.

[12] An example of such an unanticipated consequence can be found in R. Carlson, "The Influence of the Community and the Primary Group on the Reactions of Southern Negroes to Syphilis," Columbia University, 1952, unpublished doctoral dissertation.

[13] A fuller discussion appears in Wright, *op.cit.,* from which the following section is drawn.

PARTIAL FUNCTIONAL INVENTORY FOR MASS COMMUNICATIONS

| | System under Consideration | | | |
	Society	Individual	Specific Subgroups (e.g. Political Elite)	Culture
	1. MASS-COMMUNICATED ACTIVITY: SURVEILLANCE (NEWS)			
Functions (manifest and latent)	Warning; Natural dangers Attack; war	Warning Instrumental	Instrumental: Information useful to power	Aids cultural contact Aids cultural growth
	Instrumental: News essential to the economy and other institutions	Adds prestige: Opinion leadership	Detects: Knowledge of subversive and deviant behavior	
	Ethicizing	Status conferral	Manages public opinion Monitors Controls	
			Legitimizes power: Status conferral	
Dysfunctions (manifest and latent)	Threatens stability: News of "better" societies	Anxiety Privatization Apathy Narcotization	Threatens power: News of reality "Enemy" propaganda Exposés	Permits cultural invasion
	Fosters panic			

PARTIAL FUNCTIONAL INVENTORY FOR MASS COMMUNICATIONS (*continued*)

| | System under Consideration | | |
	Society	*Individual*	*Specific Subgroups* (*e.g. Political Elite*)	*Culture*
2. MASS-COMMUNICATED ACTIVITY: CORRELATION (EDITORIAL SELECTION, INTERPRETATION, AND PRESCRIPTION)				
Functions (manifest and latent)	Aids mobilization Impedes threats to social stability Impedes panic	Provides efficiency: Assimilating news Impedes: Overstimulation Anxiety Apathy Privatization	Helps preserve power	Impedes cultural invasion Maintains cultural consensus
Dysfunctions (manifest and latent)	Increases social conformism: Impedes social change if social criticism is avoided	Weakens critical faculties Increases passivity	Increases responsibility	Impedes cultural growth

3. MASS-COMMUNICATED ACTIVITY: CULTURAL TRANSMISSION

Functions (manifest and latent)	Increases social cohesion: Widens base of common norms, experiences, etc. Reduces anomie Continues socialization: Reaches adults even after they have left such institutions as school	Aids integration: Exposure to common norms Reduces idiosyncrasy Reduces anomia	Extends power: Another agency for socialization	Standardizes Maintains cultural consensus
Dysfunctions (manifest and latent)	Augments "mass" society	Depersonalizes acts of socialization		Reduces variety of subcultures

4. MASS-COMMUNICATED ACTIVITY: ENTERTAINMENT

Functions (manifest and latent)	Respite for masses	Respite	Extends power: Control over another area of life	
Dysfunctions (manifest and latent)	Diverts public: Avoids social action	Increases passivity Lowers "tastes" Permits escapism		Weakens aesthetics: "Popular culture"

Forewarned, the population might mobilize and avert destruction. Furthermore, insofar as the information is available to the mass of the population (rather than to a select few) warnings through mass communication may have the additional function of supporting feelings of egalitarianism within the society, i.e. everyone has had an equal chance to escape from danger. Second, a flow of data about the environment is *instrumental* to the everyday institutional needs of the society, e.g. stock market activities, navigation, and air traffic.

For individuals, several functions of surveillance can be discerned. First, insofar as personal welfare is linked to social welfare, the *warning* and *instrumental* functions of mass-communicated news for society also serve the individual. In addition, a number of more personal forms of utility can be identified. For example, in 1945, Berelson took advantage of a local newspaper strike in New York City to study what people "missed" when they did not receive their regular newspaper.[14] One clearly identifiable function of the newspaper for these urbanites was as a source of information about routine events, e.g. providing data on local radio and motion picture performances, sales by local merchants, embarkations, deaths, and the latest fashions. When people "missed" their daily papers they were, in fact, missing a tool for daily living. A third function of mass-communicated news is to bestow *prestige* upon the individuals who make the effort to keep themselves informed about events. To the extent that being informed is considered important by the society, people who conform to this norm enhance their prestige within the group. Often those individuals who select local news as their focus of attention emerge as local opinion leaders in their community, while people who turn to events in the greater society operate as cosmopolitan influentials.[15]

Lazarsfeld and Merton have suggested two other functions of mass communication which seem to be especially applicable to mass-communicated news: *status conferral* and the enforcement of social norms (*ethicizing*).[16] Status conferral means that news reports about a member of any society enhance his prestige. By focusing the power of the mass media upon him society confers upon him a high public status. Hence the premium placed upon publicity and public relations in modern societies. Mass communication has an ethicizing function when it strengthens social control over the individual members of the mass

[14] B. Berelson, "What 'Missing the Newspaper' Means," in Paul Lazarsfeld and F. Stanton, editors, *Communications Research 1948-1949*, New York, Harper, 1949, pp. 111-129.

[15] Cf. R. Merton, "Patterns of Influence: A Study of Interpersonal Influence and of Communication Behavior in a Local Community," in Lazarsfeld and Stanton, *op.cit.*, pp. 180-219.

[16] Lazarsfeld and Merton, *op.cit.*

society by bringing their deviant behavior into public view, as in news-paper crusades. The facts about norm violation might have been known already privately by many members of the society; but the public dis-closure through mass communication creates the social conditions under which most people must condemn the violations and support public, rather than private, standards of morality. By this process, mass-com-municated news strengthens social control in large urbanized societies where urban anonymity has weakened informal face-to-face detection and control of deviant behavior.

Surveillance through mass communication can prove dysfunctional as well as functional for society and the individual. First, uncensored news about the world potentially *threatens* the structure of any society. For example, information about conditions and ideologies in other societies might lead to invidious comparisons with conditions at home, and hence to strains toward change. Second, uninterpreted warnings about danger in the environment might lead to *panic* by the mass audience. For example, in Cantril's analysis of the effects of the radio program "Invasion from Mars," the belief that the radio story was actually a news report contributed to the panic reaction by many listeners.[17]

Dysfunctions can be identified on the individual level too. First, data about dangers in the environment, instead of having the function of warning, could lead to heightened *anxieties* within the audience, e.g. war nerves. Second, too much news might lead to *privatization*: the individual becomes overwhelmed by the data brought to his attention and reacts by turning to matters in his private life over which he has greater control.[18] Third, access to mass-communicated news might lead to *apathy*. Or he may believe that to be an informed citizen is equivalent to being an active citizen. Lazarsfeld and Merton have given this dysfunction the label of *narcotization*.[19]

One also can analyze functions and dysfunctions of mass-communi-cated news for smaller subgroups within the society. To illustrate, such news activity might prove especially functional for a political elite insofar as the free flow of news provides information which is useful to the maintenance of *power* by this group. Furthermore the publicity given to events within the society facilitates the *detection* of deviant and possibly subversive behavior, as well as providing an opportunity

[17] H. Cantril, H. Gaudet, and H. Herzog, *Invasion From Mars*, Princeton, N.J., Princeton University Press, 1940.

[18] For a discussion of the feeling of social impotence that marks privatization, see E. Kris and N. Leites, "Trends in Twentieth Century Propaganda," in G. Roheim, editor, *Psychoanalysis and the Social Sciences*, New York, International Universities Press, 1947.

[19] Lazarsfeld and Merton, *op.cit.*

to *monitor* (and perhaps control) public opinion. The attention which the news media give to political figures and their behavior can, in turn, enhance and *legitimize* their position of power, through the process of status conferral. On the other hand, mass-communicated news may prove dysfunctional to such a political group in a variety of ways. The news which reaches a mass audience may undermine or threaten the political power elite, as for instance when news of losses during wartime contradict the leaders' claims of victory or when enemy propaganda deliberately aims at undermining the rulers' power.[20]

Finally, one can canvass the impact of mass-communicated news on culture itself. Among the possible functions here are the enrichment and variety which are introduced into a society's culture through mass-communicated information about other cultures, as well as possible growth and adaptability of culture as a result of such contacts. On the dysfunctional side, such uncontrolled news about other societies can lead to cultural invasion and weakening of the host culture.

While present space does not permit a full discussion of possible functions and dysfunctions of the other three communication activities—correlation, cultural transmission, and entertainment—a few hypothesized functions and dysfunctions are illustrated in the accompanying chart. Such examples demonstrate the usefulness of this form—or some equivalent method—of organizing hypotheses and findings about the effects of mass communications.[21] We turn now to our third, and final, point of discussion: the desirability of rephrasing or formulating additional hypotheses about mass communication in terms especially central to functional theory.

FORMULATING FUNCTIONAL HYPOTHESES

Not all effects of mass communication are germane to functional analysis, only those which are relevant and important if the system under analysis is to continue to operate normally. The basic pattern of functional analysis has recently been characterized by Hempel as follows:

The object of the analysis is some "item" i, which is a relatively persistent trait or disposition (e.g. the beating of the heart) occurring in a system s (e.g. the body of a living vertebrate); and the analysis aims to show that s is in a state, or internal condition c_i, and in an environment presenting certain external conditions c_e such that under conditions c_i and c_e (jointly to be referred to as c) the trait i has effects which satisfy some "need" or "functional require-

[20] Cf. H. Speier, "Psychological Warfare Reconsidered," in D. Lerner and H. Lasswell, editors, *The Policy Sciences*, Stanford, Calif., Stanford University Press, 1951.
[21] For one instructive analysis of the effects of edited news coverage, see W. Breed, "Mass Communication and Socio-cultural Integration," *Social Forces*, Vol. 37, 1958, pp. 109-116.

ment" of s, i.e. a condition n which is necessary for the system's remaining in adequate, or effective, or proper, working order.[22]

Hempel also elaborates the basic terms in this schema. The item i, for example, may be one of several such items forming a class I, any one of which is functionally equivalent to any other; that is, each has approximately the same effect of fulfilling the condition n necessary for the system to operate properly. One can argue, that, if at any time t, system s functions adequately in a setting of kind c, and s can function adequately in setting c only if condition n is satisfied, then some one of the items in class I is present at t. The item i (or its equivalent) is a functional requirement of s, under the conditions stated.

What constitutes a state of normal operation remains, as yet, undefined and poses one of the most difficult problems in functional theory. Rather than assume that only one state represents normal operation, Hempel suggests that it may be necessary to consider a range of states, R, that defines adequate performance relative to some standard of survival or adjustment. Specification of the standard, then, poses a problem the solution to which may vary from case to case. One solution, however, may come from the study of the system itself, if the analyst employs an equilibrium model or general hypothesis of self-regulation of the system. This hypothesis, overly simplified, asserts that the system will adjust itself by developing appropriate traits which satisfy the various functional requirements that arise from changes in its internal state or environment. In the study of any given system s, then, the standard of survival or adjustment,

. . . would be indicated by specifying a certain class or range R of possible states of s, with the understanding that s was to be considered as "surviving in proper working order," or as "adjusting properly under changing conditions" just in case s remained in, or upon disturbance returned to, some state within the range R. A need, or functional requirement, of system s relative to R is then a necessary condition for the system's remaining in, or returning to, a state in R; and the function, relative to R, of an item i in s consists in i's effecting the satisfaction of some such functional requirement.[23]

To illustrate the third essential step in functional analysis of mass communication (i.e. phrasing of hypotheses and propositions) let us apply some of the above ideas about self-regulation to one aspect of mass communication: surveillance. Let the items i represent such varied forms of mass-communicated news as television newscasts, newspaper stories, radio news reports, and motion picture newsreels; together they comprise a class of items I, mass-communicated surveillance. Assume,

[22] C. Hempel, "The Logic of Functional Analysis," in N. Gross, editor, *Symposium on Sociological Theory*, Evanston, Ill., Row, Peterson, 1959, p. 280.
[23] *Ibid.*, p. 296.

for the sake of the example, that these items are functionally equivalent forms of news. Let the *individual* be the unit or system with which we are concerned. And let conditions c be those of a modern society, in which many events of importance to the individual occur beyond the immediate environment which he can observe first-hand. Then proposition 1 is:

1. If the individual s is to maintain a state of adequate or normal operation R, in a society C in which events of importance to him occur outside the immediate observable environment, then there must be available to him some sufficient form of mass-communicated news i.

Normal operation needs to be defined, of course. We might, for example, define such a state as one in which the individual has sufficient information to cope with the environment. Or we might define adequate or normal operation as a state in which the individual *thinks* that he has sufficient information about events in the environment. Arbitrarily we select the latter definition here, since our next concern will be with predicting the probable behavior of the individual when he is disturbed from the normal state. We assume that such purposive behavior is motivated by the individual's definition of the situation as well as by the objective situation itself.

With this subjective definition of normalcy, then, proposition 1 can be rephrased as follows:

2. If at any given time t an individual s is operating in a normal state R (i.e. he thinks that he has sufficient information about events in his environment), and this state can be achieved in a modern society only if the individual has access to mass-communicated surveillance I, then some form of mass-communicated news i must be present and available to him at time t.

And the hypothesis of self-regulation predicts that:

3. If the individual is disturbed from his normal state R (i.e. he comes to think that he does *not* have sufficient information about events in the environment) by the removal of or interference with i (the previously adequate form of mass-communicated news), then the individual will react by seeking the functional equivalents of i (i.e. another source of mass-communicated news), in order to return to his normal state R.

What are the circumstances under which such a hypothesis could be tested? One method consists of experimentally manipulating the forms of mass-communicated news i available to the individual, perhaps disturbing the normal pattern by removing or interfering with i for an experimental group of individuals but not for a matched control group. Then the analyst could examine the behavior of the individuals involved. The hypothesis of self-regulation would lead to the prediction that the deprived individuals would now turn to alternative i's in order to continue to meet the necessary conditions for normal operation.

A second method consists of taking advantage of natural disturbances in mass-communicated surveillance. Berelson's study of people's reactions to a newspaper strike is a case in point.[24] Surveillance, of course, is only one of the many services which the daily newspaper provides for the reader. Nevertheless, for some readers this appeared to be a very important function, and these people found themselves greatly disturbed by the loss of their customary source of information about international, national and local events. Under such circumstances of sudden deprivation, one would like to know the new communications behavior of the individuals involved.

Still a third method consists of analyzing the behavior of people who are differentially located in society with respect to their access to specific forms of mass-communicated news. What alternative form of surveillance has been employed by people for whom a certain type of mass-communicated news is not ordinarily available? Several possible groups might be compared instructively here, such as literate *versus* illiterate members of the society; immigrants knowing only their native language *versus* citizens; people wealthy enough to have television and radio receivers *versus* those who are not.[25]

To conclude our discussion of functional propositions we shall introduce one further complexity. Thus far we have treated each communication activity (surveillance, correlation, cultural transmission, and entertainment) as if it existed in isolation from the others. Obviously, in a total communication system any mass medium may perform any one or several of these activities; and the performance of one activity may have consequences for the others. Our concluding proposition is that many of the functions of one mass-communicated activity can be interpreted as *social mechanisms* for minimizing or counteracting the

[24] Berelson, *op.cit.*

[25] People also may turn to word-of-mouth sources of information as alternatives to mass-communicated news, of course. As examples of instructive analyses relevant to this point see P. Rossi and R. Bauer, "Some Patterns of Soviet Communications Behavior," *Public Opinion Quarterly*, Vol. 16, 1952, pp. 653-670; R. Bauer and D. Gleicher, "Word-of-mouth Communication in the Soviet Union," *Public Opinion Quarterly*, Vol. 17, 1953, pp. 297-310; *Communications Behavior and Political Attitudes in Four Arabic Countries*, New York, Bureau of Applied Social Research, 1952; and O. Larsen and R. Hill, "Mass Media and Interpersonal Communication in the Diffusion of a News Event," *American Sociological Review*, Vol. 19, 1954, pp. 426-443.

dysfunctions produced by another activity, in order to keep the system from breaking down.

To illustrate, suppose we accept the proposition that in a modern society the individual's need for surveillance must be met through the process of mass communication. At the same time, however, the mass-communicative features of this activity have effects on the individual that may be dysfunctional. For example, large amounts of raw news may overwhelm him and lead to personal anxiety, apathy, or other reactions which would interfere with his reception of the items of news about the environment necessary for his normal operations. What happens that helps prevent such dysfunctional effects of mass-communicated news from interfering with the basic functions? To some extent such dysfunctions are minimized by the practice in modern societies of handling the second communication activity, correlation, also by mass communication (see our chart). Not all the events in the world get reported to the listener or reader through mass communication. There is a constant process of selection, editing, and interpretation of the news as it appears in mass-communicated form, often accompanied by prescriptions on what the individual should do about the events reported.

But even edited news can have dysfunctions when mass-communicated, such harmful effects as might come from the content or nature of the information itself. For example, news about war or international events sometimes increases personal tensions and anxiety which, in turn, leads the individual to reduce his attention to the news (hence disturbing the normal state of equilibrium). From this perspective, it is significant that the same mass media which provide surveillance and correlation often serve as a source of entertainment in a mass society. Indeed, the entertainment aspects of events may be interspersed with or woven into the news itself, in such forms as human-interest stories, oddities in the news, scandal, gossip, details of private lives, cartoons, and comic strips. One function of mass-communicated entertainment, then, is to provide respite for the individual which, perhaps, permits him to continue to be exposed to the mass-communicated news, interpretation, and prescriptions so necessary for his survival in the modern world. At present, such an assertion is only conjectural. There is no reason, however, why future audience research might not bear directly upon the functional issue at hand, especially as such research illuminates the multiple uses to which the mass media are put and the varied gratifications and annoyances that people experience while getting the news.[26]

[26] For a recent discussion of some possible studies of the "uses" of mass media see E. Katz, "Mass Communications Research and the Study of Popular Culture: An Editorial Note on a Possible Future for This Journal," *Studies in Public Communication*, No. 2, 1959, pp. 1-6.

HIGH NOON
IN THE RESEARCH
MARKETPLACE
Robert O. Carlson

THIS PAPER deals with some of the problems and consequences that arise when public opinion research is bought
and sold. Surprisingly little has been written about this topic,
perhaps because it is thought too crass a subject for serious
study or perhaps because it is felt to be too controversial. The thesis I
offer for your consideration this evening can be stated in simple terms.
It holds that the ultimate fate of a piece of research in our field frequently is determined not so much by the excellence of the data collected as by the nature of the relationship that evolves between the
client and his research organization. I shall discuss some aspects of the
relationship between buyers and sellers of research in an effort to
identify the common interests as well as the divergent points of view
which each brings to this association.

I begin with a rhetorical question: Why have scholars in our field
paid so little attention to the impact of this research relationship on
the kinds of problems studied and the kinds of analysis employed
and the degree of success achieved? Certainly social scientists have
shown little reluctance to study the reasons why other kinds of relationships succeed or fail. They have commented upon the many nuances
of interaction between the employer and his employee, the merchant

Originally published in Volume 25, Number 3, 1961 of the *Public Opinion Quarterly*.

and his customer, and the communicator and his audience. I believe the relationship between the buyer and seller of public opinion research has not been studied in greater detail because each is unclear as to his self-image. Most of us would agree that the researcher is far more than a mere collector and analyzer of data, and that the client is a good deal more than simply someone in search of an answer to his problem. Yet we often operate on these relatively naïve bases.

For example, clients are likely to bring to the research relationship a wide assortment of expectations. Some are sophisticated and others are virginal in their outlook on research. Some are anxious to act on results and others are not. Some are convinced of the intrinsic value of research and others have serious doubts about it or see it, at best, as a kind of window dressing. Some have a good deal of money to spend and a willingness to part with it, but the typical client has limited funds, unlimited anxiety, and a slightly queasy feeling that he has wandered into a mysterious, dimly lit, academic world. Candor compels us to note that research agencies may vary almost as much as clients in the degree of sophistication and dedication which they bring to their task.

Thus, when the statistically average client encounters the statistically average research agency, we may expect certain chronic problems to emerge. Since I have been both a client of public opinion research agencies and a researcher, I offer these comments with full knowledge that I speak of a difficult and tremendously sensitive area. This paper singles out six propositions about the client-researcher relationship that seem relevant for understanding the cross-pressures on each. It offers them in the hope that we may take constructive action on them.

1. There often is a lack of clarity on the part of both client and researcher as to their mutual roles, obligations, and responsibilities.
2. The client and the research agency may bring different time horizons to the study of a problem.
3. Breakdowns in communication within the client organization, as well as faulty communication between the client and his agency, contribute to disappointing research studies.
4. The client-researcher relationship represents an ever-changing distribution of power, and this shifting of power affects the way research problems are structured and the extent to which research findings are accepted and utilized by the client.
5. There is considerable evidence that clients and researchers employ different criteria in evaluating a completed study, and seldom do they communicate these judgments to one another.
6. Finally, both researchers and clients are disturbed by charges that

the field of public opinion research is not a true profession, that it lacks standards for membership and performance, and that its work must therefore be viewed with a decent amount of reservation and question.

We turn now to the first of these propositions, that which asserts that both client and researcher need to define their roles more clearly. Let us translate this somewhat pretentious statement into a concrete bill of particulars. We begin by asking: What is the correct posture for the research agency to assume vis-à-vis its client? This question obtains whether we are referring to a government research bureau in Washington, a commercial office high on Madison Avenue, or the research bureau on the reputedly quiet and untroubled lane of a college campus. To what extent is the research agency something more than a mere collector of data with which its customer may do as he pleases? To what degree should it assume the role of a consultant—an advisor on action and strategy? Is its objectivity lost when it turns to policy making, or should clients expect that the implications of complex research findings will be translated into action programs for them?

An attempt to answer the foregoing question raises many more. Should the researcher try to indicate the likelihood of success before undertaking the study of a problem for his client? When the study is completed, does he have a responsibility for pointing out that his data differ in important respects from previous studies of the same general problem? Is it appropriate for him to editorialize in any measure on the implications of his findings, or does this constitute an unwarranted intrusion into the client's realm? Is the best researcher one who "just reports the facts" or is he one who deliberately tries to place his findings in a wider framework than the highly specific problem assigned to him?

There are other aspects of client-researcher relationships, almost too delicate for public discussion, which yet seem to have profound implications for the future growth of our field and must be confronted. We know, for example, that some research agencies, serving the same client for years, become confidants of management. From the purely tough-minded view of management, what are the pros and cons of retaining the same research agency for many years? Are the obvious advantages of its greater familiarity with the management's problems outweighed by the possibility of complacency and a tendency to view new problems in conventional ways? On the other hand, will calling upon a new research team actually bring in a fresh point of view or will it take up valuable time in educating the new team?

To what extent is it proper for clients to solicit a number of bids from different research groups before deciding who gets an assignment? Government, business, and foundations are conditioned to the concept of competitive bidding in granting contracts for other services. On the other hand, most researchers will argue with spirited conviction that the professional client-researcher relationship is like that between doctors or lawyers and their clients, and that competitive bidding is contrary to the ethos of a professional group. Does this contention, if it is upheld, imply that opinion research has a standing comparable to that of the medical or legal professions? Does it then become reasonable for consumers of our research to demand that we define criteria for membership in our profession and that we spell out standards of training and the manner in which we propose to enforce our standards and codes of ethics?

Regretfully, we can only raise such points as examples of the unresolved issues which cloud the self-image of both the buyer and the seller of public opinion research. Hopefully, if each recognizes them as problems, we have taken a first step toward answering them. Certainly there is considerable evidence that specialists, whether in our field or in others, are likely to be drawn increasingly into policy-making positions as they win acceptance of themselves and their disciplines, and all indications are that we in the communications research field will be increasingly cast in the role of consultants to our clients.

TIME HORIZONS FOR THE STUDY OF A PROBLEM

There appears to be a connection between the foregoing problems and point 2 of this paper, which asks whether the client and the researcher may not operate with rather different concepts concerning the time and scope appropriate for the study of a problem. By the very nature of the financial and manpower limitations under which he works, the researcher finds himself under pressure to limit the scope and the time he gives to a project. To make optimal use of his manpower, even as one research project starts he must give thought to the way his personnel and other resources will be employed when that job is completed. The deadline looms large in his perception and planning. Does this pressure ever lead him to make snap judgments or superficial decisions during the analysis of data? How often are intriguing byways of analysis left unexplored by an agency which feels impelled by economic reality to follow a safe and familiar course— one that gives promise of meeting the deadline but is almost certain to be pedestrian in its results. Too many studies in our field are produced with half-analyzed data. Can the client help to resolve this dilemma?

The question of meeting a deadline is not so much a problem as it is a symptom of a more serious matter. Seldom can the client and the researcher foresee, at the time they are developing a study design, what promising avenues of investigation will open. Pretests attempt to anticipate major substantive areas of interest, but such tests have only limited use in predicting the kinds of findings which may emerge as analysis of raw data proceeds. The client may do himself a disservice by placing too much importance on the deadline. The study deadline becomes an end in itself rather than a means. I believe that there may come a time about midway through a study when the researcher gets a gnawing feeling that, in its present form, the study just is not going to produce very interesting or useful information. I believe he should be encouraged to report these misgivings to his client, and that the client should be prepared to accept this as one of the legitimate risks of research. To the extent that a neatly bound research report presented on a given date becomes an end in itself, it probably does a disservice to both client and researcher by encouraging banal or even misleading conclusions on questions that deserve to be restudied from a new and fresh view.

COMMUNICATION

A third factor which helps to explain why some public opinion research studies appear to be more productive than others is that familiar word, "communication." Two aspects of the problem influence research results: the nature of the communication network within the client organization and the effectiveness of communication between the client and his researcher.

Frequently, research is authorized by one level in a client organization (usually a top policy-making body) but its implementation is left to persons on a lower echelon. These people are the ones who sit down with the research agency and spell out the precise definition of the problem and the universe which is to be studied. Too often, incomplete information from the policy-making level may force these people to guess at the precise reasons a project has been authorized and the use to which its data will be put. As a consequence, they may feel that a research report has fully met the needs for which it was commissioned, discovering its deficiencies only when the report reaches top management.

Until those who make policy in an organization are involved in defining its research problems and forced to translate them into a concrete study design, there will always be a fuzzy quality and a sense of remoteness to public opinion research. Only by requiring top-level approval of decisions in this area, as in the financial and legal area, can a research project get the serious thought and criticism that are needed from those in authority. When management is put in the position of having to offer better alternatives, it may appreciate the technical problems we face in our work and make more explicit the uses to which it hopes to apply research findings. It may also be forced to face the question of its motives for commissioning the research, including the possibility that it is using research to delay decisions, to spread responsibility for decisions, or to legitimize actions which it has already decided upon.

If the foregoing problems sometimes occur, as I believe they do, we must also recognize that at other times the nature of the research process generates situations in which failures to communicate clearly between client and researcher are almost inevitable. This is particularly true in cases such as the following: when the client is called upon to visualize the kind of information which will be forthcoming from projective questions or depth interviews, when a crucial part of the analysis depends on the construction of indexes, when the study results involve the use of ideal models, and when understanding the survey findings requires a knowledge of sampling theory. It is virtually impossible for the average client to comprehend these technical procedures fully, much less to hazard a guess as to whether they will meet his operational needs. The client is forced to make an intuitive judgment about the study design offered him or else to place his trust in the professional skill of his agency. He has still another alternative, of course. He may consider research sufficiently important to have a full-time research technician on his staff to counsel him on study design and evaluation. At some point, however, the client will have to surrender control of his project to his research agency, and this leads us to a consideration of point 4 of this paper.

DISTRIBUTION OF POWER IN THE CLIENT-RESEARCHER RELATIONSHIP

In theory, all power initially rests with the client, for he can decide whether or not to buy research. But even at this point appearances are deceiving, for the mores of the research profession are such that the prospective client may be inhibited from shopping around for the best buy he can find. Usually, he must decide which agency he wishes to approach. He then describes his problem to that group and learns whether they can and will undertake a study for him at a cost he finds reasonable.

Having selected his research agency, the client encounters a new aspect of the power complex. He is free to reveal as much or as little about himself and his problem as he pleases. More important, in addition to defining his problem he may also hint at what he thinks or hopes the research will demonstrate. The researcher, in such cases, must be on guard lest this revelation subtly influence his study design and analysis.

Once a research design has been agreed upon and work begun, the balance of power shifts clearly in the direction of the researcher. As work continues, he makes a whole series of critical decisions without consulting the client. These include decisions about how to code answers and how to combine them into scores and how to classify respondents into meaningful analytical categories. Seldom does the researcher call upon the client's knowledge at this stage of the analysis. Yet a strong argument can be made that, if the client has a role to play in helping set up his study design, he has an equally valid role to play in helping interpret data collected for him. I feel we in the research field should consult far more frequently with our clients during the collection and analysis of survey data. Too often we expect them to be good boys and sit with folded hands on the sidelines while we "professionals" study their problems. How different this is, for example, from the constant communication between the lawyer and his client in a legal action.

Still another aspect of this power relationship calls for comment. Too many researchers feel they must give the impression that they never entertained doubts or misgivings during the entire time they carried out a study. I suggest that the finished research report give an account (in the appendix, perhaps) of the hunches and bright ideas that did not work out. I have a feeling that the client will be almost as interested in these false starts as in those ideas which eventually paid off. The client often receives a full report on all aspects of a research project in the physical sciences, including those experiments which did not work, because this warns him of avenues of investigation that are blind alleys. Researchers in the field of human relations, perhaps lacking the public acceptance of their colleagues in the physical sciences, are more reluctant to confess that they too make false starts and at times pursue fruitless lines of inquiry.

The delivery of the finished research report represents the complete shift of power from client to researcher. At this stage, the researcher knows things about the client's problem which the client himself does not. The client, upon reading the report, may be pleased or not, the findings may be congruent with his needs or not, but it is too late for him to do much about it. He may, of course, withhold future business or even actively discourage others from patronizing the agency in question, but this, at best, is an unsatisfactory means of expressing his displeasure. This possibility, however, does lead us into a consideration of a fifth aspect of the client-researcher relationship.

CRITERIA FOR EVALUATING A RESEARCH STUDY

In practice, the most widely accepted criterion of success or failure of a project has been whether the client says he likes the finished job. This criterion makes sense only up to a point, however, because the client really is not in a position to know whether the study meets his needs until he has had a chance to translate some of the findings into action. In fact, the client's initial reaction to a study may change— it may grow more or less favorable as he has time to live with the findings, to think about their relevance, and to test out their bearing on his day-to-day operations. Yet how often are these latter-day judgments communicated by the client to the researcher—or, for that matter, how often are they solicited? We hear much about the values of secondary analysis of survey research data, and few would argue this point. But I feel we are guilty of doing too little in the way of secondary analysis of client reactions to a study—one, two, or even three years after delivery date.

Still another factor may complicate a client's efforts to evaluate a finished research report. Usually the sponsorship and supervision of a project resides with a particular individual or a department within the client organization. In a very real sense, the delivered research report will be an important basis for passing judgment on that individual or his department. This judgment by management may create pressures for the individual or his department to cover up and excuse a shoddy job of research or else face rebuke from above. It is an exceptional boss, I'm afraid, who is told by an individual or a department that it has commissioned a research job which, upon subsequent examination, turns out to be second-rate. It is also an exceptional boss whose subordinates authorize research studies which may reflect on the soundness of his judgment and prior actions. Here I confess I have no remedial suggestions to offer.

It has already been argued that management's evaluation of a research study often depends on how it feels the study contributes to the development and improvement of a specific program of action. But this is at best a rule of thumb. The danger is that many clients do not have the slightest idea how to translate research findings into action. More than one client has decided that a research study was not useful to him when, in fact, his real problem was that he did not have the personnel or the energy or the imagination to translate its findings into a program of action. And, of course, it is a rare researcher indeed who is ever given an opportunity to observe how his data are applied to specific programs. More often he is left to worry that they may be ripped out of context and applied piecemeal by an overenthusiastic client who wants action and wants it fast.

PROFESSIONALISM OF PUBLIC OPINION RESEARCH

Moving now to the sixth and final point of this paper, it is clear that a discussion of the client-researcher relationship would be incomplete without recognizing that our clients are increasingly looking for a clearer statement from us as to the professional standards to which we lay claim. Nor are they alone in this interest. Anyone who has attended the annual AAPOR business meeting knows how lovingly we agonize over this problem in public each year. One gets the impression that this annual rite-of-spring serves to blow off steam and permits us to put our worries back in a mental deep freeze for another year, but little else happens.

Critics of public opinion research, both among our clients and in the general public, are not in short supply today. There are, for example, the predictable attacks made on election polls every four years in spite of the remarkably good record of our colleagues over the past decade. More serious, perhaps, are the efforts to pass restrictive laws in a number of states. These include bills which would require interviewers to be licensed and fingerprinted, bills which would require television and radio rating services to reveal the identity of their respondents, local ordinances prohibiting any kind of door-to-door interviewing, and a host of similar harassments. Inevitably, our clients turn to us for comment on these attacks.

It is fair to say, I think, that we in the public opinion research field are being scrutinized, castigated, defended, and misunderstood almost daily in the press, in business circles, and in the academic world. We are charged with subtle manipulation of people's minds and actions or, worse yet, with turning the force of popular opinion into a bludgeon with which to intimidate the individual. We have in the last twenty years emerged from shadowy and little-known beginnings, and we stand today in the glaring light of high noon. As president of AAPOR, I have been concerned that we show signs of drifting in this warm and comfortable light, unwilling to acknowledge that our mission, as well as the ranks of our critics, has grown in the last decade, and unable to see the thunderclouds gathering on the horizon. I fear we too easily dismiss our critics as being captious and ill-informed and that we continue to delude ourselves into thinking that restrictive legislation simply cannot happen to us. We are so pleased with the informality and good fellowship of our society that we cannot believe that others outside our ranks entertain suspicions and doubts about us.

As to whether our field of public opinion research is or is not a profession at this time, this strikes me as being a bad question, for it assumes that we are dealing with an all-or-nothing situation. Quite the contrary is the case. Professions develop slowly, painfully, and often without any conscious effort. Professions are not created by legislation or by public relations gimmicks or by drawing up codes of ethics and conduct. The history of the Western world indicates that they attained this status only as they successfully met social needs with dignity and common sense. I defy anyone to state when medicine or law ceased to be bodies of specialized knowledge and emerged as professions.

This paper has detailed some of the factors that complicate the relationship between clients and research agencies. It does not suggest that these difficulties are found in every research relationship or that much has not already been done to educate both the client and the researcher to a more realistic view of each other's needs and obligations. As a field becomes professionalized, its practitioners gain self-esteem, and I see many signs that we are moving in this professional direction. The level of sophistication in both commercial and academic research is improving rapidly. More clients are spending more money each year for research to guide them in policy making and to help them evaluate programs of action. The number of university-sponsored research centers devoted to training students in public opinion research continues to grow, and the diversity of projects they undertake to study is truly impressive. Our members are moving into important policy-making posts in government, universities, and business. Our research methods are spreading with brush-fire rapidity to all parts of the world, and, as you know, some members of AAPOR are not with us tonight because they have been called to Poland, Africa, India, and Japan to help these countries develop programs of research.

All things considered, the prospects for our field are bright—as befits a view taken at high noon. On every side we see evidence of professional growth and self-assurance. With that growth I hope more of us will indulge in one of the prerogatives of maturity—the right to be a little sentimental and moralistic. Earlier I referred to some ambiguity in our self-image as researchers. Sometimes I think we pride ourselves too much on being hard-headed researchers, dealing with statements of statistical probability and busily dissecting our respondents and putting them back together again. In reality, this is but one facet of our work and its professional satisfaction. We are likely to forget that in our public opinion research we are dealing with a tradition as old as Greece and Rome. We seek to understand the concept of consensus, and the forces which facilitate or impede it. In trying to capture that elusive thing called "public opinion" we are joining in a labor which has engaged some of the best minds of our Western civilization—Plato, Rousseau, de Tocqueville, Dicey, Lowell, and Lippmann, to name but a few. Whether our research problems are as limited as determining consumer preferences for a product or as all-embracing as attitudes toward disarmament, we are dealing with a prime force in the lives of individuals and nations. It is the force for change in a world where change is exploding upon us from every side. Industry, labor unions, government, foundations, and individual scholars are seeking to discern and understand this force which changes men's allegiances, hopes, and fears. By some curious turn of history, we find ourselves in the spotlight of high noon, expected to provide some of the tools and the theories to explain these changes in the attitudes and values that men live by.

Most of you would feel embarrassed and uncomfortable if you were told that, as researchers, you have been cast in a heroic role, so I'll not tell you that. Instead, in closing, I shall be more sober in my judgment and simply remind you that, in an era when too often emotion and stereotype thinking is found in high places, the information you provide your clients, and the degree of trust and confidence you earn from them, will determine whether or not thoughtful counsel and pertinent facts are brought to bear in the making of public policy. Surely this is a task worthy of our best thought and effort.

26

**BEHAVIORAL
SUPPORT FOR
OPINION CHANGE**
Leon Festinger

THE LAST three decades have seen a steady and impressive growth in our knowledge concerning attitudes and opinions —how they are formed, how they are changed, and their relations to one another. For example, we now know a good deal about the effects on opinion change of varying the structure of a persuasive communication—whether it is one-sided or two-sided, whether it is fear-arousing or not, whether pro arguments precede or follow con arguments, and whether it is attributed to trustworthy or untrustworthy sources. Phenomena such as sleeper effects, immunization to counterpropaganda, assimilation and contrast effects, are beginning to be understood. We have also learned a great deal about attitude and opinion change in small face-to-face groups, about the relationship between personality variables and opinion change, about factors affecting resistance to persuasive communications, and so on. I do not intend to review seriously all this work. Anyone who wants to has only to start looking for the names of Hovland, Janis, Kelley, McGuire, Newcomb, Katz, Peak, Kelman—there are many others but these would do for a start.

There is, however, one important gap in our knowledge about attitude and opinion change—a gap that is doubly peculiar when seen in relation to the strong behavioral emphasis in psychology in the United States. I first realized the existence of this gap on reading a manuscript by Arthur R. Cohen. Let me read to you the paragraph that startled me. Cohen's manuscript focuses on the "... ways in which persuasive communicators and members of one's social group come to influence the attitudes of the individual." In his concluding remarks he says:

Originally published in Volume 28, Number 3, 1964 of the *Public Opinion Quarterly*.

Probably the most important and long-range research problem in the sphere of attitude theory has to do with the implications of attitude change for subsequent behavior. In general, most of the researchers whose work we have examined make the widespread psychological assumption that since attitudes are evaluative predispositions, they have consequences for the way people act toward others, for the programs they actually carry out and the manner in which they perform these programs. Thus attitudes are always seen to be a precursor to behavior, a determinant of what behaviors the individual will actually go about doing in his daily affairs. However, though most psychologists assume such a state of affairs, very little work on attitude change has explicitly dealt with the behavior that may follow upon a change in attitudes. Most researchers in this field are content to demonstrate that there are factors which affect attitude change and that these factors are open to orderly exploration, without actually carrying through to the point where they examine the links between changed attitudes and changes in learning, performance, perception and interaction. Until a good deal more experimental investigation demonstrates that attitude change has implications for subsequent behavior, we cannot be certain that our change procedures do anything more than cause cognitive realignments, or even, perhaps, that the attitude concept has any critical significance whatever for psychology.[1]

I was, at first reading, slightly skeptical about the assertion that there is a dearth of studies relating attitude or opinion change to behavior. Although I could not think of any offhand, it seemed reasonable that many of them would be scattered through the journals. Consequently, I started looking for such studies and asked others if they knew of any. After prolonged search, with the help of many others, I succeeded in locating only three relevant studies, one of which is of dubious relevance and one of which required re-analysis of data. The absence of research, and of theoretical thinking, about the effect of attitude change on subsequent behavior is indeed astonishing.

Before telling you about these three studies I would like to make sure that the problem is clear. I am not raising the question of whether or not attitudes are found to relate to relevant behavior. Let us accept the conclusion that they are related, at least to some extent, although even here relatively few studies in the literature address themselves to this question. A fairly recent study by De Fleur and Westie provides a good example of the kind of relationship between existing attitudes and relevant overt behavior that may be found under controlled conditions with good measurement.[2]

The investigators obtained measures of attitudes toward Negroes from 250 college students. The particular attitude measure employed

<hr />

[1] Arthur R. Cohen, *Attitude Change and Social Influence*, New York, Basic Books, in press.

[2] M. L. De Fleur and F. R. Westie, "Verbal Attitudes and Overt Act: An Experiment on the Salience of Attitudes," *American Sociological Review*, Vol. 23, 1958, pp. 667-673.

was apparently reliable, test-retest measures over a five-week interval yielding a correlation of +.96. They selected, from these 250 students, 23 who had scored in the upper quartile and 23 who had scored in the lower quartile, matching the two groups on a number of other variables. These two extreme groups were then compared on a rather clever measure of overt behavior with respect to Negroes. A situation was constructed in which it was believable to ask each of them to sign an authorization permitting use of a photograph of himself sitting with a Negro. The subject was free not to permit the photograph to be taken at all, or, if he signed the authorization, to permit any of a number of possible uses of the photograph ranging from very limited use in laboratory experiments to, at the other extreme, use in a nation-wide publicity campaign. The signing of the authorization was real, and may be regarded as an instance of overt commitment. As the authors say: "In American society, the affixing of one's signature to a document is a particularly significant act. The signing of checks, contracts, agreements, and the like is clearly understood to indicate a binding obligation on the part of the signer to abide by the provisions of the document."

What, then, is the relationship found between the measure of general attitudes toward Negroes and the behavioral measure? Table 1 presents a summary of the data. Clearly, there is a relationship between the attitude and the behavior. Those who are prejudiced are less willing to have the photograph taken and widely used. True, it is a relatively small relationship, although highly significant statistically. The smallness of the relationship is emphasized when we recall that we are comparing extreme groups. But nevertheless, it is comforting to know that a relation does exist. One can understand the smallness of the relationship by realizing that overt behavior is affected by many other variables in addition to one's own private attitude.

TABLE 1

RELATIONSHIP BETWEEN RACE ATTITUDES AND LEVEL OF SIGNED
AGREEMENT TO BE PHOTOGRAPHED WITH NEGRO

Signed Level of Agreement	Prejudiced Group	Unprejudiced Group
Below mean	18	9
Above mean	5	14

But data such as this do not answer the question we wish to raise here. The fact that existing attitudes relate to overt behavior does not tell us whether or not an attitude *change* brought about by exposure to a persuasive communication will be reflected in a *change*

431

in subsequent behavior. To answer this question we need studies in which, after people have been exposed to a persuasive communication, a measure of attitude or opinion is obtained on the basis of which attitude change can be assessed. Such studies must also, some time later, provide an indication of behavior change relevant to the opinion or attitude, so that one can see whether the cognitive change had any effect on subsequent behavior. We may even be content with studies in which overt behavior is not actually observed. If the subjects are asked questions about what they actually did, this may suffice.

As I mentioned before, we were able to locate only three studies reasonably close to meeting these requirements. One of these, the data from which I reanalyzed, was part of a larger series of studies conducted by Maccoby et al.[3] These investigators selected a sample of mothers whose only child was between three and twelve months old. Each of these mothers was interviewed and was asked, among other questions, at what age she believed toilet training of the child should begin. Three weeks later, each of these women was again interviewed. This time, however, two different procedures were followed. Half the mothers, selected at random, were designated as a control group and were simply re-interviewed. In this second interview they were again asked the age at which they thought toilet training of the child should begin. The other half of the sample, the experimental group, were first exposed to a persuasive communication and then re-interviewed with the same interview used in the control group. The persuasive communication was a specially prepared, illustrated pamphlet entitled "When to Toilet Train Your Child." Each mother in the experimental group was handed this pamphlet and asked to read it, then and there, while the interviewer waited. The pamphlet argued strongly for starting toilet training at the age of twenty-four months. The re-interview occurred immediately after the mother had read the pamphlet. Thus, a comparison of the results of the two groups on the first and second interviews indicated how successful the pamphlet was in changing their opinion concerning when toilet training should start.

In order to assess the persistence of the change in opinion brought about by the pamphlet, both groups of mothers were again interviewed about six months later and were again asked at what age they thought toilet training should begin. Finally, and most importantly for our present concern, about a year after the initial interviews, on the assumption that most of the mothers would have started toilet training already, they were interviewed again and asked at *what age they had*

[3] N. Maccoby, A. K. Romney, J. S. Adams, and Eleanor E. Maccoby, *"Critical Periods" in Seeking and Accepting Information,* Paris-Stanford Studies in Communication, Stanford, Calif., Institute for Communication Research, 1962.

actually started. This last may certainly be regarded as a simple, and probably truthful, report of their actual behavior. Consequently, one can look at the relationship between attitude change and behavior.

In any study in which people are interviewed and re-interviewed over a period of a year, there is an inevitable attrition. Some mothers left the area, others simply could not be reached for one or another interview, and the like. Actually, in this study the drop-out rate was remarkably small. About 80 per cent of the initial sample was actually interviewed all four times, 45 mothers in the experimental group and 47 mothers in the control group. At the time of the fourth interview 34 mothers in each of the two groups had begun toilet training their child and, consequently, it is only for these 68 mothers that we have a measure of actual behavior. The other 24 mothers (11 in the experimental group and 13 in the control group) who had not yet started toilet training by the time of the last interview were asked when they intended to start. Although for these we cannot say that we have a measure of actual behavior, we will present the results for them also.

First, however, let us look at the data presented in Table 2 for those who had started toilet training. The data are rather startling to contemplate—although perhaps not too startling. It is clear that the persuasive communication was quite effective in immediately changing the opinions of the mothers in the experimental group. The change, on the average, was to advocate toilet training 2.3 months later than on the initial interview. The control group did not change materially—actually moving slightly in the direction of advocating earlier toilet training.

TABLE 2

Attitude Change and Behavior of Mothers Who Had Started with Respect to Toilet Training
(data in months)

	Control (N = 34)	Experimental (N = 34)
Immediate opinion change (Interview 2—Interview 1)	−0.2	+2.3
Delayed opinion change (Interview 3—Interview 1)	+0.8	+1.6
Effect of opinion change on behavior (Interview 4—Interview 1)	+2.0	+1.2

Six months later the change was still maintained, although somewhat reduced in magnitude. The experimental group still advocated that toilet training begin 1.6 months later than they had on the initial interview. The control group, however, also now advocated somewhat later toilet training. Nevertheless, there was still a clear difference between the two groups.

When we examine when these mothers actually started to toilet train their child, however, we are met with a surprise. There is, if anything, a reverse relationship between attitude change and behavior. The mothers in the experimental group actually started toilet training 1.2 months later on the average than they had initially advocated. But the mothers in the control group, who had never been subjected to any experimental persuasive communication to change their opinion, started toilet training 2.0 months later than their initial opinion would have indicated. Apparently, in the usual American home, as the child gets older, events conspire to delay toilet training somewhat beyond what the mothers think is probably desirable. But the opinion change in the experimental group clearly did not carry over to affect behavior.

We can also see evidence of the same thing in the data for those mothers who had not as yet started to toilet train their children at the time of the fourth interview. These are presented in Table 3. Here again it is clear that the persuasive communication had a strong immediate effect on the opinions of the mothers in the experimental group and that, six months later, this effect had been maintained. The difference between the control and the experimental groups was almost as large after six months as it was immediately after the persuasive communication. It is also clear that events conspired to make these mothers delay the actual onset of toilet training and conspired equally for both groups. The changed opinion had no effect on the actual behavior of these mothers. The difference between their initial opinion and their intention at the time of the fourth interview was high because these data are for a selected group who had not yet started to toilet train their children. The important thing, however, is that there was no difference between the experimental and control groups.

TABLE 3

ATTITUDE CHANGE AND INTENTIONS OF MOTHERS WHO HAD NOT
STARTED WITH RESPECT TO TOILET TRAINING
(*data in months*)

	Control (N = 13)	Experimental (N = 11)
Immediate opinion change (Interview 2—Interview 1)	−1.2	+2.2
Delayed opinion change (Interview 3—Interview 1)	+0.3	+3.0
Effect of opinion change on intention (Interview 4—Interview 1)	+5.1	+5.2

Another way to look at the data is as follows. Both Table 2 and Table 3 show that the persuasive communication was effective for the experimental group and that the impact of the persuasive communication was still present six months later. If this opinion change had had any effect on behavior, we would expect that, by the time of the fourth interview, a larger percentage of the mothers in the control group would have already started to toilet train their children. More of the mothers in the experimental group, having become convinced that toilet training should start later, would *not* yet have started. Actually, the difference was negligible and slightly in the reverse direction. Thirty-four out of 45 mothers in the experimental group and 34 out of 47 mothers in the control group had already started toilet training by the time of the fourth interview. All in all, we can detect no effect on behavior of a clear and persistent change in opinion brought about by a persuasive communication.

Let us proceed to examine another relevant study. This study, reported by Fleishman, Harris, and Burtt, attempted to measure the effects of a two-week training course for foremen in industry.[4] This training course stressed principles of human relations in dealing with subordinates. Clearly, we are not faced here with the impact of one short persuasive communication but rather with a series of such communications extending over a two-week period. These persuasive communications took the form of lectures and group discussions, assisted by visual aids and role playing. For our purposes here, we may, perhaps, safely regard this two-week training session as a concerted attempt to persuade the foremen that mutual trust, warmth, and consideration for the other person are important aspects of effective leadership. (Before anyone misinterprets what I have said, let me hasten to add that undoubtedly other things went on during the two weeks. I have simply abstracted the aspect of the training session that resembles a persuasive communication.)

Given such a prolonged exposure to such a heavy dose of persuasion, we can well imagine that the opinions of the trainees would change from before to after the two-week session. The investigators attempted to measure any such opinion change in the following way. Before the training session and on its last day, the foremen were given a questionnaire measuring their opinions concerning leadership on the part of foremen. The major dimension on the questionnaire of interest to us here is one the authors label "consideration," made up of questions on such things as friendship, mutual trust, and warmth between the

[4] E. Fleishmann, E. Harris, and H. Burtt, *Leadership and Supervision in Industry: An Evaluation of a Supervisory Training Program,* Columbus, Ohio State University, Bureau of Educational Research, 1955.

leader and his group. As one would expect, the investigators found a clear, appreciable, and significant change on this dimension from before to after the training session. The two weeks of persuasion were effective and the foremen now thought that the dimension of "consideration" was more important than they had previously believed.

This study is relevant for our present purposes because the investigators proceeded to obtain a subsequent on-the-job behavioral measure relevant to the dimension of "consideration." They compared the behavior of those foremen who had attended the training session with a comparable group of foremen who had not. The results are rather surprising. In general, there were no very consistent differences in behavior between the group of foremen who had, and the group who had not, been exposed to the two-week training session. This, in itself, is worrisome. Significant opinion change brought about as a result of a two-week exposure to a series of persuasive communications shows no relationship to behavior. But the results are actually even more surprising than this. The investigators divided their group of "trained" foremen into subgroups according to how recently they had completed the training course. After all, it might be reasoned that the effect of the training disappears with time. If so, one should at least be able to observe an effect on behavior among those who had most recently completed their two-week training course. The results show that the "most recently trained sub-group" was actually *lower* in consideration *behavior* than the group that had never been exposed to any training —had never been exposed to the impact of the persuasive communications. Once more we see the hint of a slightly inverse relationship between attitude change and behavior.

We will now proceed to examine the only other study we were able to find bearing on the question of the relation between opinion change and behavior. This is the well known study by Janis and Feshbach on the effects of fear-arousing communications.[5] Because the authors of this study did not interpret their data as bearing on this question, we will have to put a different interpretation on their experiment in order to make it relevant. Perhaps this different interpretation is not justifiable. But since so few published studies could be found that bear on our problem at all, I will proceed with the re-interpretation.

Of four groups of high school students used in the experiment, one, the control group, was not exposed to the relevant persuasive communication. The other three groups each heard an illustrated lecture about proper care of teeth and gums that attempted to persuade them

[5] I. Janis and S. Feshbach, "Effects of Fear-arousing Communications," *Journal of Abnormal and Social Psychology*, Vol. 48, 1953, pp. 78-92.

that it was important to care for the teeth properly in order to avoid unpleasant consequences. The lectures each of the three groups heard differed in their emphasis on the painful consequences of improper oral hygiene. In the words of the authors:

> One of the main characteristics of the *Strong* appeal was the use of personalized threat-references explicitly directed to the audience, i.e., statements to the effect that "this can happen to you." The *Moderate* appeal, on the other hand, described the dangerous consequences of improper oral hygiene in a more factual way using impersonal language. In the *Minimal* appeal, the limited discussion of unfavorable consequences also used a purely factual style.

One might expect that the more emphasis put upon the importance of proper oral hygiene, and the more personal the importance is made, the more effective the communication would be in making the listener feel that proper oral hygiene is something to be concerned about. Thus, we might expect that the Strong appeal would be most effective, and the Minimal appeal least effective, in persuading people to be concerned about proper oral hygiene. One week before hearing the lecture, and immediately after hearing the lecture, all the subjects were asked two questions about how concerned or worried they were about the possibility of developing diseased gums and decayed teeth. The authors interpret these questions as indicating the degree of emotionality aroused by the persuasive communication, but, for the sake of our re-interpretation, let us look at the answers as reflecting opinion change. After all, the communications attempted to concern the listeners about these things. Let us see how well they succeeded. The data are shown in Table 4.

TABLE 4

PERCENTAGE WHO FELT "SOMEWHAT" OR "VERY" WORRIED
ABOUT DECAYED TEETH AND DISEASED GUMS

	Before	After
Strong appeal (N = 50)	34	76
Moderate appeal (N = 50)	24	50
Minimal appeal (N = 50)	22	46
Control group (N = 50)	30	38

As one might expect, the persuasive communications were all effective to some extent—they all succeeded in creating more change in concern about oral hygiene than appeared in the control group. Within the experimental conditions we find that the Strong appeal was, plausibly, most effective. The Moderate and Minimal appeals seem to have been about equally effective.

The three persuasive communications, in addition to attempting to persuade the listeners of the importance of oral hygiene, also attempted to persuade them about the proper way to brush one's teeth and the characteristics of a "proper" type of toothbrush. Here, however, the three communications were equal. Before and after measures were obtained concerning the beliefs in the desirability of the recommended characteristics of a toothbrush. On these issues, where the communications did not differ, the authors state, ". . . all three experimental groups, as compared with the Control group, showed a significant change in the direction of accepting the conclusions presented in the communication. Among the three experimental groups, there were no significant differences with respect to net changes."

In other words, the three experimental groups were equally persuaded about the proper procedures to use in caring for the gums and teeth, but the Strong appeal group was made to feel these procedures were more important. If there were a simple, straightforward relationship between opinion or attitude change and behavior, one would expect the control group to change their behavior least (or not at all) and the Strong appeal group to change their behavior most.

On the initial questionnaire, given one week before the students heard the persuasive communications, five questions asked them to describe the way they were currently brushing their teeth—in other words, asked them to report their behavior. A week after having been exposed to the persuasive communications they were again asked these same five questions, covering aspects of tooth brushing that were stressed in the persuasive communications as the proper way to brush one's teeth. The answers were scored in terms of whether the student did or did not use the recommended practice. Since these questions asked the students about what they actually did when they brushed their teeth, perhaps it is legitimate to regard their answers as truthful reports concerning their actual behavior. This may or may not be a valid interpretation of their responses, but, assuming that it is, let us see what the relationship is between attitude change and their reported behavior. Table 5 presents the data on the percentage of subjects in each group who changed in the direction of increased use of the practices recommended in the persuasive communication.

It is clear from even a cursory glance at the data that the results do not represent a simple relation between attitude change and behavior. It is true that those who heard any of the persuasive communications reported more change in their behavior than the control group. This, however, may simply reflect the fact that subjects in the experimental conditions learned the proper terminology and what is approved. The interesting comparison is among the experimental groups. Within the

TABLE 5

PERCENTAGE WHO CHANGED TOWARD INCREASED USE OF
RECOMMENDED DENTAL PRACTICES

	Per Cent Who Changed
Strong appeal	28
Moderate appeal	44
Minimal appeal	50
Control group	22

experimental conditions, the relation between behavior and the degree to which students were made to feel concerned about oral hygiene was actually in the reverse direction from what one would expect from any simple relationship between attitude change and behavior.

The authors offer as an explanation for the inverse relationship the hypothesis that the Strong appeal created strong fear and, hence, subjects exposed to this communication were motivated to avoid thinking about it. Perhaps this is the correct explanation, although little evidence is presented in the study to support the assertion that strong fear was aroused in the Strong appeal condition. And it is certainly not clear why people who are more concerned about something are not more likely to take action. If we think of the results of this study together with the results of the previous studies I described (and let me stress again that these are the only three studies I have been able to find that are at all relevant to the issue at hand), it seems clear that we cannot glibly assume a relationship between attitude change and behavior. Indeed, it seems that the absence of research in this area is a glaring omission and that the whole problem needs thinking through.

Let us, for the sake of the present discussion, put aside the possibility that responses to a questionnaire after having been exposed to a persuasive communication may reflect nothing more than "lip service"; that is, the person's real opinions and attitudes may not have changed at all but his responses may simply reflect a desire not to appear unreasonable in the eyes of the experimenter. This kind of thing may affect responses to questionnaires to some extent, but it seems unreasonable to imagine that it is a dominant effect or that it could account for differences among experimental conditions. Undoubtedly, to a major extent, a person's answers to a questionnaire reflect how he really feels about the issue at that moment. Then why should one not observe a clear relationship with behavior?

I would like to suggest one possible reason for a complex relationship between attitude or opinion change and behavior. I have no data to support this suggestion, but perhaps it may offer some conceptual basis for future research that will clarify the problem. I want to suggest that when opinions or attitudes are changed through the momentary impact of a persuasive communication, this change, all by itself, is inherently unstable and will disappear or remain isolated unless an environmental or behavioral change can be brought about to support and maintain it.

To illustrate and amplify this suggestion, let us imagine a person who held the unlikely opinion that giving speeches was a productive and worthwhile thing to do. Undoubtedly, such an opinion would have been developed over many years on the basis of his own experience, what other people say about it, and also his own needs and motives. For example, he has observed that many people engage in the practice of giving speeches and from this it seems clear that it must have some desirable aspects. He has even read that at A.P.A. conventions papers are held to short periods of time because so many people (more than can be accommodated) want to make speeches. Surely, giving a speech must be a good thing to do. What is more, he has observed that many people actually go to listen to such speeches—a fact that certainly supports his opinion.

There is even more to the "reality" basis he has for this opinion. Once when he gave a speech, two people came up to him afterward and told him how wonderful they thought it was. What better evidence could he have that it was indeed worthwhile to engage in this activity? Furthermore, no one ever came up to him to tell him it was a waste of time. In addition, he found that he got quite a bit of personal satisfaction out of having all those people listening to what he said. All in all, the opinion became rather well established. There was considerable evidence to support it, none to contradict it, and it was a pleasant opinion to hold.

Needless to say, such a well-established opinion would affect the person's behavior. This does not mean that at every possible opportunity he would give a speech, but rather that he would be more likely to do so than someone who did not hold the opinion that such speeches were very worthwhile. It would not be a perfect relationship, since many other factors would affect his behavior, for example, the availability of time and whether or not he really had anything to say. But, by and large, one would observe a positive relationship.

Let us now imagine that the following unhappy incident occurs in the life of this contented speechmaker. One day, shortly before he is to leave town to go to some distant place to deliver a speech, he happens to engage in conversation with a few of his friends. One of them, on learning about the imminent trip, raises the question as to why it is necessary or valuable to do this kind of thing. After all, the monetary cost and the time spent are rather large. What does an audience get out of a personally delivered speech that they couldn't get just as well out of reading it?

Let us imagine the highly unlikely event that, in the ensuing discussion, no one is able to come up with a good answer to this question and so a real impact is made on the speechmaker's opinion. If one were to give this person a questionnaire at this moment, one would discover that a change in his opinion had been brought about. He would feel less certain that it was a good thing to do. But what are the implications for the future of this change in his opinion? After this friendly but unsettling discussion, our speechmaker returns to the same environment that produced his opinion initially, and, we can consequently assume, there will be pressures to return to his former opinion. Pressures, indeed, that he has not felt in a long time. Furthermore, he is about to leave to make a speech and he goes ahead with what he is already committed to doing. This obviously further helps to restore his former opinion. The world he encounters remains the same, his experiences remain the same, and so his opinion will tend to revert. His behavior will remain the same or perhaps even intensify in an effort to restore his former opinion. The exact content of his opinion may indeed have changed somewhat and become more differentiated. He may buttress his original opinion by the notion that many people will listen to a speech who would not read it and that it is important to communicate to many people; he may persuade himself that the personal contact is in some unspecified way very important; he may even tell himself that a practice so widespread must be good even if he, at the moment, cannot see its good aspects clearly.

It is my present contention that, in order to produce a stable behavior change following opinion change, an environmental change must also be produced which, representing reality, will support the new opinion and the new behavior. Otherwise, the same factors that produced the initial opinion and the behavior will continue to operate to nullify the effect of the opinion change.

Thus far we have speculated mainly about some possible reasons for the *absence* of a relationship between opinion change following a persuasive communication and resulting behavior. We have not grappled with the perplexing question raised by the persistent hint of a slightly inverse relationship (if three times may be called persistent). I must confess that I have no very good or interesting speculations to offer here. Let me also emphasize that the data certainly do not warrant assuming that such an inverse relationship really does exist: they do no more than raise a possible suspicion. If this inverse relation is found not to exist, there is, of course, nothing to explain. If, however, it does exist, we must find some explanation for it.

What I want to stress is that we have been quietly and placidly ignoring a very vital problem. We have essentially persuaded ourselves that we can simply assume that there is, of course, a relationship between attitude change and subsequent behavior and, since this relationship is obvious, why should we labor to overcome the considerable technical difficulties of investigating it? But the few relevant studies certainly show that this "obvious" relationship probably does not exist and that, indeed, some nonobvious relationships may exist. The problem needs concerted investigation.

**SELECTIVE EXPOSURE
TO INFORMATION: A
CRITICAL REVIEW**
David O. Sears and
Jonathan L. Freedman

O NE OF THE most widely accepted principles in sociology and social psychology is the principle of selective exposure. It is a basic fact in the thinking of many social scientists about communication effects. For example, Lazarsfeld, Berelson, and Gaudet find it an indispensable link in their explanation of why a political campaign mainly activates and reinforces pre-existing preferences or predispositions.[1] Hyman and Sheatsley[2] and Klapper[3] make the more general point: information campaigns, and mass communications of any kind, rarely have important persuasive impact because, among other things, of selective exposure. In Festinger's very influential cognitive dissonance theory, selective exposure plays a central role as a prime mechanism for dissonance reduction.[4] McGuire based an extensive program of research on immunization against persuasion on the assumption that people are often quite unacquainted

---

* Preparation of this manuscript was supported by NSF grants to the authors.

[1] P. F. Lazarsfeld, B. Berelson, and Hazel Gaudet, *The People's Choice,* 2nd ed., New York, Columbia University Press, 1948.

[2] H. H. Hyman and P. B. Sheatsley, "Some Reasons Why Information Campaigns Fail," *Public Opinion Quarterly,* Vol. 11, 1947, pp. 413-423.

[3] J. T. Klapper, *The Effects of Mass Communications,* Glencoe, Ill., Free Press, 1960.

[4] L. Festinger, *A Theory of Cognitive Dissonance,* Evanston, Ill., Row, Peterson, 1957.

Originally published in Volume 31, Number 2, 1967 of the *Public Opinion Quarterly*.

with counterpropaganda, because of selective exposure.[5] Experimental psychologists and survey researchers alike agree that laboratory and field studies of mass communications often come to quite different conclusions because, in large part, of selective exposure.[6] So the theme of selective exposure runs through much of the research on attitudes and communication of the past two decades.

Nevertheless, the empirical literature on selective exposure has been rather unsatisfying. Partly this is because the term itself has been used in a confusing way. The observation of an empirical correlation between attitudes and exposure has rarely been distinguished from an active psychological preference for supportive information, although they clearly may be quite different. Perhaps more important, a substantial amount of research has been done in the last decade relating to these two questions, and the results are not as unequivocal as one might expect.[7] Under these circumstances, a thorough review and assessment of this research would appear to be in order. The purpose of this paper is, therefore, first to clarify what is meant by "selective exposure," then to characterize the evidence leading to its use, and finally to evaluate the evidence regarding whether or not there is a psychological tendency to prefer supportive to nonsupportive information.

DEFINITION

First, what is meant by "selective exposure"? How is the term generally used?

Any systematic bias in audience composition. Sometimes it is used to describe any bias whatever in the composition of a communication audience, as long as the bias can be correlated with anything unusual in communication content. So, when the audience for educational broadcasts on the radio is disproportionately composed of highly educated persons, selective or "partisan" exposure is said to be pres-

---

[5] W. J. McGuire, "Inducing Resistance to Persuasion: Some Contemporary Approaches," in L. Berkowitz, ed., *Advances in Experimental Social Psychology*, Vol. 1, New York, Academic Press, 1964.

[6] C. I. Hovland, "Reconciling Conflicting Results Derived from Experimental and Survey Studies of Attitude Change," *American Psychologist*, Vol. 14, 1959, pp. 8-17. S. M. Lipset, P. F. Lazarsfeld, A. Barton, and J. Linz, "The Psychology of Voting: An Analysis of Political Behavior," in G. Lindzey ed., *Handbook of Social Psychology*, Vol. 2, Cambridge, Mass., Addison-Wesley, 1954.

[7] Several other writers have commented upon this in passing. See D. Papageorgis and W. J. McGuire, "The Generality of Immunity to Persuasion Produced by Pre-exposure to Weakened Counterarguments," *Journal of Abnormal and Social Psychology*, Vol. 62, 1961, pp. 475-481; I. D. Steiner, "Receptivity to Supportive versus Nonsupportive Communications," *Journal of Abnormal and Social Psychology*, Vol. 65, 1962, pp. 266-267; and J. W. Brehm and A. R. Cohen, *Explorations in Cognitive Dissonance*, New York, Wiley, 1962.

ent. The same is said when broadcasts about a particular ethnic group reach more members of that group than would be expected by chance.[8]

Perhaps the most general statement has been made by Berelson and Steiner in their redoubtable collection of propositions about human behavior: "People tend to see and hear communications that are favorable or congenial to their predispositions; they are more likely to see and hear congenial communications than neutral or hostile ones." The predispositions referred to include "sex role, educational status, interest and involvement, ethnic status, political attitude, aesthetic position, and, indeed, any way of characterising people that matters to them."[9] Expressed in this form, the selective exposure hypothesis offers no explanation for *why* audiences are biased. The only assertion is that they are biased, and are biased systematically along dimensions that parallel salient aspects of the communication or attributes of the communicator. In this form, the proposition is perhaps too general to be of much use.

Unusual agreement about a matter of opinion. The most common, and perhaps most interesting, application of the previous definition has to do with matters of opinion. "Selectivity" describes audience bias in the direction of agreeing to an unusual extent with the communicator's stand on an issue relevant to the communication. Lazarsfeld *et al.* put it this way: "Exposure is always selective; in other words, a positive relationship exists between people's opinions and what they choose to listen to or read."[10] Lipset *et al.* later said that "most people expose themselves, most of the time, to the kind of propaganda with which they agree to begin with."[11] Klapper summarized the point this way: "By and large, people tend to expose themselves to those mass communications which are in accord with their existing attitudes."[12] Childs concludes: "Innumerable studies show that readers tend to read what they agree with, approve, or like."[13] These are simply descriptive statements: they only assert that communication audiences usually share, to an extraordinary degree, the viewpoints of the communicator. These statements again are noncommittal with respect to the *cause* of this bias. For that reason, this form of the selective exposure hypothesis will be referred to below as *"de facto selectivity."*

Preference for supportive, rather than nonsupportive, information.

---

[8] Lazarsfeld *et al., op. cit.,* p. 166.

[9] B. Berelson and G. A. Steiner, *Human Behavior,* New York, Harcourt Brace & World, 1964, pp. 529-530.

[10] *Op. cit.,* p. 164.

[11] *Op. cit.,* p. 1158.

[12] *Op. cit.,* p. 19.

[13] H. L. Childs, *Public Opinion,* Princeton, N. J., Van Nostrand, 1965.

The strongest form of the selective exposure proposition is that people prefer exposure to communications that agree with their pre-existing opinions. Hence, people are thought actively to seek out material that supports their opinions, and actively to avoid material that challenges them. Lazarsfeld *et al.* hypothesized: "It is likely that a desire for re-inforcement of one's own point of view exists."[14] Two decades later, the hypothesis had been confirmed: "Although self-selection of ex-posure in line with predispositions is mainly conscious and deliberate, it can also operate nonconsciously as well."[15] And the Behavioral Sci-ences Subpanel of the President's Science Advisory Committee felt the proposition was sufficiently well-documented to be included in the corpus of established social science fact: ". . . individuals engage in selective exposure. . . . If a new piece of information would weaken the existing structure of their ideas and emotions, it will be shunned . . . if it reinforces the structure, it will be sought out. . . ."[16] In this form, then, the cause of *de facto* selectivity is quite explicit. People expose themselves to communications with which they already agree and do not expose themselves to those with which they disagree, be-cause they actively seek the former and actively avoid the latter. Why? Presumably because of a general psychological preference for com-patible information.

Since the focus of this paper is upon opinions and attitudes, the first and most general of these definitions will not be discussed. Let us then consider the evidence for selective exposure in these latter two senses. For consistency of usage, they will be referred to as *"de facto selectivity"* and "selective exposure," respectively, in the remainder of the paper.

DE FACTO SELECTIVITY

Biases in the composition of voluntary audiences to mass communi-cations have been reported often in survey studies. Often these biases parallel the opinion dimension emphasized by the communicator, and are in the direction of unusual initial agreement between audience and communicator. A typical example is Senator William Knowland's tel-ethon in the 1958 California gubernatorial election. Interviews with voters immediately after the election revealed that twice as many Re-publicans as Democrats (proportionately) had seen this Republican candidate's program. Thirty per cent more viewers watched the pro-gram in Republican homes than in Democratic homes, and the aver-

---

[14] *Loc. cit.*

[15] Berelson and Steiner, *op. cit.*, p. 530.

[16] Behavioral Sciences Subpanel, President's Science Advisory Committee, "Re-port to the President," *Behavioral Science,* Vol. 7, 1962, p. 277.

age Republican viewer watched the program for about an hour longer than did the average Democratic viewer.[17]

Mass meetings also seem to attract biased audiences. A typical example is the audience of the Christian Anti-Communist Crusade School held in Oakland, California, in 1962. The Crusade is largely organized and run by white Protestants of a conservative political persuasion. And those who attended the school were over three times as likely to think the internal Communist threat to be "a very great danger" as a national sample of citizens asked the same question. Republicans were also heavily overrepresented: 66 per cent were Republicans and 8 per cent identified themselves as Democrats.[18]

Extended propaganda campaigns seem to elicit *de facto* selectivity as well. The classic finding is Lazarsfeld *et al.*'s: Of those respondents with constant voting intentions from May to October, about two-thirds were exposed predominantly to propaganda favoring their side, and less than one-fourth mainly to propaganda favoring the other side.[19] Similarly, in a study done on the University of California loyalty oath controversy, Lipset found newspaper-reading habits to be systematically related to general liberalism or conservatism, party preference, and attitudes toward the controversy. Students tended to read newspapers whose editorial policy was closest to their own opinions.[20] And in a somewhat different realm, Ehrlich *et al.* found that people, whether or not they had just bought new cars, had read a higher percentage of the available ads about their own makes than about any other make.[21]

Each of these demonstrations shares a common basis: the correlation of positions on an attitude dimension with an act, or a series of acts, of exposure to mass communications. A causal relationship has often been inferred from these correlations, although they do not permit it to be determined in any rigorous sense, of course. Data collected in experimental situations are more appropriate for that end, and will be discussed later. Yet, for it to be likely that attitudes are an important

[17] W. Schramm and R. F. Carter, "Effectiveness of a Political Telethon," *Public Opinion Quarterly*, Vol. 23, 1959, pp. 121-126.

[18] R. E. Wolfinger, Barbara K. Wolfinger, K. Prewitt, and Sheilah Rosenhack, "The Clientele of the Christian Anti-Communism Crusade," in D. E. Apter, ed., *Ideology and Discontent*, Glencoe, Ill., Free Press, 1964. These authors do not discuss "selective exposure" per se, but the data are relevant in the present context.

[19] *Op. cit.*

[20] S. M. Lipset, "Opinion Formation in a Crisis Situation," *Public Opinion Quarterly*, Vol. 17, 1953, pp. 20-46.

[21] Danuta Ehrlich, I. Guttmann, P. Schonbach, and J. Mills, "Post-decision Exposure to Relevant Information," *Journal of Abnormal and Social Psychology*, Vol. 54, 1957, pp. 98-102.

cause of selective exposure, two criteria must be met by correlational studies: (1) The correlation must be well documented. It should hold, fairly unequivocally, in most cases. (2) Attitudes should be better predictors of (i.e. correlate more highly with) exposure than other variables. These studies should be evaluated with respect to these two criteria, for if they fall short, the causal role of attitudes seems likely to be modest.

Strength and generality of the effect. It is not appropriate to review all studies yielding *de facto* selectivity, since the only point here is to see whether or not it has been established beyond much doubt. Let us consider the strength of the effect as it appears in the classic study by Lazarsfeld, Berelson, and Gaudet, since it is almost always cited as representative. They indeed found that their respondents had been exposed predominantly to propaganda supporting their predispositions. A breakdown into parties, however, reveals the fact that this finding held only for persons with Republican predispositions. Far from being selectively exposed, those with Democratic predispositions were almost evenly divided, 50.4 per cent being exposed primarily to Democratic propaganda, and 49.6 per cent primarily to Republican propaganda.[22] Thus, only the Republicans appear actually to have been selective.

However, if one considers the relative availability of pro-Republican and pro-Democratic propaganda, the finding becomes even more paradoxical. Actually, 68.8 per cent of the available partisan propaganda in the campaign was pro-Republican.[23] It is thus hardly surprising that 69.7 per cent of those with Republican predispositions were exposed primarily to pro-Republican information, and 30.3 per cent primarily to pro-Democratic publicity.[24] The exposure of those with Republican predispositions almost exactly matched the partisan division of available information. In fact, looked at from this point of view, it was the Democrats who were selectively exposed, even though actually exposed to equal amounts of Democratic and Republican propaganda, since they were exposed to considerably more Democratic propaganda than might have been expected by chance. And in the later Elmira study one finds a similar pattern: the Republicans' exposure was only 54 per cent pro-Dewey, not up to the considerable pro-Republican margin in available information. The Democrats' exposure was 57

[22] *Op. cit.,* p. 96.

[23] *Ibid.,* p. 111.

[24] *Ibid.,* p. 96. The Republican "constant partisans" were slightly more selective than would be expected from availability alone, while late-deciding Republicans were slightly less so. Constant and late-deciding Democrats, alike, were exposed to more supportive propaganda than would be expected from availability (*ibid.,* pp. 82, 164). These percentages all exclude respondents exposed equally to both sides, and exclude neutral propaganda.

per cent pro-Truman, despite the rarity of pro-Democratic items in the media.[25] So it is obvious that even in these well-designed studies the effect does not clearly hold for both sets of partisans.

Measurement problems. Even so, many reports of *de facto* selectivity may well overestimate the magnitude of the effect because of the kinds of measures used. Perhaps the most obvious problem is that only one interview has been used in most studies. If, in this interview, attitudes and exposure favor the same side of an issue, the interpretation is ambiguous: the congruence may reflect either attitude change or *de facto* selectivity.[26] It is not ambiguous, of course, when the attitude or preference has been unequivocally proven to antedate the opportunities for exposure, as, for instance, when the respondent is known to have bought a particular car before the specific ads in question appeared, or in panel studies. However, most studies do not allow this, and must simply hope the respondent is recalling accurately, ignore the possibility of attitude change altogether, or try to argue it away. None of these is a substitute for an advance measure, and each one maximizes the probability of obtaining *de facto* selectivity, since any attitude change is likely to reduce the discrepancy between communication and respondent's position, rather than increase it.

Second, almost all studies have depended upon retrospective self-reports of exposure, rather than direct and immediate observation of it. It is not possible to say with any certainty what kind of bias this may introduce (owing to selective memory, selective reporting, etc.), but it does seem highly likely to be a systematic bias in any given study. This shortcoming is, of course, a much more difficult one to remedy.

Alternative predictors. Two general possibilities arise when we consider whether other variables are better predictors of selectivity than attitudes. One is relatively straightforward: sometimes other variables simply are more strongly correlated with selectivity than are political or social attitudes. This raises the question of which is the more likely causal agent. The second possibility is that other variables, themselves associated with differences in *absolute* rates of exposure, have artifactually produced *de facto* selectivity.

As an illustration of the first possibility, let us consider a case in

[25] B. R. Berelson, P. F. Lazarsfeld, and W. N. McPhee, *Voting: A Study of Opinion Formation in a Presidential Election,* Chicago, University of Chicago Press, 1954, p. 245.
[26] Raymond and Alice Bauer take a strong position on this point. In the absence of any other information, they say, one must interpret any such correlations as "a result of *selective exposure,* rather than evidence for the effects of communications." See their "America, Mass Society, and Mass Media," *Journal of Social Issues,* Vol. 16, 1960, p. 29.

which the communications are expressly ideological, and in which one would thus think exposure to be unequivocally determined by ideological preferences. Those attending the Christian Anti-Communist Crusade were indeed unrepresentative ideologically, but also, as it happened, religiously (only one-third as many Catholics as in the Bay Area generally), racially (no nonwhites in the sample at all, as opposed to 12 per cent in the Bay Area generally), educationally (52 per cent were college graduates, as opposed to 13 per cent in the Bay Area), and so on.[27] Clearly, the school was an upper-middle-class WASP affair. Political conservatism predicted attendance rather well, but then so did a variety of other background variables. In fact, a substantial number of Crusaders ascribed their own attendance to church influence. So it may be quite arbitrary to give ideology the major credit for exposure, even in this seemingly obvious case.

To illustrate the second possibility, consider the variable that predicts differences in absolute rates of exposure to public affairs communications most powerfully, years of education. Now, clearly, *de facto* selectivity effects could be obtained with any issue about which highly educated people generally disagree with poorly educated people, if we consider only propaganda favorable to the former's position. There are numerous positions of this kind: pro–civil liberties, pro–civil rights, and internationalist positions are (at present) positively related to years of education. So, naturally, pro–civil liberties, pro–civil rights, and pro-internationalism propaganda reaches mainly those sympathetic to it. A typical example is the massive pro-UN campaign in Cincinnati in 1947-1948. As usual, those who had favored the UN at the beginning of the campaign turned out to have received most of the pro-UN propaganda. It was therefore concluded that, "if there was an increase in exposure [during the campaign], *it was their previous orientation* [i.e. attitude toward the UN] *which determined the extent to which people exposed themselves to further information about the United Nations*" (emphasis ours).[28] But the best way to be exposed to the campaign was to go to church, attend service club and PTA meetings, be a regular newspaper reader, have the radio on most of the time, and talk to one's children about what had happened in school. Thus, not surprisingly, college-educated persons were exposed to the campaign at a rate *four times* that of grammar-school-educated persons. These are all things that well-educated people are likely to do more than poorly educated people, regardless of how they feel about

[27] Wolfinger *et al., op. cit.*
[28] Shirley A. Star and Helen M. Hughes, "Report of an Educational Campaign: The Cincinnati Plan for the United Nations," *American Journal of Sociology*, Vol. 55, 1950, p. 398.

the United Nations. So exposure to the campaign is at least as well predicted by education as by internationalist attitudes, and education seems to be the more likely predictor.

Thus many reports of de facto selective exposure may represent little more than cases in which highly educated persons, who normally are overrepresented in any audience for public affairs presentations, also share a common set of political, social, and/or economic attitudes. Star and Hughes are clearly on solid ground in recommending that information campaigns be directed especially at "women, the relatively uneducated, the elderly, and the poor," since they are normally least likely to be reached.[29] However, low rates of exposure of such population groups must be distinguished from alleged avoidance of information because of discrepant beliefs.[30]

Conclusion. So, on several grounds, published reports of *de facto* selectivity fall somewhat short of representing ideal proof that people do in fact "tend to expose themselves to those mass communications which are in accord with their existing attitudes." Often it has not been established that these attitudes actually did exist beforehand, and often it is not entirely clear what the pattern of exposure actually was. The magnitude of the effect seems rather small, or limited to one set of partisans in some cases. And allegedly selective information seekers often cannot be distinguished from promiscuous information gatherers, because it is not clear that they have both high rates of exposure to friendly propaganda and low rates of exposure to hostile propaganda. Finally, "existing attitudes" often represent only one of several variables that correlate highly with exposure, and their selection as the best predictor may be unnecessarily arbitrary.

Nevertheless, it still seems likely that *de facto* selectivity holds, as a descriptive generalization, on many occasions and for many people. Clearly, demonstrations of the effect have been considerably less conclusive than one might think. But even if it had been clearly demonstrated, it would not indicate that people prefer exposure to supportive information, although that would be a very natural implication. So the next step is to examine the evidence for selective exposure defined in the third sense cited above.

[29] *Ibid.*, p. 397.

[30] In fact, sometimes well-educated groups expose themselves to discrepant propaganda even more than groups who should agree with it. Lazarsfeld reports that the "high" socio-economic class listened to two of the most important New Deal speeches at a rate better than 50 per cent greater than the "low" class. It seems unlikely that this great interest among "high" class listeners arose because they generally agreed so much with the two speakers, Franklin Roosevelt and Hugo Black. P. F. Lazarsfeld, *Radio and the Printed Page,* New York, Duell, Sloan, and Pearce, 1940, pp. 26-28.

IS THERE A GENERAL PSYCHOLOGICAL PREFERENCE FOR SUPPORTIVE INFORMATION?

If a person is given a choice between supportive and nonsupportive information, will he prefer exposure to the former, all other things being equal? This is the crucial question, and there is a considerable amount of research bearing on it. The typical procedure has been to measure a subject's opinion on an issue and then determine which of several communications on the issue he would like to read or hear. The opinions have ranged from firmly established ones, such as political preferences and ideas about child development, to those probably adopted for the first time during the experiment itself, such as preferences between verdicts in mock murder trials or essay and multiple-choice examinations. The communications have been, most often, written articles offered in a way that clearly communicates their positions on the issue. However, the choice has sometimes been between oral presentations, and sometimes actual exposure, rather than stated preferences, has been measured. The appropriate dependent variable, in all cases, is a measure of interest in supportive information relative to interest in nonsupportive information. "Supportive" information is usually defined simply as the communicator's taking the same general position as the subject, and "nonsupportive" as his taking the opposite position.

Preference for supportive information. A clear preference for supportive information was obtained in two studies. In one, persons who had recently bought a car were shown eight envelopes allegedly containing advertisements for different brands of cars, and asked to indicate which two they would most like to read. Over 80 per cent of the respondents chose an envelope containing ads for their own car (presumably supportive of their purchase), as contrasted with the chance figure of 25 per cent. The difference is highly significant.[31]

Freedman and Sears gave California citizens a choice among several pamphlets on the two candidates in the 1962 gubernatorial contest. Considering only those subjects who selected a partisan pamphlet as their first choice, 58 per cent chose one favoring their candidate. This, too, was significantly greater than chance (50 per cent).[32]

In both these studies it was possible to control for any special attractiveness of one alternative, because subjects holding various positions were tested. In a third study this was not possible, so the results are equivocal. Adams gave mothers of young children a choice between

[31] Ehrlich *et al., op. cit.*

[32] J. L. Freedman and D. O. Sears, "Voters' Preferences among Types of Information," *American Psychologist,* Vol. 18, 1963, p. 375 (abstract).

two speeches to be given later at a local university—one supporting the hereditary theory of child development, the other supporting an environmental position. The speech conforming to their own initial opinions was selected by 75.9 per cent of the mothers, significantly greater than chance.[33] Unfortunately, 94 per cent of the mothers expressed a pro-environmental view, and the few pro-heredity mothers were not considered in the analysis, thus confounding preference with initial position. A pro-environment speech would seem to be more useful and intrinsically interesting, regardless of whether or not one agreed with it: information on how environment shapes behavior is often useful to the mother of a young child, while information on the genes' impact may not be quite so timely. So, in the absence of pro-heredity subjects, it is not possible to assess whether the obtained preference for the environmental talk was due to its universal attractiveness or to its supportiveness.

The results of two other studies are even more difficult to interpret. Mills, Aronson, and Robinson gave students a choice between taking a multiple-choice exam or an essay exam, and then asked them to rank their interest in various articles favorable or unfavorable to the two kinds of exams. Some subjects were given a choice among positively oriented articles, and these subjects significantly preferred those favorable to the chosen exam. Others chose among negatively oriented articles, and these subjects slightly (not significantly) preferred articles unfavorable to the chosen exam.[34] In other words, supportive information was preferred among the former subjects, nonsupportive slightly preferred among the latter.

Rosen's attempt at replication of this study raises an important question about even these rather equivocal results. One would think that the most relevant belief to the student's choice of exam is his estimate of which one will give him the better grade. Thus, to support this belief, an article should argue that the chosen exam will give him the better mark, and, to challenge it, an article should take the position that he would have done better on the kind of test he did not choose. In fact, the article titles used by Mills *et al.* dealt with matters such as the difficulty of the tests and how much anxiety they usually aroused, and not on how well the subject would do relative to the rest of the class. It is therefore doubtful that any of the articles were supportive or nonsupportive in any meaningful sense. Rosen therefore improved the design by including two such articles. These suggested that the subject had made the wrong choice, e.g., "These

---

[33] J. S. Adams, "Reduction of Cognitive Dissonance by Seeking Consonant Information," *Journal of Abnormal and Social Psychology*, Vol. 62, 1961, pp. 74-78.

[34] J. Mills, E. Aronson, and H. Robinson, "Selectivity in Exposure to Information," *Journal of Abnormal and Social Psychology*, Vol. 59, 1959, pp. 250-253.

authors present some evidence that students who prefer essay exams generally do a lot better on objective tests." Clearly, this title is nonsupportive for those who chose essay exams.

Rosen's findings are both striking and odd. Considering all article titles, the subjects significantly preferred information favorable to the chosen exam. But 67 per cent of the subjects preferred the clearly nonsupportive new title to the other new title![35] This certainly conflicts with the over-all result of the study. And the two studies, considered together, provide evidence of about every kind: with positive articles, subjects prefer supportive information; with negative articles, they have no preference; and with titles advocating reversal of choice (and thus clearly differing in supportiveness), they strongly prefer nonsupportive information.

No preference. A series of experiments show no preference between supportive and nonsupportive information. In two separate studies, Feather found that neither smokers nor nonsmokers had any significant preference between an article suggesting that smoking causes lung cancer and one arguing that smoking does not cause lung cancer. Similarly, Mills and Ross obtained opinions on the use of television as an educational tool, and then asked the subjects to indicate their interest in reading articles for and against their position. In none of a variety of experimental conditions was there any significant preference for either supportive or nonsupportive articles. And Jecker told subjects they would play a competitive game in cooperation with a partner, and then measured the time devoted to reading favorable and unfavorable information about the partner. Exposure times for the two kinds of information did not differ, regardless of whether the subject had already chosen the partner, was about to choose the partner, or was only given limited choice in the matter.[36]

In three other studies, each subject read excerpts from a (fictitious) murder-trial transcript, and gave his verdict. He then indicated his preferences among several articles dealing with the case, two of which were pro-acquittal and two pro-conviction. Considering only these four articles, Sears found that exactly 50 per cent of the subjects preferred an article supporting their votes; Sears and Freedman found that 45.4 per cent preferred a supportive article; and the figure for the third

[35] S. Rosen, "Post-decision Affinity for Incompatible Information," *Journal of Abnormal and Social Psychology*, Vol. 63, 1961, pp. 188-190.

[36] N. T. Feather, "Cigarette Smoking and Lung Cancer: A Study of Cognitive Dissonance," *Australian Journal of Psychology*, Vol. 14, 1962, pp. 55-64; N. T. Feather, "Cognitive Dissonance, Sensitivity, and Evaluation," *Journal of Abnormal and Social Psychology*, Vol. 66, 1963, pp. 157-163; J. Mills and A. Ross, "Effects of Commitment and Certainty upon Interest in Supporting Information," *Journal of Abnormal and Social Psychology*, Vol. 68, 1964, pp. 552-555; J. D. Jecker, "Selective Exposure to New Information," in L. Festinger, *Conflict, Decision and Dissonance*, Stanford, Calif., Stanford University Press, 1964.

study was 43.1 per cent. In the three studies combined, 46.1 per cent ($N = 317$) ranked a supportive article first. This slight preference for nonsupportive information is not significant, nor do the percentages for the individual studies differ significantly from chance (50 per cent in each case). Furthermore, actual exposure was measured in the last two of these studies. Each subject was given either a supportive or a nonsupportive communication to read, and the length of time he spent reading it was recorded. In the first study, subjects spent more time reading nonsupportive articles than supportive, but in the second study there was no difference between the two types of articles.[37]

Thus, several studies demonstrate no preference between supportive and nonsupportive information. It might be argued, however, that the jury situation, in particular, is not ideal for obtaining selective exposure effects, owing to natural pressures on jurors toward impartiality and fairness. Although it would be pleasant to believe that people suddenly become impartial, fair, and objective when they become jurors, it seems quite implausible. Other data collected in these experiments indicated that the subjects reacted in a highly partisan manner to the communications they actually read: they evaluated the supportive communication much more favorably than its nonsupportive counterpart in each experiment, regardless of which verdict they had supported. So partisanship was not absent, but it operated on information evaluation rather than on information selection.

Preference for nonsupportive information. In one of the studies described above there was actually some indication of a preference for *nonsupportive* information: Rosen obtained a general preference for the nonsupportive choice-reversal article. Several other studies have produced quite convincing evidence of a preference for nonsupportive information.

In Brodbeck's study, subjects in groups of eight were led to believe that the group as a whole was evenly divided on the issue of wire tapping. Then each subject chose the group member whose opinions on wire tapping she would most like to hear. By chance 42.9 per cent of the subjects would have been expected to choose someone they agreed with, but only 20.2 per cent did so. That is, they strongly tended to choose someone with whom they disagreed; presumably they preferred to hear nonsupportive information.[38]

[37] D. O. Sears, "Opinion Formation and Information Preferences in an Adversary Situation," *Journal of Experimental Social Psychology,* Vol. 2, 1966, pp. 130-142; D. O. Sears and J. L. Freedman, "Commitment, Information Utility, and Selective Exposure," *USN Technical Reports, ONR,* Nonr-233(54) NR 171-350, No. 12, August 1963; D. O. Sears and J. L. Freedman, "The Effects of Expected Familiarity with Arguments upon Opinion Change and Selective Exposure," *Journal of Personality and Social Psychology,* Vol. 2, 1965, pp. 420-426.

[38] May Brodbeck, "The Role of Small Groups in Mediating the Effects of Propaganda," *Journal of Abnormal and Social Psychology,* Vol. 52, 1956, pp. 166-170.

Feather's results were described above only for smokers as a group and for nonsmokers as a group, without considering the most relevant belief involved: Is there convincing evidence that smoking leads to lung cancer? In the first of these studies, Feather divided each group into those who believed there was convincing evidence for the relationship and those who believed the evidence was not very convincing. Smokers of both kinds preferred the article *contradicting* their beliefs, while nonsmokers showed no particular exposure preference, regardless of their position. Hence, this again is evidence of preference for nonsupportive information, in subjects who were presumably highly ego-involved about an important issue.[39]

In two final studies, the subjects' opinions were experimentally manipulated. Sears gave subjects brief synopses of the testimony at murder trials. The content of the evidence was varied only slightly, but crucially, so that all subjects read very similar cases, but generally emerged with different verdict preferences. They then were offered either the defense or the prosecution summation. Of those given "guilty" cases, 31.2 per cent preferred the supportive summation; of those given "innocent" cases, 27.3 per cent preferred the supportive summation. Both differ significantly from chance (50 per cent), so this study, too, records a clear preference for nonsupportive information.[40]

Even more dramatic is Freedman's study. Subjects listened to a (fictitious) interview between a candidate for an overseas conference and the person in charge of the conference. For some subjects, the candidate was made to sound very good; for others, very bad. After each subject evaluated the candidate, he was offered a choice between two additional evaluations of the candidate by people who supposedly knew him well, one of which was described as very favorable, and the other as very unfavorable. Only 18 subjects were run because the results were so consistent and striking. Only 1 subject chose the evaluation that agreed with his own, and 17 chose the nonsupportive evaluation.[41]

Conclusions. By now it must be clear that there is no consistent result in this research. Five studies showed some preference for supportive information: Ehrlich *et al.* (1957), Freedman and Sears (1963), Adams (1961), Mills *et al.* (positive articles) (1961), and Rosen (positive arti-

[39] Feather, 1962, *op. cit.*

[40] D. O. Sears, "Biased Indoctrination and Selectivity of Exposure to New Information," *Sociometry*, Vol. 28, 1965, pp. 363-376.

[41] J. L. Freedman, "Preference for Dissonant Information," *Journal of Personality and Social Psychology*, Vol. 2, 1965a, pp. 287-289. Four additional articles have appeared since the completion of this paper. Brock found that smokers preferred supportive information on lung cancer more than did nonsmokers, but did not avoid nonsupportive information to any greater extent (T. C. Brock, "Commitment to Exposure as a Determinant of Information Receptivity," *Journal of Per-*

cles (1961). Eight showed no preference: Mills *et al.* (negative articles) (1959), Feather (nonsmokers only) (1962), Feather (1963), Mills and Ross (1964), Jecker (1964), Sears (1966), and Sears and Freedman (1963 and 1965). And five showed a preference for nonsupportive information: Rosen (choice-reversal articles) (1961), Brodbeck (1956), Feather (smokers only) (1962), Sears (1965), and Freedman (1965a). The conclusion seems clear. The available evidence fails to indicate the presence of a general preference for supportive information.

COGNITIVE DISSONANCE AND SELECTIVE EXPOSURE

Even if there is no general preference one way or the other, there must be conditions under which supportive information will be preferred. The most concrete specification of what these conditions might be has been made within the context of cognitive dissonance theory. Two specific hypotheses have been offered, each based on the assumption that dissonance may be reduced or avoided by selectivity in information seeking. One is that selectivity increases following a decision or a commitment to do something, and the other is that selectivity increases following involuntary exposure to nonsupportive information. Several studies have been done to test these hypotheses, each based essentially on a comparison between a high-dissonance condition and a low-dissonance condition. Since these studies have been reviewed intensively elsewhere, it is not necessary to go into detail about them here. It is enough to say that the results are again equivocal. Of the five studies specifically designed to test the first hypothesis, only one, a survey study, offers even a marginally significant difference in selectivity between high- and low-dissonance conditions. None of the three studies testing the second hypothesis provides a significant difference between two such conditions.[42]

A third hypothesis has been offered more recently, that selectivity is inversely related to the amount of confidence a person has in his initial

---

sonality and Social Psychology, Vol. 2, 1965, pp. 10-19). In only one of three experiments does Mills report respondents in a market research situation seeking supportive information, but in all three he reports avoidance of dissonant information (J. Mills, "Avoidance of Dissonant Information," *Journal of Personality and Social Psychology*, Vol. 2, 1965, pp. 589-593, and "Effect of Certainty about a Decision upon Postdecision Exposure to Consonant and Dissonant Information," *Journal of Personality and Social Psychology*, Vol. 2, 1965, pp. 749-752). Finally, in a study done in the 1964 presidential election, apparently supportive information was not significantly sought nor nonsupportive information significantly avoided (R. J. Rhine, "The 1964 Presidential Election and Curves of Information Seeking and Avoiding," *Journal of Personality and Social Psychology*, Vol. 5, 1967, pp. 416-423). So the evidence continues to be highly inconclusive.

[42] For a review of these studies, see J. L. Freedman and D. O. Sears, "Selective Exposure," in L. Berkowitz, ed., *Advances in Experimental Social Psychology*, Vol. 2, New York, Academic Press, 1965.

opinion. Two studies are directly relevant to this hypothesis. The first supported it, while the second, an attempt at an exact replication of the first, yielded no favorable evidence.[43]

Thus the use of dissonance theory to specify particular circumstances under which selectivity would occur has not been a great success. Unfortunately, it remains the only systematic theoretical effort, as well as the only one that has generated a body of empirical research.

VOLUNTARY EXPOSURE TO INFORMATION

It is possible to take an entirely different approach to the lack of support for the selective exposure hypothesis. Rather than attempt to explain, or explain away, the negative results, it might be fruitful to accept them at face value (at least for the time being) and turn instead to the more general problem of the factors that *do* affect voluntary exposure to information. In this way, it might be possible to understand more about exposure in general, and thus to determine why *de facto* selectivity occurs.

Education and social class. One class of factors is those individual differences or predispositions that are theoretically independent of partisan preferences. As indicated above, clearly the most powerful known predictor of voluntary exposure to mass communications of an informational or public affairs sort is the general factor of education and social class. Two representative studies indicate the magnitude of its predictive power. Star and Hughes report that 68 per cent of their college-educated respondents were exposed to the UN campaign in at least three media, while only 17 per cent of the grammar-school-educated respondents were, only one-fourth as many.[44] Key presents Survey Research Center data indicating that college-educated persons comprised over four times as many of those who were exposed to the 1956 presidential campaign in at least four media as did grammar-school-educated respondents. And of those exposed to the campaign in no media, 3 per cent were college-educated and 58 per cent had only grade-school educations, almost twenty times as many.[45] So, in contrast to the rather pale and ephemeral effects of selectivity, *de facto* or otherwise, education yields enormous differences. Why it produces such differences is not known and remains a provocative question, and a subtler one than might appear at first glance.[46]

[43] L. K. Canon, "Self-confidence and Selective Exposure to Information," in Festinger, 1964, *op. cit.*; J. L. Freedman, "Confidence, Utility and Selective Exposure: A Partial Replication," *Journal of Personality and Social Psychology*, Vol. 2, 1965b, pp. 778-780.

[44] *Op. cit.*

[45] V. O. Key, Jr., *Public Opinion and American Democracy*, New York, Knopf, 1961, p. 349.

[46] For example, see the discussion in R. E. Lane and D. O. Sears, *Public Opinion*, Englewood Cliffs, N. J. Prentice-Hall, 1964, pp. 62-63. Another possibility worth

Utility of information. The perceived utility of the information is another factor likely to have a major effect on exposure preferences. It is obvious that information varies greatly in the extent to which it will serve a useful, practical purpose, although this fact has often been ignored in previous research. It seems likely that the greater the perceived utility of the information, the greater will be the subject's desire to be exposed to it. Utility may have been an important variable in several exposure experiments. For example, in Adams's study mentioned earlier, in which he offered women a choice between a talk on environmental factors and one on hereditary factors in child behavior, the former was potentially of greater practical importance and was preferred by a 3-to-1 margin.[47] Similarly, Maccoby *et al.* offered housewives a pamphlet on toilet training and recorded how many requested the pamphlet; they sent the pamphlet to a different group of women and recorded how many actually read it. The subjects were divided into those who had an only child between the ages of three and twelve months (critical group), those who had an older child (post group), and those who had no children (pre group). Presumably the pamphlet was most useful to the critical group. This group expressed more interest in getting the pamphlet (71 vs. 36 per cent and 38 per cent for the other groups); and a greater percentage of them read it when it was sent to them (88 vs. 48 and 47 per cent).[48] And both Mills *et al.* and Rosen found that students were more interested in reading about the merits and demerits alike of the exam they had decided to take than about the exam they had decided not to take.[49] Finally, Canon and Freedman explicitly varied utility. The subjects made a decision on what was supposedly a case study in business and were then offered a choice of articles supportive or nonsupportive of their choice. Before rating the articles, they were told either that they would have to present their reasons for deciding on the case as they did, or that they would engage in a written debate in which they would have to rebut arguments from the opposing side. It was assumed that in the former case supportive information would be more useful, since it would provide necessary reasons for their decision. In the latter case, non-

---

mentioning is that social class or education may be directly related to selectivity. Most of the experimental studies cited here were conducted with middle-class college students, and other types of subjects might have yielded greater support for selective exposure. However, there are no relevant data available, and, given the record to date, we would hesitate to bet on these being critical factors.

[47] *Op. cit.*

[48] N. Maccoby, A. K. Romney, J. S. Adams, and Eleanor E. Maccoby, "Critical Periods in Seeking and Accepting Information," in *Paris-Stanford Studies in Communications*, Stanford, Calif., Institute for Communications Research, 1962.

[49] *Op. cit.*

supportive information would presumably be more useful, since the subject could not prepare his rebuttal without knowing what the opposition believed. In both studies, the more useful information was significantly preferred to the less useful, regardless of which was supportive or nonsupportive of the subject's decision.[50]

Thus, the evidence strongly supports the contention that information that is expected to serve a practical purpose is preferred to less useful information. And, just as with education, the effects are large and highly significant.

Past history of exposure on the issue. One would surely think that an individual's past history of exposure would influence his subsequent information preferences. Indeed, in several studies it has been shown that exposure to one side's arguments is likely to increase the chances of voluntary exposure to the other side's. As indicated above, Sears gave subjects testimony indicating, in some cases, the defendant's guilt, and in others, his innocence. After being introduced to the case in this one-sided manner, the subjects strongly preferred to see the summation given by the attorney favoring the opposite view.[51] In another study, Sears gave subjects neither, one, or both attorneys' summations from a court trial. In the no-summation and two-summation conditions, subsequent information preferences were unsystematic, and unrelated to the subject's opinions. When given a single summation, however, the subject strongly preferred information favoring the *other* side, regardless of whether or not they sympathized with it.[52] And when Freedman gave subjects material biased against a candidate for an overseas conference, subjects preferred material favorable to him; if the bias was in his favor, they preferred material unfavorable to him.[53]

These three studies give, therefore, a highly consistent picture: in each case, when subjects were exposed initially to biased or one-sided information, they later preferred information favoring the opposite position, regardless of whether it attacked or supported their own position. How far this generalization may be extended is, however, unclear at this time.

Education, information utility, and past history of exposure are but three of the many factors that no doubt influence exposure preferences and rates of exposure. These are important in the present context for two main reasons: first, they have been demonstrated to affect exposure in a powerful way, whereas demonstrations of selective ex-

[50] *Op. cit.*
[51] Sears, 1965, *op. cit.*
[52] Sears, 1966, *op. cit.*
[53] Freedman, 1965a, *op. cit.*

posure have been very weak. Hence, selectivity may at best be a rather trivial variable relative to other influences upon exposure. Second, they offer ways of explaining the occurrence of *de facto* selectivity without assuming the existence of underlying preferences for supportive information. As indicated earlier, propaganda may often reach mainly those sympathetic to it simply because it advocates positions generally shared by those who have high rates of exposure to *all* propaganda. And when supportive information is most useful, as in the case of Adams's pro-environment talk or articles describing the merits of an exam one must take, it may be preferred; but when nonsupportive information is more useful, as in the case of Rosen's choice-reversal article, it may be preferred. So *de facto* selectivity effects may occur as a result of particular combinations of variables that are themselves extraneous to the supportive-nonsupportive dimension.

CONCLUSIONS

This paper has been concerned primarily with evaluating the evidence for the existence of selectivity in voluntary exposure to information. There seems to be some evidence (although not as unequivocal as often claimed) for the existence of *de facto* selectivity. Most audiences for mass communications apparently tend to overrepresent persons already sympathetic to the views being propounded, and most persons seem to be exposed disproportionately to communications that support their opinions.

On the other hand, a considerable amount of experimental research has uncovered no general psychological preference for supportive information. Under some circumstances, people seem to prefer information that supports their opinions; under other circumstances, people seem to prefer information that contradicts their opinions. In no way can the available evidence be said to support the contention that people generally seek out supportive information and avoid nonsupportive information.

These two conclusions are paradoxical. How can it be that people are in fact selective, yet display no trace of a general preference for supportive information? A variety of answers have been provided above and need not be summarized here. Most generally, examples of *de facto* selectivity come from communication settings in which exposure is complexly determined by a great many factors that are incidental to the supportiveness of the information. We have reviewed research on only three of these factors, but many more are surely as important. Clearly, these factors can themselves on occasion produce *de facto* selectivity. One general possibility is that they do more often than they do not, presumably because in natural communication situations such variables are not randomly related to communicators' positions on various social, political, economic, religious, etc., issues. For example, those who find a particular kind of information most useful may also sympathize most with the particular editorial stance that happens, in most cases, to be paired with it. Financiers find the *Wall Street Journal*'s financial news very helpful and also (probably incidentally) tend to agree with its politics. College professors and diplomats rely upon the *New York Times*'s comprehensive news coverage and often agree with its editorials as well. These are not merely coincidences. Nor are they necessarily examples of selective exposure. However, it is beyond the scope of this paper to inquire into the reasons for such correlations.

Another possibility is that selectivity may be considerably more important on a long-term basis than at any given moment. Many people may be willing to take on the task of exposing themselves to nonsupportive information on any given occasion. Yet it may be quite tiring and aggravating, and thus something to be undertaken only at widely separated moments of particular intellectual fortitude. So dramatic selectivity in preferences may not appear at any given moment in time, but, over a long period, people may organize their surroundings in a way that ensures *de facto* selectivity. The data relevant to this point deal mostly with the acquisition of friends and spouses (rather than with information or exposure preferences), and so also lie beyond the scope of this paper. Nevertheless, the argument is intriguing and the data have been ingeniously gathered.[54]

Finally, this research suggests a change of emphasis in our thinking about how people deal with discrepant information. It has generally been assumed that selective exposure and other processes that bar information reception are prime mechanisms by which people resist influence.[55] Perhaps such processes are not very important after all. Feather reports that smokers do not avoid reading unpleasant information about smoking and lung cancer; rather, they subject it to careful and mercilessly unsympathetic scrutiny.[56] Perhaps resistance to influence is accomplished most often and most successfully at the level of information evaluation, rather than at the level of selective seeking and avoiding of information.

[54] T. M. Newcomb, "The Persistence and Regression of Changed Attitudes," *Journal of Social Issues*, Vol. 19, 1963, pp. 3-14; Berelson *et al., op. cit.*
[55] Cf. Klapper, *op. cit.*
[56] Feather, 1963, *op. cit.*

28

ATTITUDE CHANGE
AND BEHAVIORAL CHANGE
Milton Rokeach

SINCE World War II many experimental studies of opinion change, carried out within a variety of conceptual frameworks, have been designed to increase our theoretical understanding of the conditions under which men's minds and men's behavior may change. While the main *empirical* focus of these studies is on behavioral changes in the expression of opinion, their main *theoretical* concern is with the conditions facilitating and inhibiting change in underlying beliefs and attitudes. To what extent have these experimental studies actually advanced our theoretical understanding of processes leading to attitude and behavior change? And to what extent have they improved our understanding of the fundamental structure of underlying attitudes, the way attitudes are organized with respect to one another, and the way attitude and attitude change may affect behavior?

To discuss these questions I would like to begin with certain considerations, not about attitude change, but about the nature of attitude, and about the relationship between attitude and behavior. In contemporary approaches to "attitude change" the accent seems to be on the understanding of "change" rather than on the understanding of "attitude"; that is, one may note an interest in attitude theory as such only insofar as that interest is necessary to formulate testable hypotheses about attitude change. The point of view to be developed

* This is one of a series of papers on attitude organization and modification supported by a grant from the National Science Foundation. Earlier versions of this paper were presented at a Symposium on Attitude Change and Behavior Change held at the State University of New York at Buffalo in March 1965, and at the meetings of the World Association for Public Opinion Research in Dublin in September 1965.

Originally published in Volume 30, Number 4, 1966 of the *Public Opinion Quarterly*.

here will differ somewhat from that expressed by the late Arthur R. Cohen who, in the preface to his recent book, *Attitude Change and Social Influence,* wrote: "This book does not take up the definition and conceptualization of attitude, but instead assumes that there is a commonly accepted core of meaning for the term 'attitude change'."[1] I will try to show that the concept of "attitude change" can have no "commonly accepted core of meaning" apart from the concept of attitude—that, indeed, theory and research on the nature, determinants, and consequents of attitude formation and maintenance are prerequisite to and inseparable from theory and research on attitude change.

ATTITUDE AND BEHAVIOR

For purposes of this discussion let me offer the following coordinated definitions of attitude and attitude change. An *attitude* is a relatively enduring organization of beliefs about an object or situation predisposing one to respond in some preferential manner.[2] *Attitude change* would then be a change in predisposition,[3] the change being either a change in the organization or structure of beliefs or a change in the content of one or more of the beliefs entering into the attitude organization.

Especially important for the major thesis of this paper is that an attitude may be focussed either on an object or on a situation. In the first instance we have in mind an attitude-object, which may be concrete or abstract, involving a person, a group, an institution, or an issue. In the second instance the attitude is focussed on a specific situation, an event, or an activity. To say that a person has an enduring attitude toward a given object is to say that this attitude will, when activated, somehow determine his behavior toward the attitude-object, across situations; conversely, to say that a person has an enduring attitude toward a given situation is to say that this attitude will, when activated, determine his behavior toward the situation, across attitude-objects.

Social scientists have generally been far more interested in the theory and measurement of attitudes toward objects, across situations, than in the theory and measurement of attitudes toward situations,

---

[1] Arthur R. Cohen, *Attitude Change and Social Influence,* New York, Basic Books, 1964, p. xi.

[2] A detailed elaboration of the nature of attitudes is presented in M. Rokeach, "The Nature of Attitudes," in *International Encyclopedia of Social Sciences,* New York, Macmillan, 1966.

[3] A *predisposition* would be defined as a hypothetical state of the organism which, when activated by a stimulus, causes a person to respond selectively, affectively, or preferentially to the stimulus.

across objects. Thus, we have scales that measure attitudes toward the Negro, the Jew, liberalism-conservatism, and religion. But we do not have scales that measure attitudes toward such situations as managing or being a guest in a Southern hotel, being a passenger or driver of a bus, buying or selling real estate. As a result, the study of attitudes-toward-situations has become more or less divorced from the study of attitudes-toward-objects.

This separation of attitude-toward-object from attitude-toward-situation has, in my opinion, severely retarded the growth not only of attitude theory but also of attitude-change theory. It has resulted in a failure to appreciate that an attitude-object is always encountered within some situation about which we also have an organized attitude. It has resulted in unsophisticated attempts to predict behavior or behavioral change on the basis of a single attitude-toward-object, ignoring the equally relevant attitude-toward-situation. And it has resulted in unjustified interpretations and conclusions that there are often inconsistencies between attitudes and behavior, or between attitude changes and behavioral change.

A preferential response toward an attitude-object cannot occur in a vacuum; it must necessarily be elicited within the context of some social situation about which, as already noted, we also have an attitude. If you like, conceive of the attitude-object you encounter as the *figure* and the situation in which you encounter it as the *ground*. How a person will behave toward an object-within-a-situation will depend, on the one hand, on the particular beliefs or predispositions activated by the attitude-object and, on the other hand, on the particular beliefs or predispositions activated by the situation. Thus it follows that a person's social behavior must always be a function of at least two attitudes—one activated by the attitude-object, the other activated by the situation.

If one focusses only on attitude-toward-object, he is bound to observe some inconsistency between attitudes and behavior, or, at least, a lack of dependence of behavior on attitude. Most frequently mentioned as evidence of this are such studies as those by LaPiere[4] and Kutner *et al.*,[5] in which restaurant owners and innkeepers showed marked discrepancies between their verbal expressions of discrimination toward Chinese and Negroes by letter or phone and their non-discriminatory, face-to-face behavior. The present analysis suggests one possible explanation for such apparent inconsistency: the in-

---

[4] R. T. LaPiere, "Attitudes vs. Actions," *Social Forces,* Vol. 13, 1934, pp. 230-237.
[5] B. Kutner, Carol Wilkins, and Penny R. Yarrow, "Verbal Attitudes and Overt Behavior Involving Racial Prejudice," *Journal of Abnormal and Social Psychology,* Vol. 27, 1952, pp. 649-652.

vestigators did not obtain all the relevant attitudinal information needed to make accurate predictions. The subjects not only had attitudes toward Chinese and Negroes, but, as managers of businesses, also had attitudes about the proper conduct of such businesses. The investigator's methods, however, are typically focussed on attitude-toward-object and are generally insensitive to attitude-toward-situation.

The proposition that behavior is always a function of at least two attitudes (to be called A_o and A_s) has at least two implications worth noting. First, a given attitude-toward-object, whenever activated, need not always be behaviorally manifested or expressed in the same way or to the same degree. Its expression will vary adaptively as the attitude activated by the situation varies, with attitude-toward-situation facilitating or inhibiting the expression of attitude-toward-object, and vice versa. Any attitude-toward-object has the inherent property of being differentially manifested *along a range of values* rather than as a single value, depending on the situation within which the attitude-object is encountered.[6] This same property is inherent in any attitude-toward-situation. Consequently, a significant change of opinion toward an object may indicate nothing more than that a given attitude-toward-object was activated, and thus behaviorally expressed, in two different situations, S_1 and S_2, activating, respectively, two different attitudes-toward-situation, A_{s_1} and A_{s_2}.

Second, in principle there is no difference between the verbal and the nonverbal expression of a given attitude. Every expression in behavior, verbal or nonverbal, must be a confounding and a compounding function of at least two underlying attitudes. Thus, any verbal expression of opinion, like any nonverbal behavior, is also a function of at least two attitudes—attitude-toward-object and attitude-toward-situation—and ascertaining the extent to which the opinion is a manifestation of one attitude or the other, or both, requires careful inference rather than careless assumption.

COGNITIVE INTERACTION BETWEEN TWO ATTITUDES

It is not enough merely to assert that social behavior is a function of two attitudes. To predict behavioral outcome requires a model

[6] H. C. Kelman expresses a similar view: "The attitudes expressed by an individual may vary from situation to situation, depending on the requirements of the situation in which he finds himself and the motivations which he brings into this situation. What the individual says will be determined at least in part by what he considers to be proper in this situation and consonant with group norms, and also by what he considers to be most conducive to the achievement of his personal goals. . . . The amount of discrepancy depends on the situational requirements, on the person's goals, on his relation to the group, and on some of his personal characteristics."

about the manner in which the two attitudes will cognitively interact with one another. In a recent paper, Rokeach and Rothman[7] have presented such a model of cognitive interaction, called the belief congruence model, which has been shown to be approximately three times[8] as accurate as Osgood and Tannenbaum's congruity model[8] in quantitatively predicting the outcome of cognitive interaction.

Applying this model to the present context, we can then conjecture that whenever a person encounters an attitude-object within some situation, two attitudes, A_o and A_s, are activated; further, a comparison process regarding the relative importance of these two attitudes with respect to one another is also activated. The two attitudes are assumed to affect behavior in direct proportion to their perceived importance with respect to one another. The more important A_o is perceived to be with respect to A_s, the more will the behavioral outcome be a function of A_o; conversely, the more important A_s is perceived to be with respect to A_o, the more will the behavioral outcome be a function of A_s.

How can the relative importance of two attitudes be determined? One way is by strictly empirical means—for example, by the method of paired comparison. In this instance we would not be able to predict the behavioral outcome of cognitive interaction between two attitudes of varying importance because we would have no way of knowing in advance their importance relative to one another or the absolute degree of that importance. Fortunately, however, the comparison of relative importance of the two attitudes does not occur in a vacuum; it takes place within the general framework of one's total belief system, wherein all beliefs and attitudes are arranged along a central-peripheral dimension of importance. Thus, the two attitudes, A_o and A_s, can be compared as if to determine their relative position along this central-peripheral dimension. I have already presented elsewhere some tentative and admittedly incomplete conceptualizations of the types of beliefs and attitudes that may be found along this central-peripheral dimension;[9] such conceptualizations enable us to make at least some educated guesses in advance about which of two attitudes is likely to be the more important. I will have more to say about the

---

("Social Influence and Personal Belief: A Theoretical and Experimental Approach to the Study of Behavior Change," unpublished manuscript, 1958, pp. 25-26.)

[7] M. Rokeach and G. Rothman, "The Principle of Belief Congruence and the Congruity Principle as Models of Cognitive Interaction," *Psychological Review*, Vol. 72, 1965, pp. 128-142.

[8] C. E. Osgood and P. H. Tannenbaum, "The Principle of Congruity in the Prediction of Attitude Change," *Psychological Review*, Vol. 62, 1955, pp. 42-55.

[9] M. Rokeach, *The Open and Closed Mind: Investigations into the Nature of Belief Systems and Personality Systems*, New York, Basic Books, 1960; *The Three Christs of Ypsilanti: A Psychological Study*, New York, Knopf, 1964.

several types of beliefs varying along the central-peripheral dimension later on in this paper.

The question may now be raised whether it is ever possible to obtain a behavioral measure of a given attitude-toward-object that is uncontaminated by interaction with attitude-toward-situation. The extent to which this is possible is a function of the extent to which the situation is a "neutral" one—that is, a situation carefully structured by the experimenter to activate a relatively unimportant attitude-toward-situation that is, hence, of relatively little influence in the context of its interaction with attitude-toward-object. Learning how to structure the test or interview situation so that it is a neutral one is, of course, a major objective of attitude and survey research methodology. But this is only a methodological ideal to strive for and is probably rarely achieved in practice.

ATTITUDE CHANGE AND BEHAVIORAL CHANGE

The proposition that behavior is always a function of two interacting attitudes has, I believe, important and disturbing implications for theory and research on attitude change and behavioral change. If expressing an opinion is a form of behavior, then expressing a changed opinion is also a form of behavior; thus, a changed opinion must also be a function of the two attitudes previously discussed— attitude-toward-object and attitude-toward-situation. Similarly, any change in nonverbal behavior is also a form of behavior, and hence must also be a function of the same two attitudes. The question therefore arises: When there is a change in opinion or behavior, how can we tell whether or not there has also been a change in attitude and, if so, *which* attitude?

Although a reasonably clear distinction can be made between an underlying attitude and an expression of opinion (or, if you will, between a covert and overt attitude, or between a private and public attitude), and between an underlying attitude change and an expressed opinion change, one may nevertheless observe in the experimental and theoretical literature a general tendency to use these concepts interchangeably and thereby to shift the discussion back and forth between "attitude" and "opinion," and between "opinion change" and "attitude change." It thereby becomes difficult to tell whether one is dealing in any instance with phenomena involving attitude change, expressed opinion change, or both. Many writers have ridden roughshod over the distinction between attitude and expressed opinion by using the phrases "attitude change," "opinion change," "attitude *and* opinion change" and "attitude *or* opinion change" more or less arbitrarily in the context of a single discussion.

In this way the impression is created that a significant change in the expression of an opinion also represents a change in underlying attitude. For example, Hovland opens his paper, "Reconciling Conflicting Results Derived from Experimental and Survey Studies of Attitude [*sic*] Change":

Two quite different types of research design are characteristically used to study the modification of attitudes [*sic*] through communication. In the first type, the *experiment*, individuals are given a controlled exposure to a communication and the effects evaluated in terms of the amount of change in attitude or opinion [*sic*] produced.[10]

Festinger opens his article entitled, "Behavioral Support for Opinion [*sic*] Change":

The last three decades have seen a steady and impressive growth in our knowledge concerning attitudes and opinions [*sic*].[11]

Both of these writers, like many others, then employ the concepts of "attitude" and "opinion" indiscriminately in carrying forward their discussions, which are usually discussions about how some empirical data involving a change in *expressed* opinion bear on some hypothesis or theory regarding a change in attitude.

As one tries to assimilate the growing experimental literature on opinion change, he becomes increasingly aware that this literature concerns primarily the conditions affecting change in the expression of opinion. But this literature, considered as a whole, does not seem to have much to say about the conditions leading to a change in the content or structure of underlying predispositions (or, as Doob would have it,[12] of implicit responses) toward objects or toward situations.

Theories of attitude change, with certain exceptions (e.g. Kelman's work on processes of social influence, related work on the public-private variable, work on the "sleeper" effect), seem to be generally unconcerned with whether an expressed opinion change does or does not represent an underlying attitude change. Indeed, the classical paradigm employed in experimental studies of opinion change— pre-test, treatment, post-test—is not capable of telling us whether an expressed opinion change indicates an attitude change; it can tell us only whether an expression of opinion has or has not changed as a result of a particular experimental treatment. If the main theoretical concern of experimental studies on expressed opinion change is with

10 C. I. Hovland, "Reconciling Conflicting Results Derived from Experimental and Survey Studies of Attitude Change," *American Psychologist*, Vol. 14, 1959, p. 8.
11 L. Festinger, "Behavioral Support for Opinion Change," *Public Opinion Quarterly*, Vol. 28, 1964, p. 404.
12 L. W. Doob, "The Behavior of Attitudes," *Psychological Review*, Vol. 54, 1947, pp. 135-156.

the conditions leading to attitude change, then the classical paradigm is basically a faulty one and should be replaced with other or modified experimental designs (to be discussed later) more suited to deal with this issue.

A closely related point concerns the relationship among attitude change, expressed opinion change, and behavioral change. In his presidential address to Division 8 of the American Psychological Association, Leon Festinger expresses astonishment over the "absence of research, and of theoretical thinking, about the effect of attitude change on subsequent behavior."[13] He says that he could find only three empirical studies relevant to this problem and that they all show "the *absence* of a relationship between opinion change . . . and resulting behavior."[14] Festinger stresses in his closing remarks that we ought not to ignore this problem or simply assume "a relationship between attitude change and subsequent behavior. . . ." He concludes that "The problem needs concerted investigation."[15] And Cohen, in a similar vein, writes: "Until experimental research demonstrates that attitude change has consequences for subsequent behavior, we cannot be certain that our procedures . . . do anything more than cause cognitive realignments."[16] It should be noted, first, that we cannot even be certain whether the experimental procedures employed "cause cognitive realignments" and, second, that the absence of relationship noted by Festinger and Cohen is not between attitude change and subsequent behavior but between two forms of behavior—expressed opinion change, and subsequent nonverbal behavioral change. My main point, then, is that there would seem to be not one but two problems requiring "theoretical thinking" and "concerted investigation." First: Why is it so difficult to demonstrate a relationship between attitude change and behavioral change? And, second: Why is it so difficult to demonstrate a relationship between one form of behavioral change and another form?

I have proposed that expressed opinion or behavioral change is always a function of at least two attitudes. This proposition only complicates our attempts to determine whether or not a particular change in expressed opinion or behavior represents a change in attitude. Because we have to contend with two types of underlying attitudes, we now have four possible determinants of a change in expressed opinion or behavior: (1) interaction between attitude-toward-object and attitude-toward-situation, neither of which has changed, or (2) a

13 Festinger, *op. cit.,* p. 405.
14 *Ibid.,* p. 416.
15 *Ibid.,* p. 417.
16 Cohen, *op. cit.,* p. 138.

change only in the attitude-toward-object, or (3) a change only in the attitude-toward-situation, or (4) a change in both attitude-toward-object and attitude-toward-situation.

Changes in expressed opinion or behavior as a result of (2), (3), and (4) are more or less self-evident. But the first determinant of expressed opinion or behavioral change—the interaction between A_o and A_s, neither of which has changed—merits further consideration because (a) it goes against the widely held assumption that behavioral and expressed opinion changes cannot take place without a preceding change in attitude; (b) it has implications for experimentally oriented and personality-oriented studies of attitude and behavioral change; and (c) it may open up some fresh possibilities for bringing about changes in expressed opinion and behavior that do not depend on antecedent attitude change.

Let us consider a variety of instances in which a change of expressed opinion or behavior may be observed and understood without positing a change in underlying attitude. First, there are those actions which represent public conformity or compliance without private acceptance. Kelman has shown that a subject exposed to an authority who is in a position to reward and punish will display a change of opinion in the direction of authority's opinion,[17] but this change of opinion is manifested only under conditions of surveillance by authority and not under conditions of nonsurveillance. The surveillance condition represents a situation, S_1, activating the attitude, A_{s_1}. The nonsurveillance condition represents another situation, S_2, activating another attitude, A_{s_2}. A change in expression of opinion from conditions of nonsurveillance to surveillance can readily be accounted for without assuming a change in underlying attitude-toward-object. One measure of opinion toward a specified object is the behavioral result of the interaction between A_o and A_{s_1}; the other measure is a result of the interaction of the same A_o but another attitude, A_{s_2}. The change of expressed opinion toward the specified attitude-object can be best understood as a reflection of the two different situations, each activating a different attitude-toward-situation. And there is no need to assume that any one of the activated attitudes—A_o or A_{s_1} or A_{s_2}—has undergone any change.

But not all instances of expressed opinion change unaccompanied by attitude change necessarily represent acts of public compliance or conformity. Consider, for example, expressed opinion changes brought about as a result of what Orne has called the "demand char-

17 H. C. Kelman, "Compliance, Identification, and Internalization: Three Processes of Attitude Change," *Journal of Conflict Resolution*, Vol. 2, 1958, pp. 51-60.

acteristics" of the experimental situation,[18] or what Rosenberg has called "evaluation apprehension."[19] Both terms refer to methodologically unwanted situational variables that may or may not motivate compliant behavior, variables which exist during the post-test period and not during the pre-test period, and which activate some attitude-toward-situation persisting beyond that activated by the experimental treatment as such. Changes in expressed opinion toward an object from pre- to post-test thus result because two different situations activated two different attitudes, A_{s_1} and A_{s_2}; and we can therefore account for such changes without adding further assumptions regarding underlying attitude change.

Incidentally, changes in expressed opinion thus obtained are difficult to interpret because they violate a basic principle of measurement theory, namely, that repeated measurements designed to assess the effects of some experimental variable should be obtained under constant test conditions. Unlike survey research methodology, experimental studies of opinion change employing the pre-test, treatment, and post-test paradigm cannot by their very nature guarantee the required constancy of testing conditions. The post-test situation is bound to be psychologically different from the pre-test situation, the former activating different attitudes from the latter. Moreover, a post-test situation following one experimental treatment is not necessarily comparable with another post-test situation following a different experimental treatment. Orne expresses a similar view when he writes: "It should be clear that demand characteristics cannot be eliminated from experiments; all experiments will have demand characteristics and these will always have some effect."[20] Nevertheless, the proposition that behavior is a function of A_o and A_s would, if valid, require us to assess the relative effects of A_o and A_s in the pre-test and in the post-test situations separately, in order to determine the meaning of a given change in expressed opinion.

Let me turn now to another illustration, this time not of an opinion change but of a change in behavior, real-life behavior which is different from what we would ordinarily expect, which does not necessarily involve an attitude change, and which does not necessarily represent an act of public compliance or conformity.

This experiment, which was carried out in collaboration with

[18] M. T. Orne, "On the Social Psychology of the Psychological Experiment: With Particular Reference to Demand Characteristics and Their Implications," *American Psychologist*, Vol. 17, 1962, pp. 776-783.

[19] M. J. Rosenberg, "When Dissonance Fails: On Eliminating Evaluation Apprehension from Attitude Measurement," *Journal of Personal and Social Psychology*, Vol. 1, 1965, pp. 28-42.

[20] Orne, *op. cit.*, p. 779.

Louis Mezei, takes place in the natural setting of the personnel offices of two state mental hospitals near Detroit, Michigan. The subjects are twenty-six Negro and twenty-four white males applying for jobs as janitor, attendant, laundry worker, and the like. Each subject, after he has filled out his application forms, is made to wait for his interview in a room with four other people who are apparently also waiting to be interviewed. These four are really our confederates. Two of them are white and two are Negro. These four, along with the real applicant, are told that while they wait they might want to look at a mimeographed list of issues that are used in a training program for hired personnel. These issues, concerning problem situations involving difficult mental patients, can be resolved in one of two ways: by being permissive or harsh. For example, one issue concerns a mental patient who asks to be fed after dining hours. How should one deal with such a request, the subjects are asked. The confederates "spontaneously" launch into a discussion of the issues, with one white and one Negro confederate advocating the permissive solution and with one white and one Negro confederate advocating the harsh solution. The naïve subject is gradually drawn into the discussion by the four confederates so that he, too, states whether he favors the permissive or harsh solution. He is then asked which two of the four confederates he would most prefer to work with. Which two will he choose and on what basis?

One might reasonably expect that of fifty persons applying for low-status jobs a substantial number would, under the conditions described, choose two partners of their own race, given the salience of racial attitudes in our culture. But the results shown in Table 1 (which are the results from only one of three experiments reported more fully elsewhere by Rokeach and Mezei)[21] do not confirm the expectation that attitude-toward-race is at all important. There are six possible ways of choosing the two partners under the specified conditions. These are indicated in the column heads of Table 1: (1) S+O+, a person of the same race and a person of the other race, both agreeing with the subject; (2) S—O—, a person of the same race and a person of the other race, both disagreeing with the subject, etc.

Only two subjects of the fifty chose attitude-objects of the same race (pattern 3, S+S—), considerably less than would be expected even on a purely chance basis. That similarity of race is not an important criterion of choice of work partners, either for white or for Negro subjects, is indicated further in that three more subjects chose two work partners of the other race (pattern 4, O+O—). It is clear that

21 M. Rokeach and L. Mezei, "Race and Shared Belief as Factors in Social Choice," *Science*, Vol. 151, 1966, pp. 167-172.

TABLE 1

FREQUENCIES OF CHOOSING EACH INTERPERSONAL PATTERN

	(1) S+O+	(2) S−O−	(3) S+S−	(4) O+O−	(5) S+O−	(6) S−O+	Total
Negro	15	3	1	2	3	2	26
White	15	0	1	1	1	6	24
Total	30	3	2	3	4	8	50

S = same race; O = other race; + = agree; − = disagree.

the most frequent basis of choice is not similarity of race but similarity of belief—which is fifteen times more frequent. Thirty of the fifty subjects chose two work partners, one white and one Negro, both of whom agreed with the subject, as compared with only two subjects who chose on the basis of similarity of race.

Even though we have no direct pre-test and post-test data showing that there has been an actual change of behavior in the particular individuals studied here, I would nevertheless regard these data as relevant to the issue of behavioral change not preceded by attitude change. For the choice of work partners shown in Table 1 is not what we would ordinarily expect from fifty lower-class persons looking for a job, given the harsh facts of social discrimination in contemporary American culture. The data presented in Table 1 represent only a small portion of a larger body of data suggesting that the observed absence of racial discrimination is a function of the subject's knowing the stand taken by a Negro or white on an important issue. Assuming that there has been a change in behavior from discrimination on the basis of race to discrimination on the basis of belief, we are again not required to posit any changes in attitudes underlying that behavior (although such changes can come about subsequently, as dissonance theory suggests). We can more simply understand such behavior as arising from an interaction between two attitudes, activated by an object encountered within a situation in which the activated attitude-toward-situation far outweighs in importance the activated attitude-toward-object.

As a final example of behavioral change occurring without underlying attitude change, let me discuss an as yet unpublished study by Jamias and Troldahl.[22] These investigators were studying differences in willingness to adopt new agricultural practices recommended by agricultural extension agents as a function of personality and social

[22] J. F. Jamias, and V. C. Troldahl, "Dogmatism, Tradition and General Innovativeness," 1965, unpublished manuscript.

system. The frequency of adoption of recommended agricultural practices—the dependent variable—was measured by a series of questions, each designed to determine which of several alternative procedures the dairy farmer followed in the day-to-day management of his farm. On each question, one of the alternatives was the one recommended by agricultural extension agents. Personality differences in receptivity to new information were measured by the Dogmatism Scale, and social system differences in receptivity were determined by identifying two types of rural townships in Michigan, one type identified as high and the other as low in their "value for innovativeness." The two types of social systems were readily identified by agricultural extension agents on the basis of the generally positive or negative attitude of the people in the townships toward extension activities, size of attendance at extension meetings, etc. The results are shown in Table 2.

TABLE 2

MEAN ADOPTION RATE BY HIGH AND LOW DOGMATIC GROUPS LIVING IN SOCIAL SYSTEMS HIGH AND LOW IN "VALUE FOR INNOVATIVENESS"

	Social System in Which Value for Innovativeness is	
	Low	High
Low dogmatism group	7.3	6.2
High dogmatism group	4.9	6.8
Correlation between dogmatism and adoption rate	−.40	−.09

Statistical analyses show a highly significant interaction between receptivity in the personality system and receptivity in the social system. In the social system having a low value for innovativeness, the correlation between scores on the Dogmatism Scale and adoption rate is —.40; in the social system having a high value for innovativeness, the correlation is —.09. Highly dogmatic persons (scoring above the median on a modified form of the Dogmatism Scale constructed by Troldahl and Powell)[23] living in social systems having a high value for innovativeness more frequently adopt recommendations of agricultural extension agents than highly dogmatic persons living in social systems having a low value for innovativeness. But low dogmatic subjects, regardless of the social system in which they live, have a relatively high adoption rate for new practices recommended by agricultural experts.

Table 2 shows that behavioral changes in highly dogmatic persons are the result of compliance or identification with social norms, and

23 V. C. Troldahl and F. A. Powell, "A Short-form Dogmatism Scale for Use in Field Studies," *Social Forces*, Vol. 44, 1965, pp. 211-214.

behavioral changes in low dogmatic persons are the result of a generalized receptivity to new information, which is routinely internalized according to its intrinsic correctness and usefulness. Again, no change of underlying attitude need be postulated to account for behavioral change, either in the unreceptive highly dogmatic subjects or in the more receptive low dogmatic subjects. Thus, the results suggest that we can produce changes in the behavior of different individuals through knowledge of personality organization, that is, a knowledge of how a particular situation will activate different beliefs and attitudes in persons who vary in the structure of their belief systems.

In summary, I have tried to suggest that a behavioral change (and this includes an expressed opinion change) may be determined by a change in attitude-toward-object, or in attitude-toward-situation, or both, or neither. I have concentrated mainly on behavioral changes that do not involve any kind of underlying attitude change, and have cited various instances of behavioral change in real life and in the laboratory which are attributable to compliance, demand characteristics, evaluation apprehension, the activation of salient beliefs and attitudes within the context of on-going activity, or the activation of different beliefs and attitudes in persons with differing personality structures. All the illustrations cited have, I believe, a common thread. They all involve expressed opinion or behavioral changes that can be analyzed and reduced to two component attitudes, A_o and A_s, interacting within a figure-ground relationship, carrying differential weights, and affecting a behavioral outcome in proportion to their relative importance with respect to one another. And all these examples suggest that many kinds of behavioral change can be brought about by learning which attitude-object to combine with which situation, which attitudes are activated by attitude-object and situation in different personalities, and which outcome to expect from such interactions in different personalities.

Before terminating this portion of the discussion, however, let me mention one other relevant consideration that has thus far been altogether overlooked in contemporary theory and research on attitude change. If expressed opinion changes may be observed when there has been no underlying attitude change, then the converse is also true: an absence of expressed opinion change may be observed even after a change in underlying attitude has already taken place. For example, a dutiful son may continue to express pro-religious sentiments even after he has changed his underlying attitudes toward religion, in order not to hurt his parents; a disillusioned Communist may continue to engage in Party activities because he is afraid of social ostracism; a person may continue to say "I love you" even after he has stopped loving. All these examples suggest a possible constancy in expressing an opinion despite a change in attitude. The conditions under which such phenomena will occur deserve more study than they have received so far.

METHODS FOR ASSESSING ATTITUDE CHANGE

Thus far, I have tried merely to suggest that a change in behavior or expressed opinion may arise in different ways, and may or may not involve a change in underlying attitude-toward-object or attitude-toward-situation. I have also tried to suggest that the classical paradigm employed in experimental studies of opinion change cannot yield information about attitude change as such. The question is, then, how should we proceed if we wish to ascertain whether a given attitude has undergone change, or, at least, if we wish to increase the probability of correctly inferring that a given expressed opinion change represents an attitude change.

I would like to discuss three methods and I will try to illustrate each with some relevant research studies.

1. *Test for opinion change across different situations.* If verbal or nonverbal behavior toward an object is observed in only one situation following an experimental treatment, we hardly have a basis for inferring a change of attitude. Orne has pointed out: "If a test is given twice with some intervening treatment, even the dullest college student is aware that some change is expected, particularly if the test is in some obvious way related to the treatment."[24] But the more post-test situations in which a changed opinion is manifested, the more confident we may be that a change in attitude has actually taken place. Any experimental study of expressed opinion change, if it is to qualify as a study in attitude change, should demonstrate the existence of change in at least two reasonably different situations.

One research design in which there are several post-tests of opinion change is Kelman's study of three processes of social influence. Opinion change was assessed in three different post-test situations, under conditions of surveillance and salience, nonsurveillance and salience, and nonsurveillance and nonsalience. In the last condition, the post-test was administered "one or two weeks after the communication session, in a different place, under different auspices, and by a different experimenter."[25] Kelman has shown that subjects who were given the experimental treatment designed to favor compliance manifested an opinion change only under conditions of surveillance and salience, thereby suggesting that there was no change in underlying attitude.

24 Orne, *op. cit.*, p. 779.
25 Kelman, "Compliance, Identification, and Internalization," p. 56.

Subjects who were given the internalization treatment, however, manifested opinion changes in all three post-test situations.

Another illustration of repeated post-tests is my study on *The Three Christs of Ypsilanti*, which is concerned with underlying changes in delusional attitudes and beliefs among three paranoid schizophrenic patients who believed they were Jesus Christ. After several months of confrontation with each other over who was the real Christ, the youngest of the three, Leon Gabor, announced one day that he was no longer married to the Virgin Mary. Our problem was to determine whether or not this change in expressed opinion represented an underlying change in delusional belief. Our confidence that it did indeed represent such a delusional change increased as Leon Gabor repeatedly told us during the next few weeks and months in various contexts that he was about to get divorced, then that he was divorced, then that he had a new brother, then that his brother had married the Virgin Mary, then that he himself was about to re-marry, then that he had re-married another woman, and so forth. Had we relied only on one "post-test" expression of a changed opinion about whom Leon was married to, our claim of a change in delusion would have been extremely weak.

In the experimental literature on opinion change, one may find an occasional study in which two or more post-test situations are employed, but, unless I am mistaken, such studies are the exception rather than the rule. In the typical experiment the post-test is given only once, usually within a short time after the experimental treatment; thus the meaning of the expressed opinion change in relation to attitude change is highly equivocal.

The preceding remarks concern the assessment of change in underlying attitudes-toward-object in several post-test situations. I have not said anything about assessing change in underlying attitude-toward-situation because this type of attitude is typically not employed in experimental studies of attitude change. But the principle would seem to be the same: instead of testing for a change in opinion toward an attitude-object across situations, a change in attitude-toward-situation would be tested by substituting various attitude-objects which might be encountered within that situation.

2. *Test for changes of several opinions in one situation.* In the classical paradigm only one opinion is pre-tested, experimentally treated, and then post-tested. Evaluation of the nature of the opinion change is difficult because the expressed opinion is compared only with itself. But suppose several opinions that are thought to be systematically related to one another in some way were pre-tested, experimentally treated, and then assessed for change all in one post-test

situation? Suppose, further, that we find differential opinion changes and that these differential changes are systematically related to one another in the same way as the original opinions are related to one another?

In an as yet unpublished study by Rokeach, Reyher, and Wiseman, over fifty beliefs ranging from highly central beliefs about self-identity to highly inconsequential ones were subjected to change through hypnotic induction. Immediately prior to the hypnotic trance, the subject is pre-tested on these beliefs and attitudes, indicating his agreement or disagreement on an 11-point scale ranging from -5 to $+5$.

The subject is then hypnotized. By suggestion, the experimenter attempts to alter one of five types of beliefs varying in centrality. It is suggested to the subject that he will experience an impulse to respond to such statements in a manner opposite to the way he had responded previously. He is then asked to respond while still under hypnosis to one of the five types of statements to which he was subjected in the experimental treatment. He then responds again to all the statements, first under hypnosis, and again immediately after hypnosis.

On several later occasions, about a week apart, the same subject is brought back for additional testing. He is re-hypnotized and, once again through suggestion, attempts are made to alter, in turn, each of four other kinds of beliefs varying in centrality-peripherality. For example, in the first experimental session an attempt is made to alter through suggestion a subject's primitive beliefs about self-identity; in the second session, his beliefs about authority; in the third session, beliefs which he has derived from external authority, which we call peripheral beliefs, and so on, for the remaining sessions, until each of five kinds of beliefs has, in turn, been subjected to the hypnotic manipulation.

It may be helpful to give a few of the belief statements to which the subject is asked to respond before, during, and after hypnosis. Two belief statements are: "My name is [real name]," and "My name is Ivan Petrov." In the pre-hypnotic test the subject would, of course, be expected to agree strongly with the first statement and disagree strongly with the second statement. Another pair of statements reads: "My mother's name is [real name]," and "My mother's name is Olga Petrov." Again, the subject can normally be expected to accept strongly the first statement, and to reject strongly the second statement. In the same way, we presented other biographical statements, paired with fictitious biographical statements—that the subject's father is Boris Petrov, that the subject was born and lives in Moscow, that he is an atheist and member of the Communist Party. Our subjects, who were neither atheist nor Communist, strongly reject each of these latter statements in the pre-hypnotic session and strongly accept the parallel statements based on their real biographical data.

The belief statements just described are samples of one kind of primitive belief, ones we have identified as taken-for-granted beliefs supported by a unanimous social consensus. Other statements are presented to sample a second kind of primitive belief, beliefs that, we assume, do not depend on social support. For example: "I believe my mother loves me." "I can remember having been very curious and sexually excited about the thought of seeing my mother without clothes on." Statements are then presented to test a third kind of belief ranging along the central-peripheral dimension we call authority beliefs, for example, "The philosophy of Nikita Khrushchev is basically a sound one and I am all for it." Similarly worded statements are presented about such positive and negative authority figures as Hitler, Faubus, Eisenhower, Kennedy, Lincoln, and Castro.

Some examples of the fourth kind of belief, which we call peripheral beliefs, beliefs derivable from authority, are: "The Russians were justified in putting down the Hungarian revolt in 1956," "The Gettysburg Address does not really say anything important," and "I think this country would have been better off if the South had won the Civil War."

Finally, there are inconsequential beliefs, beliefs which, if changed, are not expected to produce any significant changes in other beliefs: "There is no doubt in my mind that Elizabeth Taylor is more beautiful than Dinah Shore," and "I think summer is a much more enjoyable time of the year than winter."

This experimental situation was designed to determine whether different kinds of beliefs ranging systematically along a theoretically postulated central-peripheral dimension can be changed through hypnosis and, if so, which kinds of beliefs will be the easiest to change and which the most difficult. In other words, we were interested in determining whether differential changes in several beliefs will occur as a result of a single experimental treatment.

This is not the place to present the full results, which will be contained in a technical report presently in preparation. But Table 3 shows that the hypothesized differential changes in many expressed opinions were obtained as a result of one experimental treatment. As expected, the amount of change varies in inverse proportion to centrality of belief, the primitive beliefs changing least as a result of hypnotic suggestion, authority beliefs changing more, peripheral beliefs changing still more, and inconsequential beliefs changing the most. These differential results were obtained on three occasions, I might add: immediately after the hypnotic suggestion, a short time later while the subject was still under hypnosis, and immediately after he was awakened. It would be difficult to attribute such differential changes to compliance or to the operation of any other post-test situational variable, because the post-test situation, and the attitude activated by that situation, is a constant. Yet opinion changes vary systematically in the same way the original opinions vary, namely, as a function of centrality-peripherality. To account for such differential changes we would have to infer that they are manifestations of differential changes in underlying attitudes.

TABLE 3

MEAN CHANGES UNDER HYPNOSIS OF FIVE TYPES OF BELIEFS
VARYING IN CENTRALITY

Type of Belief	As an Immediate Result of Hypnotic Suggestion	Post-test 1: While Still under Hypnosis	Post-test 2: Post-hypnosis
Primitive, Type 1 (unanimous social support)	2.48	2.66	2.56
Primitive, Type 2 (no social support)	3.50	3.52	2.82
Authority	3.54	3.47	2.87
Peripheral	3.65	3.62	3.55
Inconsequential	4.25	4.08	3.48

Another illustration from our own research program where several opinion changes are obtained in one post-test situation may again be taken from *The Three Christs* study. As a result of experimental confrontation with others over the issue of who was the real Christ, Leon Gabor reported that he had changed his name from *Dr. Domino Dominorum et Rex Rexarum, Simplis Christianus Pueris Mentalis Doktor, the reincarnation of Jesus Christ of Nazareth* to Dr. R. I. Dung. Again the problem was whether this expressed opinion change regarding a new identity represented a true underlying change. And, again, our confidence increased that it did indeed represent a true change when he expressed a network of additional differential changes in opinion that were wholly consistent with the expressed change of name.

3. *Test for other behavioral changes accompanying a given opinion change.* If a single expressed opinion change truly represents a change in underlying attitude, it is reasonable to expect that such a change will be accompanied by other changes—cognitive, affective, or behavioral—which theoretically should be related to the change in attitude. It is difficult to believe that a change in expressed opinion representing a true change in attitude would have no other behavioral

481

manifestations. That Festinger and Cohen find virtually no studies in the experimental literature showing behavioral change following an attitude change only serves to reinforce my suspicion that most current experimental studies on opinion change do not deal with true attitude change, but with superficial opinion changes.

But I would like to draw attention to some data, again from our own research program, which illustrate that behavioral changes following or accompanying opinion changes can indeed be obtained. In *The Three Christs* study, one may note many changes in Leon Gabor's behavior following changes in expressed opinion. After he verbally claimed to have a new wife, Madame Yeti Woman, his behavior with respect to money changed. He accepted, handled, and spent money when it allegedly came from Madame Yeti; these were actions we had never before observed. Furthermore, Leon Gabor, following suggestions allegedly coming from his new wife, changed the song with which he always opened the meetings on days he was chairman from *America* to *Onward Christian Soldiers*, a permanent behavioral change. Again, these behavioral changes serve to increase our confidence in the inference that Leon's expressed opinion change represented a true change in underlying delusion.

Perhaps more impressive in this respect is a study of changes in expressed values by Kemp.[26] His subjects were all religiously minded persons enrolled in a special training curriculum designed to prepare them for positions as Boy Scout executives or YMCA or YWCA secretaries. Kemp was interested in determining whether changes in values and in behavior were a function of personality. The subjects were given the Allport-Vernon Scale of Values while still in college in 1950. Six years later they were contacted again, were given the Dogmatism Scale, and were retested with the Allport-Vernon Scale. As shown in Table 4, closed, middle, and open-minded subjects all expressed identical value patterns in 1950. But in 1956, the rank order of values remained the same only for the middle group, and had changed for the closed and open groups:

Although *religious* values were still predominant in all groups, the closed group increased in *political* and *economic* values and decreased markedly in *social* values. The open group remained unchanged in its *religious* and *social* values but increased in *theoretical* values and decreased in *economic* and *political* values. . . . The vocational choices . . . follow closely these changes or non-changes in value patterns. Roughly 70 per cent of the middle group became Boy Scout executives as planned, or entered closely related professions. But most of the open and closed subjects changed their vocational choice after leaving college; the open subjects more frequently entered vocations

[26] G. C. Kemp, "Change in Values in Relation to Open-Closed Systems," in M. Rokeach, *The Open and Closed Mind.*

requiring more advanced professional training in careers involving social welfare, and the closed subjects more frequently entered military and commercial careers of an administrative nature.[27]

TABLE 4

RANK ORDER OF IMPORTANCE OF SIX VALUES FOR THE TOTAL GROUP AND FOR OPEN, MIDDLE, AND CLOSED SUBGROUPS IN 1950 AND IN 1956

	(N)	Religious	Social	Political	Economic	Theoretical	Esthetic
Test 1950:							
Open	(25)	1	2	3	4	5	6
Middle	(54)	1	2	3	4	5	6
Closed	(25)	1	2	3	4	5	6
Total group	(104)	1	2	3	4	5	6
Retest 1956:							
Open	(25)	1	2	4	6	3	5
Middle	(54)	1	2	3	4	5	6
Closed	(25)	1	5	2	3	4	6
Total group	(104)	1	2.5	2.5	5	4	6

SOURCE: M. Rokeach, *The Open and Closed Mind*, New York, Basic Books, 1960, p. 339.

That vocational changes accompanied changes in scores on the Allport-Vernon Scale of Values strengthens the likelihood that the changes in expressed values represent real changes in underlying values.

CONCLUSION

In closing, I would like to concede that the point of view I have presented will probably not appeal to those who, disliking to think in terms of genotypes and phenotypes, would insist on equating an attitude with its operational measurement by some opinion questionnaire. But, starting with a conception of attitude as a hypothetical construct, I have proposed that the literature on opinion change does indeed tell us a good deal about the social influence variables and cognitive processes affecting changes in expressed opinion. But this is a literature concerning changes which, in the main, seem to be localized in the region of the lips and do not seem to affect the mind and heart, nor the hands and feet.

The view developed here on the relations existing among attitude, attitude change, and behavioral change is incomplete, however. It has neglected other kinds of change which must sooner or later be

[27] *Ibid.*, pp. 345-346.

considered if there is to be a truly systematic consideration of antecedents and consequents of attitude and behavioral change, namely, the problem of changes in values, in ideology, in total belief systems, in therapy, and in personality. It seems to me that contemporary theory and research on opinion change, dealing as they typically do with changes in single and isolated expressions of opinion, and selecting as they typically do opinions that are, as Hovland points out, "relatively uninvolving"[28] and thus easily capable of manipulation within the context of a relatively brief experimental session, have somehow lost touch with such broader issues. I hope that the present paper will serve as a contribution toward our regaining contact with these broader and more significant kinds of change, which may affect and be affected by our everyday life in local, national, and international affairs.

[28] Hovland, *op. cit.*

29

PREDICTING BEHAVIOR
FROM ATTITUDES
Alan G. Weinstein

FOR AT LEAST five decades, researchers have looked for a link between attitudes and behavior. Fishbein has suggested that, faced with essentially negative findings, social psychologists have criticized both measuring techniques and conceptualizations.[1] He speculated that this in turn had led to a concentration of effort on scaling elegance and increasingly complex definitions of attitude, rather than upon research directed at the dynamics of the relationship itself.

Nevertheless, there have been meaningful attempts to explain this relationship.[2] To Doob, attitudes are implicit responses to external stimuli.[3] In turn, these implicit responses act as drive-producing cues with the potential of arousing numerous behavioral responses. Invoking reinforcement theory, Doob argued that behavioral responses are a function of an individual's reinforcement history and will be evoked as drive-reducing mechanisms by the aroused individual.

If, as Doob suggests, an individual develops a response hierarchy

---

* The author would like to thank Hjalmar Rosen for the inspiration and guidance he gave to this research.

1 M. Fishbein, "A Behavior Theory Approach to the Relations between Beliefs about an Object and the Attitude toward the Object," in M. Fishbein, ed., *Readings in Attitude Theory and Measurement,* New York, Wiley, 1967.

2 In addition to Fishbein (*op. cit.*) see L. W. Doob, "The Behavior of Attitudes," *Psychological Review,* Vol. 54, 1947, pp. 135-156, and D. T. Campbell, "Social Attitudes and Other Acquired Behavioral Dispositions," in S. Koch ed., *Psychology: A Study of Science,* New York, McGraw-Hill, 1963, Vol. 6, pp. 94-172.

3 Doob, *op. cit.*

Originally published in Volume 36, Number 3, 1972 of the *Public Opinion Quarterly.*

based on past reinforcement in conjunction with an attitudinal arousal, then that individual should act, given an appropriate behavioral alternative. Conversely, if the individual is faced with a behavioral alternative which is perceived to have negative consequences or one which is not functionally related to his aroused attitude, there would be little justification for predicting that response— i.e., a person will not act unless both issue and action have positive value. This becomes most important in predicting behavior from attitudes. Although an individual may evaluate an issue positively, he may act as if he did not. This is well illustrated in the political arena, where liberals may have similar attitudes toward an issue but disagree on which action to support. On the other hand, liberals and conservatives may form a coalition in support of an action despite major differences in their attitudes toward the underlying issue.

Utilizing a unidimensional concept of attitude as an evaluative or affective response (paralleling Fishbein's position) and focusing attention on whether or not a specific overt behavior will occur, the following hypotheses were developed.

Hypothesis 1 (H$_1$): The attitudinal assessment of both issue and potential action yield a superior prediction of behavior than an assessment of the issue or potential action alone.

Doob's separation of the stimulus and behavioral effects provides a model for relating a given issue (referent component) and choice of action (action component) to actual behavior. By obtaining attitude measures of referent and action components, one can assess the usefulness of the additional knowledge of attitude toward action in predicting behavior. This can be accomplished in two ways: (1) by assessing the attitude toward referent and action components as independent stimuli and combining them statistically, or (2) by assessing a combined attitude concept including both referent and action components in the same stimulus.

Hypothesis 2 (H$_2$): Predictions are *less* accurate when the referent attitude favors action than when it does not. Given an action choice *re* a particular issue, affect consistent with that choice, i.e. in favor of the action, will generate poorer prediction of behavior than will affect less favorable to the action choice. For example, students who favor militant action and who dislike having ROTC on campus may or may not take militant action against ROTC. However, if the same students are against militant action, then they are not likely to behave militantly despite their negative attitude toward ROTC.

The logic supporting this hypothesis is as follows. With regard to the combined stimulus, i.e. action in the context of a referent, if one is opposed to the action available there is little logic for taking the action. However, if one has a positive affect toward the available action this does not guarantee its choice, since it is quite possible that other choice alternatives not included within a paradigm are preferred, i.e. have more positive affect associated with them. In such a case, the subject could reject the available action choice, not because he is opposed to it, but because, relatively speaking, he does not perceive it to be an optimal way to behave.

METHOD

The questionnaire used to assess the attitude variables under consideration was a Semantic Differential Scale loaded on the evaluative dimension.[4] The subscales consisted of the following adjective pairs: good-bad, unimportant-important, approve-disapprove, dangerous-safe, desirable-undesirable, foolish-wise, positive-negative, and worthless-useful. Of these, the importance subscale was not considered in the total attitude scores. The order of the adjectives was alternated between positive and negative forms appearing first to help eliminate response set. Three concept stimuli were developed for evaluation. These are a combined concept, "Signing a petition protesting the quarter system"; a referent concept, "The quarter system"; and an action concept, "Signing a protest petition."

Two separate classes of undergraduates were used as subjects with 53 persons in Class A and 51 Class B. One third of each class were given the combined concept scale concerning signing a protest petition against the quarter system. Of the remaining two thirds, half (subgroup 2) were given the referent component scale followed by the action component scale. The remaining subjects (subgroup 3) had the sequence of the two scales reversed to check for any response bias due to sequence effects.

One week later, a different experimenter was introduced to the classes as a person interested in obtaining signed petitions protesting the quarter system. Students were told that signed petitions would be used at the discretion of this individual. The experimenter passed out individual petitions sheets to each member of the two classes. The petitions read as follows: "I, the undersigned student at ———— University, am opposed to the quarter system and recommend an alternative system." The *Ss* were told to sign their names to the upper righthand corner of the petition, and to either sign or not sign their petition forms as they chose. After a few minutes, the forms were collected. The initial sample size in each class was reduced to 48 in Class A and 46 in Class B because of absences in the second session.

[4] C. E. Osgood, G. J. Suci, and P. H. Tannenbaum, *The Measurement of Meaning,* Urbana, University of Illinois, 1957.

Point biserial correlations were computed between the semantic differential scores and the dichotomous choice behavior, i.e. signing or not signing, for each stimulus condition in classes A and B. On the basis of the correlations calculated for subgroups 2 and 3, it was found that sequence had no significant effect on the relationship between either referent or action components and signing behavior, and the subgroups were therefore combined.

In support of H_1, the data in Table 1 show that in each of the two classes, the affect score generated by the combined stimulus yielded higher correlation coefficients than did the affect score toward the referent or action stimulus alone. Also, the combined and referent stimuli predict significantly better than the action stimulus for both classes. The probability that a significant difference exists between the combined and referent groups was $p < .10$. Taken simultaneously, the probability that these two independent samples yield $p < .10$ by chance is less than 2 percent.

Table 1 offers further support for H_1, showing that the combined stimulus predicts better than the multiple correlations of both referent and action stimuli. Again, the finding is not significant at $p < .05$ but holds up under replication.

TABLE 1

CORRELATIONS BETWEEN ATTITUDE COMPONENTS AND BEHAVIOR FOR TWO INDEPENDENT GROUPS

Groups	Combined Stimulus	Referent Stimulus	Action Stimulus	Multiple Correlation of Referent and Action Stimulus	Intercorrelation between Referent and Action Stimuli
Class A	−.65*	.49*	−29	.57*	.07
Class B	−.62*	.51*	−19	.52*	.16
Total Sample	−.69	.52	−.22	.54	.12

$p < .10$ $p < .05$

* $p < .05$ from zero correlation.

The question arose whether intensity of affect or a multiplicative relationship between referent and action components would yield fruitful results. These analyses were performed and did not predict as well as the original affect measure.

Another question was raised with regard to the linearity of the relationships for the different stimulus groups. The frequency of signers increased in nearly linear fashion as affect toward the combined and referent stimuli increased. This was not so, however, for the action stimulus, which conformed more to a curvilinear relationship. A non-linear analysis of the data might reveal additional findings.

TABLE 2

BEHAVIOR IN RELATION TO NEGATIVE-POSITIVE AFFECT TOWARD REFERENT, ACTION, AND COMBINED STIMULI[a]

| | | Attitude | | |
		Positive	Negative	
Combined Stimulus "Signing a protest petition against the quarter system"	Signed	11	0	11
	Did not sign	8	9	17
		19	9	28
Action Stimulus "Signing a protest petition"	Signed	20	1	21
	Did not sign	27	11	38
		47	12	59
Referent Stimulus[b] "Quarter system"	Signed	5	18	23
	Did not sign	26	14	40
		31	32	63

[a] A median split was used to divide positive and negative affect.
[b] A positive attitude toward the referent would be consistent with non-action. A negative attitude would be consistent with action.

Table 2 exhibits data supporting H_2 for each stimulus condition. The first 2×2 table represents the combined stimulus condition. Of Ss who are in favor of signing a protest petition against the quarter system, only 11 of 19 signed the petition. This is close to chance prediction. But of those who are negative toward this issue, not one signed the petition. This relative difference in predictability is also evidenced in the other two subtables. Of those in favor of signing protest petitions, less than half signed the petition. Yet only one of the twelve having a negative attitude toward this behavior signed a petition. Finally, in the referent condition, only 5 who were in favor of the issue signed a petition. This low proportion of "misses" is contrasted with the chance prediction obtained for persons in opposition to the quarter system. A significant difference between proportions test was performed for all three tables.[5] In each case a significant difference ($p < .05$) was found in the proportion of errors.

Further support for H_2 could be found. Six errors (17%) in prediction were made for those who were either in favor of the quarter system or against protest petitions. None of these subjects should have signed according to the logic proposed. Of those who expressed negative attitudes toward the quarter system and favorable attitudes toward signing protest petitions, 6 out of 21, or 29 percent failed to sign.

DISCUSSION AND CONCLUSIONS

Both hypotheses were given support by the data. The appreciation in the variance accounted for by including an action component is one of the critical findings of this study. In terms of the correlations reported in Table 1, it is apparent that affect toward action as an independent variable, or in statistical combination with affect toward referent, accounts for a small proportion of the criterion variance. When the action component is included as part of the stimulus, however, prediction is definitely improved.

The design and results of this study support Fishbein's contention that attitude has often been measured on inappropriate stimulus objects.[6] In the terms of this study, unless the referent stimulus generates an affective response representing drive arousal (negative affect toward the existing state of affairs), no action will be forthcoming. Second, Fishbein suggests that the focal behavior may be cognitively unrelated to the focal attitude, i.e. behavior will occur only when it is perceived to serve as an adequate drive reduction mechanism for drive arousal represented by the affective response to the focal stimulus. The results of this study support such a position.

Another aspect of the findings that merits discussion is the greater accuracy of prediction based on negative affect. If the action alternatives were assessed negatively (inappropriate), this was sufficient basis for rejecting the action choice, i.e. petition signing, whereas positive affect toward action did not guarantee behavior in conformity with attitude. This finding suggests that for behavior to occur as a tension-reducing mechanism, more conditions must be fulfilled than in the case where the action (choice) is rejected. First, the available action must be appraised as being desirable. Second, it must be appraised as more desirable than alternative courses of action. Rejection *can occur if either or both* of these conditions is not met.

[5] Quinn McNemar, *Psychological Statistics,* New York, Wiley, 1962.
[6] Fishbein, *op. cit.*

This final group of articles from *the Public Opinion Quarterly* provides historical perspective on the study of public opinion. Philosophers and politicians have been particularly fascinated by the phenomenon of public opinion and over the years a vast body of literature has been addressed to the question, What is public opinion and how does it influence our lives?

Francis Wilson in *"The Federalist* on Public Opinion" makes a distinguished contribution to our understanding of how the men who were instrumental in founding this country conceived of the role of public opinion. "The maxim that all government rests on opinion became in 1788 in its way as venerable as *vox populi vox dei*. Those who framed our system of government knew both sayings, but they stressed the former more than the latter. 'If it be true that all governments rest on opinion,' we read in *The Federalist*, No. XLIX, 'it is no less true that the strength of opinion in each individual, and its practical influence on his conduct, depends much on the number which he supposes to have entertained the same opinion.' "

Although Wilson's article was written several decades ago, it has a timely observation:

> What is needed today is a frontal analysis of the function of public opinion in a revolutionary age. *The Federalist* was, in its time, just such a frontal attack, and it contains perhaps one of the few genuine theories of opnion stated in modern times. It is animated by charity toward ordinary mortals, but is also speaks with candor of the weakness of the political animal. Modern writers, like the authors of *The Federalist*, never say really that government rests entirely on opinion, or that government is justified wholly by the opinion of its citizens.   .

Wilson identified three theories of the function of opinion.

> In the first place, it may be argued that the operational basis and standard of government is what the public wants. . . . A second theory of the function of public opinion assumes the rationality of man and the binding character of the power of reason. . . . In the third place, there is what may be called the conservative theory of the function of opinion. In some respects we cannot separate this third view from the second, and like the second its adherents waver

between an unshaken confidence in popular reason and a strong element of scepticism, asserting that the majority is not always or ultimately to be followed.

He traces facets of each theory as it is reflected in the writings of those who contributed to *The Federalist*. These writings deal with fundamental questions of morality, checks and balances, and the role of the government vis-a-vis the individual.

In his second article Wilson deals with another significant discussion of the function of public opinion. "James Bryce on Public Opinion: Fifty Years Later" provides some incisive and critical comments on the theories held by the author of the classic study, *The American Commonwealth*. Wilson notes the irony of Bryce's criticism of de Tocqueville's, *Democracy in America*, which appeared approximately fifty years after the publication of *The Federalist*. Wilson thinks Bryce wrong in judging that "Tocqueville did not know the mentality of the middle class, a way of life so fundamental to nineteenth century America."

Let us turn directly now to the study of public opinion in Bryce's work. The central theme is the rule of public opinion in the United States. He viewed that sovereignty with no fear; rather he welcomed it and saw in it one of the foundations of American greatness. The whole structure of American government was interpreted in the light of the control of opinion.

In Bryce one can discover the beginning of the distinction that in subsequent years has so troubled the student of opinion, the distinction between opinion and 'real' opinion. Bryce declared that in orthodox democratic theory 'every citizen has, or ought to have, thought out certain opinions. . . .' On the other hand, there is very little individuality in American opinion (the ghost of Tocqueville?), especially among average men.

While Wilson has some critical comments on *The American Commonwealth*, he does not deny the important role it played in shaping academic discussions of the concept of public opinion for several generations of scholars. One of his final observations about Bryce has particular significance today: "Our last problem in the study of Bryce must take us from his early treatment of the issue of majority tyranny to the rude awakening of the modern class war. The mid-nineteenth century treatment of democracy was profoundly concerned with the tyranny of the majority; today we are not so sure that tyranny must always come from the majority. We know that it can also come from the expertly organized minority."

In addition to historians and political scientists, a number of other social scientists have discussed the function of public opinion in the pages of *The*

Public Opinion Quarterly. Margaret Mead brings her rich experience as a social anthropologist to bear in her article "Public Opinion Mechanisms Among Primitive Peoples." Writing of a few selected primitive societies of which she had first-hand knowledge she found it possible to distinguish three types of emphasis in the relationship between political organization and public opinion.

> The first type are those societies which depend for impetus or inhibition of community action upon the continuing response of individuals in public opinion situations, in the manner by Professor Allport—'The term public opinion is given its meaning with reference to a multi-individual situation in which individuals are expressing themselves or can be called upon to express themselves, as favoring or supporting (or else disfavoring or opposing) some definite conditions, person, or proposal of widespread importance, in such a proportion of number, intensity, and constancy, as to give rise to the probability of affecting action, directly or indirectly, toward the object concerned.'

As an example of this type Mead chooses the Arapesh, a Papuan-speaking people of New Guinea, and she provides rich data to illustrate her thesis.

Mead's second type of primitive societies are "those that depend upon the operation of formal alignments of individuals, who react not in terms of their personal opinions concerning the given issue, but in terms of their defined positions in the formal structure." She cites another tribe in New Guinea, the Iatmul, as manifesting this type of society.

Her third type of primitive societies are "those societies which do not depend for their functioning on public opinion at all—in Professor Allport's sense of the term—but which function by invoking purely formal participation in and respect for an impersonal pattern or code." She finds evidence of this type of society in Balinese mountain villages. Good scholar that she is, she closes by stating, "Although I have, for purposes of clearer exposition, distinguished these three types, it must not be supposed that the classifications are mutually exclusive or that they exhaust the possibilities."

Lee Benson's brilliant essay, "An Approach to the Scientific Study of Past Public Opinion," gives a thoughtful and balanced overview of this neglected area.

> For his purposes 'public opinion' is *arbitrarily* defined as referring only to opinions on 'political issues.' As defined here, an opinion always connotes a *position* on some specific government action or general course of action; an attitude represents a persistent, general *orientation* toward some individuals, groups, institutions, or processes, but it does not necessarily result in a specific position on specific public issues. Put another way, the concept, 'the historical

study of public opinion,' for our purposes means the use of procedures to secure data from *documents* (broadly defined) that the
researcher *locates and selects but does not create, directly or indirectly.* By selecting documents and, so to speak, 'interrogating'
their authors, historical researchers *generate* data designed to answer
questions about past public opinion.

[Benson reminds us that] non-historians may find it surprising, but the three main dimensions of the concept of public
opinion were clearly identified by a historian over two thousand
years ago. Thucydides, in his classic *History of the Peloponnesian
War*, organized his book around three closely related but different
themes, the *distribution* of public opinion, the processes of opinion
formation, and the *impact* of opinion upon government decisions. . . . Truth in history is not only what happened but what men
believed to have happened. Public officials may—and frequently
do—misperceive public opinion. For our present purposes, that does
not matter. What does matter is that the *reality*, not the *accuracy*, of
their perceptions influences their actions—to the extent that they
consciously allow public opinion to influence their actions.

He offers "a tentative system of analysis for historical opinion research
based upon (1) selection of period for measurement and (2) constructing a
narrative framework to catch public opinion."

Bernard Berelson's "Democratic Theory and Public Opinion" serves as a
perfect complement to Benson's historical review of public opinion. Berelson
says "my subject is the claim of political theory to contribute to the character of
public opinion research."

He is interested in the nature of electorate decisions.

There appear to be two requirements in democratic theory which
refer primarily to characteristics demanded of the electorate as it
initially comes to make a political decision. . . . The first is the
possession of a suitable *personality structure*: within a range of
variations, the electorate is required to possess the types of characters which can operate effectively, if not efficiently, in a free
society. Certain kinds of personality structures are not congenial to a
democratic society, could not operate successfully within it, and
would be destructive of democratic values. Others are more compatible with or even disposed toward the effective performance of
the various roles which make up the democratic political system. . . .
The distribution of such personality characteristics in the population, let alone their relationship to political behavior, is not known.

The second requirement is not only a prerequisite but also an
outcome of electorate decisions. This is the factor of *interest* and

496

participation: the electorate is required to possess a certain degree of involvement in the process of political decision, to take an appropriate share of responsibility. Political democracy requires a fairly strong and fairly continuous level of interest from a minority, and from a larger body of the citizenry a moderate-to-mild and discontinuous interest but with a stable readiness to respond in critical political situations. Political disinterest or apathy is not permitted, or at least not approved. Here the descriptive documentation provided by opinion studies is relatively good.

Berelson then describes the components of electorate decisions. "The first requirement is that the electorate must be informed about the matters under consideration. Here, information refers to isolated facts and knowledge of general propositions, both of which provide reliable insight into the consequences of the decision. The second component requires the electorate to possess a body of stable political principle or moral standards to which questions can be referred for evaluation and decision. The third set of essentials refers to the decision-making process, which has three requirements: (1) accurate observation, (2) communication and discussion, and (3) rationality.

Harold Lasswell calls upon his impressive credentials as a student of law, government, and the communications process in his article "Communications Research and Public Policy" in which he puts forth "the proposition that future advances in the study of public opinion and communication depend on the development of a sense of professional responsibility as a full-fledged member of the policy sciences." Lasswell offers "a simple model of the policy (or decision) process as a checklist for considering the interrelations of clients and research." His treatment of this relationship focuses on different aspects of this relationship from those discussed in Carlson's chapter. His checklist includes the *intelligence* phase, the *prescribing* phase, the *invoking* phase, *application activities*, and the *terminating* function. Having explored these aspects of communications research in policy formation, he turns his attention to another area of special concern to him.

> It is in connection with the *appraisal* phase that communication research plays a particularly active role. To appraise a flow of official activities is to characterize them in terms of conformity to the goals of public policy, and to impute responsibility for what has happened. Think of the torrent of information at hand about judgments of the efficiency or inefficiency, integrity or corruptness, legality or illegality of foreign and internal policies. Intelligence points forward; appraisal first looks backward as a step toward future action.

Lasswell then turns his attention to the professional status of the communications researcher.

The important thing about a profession is not conveyed by the traditional assertion that it has a distinctive literature. Today, practically every craft or trade meets this criterion. More relevant is the distinction between the exercise of a skill, and the coupling of skill with knowledge of the aggregated process to which the skill is intimately related. . . . It is not enough for communication specialists to acquire skill in surveying, content analysis, or other technical operations. A genuine profession can be said to complement skill with enlightenment. In the case of communication, this implies a common map of the trends, conditions, and projections of the entire process. It also implies the capacity to invent and evaluate policies for the accomplishment of postulated goals.

He has much more to say be way of elaborating on these points, including a suggestion for the creation of "a 'third voice' that can attract general attention for its reports on how things are going. At present the principal voices are self-serving, whether the self is a government, a political party, a business, or what. The role of a third, disinterested voice is to supply a competing appraisal of the images spread by self-serving sources."

It is fitting that the final chapter in this volume is by Paul Lazarsfeld, for he has contributed to the growth of public opinion research to a degree unparallelled by any other scholar or researcher. The first two paragraphs of his essay, "Public Opinion and the Classical Tradition," represent his statement of the state of the art of studying public opinion:

Quite possibly the emergence of empirical social science will one day be considered an outstanding feature of the twentieth century. But its birth has not been without travail. Hardest have been its struggles with what we shall call the classical tradition. After all, for two thousand years or more people have thought and written about human and social affairs. Has the empirical trend been an enriching innovation? Has it had a pernicious effect? The matter has certainly been much discussed in recent years.

The debate over the study of public opinion probably provides the best case in point. Since about the beginning of the eighteenth century a steadily increasing amount has been written on this subject by political scientists, by historians and, recently, by sociologists. Toward the beginning of the twentieth century, however, this classical tradition was confronted by the empiricists, who rallied around the notion of attitudes.

Lazarsfeld writes at length about the complexities of the classical notion of public opinion. At one point he observes:

498

It is this intertwining of matters of definition and factual problems which is so characteristic of the classical tradition. We are probably faced here by an irreversible development. Now that we have the reality of public opinion polls we will undoubtedly keep on calling public opinion a well analyzed distribution of attitudes. But certainly no one denies that we still know very little about how such complete attitude distributions come into being, and what role they actually play in the governmental process. And under the general heading of the 'mass society phenomenon' we certainly keep on worrying about the role it *should* play. Thus the issue of definition resolves itself in an interesting way. The critics of polling are worried that the joy of having found greater conceptual clarity will lead us to forget some of the grave philosophical and empirical problems with which the classics dealt (and well these critics might worry as far as some pollsters are concerned). But what is overlooked is something that has happened often in intellectual history: a new technique has permitted the sorting out of various aspects of a diffused concern and has prepared the way for a more rational approach to its different elements.

The foregoing articles offer solid and stimulating observations on the historical roots of the study of public opinion. They do more, however. They provide a very necessary perspective for all students of public opinion as to many different academic disciplines that have important contributions to make to this subject. The final essay suggests that it is possible to incorporate this rich legacy of scholarship into theoretical deliberations of today's public opinion researchers.

THE FEDERALIST
ON PUBLIC OPINION
Francis G. Wilson

T HE MAXIM that all government rests on opinion became in 1788 in its way as venerable as *vox populi vox dei*. Those who framed our system of government knew both sayings, but they stressed the former more than the latter. "If it be true that all governments rest on opinion," we read in *The Federalist*, No. XLIX, "it is no less true that the strength of opinion in each individual, and its practical influence on his conduct, depend much on the number which he supposes to have entertained the same opinion. The reason of man, like man himself, is timid and cautious when left alone, and acquires firmness and confidence in proportion to the number with which it is associated. When the examples which fortify opinion are ancient as well as numerous, they are known to have a double effect. In a nation of philosophers, this consideration ought to be disregarded. A reverence for the laws would be sufficiently inculcated by the voice of an enlightened reason. But a nation of philosophers is as little to be expected as the philosophical race of kings wished for by Plato. And in every other nation, the most rational government will not find it a superfluous advantage to have the prejudices of the community on its side."[1]

Our problem is to discuss the theoretical function of opinion as *The Federalist* states it. This issue is part of the more comprehensive theory of public opinion, but many would regard it as the initial and most essential phase of this larger subject.[2] Today, when the bald use of

[1] The numbering of the papers in *The Federalist* and the ascription of authorship follows here the Lodge edition of 1886. See introduction to Everyman edition of 1911 by W. J. Ashley.

[2] Cf. my article "Concepts of Public Opinion," *The American Political Science Review*, XXVII (1933), 371*ff.*

Originally published in Volume 6, Number 4, 1942 of the *Public Opinion Quarterly*.

amoral political techniques by our enemies has forced the democracies to re-examine the fundamentals of social morality, it is essential that conflicting theories of the function of opinion should be clarified.

Now the central propositions to be argued here are that most modern discussions of the function of opinion do not face clearly certain fundamental issues, and that *The Federalist* can throw light on these issues, as well as assist in the formulation of a coherent, conservative theory of opinion. What is needed today is a frontal analysis of the function of public opinion in a revolutionary age. *The Federalist* was, in its time, just such a frontal attack, and it contains perhaps one of the few genuine theories of opinion stated in modern times. It is animated by charity toward ordinary mortals, but it also speaks with candor of the weaknesses of the political animal. Modern writers, like the authors of *The Federalist*, never say really that government rests entirely on opinion, or that government is justified wholly by the opinion of its citizens.

THEORIES OF THE FUNCTION OF OPINION

It may be said that, broadly, there are three theories of the function of opinion. In the first place, it may be argued that the operational basis and standard of government is what the public wants. Two assumptions are vitally important to this view. Its proponent must argue that the people can do or attain what they want, either in a particular state or by a kind of consensus gentium. It must also be argued that whatever is approved by such consent is right or is the standard by which a government should be directed. It is clear that while it may be easy to argue moral relativism, or that the very idea of morality is a kind of linguistic boner, it is much more difficult to say that in practical politics the people are able to do precisely what they may want. Briefly, whenever the desires of people go counter to the patterns of political control, the consequences of behavior differ from the purposes originally accepted.

More serious in our time, however, is the view that government must be in accordance with more than human caprice, or, indeed, that justice is more than simple whim or even long-standing prejudice. The moral relativist may have an easy time of it in periods of peaceful prosperity, but the condemnation of tyranny and irresponsible oligarchy, we have found, requires more than a mere "some people do and others don't." It requires a standard of justice, a theory of morality which applies to men in general. It requires a philosophy of right which cannot be stated simply in terms of a mathematical equation or a scientific formula; it must be stated in terms of the Greek-Christian theory of morality, which has been the fortress of Western humanity in times of social disaster. When Socrates in *The Republic* denounced and vivisected the theories asserting that what the people want and can get is the basis of justice, he was stating an argument which is all but as fresh as on the day it was written. Indeed, the grossest perverters of Machiavelli have hardly reached the proposition that the standard for the conduct of the state is merely what the public wants. We may, therefore, consider this point of view as something of a straw man, needing little further attention.

A second theory of the function of public opinion assumes the rationality of man and the binding character of the power of reason. Rational opinion discovers the rights of men and the moral criteria for action by the state. Upon this assumption the right of the majority to sovereignty is clear, and opinion so guided would be able to achieve its legitimate purposes. The rising defense of democracy during the period since the Enlightenment is closely associated with this interpretation of the function of opinion. We might call to witness Rousseau's conception of the general will, the contract theory of society propounded by John Locke, or many of the defenders of a democratic philosophy in America, such as Thomas Jefferson and his followers. But how will we reconcile the assertion that men have natural rights against society when we also say that a majority of the people have a right to govern? Professor Kendall has recently shown that Locke, at least, believed men would act rationally and therefore there could be no enduring conflict between the moral capacities of men and the will of the sovereign majority. He has called this Locke's "latent premise," which should have been elaborated in the *Two Treaties* but which was not.[3] In adopting Kendall's interpretation, we argue that we have, in the second place, the latent premise theory of the function of opinion. It is the pervading reasonableness of man which gives opinion its legitimate majority authority in society.

It should be noted that this theoretical product of the age of reason did not stress the immediate participation of reason in the divine mind,

[3] See Willmoore Kendall, *John Locke and the Doctrine of Majority-Rule* (Urbana, Ill., 1941), pp. 132ff.

502

since in general a deistic attitude was assumed. In its day this theory was radical enough and is to be distinguished from the historically more conservative theory which insisted on the divine origin of the moral order and the participation of human reason in the reason of God.

CONSERVATIVE THEORY

In the third place, there is what may be called the conservative theory of the function of opinion. In some respects we cannot separate this third view from the second, and like the second its adherents waver between an unshaken confidence in popular reason and a strong element of scepticism, asserting that the majority is not always or ultimately to be followed. Thus there is no latent premise that men will act rationally, and there is in general a theistic interpretation of the relation of human reason and the moral order. One immediate implication of this position is that democracy is a form of government, depending on a social theory of justice which is applicable to any form. In other words, the principles of justice are not directly democratic as in the second theory. The criteria of justice may or may not be accepted by the majority; the norms of behavior may or may not coincide with opinion. In this statement we have, it may be argued, the historic and conservative theory of the operation of opinion in the state.

Opinion here becomes a subdivision of a general theory of justice. Our third conception of the function of opinion involves a theory of truth not essentially different from the second point of view; but it involves also a conception of the pattern or characteristics of human behavior which is widely different. Under Hamilton's statement we could not say that men will in the end act rationally under mere majority control; but we could say that they may or may not act rationally depending upon various circumstances. It might be observed that even the Jeffersonians veered toward the third view whenever the majority went against them, and in their defense of the constitutional balance they were implicitly taking the conservative view of public opinion. It hardly needs to be mentioned that what Hamilton was saying was the echo of the ancient moral tradition of the East and the West. Confucius, the Laws of Manu, Plato, the Christian Fathers, John Calvin, Leo XIII in his great nineteenth-century Encyclicals, and in part the authors of the Declaration of Independence would find nothing strange in it.

Now the American tradition as expressed by the Philadelphia Convention and *The Federalist* holds that some opinion is estimable and some is not, and that it is the function of enlightened rulers to stand against that opinion which is either erroneous or impracticable under the circumstances. Yet withal we must say that *The Federalist* was kindly in its attitude toward the common man, and that never during the formative period of our tradition was the sovereignty of the rational people denied. Most people have reasoned judiciously in response to the patriotic appeal of the Philadelphia Convention, John Jay notes in *The Federalist* No. II. And Madison declared in No. XIV: "Is it not the glory of the people of America, that, whilst they have paid decent regard to the opinions of former times and other nations, they have not suffered a blind veneration for antiquity, for custom, or for names, to overrule the suggestions of their own good sense, the knowledge of their own situation, and the lessons of their own experience?"

Yet there are special problems regarding opinion which must be faced in a republic. "As there is a degree of depravity in mankind which requires a certain degree of circumspection and distrust," we read in *The Federalist* No. LV, "so there are other qualities in human nature which justify a certain portion of esteem and confidence. Republican government presupposes the existence of these qualities in a higher degree than any other form." Further in No. LXXVI, Hamilton urges that the "supposition of universal venality in human nature is little less an error in political reasoning than the supposition of universal rectitude."

If the good and bad in opinion must be balanced by government, it is the organization of government that will reflect the principles of balance. Thus, the framers of the Constitution and the authors of *The Federalist* believed in a new application of the principle of the mixed constitution, combining democratic and aristocratic elements with a strong executive, and supported by a check and balance system or the separation of powers. In some of the discussions the separation of powers looms larger than the principle of mixed government, but it is clear that the framers wanted checks and separation in order to limit the people as well as the agencies of the government. In the government there must always be a clearly democratic element, in this case the House of Representatives which would stand in close sympathy with the people.[4]

Our concern here is primarily with the popular branch, for it was in the representative system that opinion would have its fullest expression. Madison in the famous No. X of *The Federalist* shows that the effect of representation is "to refine and enlarge the public views, by passing them through the medium of a chosen body of citizens, whose wisdom may best discern the true interest of their country, and whose patriotism and love of justice will be least likely to sacrifice it to temporary and partial considerations." Hamilton, indeed, believed that the general government would be better administered than the local ones because, as he said in No. XXVII, the extension of the spheres of election in the House will give a greater choice to the people and it will be less responsive to the temporary aberrations of the people.

The evaluation of the action of opinion in *The Federalist* centers essentially on the legislative power of the people and neglects measurably the constituent function of opinion. *The Federalist* itself was an argument directed to the latter problem, but within the document the central issue is how the people act in the choice of representatives and the laws exemplified in the conduct of the delegates of the people. It was recognized that the House of Representatives must have a common interest and sympathy with the people. Specifically, Madison or Hamilton argued in No. LIII against the proposition "that where annual elections end, tyranny begins." The general character of the Republic, the kind of work to be done, the distance to be traveled, were against one year terms and for the moderate proposal for a term of two years. Likewise, while there must be enough representatives for consultation and discussion, the membership must be limited "to avoid the confusion and intemperance of a multitude." Thus in No. LV our authors declare: "Had every Athenian been a Socrates, every Athenian assembly would

---

[4] The Declaration of Resolves of the First Continental Congress, October 14, 1774, stated "that the foundation of English liberty, and of all free government, is a right in the people to participate in their legislative council." See *Documents Illustrative of the Formation of the Union of the American States.* 69th Congress, 1st Sess., House Document No. 398, 1927, p. 3. This idea runs through the work of the Constitutional Convention, but with varying emphasis on the part of the members. Madison, Wilson and Franklin especially defended the democratic element in the Constitution. We may assert that, broadly, the framers of the state constitutions were in agreement with the framers of the national constitution and the authors of *The Federalist.*

still have been a mob." The clear admission that the people must be checked by devices they accept themselves is crucial in the third theory of opinion we have discussed, but it is an idea that more radical exponents of the power of opinion today hardly like to accept.[5]

THE PATTERNS OF POLITICS

The conservative theory of the function of opinion centers, therefore, not only upon an objective and rational theory of moral validity, but also upon the proposition that part of the theory of opinion is a statement of the patterns of political behavior. The mixed constitution is an institutional statement of the same proposition, as are the devices associated with it. In addition to the disorderly inclinations of men, because of the distortion of passion and ignorance, government must be effective, and there is a pattern of effective government which leaders may carry into effect. *The Federalist* shows little concern with what we might call naturalistic limitations on governmental effectiveness; it is chiefly concerned with the limitations on government imposed by the known operations of human opinion.

In the light of these observations we may consider briefly Madison's utterances in No. X. This document has been regarded by many as an economic interpretation of politics, but a careful reading might show that the principal theme is the passions and ignorance of men reflected in their political opinions, whether or not such passion and ignorance arise from the unequal distribution of property. Madison makes himself clear that property is not the only cause for the disorder of faction and the repudiation of the common interests of the Republic. Popular governments, he urged, tend toward the dangerous vice of faction; confusion and violence in the public counsels will be remedied by the establishment of the Union. But the latent causes of faction are sown in the nature of man. Hamilton states a similar realism in No. XXVIII when he declares that ". . . seditions and insurrections are, unhappily, maladies as inseparable from the body politic as tumours and eruptions from the natural body. . . ." Under the Constitution force will be proportionate to the need.

[5] The fact that the regulation of the right to vote was left to the states made it unnecessary to discuss this matter at length in *The Federalist*. In a sense it is outside the scope of this paper, since the suffrage is the most prominent device for defining the participating public. The framers of the Constitution were in favor, generally, of the conventional freehold qualification for voting.

This doctrine is further elaborated in No. LI. Government itself is the greatest adverse reflection on human nature, and government must first control the governed and then control itself. In controlling the governed, one part of society may need protection against another. If the majority be united by a common interest, the rights of the minority will be insecure. Thus in America we need to create "a will in the community independent of the majority—that is, of the society itself." But in addition there should be such a diversity in interest that a majority combination will be improbable.

The modern analysis of oligarchy, the government of the few or the elite, was not wholly strange to *The Federalist*. In No. LVIII it is argued that the greater the number of representatives, the fewer will be the number who control. Moreover, the greater the number in the House of Representatives, the more will be the ascendancy of passion over reason, and the more will be found representatives with weak capacities and limited information. "The people can never err more than in supposing that by multiplying their representatives beyond a certain limit, they strengthen the barrier against the government of the few. ... The countenance of the government may become more democratic, but the soul that animates it will be more oligarchic."[6]

CONSTITUTIONAL CHECKS ON OPINION

Politics must be more than mere technique, more than the manipulation of the passions of the population. Yet in the construction of the Constitution, the framers were conscious of the values of an arrangement of offices. The Senate, the President, and the judicial organization, as well as the guarantee of rights, all were related for the purpose of preventing one branch of the government, especially the predominant popular branch, from exercising a concentrated authority. That same balance in the Constitution, combined with the federal principle, served to check at the point of authority the power of opinion. Those who defended our Constitution did have a sense of political technique, but it was not, as in recent years in Europe, used for the purpose of establishing an irresponsible and concentrated authority; rather it was technique

---

[6] See Franklin's speech on June 2, 1787, in the Constitutional Convention in opposition to the presidential veto. "It will be said that we don't propose to establish kings. I know it. But there is a natural inclination to kingly government. It sometimes relieves them from Aristocratic domination. They had rather have one tyrant than five hundred. It gives more the appearance of equality among citizens, and that they like."

in the service of moderated power in order that social and moral values might be realized in our government.

A Senate is necessary, we read in No. LXII, because of the propensity of "all single and numerous assemblies to yield to the impulse of sudden and violent passions, and to be seduced by factious leaders into intemperate and pernicious resolutions." It will avoid mutability in the public counsels arising from a rapid succession of new members; likewise, another effect of instability will be checked, that is, the "advantage it gives to the sagacious, the enterprising, and the moneyed few over the industrious and uninformed mass of the people." Historically, it could be observed also that there had been no long-lived republic which did not have a senate, and Sparta, Rome and Carthage were called to witness.

Much the same argument was advanced in defense of the presidential office. In No. LXVIII, Hamilton urged that the choice of electors is less apt to convulse the community with any extraordinary or violent movements "than the choice of *one* who was himself to be the final object of the public wishes." No. LXX insists that a plural executive would, on the other hand, deprive public opinion of its power to restrain executive authority, since responsibility would be shifted from one executive official to another. Some thought that the executive should show a "servile pliancy" before the prevailing currents of politics. This Hamilton denied in No. LXXI. The deliberate sense of the community should control the government, but this did not mean compliance with "every sudden breeze of passion" or every transient impulse which may come from the arts of men "who flatter their [the people's] prejudices to betray their interests." The wonder is, thought Hamilton, that the people so seldom err, beset as they are by the wiles of parasites and sycophants, by the snares of the ambitious, the avaricious and the desperate. Men who know must stand against popular delusions and serve the people at the peril of their displeasure.[7]

Naturally, the fundamental written law would be regarded as a stabilizing force in politics, as well as the judicial interpretation of the Constitution. The people have a right to alter the Constitution, Hamil-

[7] Speaking of the veto power of the President, Hamilton said in *The Federalist*, No. LXXIII: "The primary inducement to conferring the power in question upon the Executive is, to enable him to defend himself; the secondary one is to increase the chances in favor of the community against the passing of bad laws, through haste, inadvertence, or design:"

ton affirmed in No. LXXVIII, but momentary inclination holding a majority of the people does not justify a violation of the Constitution. Only by solemn and authoritative act may it be changed; until then it is binding as it stands. Moreover, judges who interpret the Constitution should not be removed merely because of inability. "The mensuration of the faculties of the mind has, I believe, no place in the catalogue of known arts," said Hamilton in No. LXXIX.

The capstone of the conservative view of opinion is the theory of rights, rights which deserve protection in republican government against both the people and the officials of government. To the charge that the Constitution contained no bill of rights, Hamilton replied in No. LXXXIV that there are provisions protecting rights throughout the proposed instrument of government. And to the argument that there was no guarantee of the freedom of the press, he answered tartly that no such provision was to be found in the Constitution of New York. But who can define freedom of the press? Whatever security there is for the press must "depend on public opinion, and on the general spirit of the people and of the government. And here, after all, as is intimated upon another occasion, must we seek for the only solid basis of all our rights."

LIBERAL LIMITATIONS ON OPINION

Hamilton's appeal to public opinion for the protection of rights is of more than passing interest. For it is clear that the fundamental purpose of the Constitution as it came from the hands of the framers was to secure rights which social morality assigns to the individual. It is in the theory of rights of individuals or groups, i.e., minorities, that the theories of the function of opinion diverge in the final analysis most sharply. We have seen already that in fact no theory of opinion does actually accept the existing wish of a majority as the final test of what ought to be done by government. It is, as has been said, the limitation which counts.

We may take, for example, the work of V. L. Parrington, *Main Currents in American Thought*. Whenever the conservatives suggested limitations on the majority in regard to the rights of property, the Parringtonian scorn is directed against the evils of the reactionary mind. But when William E. Channing argued that the multitude could not determine what subjects ought to be discussed by the citizenry, Parrington is pleased. Here is clearly a principle of political morality above the determination of the majority.[8] The conservative would say that both the rights of property and free inquiry are morally above the determination of the majority. Edwin Mims, Jr., goes to great length in arguing the freedom and sovereignty of the majority; he asserts quite correctly that our tradition stands for the sovereignty of the people. What he seems to forget is that all defenders of majority principle were likewise defenders of rights and Constitutions as fundamental law; this situation eliminates a right of immediate revolution vested in the people. If so, the road back to the conservative theory of opinion is well-paved. Mims declares: ". . . the true alternative to the corporate will of the prince is the general will of a public-spirited, patriotic majority whose power is limited only by the stipulation that minority individuals shall be unrestrained in their efforts to form a new majority. . . ." The conservative denier of the latent premise theory would assert, first, that if there is one limitation on the majority there may be others; and, second, that the tradition of limitation on the majority in American history is broader than is stated in the above quotation, for it is based on a theory of morality and justice which guarantees other rights as sacredly as the one mentioned.[9]

The latent premise theory historically has tended toward the assertion of one natural right, the right of the majority. But even here the theory has never quite asserted that what the majority wants will really be rational. Conservatives, on the other hand, have maintained the plurality of rights inhering in the people, and have, in fact, often looked to the judiciary for the protection of rights associated with property. When John Quincy Adams in the articles signed *Publicola* in 1791 stated a theory of justice higher than a mere majority he was presenting the conservative theory of opinion. "This principle, that a whole nation has a right to do whatever it pleases, cannot in any sense whatever be admitted as true," he said. "The eternal and immutable laws of justice and of morality are paramount to all human legislation. The violation of those laws is certainly within the power, but it is not among the rights of nations."[10]

Both the latent premise and the conservative theories of opinion

---

[8] V. L. Parrington, *Main Currents in American Thought* (New York, 1927), Vol. II, pp. 336-337, for the quotation from Channing, *Works*, Vol. II, p. 161.

[9] Edward Mims, Jr., *The Majority of the People* (New York, 1941), p. 275.

[10] See *The Writings of John Quincy Adams*, edited by W. C. Ford (7 vols., New York, 1913-1917), Vol. I, pp. 70-71.

admit limitations. In recent literature the former imposes only one significant limitation, and that is the right of the minority to talk. The latter would certainly accept this limitation, since freedom of speech and press are among the rights the majority may not invade. But the basis of this right (which is not clear in radical majoritarianism) in the conservative theory is the same as the other rights which may be accepted. For there is a norm above opinion, a standard of justice and morality which assures to the individual his freedoms in society. And these freedoms are more substantial than the right to grumble against the acts of a majority which may or may not be rational.

THE FEDERALIST TODAY

Specifically, *The Federalist* recognized two general sources of limitation on the function of public opinion. There were, in the first place, the principles of social morality from which specific rights were deduced, including the right of the majority to act so long as it remains within the framework of justice. But the failure of *The Federalist* to discuss the formation of opinion, or to sense the control mechanism in propaganda, is one of its greatest weaknesses. Today we are less concerned with constitutional limitations on the majority and more with the limitations which arise from the direct formation of the majority itself. In the second place, there are tendencies in political behavior which must be guarded against, since neither the people nor those in power always respect the principles of social morality. Thus the Constitution, the elements of the mixed constitution, the separation of powers, the restraining influence of the Senate, the veto of the President, and the right of judicial review, all tend in the same direction —to introduce responsibility into government. Not only do these structures, in the theory of *The Federalist*, assure the rights of individuals but they also prevent the normal toleration of the behavior patterns which result in oligarchy, the government of the few, or the concentration of authority.

No theory of the function of opinion remains unchanged in detail from generation to generation. It would be foolish to assert that what the authors of *The Federalist* believed to be the proper constitutional position of opinion should be followed slavishly today. Yet in the form of historical continuity much that they believed remains with us today. The spirit of limitation on public opinion as stated in *The Federalist* is changed, but limitation remains. We do not believe that what the public wants is the applicable criterion of social justice; nor do we believe that the majority is always right, or that the representatives of that opinion need no enforcement of political responsibility. Today, as the civil servant becomes more and more the central issue in politics, we must assume that the principles of conservative limitation on opinion will in measure apply. Madison, Hamilton and Jay would argue no differently.

The study of public opinion must go beyond the descriptive phase through which it has been passing. Civilization, in this time of revolution, must embody principles of justice as they have been developed in Western thought, in the Greek-Christian tradition, for the past 2500 years. The norms of the people and the norms of the leaders must be subjected to rational criticism in the light of what we can know of social and individual morality. Here at least is one of the imperatives of the age of reconstruction we are sure to face. We cannot trust the mere passions of masses and leaders for the creation of a just peace.

JAMES BRYCE
ON PUBLIC OPINION:
FIFTY YEARS LATER
Francis G. Wilson

A little more than fifty years have passed since publication of Lord Bryce's *The American Commonwealth,* the work upon which the larger share of his American reputation has been based. One returns to his pages today with mixed feelings. It is clear that to Bryce's mind the existence of democracy was a closed issue; democracy itself was the final and progressive form of government toward which the peoples of the world were to struggle. His comments on public opinion must be read in the light of his resolution of the larger issue; his judgment of opinion is governed by his judgment of democracy. In discussing the political career of Robert Lowe, Viscount Sherbrooke, Bryce remarked that no one since Lowe had been an avowed enemy of democracy, and that no one since 1867, during the consideration of Disraeli's household suffrage in boroughs bill, had been a frank enemy of democratizing the government.[1] Bryce lived long enough to see the beginning flare of the contemporary anti-democratic movement, but not long enough to see the whole issue reopened as it is today.

No one can deny the importance of Bryce in the succession of important students of public opinion. In fact it can be said that Bryce was one of the most important of modern scholars in making the thinking world conscious of the problem of opinion. For

[1] James Bryce, *Studies in Contemporary Biography,* 1903, p. 309. Bryce observes (p. 310) that Disraeli was the first to reveal the secret that the masses will as readily vote conservative as liberal.

Originally published in,Volume 3, Number 3, 1939 of the *Public Opinion Quarterly*.

a generation, Bryce set the pace in the study of opinion, and while his method is now outmoded, his stimulation continues to be effective. A critical student will no doubt say that *Modern Democracies* (1921) is a work far inferior to *The American Commonwealth*; it is to the latter work that we must go to find the full-rounded and optimistic outlines of his theory of public opinion.

For almost a generation we have been busily engaged in shattering the democratic "myth"; we have been realists in the study of social behavior. Consequently, the Victorian observation of "facts," so characteristic of Bryce, seems alien to our own understanding of politics. Either the United States has changed enormously since Bryce wrote, or Bryce failed to see what the American political stage was really like. If our British statesman was correct in his method, then we have come from a period of consolidation in politics to one of sharp transition. In part this must be true, yet it seems that Bryce took all facts without distinction (there was no aristocracy of facts as Pareto claims) and painted them verbally with his myopic bias. The plain fact is that Bryce did not really see the United States; he found what he wanted to find. But optimism was characteristic of the first generation of readers of Bryce; no doubt they felt that the author of *The American Commonwealth* was a profound observer.

BRYCE ON DE TOCQUEVILLE

A touch of irony may be suggested by a comparison of Bryce's criticism of Alexis de Tocqueville's method and our similar criticism of Bryce. Tocqueville was mistaken in many of his observations, argued Bryce, since he was seeking in America the ideal or type of democracy. British institutions were insufficiently familiar to him, and therefore many things commonplace in the Anglo-American political structure appeared novel or striking. Tocqueville did not see the basic similarity between English and American democracy—this is the flat assertion of the author of the *Commonwealth*. In addition to mistaking the transitory and the permanent, Tocqueville did not know the mentality of the middle class, a way of life so fundamental to nineteenth century America.[2]

Tocqueville was an aristocrat, carrying the image of France in his mind, but attempting to observe *Democracy in America*. Now in general it is just this sort of criticism that we must make today of Bryce's study of public opinion in the United States. Just as Tocqueville, Bryce saw what he wanted to see. Perhaps today we are seeing what we want to see, but certainly it is true that we cannot see now the conditions Bryce saw when he was studying our political life.

The Johns Hopkins study cited above must have been written with either a finished or partially finished *American Commonwealth* before the author. Implicitly, Bryce recognized himself in the apostolic succession of students of American democracy. Tocqueville wrote approximately fifty years after the publication of *The Federalist,* and Bryce's work appeared approximately fifty years after the publication of *Democracy in America*. It is now fifty years since Bryce wrote, and it may be that the bitter words in defense of democracy today are not to be in the same tradition as the great trilogy of works on American politics just mentioned. Charles A. Beard, Harold J. Laski or others might be mentioned as successors to Bryce, but they may not be willing to accept the accolade.

"RULE OF PUBLIC OPINION"

Let us turn directly now to the study of public opinion in Bryce's work. The central theme is the rule of public opinion in the United States. He viewed that sovereignty with no fear; rather he welcomed it and saw in it one of the foundations of American greatness. The whole structure of American government was interpreted in the light of the control of opinion. Presidential power, for example, comes directly from the people, and the President represents the people no less than members of the legislature. Public opinion governs by and through the President, though Bryce noted that it is popular to warn against "one-man power" in the

[2] See James Bryce, "The Predictions of Hamilton and de Tocqueville," *Johns Hopkins University Studies in History and Political Science,* 5th series, Vol. IX (1887), pp. 22 ff.

United States. "Nowhere is the rule of public opinion as complete as in America, nor so direct, that is to say, so independent of the ordinary machinery of government."[3] Likewise, the Supreme Court feels the touch of public opinion, since public opinion is stronger in its influence in the United States than anywhere else. Judges are only men, observed Bryce, and when the meaning of the Constitution is in doubt, it is natural to follow the lead of public opinion.[4] Behind the legislatures, the executives and the judiciary is the power of opinion. In the end the people approve or disapprove of an interpretation of the Constitution. This is so even when the interpretation goes beyond the letter of the Constitution.[5]

In Bryce one can discover the beginning of the distinction that in subsequent years has so troubled the student of opinion, the distinction between opinion and "real" opinion. Bryce declared that in orthodox democratic theory "every citizen has, or ought to have, thought out certain opinions. . . ." On the other hand, there is very little individuality in American opinion (the ghost of Tocqueville?), especially among average men. There is, indeed, little substance in their opinions. "It is, therefore, rather sentiment than thought that the mass can contribute. . . ."[6] The upper classes, on the other hand, entertain ideas concerning their own interest, though they are often wrong, in contrast with the lower groups where there is more sentiment. In proof Bryce observed that the masses favored the attainment of national status in Italy, and in North America during the Civil War. Nearly all great political causes have made their way first among the middle or humbler classes. But it is the aristocrats who furnish the masses with ideas.[7] Opinion as sentiment, however, is fundamentally passive. In nineteen out of twenty men opinion consists chiefly of sentiments, while a small active class is busy making and sounding out opinion, along with the formative influence of education.

[3] James Bryce, *The American Commonwealth*, American edition, 1891, Vol. I, pp. 62-3.
[4] *ibid.*, Vol. I, p. 267.
[5] *ibid.*, Vol. I, p. 376.
[6] *ibid.*, Vol. II, p. 242.
[7] *ibid.*, Vol. II, pp. 243-4.

A knowledge of public opinion on the part of the leaders is, therefore, very largely a knowledge of popular sentiment. The machinery of democracy is of critical importance in this respect, and Bryce observed that in Switzerland where the initiative and referendum are in operation, the leaders have fairly constant information as to the state of the public mind. Like the pyramids, however, the excellence of popular government is not its wisdom but its strength, an observation that is sufficiently vague, perhaps, for the caustic temper of our times.[8] Our author continued by saying that "The longer public opinion has ruled, the more absolute is the authority of the majority likely to become, the less likely are energetic majorities to arise, the more are politicians likely to occupy themselves, not in forming opinion, but in discovering and hastening to obey it."[9]

There is a slight touch of melancholy in this statement, yet it did not impress Bryce at the time. Time and inevitable decay had not captured his imagination. A government, insisted Bryce, may be both free and good without being subject to continuous control by public opinion. But the tendency is toward this result in the United States; the United States is closer to the continuous governance of opinion than any other country in the world. In the end Bryce concluded that the mass of American citizens are as directly sovereign or supreme in their power as the citizens in the Assembly at Athens or Syracuse. The citizens of Republican Rome are excluded from this comparison because they left more power to the Senate and to the magistrates than did the Greek democracies.[10] Public opinion in the United States was thus regarded as the arbiter between the units of government under a check-and-balance system. But this tendency is reinforced by the fact that there is no ruling class in the United States, while in Germany, Italy, France, and England public opinion is the opinion in effect of the ruling classes.[11]

[8] *ibid.*, Vol. II, pp. 251-2.
[9] *ibid.*, Vol. II, p. 254.
[10] *ibid.*, Vol. II, pp. 255, 257.
[11] *ibid.*, Vol. II, pp. 259-60. Bryce emphasized the fact that the ruling class in England is more powerful in the formation and leading of opinion than in the United States.

FUNDAMENTAL VS. MINOR ISSUES

Today our appreciation of democracy is shadowed by persistent discussion of issues that seem in nature to be irreconcilable. In large measure the future of democratic government and the usefulness of government by public opinion depend on the solution of these issues. Bryce was not faced with fundamental issues upon which discussion rapidly degenerates into the passionate affirmation of a position. His day in America was a time of consolidation or of convalescence after the stirring times of the Civil War. Thus he could say with a clear conscience: "Questions on which the masses have made up their minds pass out of the region of practical discussion. Controversy is confined to minor topics. . . ."[12] But such a judgment would not be valid today when, in all of Western Europe, political controversy deals increasingly with fundamental rather than minor issues. Bryce may be accused of having been too optimistic, but so were all of his contemporaries. The relief of American democracy after the Civil War, the feeling that the great issues had been settled, that the future was bright with promise of political and economic advance, could not fail to infect the student of our democracy. *The American Commonwealth* appeared at a time when throughout the western world there was general agreement about the fundamental rightness of democracy. And the survival of American federalism, with its Lincolnian revival of the principles of the Declaration of Independence, only added to the prevailing attitude.

In the study of Hamilton and Tocqueville we see Bryce congratulating the United States that the ominous tendencies observed by earlier students had not continued. But as the previous scholars failed to see needed solutions, so Bryce failed to see the germs of renewed controversy on fundamental problems. When

There is, therefore, more average political intelligence in the United States than in England. In the United States opinion is not made, he said; it grows. Likewise, there is a higher percentage of the qualified electorate that votes in the United States than in England. Those who do not vote leave their will in the hands of those who do. *ibid.*, Vol. II, pp. 252, 315-17. Cf. my article, "The Pragmatic Electorate," *American Political Science Review*, XXIV (1930), pp. 17 *ff.*

[12] Bryce, *op. cit.*, Vol. II, p. 335.

the great issues of the Civil War were settled, there was less cause, said Bryce, "for ordinary citizens to trouble themselves about public affairs." The professional politicians saw their field left free; yet in spite of the organization of the country under the politicians, the citizens of the United States voted more intelligently in this period, he argued, than in any other country except Switzerland. "Thus the influence which counterworks that of the professionals is the influence of public opinion expressing itself constantly through the countless voices in the press, and more distinctly at frequent intervals by the ballot-box."[13]

No one can accuse Bryce of having a systematic approach to the study of public opinion. To use a Chinese figure of speech, his thought on the subject was like a river that overflowed everything and was of no use to anyone. We must make an effort, however, to suggest the nature of the definitions he offered. Early in *The American Commonwealth* public opinion was tied up with the political party, since parties express opinion. In turn this implied that public opinion is a problem in large measure of political participation; in this we come closest to his conception of the nature of the public, though this idea is not defined. Parties are not the ultimate force, declared Bryce, since the people stand behind them:

> Public opinion, that is the mind and conscience of the whole nation, is the opinion of persons who are included in the parties, for the parties taken together are the nation. . . . Yet it [public opinion] stands above the parties, being cooler and larger-minded than they are. . . . It is the product of a greater number of minds than in any other country, and it is more indisputably sovereign. It is the central point in the whole American polity.[14]

In another connection Bryce declared that public opinion in the United States was the opinion of the whole nation, because there was little distinction between classes. Here especially there

---

[13] *ibid.*, Vol. II, p. 64.

[14] *ibid.*, Vol. I, p. 6. In *Modern Democracies* (1921), Vol. I, p. 153, Bryce declared public opinion to be "the aggregate of the views men hold regarding matters that affect or interest the whole community. Thus understood, it is a congeries of all sorts of discrepant notions, beliefs, fancies, prejudices, and aspirations."

is no ruling class to modify the opinions of the elected representatives. The representatives themselves are unable to appeal from the classes to the masses. In support he argued that in the United States the opinions of both employers and workers on non-labor matters are essentially the same, making opinion more easily ascertained and more powerful.[15] In contrast with this view, however, Bryce argued that very little of a man's opinion is really his own, since he has been told how and what to think. Thus opinion at its simplest is "the prevalent impression of the moment." But if this is the case, opinion tends to crystallize through private discussion and through newspaper treatment. Action may be required finally, and the people called upon to vote on the issue.[16] While there may be differences of opinion and two sides expressed in the voting, there is no inclination to refuse to abide by the results of an election.

"NEWNESS" OF PUBLIC OPINION

Like other students of public opinion, Bryce was torn between its "newness" and its early historical appearance. With David Hume, Bryce recognized that opinion is the chief and ultimate power at all times in nearly all governments, that is, the opinion of the masses of the people. While military tyranny, as in some of the Green city-states, had been able to ignore opinion for a time, even in Eastern despotisms Bryce is constrained to recognize the upport the masses implicitly give the government. On the contrary, Bryce recognized that we speak of public opinion as a new force, "conspicuous" only since governments began to be popular. Only in the last generation, said Bryce, statesmen had looked on it with suspicion. He quoted a letter written in 1820 by Sir Robert Peel in which Peel spoke "with the air of a discoverer" of "that great compound of folly, weakness, prejudice, wrong feeling, right feeling, obstinacy, and newspaper paragraphs, which is called public opinion."[17]

[15] Bryce, *American Commonwealth,* Vol. II, pp. 260-1.
[16] *ibid.,* Vol. II, pp. 239-40.
[17] *ibid.,* Vol. II, p. 247.

The belief in authority and the love of order, according to Lord Bryce, are among the strongest forces in human nature and therefore of politics. In the earliest political societies opinion is passive; it gives acquiescence rather than support. In free countries, by contrast, the people consciously support the government. There are, suggested Bryce, three stages in the development of opinion, the first is the passive, the second involves conflict between the rulers and conscious opinion, and the third and last phase is the dominance of opinion. Without being prophetic or suggesting public opinion "polls," he argued that if one could know the state of opinion at all times rather than once in a while at the ballot-box, public opinion would "not only reign but govern."[18]

EXPRESSION OF OPINION

We now come to another major phase of Bryce's treatment of public opinion, namely, the expression of opinion. Under this heading we must mention those agencies which the author of the *Commonwealth* regarded as being most effective in giving expression to the prevailing trends of public thought. We must mention, briefly, elections, the press, and the political party. Bryce gave far more attention to the expression of opinion than its formation. Apparently in agreement with his times, he had no conception of the scope of propaganda, and the expression of opinion itself was simply a phase of democratic technique which, in his day, was largely solved. While there was no question in his mind as to the ultimate value of elections, some comment must be made. He observed that voting was invented by the ancient Greek and Italian city-states and from them spread to the rest of the civilized world. On the other hand, there has never been complete satisfaction with voting, since no machinery has been invented to overcome the defects readily apparent in the electoral process. The ballot-box and elections are the regalia of the sovereignty of public opinion. But he was no electoral purist, since he recognized that expression of opinion was a far more complicated problem than

[18] *ibid.*, Vol. II, pp. 248-51.

simply holding an election. Without developing the implications of his statement, he noted that plural voting based on property and educational qualifications was rejected in England because the rich had other ways than the ballot of influencing public policy.[19]

How does public opinion express itself? Are the organs of expression adequate? These questions led Bryce into the problem of the press in modern democracies. He remarked that the newspapers are the chief organs of opinion; that United States newspapers contain "more domestic political intelligence than any, except perhaps two or three of the chief English journals." On the other hand, our party press is regarded as less powerful than in Europe. We must look to the press as the chief mirror of public opinion.[20]

The American press serves the expression of public opinion and subserves the formation of opinion better than does the press of any part of the European continent. Our newspapers, insisted Bryce, are above the level of the machine politicians. While in Europe the public meeting, discussion, and conversation are more important than in the United States, our general habit of reading papers makes this less necessary.[21]

BRYCE DISCOVERS "PROPAGANDA"

It was not really until after the World War that Bryce began a more systematic examination of the press, and then it was in connection with international relations. By that time he had also discovered "propaganda," and the press was viewed in part as an agency of propaganda rather than as a mirror of public opinion. In 1922 Bryce was willing to say that the press was more frequently an influence for ill will between nations than for peaceful relations; the press is more dangerous than the politicians since it can-

[19] *Modern Democracies*, Vol. I, pp. 151, 153. *ibid.*, Vol. I, p. 286, another undeveloped idea is to be found. He makes a fundamental distinction between public opinion and the rule of the ballot, though admitting that an election is one way of ascertaining public opinion.
[20] Bryce, *American Commonwealth*, Vol. II, pp. 262-5.
[21] *ibid.*, Vol. II, pp. 267-70.

not be made responsible. He agreed that the purpose of the press is to make money, but he deplored the use of the newspapers by governments to distort the facts, as was the practice with Bismarck's "Reptile Press" which set an example for other governments. Comment is hardly necessary on the sharp change in his evaluation of the function of the newspapers.[22]

Lord Bryce was keenly aware of the corruption of party politics. But his defense of public opinion led him to assert that public opinion is on a higher level than party politics. How can this be? To explain it, he said, one must look at the total American background. It is clear that we have here another of those Brycean waverings between democratic optimism and aristocratic pessimism.[23] Perhaps it was customary in Bryce's day to be charitable to public opinion and harsh on the bosses; today we might say that a boss is just as much a reflection of public opinion as a newspaper.

The modern concern for the education of public opinion is not reflected in *The American Commonwealth*. The reason for this is to be found in the fact that he accepted almost at face value the optimism of his day in the achievements and future of democracy. Thus instead of discussing the education or elevation of public opinion we must observe some of the characteristics of the American attitude toward opinion, and some collateral influences at work in the formation of opinion. Bryce was deeply impressed with the unbounded confidence of Americans in the people and in the democratic system of government. He could not escape the proposition so casually accepted at that time that truth and justice always win out with the people in the long run. Without serious criticism he noted that Americans feel that a group is proved to be in the right if it is the majority. Sometimes the existence of the

[22] James Bryce, *International Relations* (1922), pp. 142, 143, 182.

[23] Bryce, *American Commonwealth*, Vol. II, p. 231. In *Modern Democracies*, Vol. II, pp. 118-19, Bryce noted that party spirit and spirit of "faction" are evils in that intelligent individuals are submerged or obey the party. But party government gives organization to public opinion, and party discussion is an educative force. On the other hand (*ibid.*, Vol. II, p. 544), he declared that only a small number of people really influence voting. Often public opinion is faint and uncertain, in which case the few really decide. Democratic opinion is made by a small percentage of the nation.

majority is accepted as an act of divine providence. In other cases the will of the people is accepted like the irresistible forces of nature. But reason in this position is found by Bryce in the fact that Americans on the whole are more educated than any other people, except Switzerland, parts of Germany, Norway, Iceland, and Scotland. He admitted, however, that the education of the masses is superficial. How these two estimates of our people are to be reconciled we leave to Lord Bryce.[24]

SECTIONAL VARIATION

Whatever Bryce may have thought of public opinion in general in the United States, he had little appreciation of the South. One is inclined to believe that most of the people he talked to were northerners or westerners. The South is an example of backwardness rather than of the general march of democratic progress. Hence he was profoundly impressed by the ignorance of the Negro in the southern states. "If one part of the population is as educated and capable as that of Switzerland, another is as ignorant and politically untrained as that of Russia."[25]

Following in the footsteps of Tocqueville, Bryce detected differences in American and European public opinion because of the absence of a predominant political capital in the United States. The European capital, such as Paris, becomes the central and focal point of public opinion. Paris is the chief factory where French opinion is made. Because of this fact, public opinion crystallizes less rapidly in the United States; the temperature of opinion is not so high as where there is a great capital. No one city tends to dominate the American scene.[26] Local self-government provides in the United States a welcome counterbalance to our great centers of thought and action, and particularly against the capital city.

[24] Bryce, *American Commonwealth,* Vol. II, pp. 275-8. One of the forces controlling American opinion, in Bryce's view, is Christianity, which influences us more than in the so-called age of faith.

[25] *ibid.,* Vol. II, p. 309.

[26] *ibid.,* Vol. II, pp. 660, 665. *Modern Democracies,* Vol. I, p. 296.

According to Bryce, there ought to be many important provincial cities to reflect the divergent political trends of a country.[27]

Propaganda analysis is playing an increasingly dominant rôle today in the study of public opinion, but the subject is not discussed in *The American Commonwealth*. After the World War, however, Bryce, like other students of politics, began to deal with the question. His investigations were superficial, and his observations throw little light on the subject. The issue of the manufacture of public opinion was recognized in *Modern Democracies* and in his lectures on *International Relations*. While wealth may be curbed, noted Bryce, the manufacture of opinion seems "to defy all regulation." The only remedy, in a free country, is to disprove false facts and refute fallacies. Artificially created and factitious opinion, generated through the art of propaganda, is particularly dangerous to democracy, and he observed the menace of the influence of the manufacturers of munitions. If there is a process of clarification and consolidation of opinion—chiefly its streams of sentiment— there is also an increase in the number of electors indifferent to politics, incidental to the establishment of universal suffrage. We can see the calm of the nineteenth century Bryce giving away before the uncertainties of the post-war world.[28]

Bryce's disquietude is clear in his brief analysis of the new phenomenon of "propaganda campaigns." But these campaigns were the ones organized during and after the war by peoples who desired larger political recognition. "Propaganda," he said, "is a war on opinion by opinion." It can work through non-official channels, and it is a one-sided statement appealing to opinion and prejudice. Bryce now discovered that propaganda is quite an old technique; it began with the proclamations of the French revolutionary leaders in 1792, and it had been used since in the nineteenth

---

[27] *ibid.,* Vol. II, p. 437. *ibid.,* Vol. II, p. 502, Bryce showed his appreciation of homogeneity in opinion, for "though it may not avert class wars, [it] helps each class of the community to understand the mind of the others, and can create a general opinion in a nation." Correlative to these points of view, Bryce recognized the "swing of the pendulum" in politics and the persistent trends of public opinion once it is formed. The pendulary swings concern minor principles. *ibid.,* Vol. II, p. 364; Vol. I, pp. 286 *ff.*

[28] *Modern Democracies,* Vol. II, pp. 483-4; Vol. I, pp. 154-7.

century incitement to revolution, particularly in Germany and Italy. Following the war, the anarchists and communists continued the older traditions. The most recent propaganda noted by our author was called "ethnological propaganda" in favor of Pan-Slavism, Pan-Turanianism, and Pan-Islamism. These efforts have arisen because the masses have escaped from the control of their former rulers and are seeking to gain control of public opinion. But fanaticism, warned Bryce, may be more dangerous than obedience used to be. Bryce was sensing the contrast between his latter years and the lost world of *The American Commonwealth*.[29]

MODERN CLASS WAR

Our last problem in the study of Bryce must take us from his early treatment of the issue of majority tyranny to the rude awakening of the modern class war. The mid-nineteenth century treatment of democracy was profoundly concerned with the tyranny of the majority; today we are not so sure that tyranny must always come from the majority. We know that it can also come from the expertly organized minority. But somehow Tocqueville and Bryce (in *The American Commonwealth*) missed the minority as a potential tyrant. They were impressed with what the majority might do with its power. Bryce was concerned in large measure to refute Tocqueville's charge that the majority in America was tyrannical. From Aristotle to Tocqueville the capital fault of democracy was this tyranny, and Tocqueville held it to be the chief defect of the United States. Bryce denied that the American majority mistreats the minority.[30] Tocqueville urged that he did not know any country in which there was less independence of spirit and less real liberty of discussion. Bryce replied that the

[29] Bryce, *International Relations*, pp. 20-4. Bryce believed that democracy has one marked advantage in defending itself against the submarine war of wealth: it can use publicity and the force of opinion. Democracy may rely on law and opinion, but opinion is the better prop. Opinion gives "tone" to political life, and tone can go down and it can come up, as in England in the days of Chatham and in the United States since 1890. *Modern Democracies*, Vol. II, p. 487. On this problem in South America see his, *South America, Observations and Impressions* (rev. ed., 1914), pp. 539-40.

[30] *American Commonwealth*, Vol. II, pp. 337 *ff.*

Frenchman saw the power of opinion at its heyday in America, but that since the Civil War there has been less violence in political passion and a more general tolerance among people. It may be true, admitted Bryce, that "genuine opinion is surrounded by many counterfeits," that there is a din of voices, that there is no group of persons whose duty it is to find remedies for acknowledged evils, that there is nothing to stop the power of opinion if it moves rashly, and that the American people suffer from administrative and political incompetence, but nevertheless there is no tyranny of the majority.[31]

Though public opinion is actually not tyrannical there is danger in the fact that people have "an undue confidence in their wisdom, their virtue and their freedom."

"Public opinion," said Bryce, "is a sort of atmosphere, fresh, keen, and full of sunlight, like that of the American cities, and this sunlight kills many of those noxious germs which are hatched where politicians congregate."[32] Bryce had words of praise for the minority in the United States, for in no country does a beaten minority take defeat so well. With all groups there is a feeling that public opinion must be obeyed. This is true at least in the North.

"It was far otherwise in the South before the war," he granted, "but the South was not a democracy, and its public opinion was that of a passionate class. . . . It is chiefly the faith in publicity that gives to the American public their peculiar buoyancy and what one may call their airy hopefulness in discussing even the weak points of their system."[33]

With Bryce there is always the contrast. He indicated that our people show fatalism in their submission to the majority. There being no aristocracy, all are submerged in the nation; the majority must be obeyed. "Most men are fitter," said Bryce, "to make part of the multitude than to strive against it."[34]

---

[31] *ibid.,* Vol. II, pp. 342-8.

[32] *ibid.,* Vol. II, pp. 352, 355.

[33] *ibid.,* Vol. II, pp. 358-9.

[34] *ibid.,* pp. 327 *ff.,* 335. There are few independent schools of opinion in the United States. Americans are tenacious of ideas once they are acquired, insisted Bryce, though they can be suddenly excited for short periods, e.g. the Know-Nothing Party. Bryce

The discovery of the class war must have been one of the more profound shocks in Bryce's long and active life. His understanding of it is narrow, and he did not know quite how to fit it into his cosmogony. The class war and general strike, he challenged, did not come from democracy; they are an attack on it, and the physical force that was once needed to establish democracy is now used against it.

"Public opinion restrains the selfishness of an individual," he said, "but the public opinion of a class possessed by the sense of a common interest confirms the individual in his selfishness and blinds him to his own injustice."[35] Did Bryce realize here that the great tyranny is that of the minority?

BRYCE'S FAITH

This article should be concluded with a part of Bryce's confession of faith in *Modern Democracies*. A wise and tolerant public opinion requires the interest and intelligence of the voters, but it also requires agreement on certain fundamental political doctrines. We must give Bryce credit for seeing nearly twenty years ago, if dimly, what we see so clearly today, that tolerance and disagreement on essentials go ill together. But let us also hope that Bryce was right when he said that man is not an irrational animal; that truth will win in the long run, though its victory may be long delayed by self-interest, prejudice, and ignorance; and that, as he said, the spirit of democracy may rise above that of machinery.[36]

merely noted the power of corporations, but did not, apparently, consider them much of a menace. "In no country does one find so many men of eminent capacity for business . . . who are so uninteresting, so intellectually barren, outside the sphere of their business knowledge." *ibid.*, Vol. II, pp. 282-3, 292.

[35] *Modern Democracies,* Vol. II, pp. 580-2.

[36] *ibid.,* Vol. I, pp. 158, 160.

32

PUBLIC OPINION
MECHANISMS AMONG
PRIMITIVE PEOPLES
Margaret Mead

Students of primitive societies claim that they can make contributions to the social sciences which are primarily concerned with the analysis of social processes within our society. This claim has various theoretical bases: (1) The assumption that primitive societies are representative of simpler social forms, ancestral to our own, and therefore throw light upon the probable history of an institution, and the further assumption that the history of an institution throws significant light upon its functioning; (2) The coherency of the material; the fact that the social system of a small primitive group is sufficiently simple to be grasped in all its aspects by one investigator; and (3) The importance of cross-cultural comparisons in helping to clarify, sharpen, limit, and enlarge the instrumental concepts which are being used in the analysis of our own society. It is from this third point of view that the findings from primitive society should have most interest for students of public opinion. The theoretical claims of (1) are somewhat dubious, and also it is not of great importance for students of the operation of public opinion at the present day to consider hints as to how our Stone Age ancestors may be supposed to have manipulated the opinions of the group. Consideration (2), the coherency of the material, gives the data a special claim to consideration because it is from the analysis of whole societies that we can attempt the cross-cultural clarification of concepts.

Originally published in Volume 1, Number 3, 1937 of the *Public Opinion Quarterly*.

In making cross-cultural comparisons various courses are open to us. We may take a hypothesis which has been developed from study of our own culture and subject it to negative criticism, showing how the premises upon which the hypothesis is based are invalidated by such and such facts obtaining in this or that primitive tribe. Such criticism requires the social scientist to redefine his concepts in the light of the non-agreement of these facts from other societies.[1]

This approach leaves the student of our society holding the bag. The ethnologist says: "Here are instances from other functioning social systems for which your theory is not adequate. What are you going to do about it?" In group discussions where the ethnologist plays this rôle, his major contribution is to meet every generalization with: "Yes, but . . ."

But it should also be possible for the ethnologist to make positive contributions: to analyze the social forms of primitive society and to present them in sufficiently compact and intelligible terms so as to enrich the working concepts of other disciplines. In so vast and so slightly delimited a field as that of public opinion, the focus must be narrowed to make comparative comment of any value at all. I shall confine my discussion to the relationship between political functioning and public opinion. I shall refer to only a few selected primitive societies of which I have first-hand knowledge, or upon which I have access to first-rate written and oral materials.

THREE TYPES OF EMPHASIS

Among these few societies I have found it possible to distinguish three types of emphasis in the relationship between political organization and public opinion. These types are: (I) Those societies which depend for impetus or inhibition of community action upon the continuing response of individuals in public opinion situations, in the manner defined by Professor Allport;[2] (II) Those which depend upon the operation of formal alignments of individuals, who react not in terms of their personal opinions

[1] Examples of this method are: Malinowski, B., *Sex and Repression in Savage Society* (London: Kegan Paul, 1926); Benedict, R., "Culture and the Abnormal," *Journal of General Psychology,* Vol. 10, No. 1, January 1934, pp. 59-82; Mead, M., *Coming of Age in Samoa* (New York: Morrow, 1928).

[2] "The term public opinion is given its meaning with reference to a multi-individual situation in which individuals are expressing themselves, or can be called upon to express themselves, as favoring or supporting (or else disfavoring or opposing) some definite condition, person, or proposal of widespread importance, in such a proportion of number, intensity, and constancy, as to give rise to the probability of affecting action, directly or indirectly, toward the object concerned." Allport, Floyd H., "Toward a Science of Public Opinion," PUBLIC OPINION QUARTERLY, Vol. I, No. 1, January 1937, p. 23.

concerning the given issue, but in terms of their defined positions in the formal structure; (III) Those societies which do not depend for their functioning on public opinion at all—in Professor Allport's sense of the term—but which function by invoking the purely formal participation in and respect for an impersonal pattern or code.

In our mixed and heterogeneous society all of these types of emphases appear, no one in a pure form, whereas in the greater coherence and simpler integration of primitive societies, the operation of each form can be found virtually unconfused by the presence of the others. Before discussing these extreme forms, however, it may be well to illustrate from our own society. When a group of individuals, as in a lynching mob or in a popular and spontaneous uprising demanding better working conditions, react immediately to a situation, each in terms of his own feeling on the subject, and without referring his action to considerations of party membership, church affiliations, or the relationship between his action and the forms of his society, and their action is politically effective, this constitutes a situation which is typical of societies of Type I.[3] Type II is found when individuals meet an issue, not by responding to the issue itself, but primarily in terms of party membership. As an example let us take an issue which is fortuitously present in the platform of one political party and is not a coherent part of the party program, and let us say that the individual whom we are considering is a member of his political party purely because his father was. Still he is strongly enough involved to support fiercely all moves of his own party and to condemn and execrate roundly all moves of the opposite party. The issue itself is subsidiary to its place in a scheme of opposition, in which, if the Democrat votes Yes, the Republican votes No. Type III is in a sense the most difficult to illustrate from our own society because our tradition of emotional involvement in every type of issue from the Revision of the Constitution to Daylight Saving Time is so strong. It is necessary to picture a society in which issues as vital as migration or war are settled as formally, from the standpoint of any effective expression of public opinion, as is the date of Thanksgiving Day. Here, although the behavior of the entire population is altered for a day by the yearly Proclamation, there is no issue involving public opinion. Similarly with the vagaries of the date of Easter Sunday. Although the date on which Easter falls each year is of great impor-

---

[3] I am not considering here the individual's motivations, but merely making the negative proviso that those motives should be primarily personal, and not consciously oriented to some form of group loyalty or some scheme of impersonal structure.

tance to large numbers of people whose commercial interests are involved in the seasonableness of the event, the date of Easter, arbitrarily fixed according to an outmoded method of calculation, remains outside the field of effective public opinion. With these preliminary illustrations in mind, we can look at primitive societies which exemplify these types.

TYPE I: THE ARAPESH

The Arapesh are a Papuan-speaking people of New Guinea, who occupy a mountainous country stretching between the sea coast and an inland plain. They are without any institutionalized political forms;[4] they have no chiefs, priests, sanctioned soothsayers, or hereditary leaders. They live in small communities in which residence is exceedingly shifting, and are loosely classified for ceremonial purposes into geographical districts. Between the hamlets of each district, and between adjacent hamlets of different districts, there are numerous inter-relationships based on present and past marriages, trade friendships, economic cooperation, etc. Any communal work is done by temporary constellations of affiliated persons based on the various ties of blood relationship, marriage, and residence. No man's allegiance to any group—his patrilineal kin, his patrilineal clan, his hereditary hamlet, his district, his ceremonial feasting division—is either fixed enough over time, or binding enough at any given moment, to prevent his following his own immediate impulses of helpfulness or of hostility, his tendency to avoid trouble or to plunge into it when occasion offers. The smallest event—the slaughter of a pig, the presence of a festering sore on the foot of some unimportant person, the death of an infant, the elopement of a woman—may become a political issue, and may lead to the formation of new alliances or to the declaration of new animosities. Both alliances and hostilities, however, are equally short-lived because, owing to the lack of political organization, they cannot be maintained over time; a new issue will realign everyone tomorrow.

Let us take the instance of the trespass of a pig owned by a resident in one hamlet on the gardens of a member of another hamlet. There is in existence a mode of procedure in such cases. The man whose garden has been trespassed upon kills the pig, and—if he feels friendly toward the owner

[4] It is impossible in the space of a short article to deal in any but the sketchiest fashion with the political system of these people. For a short summary, see Chapter I, Mead, M., ed., *Competition and Cooperation among Primitive Peoples* (New York: McGraw-Hill, 1937). See also Mead, M., *Sex and Temperament in Three Primitive Societies* (New York: Morrow, 1935).

of the pig, or is a quiet man and anxious to avoid trouble—sends word to the owner to come and get his pig. This results in a minimum of bad feeling as the meat can still be used to discharge debts among a meat-hungry people. If, however, the owner of the land is angered by the trespass and his feeling of outrage is not assuaged by killing the pig, he not only kills the pig but he eats it. But such an act may lead to hostilities from the pig's owner and is therefore an act of political significance upon which he will not venture without first sounding out public opinion. While the pig continues to root in his garden, or while it lies freshly bleeding from his spear, he consults his nearest age-mates and immediate associates, his brother, his brother-in-law, his cousin. If they are against eating the pig, the matter goes no further. But if they approve, the matter is carried to a slightly higher authority, the fathers and uncles who happen to be in the immediate vicinity. Finally, to clinch the matter, a Big Man, a man who has shown some rather reluctant ability to take responsibility in the organization of social life, is consulted. If he says yes also, the pig is cut up and all who have given their consent to the venture share in eating the pig, and thus affirm their willingness to share in any unpleasant consequences—an immediate scrap, a longer battle of black magic, or the severance of existing peaceful feasting relationships with the pig-owner's group. This situation fulfils, it seems to me, Professor Allport's definition, and is the crux of all Arapesh political action.[5] An Arapesh has an opinion *for* or *against* every course of action proposed, and upon the nature of these expressed opinions, who is *for* and who is *against*, depends the fate of the issue. Such a society may, perhaps, be said to represent the political importance of public opinion at its maximum, a society which depends upon personal attitudes and relies upon aggregations of emotionally involved persons to produce action.

Among other societies in which the immediate expressed responses of individuals are of maximum importance may be mentioned the Andamanese,[6] the Ojibwa,[7] and the Eskimo.[8]

[5] For the expression of public opinion in a case of suspected sorcery among the Arapesh see *Sex and Temperament*, pp. 111-121, especially p. 121.

[6] Brown, A. R. (Radcliffe-Brown), *The Andaman Islanders* (Cambridge University Press, 1932).

[7] Landes, R., "The Ojibwa of Canada," Chapter III of *Competition and Cooperation among Primitive Peoples, op. cit.*

[8] Thalbitzer, W., ed., *Meddelelser om Grönland*, Vols. 39 and 40; and Mirsky, J., "The Eskimo of Greenland," Chapter IV of *Competition and Cooperation among Primitive Peoples, op. cit.*

TYPE II: THE IATMUL

Societies of Type II are more highly organized and contain cultural forms which result in individuals acting together in groups in regard to an immediate issue, not because they have an *opinion* about the issue, but because they have an emotional allegiance to a formal group. Such societies are commonly organized upon a dual basis. This duality may be based upon differences as simple as that between the people born in winter and those born in summer, or between those who are forbidden to eat hawk and those forbidden to eat parrot, or between those who live south of the cemetery or those who live north of it. But upon such a simple and formal base, ideas of social opposition may be built which are sufficiently well organized to become the structural principle of action within a society. When membership in a group which is by definition opposed to another group has become of prime importance, any political issue instead of raising the question: "How do I personally feel about it?" raises the question: "What does my Group A think about this? Have they taken up a position in favor of it? If so, I, as one of the Group A, support it against Group B who will of course oppose it." In such societies the success of any attempt to influence the group toward action depends not upon the personal opinion of individuals, but upon the functioning of these formal antagonisms.

The Iatmul people[9] of New Guinea are a tribe of head-hunters who live in large, independent villages on the Middle Sepik River in New Guinea. Without any form of chieftainship or centralized authority, they are able to integrate for peaceful community living and action against outsiders as many as a thousand people—the Arapesh district seldom included more than two hundred persons, a hamlet averaged about forty. Iatmuls depend upon a system of cross-cutting groups in terms of which individuals act as members of patrilineal clans, as members of matrilineal groups, as members of opposed age grades, as members of one of two opposed totemic moieties. Considerations of inter-group relationships, of defending one's mother's clan against all others, or of always meeting a challenge from the opposing age grade, supersede the merits of actual issues. The communities are held together only by the fact that these various loyalties overlap and contradict each other so that the man who is one's formal foe today—*qua* group membership—is one's formal ally tomorrow.

[9] See Bateson, G., "Social Structure of the Iatmul People," *Oceania,* Vol. II, Nos. 3 and 4; Bateson, G., *Naven, A Survey of the Problems Suggested by a Composite Picture of the Culture of a New Guinea Tribe, Drawn from Three Points of View* (Cambridge University Press, 1936).

Let us consider, then, examples of the functioning of public opinion among the Iatmul, in the play of group attitudes. The elder age grade of Moiety A[10] were initiating the novices from Moiety B. Initiation ceremonies among the Iatmul are marked by a series of irresponsibly executed brutalities. On this particular occasion, an innovator, a member of the elder group of Moiety A, proposed that one bullying episode should be omitted from the series. This was an occasion upon which public opinion could be expressed. A member of the elder age grade of Moiety B, the group which would presently initiate the novices of Moiety A, immediately turned the proposal into an occasion for ceremonial hostility, completely ignoring the issue at hand, and accusing Moiety A of being afraid of what *his* moiety, B, would do later when they had to initiate the A novices. Moiety A, in response to this taunt, carried out the rite with particular cruelty. The fact that the proposed change would have softened the fate of their own children was ignored by Moiety B in favor of the chance to make a point of ceremonial hostility.

Here it is necessary to recognize a peculiarity of Iatmul culture. Any rite once neglected is regarded as gone forever. If the proposed omission had been carried through, the initiatory system would have been impoverished by one episode. Had the member of Moiety B been interested in preserving an item of ceremonial he could have chosen no more effective method than to invoke the rivalry feeling between the two groups. So a Iatmul who wished to organize a head-hunting raid in which other people were not yet interested, might start a proposal for the raid with a taunt to the other side about the paucity of heads which they had taken in the past year. This taunt would be flung back with interest, and in the end the jealous pride of each moiety would be involved in going on the same raid.

Thus in societies so organized the impetus to action is given not by an appeal to the direct opinion of individuals on an issue, but indirectly through the invocation of group loyalties and group rivalries. Where an individual is a member of a series of concentric groups—so that, as a member of his family, of his household, his clan, his village, his dual organization, his district, he is consistently associated with the same people—there is danger of these group attitudes hardening into hostilities which will split the society. Unless there is a central authority at the head to which all are bound, this danger is especially great if opinions become organized instead

[10] I have considerably simplified this statement. The more intricate details may be found on p. 135 of *Naven, op. cit.* I have translated Ax3 as "elder brother grade of Moiety A"; Ay3 as "elder age grade of Moiety B"; By4 as "novice group of Moiety B," etc.

of fortuitous. This condition hardly obtains among the Iatmul because the cross-cutting of loyalties prevents the formation of permanent antithetical attitudes within the community.[11]

TYPE III: THE BALINESE

In the third type of society the individual is not emotionally involved with the immediate issue, or in his loyalty to a group or to series of groups with overlapping and cross-cutting memberships. The community is not composed of political individuals, but of a certain number of house sites, seats in the council houses, recurrent duties to the temple. Into these cubbyholes in a spatially and calendrically defined social organization individuals are fitted as occasion dictates. Their whole dependence is on the preservation of the impersonal pattern.

In a Balinese mountain village, all able-bodied men are members of the village council and progress in turn toward greater and greater official importance until at last they are superannuated and replaced. In this scheme each human unit is a cipher; he fits into a cubbyhole which is successively filled by a series of human beings, each one of whom has been trained from childhood to feel that his whole safety depends upon the continuance of the pattern. Whereas in societies of Type I, the question is: "How do I feel about it?" and "How do A, B, and C feel about it?" and in societies of Type II the question is "Does my group support this?" or "Does the opposite group oppose it?", and the issue itself becomes irrelevant except to a few individuals who may consciously or unconsciously exploit these loyalties to produce results, in societies of Type III the question is only: "What is the place of this new proposal in our pattern of decreed and traditional behavior?" This question is asked as seriously and as self-consciously as the constitutionality of a proposed act of Congress might be discussed by a professor of jurisprudence. The process of rejection or acceptance, however, is as colorless as the placing of a name in a decreed alphabetical order.

For example, a new form of incest is committed in a village; a man marries his first cousin twice removed, his classificatory grandmother. In this

---

[11] But in such societies decisions are not reached by majorities, but by balancing and discarding irrelevant loyalties. This throws light, I think, upon one of the puzzling aspects of American Indian political procedure, the requirement that any decision of a council should be unanimous. This requirement among a people trained to feel *for* or *against* an issue only when the issue was translated into group terms, meant that members refrained from invoking irrelevant group loyalties and so left the few who were interested or capable to decide the current issue on its merits. [The reader may be interested to note that in the article "Peasants and Propaganda in Croatia" in this issue Dinko Tomasic refers (p. 72) to the customary unanimity of decisions in the Croats' village councils.—ED.]

village it is not permitted to marry a first cousin. In other villages of which the people have heard, it is forbidden to marry a person reckoned as two generations removed. The council meets and deliberates. The head men hesitate and demur; they do not know the answer. Relatives of the girl and of the boy are called before them and say merely: "We will follow whatever decision is made." The village law about first-cousin incest is that both persons shall be expelled from the village and placed on "Land of Punishment" to the south of it, and forbidden to participate in village land or worship other than the Gods of Death. No one pleads the cause of the boy or the girl. No one speaks of the outrage. Neither family attempts to gather adherents and form a party. The calendrical expert who is the greatest authority on village law points out: (1) that they might consider whether a first cousin twice removed is nearer than a plain second cousin, with whom marriage is permitted; and (2) that if the couple are expelled the village will have to undergo a taboo period of forty-two days and that such and such of the various feasts which are scheduled will have to be postponed and such and such feasts will have to be omitted entirely. The day drags on. Occasionally someone points out to the head man: "You are the heads. It is your business to decide what the law is." Finally it is decided that, no matter how far removed, a first cousin is a *first* cousin, and the law of the village is clear. The villagers are apportioned and half are sent to each house to lift the house and set it outside the village. The relatives of the girl worry about the cost of the purification ceremonies; the relatives of the boy weep a little quietly at home. No one takes sides; they follow the law, and for forty-two days no one may pray to the gods or consult a soothsayer about his illness. In Professor Allport's sense there is no public opinion situation. No one can be said to "favor or support" or to "disfavor or oppose" "some definite condition, person, or proposal of widespread importance." The only political feeling the people possess is in favor of the preservation of the pattern. Not *How do I feel?* or *How does my group feel?*, but *How does this issue fit in?* That is the only question.

It is as if the body politic to which a new issue had to be referred in each of the three types of society might be likened to three types of officials to whom one applied for some relaxation of a regulation. The first type would act as he felt, according to whether he liked or disliked the applicant, whether he wished to appear to be a jolly good fellow, whether he feared the consequences in terms of a rebuke from a superior, etc. The second type would refer his behavior to such considerations as that he and the applicant were both Masons or both Catholics or to a difference of race, nationality, or class. The third type of official merely looks up the code book to find whether or not the law which he is administering permits the granting of the request, and quite impersonally and coolly he replies that it can or cannot be done. He is involved in neither permission nor refusal; he merely administers the law.

INNOVATION IN THE THREE TYPES

An innovator or importer among the Arapesh must suit the new item to the feeling of the people. There is no body of law to which an innovation may be referred. The people are so easy-going that they are quite ready to accept as already customary[12] an act which has occurred twice. There is no group sufficiently powerful and organized to defend an innovation, or to impose it on the community. There is no group pride which can be invoked to support an innovation otherwise unsupported. There is nothing whatsoever to determine the issue except the congruence of the proposed innovation with the feeling of the individual Arapesh who are immediately concerned.

For example, a new ceremony was being purchased by an Arapesh village, a ceremony which had been brought from afar. It contained new masks, new songs, new dances, new styles of clothing, and bits of associated magic. One of these bits of magic provided that the owners would become so desirable that all the women within many miles would run away to them. Now the village of Kobelen had paid a great deal for the ceremony, straining its resources to the utmost. But this last observance they rejected; they refused even to hear this charm. The idea of being pursued by strange and amorous women was thoroughly discordant with the mild, highly domesticated love ideals of the Arapesh. They said: "You may keep that spell. It would only bring us trouble."

An examination of Arapesh importations from surrounding cultures shows that this is typical; every importation is pruned and toned down until it is congruent—not with the articulate form of the culture, but with the feeling of individuals.

On the other hand, in the Iatmul village of Komindimbit, a strange wooden mask was introduced into the initiatory ritual. A group of men from that village had found it resting as a trophy of war in a foreign village and

[12] This happened, for instance, in the district of Alitoa when two men of the hamlet of Ahalesimihi each married first a young woman, and then that young woman's widowed mother. No one was offended, and they began to speak of "the marrying fashion of Ahalesimihi."

had stolen it and taken it home with them. They decided to make it into one more symbol in terms of which they could score off the other moiety. At the next initiation, the mask was duly treated as a mystery, housed in a special house, the novices of the other moiety were all whipped before they could see it. After this it was duly entrenched as part of the initiatory system.

As a third contrast, consider this problem arising in a Balinese mountain village: Can the village priestess wear black and white striped velvet? She is a sacred person, surrounded with taboos concerning what she may dare to wear, eat, carry, whom she may safely visit, under what type of roof she may safely sleep. It is a good piece of cloth, but can she wear it? The matter is referred to those who are wise in the law, and their decision takes into account (a) all black cloth is forbidden to religious functionaries in that village; (b) silk is forbidden; (c) this cloth is neither all black nor exactly silk. Can she wear it? Once the problem is settled, legalistically, in terms of how much black makes a piece of cloth black, how much softness may be assumed to be analogous to silk, she is still free to wear it or not. But if the decision is incorrect, she herself—not the village, not her kin, but she herself—will be punished by the Gods, and in any case no one else will be interested. The slightest break in the pattern must be viewed with great caution, and if adopted must be rationalized.[13]

It may be objected that these instances are curiously incomparable; in one case I describe the rejection of an imponderable bit of magic, in the second case the incorporation of an alien religious object, and in the third a decision about wearing a piece of cloth. But I can plead, in extenuation, that I am following here the facts as I know them. Societies like the Arapesh which depend upon the emotional organization of their members to integrate their institutions can afford to risk the importation of whole institutions, whereas more tightly organized societies have to find a formal place for the importation, while the Balinese habitually deal with items of culture in small discrete bits.

Although I have, for purposes of clearer exposition, distinguished these three types, it must not be supposed that the classifications are mutually exclusive or that they exhaust the possibilities. The society of Zuni may be

[13] So a Brahman priest in Bali has been forbidden from time immemorial to walk under running water, and Balinese roads are frequently crossed by irrigating aqueducts. As motor roads were built and priests fared further afield, getting out and climbing steep road banks became more and more of a nuisance. And now one famous priest has decided that he may sit in a closed car and not get out when the car goes under an aqueduct, because the car is really his house, and he is not on the road at all.

said to lie between that of Iatmul and Bali; they possess a series of cross-cutting and overlapping groups, as do the Iatmul, but their emotional involvement in any group is much less, and they rely a great deal, as do the Balinese, upon devotion to an impersonal pattern. But unlike the Balinese, the judgment of one man upon his neighbor is continually invoked—among the Zuni—as a socially regulating mechanism, and so public opinion is a constantly present negative sanction, slowing down and preventing action. But the terms in which a judgment is rendered in Zuni are reminiscent of the impersonal legalism of Bali. For example, a Zuni family murdered a Navajo guest. This was articulately condemned because the man who committed the murder did not have the ceremonial right to kill people.

CONCLUSION

This brief consideration of divergent social systems suggests that each of the different types of appeal to public opinion or ignoring of public opinion which we find in modern society presupposes a different relationship between the character formation of the citizen and the political system of which he is a unit. Each appeal: "How do *you* personally feel about this?" "Every member of X group will of course support . . ." or "The Y group are supporting this, therefore you, as a member of the opposed X group, must oppose!" "The proposed change will introduce such and such discrepancies in the legal structure upon which our society is based"—each of these designates the recipient of the appeal as a different sort of political animal. In an integrated primitive society, one type of appeal is reiterated until it becomes a factor in further integrating the individuals. In our diverse and disintegrate society, the incommensurability of these types of appeal may possibly stimulate some individuals to critical thought which transcends any of them. But it is even more possible that a continued exposure to such incomparable assumptions may be an important influence in the fragmentation and distintegration of the average citizen.

Bajoeng Gede,
Bali, Netherlands East Indies.

33

AN APPROACH
TO THE SCIENTIFIC
STUDY OF PAST
PUBLIC OPINION

Lee Benson

L ACKING relevant opinion surveys or polls, can contemporary researchers study past public opinion scientifically? Yes. Has past public opinion been studied scientifically? No. If I answer "No" to the second question, how can I responsibly answer "Yes" to the first? That is *the* question this essay tries to answer. A final question-answer set completes our agenda: Should social scientists other than historians seriously concern themselves with the study of past public opinion? Yes.[1]

I. DEFINING CONCEPTS

Some definitions may help to minimize communication difficulties. They are presented here, it cannot be overemphasized, as working "specifications of meaning," not as definitive statements.[2]

A. Public Opinion

"VOX POPULI may be Vox Dei, but very little attention shows that there has never been agreement as to what Vox means or as to what Populus means." Coined many years ago by Henry Maine,[3] that epigram wittily suggests the confusion still beclouding the concept of public opinion. The confusion stems partly from the concept's moral implications. Particularly in societies boasting democratic forms of government, it seem mandatory that the will of the people prevail. The claim that public opinion supports one side has considerable potency, and the question of "who" constitutes the public represents, therefore, more than a scholastic exercise in concept clarification. Not surprisingly, political theorists, statesmen, and as-

---

[1] During the 1950's, Paul Lazarsfeld stimulated my interest in the problems considered in this essay. He bears no responsibility, of course, for the particular solutions proposed here. I am glad to have this opportunity, however, to acknowledge my intellectual indebtedness to him.

[2] In this connection, see Abraham Kaplan, *The Conduct of Inquiry,* San Francisco, Chandler, 1964, pp. 71-78.

[3] As quoted in A. Lawrence Lowell, *Public Opinion and Popular Government,* New York, Longmans, 1914, p. 3.

Originally published in Volume 31, Number 4, 1967 of the *Public Opinion Quarterly*.

sorted pundits have displayed marked ingenuity in answering it according to different predispositions and interests.[4]

In similar fashion, the concept's moral connotations have provoked other difficult questions: What is meant by "opinion"? When is "opinion" simply the product of habit rather than thought? When is it a "real opinion" instead of a "mere prejudice or meaningless impression"? About what subjects is the "public" capable of having opinions worth consideration by public officials? What degree of coercion by government, or by other agencies or agents, makes it invalid to speak of the existence of public opinion? Under what conditions, and in respect to what type of issue, should a minority submit to majority opinion?

The last question suggests another possible source of conceptual confusion. "Public opinion" sometimes is equated with consensus. Does "public opinion" imply unanimity, near-unanimity, or numerical majority? Does it refer to the "effective" rather than the numerical majority? Differences on these and similar questions have confused the concept and provoked heated but unilluminating controversies.

The final source of confusion considered here illustrates the validity of Gresham's Law, whether applied to the minting of currency or of concepts. Pollsters have become so ubiquitous, man-in-the-street interviews so commonplace, that the concept of "public opinion" has lost its original meaning. Instead of referring only to political issues of consequence to governments, "public opinion" now connotes views on questions of such different mettle as: Do Europeans make better lovers than Americans? Should teenagers "go steady"? Should the United States halt the bombing of North Vietnam?

As Harwood L. Childs persuasively argues, despite numerous attempts, no *intrinsic* reasons can be found to restrict the term "public opinion" to opinions of a certain type held by individuals of a certain type.[5] But scientific disciplines, and fields of specialization

---

[4] Excellent historical reviews of the public opinion concept that deal with this question, and with other questions posed below, are presented in Paul A. Palmer, "The Concept of Public Opinion in Political Theory," in Bernard Berelson and Morris Janowitz, eds., *Reader in Public Opinion and Communication*, Glencoe, Ill., Free Press, 1953 ed., pp. 3-13; Hans Speier, "Historical Development of Public Opinion," *American Journal of Sociology*, Vol. 55, January 1950, pp. 376-388; Paul F. Lazarsfeld, "Public Opinion and the Classical Tradition," *Public Opinion Quarterly*, Vol. 21, 1957, pp. 39-53; Harwood L. Childs, *Public Opinion: Nature, Formation, and Role*, Princeton, N. J., Van Nostrand, 1965, pp. 12-41. See also George Carslake Thompson "The Evaluation of Public Opinion," in Berelson and Janowitz, eds., *op. cit.*, pp. 14-20; A. V. Dicey, *Lectures on the Relation Between Law and Public Opinion in England During the Nineteenth Century*, 2nd ed., London, 1914, pp. 1-47; Lowell, *op. cit.*, pp. 3-54; James Bryce, *Modern Democracies*, New York, 1921, Vol. 1, pp. 151-162.

[5] Childs, *op. cit.*, pp. 14-26.

within a discipline, seem to progress most rapidly when, at any given time, they abstract from "total reality" a limited range of phenomena for intensive study. As noted in more detail below, historians have not yet generally even *begun* to try to develop scientific procedures to study past public opinion. It seems good strategy, therefore, to begin that job by sharply restricting attention to one type of opinion—and one that historians are likely to find *relatively* easy and congenial to study systematically. At any rate, that is the strategy advocated by, and adopted in, this essay. For our purposes, "public opinion" is *arbitrarily* defined to refer only to opinions on "political issues." It has neither moral, majoritarian, nor effective connotations, and does not imply legitimate, correct, or informed opinion, which should prevail.

In the sense of "who," the "public" is defined as referring to all inhabitants of a specified political entity having the right, *or claiming the right,* explicitly or implicitly, to influence government actions, directly or indirectly. (The famous "strong-minded" women of the pre–Civil War period had no right to vote, but few American historians would deny that they exercised more influence than many men legally entitled to participate in the decision-making process.) In the sense of "what," "public" refers to government "actions" of concern to members of the political entity and about which they hold opinions—including no opinions. "Actions" are broadly defined to encompass the laws, policies, rulings, personnel, and structure of government. "Opinion" is taken to mean the *position* or *stand*—favorable, unfavorable, undecided, and variations thereof—held by individuals (or groups) on proposed, future, present, or past government actions. It refers either to action on a specific issue or to some over-all course of action on related issues. Clearly, therefore, as defined here, government action forms the core of the public opinion concept.[6] But conceptual clarification also requires us to distinguish explicitly between "opinions" and "attitudes."

As defined here, an opinion always connotes a *position* on some specific government action or general course of action; an attitude represents a persistent, general *orientation* toward some individuals, groups, institutions, or processes, but it does not necessarily result in a specific position on specified public issues.[7] A substantive example may highlight the distinction. Americans' positions during the 1840's relevant to government actions to abolish, restrict, or foster slavery

[6] I have freely adapted the definition of public opinion suggested by Speier, *op. cit.,* p. 376.

[7] Once again, I have freely adapted a definition offered elsewhere. See Theodore M. Newcomb, Ralph H. Turner, Philip E. Converse, *Social Psychology*, Holt, Rinehart and Winston, New York, 1965, pp. 47-114.

are, according to our definition, viewed as their *opinions* on issues relating to the institution. Their evaluations of slavery as "good or bad," "moral or immoral," are viewed as their *attitudes* toward the institution. (At the boundary line betweeen opinions and attitudes, blurring occurs, of course, but that familiar classification problem need not detain us.)

Distinguishing between opinions and attitudes is more than a semantic exercise. The claim that a large majority of Northerners had antislavery attitudes during the 1840's, for example, may well be credible. But it may also provide little credible information about the distribution of Northern opinion on specific public issues related to slavery and may, in fact, encourage a highly distorted description. It is easily conceivable that men had similar *attitudes* toward slavery and directly contradictory opinions on, for example, the annexation of Texas. They may have disagreed on the consequences of that action, they may have differed in their views on the powers of the Federal government or the importance of national unity, they may have differed in their political or economic interests, and so on. Equating an antislavery or proslavery attitude with an opinion for or against annexation, therefore, confuses very different things. To say that is not to deny that attitudes may *help* to shape opinions and that both may be used as indicators of each other. The argument is that the complex interrelationships between opinions and attitudes can perhaps be uncovered and disentangled after painstaking investigation; they cannot be automatically assumed, a priori, to take a particular form. This problem will be further discussed below. But it seems worth emphasizing at the outset that, in my judgment, failure to distinguish sharply between opinions and attitudes hampers public opinion research in general and research on past public opinion in particular.

B. Historical Study of Public Opinion

As defined here, "historical" study of public opinion connotes more than the study of past phenomena, it connotes research carried out by procedures that secure data by means other than personal interviews, mail questionnaires, or direct observation. Put another way, the concept, "the historical study of public opinion," for our purposes, means the use of procedures to secure data from *documents* (broadly defined) that the researcher *locates and selects but does not create, directly or indirectly*. By selecting documents and, so to speak, "interrogating" their authors, historical researchers *generate* data designed to answer questions about past public opinion.

Contemporary opinion researchers also generate data, but they do so by conducting more or less structured interviews with respondents selected according to some specified sampling criteria. When they use documents not created by researchers for that purpose as data sources, they are, according to our definition, engaged in the historical study of public opinion. In short, it is not the "distance" from the present that determines if a study is historical in character, it is the procedures used to generate data about some dimension of public opinion. Can historical procedures be scientific, however, or must that term be restricted to procedures that, to quote Daniel Lerner, yield "largely quantified data accumulated by structured observation in empirical situations approximating (with specified deviations) the model of controlled experiment"?[8]

C. Scientific Historical Study of Public Opinion

Is history art or science? An old question, much chewed over, never resolved—never to be resolved because it is a badly formulated old question. A better question, I think, is: Can past human behavior, e.g. past public opinion, be described and explained "scientifically," as well as "artistically"? That question poses a prior one: What is science? More precisely: What do we mean by "science"?

In my judgment, Ernest Nagel's definition of science can help us develop a fruitful approach to the study of past public opinion. According to his liberal definition, the enterprise has two main dimensions, goals and means. The main goal, or "the distinctive aim of the scientific enterprise is to provide systematic and responsibly supported explanations [of phenomena]." The main means to achieve that goal is the practice of scientific method: more specifically, "the persistent critique of arguments, in the light of tried canons for judging the reliability of the procedures by which evidential data are obtained, and for assessing the probative force of the evidence on which conclusions are based."[9]

As Joseph Strayer has noted, historians have "been talking about the importance of public opinion for several generations, longer perhaps than any other professional group."[10] It seems indisputable, however, that they have not yet developed "tried canons for judging

---

[8] As quoted in Allen H. Barton and Paul F. Lazarsfeld, "Some Functions of Qualitative Analysis in Social Research," *Frankfurter Bertrage Zur Soziologie*, Band 1, 1955, p. 321. This important methodological essay is particularly relevant to historical research and is conveniently reprinted as "S-336," in the Bobbs-Merrill Reprint Series in the Social Sciences.

[9] Ernest Nagel, *The Structure of Science*, New York, Harcourt, Brace & World, 1961, pp. 1-15.

[10] Joseph Strayer, "The Historian's Concept of Public Opinion," in Mirra Komarovsky, ed., *Common Frontiers of the Social Sciences*, Glencoe, Ill., Free Press, 1957, p. 263.

the reliability of the procedures by which evidential data [relevant to public opinion] are obtained," nor "tried canons . . . for assessing the probative force of the evidence on which conclusions are based."[11] Why not?

One answer may be that such canons or principles cannot be developed, given the nature of public opinion and the kinds of documents available for historical research. That may turn out to be the right answer. At present, however, no warrant exists for it other than as a hypothesis that, ultimately, may or may not be confirmed. A more optimistic, and in my judgment a more compelling, answer is that "tried canons" for research on historical public opinion have not been developed because historians have not systematically tried to develop them.[12] Instead, historians studying public opinion have strongly tended to rely upon "historical method" to perform tasks for which it was not designed and for which, as it now stands, it is grossly inadequate.

My basic assumptions are that historical method, as developed to date, cannot satisfy the demands made upon it by researchers interested in mass behavior, and that a serious methodological gap therefore exists in historiography that will require large-scale, sustained efforts to close. Widespread recognition of the gap, I further assume, must precede its eventual elimination—an assumption consonant with my fond hope that this paper will be viewed as an essay in constructive criticism.

As is well known, modern historical method was founded in Germany during the early nineteenth century. Trained in philology, Barthold Niebuhr, Leopold von Ranke, and others then brilliantly applied that discipline's critical method to ancient, medieval, and early modern documents. As a result, "scientific history" came into

11 *Ibid.*

12 See the stimulating critiques in Ernest R. May, "An American Tradition in Foreign Policy: The Role of Public Opinion," in William H. Nelson, ed., *Theory and Practice in American Politics,* Chicago, University of Chicago Press, 1964, pp. 101-122; Robert A. Kann, "Public Opinion Research: A Contribution to Historical Method," *Political Science Quarterly,* Vol. 73, September 1958, pp. 374-396. Though focused on foreign policy, May's essay provides an excellent overview of the American literature relevant to the study of public opinion. For a comprehensive bibliographic guide to the literature, see the chapter notes and supplementary reading suggestions in Childs, *op. cit.*

May has carried further his study of the impact of public opinion upon American foreign policy in his "American Imperialism: A Reinterpretation," in Donald Fleming and Bernard Bailyn, eds., *Perspectives in American History,* Cambridge, Mass., Harvard University Press, 1967, Vol. I, pp. 123-286. It appeared too late for consideration in this essay. Another essay in the same volume, Donald Fleming, "Attitude: The History of a Concept," *ibid.,* pp. 287-365, also appears to warrant intensive study.

being—a term that primarily meant the critical study of primary sources, not science in Nagel's sense. Essentially, the rules laid down by the founding fathers of the discipline focused attention upon the authentication of documents and the evaluation of testimony that credibly could be extracted from different kinds of authentic documents. A quotation from the preface of one of Ranke's major works illustrates the point:

The basis of the present work, the sources of its material, are memoirs, diaries, letters, diplomatic reports, and original narratives of eyewitnesses; other writings were used only if they were immediately derived from the above mentioned or seemed to equal them because of some original information.[13]

Later scholars added important refinements to the rules laid down by Niebuhr, von Ranke, and other pioneers but did not greatly extend the boundaries originally mapped out for the "new science." And it is equally well known that historical method in the United States today differs little from that taught in European universities during the late nineteenth century.

Though the *methods* taught today in seminars and described in manuals essentially remain unaltered, historians' *interests* have shifted radically. Since Western historians no longer focus primarily upon ancient, medieval, and early modern events, research necessarily is not confined to the activities of relatively homogeneous, small, elite groups in a highly stratified society. In particular, American historians largely concern themselves with mass behavior in a dynamic, pluralistic, mass society. Thus a serious gap between historiographic theory and practice has resulted; the traditional rules of historical method were not devised by scholars dealing with mass behavior and have not been amended in any systematic form by later scholars concerned with such phenomena. It follows, therefore, that historical method, as developed to date, can have only limited value as a guide to researchers trying to study public opinion in a mass society.

Instead of directing criticism against the general principles of historical method, the purpose here is to call attention to the necessity of extending them. For example, one will search in vain through the manuals of historical method for observations that offer anything but elementary guidance to researchers engaged in studying public opinion. Moreover, the task of prying out useful procedures from specialized studies is greatly complicated by the tendency of historians to avoid making them explicit. In sum, good ground is believed to

---

[13] As quoted in Fritz Stern, ed., *The Varieties of History,* New York, Meridian, 1956, p. 57.

exist for the assumption that historical method, as now codified, is inadequate to the demands made upon it by scholars interested in an aspect of mass behavior such as public opinion. A recent statement on the advantages of codifying the research procedures employed in different disciplines is put so cogently as only to require repetition.

The advancement of research procedure in social science as elsewhere depends on making explicit what researchers actually do, and systematically analyzing it in the light of logic and of substantive knowledge. Such a 'codification' of procedures points out dangers, indicates neglected possibilities, and suggests improvements. It makes possible the generalization of methodological knowledge—its transfer from one specific project or subject matter to others, from one researcher to the scientific community. Finally, it makes possible a more systematic training of students, in place of simply exposing them to concrete cases of research in the hope that they will somehow absorb the right lessons.[14]

As discussed in Section V below, an implicit pattern can be seen in the procedures American historians have spontaneously and intuitively developed to study past public opinion. Those procedures, used painstakingly and imaginatively, as the three articles in this issue by Helbich, Lancaster, and Maxwell on public opinion and the Versaille Treaty concretely suggest, can yield data that significantly improve our understanding of the role public opinion played in past governmental decisions. In my judgment, however, if we hope to make major advances in the historical study of public opinion, we must sharply reverse our priorities and concentrate primarily upon methodological rather than substantive problems.

Codification of *existing* procedures, although helpful, will not get us very far. Until we consciously try to develop a general analytic model, or system of analysis, and seriously engage in theory construction and concept and index formation, we are not likely to develop a genuinely scientific study of past public opinion. Bluntly stated, we historians need to move beyond that "brute empiricism" which relies upon "saturation" in primary sources unguided by canons for generating data and for making inferences from the data generated. Before sketching an approach that at least points in that direction, it seems useful to suggest that non-historians also have a vital stake, and should therefore participate vitally, in the enterprise.

II. SOCIAL SCIENTISTS AND THE HISTORICAL STUDY OF PUBLIC OPINION

Bernard Berelson and Morris Janowitz, in the second edition (1965) of their *Reader in Public Opinion and Communication*, optimis-

---

[14] Barton and Lazarsfeld, *op. cit.*, in Bobbs-Merrill Reprints "S-336," p. 321.

tically observed that significant progress had beeen made in developing a "generally accepted theory of public opinion" since the first edition appeared fifteen years earlier. "It is still true," they conceded, however, "that there is no generally accepted theory of public opinion, nor does it appear likely that one will emerge in the immediate future." Lack of long-term trend data, they suggested, seriously retards theoretical progress:

The main contribution of opinion polling to the understanding of opinion formation is through the accumulation of trend data over time. After public opinion polling had provided a body of answers to standardized opinion questions, it became possible to chart trends in the gross development of opinions and relate them to external political and military events. Unfortunately, the number of such long-term bodies of data is limited because survey organizations have generally not accepted responsibility for this task.[15]

Almost a decade earlier, in the twentieth-anniversary issue of this journal, Herbert Hyman had similarly pointed to the "deficiencies of discontinuous data" as:

perhaps the most crucial deficiency for the growth of a theory. The absence of data which provides a sound description of even the *lack* of public opinion on a problem, at a time when it is not under discussion, means that there is no basis for developing adequate theory as to the formation of public opinion. Similarly, the waning of an issue has generally meant the neglect of it by survey research. Thus, no theory can really be built as to either the formation or decline of public opinion. . . . Obviously, what would be desirable would be to extend public opinion research from the *ad hoc* description of whatever part of the current social world is hot to the systematic description of both the hot and the cold. With such an extension, theory could develop in a number of fruitful directions. Taking any point in time, the *structure* of public thinking, the *mental organization* of public attitudes, would be better understood by seeing the connections between different bodies of opinion. And if these same areas were dealt with over long spans of time, providing trend data, a theory of public opinion formation and opinion change would be well on its way to formulation. As a result of the rise of panels, part of that theory is now available, but only that part which deals with the flux of opinion over short ranges of time in relation to very specific stimuli or psychological factors. By contrast, long term trends in the systematic description of public opinion would enable us to relate opinion processes to much more macroscopic determinants: for example, law, social change, demographic processes, and the like. And such trend data in juxtaposition with political analysis would lead not merely to theories of opinion formation, but also to theories about the *consequences* of popular opinion for political actions.[16]

[15] Berelson and Janowitz, *op. cit.*, 2nd ed., New York, Free Press of Glencoe, 1965, Vol. 1, pp. 65-66.
[16] Herbert H. Hyman, "Toward a Theory of Public Opinion," *Public Opinion Quarterly*, Vol. 21, 1957, pp. 56-57.

Paul Lazarsfeld, probably more than any other individual, has focused attention on the value of long-term trend studies for opinion research. Beginning at least as early as his 1950 presidential address to the American Association for Public Opinion Research, he repeatedly called for such studies, and urged establishment of a "'commission for the utilization of polls in the service of future historiography,' whose specific task it would be to furnish us [pollsters] with appropriate ideas [on significant questions to ask]."[17] But, as the recent observation by Berelson and Janowitz suggests, the programatic statements of Lazarsfeld and Hyman have had relatively little effect. Historians certainly have not joined with pollsters in the service of future historiography and survey organizations have generally not accepted responsibility for the task of developing long-term bodies of data.

The situation may change to some extent, of course. But it seems reasonable to believe that the Lazarsfeld-Hyman-Berelson-Janowitz statements, by restricting attention to public opinion research carried out by survey methods, do not go far enough. That is, serious deficiencies in long-term trend data, in my judgment, must continue to exist and handicap theory construction if public opinion research continues to depend exclusively, or primarily, upon *non-historical sources of data*.

For one thing, macroscopic social and cultural changes tend to take a very long time indeed to develop and make their consequences felt. Only extraordinarily long-lived and patient pollsters or survey organizations, therefore, might be expected to devote the resources needed to measure continuously the impact of macroscopic changes on opinion formation, and, in turn, the impact of opinion change over time on government policies. For another, lacking the perspective gained by "20-20 hindsight," it is doubtful that any group could identify in advance most of the issues that, in time, would come to be recognized as important. And it is even more doubtful that significant opinion-forming events (broadly defined) could be recognized, as it were, on the spot, and surveys quickly organized and conducted to secure *valid* retrospective before-and-after data. Moreover, even under the best circumstances, contemporary researchers surely find it difficult to secure valid data about the impact of public opinion on government action. Not only are contemporary researchers unlikely to have continuous access to decision makers and get truthful answers to probing questions, but government officials and political influentials are highly unlikely, *retrospectively*, to provide comprehensive,

[17] See Lazarsfeld's essay in the "Debate" on history and public opinion research, "The Historian and the Pollster," in Komarovsky, ed., *op. cit.*, pp. 242-268.

candid, accurate answers—even if they really tried hard to do so. In respect to this dimension of public opinion research, non-historians could profit from the emphasis historians place upon the painstaking procedures needed to extract reliable and valid data from primary sources.

Other difficulties could be sketched but would only belabor the main argument: If we need many "long-term bodies of data" to develop a powerful general theory of public opinion, heavy, although certainly not exclusive, reliance will have to be placed upon historical studies. The argument should not be caricatured as maintaining that historical procedures can be developed to secure all the types of data that can be secured by contemporary opinion research. Under the best of foreseeable circumstances, serious gaps will remain, e.g. historical data about the influence of primary groups and personality traits upon opinion formation. But historical study of public opinion can be significantly improved and its improvement would contribute significantly to the general study of public opinion. If that argument has merit, it follows that all social scientists interested in public opinion have a vital stake in developing the scientific character of its historical study.

III. THE CONCEPT OF PUBLIC OPINION: MAIN DIMENSIONS AND SUBCATEGORIES

Non-historians may find it surprising, but the three main dimensions of the concept of public opinion were clearly identified by a historian over two thousand years ago. Thucydides, in his classic *History of the Peloponnesian War,* organized his book around three closely related but different themes, the *distribution* of public opinion, the processes of opinion *formation,* and the *impact* of opinion upon government decisions.[18] Unfortunately, historians did not exploit the lead Thucydides provided and did not go on to develop a classification system for the different phenomena subsumed under the over-all concept, "public opinion." As a result, the historical study of public opinion has been seriously handicapped by lack of a good classification system to (1) distinguish among different types of phenomena; (2) provide a logical framework for ordering data; (3) suggest the need to devise different procedures to study different phenomena; (4) help bring complex relationships into focus; and (5) illuminate uniformities and differences. On the assumption that a good classification system is indispensable to fruitful research dealing with complex phenomena, it seems useful to try to develop one

[18] See the discussion of Thucydides in Lee Benson, "Causation and the American Civil War," *History and Theory,* Vol. 1, No. 2, 1961, pp. 167-168.

based upon Thucydides' dimensions as, in effect, elaborated by modern opinion researchers.[19]

A. Distribution of Opinion

"Spartans, those of you who think that the treaty [with Athens] has been broken and that the Athenians are aggressors, get up and stand on one side. Those who do not think so, stand on the other side," and he pointed out to them where they were to stand. They then rose to their feet and separated into two divisions. The great majority were of the opinion that the treaty had been broken.[20]

That is how Thucydides described the decision taken at the climactic meeting of the Spartan Assembly that declared war on Athens in 431 B.C. As the quotation indicates, he provided some explicit information about what we can call the "direction of opinion" but none about the "quality of opinion." Those two categories constitute the main subdivisions of the proposed classification system's first dimension, "distribution of opinion." In turn, each can usefully be subdivided to permit more precise categories for differentiating, ordering, and relating phenomena.

1. Direction of opinion. What do we want to know about the direction of public opinion on an issue over time and place? At least two very different things: (a) the quantitative *divisions* of opinion among the public; (b) the *attributes,* or *characteristics,* of the individuals who held different positions on the issue. We can combine them, of course, to make statements about the distribution of opinions among members of specified groups, or the group characteristics of the individuals holding a specified position. But the two categories are significantly different, a simple observation that forcefully points up the limitations of the information Thucydides provided, as well as the desirability of developing a good classification system for research on public opinion, past or present.

We know from Thucydides—assuming his account to be accurate—that "the great majority [of the Spartans] were of the opinion that the treaty had been broken." But we know nothing else about them. For example, we do not know how, if in any way other than their different positions on the issue, they differed from the small minority of Spartans who believed that the treaty had *not* been broken. As a result, although this essay is not the appropriate place to do so, I

[19] They differ somewhat in emphasis, but see the classification systems in, V. O. Key, *Public Opinion and American Democracy,* New York, Knopf, 1961; Robert E. Lane and David O. Sears, *Public Opinion,* Englewood Cliffs, N. J., Prentice-Hall, 1964; Childs, *op. cit.*

[20] Thucydides, *History of the Peloponnesian War,* Rex Warner translation, Great Britain, Penguin Books, 1956, Book I, p. 61.

think it could be shown that Thucydides' explanation of the Peloponnesian War can neither be confirmed nor disconfirmed. The relevant point is to observe that systematic research requires us to get data about both the quantitative divisions of opinion *and* the attributes of the members of a public who hold different positions. This observation gives us two categories, "Positions" and "Attributes," under the more general heading, "Direction of opinion."

a. Positions. For each of the different possible positions on a specific issue, we want to know the distribution of opinion of the members of the groups we designate as constituting "the public." Such information would permit us to identify who held what position, to state the distribution of opinion *within* a specified group, and to compare the distributions *between* different groups. Giving the "Ayes and Nays," as, in effect, Thucydides did, is the simplest form of stating divisions of opinion. Though numerous positions might be created, the range of useful variations on the "aye-nay" formula is narrow; it is hard to go much beyond some variant of "Favorable, Neutral, Undecided, No Opinion, Unfavorable." In short, when the qualitative content of opinion is ignored and each head is counted as an equal unit, there are not many ways to count heads on an issue.

b. Attributes. We can identify only a limited number of different positions on an issue, but, at least in theory, no limit exists to the number of attributes or characteristics we can use to stratify (or divide) a public into different groups. In practice, particularly in historical research, the range of choice tends to be much more restricted. For example, we might wish to group individuals according to personality type because we believe that significant relationships exist between personality type and opinion formation. Obviously, we cannot do so "historically," except perhaps with individual members of elite groups for whom we happen to have the requisite personal documents. Such limitations upon some aspects of historical opinion research need only induce caution, however, not paralysis.

It seems unlikely that personality characteristics are the only, or even the most significant, attributes relevant to opinion formation. Moreover, it seems reasonable to assume that significant relationships exist between some types of group membership (i.e. "interacting" rather than "categorical" groups) and personality characteristics. As John J. Honigman, a specialist on culture and personality, observes, "the members of any enduring group tend to manifest certain relatively common personality characteristics." That proposition, by enabling historians to treat personality, in effect, as only *one* "intervening variable" between group membership and opinion formation, puts our inability to secure data about individual personalities in much less alarming perspective—particularly if we sensibly restrict our claims about public opinion to those dimensions for which we can secure empirical data, do not pretend to offer exhaustive reconstructions and explanations, and do not feel compelled to imply perfect confidence in our claims. Nevertheless, given the past tendency of historians to ignore personality characteristics in opinion research, it seems useful to emphasize that we do not exhaust the range of possible determinants when we group men according to "external" attributes.[21]

To help overcome the "deficiencies of discontinuous data" pointed to by Hyman, it clearly would be highly desirable for studies of past (and present) opinion to use *comparable* (not necessarily identical) attributes to stratify the publics studied. But the choice of attributes inevitably is influenced by the specific issue(s) involved, the source materials available, the degree of precision desired, and the hypotheses being tested. Only a specialist in Greek history, therefore, could identify the attributes that Thucydides, ideally, would have used to study the relationships between public opinion and the coming of the Peloponnesian War. It is possible, nevertheless, to identify four *types* of attributes generally relevant to opinion studies. Because the papers in this issue that deal with public opinion and ratification of the Versailles Treaty provide concrete examples of how they are used in substantive research, the attributes will be identified in American terms. With appropriate changes in terms, however, the typology seems widely applicable.

Place is the type of attribute perhaps most commonly used to divide "a public" into "publics." That is, researchers can try to ascertain the quantitative divisions of opinion on specified issues at specified times among Americans as a group, or among the inhabitants of different sections, states, localities, and the like.

"Political role" identifies another type of attribute. "Formal political roles" permit researchers to distinguish members of the electorate, voters from eligible nonvoters, *et al.* "Informal roles" in principle—that is, if the requisite data can be obtained—permit researchers to distinguish the members of a political system according to party or faction, "liberal" or "conservative" attitudes, differential power to influence decisions (e.g. "elites" and "masses"), or other attributes that seem theoretically relevant.

Demographic attributes can be used to stratify "the public" into

21 For a somewhat less optimistic view of the problems personality variables pose for historical opinion research, see May, *loc. cit.* On the relationships between personality and culture, see John J. Honigmann, *Culture and Personality*, New York, Harper & Row, 1954, pp. 195-225; and, a particularly relevant essay for historians, Anthony F. C. Wallace, "The Psychic Unity of Human Groups," in Bert Kaplan, ed., *Studying Personality Cross-culturally*, New York, Harper & Row, 1961, pp. 128-163.

a very large number of smaller "publics." Relevant demographic attributes vary according to time, place, issue, *and theory,* but the standard divisions are some variant and combination of economic, ethnic, religious, urban-rural, educational, age, and sex differences.

Formal voluntary association is the last type of attribute identified in the typology sketched here. To some extent, these attributes overlap with demographic ones, but the difference is that they connote "voluntary" membership (or nonmembership) in formal *organizations* (e.g. Chambers of Commerce, trade-unions, farmers' organizations, veterans' organizations, religious organizations, ethnic societies) rather than "categorical" membership in some group identified by a demographic attribute.

In principle, of course, the four types of attributes can be combined into an extraordinarily large number of subdivisions among "the American public." In practice, limitations of resources and data sharply restrict the ability of researchers to deal with all publics that might be theoretically relevant. This observation again need induce only caution, not paralysis. To know what theoretically ought to be done, even if historians cannot do it, is useful—and chastening. But inability to do *everything* worth doing is not equivalent to inability to do *anything.*

2. *Quality of opinion.* Attention thus far has been restricted to *quantitative divisions* of opinion among the members of different groups. Two assumptions, however, seem reasonable: heads do not count equally in determining the impact of public opinion on government actions; the *qualities* of men's opinions form a significant component of their relative will and power to influence government actions. If we accept those assumptions, it seems useful to create subdivisions under the general category, "Quality of opinion."

a. State (or crystallization) of opinion. At any given time, have the members of a group crystallized their positions on a given issue or are opinions in a formative state? The two main states have been termed "latent" and "manifest." That historians feel both compelled and able to distinguish between these states is nicely illustrated in the paper by James L. Lancaster on "The Protestant Churches and the Fight for Ratification of the Versailles Treaty," in this issue. In effect, one of his basic themes is the transition of opinion from a latent to a manifest state. For example, he emphasizes that specified types of Protestant leaders, those of "liberal theological persuasion," were overwhelmingly sympathetic to the general idea of a league of nations but not necessarily favorable to "whatever specific plan emerged from Versailles." He then advances and supports the claim that three specific events helped to crystallize their latent support into manifest support: "the release of the text of the Covenant, the speeches made by . . . President [Wilson] on its behalf, and the debate in Boston on March 19, 1919, between President A. Lawrence Lowell of Harvard University and Senator Henry Cabot Lodge" (p. 6).

b. Saliency of opinion. For the members of specified groups, how "salient" (important) is a given public issue *compared* either to other public issues or to other "issues" affecting their lives? That question points up the need to study opinion on an issue not in isolation from opinions on other issues, but as one strand of an interrelated web of opinion. Men may share the same position on an issue but vary enormously in the importance they attach to it. Historians, therefore, must grapple with the problem of ascertaining the relative saliency of an issue to different groups at the same time, or to the same group at different times.[22] That dictum can also be illustrated by Lancaster's paper.

In effect, Lancaster explains the tremendous *activity* certain Protestant leaders engaged in to secure ratification of Wilson's plan by noting its extraordinary *saliency* for them. For one minister, "the League [of Nations] was the practical application to the whole world of Christ's teachings concerning individuals"; for another, it was "cementing the nations of earth so that the Kingdom of God may come" (p. 602).

c. Intensity of opinion. How convinced are men that their position on an issue is the right position? That is, in addition to wanting to know something about the saliency of an issue to members of a group, we want to know something about the relative intensity (or strength) of their convictions concerning the positions they favor. Depending upon the data available and the precision desired, we can try to group men in categories ranging from some variant of "strongly favorable" to "strongly unfavorable."

d. Duration of opinion. One determinant of the strength of an opinion, it seems reasonable to postulate, is how long an individual holds it. To treat "duration" separately from "strength," however, is not to engage in conspicuous creation of categories. Duration is by no means the only determinant of strength of conviction. Moreover, if we treat determinants separately, we improve our ability to measure and explain their relative contributions to the strength of opinion. Still another consideration is that when we deal with opinion formation, we particularly need to secure data about the durability of opinions.

e. Knowledgeability of opinion. As conceived here, no more legiti-

[22] In this connection, see the chapter, "Texas Annexation and New York Public Opinion," in Lee Benson, *The Concept of Jacksonian Democracy: New York as a Test Case,* Princeton, N. J., Princeton University Press, 1961, 254-269.

macy is attributed to "informed" than to "uninformed" opinion. But the assumption seems reasonable that informed opinions tend to be stronger and more durable than uniformed ones, and that government officials take those qualities into account when considering opinion distribution on an issue. The "Knowledgeability" category is therefore included in the classification system, although I cheerfully concede that it may be difficult to secure relevant historical data.

B. Formation of Opinion

The papers in this issue focused on the Versailles Treaty provide answers to a wide variety of questions related to opinion formation. To order such questions systematically and comprehensively, the dimension can conveniently be subdivided into five categories: (1) Formative agents, (2) Agents' motives, (3) Agents' actions, (4) Impact of agents' actions, and (5) Explanation of impact of agents' actions. Those categories, although interrelated, are analytically distinct. To secure historical data about the different types of phenomena assigned to them requires, therefore, different procedures and, in Nagel's terms, different "tried canons" for judging both the reliability of the procedures and "the probative force of the evidence on which conclusions are based."

1. Formative agents. "Every factor that makes the individual what he is attitudinally enters into the formation of political opinion."[23] That all-encompassing proposition may be true, almost by definition, but it gives little guidance to researchers trying to develop an operational strategy for the study of opinion formation. Rather than begin by trying to identify either the diverse environments in which members of the public form their opinions or their even more diverse predispositions, historians might better begin by trying to identify the relatively small number of individuals or groups actively working to form opinions on specific issues. The basic assumption here is that public opinion on an issue (broadly defined) does not evolve spontaneously but strongly tends to be "made" by the conscious actions of a relatively small number of "formative agents." Once we explicitly identify the issues that concern us in our research, it seems reasonable to assume—and the three papers support the assumption—that we can systematically identify the "leading agents" if we consciously try to do so and saturate ourselves in the historical situation. And once we systematically identify the leading agents, it can be further assumed, we place ourselves in a better position to try to reconstruct and explain the complex processes of opinion formation.

No implication is intended that formative agents either act with

23 That sentence begins the section on "Formation," in Key, *op. cit.*, p. 291.

perfect knowledge and rationality or achieve the precise results they want or expect. On the contrary, I assume that all agents fall considerably short of perfection, that they display wide variations in knowledge and rationality, and that their actions frequently "boomerang." Moreover, I assume that the actual distribution of opinion on any given issue at any given time represents the outcome of conflicting actions whose impact could, at best, have been predicted only within wide limits—if for no other reason than the occurrence of uncontrollable changes in the general historical situation. But my operative assumption is that if we begin with *conscious agents acting purposively*, we stand on solid theoretical ground and can conduct research according to a workable design.

Granted that assumption, it seems useful to try to develop a standard typology of formative agents. Among other advantages, its development and adoption would tend to produce comparable, cumulative studies and thereby contribute to both theoretical and substantive progress. The typology sketched below obviously is neither elegant nor exhaustive. It represents a beginning rather than an end; its deficiencies, I trust, will stimulate other researchers to repair them rather than to dismiss the enterprise as hopeless.

a. Government officials. Of the different types of formative agents, government officials head the list. We can safely assume that, to some extent, they always consciously try to form public opinion on all "major" issues because we can safely assume that, to some extent, public opinion always affects their operations. Depending upon the subject, officials can be differentiated according to position, level, branch, unit of government, etc. A less obvious but significant differentiation is between "official role" and "nonofficial role." That is, in addition to opinion-making power derived from their government positions, officials may also have influence on various groups, organizations, or individuals, and they may use their influence to help shape public opinion. To cite only one possible reason for making the distinction: It may help us to understand why different men occupying the same position, or similar positions, differ markedly in their ability to influence the distribution of opinion.

b. Political leaders. In this context, "political leaders" connotes men who either do not hold public office or who function as officeholders in one type of nonofficial role. Like government officials, political leaders have a vital stake in the distribution of public opinion and can reasonably be assumed, therefore, to act constantly to shape it. Distinctions between government officials and political leaders may not be universally applicable, but the latter term is not restricted to the modern era. In any era, I assume, a relatively small group of men lead "parties," "factions," "cliques," "circles," and variants thereof.

c. Mass media directors. This term is restricted to the modern era. It designates men who own, operate, or significantly influence the mass media used to communicate information and views. Actually, sharp distinctions between "information" and "views" tend to be somewhat misleading. As George Gerbner suggests, the best proposition to adopt in studying opinion formation is, "all news are views."[24] But it is important to recognize that the opinion-forming power of any communication medium varies widely over time, place, and type of issue, an observation particularly relevant to the problem considered in Section V below of constructing *indicators* of opinion distribution.

d. Leaders of nonpolitical formal organizations. We might extend Gerbner's proposition to claim that, at least in the United States, all major formal organizations (e.g. National Council of Churches, National Association of Manufactures, AFL-CIO) are political organizations. To do so, however, would be to engage in reductionism and obliterate the boundaries between a political system and its environment. A more reasonable position is to assume that the leaders of all major organizations *consciously* act to form public opinion at some times, on some issues. Depending upon the issue and situation, therefore, we could estimate the likelihood that the leaders of specified organizations acted to form opinion, and design our research operations accordingly. To illustrate the point concretely Lancaster's paper can again be cited, although the other two papers, by Maxwell and Helbich, also provide striking examples.

Given the long history of participation by American Protestant organizations in the "crusade for peace," dating from 1815, and the specific work of the Federal Council of Churches of Christ in America during 1917-1918, Lancaster "naturally" (my term) focuses on that organization's efforts to gain support for the League of Nations. Accordingly, he finds (pp. 598-599):

The Executive Committee of the Federal Council of Churches issued on December 12, 1918, a ringing endorsement of President Wilson's plan for a league of nations. Acting on the recommendation of its Commission on International Justice and Goodwill, the committee challenged its affiliates to strengthen the President's position in Paris and at home. . . . The Federal Council asked local churches to provide suitable courses of study on the League of Nations and directed its Commission on Inter-Church Federations to secure expressions of approval of the League by public vote in local con-

24 George Gerbner, "Ideological Perspectives and Political Tendencies in News Reporting," *Journalism Quarterly,* Vol. 41, Autumn 1964, p. 495.

gregations. Sunday, January 12, 1919, was designated a day of prayer for the establishment of a league of nations.

In similar fashion, his paper, essentially a study of opinion formation, focuses on the activities of other religious organizations that, given their nature and history, might have been expected to support or oppose Wilson's plan.

e. Pressure-group leaders. To a considerable extent, the analytic distinction between "pressure-group leaders" and "leaders of non-political formal organizations" is arbitrary and not easily applied in practice. The main criterion suggested for assigning organizations to different categories is neither their size nor power but the range of issues likely to concern their leaders and members. The National Council of Churches and the American Medical Association, for example, both function today as pressure groups. But the activities of the latter are far more circumscribed—if less circumspect—than those of the former. I would therefore classify the AMA leaders, in their opinion-making roles, as "pressure-group leaders," the leaders of the National Churches of Christ as "leaders of nonpolitical formal organizations." Since one aim of the classification system proposed here is to help provide operational guidelines for opinion researchers, it seems useful to create categories that distinguish between men who lead such different kinds of pressure groups.

f. Influentials. "Influentials" is the label for the final type of formative agent considered here. Following Robert Merton, they can be further subdivided into "cosmopolitan" and "local" influentials.[25] The characteristic that differentiates them from other opinion leaders (who, of course, can also be viewed as "influentials"), is that their power derives from their personal qualities rather than their control of governmental or organizational resources.

Walter Lippmann serves as a convenient example. Hundreds of other individuals also write columns designed to influence public opinion, and many of them are more widely syndicated. It seeems safe to say, however, both that he is the most influential publicist in the United States today and that his influence derives from his reputation and persuasiveness rather than from his relationships to the media that present his views.

In short, the "influentials" assigned to this category influence public opinion through their control of personal rather than corporate resources.

2. *Agents' motives.* As the three papers below by Helbich, Lancaster, and Maxwell concretely suggest, different agents, impelled by different

[25] Robert K. Merton, *Social Theory and Social Structure,* rev. and enlarged ed., Glencoe, Ill., Free Press, 1957, pp. 387-420.

motives, can try to move public opinion in the same direction. The "liberal" editors of the *Nation* and the "hyphenated" leaders of Irish-American groups, for example, both worked to defeat ratification of the Versailles Treaty. But their motives differed significantly. To ignore this dimension would make any study of their activities seriously incomplete. Questions about *why* men wanted to form public opinion in specified ways force historians (and other researchers), of course, to explore motivational thickets abounding in thorns and pitfalls. Their exploration can be avoided, however, only by sharply reducing a study's explanatory power and theoretical interest.

3. Agents' actions. It is relatively easier to reconstruct the actions agents take to form opinion than to reconstruct their motives for wanting to do so. But some difficult questions need to be answered about phenomena assigned to this category: In addition to *overt* actions to form opinion, what *covert* actions did specified agents take? Which groups constituted the main targets for specified activities by specified agents? Which groups constituted the "real" targets as distinct from the "nominal" targets? (For example, in the current controversy over "open housing," do the groups opposed to "fair housing laws" *nominally* address themselves to "property owners" but *really* aim at "whites," irrespective of their propertied status?).

4. Impact of agents' actions on specified groups. Apart from other considerations, we need answers to the questions posed immediately above if we are to assess the relative success of different agents. The main question posed here is really a composite question: In relation to specified issues, which agents influenced which groups how much? The groups influenced can be characterized as "nominal target," "real target," "unintended target" ("boomerang" or "windfall" effects). "How much" refers to both the direction and the quality of opinion.

5. Explanation of impact of agents' activities. After we have answered the questions posed immediately above, *and only then,* we can tackle the hard job of explaining the differential success achieved by different agents. In other words, we need to secure data that permit us to say who took what actions, which had what impact, on what groups, in relation to what issue, *before* we can hope to develop systematic and responsible explanations of opinion formation. We may not be able to do so in any event, of course, but, if we first secure the specified types of data, our chances improve considerably.

Six types of determinants can be identified as helping to explain the impact of agents' actions upon public opinion. Again the topology is neither elegant nor exhaustive. But the brief notes below at least provide a beginning.

561

a. Group receptivity. It seems reasonable to assume that the predispositions of the members of a group are the most important determinants of their response to the actions taken by different agents.

b. Group attitudes toward agents. Contemporary studies support the proposition that "who" says something to someone significantly influences the response to what is said.[26] No reason exists to assume that the proposition applies uniquely to the present.

c. Agents' resources. One obvious determinant of the differential success agents enjoy is the differences in the financial and organizational resources available to them.

d. Arguments used. I assume that, except in unusual cases, the arguments used by agents have *some* significant weight in determining the opinions members of a group form on an issue. Another assumption: Persuasive arguments need not be "rational"—whatever we mean by "rational"—but researchers can hope to identify at least some of the reasons arguments *seem* rational and persuasive to the groups influenced by them. Put another way, I assume that, to respond favorably (or unfavorably) to arguments, most individuals need to perceive them as rational (or irrational). If that assumption is accepted, historians need not try to demonstrate that arguments *were* rational, they need only (*sic*) try to explain why specified arguments *seemed* rational to specified groups.[27]

e. Agents' skill in presenting arguments. Except to make explicit the assumption that skill is a significant determinant of success in opinion formation, no comment seems necessary.

f. Historical situation. Here I refer to phenomena that occur independently of actions agents take to form public opinion. For example, Maxwell points to "events in Ireland" as one of three sets of factors helping "to provide the framework within which Irish-American opposition to the League of Nations was to emerge and grow" (p. 620). In effect, what might be called the "specific historical situation" relevant to a particular issue or group, and the "general historical situation" relevant to all issues and groups, strongly tend to *condition* responses to actions designed to form opinion.

C. Impact of Public Opinion on Government Decisions

That public opinion significantly influences public policy has long

[26] See M. Brewster Smith, "Opinions, Personality, and Political Behavior," *American Political Science Review*, Vol. 52, March 1958, pp. 1-17. This article seems particularly useful for historians since it provides, in reasonably clear terms, a review of the "major foray[s] by psychologists into the personal determinants of opinion. . . ."

[27] The perspective adopted here leads to a more optimistic and less relativistic position than the one suggested in May, *op. cit.*, pp. 103-108.

been assumed. In fact, that assumption probably serves as the main scholarly justification for opinion research in general and historical opinion research in particular. How much hard evidence exists to support it, however? Rather little, according to V. O. Key, Ernest May, and Harwood L. Childs. All three have specifically focused on that question and all three essentially agree.[28] To quote the most recent (1965) statement by Childs:

. . . notwithstanding the accumulation of much data regarding voting behavior in elections and referenda, mounting quantities of opinion survey data, and many specialized studies of pressure groups, the mass media, and other links between citizens and government, few of the many hypotheses and speculations on the influences of public opinion on government found *concrete, empirical verification.* Specifically, even though public opinion is expressed regarding a specific public policy, it is seldom known which officials or agencies were aware of this state of public opinion, and what, if anything, was done about this awareness. [Emphasis added.]

Agreeing with Key that "the sharp definition of the role of public opinion as it affects different kinds of policies under different types of situations presents an analytical problem of extraordinary difficulty," Childs observed that:

For more than twenty-five years polling agencies have been making nationwide surveys of public opinion, and a wealth of opinion data has been collected regarding the views of the American people on issues of domestic and foreign policy. The question arises to what extent, if at all, public opinion actually influences public policy. There has been much theoretical speculation regarding the answer but very few hard facts.[29]

Historians might be tempted to adopt a superior tone to "pollsters" on the ground that historical method, applied to manuscript and other primary sources, has yielded the hard data so elusive to researchers lacking access to such sources. Any historian yielding to that temptation, however, would find it a chastening experience to read May's devastating critique.

[28] Key, *op. cit.*, pp. 409-431; May, *op. cit.*, pp. 102-103, 113-122; Childs, *op. cit.*, pp. 291-319.

[29] *Ibid.*, pp. 291-292, 309-310. It should be noted, however, that Childs reports upon six case studies directed by him that were explicitly designed to secure some "hard facts" to answer the question "to what extent, if at all, public opinion actually influences public policy." As he summarizes those studies, they provide highly interesting and suggestive answers to the question. But it is not another incident in interdisciplinary warfare, I trust, to observe that historians would strongly tend to doubt that firm conclusions can be drawn from case studies not based on intensive examination of correspondence and other personal documents of the government officials involved. No implication is intended that Professor Childs presents the studies as conclusive; on the contrary, my point is to reinforce his observation about the difficulty of securing relevant and significant "hard facts."

Relationships between public opinion and American foreign policy have long concerned historians, May observed, but we still have little credible knowledge about them. That embarrassing state of affairs, he suggested, and my researches on the historiography of the annexation of Texas and other pre–Civil War issues lead me to agree strongly, in large measure derives from the fact that historians have "scarcely . . . raised, let alone answered," the key questions. His concluding paragraph is particularly pertinent for our purposes:

Our chief reason for believing that public opinion has influenced and does influence foreign policy is our knowledge that American statesmen have traditionally thought themselves responsible to, and supported or constrained by, some sort of general will. The national tradition is to accept as true the definition attributed to William of Malmesbury: *vox populi, vox Dei.* American political leaders have hearkened to the voice of the people as their seventeenth-century forebears did to the voice of God. Perhaps scholars, instead of listening for these voices themselves, ought to begin by inquiring what it is that these men thought they heard.[30]

In effect, May observed that historians have strongly tended to assume that something like one-to-one relationships exist among the *distribution* of opinion, the *perception* of opinion by government officials, and the *decisions made* by government officials. But it is very difficult, he suggests, for anyone, contemporary official or later historian, to ascertain the actual distribution of public opinion at any specified time on any specified issue. Historians therefore would be better advised to begin research by focusing on decision makers' perception of public opinion rather than by "listening for these voices themselves. . . ."

As indicated in Section IV below, I incline toward a different research strategy from the one advocated by May. But he has made a significant contribution to historical opinion research, I believe, by forcefully directing attention to the problem of identifying the main categories of the dimension variously referred to by different authorities as "linkage," "influence," or "impact."

In the classification system suggested in the present essay, the "impact" dimension is subdivided into four main categories: (1) Communication of opinion to officials; (2) Impact of opinion on distribution of political power; (3) Officials' perception of opinion; and (4) Impact of perception on specified decisions.

   1. Communication of opinion to officials. Although the term "communication" has some misleading connotations when used to identify the phenomena assigned to this category, I have thus far been unable to find or devise a better one. To minimize misconceptions arising

[30] May, *op. cit.,* p. 122.

from the term's connotations, it is useful to emphasize that the category contains data designed to answer three questions: (a) Who *initiates* the processes by which government officials ultimately receive "information" about the distribution of opinion on issues? (b) What are the sequences of *"steps"* by which information about specified issues reaches officials? (c) What *"media"* are used to convey information on specified issues to officials?

Data relevant to each of those questions, I believe, are best grouped in a separate subcategory. They are identified here only in broad terms since different studies will require different sets of more or less detailed subcategories.

a. Initiators of communication process. For reasons previously suggested, I assume that, generally speaking, government officials actively try to form public opinion. For the same reasons, I assume that officials actively seek information about the distribution of opinion on issues over time. It would severely distort reality, I believe, to depict public officials only, or even primarily, as passive recipients of information. On the contrary, American public officials have always used a wide variety of devices (e.g. consultation with "expert" observers, analysis of newspapers, commissioning of "surveys") in their hot pursuit of information about public opinion.

An astonishing variety of "nonofficials" also exercise initiative in communicating information about the distribution of opinion on an issue to relevant or potent officials. One main type of "initiator" can be characterized as "spokesman" (authorized or self-appointed) for specific groups; another main type can be labeled "middleman." The "middleman" category connotes some on-going institution such as, for example, newspapers which poll the "man on the street" and *publicly* report their "findings," organizations that purport to have studied the distribution of opinion on specific issues and *privately* report their "findings" to selected officials, and so forth.

What difference does it make who initiates the processes that culminate in officials having specific perceptions of opinion distribution on an issue? Hard data to answer that question are lacking, it must be confessed. But the assumption seems reasonable that official perceptions vary considerably depending upon who initiates the communication processes and who thereby helps to determine the selection of information communicated. Granted that assumption, it follows that researchers ought to try to identify "initiators" of information on specific issues.

b. Sequence of steps in communication process. In addition to variations in official perceptions depending upon variations in who initiates the process, I assume that perceptions will vary significantly, depending upon (1) which officials receive the information in what order, and (2) the number, kind, and sequence of steps in the communication process.[31] For example, spokesmen for a group may directly communicate their perception of its opinion to one official rather than another, they may communicate it to party leaders who in turn communicate their *perceptions* to one official rather than another, they may communicate it to specific mass media, and so forth.

No implication is intended that historians (or contemporary researchers) can reconstruct all the steps in any sequence of communication flows by which specific officials receive information about public opinion on a specific issue. But it seems axiomatic that historians ought to *try* to reconstruct such sequences if they hope to reconstruct official perceptions with any reasonable degree of precision and credibility, or hope to understand and explain how those perceptions came about. May's point, in effect, is that historians have not acted upon that axiom; my point is that, to do so effectively, they need to develop and use a classification system that explicitly indicates the kinds of data to secure relevant to officials' perception.

c. Media of communication. Marshall McLuhan's guru-like dictum about "the medium is the message" at best represents only a half-truth. But opinion researchers have long been aware that the type of media used to communicate information to officials does significantly influence their perceptions of the messages communicated. No need exists to present a long list of the different media that can be used in different sequences of steps in the communication process from public to official. Two points, however, seem worth making: (1) Not only the source of information about public opinion and the circumstances under which the information is received, but the form (or media) of communication must be taken into account when we try to reconstruct and explain how the voice of the people sounded to specified officials. (2) In addition to written and verbal forms of communication, various types of action, e.g. riots, demonstrations, meetings, serve the same function—and frequently speak louder, and more persuasively, than words.

2. *Impact of opinions on distribution of political power.* Voting can be regarded, of course, as simply another form of communication of information about public opinion to public officials. It is important and complex enough, however, to warrant separate treatment.

[31] For a stimulating analysis of the way information flows influence opinions and decisions, see Elihu Katz, "The Two-step Flow of Communication: An Up-to-date Report on an Hypothesis," *Public Opinion Quarterly*, Vol. 21, 1957, pp. 61-78. See also Key, *op. cit.*, pp. 411-431.

We need not assume perfect democracy in a political system to recognize that voting is a particularly potent form of communication. Its potency stems from its dual character. Voting may simultaneously function as a form of communication of opinion to public officials and an act which, in a formally democratic system, formally determines who the officials ultimately are to whom opinions are to be communicated. The problem, of course, is that opinions on any specified issue, or set of issues, do not *necessarily* play any significant role in determining voting behavior; they may, but then again they may not.

Put another way, we are entitled to assume that voting can function as a form of communication about public opinion. But how do we know when it actually does perform that function to any significant degree and how do we know what information it actually does convey? Those questions have long bedeviled politicians and researchers. Further discussion of them is best reserved for Section V, which deals with the general problem of constructing indicators and indexes of public opinion.

3. Officials' perception of public opinion. Truth in history is not only what happened but what men believed to have happened. Public officials may—and frequently do—misperceive public opinion. For our present purposes, that does not matter. What does matter is that the *reality*, not the *accuracy*, of their perceptions influences their actions—to the extent that they consciously allow public opinion to influence their actions. "Reality" here means what they "really" think they perceive, not what they *say* they perceive.

Which officials? What is perceived? Those are the two main questions relevant to this category.

Different officials, it is obvious enough, may have radically different perceptions of the distribution of public opinion on an issue, or set of issues. Researchers, equally obviously, must therefore specifically identify the officials about whose perceptions they make claims; if they cannot do so with some reasonable degree of specificity, they are not entitled to make claims about the impact of public opinion on public policy.

The problem of identifying what is perceived by specified officials is more complex. As indicated previously, the dimension "Distribution of opinion" contains numerous and radically different components. It is not very useful, therefore, to describe the perceptions of specific officials in vague terms, e.g. "public opinion favored (or opposed) Texas Annexation." Since it seems reasonable to assume that offiicals are influenced by perceptions of both the "direction" and "quality" of opinion, data are needed relevant to the different subcategories of those broad headings. Again, no counsel of perfection is being urged here. Such data may be impossible to get, even if one really tries hard to get them. The point is, one really ought to try hard—and to recognize the implications for one's study if one does not succeed.

4. Impact of officials' perception of public opinion on specified decisions. This category is the "pay-off" one for studies focused on the relationships between public opinion and public policy. In a sense, research carried out in respect to all other categories of the proposed classification system can be regarded as preliminary research to help answer two main types of questions:

a. *What kind* of impact did officials' perception of public opinion have on the *timing* (e.g. accelerate, delay) of specified decisions? On the direction (e.g. reinforce, or weaken, an official's adherence to his own perferred position)?

b. *How much* impact, i.e. how much "weight," did officials' perception of public opinion have on both the timing and direction of specified decisions?

Posing those questions gives rise to another: Can historians really be expected to answer them systematically with any reasonable degree of credibility? For reasons indicated previously, I do not think historians can *now* be expected to do so, but I do think that eventually they may be able to do so. Development and wide *use* of a classification system of the type sketched in this essay, I have tried to suggest, would contribute significantly to the coming of that happy day. But an even more important contribution, I suggest, would be development and wide use of a general research strategy and system of analysis for the historical study of public opinion. It is to that problem that attention can now be appropriately directed.

IV. A RESEARCH STRATEGY AND TENTATIVE SYSTEM OF ANALYSIS FOR THE HISTORICAL STUDY OF PUBLIC OPINION

A. A Research Strategy

The strategy advocated here assumes that historians who undertake opinion research should schedule their operations according to the classification system sketched above.[32] That is, researchers should, *in sequence,* try to (1) reconstruct the distribution of opinion on specified issues over time, (2) reconstruct and explain the formation of opinion, (3) reconstruct and explain the impact of opinion upon policy.

---

[32] I make a sharp distinction between the operations involved in *conducting* research and those involved in *reporting* the results of research; my comments refer only to the former set of operations.

Like all research strategies, the one advocated here derives from a particular theoretical orientation that should be stated explicitly. No implication is intended, of course, that I have developed anything resembling a general theory capable of stating the conditions under which public opinion has varying degrees of impact upon specified types of public policies. My "theoretical orientation," if the term does not seem overblown, simply assumes that public officials strongly tend to play the most important roles both in consciously forming public opinion and in determining its impact upon government decisions. Given that orientation, the research strategy advocated here seems to follow logically.

How can we hope to find out who played significant roles in forming public opinion, or to explain their ability and desire to do so, if we do not *first* reconstruct the distribution of opinion over time? Similarly, how can we reconstruct and explain the impact of opinion on policy if we do not first reconstruct the distribution of opinion?

Granted that what "counts" in decision making is not the "real" distribution of opinion but officials' perception of the distribution of opinion. Surely, however, a systematic and responsible explanation requires us to make some estimate of the relationships between reality and officials' perception of reality. If officials misperceived the distribution of opinion and acted to some significant extent on their misperceptions, did those misperceptions derive from the officials' having already decided on the policies they wanted to follow, or from poor channels of communication, or both? And *before* we try to estimate the extent to which officials acted on what they thought they heard as "the voice of the people," shouldn't we try to find out whether they essentially were listening only to their own voices as echoed by people who, in effect, they had taught what to say?

Put another way, the research strategy advocated here derives from the following line of argument:

Verifying claims about popular support for, or opposition to, specified government actions is a crucial *preliminary* step in the verification of explanations that emphasize the impact of public opinion upon public decisions. No causal relationship *necessarily* exists between the distribution of public opinion and the occurrence of a particular decision, or set of decisions. If a researcher asserts that such a relationship exists, it therefore seems reasonable to ask him to justify his description of public opinion before evaluating his argument about its impact upon events. In short, it seems logical to evaluate the data and procedures used to *ascertain* public opinion on given issues before evaluating the data and procedures used to *assess* its effect. Paraphrasing Mrs. Glasse's celebrated advice on how to cook a hare, the recipe suggested here for assessing the causal role of public opinion begins, "First, catch your public opinion."[33]

B. A Tentative System of Analysis for Historical Opinion Research

How can historians—or anyone doing historical research—proceed to "catch" public opinion? To begin with, I suggest, by recognizing the implications of an obvious "fact": the distribution of opinion on an issue changes constantly. It may not change much, it may fluctuate wildly. Over time, it changes. Indeed, measured finely enough, we can assume that opinion distribution changes daily. But no researcher, of course, is likely to want to try to "catch" it on a daily basis, except for extremely limited periods of time.

1. Selection of periods for measurement. From those elementary observations, a basic problem emerges for historical opinion researchers: Which "poll days" or "poll periods" should be chosen to measure trends in the distribution of opinion on an issue over time? Depending upon the general nature of the study and the specific claims made, the poll periods might vary in length from a single day, to a month, or, in unusual cases, to a year (if the study focused on long-lived, relatively unchanging issues such as "the tariff" prior to the Civil War). But, in systematic opinion research, some specific dates must be selected on which public opinion must be described as having had some specific distribution. Obviously, to perform the operations required to develop valid descriptions of opinion distribution over time, some principles of selection must be used to minimize distortions due to "accidental circumstances" affecting opinion at certain times. "Accidental circumstances," in this context, are those not covered by the principles of selection.

One solution to the problem of identifying *valid* poll periods, i.e. periods when a researcher can reasonably expect to measure what he says he is measuring, is to use a sampling formula designed to lessen the chances of "accidents" distorting opinion distribution. For example, beginning with a carefully selected date, "polls" might be taken every five or seven or eleven months, or any other interval that rotates the dates in different years. Such solutions undoubtedly tend to lessen distortion due to chance factors and increase reliability; i.e. different researchers using the same formula, and using the same procedures and sources with comparable skill, would get similar results. But to use such solutions we must pay a heavy price; we must sacrifice

[33] It may be pedantic to note that the recipe was attributed to Mrs. Glasse erroneously; it actually appeared in a *Cook Book* published in 1747. See Kate Louise Roberts (reviser), *Hoyt's New Cyclopedia of Practical Quotation*, New York, 1922, p. 138. The recipe goes, "To make a ragoût, first catch your hare."

the flexibility that constitutes one of the great advantages historians enjoy over contemporary researchers.

As noted in the discussion of Hyman's incisive observations about the "deficiencies of discontinuous data" that retard theoretical development, contemporary researchers lack the "20-20 hindsight" enjoyed by historians. Unless they resort to retrospective interviews, of dubious validity even after short periods of time and ever more dubious thereafter, they are *"locked into"* the questions that happened to be asked about particular issues at particular times. In contrast, historical researchers, given the availability of relevant documents—a large "given," I concede—have unlimited flexibility to benefit from historical perspective and range over issues and events, as well as choose any poll periods they regard as best suited to test any theories or hypotheses they (or others) have formulated. (The "relevant document" problem is discussed in Section V below).

By unlimited flexibility to choose dates, I mean, of course, unlimited flexibility to choose poll periods *controlled by some objective criteria*. Put another way, systematic opinion research requires historians to develop a "chronicle of events," or "narrative framework," for the issue(s) studied that specialists would strongly tend to agree was based on reasonable, unarbitrary criteria.

Once historians have developed an objective narrative framework appropriate to their particular studies, they can systematically proceed to identify the poll dates (or periods) on which to measure opinion distribution. Having done so, they can try to carry out, in sequence, research designed to secure the data called for by a classification system of the type sketched above. (The question of whether we have, or can develop, methods capable of securing those data is also postponed until Section V below).

If the argument thus far is accepted, or merely granted for the sake of argument, it follows that development of an objective narrative framework is the indispensable first operation required by the proposed system of analysis for historical opinion research. Do we now know how to perform that operation?

2. Constructing a narrative framework to catch public opinion. My unpublished research on Texas Annexation has convinced me that it is possible to construct an objective narrative framework for historical opinion research; alas, I cannot yet cite published work to support the claim. What I can do now, however, in addition to emphasizing the importance of the problem, is to identify three main types of events (broadly defined) that can be combined to construct a narrative framework for any historical opinion study: (a) sequence of relevant government *decisions;* (b) actions (other than government decisions) taken by agents to form opinion; and (c) events contributing to significant changes in the historical situation. For convenience and clarity, my illustrations are all drawn from the Texas Annexation issue, but the typology and operations seem generally applicable.

a. Government decisions. On December 29, 1845, President James K. Polk signed the congressional resolution that formally made Texas the thirtieth state in the Union. To what extent, and in what ways, did public opinion influence the sequence of events that culminated in that decision? The volume of historiographic literature touching on that problem is large—and shallow. Its shallowness, I suggest, stems from the general lack of recognition among historians that to solve the problem we must begin by trying to construct a narrative framework. Failure to recognize the importance of that operation, I maintain, is primarily responsible for the failure to perform it. Put another way, the argument here is that if historians doing research on the Texas Annexation issue made a concerted and systematic attempt to construct such a framework, they would be able to achieve substantial agreement on its main parts and basic shape.

If we begin by explicitly designating Polk's action on December 29, 1845, as the decision that we ultimately have to explain, we can reasonably regard it as the terminal decision in a series of government decisions that began on February 22, 1819, with the signing of the "Transcontinental Treaty" between the United States and Spain. That treaty dealt with the southwestern boundaries of the United States, including its claims to Texas as far south as the Rio Grande. Just as it is reasonable and unarbitrary to designate the Transcontinental Treaty as the initial decision, it is possible to designate other actions, on various governmental levels, as constituting the sequence of "main decisions" between the initial and terminal decisions.

The argument can be summarized and extended as follows: Using reasonable criteria, we can identify a sequence of governmental decisions from February 22, 1819, to December 29, 1845, as "the decision to annex Texas." We can then go on to designate those decisions as major parts of an objective narrative framework for studies dealing with some aspect of public opinion and Texas Annexation. Their major role stems from their dual character; they are the decisions upon which public opinion may have had some impact and, once made, we can assume, they had some impact upon the formation of public opinion.

b. Agents' actions. Government decisions do not constitute the only parts of a narrative framework for historical opinion studies; actions taken by agents consciously trying to form opinion on an issue must also be included. We need not expect specialists unanimously to agree on all actions to be included. It seems reasonable, however, to expect that substantial agreement would be reached if an explicit, systematic, sustained attempt were made to identify the "main actions" agents took to form opinion on an issue.

Based upon a survey of the relevant secondary literature, I am confident that specialists on Texas Annexation would unanimously agree that its narrative framework should include, for example, the following actions: Senator Robert J. Walker's "immediate annexation" letter, published on February 3, 1844; Henry Clay's "anti–immediate annexation" letter, published on April 27, 1844; Martin Van Buren's "anti–immediate annexation" letter, also published on April 27, 1844; the Democratic national convention's nomination of Polk for President on an "immediate annexation" platform, May 29, 1844. In similar fashion, it seems reasonable to suggest, agreement could be reached to include many other "main actions" between 1819 and 1845.

Given the proverbially disputatious temperament of historians and the nature of the problem, some disagreements undoubtedly would persist on whether specific actions should be included in the narrative framework for a specific issue. But no need exists to belabor the point that such disagreements do not alter the basic argument made here, and that a variety of means could be used to handle the problem of what might be called "marginal actions." In general, if disagreement continued after direct and conscious confrontation of specialists, I would favor including "marginal" actions on the ground that an overly inclusive framework is preferable to an overly restrictive framework.

c. Events that change the historical situation. In relative terms, specialists trying to construct a common narrative framework for a specific issue would probably find it most difficult to agree on the type of event included in this category. Again it seems reasonable, however, to expect substantial agreement if attention is explicitly focused on the problem of deciding which events should be included and the grounds for inclusion (or exclusion) are made explicit.

For example, in respect to Texas Annexation, I think agreement could be secured among specialists that the narrative framework for the issue ought to include the 1835-1836 Congressional conflict over antislavery petitions and President Tyler's break with the Whig Party in August 1841. Neither set of events originated as conscious actions taken to influence public opinion on Texas Annexation. But those events significantly contributed to changes in the historical situation that made it both necessary and possible for agents favorable to, and opposed to, Texas Annexation to take certain actions consciously designed to influence public opinion—actions that probably would *not* have been taken if the events specified had not occurred. Moreover, without now attempting to support the claim, I think it could be shown that the distribution of public opinion on Texas Annexation differed significantly before and after each set of events cited above.

In short, the argument here is that a narrative framework designed to facilitate systematic reconstruction and explanation of opinion distribution and formation should not be restricted to government decisions and agents' conscious actions. It should also include events that, in effect, conditioned "the climate of opinion" by producing changes in the historical situation relevant to specific issues.

V. OPERATIONS TO MEASURE THE DISTRIBUTION OF OPINION

According to the research strategy advocated here, after constructing a narrative framework relevant to some specified issue(s), researchers proceed to perform operations designed to secure, in sequence, the data called for by the three main categories of the classification system. Although my own work has not progressed to the point where I can try to deal systematically with all three categories, it seems useful to make a start on the operational problems they pose by restricting attention to the first category and trying to codify, on a fairly primitive level, the procedures historians have used to find out the distribution of opinion. The discussion that follows is based on an analysis of the historical literature specifically dealing with the Civil War but it holds, I believe, for American historiography in general.[34]

A definite pattern can be detected in the procedures historians have intuitively and implicitly developed to study the distribution of opinion relevant to the coming of the Civil War. In general terms, they have acted on the assumption that information about the distribution of opinion *can reasonably be inferred* from data found in contemporary documents not originally designed for that purpose. Put another way, historians have extracted related "facts" from a wide variety of sources and grouped them together to form *indicators* of public opinion.

[34] Part of this study was reported in Lee Benson and Thomas J. Pressly, "Can Differences in Interpretations of the Causes of the American Civil War Be Resolved Objectively?" New York, Columbia University, Bureau of Applied Social Research, 1956, pp. 43-63, mimeographed.

For example, newspaper editorials dealing with a proposed law are frequently taken to reflect some aspect of public opinion regarding it, and historians use those editorials to buttress or justify their claims about public opinion. Instead of relying on a single indicator, however, historians have tended to combine several of them to form an index. Thus, if editorials are used as one indicator, the public speeches or private views of influential or "representative" men might be a second, mass meetings on the issue a third, and so on. Many different indicators have been devised and an even larger number of different indexes constructed. But the pattern invariably has been the same: (1) attempts are made to establish certain facts from source materials; (2) certain *inferences* are then drawn from those facts about the distribution of public opinion.

If some contemporary researchers believe that personal interviews are the only means by which reliable and valid information can be secured about public opinion, they would be impressed, perhaps appalled, by the astonishing variety of sources historians have ransacked in their search for opinion indicators. Unfortunately, the ingenuity displayed by historians in creating such indicators is matched by their casualness and reticence concerning their procedures. Only rarely does one find an explicit statement of the logical considerations dictating the choice of sources or justifying the inferences drawn from the factual data.

Such an individualistic, spontaneous approach to the creation and use of indicators might suggest that historians follow no rules in trying to reconstruct the distribution of public opinion on an issue. At first sight, the motto appears to be "anyone can play." Closer examination reveals that "historical opinion indicators" can be arranged into three distinct types and that some unarticulated, but loosely understood, rules govern their creation and use. The incomplete, tentative, and compressed classification system sketched below is designed to be suggestive, not exhaustive. Its purpose is simply to identify the main types of indicators created by American historians; no attempt will be made to discuss the considerations governing their formation and use. But one general point can be stressed. *Indicators are made, not found.* That is, a fact (or set of facts) extracted from historical documents does not constitute an indicator of public opinion. *It becomes an indicator only when an inference is drawn from it.* Granted this point, it will be unnecessary to distinguish hereafter between an indicator and the documents from which it is created.[35]

[35] In the classification scheme presented here, an effort has been made to demonstrate that distinctions can be drawn not only between types of indicators, but between the same indicators when different kinds of sources are used. As a result,

A. Types of Historical Opinion Indicators and Rules to Use Them

I. Actions or events
  A. Official government actions
    1. Legislative
      a. Laws
      b. Resolutions
      c. Etc.
    2. Executive
      a. Actions on legislation
      b. Recommendations in prescribed or customary addresses
      c. Etc.
    3. Judicial
      a. Formal decisions
      b. Charges to juries
      c. Etc.
    4. Etc.
  B. Official actions, nongovernmental institutions
    1. Resolutions or platforms adopted
    2. Literature published
    3. Etc.
  C. Individual, customary, or prescribed actions
    1. Voting at elections for public office
    2. Voting at elections for private office
    3. Etc.
  D. Individual, spontaneous, nonprescribed actions
    1. Demostrations or riots not planned by existing organizations
    2. Acts of violence against officials
    3. Etc.
  E. Etc.
II. Expert estimates of the distribution of public opinion
  A. Official estimates made in performance of duty
    1. Government officials in reports
    2. Nongovernment officials in reports to their organizations
    3. Etc.
  B. Estimates made for, or published in, mass media
    1. Newspaper surveys (as distinct from editorial expressions of opinion)
    2. Expert estimates reported in mass media
    3. Etc.
  C. Private estimates of knowledgeable individuals
    1. Politicians or "unbiased" observers
    2. Foreign travelers or visiting experts
    3. Etc.
  D. Etc.

---

the compressed classification scheme is not presented uniformly. In dealing with the problem of devising historical opinion indicators, I have benefited heavily from two articles by Paul F. Lazarsfeld and Allen H. Barton: "Qualitative Measurement in the Social Sciences: Classification, Typologies, and Indices," in Daniel Lerner and Harold D. Lasswell, eds. *The Policy Sciences,* Stanford, Calif., Stanford University Press, 1951, pp. 155-192, and Barton and Lazarsfeld, *op. cit.,* pp. 321-361.

III. Expressions of opinion (oral or written in origin)
  A. Influential men
    1. Private opinions (letters, diaries, etc.)
    2. Public opinions (speeches, publications, etc.)
  B. Representative men (merchants, farmers, workers, etc.)
    1. Private opinion (letters, diaries, etc.)
    2. Public opinions (petitions, letters to editors, etc.)
  C. Sensitive men (writers, artists, intellectuals, etc.)
    1. Private opinion (letters, diaries, etc.)
    2. Public opinions ("works of art," books, articles, etc.)
  D. Mass media
    1. Influential media (prestige papers, large circulation papers, etc.)
      a. Newspaper editorials
      b. Magazine editorials
      c. Etc.
    2. Representative media (class, section, ethnic group, etc.)
      a. Newspaper editorials
      b. Magazine editorials
      c. Etc.
  E. Etc.

One example may be enough to support the assertion that some informal rules govern historians engaged in studying the distribution of public opinion. Suppose the issue is repeal of the Fugitive Slave Act after 1850. Suppose the assumption is granted that newspaper editorials can be analyzed in such a way as to form a "good" indicator of opinion, i.e. that the opinions expressed in specific newspaper editorials varied as the opinions of specific groups varied. Let us further suppose that a historian relied heavily on newspaper editorials as an indicator of the distribution of "Northern" public opinion. Finally, let us suppose that the newspapers used consisted exclusively of the *New York Tribune* ("rabidly antislavery"), the *Liberator* (William Lloyd Garrison's abolitionist paper), and several semi-official organs of the Free Soil Party. Clearly, the indicator created could not be a *valid* one. At best, it did not measure "Northern" public opinion but only an extremely unrepresentative segment of it.

Though no explicit standard operating procedures have been agreed upon by historians, it is *taken for granted* that a representative, weighted sample of extant newspaper files should be used in creating an indicator.[36] And it would be possible to cite other informal "rules" that historians are supposed to observe while using newspaper editorials to construct an opinion indicator. In fact, those "rules" are so much taken for granted that they are sometimes ignored and

[36] Some interesting but general comments on newspaper editorials and public opinion are found in Lucy M. Salmon, *The Newspaper and the Historian,* New York, 1923, pp. 252-253, 270-286, 439-440, 470-471.

violated by historians who probably would subscribe to them in theory.

This last observation enables us to answer, in general terms, the basic question posed by this section of the essay. A logical way for historians to try to reconstruct the distribution of public opinion is to do systematically, explicitly, and precisely what has tended to be done impressionistically, implicitly, and vaguely. For there can be little doubt that even impressionistic methods have enabled historians to secure a great deal of information about the distribution of opinion over time and place.[37] The assumption seems logical, therefore, that an attack upon the problems that historians encounter in systematically creating and using opinion indicators is at least likely to yield modest returns. Couched in such general terms this answer does not get us very far, but it leads to consideration of other questions that may.

The methodological problems historians face in trying to reconstruct the distribution of public opinion can be identified broadly as follows: (1) What indicators are most appropriate for a particular study? (2) Given a number of appropriate indicators, how can they be combined in one index that maximizes their individual advantages and minimizes their disadvantages? (3) How does one actually go about creating and using opinion indicators and indexes? (4) What sampling principles can be devised to govern the selection of documents from which data can be extracted to form an indicator? A few general observations relevant to the first problem will be offered below; the other three are best treated specifically in relation to substantive events and will be dealt with in a future book, tentatively titled "New York Public Opinion and American Civil War Causation."

B. Choosing the "Best Indicator" for a Study

Under ideal conditions historians might use all the indicators in the classification system sketched in the preceding section. If the requisite source materials were available, and if enough time and effort could be given to the task, every indicator probably would yield *some* information about public opinion. But since conditions never are ideal, historians always must choose among possible indicators. In effect, they must decide upon a hierarchical rank order of

[37] See the discussion in Henry David, "Opinion Research in the Service of the Historian," in Komarovsky, ed., *op. cit.*, pp. 270-271. But, in my opinion, that commentary exaggerates the methodological differences between historians and contemporary researchers engaged in studying public opinion. In this connection, see the two articles by Lazarsfeld and Barton cited in note 35.

"best indicators" for the particular aspects of public opinion that concern them. An example might make the point more clearly than an abstract definition.

His terminology was different but James Bryce was essentially dealing with the problem of "best indicator" when he posed the question, "How is the drift of Public Opinion to be ascertained?" After analyzing the advantages and disadvantages of several different indicators, Bryce concluded, in his famous chapter on "Public Opinion":

> The best way in which the tendencies at work in any community can be discovered and estimated is by moving freely about among all sorts and conditions of men and noting how they are affected by the news or the arguments brought from day to day to their knowledge. In every neighborhood there are unbiased persons with good opportunities for observing, and plenty of skill in "sizing up" the attitudes and proclivities of their fellow citizens. Such men are invaluable guides. Talk is the best way of reaching the truth, because in talk one gets directly at the facts, whereas reading gives not so much the facts as what the writer believes, or wishes to have others believe. Whoever, having himself a considerable experience of politics, takes the trouble to investigate in this way will seldom go astray. There is a *flair* which long practice and "sympathetic touch" bestow. The trained observer learns how to profit by small indications, as an old seaman discerns, sooner than the landsman, the signs of coming storm.[38]

Translated into our terms, Bryce designates as the best indicator of opinion distribution some version of "private estimates of knowledgeable individuals." And examination of the literature dealing with causes of the Civil War demonstrates that historians have viewed private estimates of knowledgeable individuals as a good indicator of opinion. But the literature also demonstrates that historians have relied much more heavily upon an indicator that Bryce and other theorists tend to deprecate—voting for public office.[39] The literature, in fact, demonstrates that historians have depended much more heavily on voting than upon any other indicator for evidence to "prove" their claims about the distribution of public opinion in the pre-war period. To anyone familiar with the ruggedly individualistic traditions of American historiography, this similarity in research design appears highly suggestive. Together with other considerations, it tends to support the following conclusion: Given the American political system and the actual course of events, *as a general rule,*

[38] Bryce, *op cit.*, Vol. 1, pp. 155-160. The quotation is from p. 156.

[39] The reader can test the statement's accuracy by picking up at random works dealing with the coming of the Civil War and examining them in the light of this analysis. In addition to Bryce's criticisms of voting as an opinion indicator, see Lowell, *op. cit.*, pp. 24-25, 70-128; Walter Lippman, *Public Opinion*, New York, 1922, pp. 193-197.

voting for public office provides the single best indicator of public opinion.

1. Advantages of voting behavior as an observable indicator of opinion distribution. An objection to this line of reasoning is immediately apparent. Because historians have taken voting to be the best indicator of opinion, it does not necessarily follow that they are correct. Consensus is not the only criterion of validity and reliability. But in this case consensus has resulted from the independent and continuous efforts of historians to reconstruct the distribution of opinion rather than from routine adherence to standard procedures. Unless convincing arguments to the contrary are presented, their collective experience supports the proposition that voting is the historian's best indicator of American opinion distribution.

"But," critics may immediately reply, "haven't leading theorists— Bryce, Lowell, Lippmann—presented just such convincing arguments, and don't they apply to the pre–Civil War period in the United States, as well as to other times and places?"[40]

Without analyzing the arguments of these men in detail, four points can be made in rebuttal. In the first place, they were not writing about historical studies and their judgments cannot be applied mechanically to historical source materials. Second, some of their criticisms demonstrate only that voting is not a perfect indicator, not that other indicators are relatively better. Third, to some extent their criticisms derive from moral judgments as to *what public opinion should be and how it should be formed;* such judgments are not applicable to the study of public opinion as defined here. Finally, their most telling points are directed against faulty and impressionistic use of election results as an opinion indicator, not against the potential value of voting records studied systematically.

That American voting behavior has been imperfectly studied as an indicator of opinion is readily conceded, and the present essay partially stems from a long-range, continuing research project which attempts to document that conclusion in detail. But the project has also led to the conclusion that systematic procedures can be devised to increase the value of voting records as an opinion indicator. In works already published, I have tried to support the conclusion in practice; here the aim is to suggest some general advantages they offer compared to other opinion indicators.[41]

---

[40] *Op. cit.*

[41] The project was partially reported in Benson, "Research Problems," in Komarovsky, ed., *op. cit.*, pp. 113-181. A substantive demonstration of how voting behavior can be systematically used to reconstruct opinion distribution on an issue is presented in Benson, *Concept of Jacksonian Democracy*, pp. 254-269. But the major

Voting records have at least one unique advantage; they are the only documents left by the American public from which inferences can *directly* be drawn about mass opinions concerning public policies. All other documents from which indicators can be created require making two different types of inferences. Like voting records, other historical documents require drawing an inference from them about the distribution of opinion. But other documents require the additional inference that they actually reflect the views of the public *en masse,* not merely the views of the men responsible for the particular documents *selected* by historians as sources of opinion data.[42]

For example, when used as an indicator, newspaper editorials are assumed to reflect the opinions of "publics" that actually had no part in their composition or publication. The serious problems that arise in connection with that type of inference need little comment except to note that the problems would exist even if all relevant newspaper files were extant, equally accessible, and good sampling methods were used. But the hard job of finding out whose opinions are reflected in editorials—the publisher, the editor, the readers, the public in general—is complicated by the fact that extant files frequently are not a representative or adequate sample of the newspapers published at a given time and place. It seems to be a law of history that the party which ultimately dominates a particular area gets its papers preserved more frequently, and in more accessible places, than the losing party. In contrast, both the winners and the losers—even the very minor parties—secure immortality (sic) in the voting records. The argument here is that voting records usually are more complete, detailed, and precise, and *comparatively* more easily worked, than the materials from which any other indicator can be formed—and that those advantages will increase enormously when a major project now well under way is completed.[43]

"demonstration" belongs to that familiar category of scholarship known as "research in progress." According to present plans, it will be reported in a book jointly written with Professor Joel Silbey, tentatively titled, "New York Public Opinion and American Civil War Causation: An Essay in the Logic and Practice of Historical Explanation."

[42] In a somewhat different context and formulation, the same point has been strongly emphasized by the Social Science Research Council's Committee on Historiography. See Thomas C. Cochran, "Methods: Theory and Practice," in *Bulletin 64, The Social Sciences in Historical Study*, New York, Social Science Research Council, 1954, pp. 158-164.

[43] Thanks to the joint efforts of the Inter-university Consortium for Political Research and the American Historical Association's Committee to Collect the Quantitative Data of History, the county voting and relevant demographic statistics from 1824 to date will be available in machine-readable form in the near future. When that day arrives, and when historians have acquired the methodological training needed to make good use of those data, I predict that major advances will be made in the use of voting behavior as an opinion indicator.

An analogy may suggest the serious disadvantages of other historical opinion indicators compared with those based upon voting for public office. Suppose contemporary researchers wish to reconstruct the distribution of public opinion on given issues. They first have to draw up a representative sample of the public. Failure to meet that requirement would open the study to serious criticism and probably invalidate it. Having drawn up their sample, they try to interview all its members. Some *reasonable* degree of incompleteness is not fatal; the operative word is "reasonable." But if the sample design was poorly drawn, or if the design was poorly executed, the study's findings would be given little credence.

Now let us suppose that contemporary researchers were forced to draw their sample of people to be interviewed from the same "elite" groups whose records constitute the historian's sources. (On any social level, the records of unusual or atypical individuals are the only ones available to historians.) And let us further suppose that interviews could be secured only with a small, unrepresentative fraction of the original sample. Under those conditions, historians undoubtedly would view contemporary findings about public opinion with even greater skepticism than they do at present. Yet those are the conditions under which historians ordinarily work when they use opinion indicators other than voting behavior. That historians have been able to obtain useful information by using such indicators testifies only to their ingenuity in overcoming difficulties and to the insights gained from "saturation" in source materials.

The difficulties suggested above apply most strongly to the type of indicator classified as "Expressions of opinion," but they are also encountered in using "Expert estimates." Bryce claimed that a talk with experts was the "best way" to learn the drift of opinion, but he was careful to emphasize the necessity of "moving freely about among all sorts and conditions of men. . . ." Historians do not have that freedom. Except in rare cases, the highly unrepresentative nature of "surviving" historical documents prevents historians from following Bryce's research design.[44]

For any period, the expert estimates available to historians were made by men who cannot be viewed as representative of all groups comprising the "American public." Historians have learned enough about their own "frames of reference," and other scholars enough

[44] Historians may occasionally unearth a fairly complete file of documents written by government officials charged with the responsibility of reporting the distribution of public opinion. That excellent public opinion indicators can be created from such documents is demonstrated in Lynn M. Case, *French Opinion on War and Diplomacy during the Second Empire*, Philadelphia, University of Pennsylvania Press, 1954.

about the "sociology of knowledge," to recognize that the truly "unbiased observer" is an extremely rare bird. When expert estimates are contradictory, as they frequently are, the differences tend to be closely associated with the different group characteristics of the men making the estimates.

Unless logical or factual flaws can be demonstrated in one set of conflicting estimates, the only way to decide between them is to check them all against other opinion indicators. But if those indicators also simply represent expressions of opinion, we run into the same problem of establishing their representative quality. In practice, historians implicitly try to find some act or event against which conflicting expert estimates can be checked. But this is a circular procedure, for it first must be established that the acts or events really do indicate something specific about public opinion. Carefully staged and costly "spontaneous demonstrations," for example, have been known to occur in places other than opera houses. Thus, *whenever possible*, it seems more logical to start with acts or events as indicators of public opinion, and to use "expert estimates" and "expressions of opinion" to supplement them. Additional arguments can be offered to support this line of reasoning.

2. *Action the best test of opinion.* Attention has been directed thus far to the advantages voting data have in respect to the representative quality of documents from which inferences can be drawn about past opinion. But such data also have advantages in respect to the validity of the inferences about public opinion that can reasonably be drawn from any document.

In the classification scheme outlined above in section V.A., it will be recalled, voting for public office is designated as an "Action or events" type of indicator. Simply on the face of it, the claim seems reasonable that, other things being equal, men's actions are better *tests* of their opinions than verbal or written expressions and better *measures* of opinion than expert estimates.[45] The key phrase is, of course, "other things being equal."

Things never are exactly equal. Judgments must always be made about the degree of inequality that permits meaningful comparisons, and borderline cases inevitably produce differences in judgment. But substantial agreement is not always difficult to achieve. If life, fortune, or liberty had to be risked to "express" an opinion through a public act such as voting or signing a petition, and a "private" written or

[45] See, in this connection, Strayer, *op. cit.,* pp. 264-265. But I have somewhat changed Strayer's emphasis upon action as a test of opinion and tried to suggest the conditions under which the assumption is likely to hold.

verbal expression of opinion posed no such risk, hardly anyone would dispute the claim that things were not equal. When such dangers are not attached to public acts, however, things frequently are equal *enough* to warrant the claim that action is a better test of opinion than written or verbal expression. Moreover, if acts do entail much heavier risks *and men do act,* more valid inferences can be drawn about the *saliency* and *intensity* of their opinions from their acts than from their verbal or written expressions.

Recognizing that many exceptions to the rule exist, and that it can never be automatically assumed to hold, the claim seems warranted that in American history the act of voting is the best single *test* of opinion. Under the American political system, even with nonsecret ballots, voting *ordinarily* does not entail a heavy risk, nor are extremely heavy external pressures (governmental or social) brought to bear upon men to vote a given ticket. Some social pressures undoubtedly are brought to bear upon voters almost everywhere and at all times; but those pressures usually do not prevent some reasonable degree of "free choice." Moreover, the fact that Americans are not completely free agents in their political behavior increases rather than decreases the value of voting as a test of opinion.

To change allegiance after long attachment to one party usually forces a voter to overcome considerable social pressures. Such pressures are especially heavy when voters change to a new party, or to a minor party challenging the *status quo* (however defined). Pronounced changes in an area's voting patterns, therefore, usually are excellent clues to the saliency and intensity of opinion and indicate that "something is up." But long periods of stability are also revealing, for they suggest the absence of intense discontent.

Skeptics may not be convinced that the American people exercise their theoretical power to control government actions; only uninformed cynics fail to recognize that they attach great importance to it. In theory, at least, the American political system is dominated by the voting process. The political realities may not strongly resemble the theory, but being a "good citizen" to an American means that *he is supposed to make his opinion count.* That supposition is so basic to the democratic ideology that not having the right to vote condemns one to inferior social status.

For the vast majority of Americans, it can be assumed, voting has been the only direct means used to make opinions count. Whether their opinions were worth counting, or whether they made them count for much, are irrelevant for our present purposes. What is relevant is that the record of American history convincingly demonstrates that the masses occasionally have exercised considerable control over government actions. Even the Supreme Court, the irreverent Mr. Dooley observed, follows the election returns.

Unlike verbal or written expressions of opinions or expert estimates, voting produces some direct consequences that can be credibly reconstructed, even if the consequences are only to continue the same administration in power by the same majority. Government officials may not want to heed public opinion. They are acutely aware, however, that it *can* make itself felt through the voting process. Failure to win newspaper approval, for example, need not affect an administration's actions; failure to win voters' approval on election day inevitably affects the administration's power to act. The direct link between voting and government action is summed up in the aphorism, "Before you can be a statesman, you gotta get elected—and re-elected."

Because voting for public office directly indicates the opinions of the masses, and because it has direct consequences that can be traced, we can say that American historians have acted reasonably in implicitly treating it as the single best indicator of public opinion in the pre–Civil War period. But the discussion cannot end here. In effect, historians have agreed that the act of voting is the best *test* of opinion but they have sharply disagreed about the opinions *indicated* by the election returns. This observation might lead to the paradoxical conclusion that although voting is the best test of opinion, Bryce and others are right that it is not a good indicator of opinion. That conclusion, however, does not necessarily follow.

Like all sensitive instruments, to produce accurate results opinion indicators formed from voting records must be carefully constructed and skillfully used. Disagreement among historians and contemporaries over the "meaning" of an election outcome only underscores the central propositions of this section: (1) opinion indicators are made, not found; (2) systematic procedures have to be developed to obtain reasonably accurate results from them. In short, voting records cannot be studied casually and impressionistically, for they do not automatically yield correct inferences about the distribution of opinion on specific issues. But a marked difference exists between using the results of one election as the basis of inferences about public opinion and using the entire range of voting behavior displayed in a number of successive elections. In other words, contradictory answers can be given to two questions which frequently are treated as the same but which are essentially different. What can be learned about the distribution of opinion on given issues from an election outcome? Frequently, very little or nothing. What can be learned from *the entire range of voting behavior in a number of elections?* If the data are studied systematically, almost invariably a good deal can be learned about the distribution of opinion and, under certain conditions, a great deal.[46]

It would only belabor the point to show in detail that similar observations can be made about all other types of documents used as sources of data to construct indicators of opinion distribution. The point is that they yield remarkably different results depending upon whether systematic or impressionistic procedures are used.

The basic argument can now be stated: To practice scientific method and develop good indicators of opinion distribution, historians must consciously and systematically tackle the hard job of developing valid and reliable procedures to "generate" specific types of data from specific types of documents. In similar fashion, historians must tackle the even harder job of developing principles, in Nagel's words, "tried canons," that permit them reasonably to judge the validity of inferences drawn from the data generated.

This essay can appropriately end with a restatement of its basic argument: Historians have not yet scientifically studied past public opinion, not because it is impossible to do so, but because they have not yet tried to do so. The approach sketched here, I trust, at least focuses attention upon the problem and suggests a specific course of action that might ultimately lead to its solution or, more precisely, might stimulate other researchers to propose courses of action that might ultimately lead to its solution.

[46] I have tried to demonstrate that argument concretely in my *Concept of Jacksonian Democracy*, pp. 254-269, and *passim*. The tendency of historians to focus attention upon election results rather than upon voting behavior patterns is cogently treated in Robert T. Bower, "Opinion Research and Historical Interpretation of Elections," *Public Opinion Quarterly*, Vol. 12, 1948, pp. 457-458. In this connection, see the incisive critique of historians' use of congressional voting as an indicator of public opinion in Joel Silbey, "The Civil War Synthesis in American Political History," *Civil War History*, Vol. 10, June 1964, pp. 130-140. And for an incisive critique of historians' use of legislative resolutions, as well as a demonstration of how they can systematically be used as an indicator of public opinion, see an unpublished masters' thesis written under my direction by Madeleine S. Shapiro, "Michigan Public Opinion, the Mexican War, and the Wilmot Proviso: A Study of Legislative Resolutions as Opinion Indicators," Detroit, Wayne State University, 1964.

political theory of democracy, all of them are mentioned in one or another theory.

There appear to be two requirements in democratic theory which refer primarily to characteristics demanded of the electorate as it initially comes to make a political decision. These are the preconditions for electorate decisions.

The first is the possession of a suitable *personality structure*: within a range of variations, the electorate is required to possess the types of character which can operate effectively, if not efficiently, in a free society. Certain kinds of personality structures are not congenial to a democratic society, could not operate successfully within it, and would be destructive of democratic values. Others are more compatible with or even disposed toward the effective performance of the various roles which make up the democratic political system. Among the characteristics required—and this is not intended as anything more than an illustrative list—are a capacity for involvement in situations remote from one's face-to-face experience; a capacity to accept moral responsibility for choices; a capacity to accept frustration in political affairs with equanimity; self-control and self-restraint as reins upon the gross operation of self-interest; a nice balance between submissiveness and assertiveness; a reasonable amount of freedom from anxiety so that political affairs can be attended to; a healthy and critical attitude toward authority; a capacity for fairly broad and comprehensive identifications; a fairly good measure of self-esteem; and a sense of potency.

The distribution of such personality characteristics in the population, let alone their relationship to political behavior, is not known. What is more or less known is only a beginning of the problem. We know, for example, that contrary to common belief the incidence of psychosis has not increased in this country over the past century (Goldhamer and Marshall); on this score, at least, we are not less capable than past generations of governing ourselves. We know that the authoritarian personality is associated with social prejudice and restrictive politics (the Berkeley study of Adorno, Frenkel-Brunswick, *et al.*); that neuroticism limits attention to political matters (Elmira study); that a wide discrepancy between aspiration and achievement leads some persons to over-aggressive acts against the political environment and lowers their respect for political leaders (Bettelheim and Janowitz); that the "democratic character" is more flexible and adaptable than the authoritarian character (Lewin and Lippitt).

There is a great deal of work to be done on this problem; and it is here particularly that the psychologists can make an important contribution to the study of political behavior. The influence of character on political democracy has been perceived in general terms by a number of theorists, and some psychologists and sociologists have begun to work on the topic. The dependence of democratic processes upon the "democratic character" seems clear in general, but the nature of this relationship has been only slightly documented in the literature. Without doubt, a sympathetic and imaginative study of the literature of democratic theory will generate many important hypotheses for empirical investigation.

The second requirement is not only a prerequisite but also an outcome of electorate decisions. This is the factor of *interest and participation*;[1] the electorate is required to possess a certain degree of involvement in the process of political decision, to take an appropriate share of responsibility. Political democracy requires a fairly strong and fairly continuous level of interest from a minority, and from a larger body of the citizenry a moderate-to-mild and discontinuous interest but with a stable readiness to respond in critical political situations. Political disinterest or apathy is not permitted, or at least not approved.

Here the descriptive documentation provided by opinion studies is relatively good. The amount of political interest in the community, its fluctuations through time, its incidence among various population groups, its causes and its consequences—on all these topics we have reasonably systematic data. Less than one-third of the electorate is "really interested" in politics, and that group is by no means a cross-section of the total electorate. The more interested people are more likely to affect others and thus to exercise a greater influence upon the outcome of elections. The decreasing political interest in the population, viewed with alarm by some people who are distressed by the fact that a smaller proportion of eligible people vote now than did fifty years ago,

[1] Included here is acceptance of the political sphere as one of the legitimate elements of social life. In a democratic society the political sphere must not be widely viewed as unclean or degraded or corrupt. Opinion studies have produced some data on the image of politics and of politicians among the citizenry.

is to some extent due to the increasing feeling people have that they are impotent to affect political matters in the face of the complexity and magnitude of the issues. Participation in the actual election is not only segmental but also partial; if everybody eligible to vote actually did vote, the distribution of support in recent national elections would have been measurably different. Finally, interest is not a simple unidimensional factor. A recent analysis identified three kinds of interest: spectator interest (regarding the campaign as a dramatic spectacle); citizen interest (deciding how to vote); and partisan interest (securing the election of one's own candidate). Of these, only the second is "pure" interest according to some theorists.

The major question raised by this requirement, both for political theory and for opinion research, is the fundamental one of its universality and intensity. People have always argued whether the vote is a duty or a privilege, and there have always been advocates of an unlimited and continuous requirement of interest. As early as the Athenian democracy it was said that "we regard a man who takes no interest in public affairs not as a harmless but as a useless character." But is he really so useless to the operation of democracy? Some recent theorists and studies have suggested that a sizable group of less interested citizens is desirable as a "cushion" to absorb the intense action of highly motivated partisans. For the fact is that the highly interested are the most partisan and the least changeable. If everyone in the community were highly and continuously interested, the possibilities of compromise and of gradual solution of political problems might well be lessened to the point of danger. It is an historical axiom that democracy requires a middle class for its proper operation. Perhaps what it really requires is a body of moderately and discontinuously interested citizens within and across social classes, whose approval of or at least acquiescence in political policies must be secured.

THE COMPONENTS OF ELECTORATE DECISIONS

The political theory of democracy also makes requirements regarding the components of electorate decisions; that is, the content of the decision.

The first requirement of electorate decisions is the possession of *information and knowledge*; the electorate must be informed about the matters under consideration. Information refers to isolated facts and knowledge to general propositions; both of them provide reliable insight into the consequences of the decision. This is a requirement nearly everyone sets down for a democratic electorate; politicians and statesmen, adult educators, journalists, professors of political science—all of them pay deference to the need for "enlightened public opinion."

This is another factor on which opinion researchers have assembled a good deal of data. What do they show? One persistent conclusion is that the public is not particularly well informed about the specific issues of the day. A recent survey of the current status of American public opinion states that "tests of information invariably show at least twenty per cent of the public totally uninformed (and usually the figure is closer to forty per cent)." And at that, most of the studies have been based upon simple and isolated questions of fact (i.e., information) and only seldom, if at all, upon the historical and general propositions (i.e., knowledge) which underlie political decisions. Perhaps the proportion of the knowledgeable would be even lower than the proportion of the informed. At the same time, it must be recognized that there is a significant middle ground—a kind of vaguely perceived impression which reveals to the possessor certain relationships which are very "real" to him, which form "reasonable" bases for his decision, yet which cannot be explicitly articulated by him in any detail. An obvious example is the difference between the Republican and Democratic parties, a difference visible to many partisans of both.

Thus it often appears that people express opinions on issues when they seem to know very little about them. Lack of information may be a bar to the holding of an opinion in the minds of the theorists but it does not seem to be among the electorate (where, of course, it is not experienced as lack of information at all). In most campaigns, whether political or informational, the people best informed on the issue are the ones least likely to change their minds. Much of this represents attitudinal stability; some of it may represent rigidity.

Information and knowledge are required of the electorate on the assumption that they contribute to the wisdom of the decision; informed citizens make wiser decisions. In this country it is clear that the better-educated people are the best informed and most knowledgeable, yet it is also clear that other variables are involved in the development of wise decisions, e.g., flexibility of predispositions, a wide range of identifications, a low level of aggressiveness, etc. Finally, it appears from most studies that information and knowledge are sought and used more often as rationalization and reinforcer than as data to be used in making what might be called a free decision.

The requirement thus does not seem to be met in any direct way. But this is really an oversimplified statement of the requirement. How can an electorate be expected to be informed on the wide range of issues which confront the modern public? For example, the front page of *The New York Times* for one day alone recently contained stories on the following events, in each of which is embedded an issue on which the public might be expected to inform itself: price ceilings, the Korean war and the British position in it, the American defense build-up, Communist riots in France, the Berlin crisis, a new disarmament proposal, American military aid to France, official Soviet spies in this country, and the Mutual Security Aid Bill. Clearly there is too little time for simply getting the relevant information, let alone digesting it into a generalized system of political opinions. Actually the major decisions the ordinary citizen is called upon to make in a modern representative democracy involve basic simplifications which need not rest upon a wide range of information so long as they are based upon a certain amount of crucial information, reasonably interpreted. After all, the voter's effective choice is limited; he can vote Republican, he can vote Democratic, or he can refrain from voting, and becoming informed on a number of minor issues usually does not tip the scales against the weight of the few things that really matter—employment, social security, the cost of living, peace.

If the theoretical requirement is "full" information and knowledge, then democratic practice does not conform. But for some theorists the requirement is more differentiated than that. Representative government with large-scale political organization does not require that everyone be equally informed on everything all the time. To such a differentiated standard, actual practice may conform reasonably well. Opinion studies should not only document this requirement, but also refine their inquiries into the actual ways in which information and knowledge are held and used by the citizen in his vote decision. At the same time, theorists should differentiate and elaborate their conceptions of the intellectual requirements for a democratic citizenry.

The second component required of decisions is the possession of *principle*; the electorate is required to possess a body of stable political principle or moral standards, in contrast with fluctuating impulses or whims, to which topical questions can be referred for evaluation and decision.

Such principles are of two kinds. In the first place, there are the principles which refer to democratic procedures (as distinguished from the content of democratic decisions) and on them there must be consensus. Everyone, or nearly everyone, must agree on the rules of the political game and accept them in advance of the controversy so that they will obtain even in defeat. Among such principles are the rules that violence must not be involved in the making of electoral decisions; that the majority decision must be accepted as final in any particular instance, until legitimately appealed to a court, a legislative body, or the citizenry; that the citizen must have due respect for constituted authority; that the citizen must share respect with other parts of the community and thus be ready for political compromise. Few data on such questions have been collected in opinion studies, perhaps because their wide observance seems so obvious. It would be instructive to describe more precisely the citizenry's image of desirable and actual processes of democracy and to analyze the factors responsible for it.

The other kind of principle refers to the substantive bases of political decisions—the underlying moral or political ends in terms of which particular issues are determined at particular times. Just what they are for different parts of the population is difficult to say in the absence of more systematic research devoted to this purpose. At this time, however, it would seem at least likely that the *same* avowed principles underlie political positions at every point on the continuum from left to right. Full employment, a high standard of living, freedom, a better life for one's children, peace—these are the types of answers we have now, and we get them from persons of every political persuasion. Now this is not so empty as it sounds. Democratic theorists have pointed out what is often overlooked because too visible, namely, that an effective democracy must rest upon a body of political and moral consensus. If splits in the population are too sharp or too great, democratic processes cannot be maintained because of actual, threatened, or suspected conflict among partisans. In this circumstance, a seeming consensus which is accepted at its face value is far better than no consensus—and a seeming consensus is sometimes reflected in loyalty to the same symbols even though they carry different meanings. A sense of homogeneity is often an efficient substitute for the fact of homogeneity. Thus it is not an empty assertion to say that the role of substantive principles—like that of some information—is both to rationalize and to guide the choice simultaneously. Rationalization has a social function, too. What this means, then, is that the selection of means to reach agreed-upon ends is more likely to divide the electorate than the selection of the ends themselves.

At the same time, however, the principles must be applicable to current political life. Political decisions made today in the light of principles which support or oppose the major social reforms identified as the "New Deal" or the "welfare state" are relevant. But decisions made *simply* in conformity to an historical regional loyalty or to a primary group loyalty are of dubious relevance; and those made *only* in conformity to an ancestral loyalty or a religious loyalty are of no relevance at all. When theorists insist that public decisions in a democracy must be based upon principle and doctrine, they mean principle and doctrine which can confront and cope with the major problems of the age. Yet the studies show that a large proportion of the party vote today is by this test unprincipled.

If it is nothing more, then, the requirement of principle or doctrine means that the electorate must genuinely accept the procedures and rules involved in democratic processes, that it must at least share the symbols describing the substantive ends to which political action is directed and in terms of which it is justified, and that it must make political decisions on the basis of relevant standards. The first two requirements are met to a greater extent than the third.

THE PROCESS OF ELECTORATE DECISION

The third set of essentials in democratic theory refers to the process by which decisions are made. Here there seem to be three requirements.

The first of the requirement relates to the process of perception of which information and knowledge are the end products. This is the requirement of *accurate observation*; the electorate is required to perceive political realities clearly and objectively, with an absence or only a small amount of subjective distortion. It is difficult indeed to see life steadily and see it whole, and in politics clarity of perception is made doubly hard on the one hand by the predispositional strength which the citizen brings to the matter and, on the other, by the deliberate and in many cases inevitable ambiguity which the political leader brings there.

There is no need to labor this point. Walter Lippmann made a reputation for himself thirty years ago by elaborating the differences between the "world outside and the pictures in our heads." For the most part, he said, "we do not first see and then define, we define first and then see." Recent studies provide some documentation which refines this general observation. According to data from the Elmira study, not only is the citizen's image of the candidate and the campaign subject to the influence of preconception, but so is his view of group support for the candidates and even of the candidates' stand on political issues. Given just a minimum of ambiguity to work with—and that is usually available—people tend to think their candidate agrees with them, or at least they manage not to know where he stands on the particular issue when they stand on the other side. The stronger the party affiliation, the greater the misperception.

The consequences of such misperception are interesting to speculate about. It seems to decrease the tension within the individual since it enables him to bring his opinions into an internal consistency without disturbing his basic position. At the same time, it increases the internal solidarity of the parties and thus increases political tension within the community by seeming to sharpen the differences between the parties, particularly under the stress of a political campaign. Thus political perception is by no means simply a matter of concrete observation; it also involves protective coloration from a total position. And hence, that democratic theory which assumes clarity and objectivity of political perception must be qualified at the outset.

The second important requirement of democratic process is *communication and discussion*; the electorate is required to engage in discussion and communication on political affairs. Democratic decision-making requires free examination of political ideas, and this means discussion. Democratic citizens are supposed to listen to their political leaders arguing with one another, to listen to them when they speak directly to the electorate, to talk back to them, and to discuss among themselves the public issues of the day. According to many modern theorists, this requirement stands at the heart of the democratic process.

"Above all, if it is to be true to its own peculiar nature, democracy must enlist the effective thought of the whole community in the operation of discussion."

Now here again, as in the case of information, public opinion researchers have assembled a sizable body of data, not only on the amount and kind of communication and discussion within the community but also on the conditions under which it takes place. The overall picture presented by the opinion studies looks something like this: There is a 20 per cent nucleus of people who are active and regular political discussants, another group of 25 per cent who engage in political discussion on occasion, another 25 per cent who are activated into discussion only by dramatic political events, and a residual group of 25 or 30 per cent who do not engage in political discussion at all. Furthermore, it is particular groups within the community that give most attention to politics: the better-educated, the men, the "joiners"—in short, those groups most subject to social pressure translated into expectations of how "our kind of people" should behave in this respect. And the people who read and listen to political content in the mass media also talk and listen to other people, and thus the concentration of political communication and discussion is carried one step further.

To complete the picture we need to ask two other questions which together bring into consideration another aspect of this requirement. Democratic citizens are required not simply to discuss politics, but to discuss political alternatives in a genuine effort to clarify and refine public policy. The first question is, "Who talks to whom?", and the answer is that people mostly discuss politics with other people like themselves—"like" in such characteristics as social position, occupation, and attitude. Mainly this goes on inside the family, but even outside it there is a clear tendency for political discussions to be carried out intra- rather than inter-social groups. The second question is, "What do they see and hear and talk about?" The broad answer is, "What pleases them"; i.e., what is congenial to their own point of view. People usually read and listen to their own side. In person-to-person discussion of politics, about a third or more of the talk centers upon topics not directly involving political preferences—for example, predictions of and arguments about who will win an election—and the remainder consists overwhelmingly of exchange of mutually agreeable remarks. What this all means—and this is clearly documented—is that the people who do the most reading and listening and talking are the people who change their minds the least. Lowell did not say it first but he said it well: "To a great extent, people hear what they want to hear and see what they want to see. They associate by preference with people who think as they do, enter freely into conversation with them, and avoid with others topics that are controversial, irritating or unpleasant. This is not less true of what they read. To most people, that which runs counter to their ideas is disagreeable, and sought only from a sense of duty."

In summary, then, genuine political discussion—not acrimonious argumentation on the one hand or mutual admiration for right thinking on the other, but free and open discussion devoted to finding a solution to a problem through the clarification and modification of views—this is not marked by its magnitude. Perhaps it is naive to point this out once more; perhaps it is naive to require it in the first place. We cannot inquire here into what the requirement of discussion can really mean in a modern democracy; whether self-interested argument is improper, whether genuine discussion goes on a different level in the political process. But certainly democratic practice does not conform fully to the requirements of some theorists: "The person or party formulating political principles or policies in advance of discussion, and refusing to compromise under any circumstances; or settling such principles or policies before the process of discussion is completed and refusing to compromise further; renders discussion a farce in the first place, and in the second, limits its usefulness."

The third requirement under process is *rationality*; the electorate is required to exercise rational judgment in political decisions.

Philosophers and economists still talk professionally about "rational behavior," but sociologists never really used the concept, psychologists have given it up, and political scientists seem to be in process of doing so. The problem of giving the term a clear meaning acceptable to others is partly responsible for this state of affairs. The term, says a recent writer on rational conduct, "has enjoyed a long history which has bequeathed to it a legacy of ambiguity and confusion. . . . Any man may be excused when he is puzzled by the question how he ought to use the word and in particular how he ought to use it in relation to human conduct and to politics."

The difficulty, of course, is not that there is no reasonably clear definition for the term but that there are several definitions describing several different kinds of rationality. And the conformity of democratic practice varies with each definition. Let us review a few major meanings and their relationship to democratic practice. In the first place, we may distinguish between the rational decision as outcome and the rational decision as process. In the former case we speak of rationality as equivalent to a "right" decision. This assumes that there is one right answer to every problem, and that the power of reason can arrive at truths of policy which should be evident to all—all, that is, except those ruled by prejudice or emotion. When this is not simply a euphemism for describing decisions of which we approve, it presumably refers to a decision taken in conformity with an estimate of desirable ends (it thus assumes a valid analysis of whose interest lies where) and also in conformity with a correct estimate of which means will achieve the given ends. If we leave determination of self-interest up to the individual involved, then virtually all electorate decisions are rational by this definition; if we leave it up to the "objective observer" then the proportion will vary arbitrarily with his estimate of the present situation and the future. Even in philosophy, this meaning appears to be so ambiguous that it is difficult to see how we can design empirical research to test the extent of its observance by the electorate.

If we take rationality as referring to the process of decision—a more likely definition—then various possibilities are available. One meaning requires a certain independence of the rational process from the influence of predispositions broadly defined. Here rationality becomes the "free decision"—free from coercive imposition; free from blinding institutional loyalties; free from personal position (such as class or race); free from passions and impulses; free, in short, from any distorting or distracting pressures which prevent clear observation and calm, sober reflection. Here the term refers to logical, syllogistic ratiocination. But this seems to be an impractical, untenable, undesirable, and quite unreasonable definition; it takes the content heart out of politics and leaves the voter with no real basis on which to evaluate political proposals. By this standard, at least in its extreme version, there are almost no rational voters. As a social philosopher says, "individuals who on their own initiative form or change their fundamental beliefs through genuine critical reflection are so rare that they may be classed as abnormal."

A second meaning of rationality is close to, if not identical with, our requirement of information and knowledge: the voter should be aware of the correct state of public affairs at the present and of the "reasonable" consequences of alternative proposals for action. By this definition someone who made up his political mind on the basis of ends for which there are no present means of attainment would be making a non-rational decision, and so would the person whose estimates of the present situation or of the future were wrong. Also by this meaning the voter should be capable of indicating some relevant grounds for his decision, and most voters can cite such grounds. Here we meet the difficult question of rationalization, as against rationality, but we can suggest a partial answer. Rationality is limited by the individual's incapacity to deal with the real world in all its complexity, so it must allow for the legitimacy of dealing with simplified models of reality. In politics, the voter may "really" decide on the basis of one or two issues which are dominant for him (for example, peace or the New Deal) and use other issues as reinforcing rationalizations (for example, the military background of a candidate or corruption in the Federal administration).

A third definition requires the presence of convincibility or open-mindedness in consideration of political issues. This does not require the citizen to change his mind but only to be genuinely open to a change of mind. Here the time involved seems crucial. If this means, for example, that the citizen should be open-minded between June and November of an election year, then probably fewer than half the electorate is rational, and very few indeed in the South and parts of New England. If it includes the four years of a presidential administration or the "natural history" of a major political issue, from birth in controversy to death in near-unanimity, then the figure would become quite higher. It is hard for the researcher to be more specific because of the difficulty of determining just when "genuine consideration," as against rationalization, goes on.

Still another meaning of rationality as process requires that the decision be made in a state of low psychic tension; that is, that the decision not be an emotional one but be marked by a certain amount of detachment and freedom from passion. This poses a nice democratic dilemma; the people most rational by this definition are the people least interested in the political process and least involved in its outcome.

The more interested people are the more emotional, in this sense, and the least detached; they are the ones who ascribe important consequences to the outcome of the decision and thus find enough psychic energy to be active about the matter. Here the rational voter is the independent voter, that is, the one without sufficient interest or investment in the election to get excited about it.

Still other meanings are available. There is the meaning in which rationality refers to the presence of deliberately directed behavior to consciously formulated purposes. Here again, almost all voters could qualify. There is the meaning in which rationality refers to a choice of behavior that is optimal in some sense, and this definition can be readily satisfied on the grounds of a subjective optimum if nothing more. There is the meaning in which a rational decision is a self-consistent decision. There are undoubtedly other meanings.

If it is not easy to say what is meant by a rational decision, it is somewhat easier to say what is not meant by it. A rational decision is not a capricious decision, or an impulsive one, or an unprincipled one, or a decision guided by custom or habit or tradition or sentiment alone. But the central problem is to relate the demand of rationality to the analysis of decision-making in terms of such sociopsychological concepts as the reference group; that is, to see the "rational decision" as imbedded in a social context which limits it at the same time that it gives it political meaning. While the types of rationality are not easy to define and while they are certainly never present in a pure or extreme form, they can be isolated empirically, clarified, and investigated as to their frequency, their functions, and their preconditions.

THE OUTCOME OF ELECTORATE DECISIONS

Finally, there is one basic requirement which might be included under the need for principle but which seems to deserve independent treatment in view of its central importance with reference to the outcome of the decision. This is the requirement of *community interest*; the electorate is supposed to come to political decisions on consideration of the common good rather than, or in addition to, self-interest.

In several formulations of democratic theory, the electorate is required to devote thought to what is good for the community as a whole instead of relying exclusively upon calculation of what is good for oneself or one's own group. The classical formulation comes from

John Stuart Mill: "In any political election . . . the voter is under an absolute moral obligation to consider the interests of the public, not his private advantage, and give his vote, to the best of his judgment, exactly as he would be bound to do if he were the sole voter, and the election depended upon him alone."

Now here again the problem of definition is a central one. How is the researcher to distinguish between honest conclusion and forced rationalization, as in the slogan, "What's good for me is good for the country"? How distinguish the "immediate and apparent interest" from the "ultimate and real interest"? Does self-interest refer only to the criterion of direct self-gain or to that of benefit to one's group or class, and over what period of time? Does community interest refer to agreement on procedures, or to an outside criterion (and if so, what), or to the residual decision after the various self-interests have balanced themselves out, or to genuine concern for other groups, or to restraint upon self-interest, or to deviation from the predominant vote of one's group? The more one looks into the matter, the more it appears that one man's self-interest is another man's community interest, and that many people sincerely identify the one with the other. Nor have the theorists overlooked this. "Men come easily to believe that arrangements agreeable to themselves are beneficial to others," said Dicey. "A man's interest gives a bias to his judgment far oftener than it corrupts his heart." And from Schumpeter: "To different individuals and groups the common good is bound to mean different things. This fact, hidden from the utilitarian by the narrowness of his outlook on the world of human valuations, will introduce rifts on questions of principle which cannot be reconciled by rational argument."

In a current study of opinion formation (the Elmira study), we concluded that it is more satisfactory to analyze this question in terms of the forces making for political cleavage and political consensus within the community. The health of a democratic order depends on achieving a nice balance between them: enough cleavage to stimulate debate and action, enough consensus to hold the society together even under strain. Political parties in a democracy should disagree—but not too much, too sharply, nor too fundamentally. The evidences of cleavage are clear to everyone. Cleavage along class and religious and regional lines in addition to direct attitudinal differences on basic issues of foreign and domestic policy—these are so familiar as to require no

602

elaboration. At the same time there are important evidences of consensus, of political cohesion, which deserve more attention than they usually get. In the first place, there is the basic fact that group memberships and identifications overlap political choices; sizable political minorities are found in various social groups and this provides a kind of glue to hold the community together. In addition, even at the height of a presidential campaign there are sizable attitudinal minorities within each party and each social group on political issues, and thus sizable attitudinal agreements across party and group lines. Such overlappings link various groups together and prevent their further estrangement. All of this means that democratic politics in this country is happily not total politics—a situation where politics is the single or central selector and rejector, where other social differences are drawn on top of political lines. Cross-pressures in political allegiances, based upon a pluralistic system of values, are thus highly important to the society.

So the question of self and community interest may best be seen as the question of cleavage and consensus. The multiplicity and the heterogeneity of identifications and associations in the great society develop an overlapping, pluralistic social organization which both sharpens and softens the impact and the consequences of political activity.

CONCLUSION

The political theory of democracy, then, requires that the electorate possess appropriate personality structures, that it be interested and participate in public affairs, that it be informed, that it be principled, that it correctly perceive political realities, that it engage in discussion, that it judge rationally, and that it consider the community interest.

Now this combination of requirements sets a high—an ideal—standard for the political process. And since this is a composite list, from a variety of sources, it is not necessarily a matter for disillusionment or even disappointment that the democratic electorate does not conform to every requirement in the full degree. There is always an appropriate observation from Lord Bryce:

"Orthodox political theory assumes that every citizen has, or ought to have, thought out for himself certain opinions, for example, ought to have a definite view, defensible by arguments, of what the country needs, what principles ought to be applied in governing it, of the men to whose hands the government ought to be entrusted. There are persons who talk, though certainly very few who act, as if they believed this theory, which may be compared to the theory of some ultra-Protestants that every good Christian has or ought to have, by the strength of his own reason, worked out for himself from the Bible a system of theology."

Opinion studies in recent years have done much to fill in the picture of what actually happens in democratic decision-making. As is evident even from this brief survey, they have done so in three ways: first, by documenting the theoretical assumptions with facts about actual political behavior; second, by clarifying the concepts and assumptions of democratic theory, if in no other way simply by insisting upon researchable formulations; and third, by differentiating and reformulating the general theoretical propositions in more exact terms. Further systematic exploration of this subject within a sharper, more valid, and more sophisticated framework of political theory should make a rich contribution to each side. The difficulties of collaboration between political theorists on the one hand and opinion researchers on the other must not be allowed to stand in the way of joint work, for the theorists can provide a systematic statement in terms of which public opinion studies can be meaningfully organized, and the empirical researchers can document the theoretical requirements. The theorists can suggest new concepts and hypotheses to the researcher, and the researcher can force the theorists to sharpen and differentiate—yes, and quantify—their formulations.

Of course there are problems but they should be negotiated or overcome. For example, the theorists tend to use descriptive categories (e.g., rationality) and the researchers prefer predictive categories (e.g., group memberships) in "explaining" political preferences. Hard and joint thinking on such problems should bring returns.

The investigation of the realities of democratic processes at the level of the electorate is a useful service and it should be carried forward. Opinion studies can help a democracy not only to know itself in a topical and immediate way but also to evaluate its achievement and its progress in more general terms. In this framework, the study of public opinion can make a telling contribution in the basic, continuous struggle to bring democratic practice more and more into harmony with the requirements and the assumptions—that is, with the ideals—of democratic theory.

35

**COMMUNICATIONS
RESEARCH AND
PUBLIC POLICY**
Harold D. Lasswell

W HEN I FIRST became acquainted with the field of public opinion and communications research there was no Roper, no Gallup, no Cantril, no Stouffer, no Hovland. Lazarsfeld was neither a person, nor a measuring unit; or even a category. There was no survey research, content analysis, or quantified depth analysis; no computerized systems of storage, retrieval, and utilization; no inter-university networks of cooperation; no training institutes, research bureaus, professional bibliographies, magazines, or associations. So far as that goes, there was practically no radio or television broadcasting, no instant photography, either in black or in color; and no sonar, radar, infrared or laser.

Lest you should think that we were living in a wholly undeveloped country, I ought to acknowledge that the horseless carriage had been invented. The cable, telegraph, and telephone were fully operational. Mr. Griffith was already midwife at a spectacular rebirth of a nation. The gas balloon was as well known at country fairs as it had always been in politics. Heavier-than-air craft weren't worth hijacking. You could take a deep breath in Central Park without inhaling lethal chemicals, swallow a clam with no fear of hepatitis, and smoke marijuana in a jazz joint without alarming the FBI. Highways were unpolluted. They were, on the contrary, enriched by the nostalgic smell of horse manure, and twittering English sparrows. Men and women smoked cancerettes with peace of mind, with no apprehension that every body swelling or sore throat signified a malignant growth. Beards and moustaches were on the way out as unhygienic and offensive to women and children.

Originally published in Volume 36, Number 3, 1972 of the *Public Opinion Quarterly*.

Modern public opinion and communications research developed in response to a remarkable convergence of favoring conditions. The social sciences were in a spasm of inferiority when they compared themselves with their brothers, sisters, and cousins in the physical and biological sciences. Many of the leading figures were convinced that, unless the specialists on society were able to "quantify" their propositions, they were doomed to the permanent status of second-class citizens in the universe of secular knowledge.

SKILL DEVELOPMENT

No need to recapitulate the technical advances that have been made in surveying, depth interviewing, content analysis, or in other modes of gathering and processing data. Miscellaneous polling at election time was an old American custom. The same was true of merchandising canvasses. Information testing was a well-established pedagogical device that could be adapted to the task of discovering what, if anything, people got out of reading newspapers, or exposing themselves to other material. Churches, lodges, hospitals, and many other private associations made extensive use of questionnaires and contributed to the predisposition of Americans to play the guinea pig.

So far as content analysis is concerned, there were many precursors of quantified semantic studies. The most obvious was cryptography. But the preparation of biblical concordances, of subject catalogs in libraries, and of standard guides to legal cases and opinions were of undoubted relevance.

Developments were held back by the magnitude and repetitiousness of the material to be covered. Hence the great and, in this instance, permanent leap forward with the emergence of the computer. A glance at the Annenberg Symposium volume is a sufficient reminder of the versatile uses to which content analysis can now be applied.[1] Whether the problem is defined in terms of style or of syntactic and semantic categories, every channel is brought into the scope of research (e.g. language, dreams, poetry, fiction, argumentation, music, pictures, voice, gesture). There are plenty of unresolved issues (e.g. the measurement of intensities of involvement, the interplay of collective mood and image). In this subdivision of the field, the possibilities are as varied as they are in examining the structural linkages that can be made visible by the use of observational standpoints of different degrees of intensity. We are still a long way from predicting the differences in the data that will be dis-

[1] George Gerbner *et al., The Analysis of Communication Content: Developments in Scientific Theories and Computer Techniques,* New York, Wiley, 1969.

closed by exploring "the same" phenomena by the use of depth and surface interviewing of varying degrees of complexity.

We are on sound ground in predicting that the hundreds, indeed thousands, of trained researchers on public opinion and communication will continue to proliferate sophisticated instruments of investigation. There will be no equivalent of the nuclear test ban so long as the society allows scientific inquiry to continue. We shall see more and more serious work on such conventionally regarded "far-out" phenomena as collective parapsychological linkages, and the potential fluctuation of collective moods of quiet or assertion in synchronization with changes in the environment such as the recently reported lunar cycle.

These are not the developments, however, that I have in mind when I put forward the proposition that future advances in the study of public opinion and communication depend on the development of a sense of professional responsibility as a full-fledged member of the policy sciences.

CLIENTS IN POLICY PROCESSES

Not that technicians in the public opinion field are without ties to the processes of policy formation and execution in both governmental and private sectors of society in this and in many other countries. Official and unofficial clients abound, and there is every ground for asserting that the inflow of research results and interpretations has *some* effect on what at least some clients occasionally do.

This conclusion is clear enough if we employ a simple model of the policy (or decision) process as a checklist for considering the interrelations of clients and researchers.

Consider the *intelligence* phase of government, law, and politics. Intelligence is the obtaining, processing, and dissemination of factual information, of projections of future developments, and of the costs, gains, and risks of alternative goals and strategies. All of this is dead-center so far as public opinion research is concerned, and it is no surprise to find that official agencies of intelligence rely on in-house personnel or outside contracts to execute the tasks involved. Whether we refer to overt or covert agencies of diplomatic, military, economic, or ideological intelligence, we are the servants of the CIA, the armed forces, the foreign trade and development agencies, the broadcasting services (together with their counterparts in other governments, and in the domestic branches of national government). At state and local levels, the planning agencies may be the most significant clients.

Actually some of the organizations referred to above may be

classed primarily as *promotional* rather than intelligence-planning agencies. The foreign broadcasting services, for instance, are disseminators of particular viewpoints on controversial matters, rather than outfits chiefly charged with finding and telling it "like it is." However, the most conspicuous link between researchers and clients in the policy process of the organized body politic is the tie with political parties and candidates. For better or worse, public opinion surveys feed the handicappers (and everybody else) in national and local electoral derbies.

The connection with the *prescribing* phase of decision is less direct. At the prescribing phase the norms and the presumably enforcible sanctions of public policy are crystallized. Legislatures and councils carry official responsibility for statutes and ordinances. Usually they ask for no help from researchers. They do, however, expect to benefit from the data obtained by political party and pressure associations who report on public assumptions and preferences about what "the law" is or ought to be, and how it has worked or will work. As public opinion specialists are aware, the publication of surveys that report what people assume the norms to be is itself part of the process by which expectations crystallize, and become the accepted definition of norms and sanctions. It is evident, therefore, that public opinion surveys play a role—though not necessarily a premeditated role—in the prescribing (legislating) process itself.

The *invoking* phase of decision is a provisional characterization of a concrete situation in terms of a prescription. It happens every time a police officer makes an arrest, a private person initiates a complaint of illegality, or an administrator explores his obligations under a new regulation. These individual acts do not typically call for information about public opinion. They would, however, do precisely that if police chiefs and prosecutors were candid enough to seek public advice on which laws should be enforced with vigor, or allowed to disappear. We know, for instance, that in response to neighborhood sentiment, anti-gambling, anti-prostitution and anti-drug measures may be invoked in some localities, while suffering neglect elsewhere. It is in the large governmental areas that surveys could help.

Application activities include continued and final characterization of concrete situations in reference to prescriptions. Often the operations in question are sufficiently large scale, and continue for a long enough time, to motivate administrators (and private participants) to request research data from survey or other specialists. Think of the conduct of a drawn-out war, or the administration of price and other controls.

The *terminating* function is explicitly focused when a prescription is repealed and measures are taken to compensate those who developed legitimate expectations of advantage when the terminated arrangement was in force. When the policy of permitting private investment in housing is changed, for example, compensation takes the form of money; or equivalent facilities may be made available. When research shows that particular norms are not enforced, and are actively opposed, the dissemination of these results may actually expedite termination. The exceptions occur in ethically charged areas, such as adultery and homosexuality, regarding which legislative action may be much delayed.

It is in connection with the *appraisal* phase of policy that communication research plays a particularly active role. To appraise a flow of official activities is to characterize them in terms of conformity to the goals of public policy, and to impute responsibility for what has happened. Think of the torrents of information at hand about judgments of the efficiency or inefficiency, integrity or corruptness, legality or illegality of foreign and internal policies. Intelligence points forward; appraisal first looks backward as a step toward future action.

For the most part, our examples have been from the political power-institution sector. They have referred to structures relatively specialized to perform phases of the policy process. It should be made explicit that each structure in a body politic participates in varying degree in all functions, and that each structure has an internal policy process that entails intelligence, promotion, prescription, invocation, application, termination, and appraisal. Furthermore, each phase is carried on through formal as well as informal structures.

Note further that what has been said about the institutions specialized to participate in the shaping and sharing of *power* is equally relevant to every other sector in society. An inclusive inventory of public opinion clients would cover producers, distributors, investors, and consumers in the *wealth-market* sector; the information gatherers, publishers, and audiences in science and the mass media of *enlightenment;* and comparable participants in other processes such as *well-being* (institutions of safety, health, and comfort), *skill,* (e.g. schools), *affection* (e.g. family, friends, loyalties), *respect* (e.g. social and class distinctions), *rectitude* (e.g. moral and religious institutions).

In spite of the impressive evolution of research skills, and the cultivation of clients throughout society, the current situation is not entirely satisfactory, which is why I want to return to an old theme and explore it anew. Are specialists in the study of communication, public opinion, propaganda, and related matters developing a truly professional identity and sense of responsibility?

609

The important thing about a profession is not conveyed by the traditional assertion that it has a distinctive literature. Today, practically every craft or trade meets this criterion. More relevant is the distinction between the exercise of a skill, and the coupling of skill with knowledge of the aggregated process to which the skill is intimately related. Consider the difference between the businessman and the economist. Successful businessmen are in command of skills that pay off in operating an enterprise. Economists are properly considered professionals because they have a verifiable image of the production, distribution, investment, and consumption of wealth. Physicians belong to the professional category because they are supposedly guided by a cognitive map of the individual and collective process of health and disease.

It is not enough for communication specialists to acquire skill in surveying, content analysis, or other technical operations. A genuine profession can be said to complement skill with enlightenment. In the case of communication, this implies a common map of the trends, conditions, and projections of the entire process. It also implies the capacity to invent and evaluate policies for the accomplishment of postulated goals.

PROFESSIONAL AUTONOMY

Implied in this conception of a profession is a degree of autonomy that goes beyond the cultivation of the capabilities that enable individual clients to be discovered and served. Since a professional possesses an image of the whole, and since he is a participating member of society, it has usually been assumed that he would function responsibly. Among both medicine-men and physicians the norm continues to be that the welfare of the client must be primary, and that initiatives should be taken to protect the welfare of the entire community by calling attention to emerging threats, and by doing what one can to cope with them.

So far as specialists on communication are concerned, a professional outlook and identity have appeared rather slowly. Professional associations, for example, have not taken many steps to clarify the goals and criteria in terms of which the role of communication can be effectively appraised. Professional societies have rarely taken the initiative to bring together the many fragmentary packets of data for the purpose of reporting on the performance level of the institutions specialized in communication. Many bar associations, however, take such initiatives and report, for example, on the level of criminal justice administration. Medical societies often assess the level of health care provided in schools, families, and hospitals; and they report on the adequacy of the water supply and the sanitation services. Biological and physical science associations have recently bestirred themselves to describe the changing levels of environmental damage that result from human activities. And there are regular and partial summaries of the state of official censorship, and the territorial coverage in selected news media. It cannot be shown, however, that a communications profession has taken the lead in probing and reporting, on a sampling basis, how communications are living up to rather widely accepted criteria of performance.

THE THIRD VOICE

Nevertheless, American as well as world society needs a "third voice" that can attract general attention for its reports on how things are going. At present the principal voices are self-serving, whether the self is a government, a political party, a business, or what. The role of a third, disinterested voice is to supply a competing appraisal of the images spread by self-serving sources.

Not that a communications profession is without conscious and unconscious preferences, expectations, and identities. A profession has the responsibility to use candor, and to disclose both the normative criteria employed in a set of statements and the procedures by which data are gathered, processed, and interpreted. We also allow for the possibility that some members of a professional society are so committed to a political party program, or to some already organized and active participant in the public policy process, that they are unwilling or unable to encourage or to act as a third voice. The chances are, nevertheless, that enough members of this emerging profession are able to perform the indicated task.

SCOPE AND TIMING

There is little doubt of the crucial importance of a third voice during the next few years. The computer revolution has produced an instrument that can be employed by centralized elite structures to consolidate their position. It is no news that knowledge is power, especially knowledge that is promptly available and includes information about individuals and groups that lays open their vulnerabilities to blackmail or to tactics of positive inducement. A question is whether those who organize a third voice can act quickly enough to join with leaders of pluralistic groups who are also demanding access to available systems of storage and retrieval, and who are willing to assist in policing the use of information in ways that guard against abuse of power.

At first the scope of the third voice can be circumscribed. If it succeeds in winning confidence, the scope will presumably expand enormously. At the start, the third voice would contribute to the flow of public communication that we have labeled the "appraisal" component of decision.

It is not difficult to indicate briefly some of the criteria in terms of which an appraisal of the public decision process can be made at regular intervals. Think first of the "intelligence" function. Any flow of statements through an information network can be assessed according to "dependability, comprehensiveness, selectivity, creativity, and openness." "Promotional" activities are particularly important in the dissemination of programs of action if they are in time to obviate resort to violence. "Prescriptive" decisions can be usefully appraised by selective surveys of lawyers and other directly interested groups for the purpose of discovering the pattern of expectation about the level of enforcement or nonenforcement. The "invocation" function can be appraised, among other criteria, by the degree to which deprived groups in the body politic believe that their claims are actually heard. A critical matter for "application," especially by the courts, is the degree to which all strata of society have confidence in the impartiality of the process. Appraisals of "termination" can discover the degree to which various prescriptions are assumed to be inoperative. Clearly, the "appraisal" of public attitudes is a direct contribution when it discovers the sources that shape judgments of policy success or failure.

SCIENCE AND POLICY

It should not be assumed that by cultivating the third voice the scientific study of communication will suffer. On the contrary, the development of more operational models of the decision process, and of its interrelationships with the whole social process, will encourage the systematic gathering of trend and distribution data. In turn these data will emphasize the much neglected *time* factor in scientific models of interdetermination. By projecting probable future developments, plans can be made to obtain better data in the future than have been available in the past. Significant feedback will be obtained for reformulating models of all problem-solving tasks, such as explanation, projection, and the comparison of strategies for goal achievement.

Scientific attention would probably be directed toward characteristics of communication whose implications have received relatively little notice. For example, policy problems connected with programs of development, especially national development, are taking a new turn. Formulated goals were initially phrased in terms of investment in capital-intensive industries employing the most advanced available technology. National goals of this kind are subject to rising currents of doubt because they have so often stimulated political and social instability. They have had such results as the excessive migration of peasants to join the unemployed in metropolitan slums, and the excess "warehousing" of students in educational institutions that provide inadequate education in preparation for largely nonexistent opportunities. Hence a search for an "intermediate technology" that allows village clusters and small urban centers to provide a more gratifying flow of value indulgences (preferred outcomes.)

The new development goals are articulately related to value outcomes that are connected with the realization of preferred levels of other values, especially those we have labeled affection, respect, or rectitude (ethical-religious). The demand is for a more satisfactory quality of life that gives up the hypothetical advantages of high technology for the readily realizable gains of comradeship, neighborliness, love, and loyalty toward visualizable territories and pluralistic groups.

An intriguing question is whether the changing demands in some developing countries, taken in conjunction with certain changes in the United States and in similar societies, are precursors of a world-wide evolution toward de-emphasizing the styles of life that are resource-luxurious rather than resource-parsimonious. Collective deeds, such as fiestas of a secular or sacred character, belong to the latter category. The same point can apply to exchanges of affection, respect, and other value forms. We can speak of tendencies toward *internalization* rather than *externalization,* meaning that the involvement of the resource environment at the level of "enjoyment" is kept down. In this country one thinks of the general, though uncertain, trend toward a "rural coalition," toward communal living, and toward the cultivation of skill on musical instruments that are parsimonious of material.

Do the global trends to be revealed as communication professionals share their data indicate that these tendencies are actually significant? Do our theories of change in communicated values adequately explain what is going on? Do we actually face a future that includes the continuation of a divided, militant, and fearful globe in which new technologies of information are monopolized for the primary benefit of the top elites? And where failures of symbol-sign indoctrination will probably lead to the progressive abandonment of reliance on communication as an instrument of mass control, and to the substitution of chemico-physiological means of caste consolidation?

You may observe from these less than optimistic reflections that the changes of recent years have not led me to substitute a sanguine for an apprehensive image of the future. On the other hand they have not deprived me of a certain hope that instruments of public policy can be seized and pluralized for the common good. I trust that I am wrong in my foreboding, and that I am right in suspecting one cannot be absolutely certain of the future. In any event, the emerging profession of communication is strategically situated to take some of our destiny in hand. I therefore pose the question: Do you think that you will get on with it?[2]

[2] Those who are unacquainted with the approach that is partially exemplified in the foregoing may wish to consult: H. D. Lasswell, *A Pre-View of Policy Sciences*, American Elsevier, New York, 1971; H. D. Lasswell and Allan R. Holmberg, "Toward a General Theory of Directed Value Accumulation and Institutional Development," in *Political and Administrative Development*, Ralph Braibanti, ed., Durham, N.C., Duke University Press, 1969; J. Zvi Namenwirth and H. D. Lasswell, *The Changing Language of American Values: A Computer Study of Selected Party Platforms*, Comparative Politics Series No. 01-001, Berkeley Hills, California, Sage Publications, 1970.

PUBLIC OPINION
AND THE CLASSICAL
TRADITION
Paul F. Lazarsfeld

Q UITE possibly the emergence of empirical social science will one day be considered an outstanding feature of the twentieth century. But its birth has not been without travail. Hardest have been its struggles with what we shall call the classical tradition. After all, for two thousand years or more people have thought and written about human and social affairs. Has the empirical trend been an enriching innovation? Has it had a pernicious effect? The matter has certainly been much discussed in recent years.

The debate over the study of public opinion probably provides the best case in point. Since about the beginning of the eighteenth century a steadily increasing amount has been written on this subject by political scientists, by historians and, recently, by sociologists. Toward the beginning of the twentieth century, however, this classical tradition was confronted by the empiricists, who rallied around the notion of attitudes.

The empirical tradition in opinion and attitude research began modestly enough in Germany with simple laboratory experiments on problem solving, in which the notion of "mental sets" was carved out. It gained strength from the work of the Chicago school of sociologists, which brought the study of attitudes and values into play. Immediately thereafter, the psychometricians under the leadership of Thurstone introduced the portentous problem of measurement. And finally came the public opinion research people who, on

* This may be identified as publication No. A-230 of the Bureau of Applied Social Research, Columbia University.

Originally published in Volume 21, Number 1, 1957 of the *Public Opinion Quarterly*.

the one hand, narrowed the conceptual range but, on the other, greatly extended the field of practical applications.[1]

About ten years ago the aspiring new science and the classical tradition confronted each other like petulant antagonists. Our professional organizations certainly took cognizance of the matter. Three presidential addresses delivered at AAPOR annual meetings since 1950 have been devoted to the discussion of the relation of public opinion research to history, political theory and social theory, respectively. Nor did exponents of the classical tradition let us forget their claims: Lindsay Rogers made violent attacks, Herbert Blumer articulated his complaints, and the historians showed their contempt for public opinion research by their neglect, speaking about it only occasionally and upon request. This contentious situation has been ably summarized by Bernard Berelson in an unusually thoughtful and informative paper.[2] Were we to review where we stand now, hardly anything could be added to Berelson's remarks, and if we want to discuss how to proceed from here his essay is still the most suggestive.

Berelson sees the present state of public opinion research as the seventh phase of an unfolding process which began with a general feeling that something called public opinion was important. As a result, prominent writers developed broad speculations about it during a second phase of development. In a third phase empirical data were drawn on wherever they were available: magazine articles, speeches, or other documents. The shortcomings of these data led, fourthly, to intense interest in the methodology of the field. At this point a fifth phase set in, during which specialized commercial agencies as well as university institutes took the lead in research. Next, contact was made with intellectual neighbors such as anthropology and psychology. This makes possible the seventh phase, into which we are just entering, a phase in which systematic propositions on public opinion are being developed: public opinion research has become an empirical social science.

If we were dealing with a field like chemistry, or any other natural science, we would be rather confident that any new phase incorporated what was of value in past work; only the historian of natural science must actually turn back to earlier stages. In the social sciences the situation is not as simple. Progress in the clarity of formulations and the respect for evidence is often accompanied, at least temporarily, by an insensitivity to the broader visions and the more general concerns characteristic of an older tradition.

The resulting clash between modern empiricists and spokesmen for the classics recurs in many other fields, and is almost always productive. This is

[1] For an excellent brief history of the empirical position see Gordon Allport's essay on "Attitudes" in the *Handbook of Psychology*, edited by Carl Murchison, (Worcester, Mass.: Clark University Press, 1935).

[2] In *The Study of the Social Sciences*, edited by Leonard White, (Chicago: University of Chicago Press, 1956).

true for three distinct reasons. First, empirical development usually furnishes sharper conceptual tools that enable us to see the classics from a new vantage point: what was only dimly perceived before can now often be discerned with clarity and, as a result, new implications of all sorts can be brought to light. Secondly, the very act of inspecting this classical material brings to our attention ideas which might otherwise have been overlooked, either because of preoccupation with the work of the day, or because empirical researchers are likely to be guided too much by what is a manageable topic at the moment, rather than by what is an important issue. Finally, the classical tradition, as exemplified by Berelson's first two phases, is by no means over. We hope that scholars will keep on thinking about problems with a broad scope, irrespective of whether data or precise modes of reasoning about these problems are available. Theorizing itself can make progress, and the logic of empirical research can contribute to it. Thus, our conceptual task is to bend Berelson's phases into a loop to see how the early phases mesh with the later ones.

COMPLEXITIES OF THE CLASSICAL NOTION

We may profitably begin by paying heed to the discussions centering around the definition of public opinion. It is no coincidence that both Blumer and Rogers make this big point: when the pollsters use the term public opinion, they do not know and cannot say what they mean. Now, in principle, this is not a picayune objection. Definitions, whether implicit or explicit, do indeed have great influence on scholarly activities. In another respect, however, the objection is a strange one. Neither of the two authors proposes a definition. And if one looks at the collection of quotations which Rogers provides in one of his chapters in *The Pollsters,* one is impressed by the fact that few of the classics offered a definition. As a matter of fact, earlier writers overflow with comments about the mysterious and intangible character of public opinion.

Why is public opinion so difficult to define? It is generally agreed that it was the rise of the middle class, the spread of democratic institutions, the expansion of literacy, and the growth of mass media of communication which gave rise to concern with what was loosely called public opinion. By this term many authors of the classical school referred to people who did not belong to the ruling classes from which the government personnel was recruited and yet claimed a voice in public affairs.[3]

[3] In a book by Emden on the people and the constitution, to which we shall come back later, an interesting appendix on this history of the term "The People" can be found. He shows that at various periods in English history the people were always those who hadn't yet the right to vote but were about to get it at the next turn of parliamentary reform. In Germany, prior to the First World War, the liberal intellectuals were, for all practical purposes, excluded from government. It is therefore not surprising that the German sociologist Toennies defined

But two matters became puzzling. One is a normative problem: What is the best relation between this "public opinion" and the government? The second is a descriptive problem: How does public opinion actually exercise its influence? The term "public opinion" came into use in just the casual way in which we have introduced it now. While ostensibly a concept, it actually signified only a complicated congeries of observations, practical problems, and normative concerns. It is very much worth while to follow closely this startling piece of intellectual history: how the complexity of a developing historical situation was experienced as a linguistic difficulty because no appropriate logical categories existed to cope with it. In modern parlance one would say that there was a confusion between the subject language dealing with factual observations, and the meta-language dealing with the way the observations should be analyzed.[4]

We shall take our main example of this problem from an essay by the German historian Herman Oncken on "The Historian, the Statesman, and Public Opinion." According to Oncken, the statesman is concerned mainly with the enduring interests of his country; therefore when he writes history he should be mistrusted. The historian is mainly concerned with truth; he should not become too involved in politics or he runs the risk of a conflict of values. "Public opinion"—watch the personification—stands for the ever-shifting qualities of the human mind not encumbered by either scholastic or national responsibilities.

Oncken goes on to discuss public opinion as follows:

The vague and fluctuating cannot be understood by being clamped into a formula; certainly not when it is a very characteristic of the concept that it embodies a thousand possibilities of variation. But when all is said and done, everyone knows, if put to it, what public opinion means. If it must be set in words, then it can only appear hedged around by many restricting clauses: public opinion is a complex of similar utterances of larger or smaller segments of society concerning public affairs (1, 2); at times spontaneous, at times artfully manipulated (3); expressed in a multitude of ways, in clubs, assemblies, above all in the press and in journals, or perhaps only in unspoken feelings of each one of us (4); of the common man in the street or of a small circle of the cultured (8); here a true power factor, which statesmen must take into account, or something of no political significance (5); something again to be evaluated differently in every country (5 or 6); sometimes united, rising up like a tidal wave against the government and the experts, sometimes divided, concealing conflicting tendencies (7); at one time bringing out the simple and natural sentiments of the people, at another time being the rowdy thoughtless manifestations of wild instincts (6); always leading and

---

public opinion as the opinion of experts (*Gelehrte*), the men who thought about public issues but did not have direct access to the centers of power. Cecil S. Emden, *The People and the Constitution*, 2nd edition (London: Oxford University Press, 1956).

[4] Interestingly enough, at least one historian has dealt in detail with a similar difficulty for an earlier epoch. Lucien Febvre makes the point that in 16th century France it was impossible to develop a system of religious scepticism because the language did not provide the necessary intellectual base for it. See his *Le Probleme de l'Incroyance en XVI* Siecle*, pp. 383-401.

always being led (5, 3); looked down upon by the sophisticated, yet forcing the hands of men (6, 5); contagious like an epidemic (10); capricious, treacherous (9); and power mad (resembling man himself) (6); and then again only a word by which those in power are bewitched (5).[5]

[We have inserted numbers after the sentences in this passage so that we can refer to them easily.] Now, what is interesting about this bewildering formulation is that it can be disentangled easily as soon as one matches it against what one might call a complete attitude distribution. It is a commonplace for most of us that polling does not consist merely in finding out how many people are for or against something. We need to know the social and demographic characteristics of the respondents, and we take great care to distinguish between people who are informed and concerned with the problem and those who are not. In other words, a good public opinion poll ends up not with one distribution of attitudes but with many of them for different sectors of the population. In this sense, Oncken undoubtedly gives a definition of public opinion. It is a statistical distribution of utterances (No. 1 and No. 7), expressed by various segments of the population (No. 2), and these segments can and should be classified by the degree of their competence (No. 8).

But intermingled with this definition are a number of empirical problems which are encountered in investigations more complicated than cross-sectional surveys. What factors determine a given attitude distribution at any given time (No. 3)? What effect does it have on statemen and on the legislative process in general (No. 5)? How are opinions communicated and diffused (No. 10)?

Two further elements in this passage foreshadow topics which are now of great technical concern to us. How should one choose among the various sources and devices which can be used to ascertain an attitude distribution (No. 4)? Oncken mentions only expressions at meetings and in the printed mass media. Today we would add questionnaires and other more systematic research procedures. And we would now translate the phrase "capricious, treacherous" (No. 9) into the terminology of panel techniques, distinguishing people who upon repeated interviews show constant attitudes from those whose attitudes fluctuate. Finally (No. 6), Oncken is obviously concerned with the normative problem of how certain opinions should be evaluated— a matter to which we shall return subsequently.

It is this intertwining of matters of definition and factual problems which is so characteristic of the classical tradition. We are probably faced here by an irreversible development. Now that we have the reality of public opinion polls we will undoubtedly keep on calling public opinion a well analyzed distribution of attitudes. But certainly no one denies that we still know very little about how such complete attitude distributions come into being, and

[5] *Essays on Politics and History* (Berlin, 1914), Vol. I, pp. 203-204.

what role they actually play in the governmental process. And under the general heading of the "mass society phenomenon" we certainly keep on worrying about the role it *should* play. Thus the issue of definition resolves itself in an interesting way. The critics of polling are worried that the joy of having found greater conceptual clarity will lead us to forget some of the grave philosophical and empirical problems with which the classics dealt (and well these critics might worry as far as some pollsters are concerned). But what is overlooked is something that has happened often in intellectual history: a new technique has permitted the sorting out of various aspects of a diffused concern and has prepared the way for a more rational approach to its different elements.[6]

THE "PUBLIC OPINION SYSTEM" AS A BRIDGE

There has recently been an interesting effort to find a formulation which will bridge the gap between the classical tradition and the modern turn of events. MacIver has introduced the term "public opinion system."[7] It implies a clear understanding that the multiplicity of facts and problems by which earlier writers were confused can be structured only by distinguishing different dimensions in the concept of public opinion. One is "the opinion alignment," corresponding to the type of information which modern public opinion polls provide. The second dimension is the "structure of communication." This refers to a set of questions with which many sociologists are concerned: the role of associations and leadership; the way in which the mass media and their public influence each other. The third dimension is "the ground of consensus" which takes account of a distinction that has perturbed other writers. Some of the attitudes relevant to the study of specific historical situations are of long enduring character: people are hardly conscious of them, take them for granted, and they come to the fore only in situations where these basic sentiments are somehow threatened. Such "grounds of consensus" should be distinguished from opinions on current controversial issues.

The three components together form the "public opinion system." Two of them are clearly parallel to the two groups of elements we found in Oncken. The third component aims at taking care of another difficulty which has plagued writers during the last century: What aspects of popular sentiment

---

[6] An interesting parallel could be developed with the invention of the Arabic number system. This was also of a highly technical nature, but it permitted the formulation and later the solution of problems which were unmanageable with the numerical symbolism of antiquity.

[7] Robert M. McIver, *Academic Freedom in the United States* (New York: Columbia University Press, 1954). The "structure of communication" as part of the "public opinion system" is a felicitous way to bring out a feature common to many writers steeped in the classical tradition. Hans Speier, *e.g.* (in the American Journal of Sociology, 1950) takes an "historical approach to public opinion;" he mainly provides valuable material on ways in which opinion was formed, for instance, in coffee houses, salons, etc. Only tangentially is he concerned with "opinion alignment."

are significant for the analysis of social events? The French social psychologist, Gabriel Tarde,[8] has proposed a three-way distinction: tradition, opinion, and fashion. The German sociologist, Toennies, has paralleled the well known distinction between *Gemeinschaft* and *Gessellschaft* by coordinating religion with the former and opinion with the latter. The problem was always to place "public opinion" somewhere between the rather permanent and subconscious value system of a society and the fleeting reaction of a people to the passing events of the day.

Probably the most productive formulation of this kind has been taken over and developed by historians under the term "climate of opinion."[9] This concept became fashionable in the seventeenth century, and acquired prominence through Carl Becker's analysis of the eighteenth century Enlightenment in France. It is often drawn on by historians when they explain why they are not interested in contemporary polling: they assert that we do not investigate quasi-permanent sentiments out of which grow opinions on specific events. A sociologist giving the presidential address at the annual meeting of AAPOR recently acknowledged the existence of the issue by admonishing us to pay more attention to the study of "mentality."

RESEARCHING THE "CLIMATE OF OPINION"

Now this is indeed a topic on which the classics have much to teach us. Here they were certainly in their element, because historical documents, laws and customs are an important source of insight into climates of opinion. But again, the situation is rather complex. Some of our more sophisticated contemporaries like to answer that we can discover the basic values of any population group by applying methods like projective tests; anthropologists, especially, incline toward this point of view. But such procedures are costly, even on a small scale, and almost unmanageable with a reliable sample. There is, however, a possible compromise; this consists in the development of fairly simple projective *items* which can be handled within the frame of a sampling survey procedure. We have not yet made a great deal of progress along this line, and it is therefore worthwhile to review where we stand.

Some examples can be taken from current studies of "national character." We find considerable differences between nations if we ask such questions as: Can people be trusted? Is it possible to change human nature? Should children consult their parents before they get married? Is it dangerous to contradict one's superiors? Should clergymen or teachers be more respected in the

---

[8] His book on *Opinion and the Crowd* has never been translated. It is, however, well summarized in Sorokin's *Survey of European Sociology*. Herbert Blumer's paper on "mass and opinion" is a rendition of the Tarde point of view. (See "The Mass, the Public, and Public Opinion," included in *Reader in Public Opinion and Communication*, edited by Bernard Berelson and Morris Janowitz. Glencoe, Ill.: The Free Press, 1953.)

[9] For some historical references on the term "climate of opinion" see R. K. Merton's essay on *Social Structure and Anomie* (Free Press, Glencoe, Illinois), p. 378, footnote 6.

community? Would you rather live in another country? What do you approve or disapprove of most in your neighbors?

Within a single country, class differences have been made the object of special investigation. What should children be punished for? How much do adolescents confide in their parents? What decisions does the huband make without consulting his wife? The answers indicate whether the "mores" vary between social strata. In addition, tensions between classes can be investigated using projective items. Are the courts and the police considered impartial, or do they favor the rich? Does a worker or a business man feel he has more in common with people of the same class in other countries, or with people of a different class in his own country? Is it especially interesting to read stories and books about people of one's own class? [10]

Attention should be drawn to findings which deserve to be followed up as the historical scene changes. In a survey conducted in Germany in 1946, a sample of the population was asked whether they considered physical courage an important quality in a man. More than 90 per cent said "no." This probably reflected disillusion with the Nazi ideology, as well as an effort to guess what the American interviewer wanted to hear. It would be highly instructive to repeat this question a few years after the revival of a German army. If physical courage gains rapidly in prestige, we may have to start worrying about the consequences of German rearmament.

DICEY REVISITED: THE FEED-BACK EFFECT

Behind the battle over definitions, then, lie the serious difficulties involved in selecting problems that are important. The choice of problems, in turn, helps determine what type of techniques need development and what data should be gathered. But there is also another relationship between the style of thinking in a social science and its technical development. The propositions which the classics developed were of a broader and altogether different nature from the more microsopic findings with which we concern ourselves today. Only rarely is the discrepancy small enough to allow the problems of interest in the older tradition to be approached with the techniques and orientations of the newer one.

An exception is found in one of the most famous of the older books: Dicey's *The Relations Between Law and Public Opinion in England During the 19th Century.*[11] The title clearly presents the scope of the work. The author's main interest is in the changes which came about in England between

[10] The general role of such questionnaire items is discussed and exemplified by Jean Stoetzel in an article on the use of polls in social anthropology (UNESCO *International Social Science Bulletin*, Vol. V, No. 3). Stoetzel, incidentally, was the first, in his dissertation in France, to stress the relation of history and political science to attitude research.

[11] Second edition (London: MacMillan Co., 1920).

1840 and 1880. The earlier date represents the peak of *laissez faire,* when efforts were made to minimize governmental intereference with economic affairs. By 1880 a great deal of social legislation had been enacted, and an era had started which Dicey dislikes, and interchangeably calls the era of collectivism or of socialism. He not only tries to trace the effects of prevailing trends of opinion on legislation; he also seeks to account for changes in opinion, and formulates a number of "characteristics"—generalizations purporting to explain the ways such changes come about. One of these rules covers what we today might call a feed-back effect: "laws foster or create opinion."

Now it happens that we have by now a considerable amount of data showing that Dicey was right. Cantwell and Hyman have demonstrated that immediately after Congress enacts a law there tends to be an increase in the number of people who approve of it. (Their examples range from the debates on enlarging the Supreme Court to the Marshall Plan.) Planck gives us similar data from France, where public opinion polls showed increasing approval of a series of international agreements right after they had been signed. But how did Dicey know this when obviously no such evidence was available to him? Again, a careful reading of his argument permits separation of the "old-fashioned" from the creative and enduring element. On the one hand, he calls his rule an "undeniable truth" and seems to think that he can derive it from basic principles. On the other hand, he supports his contention with examples, developing various interesting ideas in the course of his argument. According to him, most people are sufficiently uncertain enough about their opinion, so that when a law is enacted "its underlying principle derives prestige from its mere recognition by parliament." As a matter of fact, he says, the less clearly this underlying principle is formulated the more likely it is to be accepted. Casual legislation on marginal matters often "surreptitiously introduces ideas which would not be accepted if brought before the attention of the nation" in a more explicit form.

Here is something like the beginning of a theory of how an accomplished fact finds support. Modern notions like "legitimation," "redirection of attention" and "the nature of an unstable equilibrium in a weak opinion structure" can easily be read into Dicey's discussion. But the most interesting fact from our point of view is that in none of the modern publications presenting data on this feed-back phenomenon has there been the slightest effort to explain it. Thus "Dicey revisited" shows a serious gap in our contemporary approach and gives the first hint on ways to fill it.

EMPIRICAL VERIFICATION OF CLASSICAL INSIGHTS

Sensitized by one such episode, we can now again raise the question of where we can find further material to apply to the observations of classical authors. Obviously this material cannot come from one single public opinion poll, and the time periods covered by empirical research are usually too short to be of much help. But we are now beginning to collect *comparative* public opinion data, and these are likely to lead to broader generalizations. The impetus for this has come largely from other fields. The cross-cultural files gathered at Yale by anthropologists have yielded a number of interesting books comparing the social structure or the child rearing practices of a large number of primitive tribes. Industrial sociologists have compared the productivity of work teams under varying conditions of leadership and personal interaction among members. Political scientists have begun to use the forty-eight states as a kind of political laboratory. A very interesting example is a study which attempts to show that the weaker the two party system is in a state the more influential are the pressure groups.[12]

Slowly, attitude research is being included in this new movement. One of the ways in which Bryce compared England with America was in regard to political participation. He felt that in each country one could distinguish three strata: those who make political decisions; those who seriously discuss them and influence the decision makers through the press, books, meetings, and so on; and finally, the politically inert and uninterested masses. Bryce thought that the middle group was considerably larger in the United States than in Europe; but he had no evidence.[13] Today it might, however, be supplied by the "index of political activity" constructed by Julian Woodward and Elmo Roper.[14] They obtained information on their respondents' activities in parties and pressure groups, the extent to which they discussed politics with friends, their frequency of voting, etc. Finally, they divided the American population into four groups: Those who were very active (10 per cent), those who were active (17 per cent), those who were inactive (35 per cent), and those who were very inactive (38 per cent). Probably the real decision makers were not included in their sample, but reasonable reading of the questions asked by Woodward and Roper would make the active 27 per cent correspond to Bryce's second group and the inactive 73 per cent to his third. As usual, the division has to be somewhat arbitrary, but such an index, once constructed, would be suitable for making comparisons over time and space.

In the international field, our best example comes from an attitude survey which UNESCO carried out in nine countries during 1948.[15] We select one phase of this study because it relates attitudes to an economic index. The respondents in nine countries were asked which country in the world would

[12] *"Report of the Committee on American Legislatures,"* Belle Zeller, editor, American Political Science Association. See also P. T. David "Comparative State Politics and the Problem of Party Realignment" in *Research Frontiers in Politics and Government,* The Brookings Institution, 1955.

[13] *American Commonwealth,* Part IV, Ch. X.

[14] "Political Activity of American Citizens," *American Political Science Review,* Vol. XIV, December 1950, p. 872.

[15] Buchanan and Cantril, *How Nations See Each Other,* Urbana: Univ. of Ill. Press, 1953.

give them the life they wanted to live. For each of the nine nations the proportion of respondents who named their own country was computed as an "index of satisfaction." This then was related to a set of statistics made available by another agency of the United Nations showing the "per capita calory supply." The measure of economic well-being had a correlation of .75 with the index of satisfaction. Even the deviations suggest interesting speculations. For instance, Mexico had the lowest food standard but was relatively high in the satisfaction of its citizens. Perhaps this may be explained by the high morale possibly engendered by the revolution and also by an improvement over past standards of living. The Netherlands, on the other hand, were low in satisfaction in spite of a relatively good food supply. This might be due to war devastation, the loss of Indonesia, or the high population density in Holland.

We now must return to one element in the picture which we bypassed before. The classical tradition is very much concerned with the problem of what the proper relation between public opinion and democratic government *should* be. Rogers' most valid objection against contemporary pollsters is exactly on this issue: they either do not think about it or they make naive statements to the effect that the government should actually do what the public opinion polls tell them the people want. This is a normative problem, and therefore it is important to know what the relation between the discussion of values and the factual findings of empirical research can be. The more we know about the probable consequences of various measures, the more certain can we be as to whether they will realize the values we strive for, and the more wisely can we choose among the conflicting values themselves.[16]

In the earlier writings on public opinion, value problems such as this one were discussed in a pseudo-factual language which made communication between generations especially difficult. Consider, for example, the first major American book on the topic: A. Lawrence Lowell, *Public Opinion and Popular Government*.[17] In the initial eighty pages or so of this book, Lowell proposes to find out what "true" opinion is. The first reaction of a modern reader is to think the question absurd (what is true electricity?), and to discard the book. This, however, would be a mistake. For, upon considerable effort, one learns that by "true" Lowell means the kind of public opinion which a democratic government should take into account.

Following this lead, one discovers that Lowell has three very different

16 While there is agreement on the general logic of the problem, little work has been done to analyze in detail how arguments are actually supported by facts in the discussion of social affairs. Obviously this is not identical with the rule of formal logic. But we also do not mean the misuses of propaganda, which have been described by content analysts. What we have in mind is the systematic description of efforts to come to reasonable conclusions from necessarily insufficient data. The problem is similar to the question of how policy decisions are related to factual information in government and business. This has not been well investigated either.

17 (New York, 1913.)

criteria of "true" public opinion. In modern terminology they are: (a) opinions should count only after proper general discussion, and only those people should be included who have given the matter considerable thought. Applied to currect polling practices, this means that while thoughtful persons can readily be identified by good polls, the *timing* of polls, if they are to be used by government officials, raises quite a number of important problems. (b) Neither elections nor referenda really ascertain people's attitudes properly; the former fail because they are not centered around issues, and the latter because we do not know whether the "right" (informed) people participate. Clearly, Lowell would have welcomed polls if properly analyzed and interpreted. (c) Certain topics should never be the subject of legislation and, therefore, cannot be objects of "true" public opinion; religion is an example specifically mentioned by the American constitution. Here the intricate decision of excluding certain topics confronts us. Should "true" opinion in these areas be ascertained by a public opinion poll, historical analysis of the tradition of a country, or by general philosophical consideration? Lowell does not raise or answer these questions, but he suggests interesting problems about what people consider private and what they consider public issues under various circumstances.

PUBLIC OPINION AND GOVERNMENT POLICY

The relationship of opinion to government policy has been discussed in another type of literature, to which we could profitably pay more attention than we have previously. There are writers who try to approach normative questions by the careful analysis of historical events where the consequences of measure actually taken were first described and then judged. Before considering concrete examples, attention should be drawn to the historical aspect of the problem itself. Emden's history[18] reveals the big changes which came about in the British climate of opinion on such matters. A century-and-a-half ago, for instance, it was illegal to publish any reports on the debates of the British parliament. After a while summaries were permissible, but the votes of individual members could not be published. Only since 1845, and after serious debate, were official reports issued. Conversely, up to about 1880 it was considered inadmissible for politicians, including cabinet ministers, to address the population at large. They could appeal to their own constituencies, but otherwise only parliament itself was thought to be the proper place for debate.[19]

[18] See footnote 3. This book contains much interesting information, for instance, the history of petitions in the 19th century (pp. 74 ff). Petitions fell out of usage because it was impossible to know which sector of the population the signers represented. A reading of the controversy, almost a hundred years old, shows that everyone was groping for something like representative sampling carried out by politically neutral agencies.

[19] Even today the English tradition is quite different from the American. If a law is under discussion in Congress radio and television overflow with panel debates and press interviews on

Three detailed monographic studies have analyzed the relation between governmental policy and contemporary expression of opinion in an especially interesting way. One was published in 1886 and is often quoted, but it is rarely read because of its inordinate length.[20] Its setting is the Russian-Turkish conflict in the late 1870's which led up to the Congress of Berlin. The issue between the two countries was the protection of the Christian population of the Balkans, then part of the Turkish Empire. According to the author, the British people were for the liberation of the Balkan provinces, a wish which corresponded to the demands of the Russian Government. Disraeli (Lord Beaconsfield) feared an extension of Russian influence into Europe, and his policy was essentially to help the Turks. Thus a situation arose in which the British government acted avowedly against the advice of the majority of the British press and of most civic organizations concerned with foreign affairs. Thompson gives a vividly documented description of the dramatic interplay of the two partners to the conflict: how events sometimes strengthened the one and sometimes the other and how they reacted to each other's moves. The normative problem with which the author is concerned is whether even if a government has the majority support of its own party in parliament, it shall be required to resign when there are unmistakable signs that the population at large does not agree with its policy. In the 1880's this was not yet the British tradition; it probably would be today.

The data on which Thompson drew are speeches, resolutions, editorials, and similar documents. His contribution consists in the minute analysis of the different phases of the conflict. But he has to look at the matter, so to say, from the outside; he has no information on how the decisions were made in either the British cabinet or in the various groups which organized what he called the "agitations," the anti-Turkish movement.

A much more recent book by Lynn M. Case is outstanding because it has just this kind of information.[21] Under the second Empire the French government had a detailed system for obtaining reports on public opinion from its administrative officials in all parts of the country. These were not the usual reports of the Secret Police, denouncing individuals, but rather were detached impressions of how various social groups responded to the policy of Napoleon III.[22] In times of crisis these reports came in as often as once a week. Case

---

the issue. The British Broadcasting Corporation does not permit a discussion of laws within a period of two weeks prior to a parliamentary debate to prevent the influence of the public voice on the deliberations of the legislature.

[20] Geo. C. Thompson, *Public Opinion and Lord Beaconsfield 1875-1880*, (London: Mac-Millan Co., 1886).

[21] *French Opinion on War and Diplomacy During the Second Empire*, University of Pennsylvania Press, 1954.

[22] In the historical part of his book, Toennies has a section on France (pp. 375-401). He quotes there a letter by Mirabeau urging Louis XVI to set up just this kind of an organization. Whether the reporting system of Napoleon III goes back to these early stages cannot be seen from Case's book.

not only gives a very good picture of these interesting reports; he also tells of the effect they had on the foreign policy of the Second Empire, citing minutes of cabinet meetings during which these reports were discussed and used as arguments by the participants.

This book includes one dramatic episode in which the normative implication comes out with particular clarity. In 1866, Napoleon wanted to interfere in the Austro-Prussian War, in order to avoid a Prussian victory. Public opinion reports, however, indicated such a strong desire in the population for peace and so much danger of a revolution in case of war that the group in the cabinet which was against intervention prevailed. As a result, Prussia became so powerful that four years later it could provoke war with France which, in turn, led to the defeat of Napoleon III and to the end of his regime. Case calls into doubt the wisdom of having a foreign policy guided by public opinion.[23]

Finally, we have W. P. Davison's study of the Berlin Airlift. There he reports actual polling data from Berlin cross-sections and interviews with policy makers on various levels among Americans as well as Germans. He shows how public reaction went from incredulity through hesitancy to a decision to stick it out on the side of the Western powers. Davison stresses a complex interplay: American determination was strengthened by favorable German attitudes; in turn, the Airlift increased the German expectation that the Allies would not desert them and that the Russians would not be able to take over the city. This made many cautious souls willing to take part openly in anti-communist activities. The main practical applications of this study turn on the relation of leadership and public opinion in a crisis; because of the need for swift action, Davison feels that those in command of the administrative machinery have to take chances and trust that the people at large will support them eventually.[24]

NEED FOR A CLASSICAL-EMPIRICAL SYNTHESIS

In sum, valuable thinking on the relation between governmental decision and public opinion is available. It falls short of an ideal type of research only insofar as the information on public opinion itself is more or less inferential. Undoubtedly, it will take a considerable length of time before we have a joining of the two trends: a careful analysis in the classical tradition supported by modern empirical data. Still, it does not seem unjustified to conclude these remarks in a somewhat Utopian mood. During a debate on the relation between history and public opinion, a historian remarked that even in the

[23] He takes a position quite similar to that of Almond and Speier in their writings on the topic.

[24] In its yet unpublished form the study is the first to combine poll data with traditional historical analysis. A preliminary summary of some of the findings is available from a paper identified as P-851, The RAND Corporation, Santa Monica, California.

future his colleagues will not need attitude studies; they will know what actually has happened and from that they can infer what "effective public opinion" was at the time. However, the French economic historian Ferdinand Braudel provides us with the pertinent rejoinder:

Victorious events come about as a result of many possibilities, often contradictory, among which life finally has made its choice. For one possibility which actually is realized innumerable others have drowned. These are the ones which have left little trace for the historians. And yet it is necessary to give them their place because the losing movements are forces which have at every moment affected the final outcome, sometimes by retarding and sometimes by speeding up its development. The historian should also be concerned with the opposing elements, its incipent waves which at the time were not easily arrested. Ideas which couldn't be realized at one time still might have made the subsequent victory of another idea possible.[25]

In other words, if an event is the result of several potential trends, none of which have been fully realized, then it cannot be really understood unless the "tendencies" are known. It is illogical to reverse the analysis and to derive the potential from the actual, because various combinations of trends might have led to the same outcome. Only attitude data can provide the components which produced the final result.

Thus, from all sides the need for broad gauge opinion studies becomes increasingly obvious. But the complexity of this task also becomes more evident. While modern empiricists have reason to be pleased with their progress, there is no doubt that they can gain much from close contact with the classical tradition. We should not be deterred by the classicists' sometimes outmoded style of reasoning. The essence of progress, it has been said, consists in leaving the ashes and taking the flames from the altars of one's forebears.

[25] From a discussion remark on "historical economics" contributed to the French *Revue Economique*, 1952.

INDEX

ROBERT O. CARLSON is Dean of the School of Business Administration at Adelphi University, and for many years was Chairman of the Editorial Board of the *Public Opinion Quarterly*.

For eighteen years he served as an executive of Standard Oil Company of New Jersey (now EXXON) working on management problems of the parent company and its operating affiliates in the Middle East, Africa, the Far East, Australia, and Europe. Dr. Carlson is a former Executive Officer of the American Sociological Society and a former President of the Public Relations Society of America. He has taught at Columbia, Fairfield and New York Universities and is a consultant to the Rand Corporation. He directed the Columbia University Bureau of Applied Social Research's study of communications patterns in the Middle East leading to Daniel Lerner's book, *The Passing of Traditional Society.*

FLOYD ALLPORT was for many years at Syracuse University, where he was Professor of Social and Political Psychology. Since his retirement in 1957, Dr. Allport has been living in the Bay Area of California, and has been studying and writing on the problems of "structures in nature"—in psychology, biology, behavior, and the social order.

KURT W. BACK is Professor of Sociology and Psychiatry at Duke University. His current interests include style and communication, social influences on human behavior, and population policy.

LEE BENSON is Professor of the History of the American Peoples at the University of Pennsylvania. He is currently using American history as a "natural experiment" to develop and test a Marxian-Tocquevillian theory of social conflict and the relationships between society and consciousness.

BERNARD BERELSON'S most recent position was as President of the Population Council, Inc. He is currently President Emeritus and Senior Fellow of the Council. Among his well-known works in the field of public opinion are *Content Analysis* and *Voting*, (with Paul F. Lazarsfeld and William N. McPhee.)

LEO BOGART is Executive Vice President and General Manager of the Newspaper Advertising Bureau, Inc. His article in this volume which was adapted from his Presidential Address before the American Association for Public Opinion Research, has also been incorporated in his recent book: *Silent Politics: Polls and the Awareness of Public Opinion* (Wiley Inter-science, 1972).

HARWOOD L. CHILDS, who died in 1972, was the founder of the *Public Opinion Quarterly* and for many years Professor of Politics at Princeton University. He was among the first to organize a course devoted entirely to the study of public opinion and his *Public Opinion: Nature, Formation, Role* has been one of the leading texts in the field.

PHILIP E. CONVERSE is Professor of Political Science and Sociology at the University of Michigan and a Program Director at the Institute for Social Research. He has continued his inquiries into mass electoral politics in the United States and other countries, and has more recently studied time use and subjective indicators of the quality of life.

W. PHILLIPS DAVISON is Professor of Journalism and Sociology at Columbia University, and a former Editor of the *Public Opinion Quarterly*. His most recent book is *Mass Communication and Conflict Resolution.* (Praeger, 1974).

JOHN DOLLARD retired from his chair in Psychology at Yale University in 1969, and has more recently organized a new type of research on magazines and newspapers, based on ideas developed at Yale's Institute of Human Relations. He calls it "editorial research." Professor Dollard writes that he considers the article reprinted in this volume to be one of his best, and regrets that he never had time to validate it.

LEON FESTINGER has been Professor of Psychology at the New School for Social Research since 1968, and prior to that was Professor of Psychology at Stanford University for 14 years. He is a recipient of the Distinguished Scientist Award of the American Psychological Association, and is currently studying visual perception.

JONATHAN L. FREEDMAN is Professor of Psychology at Columbia University and previously taught in the Psychology Department at Stanford. He and David C. Sears have also collaborated on a social psychology text. Professor Freedman's most recent book is *Crowding and Behavior* (Viking, 1975).

KENNETH J. GERGEN is Professor of Psychology and Chairman of the Department of Psychology at Swarthmore College. Among his current research interests are reactions to foreign aid—particularly the conditions under which people show resentment or hostility to assistance. He is a member of the Executive Board of the Roper Center's International Survey Library Association.

NATHAN GLAZER is Professor of Education and Social Structure at Harvard University and Co-Editor of *The Public Interest*. His publications include *The Lonely Crowd* (with David Riesman and Reuel Denney) and *Beyond the Melting*

Pot (with Daniel P. Moynihan). Professor Glazer's current research is in the areas of ethnicity and social policy.

HERBERT H. HYMAN is Professor of Sociology at Wesleyan University. His recent work, *Secondary Analysis of Sample Surveys* reflects his current concern that accumulated survey data contribute to the growth of theory. This concern is also reflected in Professor Hyman's forthcoming book entitled *The Enduring Effects of Education* (with Charles R. Wright and John S. Reed), which applies secondary analysis to a major policy issue.

DANIEL KATZ is Professor of Psychology Emeritus, University of Michigan, and a recipient of the Kurt Lewin Memorial Award of the Society for the Psychological Study of Social Issues. His books include *The Social Psychology of Organizations* (with Robert L. Kahn) and *Political Parties in Norway* (with Henry Valen).

ELIHU KATZ is Professor of Sociology and Communications, and Director of the Communications Institute at the Hebrew University of Jerusalem. Professor Katz has been in the forefront of the development of the "uses and gratifications" approach to the study of communication and is currently working on a comparative study of the use of mass media in nation-building.

HERBERT C. KELMAN is Richard Clarke Cabot Professor of Social Ethics at Harvard University. He received the Kurt Lewin Memorial Award of the Society for the Psychological Study of Social Issues in 1973. His current interests are in the areas of political ideology, international conflict resolution, and the relationship of action to attitude. Some of his recent research has dealt with "crimes of obedience."

JOSEPH T. KLAPPER is Director of the Office of Social Research, CBS, Inc., and has been conducting research on the effects of mass communication for more than 25 years. The substance of his article in this volume was also included in his well-known book, *The Effects of Mass Communication* (Free Press, 1960). Dr. Klapper has taught at several universities and was a member of the Surgeon General's Scientific Advisory Committee on Television and Social Behavior.

HAROLD D. LASSWELL is Ford Foundation Professor Emeritus of Law and the Social Sciences, Yale University. His article in this volume is one of an impressive series of publications on the policy implications of the social sciences, another recent one being *A Preview of Policy Sciences* (American Elsevier, 1971). Professor Lasswell is currently co-chairman of the Policy Sciences Center in New York.

PAUL F. LAZARSFELD is Quetelet Professor of Social Science Emeritus, Columbia University, and currently University Professor at the University of Pittsburgh. He was the founder of the Bureau of Applied Social Research and for many years has been a pioneer in the development and application of empirical social research. Among his recent publications is *Continuities in the Language of Social Research* (Free Press, 1973). He is currently preparing a volume to be entitled *Introduction to Applied Sociology* (Elsevier, 1975).

ELEANOR EMMONS MACCOBY is Professor of Developmental Psychology and Chairman of the Psychology Department at Stanford University. Her current research interests include study of the relationship between the sex hormone make-up and the behavior of newborn infants. Among her recent publications is *The Psychology of Sex Differences* (with Carol Nagy, Stanford University Press, 1974).

NATHAN MACCOBY is Professor of Communication and Director of the Institute for Communication Research at Stanford University. He is also Co-Director of the Stanford Heart Disease Prevention Program and is exploring methods of inducing behavior that will reduce the risk of disease. Among his other research interests is the cognitive processing of arguments and counter-arguments in attitude change.

MARGARET MEAD is Curator Emeritus of Ethnology at the American Museum of Natural History and Adjunct Professor of Anthropology, Columbia University. She is also President of the American Association for the Advancement of Science. Her latest book is *Ruth Benedict: A Biography* (Columbia University Press, 1974). Dr. Mead is now completing a book to be entitled *This Changing World* (with Ken Heyman). She is also involved with United Nations conferences on major issues, such as food, population, and human settlements.

PETER ODEGARD, who died in 1966, was for many years Professor of Political Science at the University of California, Berkeley. He also served as an advisor to the U.S. Atomic Energy Commission for seven years and as President of Reed College for three years. One of his best-known books is *Pressure Politics: The Story of the Anti-Saloon League*.

DAVID RIESMAN is Henry Ford II Professor of the Social Sciences in the Sociology Department of Harvard University. His recent work has been in the field of higher education, but he has had a continuing interest in the use and interpretation of survey data, as shown in his methodological appendix to *The Academic Mind* (by Paul F. Lazarsfeld and Wagner Thielens, Jr.) and in *The Lonely Crowd* (with Nathan Glazer).

MILTON ROKEACH is Professor of Sociology and Psychology at Washington State University, Pullman, and a former President of the Society for the Psychological Study of Social Issues. His research interests have included long-term attitude, value, and behavioral change, race prejudice, belief systems, and personality. Among his recent publications is *The Nature of Human Values* (Free Press—Macmillan, 1973).

ARNOLD ROSE, who died in 1968, taught Sociology at Bennington College, Washington University, and the University of Minnesota. He was President of the American Sociological Association and served a term in the Minnesota State Legislature. One of Professor Rose's best-known works is *The Negro in America*. He also collaborated with Gunnar Myrdal in writing *An American Dilemma*.

GARY I. SCHULMAN is Associate Professor of Sociology at the University of California in Santa Barbara. He is co-author of *Experiment as a Social Occasion* (with Paul L. Wuebben and Bruce C. Straits, Glendessary Press, 1947). His current research includes the study of willingness to do violence, sexism, and conformity processes.

DAVID O. SEARS is Professor of Psychology and Political Science at the University of California, Los Angeles. His current research interests include political socialization and political persuasion. Among his recent publications is *The Politics of Violence: The New Urban Blacks and the Watts Riot* (with John B. McConahay, Houghton Mifflin, 1973).

DON D. SMITH is Professor of Sociology at the Florida State University, Tallahassee. Some of his recent research has concerned international political communications and their effects on opinions and attitudes. Two articles by Professor Smith on the audience for short-wave broadcasts in the United States were published in the *Public Opinion Quarterly* in 1969 and 1970.

M. BREWSTER SMITH is Professor of Psychology and Vice Chancellor for the Social Sciences at the University of California, Santa Cruz, having previously taught at Harvard, Vassar, New York University, Berkeley, and Chicago. His current research interests are in political psychology and also in theories of the self that combine "humanistic" and scientific psychology.

PERCY H. TANNENBAUM is Professor in the Graduate School of Public Policy and Research Psychologist at the Institute of Human Learning, both at the University of California, Berkeley. As one of those involved in the formation of the School of Public Policy, he has recently specialized in developing methods of evaluation research and in designing communication-information systems for improving policy implementation in a range of substantive fields.

ALAN G. WEINSTEIN is Associate Professor of Management in the School of Economics and Management at Oakland University, Rochester, Michigan, and previously taught at Carnegie-Mellon University. His primary research emphasis is on organizational behavior and consumer behavior.

GERHART D. WIEBE retired in 1974 from the post of Dean, School of Public Communication, Boston University, and is currently residing in Costa Rica. He is a former research associate of Elmo Roper and for several years was Chairman of the Joint Committee for Research on Television and Children.

FRANCIS G. WILSON is presently retired and observes politics and human behavior from the vantage point of the Cosmos Club in Washington, D.C. He was for many years Professor of Political Science at the University of Illinois and authored the well-known text in the field of political theory, *Elements of Modern Politics*.

CHARLES R. WRIGHT is Professor of Communications and Sociology at the University of Pennsylvania and a member of the Editorial Board of the *Public Opinion Quarterly*. Among his recent publications in the area of sociology and communication is *Mass Communications: A Sociological Perspective* (Random House, second edition in 1975).

MASS COMMUNICATION RESEARCH: Major Issues
and Future Directions

> Edited by W. Phillips Davison and
> Frederick T.C. Yu

THE USES OF COMMUNICATION IN DECISION-
MAKING: A Comparative Study of Yugoslavia and
the United States

> Alex S. Edelstein

MASS COMMUNICATION AND CONFLICT
RESOLUTION: The Role of the Information Media
in the Advancement of Human Understanding

> W. Phillips Davison

SOVIET POLITICAL INDOCTRINATION:
Developments in Mass Media and Propaganda Since
Stalin

> Gayle Durham Hollander

THE ROLE OF COMMUNICATIONS IN THE
MIDDLE EAST CONFLICT: Ideological and
Religious Aspects

> Yonah Alexander